KU-680-026

20 19004 720

NEW COLLEGE, SWINDON

YOUTH, EDUCATION, AND SEXUALITIES

Advisory Board

William F. **Pinar**
Professor William F. Pinar
Department of Curriculum Studies
Faculty of Education
University of British Columbia
2125 Main Mall
Vancouver, British Columbia V6T 1Z4
CANADA

John P. **Elia**
Associate Professor, Associate Chair &
Co-Graduate Coordinator of the MPH Program
Department of Health Education
College of Health & Human Services
HSS Bldg. 321
San Francisco State University
1600 Holloway Avenue
San Francisco, CA 94132-4161

Tara Lynn **Fulton**
Dean of Library and Information Services
Lock Haven University
Lock Haven, PA 17745

Arthur **Lipkin**
Independent Scholar
16 Chatham
Cambridge, MA 02139

Michael **Reiss**
Professor of Science Education and Head of the
   School of Mathematics,
Science & Technology
Institute of Education
University of London
20 Bedford Way
London WC1H 0AL
UK

Will **Letts**, IV
Lecturer, School of Teacher Education
Associate Director, Centre for Research into
   Professional Practice, Learning, and
   Education
School of Teacher Education
Charles Sturt University
Bathurst NSW 2795 Australia

YOUTH, EDUCATION, AND SEXUALITIES

AN INTERNATIONAL ENCYCLOPEDIA

Volume Two
K–Z

SWINDON COLLEGE

WITHDRAWN

LEARNING RESOURCE CENTRE

Edited by
James T. Sears

Greenwood Press
Westport, Connecticut • London

1st SEPTEMBER 2008
54050000300111

Library of Congress Cataloging-in-Publication Data

Youth, education, and sexualities : an international encyclopedia /
  edited by James T. Sears.
    2 v. cm.
  Includes bibliographical references and index.
  ISBN 0-313-32748-3 (set : alk. paper)—ISBN 0-313-32754-8 (v. 1 :
alk. paper)—ISBN 0-313-32755-6 (v. 2 : alk. paper)
    1. Homosexuality and education—Encyclopedias.   2. Sex differences
in education—Encyclopedias.   3. Gay youth—Education—Encyclopedias.
    4. Gay youth—Social conditions—Encyclopedias.   5. Sexual orientation—
Encyclopedias.   I. Sears, James T. (James Thomas), 1951–   .
  LC192.6.Y68   2005
  371.826′6′03—dc22   2005018961

British Library Cataloguing in Publication Data is available.

Copyright © 2005 by James T. Sears

All rights reserved. No portion of this book may be
reproduced, by any process or technique, without the
express written consent of the publisher.

SWINDON COLLEGE

LEARNING RESOURCE CENTRE

Library of Congress Catalog Card Number: 2005018961
ISBN: 0-313-32748-3 (set)
      0-313-32754-8 (vol. I)
      0-313-32755-6 (vol. II)

First published in 2005

Greenwood Press, 88 Post Road West, Westport, CT 06881
An imprint of Greenwood Publishing Group, Inc.
www.greenwood.com

Printed in the United States of America

The paper used in this book complies with the
Permanent Paper Standard issued by the National
Information Standards Organization (Z39.48-1984).

10   9   8   7   6   5   4   3   2   1

Table of Contents

Alphabetical List of Entries

Alphabetical List of Entries

Guide to Related Topics

Colleges and Universities

Administrators
College Age Students
College Campus Organizing
College Campus Programming
College Campus Resource Centers
Community and Technical Colleges
Counseling
Curriculum, Higher Education
Fraternities
Johns Committee
Lavender Graduation
Residence Life in Colleges
School Climate, College
Single-Sex Schools
Sororities
Women's Colleges

Communities

Community LGBT Youth Groups
HIV Education
Identity Politics
Internet, Gay Men and the
Internet, Lesbians and the
Queer Zines
Race and Racism Social Class

Curriculum and Pedagogy

Art, Teaching of
Australia, Sexualities Curriculum in
Biology, Teaching of
Campus Resource Centers
Career Counseling
Children of the Rainbow Curriculum
Cocurricular Activities
College Campus Organizing
College Campus Programming
Communication
Counseling
Counselor Education
Curriculum, Antibias
Curriculum, Early Childhood
Curriculum, Higher Education
Curriculum, Primary
Curriculum, Secondary
Dance, Teaching of
ESL, Teaching of Geography, Teaching of

History, Teaching of
HIV Education
Language Arts, Teaching of
LGBT Studies
Literature, College
Literature, Early Childhood
Literature, Middle School
Literature, Secondary School
Men's Studies
Multicultural Education
Music, Teaching of
New Zealand, Teaching of Sexualities in
Philosophy, Teaching of
Physical Education, Teaching of
Poetry, Teaching of
Political Science, Teaching of
Psychology, Teaching of
Queer Pedagogy
Queer Studies
Science, Teaching of
Sexuality Education
Social Work
Theater, Teaching of
Women's Studies

Educational Associations and Organizations

Gay, Lesbian, and Straight Education
    Network (GLSEN)
GLBT Educational Equity (GLEE)
Professional Educational Organizations Scouting

Educational Policies and Practices

Antidiscrimination Policy
Disabilities, Intellectual
Disabilities, Physical
Discrimination
Educational Administration
Educational Policies
Gay–Straight Alliances
Gifted Education, LGBT Youth in
Harassment
Heteronormativity
Heterosexism
Homophobia
Lavender Graduation
Multicultural Education

Guide to Related Topics

Project 10
School Safety and Safe School Zones
Secondary Schools, LGBT
Sexism
Sexual Harassment
Sexuality Education
Single-Sex Schools
Special Education, LGBT Youth in
Workplace Issues

Educators and Professionals

Activism, LGBT Teachers
Allies
Administrators Coming Out, Teachers
Counseling
Educational Administration
Films, Youth and Educators in
Licensure
Mentoring
Professionalism
Social Work
Teachers, LGBT and History
Workplace Issues

Elementary and Secondary Schools

Administration, Educational
Administrators
Catholic Education and Youth
Counseling
Curriculum, Early Childhood
Curriculum, Primary
Curriculum, Secondary
Gay–Straight Alliances
Project 10
Proms
Rural Youth and Schools
School Climate, K-12
Secondary Schools, LGBT
Single-Sex Schools
Urban Youth and Schools

Ethnicity and Ethnic Groups

African American Youth
Asian American Youth
ESL, Teaching of
Ethnic Identity
Latinos and Latinas
Native or Indigenous LGBT Youth
Race and Racism
Racial Identity
Rural Youth and Schools
Urban Youth and Schools
White Antiracism

Government Policies and Practices

Acquired Immune Deficiency Syndrome
(AIDS)
Britain, Section 28
Colonialism and Homosexuality
Discrimination
Domestic and Relationship Violence
Hate Crimes
Licensure
Sexual Harassment
Workplace Issues
Youth, Homeless

Health

Acquired Immune Deficiency Syndrome
(AIDS)
Adolescent Sexualities
Agency
Alcoholism
Behavior Disorders
Bullying
Canada, HIV/AIDS Education in
Counseling
Deaf LGBT Youth
*Diagnostic & Statistical Manual of Mental
Disorders* (DSM)
Disabilities, Intellectual
Disabilities, Physical
Domestic and Relationship Violence
Drug Use
Eating Disorders and Body Image
Gender Identity Disorder
Homophobia
Identity Development
Japan, HIV/AIDS Education in
Mental Health
Pregnancy, Teenage
Prejudice
Prostitution or Sex Work
Religion and Psychological
Development
Reparative Therapy
Resiliency
School Safety and Safe School Zones
Sexual Abuse and Assault
Sexual Health, Gay and Bisexual
Sexual Health, Lesbian and Bisexual
Substance Abuse and Use
Suicide
Transsexuality
Youth, At-Risk
Youth Risk Behavior Surveys

History

Activism, LGBT Teachers
Administrators
Feminism
Johns Committee
Lesbian Feminism
Pink Triangle
Rainbow Flag and Other Pride Symbols
Stonewall
Teachers, LGBT and History
Women's Colleges
Women's Movement

Legal Matters

Boy Scouts of America et al. v. Dale
Discrimination
Domestic and Relationship Violence
Harassment
Hate Crimes
Lawrence v. Texas
Legal Issues, Students
Sexual Abuse and Assault
Sexual Harassment
Teachers, LGBT and History
Workplace Issues

Parents

Adoption
Allies
Children of LGBT Parents Families, LGBT
Parents, LGBT
Parents, Responses to Homosexuality

People

Butler, Judith
Foucault, Michel
Freud, Sigmund
Hall, G. Stanley
Hirschfeld, Magnus Kinsey, Alfred
Lacan, Jacques
Shepard, Matthew

Popular Culture

Camp
Cartoons
Comics
Dating
Films, Youth and Educators in
Graffiti
Identity Politics
The L Word

Music, Popular
Popular Culture
Queer as Folk
Queer Zines
Sports, Gay Men in
Sports, Lesbians in
Stereotypes
Tong-zhi
Youth Culture

Regions and Countries

Africa, LGBT Youth and Issues in
Asia, LGBT Youth and Issues in
Australia, LGBT Issues in
Australia, LGBT Youth in
Australia, Research on Sexual Identities
Australia, Sexualities Curriculum in
Brazil, LGBT Youth in
Britain, Section 28
Bulgaria, LGBT Youth in
Canada, HIV/AIDS Education in
Canada, LGBT Issues in
Canada, LGBT Youth in
China, LGBT Issues in
China, LGBT Youth in
Egypt, LGBT Youth and Issues in
Europe, LGBT Youth and Issues in
France, LGBT Youth and Issues in
India, LGBT Youth and Issues in
Ireland, LGBT Youth and Issues in
Israel, LGBT Issues in
Israel, LGBT Youth in
Japan, Gay and Transgender Youth in
Japan, HIV/AIDS Education in
Japan, Lesbian and Bisexual Youth in
Japan, LGBT Issues in
Mexico, LGBT Youth and Issues in
New Zealand, LGBT Youth and Issues in
New Zealand, Teaching of Sexualities in
Russia, LGBT Youth in
South Africa, LGBT Issues in
South Africa, LGBT Youth in
South America, LGBT Youth and Issues in
United Kingdom, LGBT Youth in

Religion

Catholic Education and Youth
Christian Moral Instruction on Homosexuality
Jewish Moral Instruction on Homosexuality
Muslim Moral Instruction on Homosexuality
Religion and Psychological Development
Religious Fundamentalism
Spirituality

Guide to Related Topics

Sexuality and Gender

Australia, Research on Sexual Identities
Bisexuality
Compulsory Heterosexuality
Cross-Dressing
Crush
Dating
Desire
Gender Identity
Gender Roles
Intersex
Multiple Genders
Prostitution or Sex Work
Sexism
Sexual Abuse and Assault
Sexual Harassment
Sexual Identity
Sexual Orientation
Sissy Boy
Stereotypes
Tomboy
Transsexuality

Symbols and Celebrations

Day of Silence or Silencing
Lavender Graduation
National Coming Out Day
Pink Triangle
Rainbow Flag and Other Pride Symbols

Teachers

Activism, LGBT Teachers
Coming Out, Teachers
Teachers, LGBT and History

Technology

Internet, Gay Men and the
Internet, Lesbians and the
Queer Zines
Virtual Schooling

Theory and Philosophy

Critical Social Theory
Feminism
Heteronormativity
Lesbian Feminism
Poststructuralism
Psychoanalysis and Education

Psychoanalysis and Feminism
Queer and Queer Theory

Youth

Activism, LGBT Youth
Adolescence
Adolescent Sexualities
Agency
Bisexual Youth
Childhood
Children of LGBT Parents
College Age Students
Coming Out, Youth
Dating
Deaf LGBT Youth
Drug Use
Eating Disorders and Body Image
Families, LGBT
Films, Youth and Educators in
Gay Youth
Gender Identity Disorder
Gifted Education, LGBT Youth in
Identity Development
Intersex
Lesbian Youth
Mental Health
Mentoring
Passing
Pregnancy, Teenage
Prostitution or Sex Work
Research, Qualitative
Research, Quantitative
Racial Identity
Resiliency
Rural Youth and Schools
Scouting
Sexual Identity
Sexual Orientation
Sissy Boy
Special Education, LGBT Youth in
Substance Abuse and Use
Suicide
Tomboy
Tong-zhi
Transgender Youth
Urban Youth and Schools
Youth, At-Risk
Youth Culture
Youth, Homeless
Youth Risk Behavior Surveys

Kinsey, Alfred (1894–1956)

Shawn M. Coyne

Using new techniques and facing formerly taboo topics, Alfred Kinsey changed the field of sex **research**, expanded the knowledge of American sexual practices, and laid the groundwork for changes in attitudes about sexuality. Although Kinsey's background as a scientist was in **biology**, he entered the field of sex research with equal zeal for this new field. Beginning his work in the late 1930s and completing his first book on the subject in 1948, he was a pioneer in the field. Not only did he face controversy over his brazen attitude about the topic, but his methods and personal life also fell under scrutiny. Nonetheless, his research had a powerful impact on United States' sex research; on basic knowledge of sexual activity, particularly homosexual activity; on how sexual activity and **sexual orientation** are defined; and on sexual attitudes in the culture.

Alfred Kinsey was a biologist. His area of expertise centered on the gall wasp, and he published extensively in this area. After completing his Ph.D. at Harvard, he taught at Indiana University (IU) where he began to develop a personal interest in human sexuality. Kinsey grew up in a religiously conservative family and during a time in which sexuality was considered for procreative purposes only and restricted to marriage. Yet Kinsey and his wife, Clara (affectionately known as Mac), had very open attitudes about sexuality.

At the end of the 1930s, the entire country was facing critical levels of venereal disease infection. As a consequence, **sexuality education** courses focused on hygienic information. While there is some disagreement as to the actual course of events, it appears that the Association of Women Students at IU approached the university president (after consulting Kinsey and on his advice) and requested a marriage course. Either because the president asked who they would recommend teach it or because Kinsey had strategically positioned himself to be the most appropriate and ready instructor, Kinsey was asked to teach the course. The course, originally designed only for college seniors, was actually attended by seniors, married or engaged students, and some faculty; men and women took it together.

From his limited research on human sexuality and his conversations with current students, Kinsey quickly learned that there was great sexual ignorance. This ignorance, he believed, led to anxiety, which sometimes prohibited healthy sexual functioning. Kinsey felt the best way to combat this was to gather information. His lectures in the marriage course—despite their great controversy and shocking use of formerly forbidden vocabulary such as "sexual intercourse," "masturbation," "clitoris," and "orgasm"—were very popular.

Through this course, Kinsey found a tremendous pool of potential data sources for his research on human sexuality. He invited students to submit to an interview, during which he confidentially recorded their sexual history. Thirty-five males and two females participated. While it might have been expected that few would be willing to participate and those who participated would be hesitant, what Kinsey found was that students appeared quite willing and were very forthcoming with details.

See also Adolescent Sexualities.

With such great ignorance and sexually transmitted infections on the rise, there was recognition for the need for accurate information. Kinsey's scientific background and stable married family life allowed him to be a perfect candidate for a grant from the Committee for Research in the Problems in Sex, which operated under the National Research Council. In 1940, it awarded Kinsey his first grant of $1,600. A much smaller amount than anticipated (even with IU matching funds in the amount of $1,200), grant dollars did increase as the project grew.

The interview method, developed in 1938 and early 1939, was central to Kinsey's groundbreaking research. Kinsey believed that anonymous survey forms could not accurately collect data. Many criticized his technique, suggesting it might allow bragging or other false representations. Kinsey resolved this concern by building in a number of questions to "check" the accuracy of the speaker. An additional criticism was that he only obtained data from volunteers. It was argued that this lack of a random sampling could skew results. Kinsey countered that random sampling would not provide full accounts of data. Many who were selected either would not participate fully or would waste too much of Kinsey's time as he tried to persuade them. Kinsey also developed a technique he called "the 100 percent group." He would contact a group—such as a local YMCA, PTA, or prison—and introduce himself. With use of many persuasion techniques, he would convince the group that they needed participate at a 100 percent rate. In the early 1950s, he used the support of the Mattachine Society, an organization with chapters in major cities of the United States, to gain access to groups that contained noncriminal gays and lesbians. While this technique was not without flaws and did have its own bias, it was ingenious. In all, Kinsey and his small trained research team conducted 18,000 interviews before losing funding. Kinsey himself conducted 8,000.

While Kinsey's techniques may have been innovative and his research field was relatively novel (**Magnus Hirschfeld** had pioneered the field), he is most recognized for the results of his two major works: *Sexual Behavior in the Human Male*, published in 1948; *Sexual Behavior in the Human Female*, published five years later. At a time when discussions and values regarding sexuality could still be considered to be puritanical, Kinsey demonstrated that sexual practices were far from the expected. First, he reported that homosexual activity, then a crime in all fifty states, was far more common than anticipated. In fact, he estimated that nearly one in three men had engaged in homosexual acts, either in fantasy or in reality. He also estimated that one in ten adults predominantly engaged in homosexual behavior, a statistic that was leveraged by gay-rights activists and their organizations, including youth groups like **Project 10**.

This led to his second important result, a new concept of sexuality. Kinsey did not recognize sexual identities; he only saw sexual acts. This was a groundbreaking perspective. He believed that nearly all people were capable of either homosexual or heterosexual acts, a slighter weaker statement than his bold belief that, "We're all bisexual, it's just a matter of degree" (Robinson 1976, 117). With many married men reporting homosexual acts at some point in their lives, to define them as one **sexual identity** or another was problematic. To demonstrate this range of sexual behavior, Kinsey developed his famous Kinsey Scale. This was a seven-point continuum scale, ranging from zero to six, used for classifying a person's sexual experience. Zero stood for exclusively heterosexual; three stood for equally heterosexual and homosexual; and six stood for exclusively homosexual. Other discoveries that were made in his research included the sexual responses of women, the great variety of sexual practices, and the significant frequency of reported masturbation.

More than just presenting scientific knowledge, Kinsey's publications had a significant impact in popular culture. Discussed and detailed in every major popular magazine and news source of his day, Kinsey's research broadened our cultural understanding of sex and sexuality. He popularized and extended the scientific field of sex research. Previously, most persons held that sex was a moral topic, unable to be researched scientifically. Kinsey created ways to define sexual acts (he based it solely on orgasm achievement) and methods to gather the information. He felt that moral values did not belong in the field of sex research. His data indicated to the public that there was indeed a wide chasm in American culture between moral and legal codes and the actual behavior of the culture's people.

Perhaps most significantly, Kinsey laid the foundation for changes in attitudes, particularly among professional groups, about sexual acts and sexuality, in particular homosexuality. He normalized homosexual behaviors by showing their common nature. With so many variations in sexual activity, he argued, one could hardly define a norm or what is normal. Kinsey's approach was to avoid definitions of people, but to instead maintain an open attitude regarding understanding sexual behavior. As a result, Kinsey, unlike many other researchers, did not attempt to explain homosexuality. Seeing homosexual possibilities for all people, he felt there was nothing to explain.

From these ramifications of his research, Kinsey's work helped to energize the "homophile" movements of the 1950s, a precursor to the gay-rights movements that developed post-Stonewall. Kinsey unofficially advised leaders of the Mattachine Society and routinely allowed his work to be disseminated in their publications, principally aimed at homosexuals and professional groups such as psychologists, ministers, and attorneys.

Kinsey's research may be over fifty years old, but it is still a source of occasional controversy. His methods are still questioned and thus the results are argued flawed. While Kinsey kept a very private life to his death, biographers have since documented his **bisexuality**, leading some to question his research as personally biased. The Kinsey Institute and Library that he started at Indiana University houses these data and collection of sexual artifacts that were collected. Like Kinsey, the Institute is a target for debate and protest even today.

An historical inclusion of Alfred Kinsey and his groundbreaking research is only a beginning step for educators. Equally significant and important is a presentation of how the ideas that flowed from Kinsey's research impacted culture, **activism**, self-definitions, and awareness of the **lesbian, gay, bisexual**, and **transgender** (LGBT) population. Understanding these concepts themselves, educators should find themselves with a greater awareness and recognition for the complexity surrounding sexuality as it is expressed and self-experienced versus how the culture defines it.

Bibliography

Bullough, Vern L. 1998. "Alfred Kinsey and the Kinsey Report: Historical Overview and Lasting Contributions." *The Journal of Sex Research* 35: 127–131.

Gathorne-Hardy, Jonathan. 1998. *Sex the Measure of All Things*. Bloomington: Indiana University Press.

Jones, James H. 1997. *Alfred C. Kinsey: A Public/Private Life*. New York: Norton.

Kinsey, Alfred, Wardel B. Pomeroy, and Clyde E. Martin. 1948. *Sexual Behavior in the Human Male*. Philadelphia: Saunders.

Kinsey, Alfred, Wardel B. Pomeroy, Clyde E. Martin, and Paul H. Gebhard. 1953. *Sexual Behavior in the Human Female*. Philadelphia: Saunders.

Pomeroy, Wardel B. 1972. *Dr. Kinsey and the Institute for Sex Research*. New York: Harper and Row.

Robinson, Paul. 1976. *The Modernization of Sex*. New York: Harper and Row.

Web Site

The Kinsey Institute for Research in Sex, Gender and Reproduction. 2004. The Kinsey Institute. Accessed December 14, 2004. http://www.indiana.edu/~kinsey. The Kinsey Institute carries on Kinsey's tradition of scientific research and education regarding human sexuality. The Institute maintains a library, provides graduate-level instruction, and sponsors services and events.

The L Word

Denise Tse Shang Tang

The L Word is a thirteen-episode Showtime television series that premiered on January 18, 2004, in the United States. Executive Producer Ilene Chaiken created the series and, to a certain extent, based the characters and stories on lesbians and bisexual women she had known in her life. Although it took five years for Chaiken to convince network executives that a lesbian television series was worthy of investment, the popularity of *The L Word*'s first season resulted in the fastest renewal of television series in Showtime's twenty-eight-year history. Unlike another Showtime television series **Queer as Folk**, there has not been a significant youth-identified character like Justin (Randy Harrison) and Hunter (Harris Allan). It is too early to measure the impact of the series, but *The L Word* provides queer women with representation on television and presents lesbian visibility for **bisexual** female and **lesbian youth**.

Worldwide younger lesbian and bisexual female audiences have engaged in the discussion about the series' first season. In Hong Kong and Shanghai, they have downloaded the episodes from the **Internet**. Copies have been shared among friends and openly discussed on Internet forums throughout **Asia**. In contrast, **gay youth** message boards in the United States and the **United Kingdom** have not seen many messages posted about *The L Word*. The absence of a youth element may be one explanation.

The L Word (Showtime) Season 1, Spring 2004. Shown: Jennifer Beals (as Bette), Laurel Holloman (as Tina). Showtime/Photofest

The *The L Word* revolves around love relationships, career ambitions, sex, and friendships among a group of glamorous lesbians and bisexual women in their thirties who reside in Los Angeles. Bette Porter (Jennifer Beals) and Tina Kennard (Laurel Holloman), who enjoy a seven-year relationship, are considered role models by their friends. Bette is a career-oriented woman, and Tina left her job at a movie studio to become pregnant and start a family with Bette. The cast features a bisexual journalist (Alice, Leisha Hailey), a professional tennis player (Dana, Erin Daniels), a sexy hairstylist (Shane played by Katherine Moennig), a café owner (Marina, by Karina Lombard), a writer (Jenny, Mia Kirshner) and her boyfriend (Tim, Eric Mabius).

The L Word's cast, "full of beautiful people" has significantly contributed to the success of the series (Warn 2004). In particular, two actresses have been steady favorites of lesbian spectators: Laurel Holloman from *The Incredibly True Adventures of Two Girls in Love* (1995) and Katherine Moennig from *Young Americans* (2000). Jennifer Beals from *Flashdance* (1983) and Mia Kirshner from *Exotica* (1995) have also secured a fan base. However, apart from Jennifer Beals and Pam Grier, the

See also Films, Youth and Educators in; Religious Fundamentalism; Stereotypes.

only other women of color represented are Ion Overman, who has an affair with Beals' character, Bette, and Karina Lombard, who identifies as Native American. Discussions on the Internet and on print media have center around the inclusion of more diverse characters, including suggestions for **Asian** and **Latina** representations.

There has been a similar lack of diversity in terms of **body image** and **social class**. Aside from the drag king character Ivan (Kelly Lynch), there have been no butch characters. In a much heated debate about the series, some viewers felt that it was an important change for lesbians not to be stereotypically represented as masculine women wearing flannel shirts and black leather boots, yet others argued that these butch women are very much part of lesbian communities. Using Ellen DeGeneres and *ER*'s Sandy Lopez as examples, Warn (2004) reminds us that "Americans prefer their women—gay and straight—to adhere to traditional notions of femininity." Similarly, the show's lack of working-class characters and the absence of social class in the storyline have been noted. The characters are young, urban professionals who reside in grand houses and lead relatively comfortable lifestyles. Finally, some viewers were embittered that only one cast member, Leisha Hailey, is an out lesbian in reality, even though Troche and Chaiken (producers) are lesbians. Nevertheless, most viewers would agree that *The L Word* could never be representative of the diversity for lesbians, bisexuals, **queer**, and questioning women of all ages.

Rose Troche, the coexecutive producer, writer and director of *The L Word*, has a long history of putting lesbians on screen. She directed *Go Fish* (USA 1994), a story about love and friendship among Chicago lesbians. Hailed as "the darling of New Queer Cinema," the success of *Go Fish* propelled Troche's career to direct two feature films *Bedrooms and Hallways* (UK 1998) and *The Safety of Objects* (UK 2001), as well as being the director for an episode of the HBO television series *Six Feet Under* (Rich 2004). In 2004, Troche became the recipient of the 2004 Frameline Award presented by the twenty-eighth San Francisco International Lesbian and Gay Film Festival.

However, positive representations of lesbian and bisexual women in television and film are rare and have generally been less than well-received by audiences. Ellen DeGeneres broke new ground when she publicly came out and then did likewise with her character in *Ellen*, which was then cancelled due to loss of audience share. As a lesbian single mom, Rosie O'Donnell's coming out also was met with mixed reactions by gay and mainstream audiences alike. One of the problems, *L Word* producer Chaiken observes, is that "lesbian characters we've seen were mostly created by men. We've been marginalized from the culture for a very long time, and I think that we're ready to claim our rightful place" (Bolonik 2004).

Praise and criticism flooded Web site message boards immediately after the first episode of *The L Word* aired. In the plot, Bette and Tina approach a straight man for sex with the purpose of getting Tina pregnant. They ask the man to abstain from using a condom. The threesome scene not only stirred up controversy concerning unprotected sex, but criticism swirled around the "blatant hetero involvement throughout the show," and this first episode catered to a heterosexual male audience (Lo 2004). The season's finale was no less shocking as Tina discovers that Bette had an affair, leading to a raw, borderline violent sexual encounter between Bette and Tina.

At the end of the first season, *The L Word* characters emerged with much-needed emotional depth. The series also sets a new trend by formalizing on television a vintage look that relies heavily on expensive designers like Gucci, Marc Jacobs, and Courreges, thus challenging viewers to a "mix and match" of the old and new styles of fashion. Valerie Steele, the museum director at the Fashion Institute of Technology, points out that lesbian fashion has evolved from butch-femme style of dress in the 1940s, androgyny in the 1960s and 1970s, lipstick lesbians in the 1980s to the rise of drag kings in the nineties (Trebay 2004).

The L Word has been broadcast via satellite and cable channels in Australia, Canada, Denmark, Israel, Norway, and the United Kingdom. The marketing campaign for the United Kingdom's premiere included television and print advertisements along with billboards in central London's Underground stations and on buses. But it has also created controversy in Australia where major advertisers pulled out, despite their public statements that they were reacting more to the advertising policy of Channel 7 (advertisers were not notified appropriately) than to the write-in campaign against the advertisers orchestrated by Salt Shakers, a Melbourne-based Christian right group (http://libertus.net/censor/odocs/pj-lword.html). The series is scheduled to air in France, Italy, and Sweden, and the pilot episode was selected for inclusion in the 2004 Hong Kong Lesbian and Gay Film and Video Festival.

Bibliography

Bolonik, Kera. 2004. "Not Your Mother's Lesbians." New York Metro.com. Accessed June 9, 2005. http://www.nymetro.com/nymetro/news/features/n_9708/index.html.

Lo, Malinda. 2004. "Does *The L Word* Represent? Viewer Reactions Vary." Accessed June 9, 2005. http://www.afterellen.com/TV/thelword/reaction.html.

MacDonald, Elizabeth. 2004. "Is America Finally Ready For Gay TV?" Accessed June 9, 2005. http://www.forbes.com/services/2004/06/07/cz_em_0607viab.html.

Rich, B. Ruby. 2004. "Touché Troche." Accessed June 9, 2005. http://www.sfgate.com/cgibin/article.cgi?f=/g/archive/2004/06/25/troche.DTL.

Taylor, C. 2004. "Candace and Lesbians of Color on *The L Word*." Accessed June 9, 2005. http://www.afterellen.com/TV/thelword/candace.html.

Trebay, Guy. 2004. "The Secret Power of Lesbian Style." Accessed June 9, 2005. http://www.thelwordonline.com/lesbian_style.shtml.

Warn, Sarah. 2004. "Too Much Otherness: Femininity on The L Word." June 9, 2005. http://www.afterellen.com/TV/thelword/femininity.html.

Web Site

Showtime—The L Word. 2005. Showtime. Accessed June 9, 2005. http://www.sho.com/site/lword/. An official site from the cable network that provides episode guides and related information.

Lacan, Jacques (1901–1981)

jan jagodzinski

Lacan's importance for **lesbian, gay, bisexual,** and **transgender** youth (LGBT) and education lies mainly in his theory of the subject and his radical stance on theorizing sex/gender. His notion of a "split subject" offers an alternative to **Michel Foucault**'s

See also Gender Identity; Poststructuralism; Psychoanalysis and Education; Psychoanalysis and Feminism; Queer Studies; Sexual Identity.

view of the poststructuralist "decentered surface" subject theorized by a hypercom- plexity of various discourses that come together to "articulate" self-identity as a multitude of subject positions. Queer theorists are often divided between Foucault who rejected **Sigmund Freud**'s "repression hypothesis," and Lacan, whom other the- orists claim can provide LGBT subjectivities with renewed possibilities (Dean 2000).

Jacques Lacan is often referred to as the "French Freud" because of his attempt to update Freud, using the structural linguistics of the 1950s. He famously said that the unconscious was structured "like" a language. His latter work in the 1970s concentrated on formalizing an open systems approach to the unconscious. A con- troversial figure in French psychiatry, he was expelled in 1953 from the Inter- national Psychoanalytic Association for his unorthodox analytical practices. Lacan then created the *Societé français de Psychoanalyse* and founded the *École Freudienne* in Paris, in 1964. The publication of his collected papers, *Écrits*, in 1966, gained him an international reputation. He dissolved his school in 1980 on the grounds that it was losing its integrity.

Lacan's view of the subject is based on three interrelated psychic registers (Symbolic, Imaginary, Real) which circle around a subject's unconscious desires. The subject is, therefore, "split" into a conscious and an unconscious self, which means that a certain part of the self is always unknown. In this view, a subject is always "lacking." There is a missing piece that would make him or her "whole" or complete. There is a "hole" in the conscious **desire** to be "w(hole)." "This is the place of unconscious desire referred to as the Real. It is capitalized as a pun so as not to confuse it with the "real." Lacan calls this part of the self—*Je*, which in the French is "I." This is distinguished from the ego, or "me" (*moi* in French) which forms the imaginary notion of the self. The ego forms the Imaginary psy- chic register. Lacan refers to this ego as a place of "misrecognition." It is a fan- tasy formation of the way we think of ourselves and the way others perceive us. This means that the *preconscious* image of oneself, that is, our "alter ego," can be completely inaccurate. The ego uses many defense mechanisms to maintain a stable "picture" of itself. This "picture frame" of the self is maintained by the un- conscious desires of which we know very little about. Since we are language- using beings, Lacan refers to the Symbolic psychic register as the level of the conscious use of language. When we speak and write, language at the same time "writes us." We must use the language of the culture we are born into to try to communicate with our parents, friends, and societal institutions. Often this Sym- bolic realm is referred to as the big Other. The capitalization refers to a realm of symbolic discourses, which demarcate the laws as to how we should live. Lacan's subject, therefore, is structured by the hypercomplex relationships of these three psychic registers. The Real (or *Je*) forms the "truth" of the subject. It is the place of his or her unconscious desire, which is "beyond" both the imaginary represen- tations of the self (the Imaginary), as well as "beyond" language (Symbolic). When we imagine or talk there is always this *excess* of unconscious desire that "spills" beyond the words and images we use, which lies in the unconscious Real. **Judith Butler** (1993) rejects the Lacanian Real and claims that *sex* is just another discursive construct, while the **transsexual** theoretician Prosser (1998) chastises Lacan for not fully developing the skin-ego. For him *gender* is just another con- struct. The issues all circle around the body. Just how is it to be theorized? Is the sexual and gendered body merely a discursive construct, or is a body formed first and foremost *through unconscious desire* in the Real?

Lacan does not reduce experience to the level of discourse—Imaginary (imagination) and Symbolic (language) psychic levels—as do queer theorists who draw on a Foucauldian foundation. Unconscious desire remains in excess of language and the imagination—in the Real. The queer theorist, Tim Dean (2000) punningly refers to this unconscious desire as "bodies that mutter." "The difference between muttering and speaking concerns the distinction involved in a notion of desire as something in language but not itself linguistic. While speech comprises signs and signifiers, muttering comprises the symptom, which represents a literally unspeakable desire" (203). Such critique has caused some consternation. Butler (1997), for instance, has tried to "save" Foucault from himself. In *The Psychic Life of Power* (86–87), she attempts to rescue this elision of the unconscious by rethinking Foucault's notion of the "soul" as the psyche which includes the unconscious *as well as the ideal ego*. It is the unconscious in the psyche which resists normalizing discourses.

One way out of this quagmire is to take seriously Lacan's claim that an impossible Real gap exists when theorizing sexual difference. Theorizing LGBT's unconscious desire as it circulates between sex and gender ends up being either "too little," and therefore "abstract" since an answer can never be found; or "too much" and seemingly "crass" in its attempt at formulating positive body identity based on same-sex preferences. LGBT subjectivity constituted only through the Symbolic and Imaginary registers can become a closed system way of thinking as the history of radical gay and lesbian identity politics in particular has shown. Education needs to work simultaneously on two tiers: keeping the representational categories of LGBT subjectivities fluid and open under the master signifier "**queer**," as well as continuing to theorize the unconscious Real of desire.

Bibliography

Butler, Judith. 1993. *Bodies that Matter: On the Discursive Limits of "Sex."* New York & London: Routledge.

———. 1997. *Psychic Life of Power: Theories in Subjection*. Stanford: Stanford University Press.

Dean, Tim. 2000. *Beyond Sexuality*. Chicago: University of Chicago Press.

Prosser J. 1998. *Second Skins: The Body Narratives of Transsexuality*. New York: Columbia University Press.

Language Arts, Teaching of

Mollie Blackburn

Examining sexualities in the teaching of language arts—which include reading, writing, listening, speaking, viewing, and visual representation—in middle and elementary school classrooms is one way of working against **heterosexism** and **homophobia**. This can be accomplished through the integration of lesbian, gay, bisexual,

See also Adolescent Sexualities; Cartoons; Children of LGBT Parents; Children of the Rainbow Curriculum; Comics; Coming Out, Teachers; Parents, LGBT; Poetry, Teaching of.

and transgender (LGBT) content, which is important for students who identify as LGBT or have friends and family members who do. Including such content into the language arts **curriculum** validates the lives of LGBT people as complicated and diverse ways of being something other than straight. Learning about LGBT people can make it easier for **queer youth** to accept themselves, and it helps everyone who shares relationships with them. The integration of this content is also important for homophobic students in that it can help them to relinquish their hate, open their minds, and thus improve their education.

According to the *Standards for the English Language Arts* (NCTE/IRA 1996), one of the purposes of teaching the language arts is for students to understand not only texts but themselves and others, as well as to understand the many dimensions of human experience. It is intellectually dishonest to exclude LGBT content from language arts curricula "simply because some faction or other may object to them" (Lipkin 1994, 106). Furthermore, working for a more socially just world demands including all voices in elementary and middle school curricula and materials.

Epstein (2000) argues that a teacher cannot count on the mere inclusion of LGBT content through **literature** to work against **stereotypes**. Teachers need to facilitate small and whole group discussions. She conducted a study of the understandings of sexuality and gender held by nine and ten year-olds in a classroom in London taught by a politically active, out, gay man. Children in small groups read texts with lesbian and gay characters (there were no bisexual or transgender characters). They talked first in small groups and then as a whole class. A pair of boys who examined a photograph of lesbian mothers was unwilling to acknowledge the nature of the women's relationship. In contrast, a small group of girls understood this relationship without condemnation in the small group, but they did not talk about it in the whole class discussion. The teacher then came out to his class, with the support of the school's governing body. The pair of boys stated that there was nothing wrong with being gay. Epstein argues that even if students only articulate antihomophobic messages to please the teacher, it requires them to try on this worldview, if only for a moment, and, in doing so, they create the possibility of returning to such a view.

In another study, Hamilton (1998) read *Jack* with a diverse group of students in a public middle school in New York City. *Jack* (Homes 1989) is a young adult novel about a teenager who struggles to understand his parents' divorce and his father's homosexuality. Hamilton describes the students' responses to the text as cacophonous. Some stated that they suspected that the father was gay, others expressed surprise, and a few reconsidered the behavior of other characters given this new information. Their responses "created a myriad of superhighways where acceptance and denial, understanding and criticism, and love and hate existed together" (37). Hamilton concluded that integrating gay content into his teaching of language arts was important because it provided his students with opportunities to challenge and be challenged, to grapple with their understandings of secrets, and to examine and practice coping with change.

Schall and Kauffmann (2003) integrated lesbian and gay content through literature in Kauffman's fourth and fifth grade multiage class in Tucson. As in the Epstein study, the students read gay- and lesbian-themed picture books in small groups. The teacher intended for the class to then talk about the issue of name-calling in a thematic unit on survival. However, the students focused on family, relationships, and community, discussing how, when they were "confronted with situations they didn't understand, they responded in negative ways" (41). The students communicated their desire to understand all kinds of relationships, including lesbian and gay relationships, and asked why they had not been told about them. They reported that no adults in their lives provided information about being gay or lesbian and that they did not know whether it was appropriate to talk about this issue with family members. Although some adults question whether this topic is an appropriate topic in **childhood**, Schall and Kauffmann (2003, 31) found that "[c]hildren are capable of reading about and discussing sensitive social issues such as homosexuality when the children are a part of a classroom community that values dialogue and critical thinking." In fact, these students suggested that lesbian and gay literature be integrated throughout the school year through themes such as family, identity, relationships, and **discrimination**.

Literature can be used to integrate topics of sexual diversity into the classrooms of even the youngest children, as shown in the documentary film, *It's Elementary: Talking about Gay Issues in School* (Cohen and Chasnoff 1997). This video portrays teachers and students discussing lesbian and gay people in **urban** and suburban schools, both public and private, and in various content areas and grade levels. In one scene, teachers read aloud and discussed with their students *Asha's Mums* (Elwin and Paulse 1990), a picture book about a little girl whose teacher questions the fact that she has two mothers. Using developmentally appropriate pedagogy, these students understood and discussed the issues confronted by this girl.

Examining sexualities in the teaching of language arts requires small and large group discussions, that incorporate thinking *and* feeling and that are led by teachers who are active, honest, and intellectually oriented. In these settings, teachers allow for and create opportunities for students to play active roles in discussions, while listening intently to what their students have to say. The most effective discussions about same-sex desire are incorporated into larger discussions about diversity and sexuality.

Operating from a **queer theory** perspective, Sumara and Davis (1998) participated in a project in a grade five and six urban Canadian class. Students were reading *The Giver* (Lowry 1993). Although this novel does not have any character identifying as LGBT, it addresses the sexual **desire** of a twelve-year-old boy for one of his female peers. These desires, called the "stirrings," are forbidden in the community, except to this particular boy because of the particular role he has been assigned. Sumara and the classroom teacher facilitated discussions in which the children talked about the "stirrings," the suppression of them, and the main characters experiences with them. They also discussed their experiences of sexual desire and suppression. Although these discussions were centered on heterosexuality, the creation of classroom space for an honest and thoughtful examination of sexualities is critical in the development of an **antibias curriculum**.

While children's and young adult literature is often used as a catalyst for such discussions—thus incorporating the reading, speaking, and listening aspects of the language arts—it is also important to view films and other media and respond to these texts through discussion and writing. However, the existence of such media appropriate for elementary or middle school students is very limited. Two appropriate films for early adolescents are *The Truth about Jane* (Rose 2000) and *Out of the Past: 400 Years of Lesbian and Gay History in America* (Dupre 1997). The former is a about a fifteen-year-old girl who knows and comes to accept her lesbianism and then struggles to help her mother accept her as well. The latter is a historical overview of the many ways in which lesbian and gay people have been excluded from educational accounts of events in U.S. **history**.

In order to challenge **heterosexism** and **heteronormativity**, teachers need to be prepared to examine sexualities through their teaching of language arts in middle and elementary classrooms. This preparation includes knowledge about curriculum materials and educational resources, methods for integrating such content into their teaching of language arts, and a theoretical grounding for antioppressive pedagogies.

Bibliography

Cohen, Helen S. (Producer), and Debra Chasnoff (Producer and Director). 1997. *It's Elementary: Talking About Gay Issues in School* [Film]. (Available from Women's Educational Media, San Francisco, CA).

Dupre, Jeff (Producer/Director). 1997. *Out of the Past* [Motion picture]. United States: Out of the Past Film Project, Inc.

Epstein, Debbie. 2000. "Reading Gender, Reading Sexualities: Children and the Negotiation of Meaning in 'Alternative' Texts." Pp. 213–233 in *Lesbian and Gay Studies and the Teaching of English: Positions, Pedagogies, and Cultural Politics*. Edited by William J. Spurlin. Urbana, IL: National Council of Teachers of English.

Hamilton, Greg. 1998. "Reading *Jack*." *English Education* 30, no. 1: 24–43.

Letts, William J., and James T. Sears, eds. 1999. *Queering Elementary Education: Advancing the Dialogue about Sexualities and Schooling*. Lanham, MD: Rowman and Littlefield.

Lipkin, Arthur. 1994. "The Case for a Gay and Lesbian Curriculum." *The High School Journal* 77, nos. 1 and 2: 95–107.

National Council of Teachers of English and International Reading Association. 1996. *Standards for the English Language Arts*. Urbana, IL: National Council of Teachers of English.

Owens, Robert E., Jr. 1998. *Queer Kids: The Challenges and Promise for Lesbian, Gay, and Bisexual Youth*. Binghamton, NY: Harrington Park Press.

Rose, Lee (Director). 2000. *The Truth about Jane* [Motion picture]. United States: Starlight Home Entertainment.

Schall, Janine, and Gloria Kauffmann. 2003. "Exploring Literature with Gay and Lesbian Characters in the Elementary School." *Journal of Children's Literature* 29, no. 1: 36–45.

Sumara, Dennis, and Brent Davis. 1998. "Telling Tales of Surprise." Pp. 197–219 in *Queer Theory in Education*. Edited by William F. Pinar. Mahwah, NJ: Lawrence Erlbaum.

Web Sites

Center for Anti-Oppressive Education. May 2005. Accessed June 7, 2005. http://www.antioppressiveeducation.org/. Conducts teacher workshops catered to a particular school or district's needs that examines the intersections of various oppressions, including sexual.

Gay Lesbian Straight Education Network. June 2005. Accessed June 7, 2005. http://www.glsen.org/cgi-bin/iowa/home.html. Site has a "Resource Center" with a link to "Curricula" where there is a list of curricular topics that could be used to integrate LGBT content into the teaching of language arts. GLSEN also sponsors an annual national conference, "Teaching Respect for All," which is attended by educators as well as students.

The National Council of Teachers of English. 2005. Accessed June 7, 2005. http://www.ncte.org/. The National Council of Teachers of English has an Interest Action Group focused on Gay and Lesbian Issues in English and language arts education.

Latinos and Latinas

Jesse G. Monteagudo

Americans of Hispanic descent, now the largest ethnic minority in the United States, represent almost every known race, ethnic background, and religion. Therefore, Latinos and Latinas in the United States defy categorization. What ties them together is a common heritage, inherited from the Spaniards who conquered most of the Americas in the sixteenth century. Young **gay, lesbian, bisexual,** or **transgender** Latinos or Latinas—like heterosexual Latinos or Latinas—are heirs to this tradition; and their development as LGBT people is affected to a large extent by that tradition. Furthermore, as ethnic or racial minorities, Latinos and Latinas are victims of racist **prejudice, discrimination,** and **stereotypes.**

Unlike Anglo-Saxon colonists in North America, who only married within their racial or ethnic group, many Spanish colonists mated with Native Americans who they conquered or with the Africans whom they brought as slaves to "the New World." Thus a large part of the Latino/a population is mestizo (Native/European) or mulato (African/European). However, this does not take into account Latinos/as whose ethnic makeup is completely Native American, African, or Spanish (Creole); not to mention those whose ancestors came from other European nations, the Middle East, or Asia. In short, Latinos and Latinas represent a rainbow of races and ethnicities; and any attempt to classify or categorize Latinos or Latinas must take this mix into account. North Americans of Hispanic descent are also divided by religion, **social class,** politics, and circumstances; so that the experience of growing up as a working-class Mexican-American in Sacramento, California, is different from the experience of growing up as a middle-class Cuban-American in Miami, Florida (Monteagudo 1991; Nava 1991).

In spite of their differences, North American Latinos and Latinas share a set of cultural traditions inherited from Spain. Among other aspects of life, these traditions affect the ways that Latinos and Latinas view homosexuality. In this regard, the most important tradition is religious. When the Spanish conquered the land that is now Latin America, they imposed their Roman Catholic faith on the Native populations and on the newly-arrived African slaves, even as the new converts secretly kept aspects of their former faiths. As a result, an overwhelming majority of Latinos and Latinas are **Catholic,** if only formally so. And while many Latinos and Latinas have broken with their Catholic past, they retain the Church's negative view of homosexuality, which holds that homosexual acts are contrary to natural law.

Another cultural tradition that Latinos and Latinas inherited from Spain is the centrality of *La Familia* (The Family). As a rule, young Hispanics live with their

See also Activism, LGBT Youth; Adolescent Sexualities; Brazil, LGBT Youth and Issues in; Christian Moral Instruction on Homosexuality; Mexico, LGBT Youth and Issues in; Sexism; South America, LGBT Youth and Issues in.

biological relatives until marriage. Those who do not marry—unless they enter the priesthood or a religious order—continue to live "at home" indefinitely. This has a major impact on young LGBT Latinos or Latinas, who must place the needs and wishes of their biological families above their own gender, sexual, or social needs. Though many young Latinos and Latinas in the United States have adopted the Anglo tradition of living on their own after they reach majority, many others continue to follow the old tradition.

LGBT Latino and Latina youth are also adversely affected by the rigid gender system that Latin society inherited from Spain. Hispanic attitudes about **gender roles** are commonly referred to as *machismo*; however, it affects all genders. Basically, *machismo* holds that men are superior to women and that both men and women have specific gender roles and character traits that they must maintain. This attitude is carried over into sexual relations, where the male is the dominant and the female is the submissive partner. Any sexual or gender deviation is frowned upon, if not actively suppressed.

A traditional definition of sex on the basis of gender roles leads to a definition of homosexuality based on gender roles. Many Latino men who have sex with other men do not identify themselves as gay or even bisexual, as long as they assume the "male" or dominant role in sex. In fact, "topping other men (usually verbally or symbolically, but occasionally physically) is central to machismo, perhaps as important as maintaining the subordination of women" (Murray 1995, 55). Thus, in the Latino tradition, a homosexual male is a man who subverts *macho* norms. And while many young LGBT Latinos and Latinas in the United States (and in major Latin American cities) have managed to break with their traditions, *machismo* continues to have a major impact on the identity development of queer Latino youth. For many young gay Latinos, growing up gay is an act of rebellion against their communities' *macho* norms (Monteagudo 1991; Muñoz 1996; Nava 1991).

In addition to inhibiting the **identity development** of young Latino men, the *macho* tradition contributes to the spread of HIV/**AIDS** in Hispanic communities. Though Hispanics are only 13 percent of the population in the United States, they account for 19 percent of all new AIDS cases (Marchant 2004). According to recent studies, Latino "YMSM" (young men who have sex with men), especially those who do not self-identify as gay, are twice as likely to become HIV-infected as white YMSM. To many of these young men AIDS—when they think of it at all—is strictly a "gay disease," and they believe that they are personally "immune" from HIV (Franka 2002). Latino AIDS educator Rafael M. Díaz lists machismo, **homophobia**, family loyalty, sexual silence, poverty, and **racism** as factors that lead to high incidents of unprotected sex and HIV transmission among young Latinos. Thus, any **HIV education** program aimed at Latino YMSM needs to be "appropriate in both language and culture and that address their specific Latino community" (Franka 2002).

Though most Latina lesbians are not directly affected by HIV/AIDS—except through their loved ones—their development as autonomous, women-loving-women is also affected by Catholic, family, and *macho* traditions. Unlike young Latinos, who are allowed a great degree of freedom from an early age, Latinas grow up with many physical and emotional restrictions. "As Latinas," wrote the Chilean-American author Mariana Romo-Carmona, "we are supposed to grow up submissive, virtuous, respectful of elders and helpful to our mothers, long suffering, deferring to men, industrious, and devoted. We also know that any deviation from these expectations constitutes an act of rebellion, and there is great pressure to conform. Independence is discouraged, and we learn early that women who think for themselves are branded 'putas' or 'marimachas'" (Ramos 1987, xxvi).

Of course, not all the problems that queer Latino and Latina youth face come from their Hispanic communities. As racial or ethnic minorities in a mostly "Anglo" society, LGBT Latinos, like other minorities, must deal with white racism and its effects on their lives, including occasional violence and more frequent discrimination, especially against poor or immigrant Latinos. Latinos also suffer disproportionately from anti-immigrant sentiment, as expressed in laws or initiatives against bilingual education or against providing education or social services to illegal aliens. Added to these are various acts of social bigotry commonly experienced by all minorities. Within the mostly-white, queer community, anti-Latino/Latina prejudice is expressed in various ways, from outright hatred to the objectification of Hispanics as "hot Latin lovers" and exotic fantasy objects.

Despites these obstacles, Latinos and Latinas have contributed to their LGBT communities. Drag entertainer José Sarria, of Colombian and Nicaraguan parentage, was the first out LGBT person (of any race) to run for San Francisco City Supervisor (1961). The late Pedro Zamora, a Cuban-American, raised AIDS awareness on MTV's *The Real World*. An openly-gay Puerto Rican, Anthony D. Romero, is Executive Director of the American Civil Liberties Union (ACLU). America's LGBT literature would be poorer without the contributions of Chicanas/os John Rechy, Gloria Anzaldúa, Arturo Islas, Cherríe Moraga, and Michael Nava; Puerto Ricans Carmen de Monteflores, Luz María Umpierre, and Emanuel Xavier; Colombian Jaime Manrique; and Cuban-Americans Rafael Campo, Elías Miguel Muñoz, and Achy Obejas. Other well-known LGBT Latinos/as include community organizer Dilia Loe, Rev. Mari Castellanos, comic Marga Gómez, figure skater Rudy Galindo, artist Phil Jimenez, leather activist and author Mauro Montoya, and actors Guillermo Diaz and Wilson Cruz.

Though Latinos and Latinas play important roles in the LGBT movement, many are also involved in building independent, Latino/Latina LGBT organizations. In 1977 Miami's lesbian and gay Latinos formed *Latinos pro Derechos Humanos* (Latins for Human Rights) to combat Anita Bryant's "Save Our Children" campaign. Other historic LGBT Latina/Latino groups include *El Comité Homosexual Latinoamericano* (1978), *Lesbianas Unidas* (1980), and the Latina Lesbian History Project formed to publish the *Compañeras* anthology (Ramos 1987).

Since 1987, the most important LGBT Latino-Latina organization has been LLEGÓ (The National Latina/o Lesbian, Gay, Bisexual & Transgender Organization), a national organization that represents Latina/o LGBT communities and addresses their unique needs. LLEGÓ's *FuturoAqui* (Future's Here) and *Projecto Fénix* (Phoenix Project) deal with the special needs of LGBT Latina/o youth. Other valuable resources for young LGBT Latinos and Latinas are the "Latino/a Youth" section of youthresource and *qvMagazine: The Latino Men's Journal*.

Bibliography

Díaz, Rafael M. 1998. *Latino Gay Men and HIV: Culture, Sexuality, and Risk Behavior*. New York: Routledge.
Marchant, Robert. 2004. "AIDS Outreach Project Focuses on Hispanics." *The Journal News*. Accessed August 2, 2004. http://www.thejournal.com/newsroom/071204/a0112aids.htm.

Monteagudo, Jesse. 1991. "Miami, Florida." Pp. 11–20 in *Hometowns: Gay Men Write About Where They Belong*. Edited by John Preston. New York: Dutton.

Muñoz, Elías Miguel. 1996. "From the Land of Machos: Journey to Oz with My Father." Pp. 17–33 in *Muy Macho: Latino Men Confront Their Manhood*. Edited by Ray González; New York: Anchor Books.

Murray, Stephen O. 1995. "Machismo, Male Homosexuality, and Latino Culture." Pp. 49–70 in *Latin American Male Homosexualities*. Edited by Stephen O. Murray. Albuquerque: University of New Mexico Press.

Nava, Michael. 1991. "Gardenland, Sacramento, California." Pp. 21–29 in *Hometowns: Gay Men Write About Where They Belong*. Edited by John Preston. New York: Dutton.

Ramos, Juanita, ed. 1987. *Compañeras: Latina Lesbians (An Anthology)*. New York: Latina Lesbian History Project.

Trujillo, Carla, ed. 1991. *Chicana Lesbians: The Girls Our Mothers Warned Us About*. Berkeley: Third Woman Press.

Web Sites

Franka, Alex. 2002. "Latino Young Men Who Have Sex with Men: Unique Needs and Challenges." Advocates For Youth. Accessed May 30, 2005. http://www.advocatesforyouth.org/publications/transitions/transitions1404_8.htm. This essay, originally appearing in *Transitions*, Volume 14, No. 4, June 2002, is a concise study of the causes of, and the solutions for, the problem of HIV transmission among Latino YMSM.

LLEGÓ—The National Latina/o Lesbian, Gay, Bisexual, and Transgender Organization. October 2004. Accessed May 30, 2005. http://www.llego.org. Lists group's policy, upcoming events, programs and resources. Good source of news by and for the Latina/o GLBT communities.

qvMagazine: The Latino Men's Journal. 2005. Accessed May 30, 2005. http://www.qvmagazine.com. *qvMagazine: The Latino Men's Journal* is the United States's leading publication by and for gay Latino men. This site has articles from the magazine as well as links to other GLBT Latina/o sites.

youthresource: A Project of Advocates for Youth. 2005. "Latino/a Youth." Accessed May 30, 2005. http://www.youthresource.com/community/youth_of_color/latino/. The "Latino.a Youth" page is especially relevant to GLBT Latina/o youth.

Lavender Graduation

Laura E. Strimpel and *Ronni Sanlo*

Lavender graduation is a commencement celebration that honors the lives and achievements of **lesbian, gay, bisexual, transgender,** and queer (LGBTQ) students in colleges and universities in the United States. Lavender graduations recognize their accomplishments as they complete their education and establish community among LGBTQ students, faculty, and staff. The first lavender graduation occurred at the University of Michigan in 1995 after Ronni Sanlo, then director of the University of Michigan LGBT center, noticed the ethnic celebrations during commencement ceremonies the previous year. Sanlo named the event to commemorate the history of LGBTQ people, particularly homosexuals who were forced to wear

See also Agency; College Campus Programming; Identity Development; Mentoring.

the **pink triangle**s (black for lesbians) in Nazi concentration camps. By 2003, there were forty such events nationwide. There are no reports of lavender graduation celebrations occurring in high schools or in countries other than the United States.

Celebratory events such as commencement ceremonies place a sense of value on the lives and achievements of those students being honored. These are particularly important for lesbian, gay, bisexual, transgender, and queer students who have faced the challenge of developing identities as college students in addition to maturing as LGBTQ individuals. For many **college age students**, these special events reward students for persisting to graduation, for staying in school, despite the hardships, the marginalization, and the isolation they may have experienced.

With the development of LGBTQ **college campus resource centers**, **educational policies** that include **sexual orientation** and gender expression in **antidiscrimination policy**, and **school climates** that are generally supportive of LGBTQ students, these youth are searching for those institutions that have opportunities for developmental advancement. Institutions which host some form of lavender graduation ceremony acknowledge these students' accomplishments and further contribute to a more positive campus climate.

There are numerous components to hosting a lavender graduation. Advertisements are designed, food and decorations prepared, invitations created for students and their families and friends, as well as arrangements made for speakers, musicians, and special guests, such as political and social dignitaries. Various university departments and student affairs professionals show their support for the event by promoting lavender graduation among students, faculty, and staff. At the University

2004 Lavender Graduation, UCLA. Photograph by and Courtesy of Ronni Sanlo.

of California-Los Angeles (UCLA), lavender graduation is a collaborative event involving the LGBT Campus Resource Center, the LGBT Studies Department, the LGBT Faculty-Staff Network, the Lambda Alumni Association, and the LGBT student organizations. The Los Angeles and Ventura chapters of Parents and Friends of Lesbians and Gays (PFLAG) also participate in the event sponsorship.

Like many university commencement ceremonies, lavender graduations begin with a procession of faculty and staff who wear degree-appropriate regalia. Next, graduating students—from undergraduates to the professional schools—march to their seats to the music of Vox Femina Los Angeles, the lesbian and bisexual women's chorus. Students who earn the **LGBT Studies** minor receive their certificates. Community awards, leadership awards, and scholarships are also presented. Each graduate is given a rainbow tassel for their cap in addition to a Certificate of Distinction that reads:

> On the occasion of this UCLA Lavender Graduation ceremony, the Lesbian Gay Bisexual Transgender Campus Resource Center awards this Certificate of Distinction for outstanding contributions to our community as a scholar and a person of pride, integrity, and honor, to Joe Gay Bruin on this ___ of June, ____.

A reception follows.

Because LGBTQ students cross all lines of **race**, nationality, **ethnic identity**, gender, ability, and **social class**, this unique multicultural event acknowledges a population of students who are often invisible on college campuses. Lavender graduation, too, is an opportunity for institutions to acknowledge the diversity of the LGBTQ population on campus, to allow LGBTQ students a graceful exit, and to invite them to return as valued and generous alumni.

In 1999, the UCLA ceremony was nominated for the Outstanding Program Award by American College Unions International (ACU-I). In 2002, the National Association of Student Personnel Administrators named the UCLA Lavender Graduation as one of the top ten exemplary programs nationally in student affairs.

Bibliography

Kuh, George. D., John. H. Schuh, and Elizabeth Whitt. 1991. *Involving Colleges: Successful Approaches to Fostering Student Learning and Development Outside the Classroom.* San Francisco: Jossey Bass.

Sanlo, Ronni L., ed. 1998. *Working with Lesbian, Gay, Bisexual, and Transgender College Students: A Handbook for Faculty and Administrators.* Westport, CT: Greenwood.

———. 2000. "Lavender Graduation: Acknowledging the Lives and Achievement of Lesbian, Gay, Bisexual, and Transgender College Students." *Journal of College Student Development* 41, no. 6: 643–647.

Sanlo, Ronni L., Sue R. Rankin, and Robert Schoenberg. 2002. *Our Place on Campus.* Westport, CT: Greenwood.

Wall, Vernon, and Nancy Evans, eds. 2000. *Toward Acceptance: Sexual Orientation Issues OnCampus.* Lanham, MD: University Press of America.

Web Sites

National Consortium of Directors of Lesbian, Gay, Bisexual, and Transgender Resources in Higher Education. Accessed December 15, 2004. http://www.lgbtcampus.org/faq/lavender_graduation.html. The mission of the National Consortium includes

advocating for LGBT program development and the establishment of LGBT Office/
Centers; the Consortium supports the development of lavender graduation as a
program of campus LGBTQ resource centers and has information links to these
ceremonies on its Web site.

UCLA Lesbian Gay Bisexual Transgender Campus Resource Center. Accessed December 15,
2004. http://www.ucla.lgbt.edu/. The UCLA LGBT Center offers education,
information, and advocacy for LGBT issues. The Center encourages an inclusive and
safe environment for lesbian, gay, bisexual, transgender, same gender loving, and queer
students, staff, faculty, and their friends and families.

Lawrence v. Texas

James Anthony Whitson

In *Lawrence v. Texas* (2003), the Supreme Court of the United States struck down a
Texas law that criminalized sexual activity between consenting adults of the same
sex. The case itself does not give the same protection to minors that it provides for
adults engaging in private, consensual activity. However, the Court's action in another case, the day after it decided *Lawrence*, suggests that the *Lawrence* decision
may offer some protection for young people when government attempts to treat
sexual activity between same-sex couples differently than sexual activity between
young heterosexual couples. In *Kansas v. Limon* (2004), a case involving two
teenagers, the American Civil Liberties Union has argued that *Lawrence* actually
provides a much broader range of protections for sexual minorities, including
young people as well as adults, beyond matters just involving sexual activity. Moreover, even the protections that directly apply only to adults still have important
consequences for young people, since they affect programs, teachers, and others
serving young people of any and all sexual identities. Also important is the strong
and sweeping language of the opinions in *Lawrence*, which may have broad significance even beyond the legal consequences of the Court's decision.

The *Lawrence* case arose out of the prosecution of two adult men in Houston,
Texas. After someone had falsely reported a weapons violation, Houston police entered a home where they discovered John Lawrence and Tyrone Garner engaged in
private, consensual sexual activity. The two men were then arrested and found guilty
of violating a Texas law that made it a crime for anyone to engage in "deviate sexual
intercourse with another individual of the same sex." The men appealed their conviction, arguing that the criminal statute used to convict them violated two different
clauses of the Fourteenth Amendment to the Constitution of the United States.

In their appeal, Lawrence and Garner argued that the Texas law violated a fundamental right that is protected by the Due Process Clause of the Fourteenth
Amendment. Although they could make a logical argument for this conclusion, the
chances that this argument would succeed in the appellate courts were clouded by
the precedent of *Bowers v. Hardwick* (1986), a case in which the U.S. Supreme
Court upheld a Georgia law that made it a crime for anybody to engage in
"sodomy." In *Bowers*, the Supreme Court ruled that privacy rights protected under

See also Boy Scouts of America et al. v. Dale; Disabilities, Intellectual; Legal Issues, Students.

the Due Process Clause do not include any "fundamental right [of] homosexuals to engage in sodomy" (190).

The Texas law challenged in *Lawrence* was different in an important way from the law that was upheld in Georgia. The Georgia law made it a crime to engage in "sodomy" no matter whether the people involved were of the same sex or different sexes. The Texas law made it a crime if a person was the same sex as his or her partner, but not if they were different genders. This feature of the Texas law was challenged in the *Lawrence* appeal as a violation of the Equal Protection Clause of the Fourteenth Amendment, since it meant that whether or not someone was committing a crime did not depend on the activity, but on whether the person doing that activity was male or female, gay or straight.

When the Supreme Court decided the *Lawrence* case, Justice Sandra Day O'Connor wrote (in a decision concurring with the judgment of the Court) that the Texas law should be ruled unconstitutional because it did violate the Equal Protection Clause. In the majority opinion, Justice Kennedy agreed with O'Connor's conclusion that there was a violation of Equal Protection which, by itself, would be enough reason to strike down the Texas law; but Kennedy, joined by four other members of the Court, concluded that a decision based only on this Equal Protection violation would not go far enough. Instead, the majority in *Lawrence* not only threw out the Texas law, but also overruled *Bowers*.

Kennedy's opinion explained that there is, in fact, a fundamental right to liberty that was violated by both the Texas law in this case and the Georgia law in *Bowers*. Kennedy explained that the right in question is not just a right to engage in "homosexual sodomy," as the Court in *Bowers* had mistakenly assumed. Broader and more fundamental rights were violated by such statutes, which the Court now recognizes as seeking "to control a personal relationship that . . . is within the liberty of persons to choose without being punished as criminals" (*Lawrence*, 2478).

Kennedy marshaled an array of sources to show that intolerance of homosexuals and homosexuality is not so deeply rooted in our history and culture as proponents of these laws have claimed, and that in any case, opinions on these matters have been changing dramatically in the United States and around the world in recent years. Ultimately, however, constitutional rights are defined on the basis of principles inscribed in the Constitution, and not on cultural prejudices and ever-changing public opinion. Based on these principles, Kennedy spelled out the Court's conclusions:

> The present case does not involve minors. . . . The case does involve two adults who, with full and mutual consent from each other, engaged in sexual practices common to a homosexual lifestyle. The petitioners are entitled to respect for their private lives. The State cannot demean their existence or control their destiny by making their private sexual conduct a crime. Their right to liberty under the Due Process Clause gives them the full right to engage in their conduct without intervention of the government. (*Lawrence*, 2484)

Although the Court was careful to indicate that its decision applies directly only to adults, it followed this decision, the next day, by sending a case involving two teenagers back to the Kansas State Court of Appeals for reconsideration in light of the *Lawrence* ruling. *Kansas v. Limon* (2004) involves a young male,

Matthew Limon, who was convicted for having consensual oral sex with a younger male, at a time when Limon had just turned eighteen years old, and was just slightly more than three years older than his fourteen-year-old partner. For this act, Limon was convicted and given a seventeen-year prison sentence. If his partner in these same sorts of activities had been a fourteen-year-old girl rather than a boy, or if he had been a female eighteen-year-old engaged in these same activities with the same male partner, the maximum sentence possible under Kansas law would have been fifteen months in jail. The American Civil Liberties Union (ACLU) argued that this discrepancy in sentencing was unconstitutional under the Equal Protection Clause, since it discriminated against Limon on the basis of his gender and his homosexuality.

When the case was sent back to the state court for reconsideration after *Lawrence*, the ACLU argued that *Lawrence* establishes a broad scope of protection against unequal treatment of sexual minorities, both adults and minors, not only for private sexual activity but in a wide range of other areas as well. They argued that young people have a Constitutionally-protected interest in sexual liberty that the states do have the power to restrict, but only if the state has some reasonable basis for its legislation, and that discrimination against homosexuals cannot be recognized as a rational basis for legislation, especially in light of *Lawrence*.

On January 30, 2004, the Kansas Court of Appeals ruled that Limon's case would not be affected by the U.S. Supreme Court decision in *Lawrence*. The ACLU quickly announced that it would appeal the Kansas state court decision, which affirmed Limon's seventeen-year sentence, and upheld the state law's unequal treatment based on whether those engaged in sexual activity are of the same or different sexes. Oral arguments were heard by the Kansas Supreme Court in August 2004, but no decision has been announced.

Among the most important consequences of *Lawrence* for young people is that it demolishes a widely-used rationale for discriminating against homosexuals as teachers or other youth workers, and for banning services and activities supporting LGBTQ youth. In states with laws against homosexual activity, especially after *Bowers* but before *Lawrence*, it was claimed that homosexuals could be presumed to be engaged in criminal activity, and homosexual support efforts were supporting criminal activity; and these claims were used as justification for employment **discrimination** and program bans (see O'Connor, concurring in *Lawrence*, 2485–2486.) After *Lawrence*, such far-reaching consequences of laws against homosexuality will no longer be supported by the courts.

Bibliography

ACLU Lesbian & Gay Rights Project. 2002. *Making Schools Safe*. 2nd ed. Washington, D.C.: American Civil Liberties Union. Accessed June 9, 2005.PDF version available for downloading at http://www.aclu.org/LesbianGayRights/LesbianGayRights.cfm?ID=11187&c=106#FileAttach.

American Civil Liberties Union. Appellant's Opening Brief on Rehearing, before the Court of Appeals of the State of Kansas, in *Kansas v. Limon*. September 11, 2003. Accessed June 9, 2005. http://www.aclu.org/LesbianGayRights/LesbianGayRightsList.cfm?c=41&ContentStyle=6.

Bowers v. Hardwick, 478 U.S. 186 (1986).

Kansas v. Limon, Case No. 85,898. January 30, 2004. Court of Appeals of the State of Kansas. Accessed May 30, 2005. http://www.kscourts.org/kscases/ctapp/2004/20040130/85898.htm.

Lawrence v. Texas, 123 S. Ct. 2472 (2003).

Web Sites

ACLU Lesbian & Gay Rights Project Main Web page. May 2005. Accessed June 9, 2005. http://www.aclu.org/LesbianGayRights/LesbianGayRightsmain.cfm. One of the best sources for information about their own cases as well as news and background on struggles for equal rights.

Index of Archive, 2004 Court Hearings. August 2004. Accessed May 31, 2005. http://judicial.kscourts.org:7780/Archive/2004%20court%20hearings/Aug-Sept%202004/Tues%208-31-04/. Oral arguments in the Kansas Supreme Court of the Limon case available on-line (to download click 85898.mp3).

Legal Issues, Students

Benjamin Baez

Legal issues relate to principles contained in laws created by statutes or court cases. Such laws encompass many matters indirectly affecting queer students, such as mandatory schooling, but some relate directly to **lesbian, gay, bisexual** and **transgender** (LGBT) youth and establish specific legal rights. A legal right is granted by statute or created by courts to resolve disputes. A legal right offers LGBT youth protection from private individuals, as do **hate crimes** laws, or from schools or government officials, such as laws prohibiting **discrimination**. LGBT students are increasingly relying on courts for protection against discrimination, invasions of privacy, and violations of their freedoms of expressions and association—the three areas of law involving the most litigation.

In the United States, the Fourteenth Amendment of the federal Constitution prohibits discrimination by public schools; private schools are free from constitutional requirements. State constitutions similarly prohibit discrimination. Discrimination happens when students are denied rights or benefits guaranteed by law or school policy. LGBT students have little federal-constitutional protection against discrimination, but they have slightly more protection under state constitutions. But because federal constitutional law is paramount, it warrants specific discussion.

The lack of federal constitutional protection against discrimination for LGBT students may be explained partially by principles which require courts to review discrimination claims differently depending on the type of discrimination. For example, courts treat racial discrimination more seriously than they do other kinds of discrimination. Further, although gender discrimination is not treated as seriously as racial discrimination, it is also given special protection. The courts, however, do not treat **sexual orientation** as "gender," and so they have ruled that sexual orientation discrimination does not warrant special protection.

See also Activism, LGBT Teachers; Activism, LGBT Youth; College Campus Organizing; Educational Policies; School Safety and Safe School Zones.

On rare occasions, courts have struck down discriminatory policies. For example, in 1996 the U. S. Supreme Court, in *Romer v. Evans*, ruled unconstitutional a Colorado law removing protection for homosexuals in public agencies. LGBT students would have been penalized by such a law since public schools are public agencies. Sixteen years earlier, a federal court, in *Fricke v. Lynch*, upheld the right of a gay student to take another boy to his **prom**. This case, however, hinged more on the student's freedom of expression than his antidiscrimination rights. In 1996, another federal court held, in *Nabozny v. Podlesny*, that a school that failed to protect a gay student from pervasive **harassment** by other students violated the Fourteenth Amendment.

The Fourteenth Amendment, however, is not the only law prohibiting discrimination. The federal government often has extended rights beyond those guaranteed by the Constitution, protecting, for example, the rights of students with disabilities under such laws as the Individuals with Disabilities in Education Act of 1975 and Section 504 of the Rehabilitation Act of 1973. Thus, LGBT students with HIV or **AIDS** are protected against discrimination in schools.

No federal law exists specifically prohibiting discrimination against LGBT students, but such students have gained limited rights under Title IX of the Education Amendments of 1972, prohibiting gender discrimination. Since Title IX requires schools to protect students from **sexual harassment**, LGBT students have protection against sexual-orientation harassment—if such harassment is severe and pervasive *and* if school officials deliberately failed to prevent it. For example, a federal court held in *Henkle v. Gregory* in 2001 that students can recover damages under Title IX from schools that fail to control such harassment.

Despite Title IX, LGBT students have little protection against discrimination under federal law. Some states, however, specifically prohibit sexual-orientation discrimination in certain situations. Massachusetts, for example, specifically prohibits sexual orientation discrimination in any school activity or benefit. In addition, "public accommodation" laws in California, Connecticut, Hawaii, Massachusetts, Minnesota, New Jersey, Wisconsin, and the District of Columbia prohibit such discrimination by agencies serving the public, such as schools. These laws can be used by LGBT students to prohibit sexual-orientation discrimination in certain school activities. For example, a federal court in the 1987 case of *Gay Rights Coalition of Georgetown University Law Center v. Georgetown University* used such a law in the District of Columbia to prohibit Georgetown University from denying access to a progay student group.

Furthermore, LGBT students can assert state constitutional rights against school districts for discrimination in guaranteed academic activities. Unlike gay teachers in some states, LGBT students cannot be dismissed from school or be denied an educational benefit, such as textbooks, transportation, and **physical education**, because of their sexual orientation. All state constitutions give children the right to a free education and its benefits, at least up until the age of sixteen. LGBT students thus gain substantial rights in public schools, simply because they are students, such as being protected from dismissal simply because they are gay (whereas teachers in some states can be so dismissed).

In some cases, however, a state law or school district policy specifically barring sexual orientation discrimination can be overridden by federal law. For example, Congress' "Don't Ask, Don't Tell" policy for the military allows discrimination against **college students** seeking ROTC participation if they are suspected of being gay. This policy applies only to active service persons, so technically the Junior Reserve Officer Training (JROTC) programs in high schools are not subject to such a policy and should not be able to discriminate, even though they often do. A number of colleges, such as Columbia University and Harvard University, have applied their **antidiscrimination policies** to bar ROTC from their campuses, and similar policies at the public school level, such as that in the St. Paul public schools, have prevented establishment of JROTC programs. But lawmakers have threatened to remove financial support to those institutions that prohibit ROTC or JROTC.

Unlike the right to be free from discrimination, the right to privacy is not specifically mentioned in the Constitution but arises from other specific rights, such as the freedom from unwarranted searches and the right to due process, which prohibits the denial of rights without legitimate reasons. No court has granted LGBT students a constitutional right to privacy, but LGBT students have indirectly gained some privacy rights. For example, the Family Educational Rights and Privacy Act of 1973 protects students' educational records from illegal disclosure. With regard to LGBT students, information in school records may include notes by counselors and teachers, incidents of harassment against LGBT students, and other matters suggesting their sexual orientation. This law, however, also gives parents of minors equal access to their children's records.

Whatever privacy rights exist, LGBT youth have fewer rights than adults. For example, many states require parental notification for minors seeking HIV testing. Also, student lockers and personal belongings can be searched easily by school officials. Furthermore, **Internet** use by students can be restricted. Filtering technology allows schools to limit students' access to Web sites, a practice justified by the Children's Internet Protection Act of 2000. Courts recognize the authority of legislators and school officials to protect children from "obscene" or "profane" materials. Since expressions of nonheterosexuality, whether or not sexual in nature, are often considered obscene or profane, these filtering policies affect LGBT students more negatively than other students. Thus, students who would otherwise have access, through schools computers, to hundreds of Web sites that speak frankly about homosexuality (information often unavailable in classrooms), are denied access.

The question of whether students have rights to express themselves over the Internet, as opposed to merely receiving information, is a bit more complex. Courts usually recognize students' limited rights to express themselves in other venues. While courts uphold censorship of sexually-explicit or threatening expression, they are less likely to support restriction of other viewpoints. Therefore, if access to a Web site is permitted by schools, then expressing progay views probably cannot be prohibited.

The right to express oneself over the Internet relates to both privacy and freedom of expression or speech. Ever since *Tinker v. Des Moines Independent Community School District*, in which the Supreme Court upheld students' rights to protest the Vietnam War, students have had a First Amendment freedom of expression. The Court has since narrowed this freedom, giving school officials extensive authority to censor expression in student newspapers and other school-sponsored activities, a practice permitted by the 1988 case, *Hazelwood School District v. Kuhlmeier*. Thus, school officials can restrict or prohibit discussion of LGBT issues in classes and other school-sponsored activities. Courts have also given schools authority to dictate attire and to limit symbols on clothing, allowing schools to forbid **queer** youth from expressing themselves through their clothing (e.g., wearing a **pink triangle**). But in such cases, the schools would have to prohibit all forms of expression in clothing since singling out progay (or even antigay) expression would likely be illegal censorship of particular viewpoints.

Similarly, while schools may not prohibit progay expression in clothing if they permit other forms of expression, the Equal Access Act of 1984 makes it illegal for public schools receiving federal financial assistance to deny access during non-instructional time to student-initiated groups because of their religious, political, or philosophical beliefs, *if the schools also give access to other groups.* Unless all groups are barred, LGBT students may form organizations and hold meetings during noninstructional time. Nevertheless, some school officials have tried to prohibit pro-LGBT groups, but public school students have gained rights under the First Amendment's freedom of association principles. In an illustrative case, a federal court in 2000 (*Colin v. Orange Unified School District*) prohibited the school from denying access to a **gay–straight alliance**.

The public school cases follow closely those in higher education a generation earlier in which courts ruled in favor of LGBT groups. Furthermore, it is unlikely that courts will support denial of funding to LGBT groups, and they have upheld the rights of schools to fund LGBT organizations despite challenges by students claiming to be offended by them. For example, the 2000 Supreme Court case of *Board of Regents of the University of Wisconsin System v. Southworth* upheld a university's mandatory student fees after it was challenged by students refusing to pay for groups "offensive to their personal beliefs," such as progay campus groups.

Courts have been less supportive of LGBT students when it comes to **curriculum** decisions, such as those regarding books for inclusion in libraries. There have been repeated attempts by public schools to ban **literature** with "gay" themes. For example, a school district in California was sued recently for pulling biographies of gays and lesbians. Despite students' challenges to schools' authority to ban books, courts generally give schools the right to choose its books, although the 1982 Supreme Court case of *Board of Education v. Pico* indicated that school boards cannot simply ban books with which they disagree, and they must have a legitimate educational reason for doing so. This case related to books in the school library; in matters of curricula, however, school boards are given extensive discretion. Schools likely can ban the discussion of LGBT issues, a practice permitted by the *Hazelwood* case discussed previously.

Finally, the freedom of expression plays an important role in challenges to "hate speech" policies, which prohibit harassment against particular social groups, such as LGBT students. While some courts have upheld antiharassment policies in public schools under the rationale that schools may legitimately promote respect and civility, courts usually are uncomfortable with what they deem to be censorship of particular views and sometimes rule that such policies violate the freedom of students to express their views. School policies that increase the penalty for violence motivated by **prejudice**, however, are legal. Thus, a school may not be able to censor antigay expression but it can impose a stricter penalty on a student who abuses another because of the other's sexual orientation.

Much of this discussion applies to both LGBT college students as well as those in K-12 schools. College students, however, are often considered adults by courts, and thus they are entitled to greater privacy rights and greater freedom to choose courses of study and books. But unlike students in public schools, college students are not guaranteed their education by law. Barring laws prohibiting discrimination against LGBT students, they are not entitled to college benefits.

Bibliography

Cameron-McCabe, Nelda, Martha McCarthy, and Stephen B. Thomas. 2004. *Public School Law: Teachers' and Students' Rights*, 5th ed. Boston, MA: Allyn and Bacon.
Conte, Alba. 1998. *Sexual Orientation and Legal Rights*, New York: Wiley.
Fricke, A. 1980. *Confessions of a Rock Lobster*. Boston, MA: Alyson.
Rubenstein, William. 1994. "Since When is the Fourteenth Amendment Our Route to Equality? Some Reflections on the Construction of the "Hate Speech." Pp. 280–299 in *Speaking of Race, Speaking of Sex: Hate Speech, Civil Rights, and Civil Liberties*. Edited by Henry Louis Gates, Jr., Anthony Griffin, Donald E. Lively, Robert C. Post, William B. Rubenstein, and Nadine Strossen. New York: New York University Press.

Web Sites

Lesbian and Gay Rights. December 2004. American Civil Liberties Union. Accessed December 7, 2004. http://www.aclu.org/LesbianGayRights/LesbianGayRightsMain.cfm. This comprehensive site detailing the activities of the ACLU includes information about the legal rights of LGBT youth.
Youth and Schools. December 2004. Lambda Legal Defense and Education Fund. Accessed December 7, 2004. http://www.lambdalegal.org/cgi-bin/iowa/issues/record?record=12. Provides information about school-related court cases filed by the Lambda Legal Defense and others.

Lesbian Feminism

Glorianne M. Leck

Lesbian feminism is a movement that merges feminist thinking with lesbian **identity politics**. The actions of lesbian feminists reflect resistance to the assumption that if you are born female you should "naturally" and/or always be sexually attracted to males and devoted to their emotional needs. In the past generation, lesbian feminism often bridged two groups, lesbians and feminists, and it positioned itself in contrast to each. They contrasted with women's rights advocates who were heterosexual and inclined to work for women's rights while still investing most of their energy in their intimacy with men. The lesbian feminists were also unlike women who identified as gay and not as feminist. Lesbian feminists worked for the rights of all women. A new generation of lesbian feminists has been building on this legacy as these feminists challenge the **school climate** with its singular focus on heterosexual **dating** rituals and the narrow teaching of patriarchal history, which devalues women's culture and the historical conditions of the oppression of women and children. As in the emphasis of **gay–straight alliances**, the lesbian feminists brought together two groups with a shared concern, liberation from gender **stereotypes** and the rules that privilege boy–girl dating over all other social arrangements, sexual partnerships, friendships, and families.

Feminist **philosophy**, put most simply, argues that one's birth should not (and need not) determine one's social status and social worth. (It is important to note that **feminism** logically extends to other birth features such as **race**, **social class**, body appearance, **disabilities**.) The feminist effort has been to raise consciousness about and alter the way society, through its educational, political, and religious

See also Internet, Lesbians and the; Psychoanalysis and Feminism; Women's Colleges.

institutions, has privileged heterosexual male persons and so-called masculine be-haviors. Consciousness-raising has resulted in and come from **women's studies** re-search and courses, community projects organized around battered women centers and efforts for pay equity, and through the arts of **poetry**, **literature**, and **film**.

A French existentialist, Simone deBeauvoir, wrote a very significant book, *The Second Sex*, read by many college students during the early 1960s. From deBeauvoir's concerns about gender equity and human freedom arose feminist concerns about sexual freedom. Feminists fought for the availability of birth control and encour-aged safe and legal abortion. These issues merged nicely with lesbian feminist con-cerns about sexual choice and freedom in **gender role** expression. The movement for control over one's body as well as economic circumstances was vital to women's liberation, feminism, and lesbian feminism.

It was in this effort to change the patriarchal assumptions about birth features and social worth that feminists, womanists, and lesbian feminists merged in their actions. Regardless of the basic belief as to whether lesbianism is a birth-given char-acteristic or an acquired sexual preference, most lesbian feminists came to an agree-ment that just acknowledging one's lesbianism or lesbian sexual preference and making that **sexual identity** public (**coming out** of the closet) was, and is, a chal-lenge to patriarchy and institutional controls over women's sexuality. It is on and around this point that much of lesbian feminist culture has developed.

Coming out and saying that you are a lesbian, or even saying you are **bisexual** can be an important lesbian feminist political act. It has been important that some women with a lot of visibility with the public in **sports** and entertainment have done that kind of coming out. Some of the best known of these have been Martina Navrat-alova, Rita Mae Brown, Deidre McCalla, Ellen DeGeneris, Melissa Etheridge, k.d. lang, Ani Difranco, Alix Dobkin, Holly Near, Alice Walker, Chastity Bono, and Rosie O'Donnell.

Lesbian feminism has drawn from a number of political movements that began to gain momentum or developed fully after World War II, notably lesbian/gay rights, civil rights, and **women's rights movements**. Each is relevant to and has con-tributed to the political development of lesbian feminism. Prior to some of these mid-century developments, liberation occurred in many countries, such as the work of young and energetic women in turn-of-the century Europe like Anna Rueling (Faderman 1980), suffragettes in England and the United States, and the many women who fought for their human and female dignity in many and varied inter-national workplace and political settings.

In the United States, names and stories that testify to courage in the face of conflict are those of Phyllis Lyon, Del Martin and others who in the 1950s devel-oped a lesbian organization, the Daughters of Bilitis, which published a national magazine. Editorial responsibilities for publication of *The Ladder* were assumed by Barbara Giddings in 1962. Writers such as Barbara Grier wrote in *The Ladder* under the name of Gene Damon. (Grier and her partner later founded Naiad Press, and that became a primary source for much of lesbian fiction writing.) *The Ladder* was made available nationally to women eager to learn and understand more about their own and other lesbian lives And the Daughters of Bilitis, with chapters in var-ious cities, provided scholarships to young lesbians. Many of these lesbians were feminists, and later their politics helped form coalitions with others from move-ments for civil rights and human rights. These lesbians began a movement that an-nounced a certain politic and pride in accepting their nonheterosexual identities.

A second movement of the 1950s and 1960s, influencing the political climate in the United States and fostering lesbian feminism, was the civil rights movement. These activists challenged **discrimination** based on racial features and skin color. There were womanists (a name preferred by some feminists of color) and women "in the life" who were active in civil rights and who saw connections between the racial and sexual **prejudices** that compounded their circumstances. Gay men and lesbian women who took their place along side other civil rights marchers included Bayard Rustin and Audre Lord. Lesbian feminists also recognized and promoted the pioneer writings of Barbara Smith, Maria Lugones, Cherrie Moraga, Gloria Anzaldua, Minnie Pratt, and bell hooks as each described some of the connections between and among oppressed groups of women.

The women's liberation movement of the 1960s was a third force that called people to a consciousness about the consequences of denying women equal economic and leadership opportunities. Lesbians quickly learned about heterosexual privilege. Some rather vocal women in the National Organization for Women actually referred to lesbians as the "lavender menace." Nevertheless, this movement set the stage for lesbian feminists to make their case to other women who were at least somewhat familiar with feminism and most of whom were ready to stand side-by-side with lesbians in the feminist struggle.

Lesbian feminists in the 1970s drew from each of the political movements of the previous two decades, but drew most strongly from feminist philosophy. One's **sexual orientation**, gender, availability for or interest in reproduction and/or one's sexual **biology**, they argued, should not determine one's social worth.

Not all who identified as lesbian feminists agreed on political strategies. There were (and are) particularly difficult disputes about whether lesbianism is to be understood as a sexual preference or a genetic predisposition. These differing viewpoints play out in many ways in lesbian lifestyle including disputes about what we call ourselves: wimmin, womyn, dykes, qweer, feminist, womanist, lesbians.

Among the early young lesbian feminist activists were those in groups such as the Furies and the Radicalesbians, who took the word "dyke," arguing that we must not let others use such words to intimidate and scare. Radicalesbians and other lesbian feminists were sometimes known to argue that any woman who truly wanted to change the system of male dominance should show her resistance either by joining intimately with women or at the least by standing apart from the patriarchal system of **compulsory heterosexuality** that had created the problems of sex role stereotyping and gender inequity. Withholding sexual favors was seen by some women (and many men) as lesbian feminist recruiting. Invested in heterosexuality, many women had difficulty believing in or being interested in this sexual freedom.

This rejection of lesbian feminists within some parts of the women's rights movement certainly encouraged lesbians within the movement to plant their feet in the lesbian feminist activists' circle. With the publication by Daughters Inc. Press of Rita Mae Brown's novel, *Rubyfruit Jungle* in 1973, Meg Christian's performance of her "Ode to A Gym Teacher" outside of the convention of the National Organization for Women in Philadelphia in 1975 and the Michigan Women's Music Festival, which began in 1976, lesbians clearly announced the presence of a culture apart from the mainstream women's liberation movement. These cultural events were an invitation to many who entered the women's rights arena to get in touch with their early **crush**es on their role models, and on the women they loved and those who had loved them.

Such a significant movement has produced a niche within Western culture and it has many whose names and work deserve recognition for their contributions to the beginnings as well as the furtherance of lesbian feminist culture. Early daring political writers, performers, and movement activists such as Radicalesbians, Rita Mae Brown, Ti grace Atkinson, Charlotte Bunch, Mary Daly, Kate Millett, Adrienne Rich, Cheryl Clark, Pat Parker, Diedre McCalla, Chris Williamson, Olivia Records, *Lesbian Connection*, and *Off Our Backs* have earned their place in lesbian feminist "herstory." Their politics are being carried on by many contemporary lesbian feminists such as singer Jamie Anderson, performance artist Alix Olson, comic strip developer Alison Bechdel, and comedians Kate Clinton, Karen Williams, Margo Gomez, and Margaret Cho.

Lesbian feminism continues to thrive through movies, television, the visual arts, stage performance, poetry, newsletters, **zines**, novels, dress, and body art. Perhaps the most reliable place to find an appreciation for and reflections upon lesbian feminism is by taking women's studies courses and attending lesbian feminist concerts, readings, and theatrical events. There, too, are those who want to live and work only with other lesbians (separatism). They have created many strong, vocal, and active lesbian feminist separatist communities and events, which also generate a significant part of lesbian political culture (Hoagland & Penelope 1988).

In other lesbian communities, lesbian feminist politics are viewed negatively. Some lesbians are more inclined to simply try to slip between the cracks of the gender wars and climb the ladders of economic success individually, on their merit, in their closet. Those lesbians, like their heterosexual women's rights counterparts, often see association with "out" lesbians as a risk to their social and political well-being.

Although lesbian feminists have long been seen as the more mainstream political activists in the lesbian community, lesbian feminists dispute this, arguing that all personal actions and sexual choices by women are political and have political consequences. What defines most of lesbian feminist politics is the effort to remove patriarchal values that give social and economic privileges exclusively for the promotion of male power and compulsory heterosexuality. Everyday efforts to call attention to the sexism in our school **curriculum** and in school social life promotes a change in perspective which in turn can generate more choices and possibilities for both women and men.

Bibliography

Abbott, Sidney, and Barbara Love. 1973. *Sappho Was a Right-on Woman*. New York: Stein and Day.

De Beauvoir, Simone. 1953. *The Second Sex*. New York: Knopf.

Faderman, Lillian. 1991. *Odd Girls and Twilight Lovers*. New York: Columbia University Press.

Faderman, Lilian, and Brigette Erikson. 1980. *Lesbian-Feminism in Turn-of-the-Century Germany*. Weatherby Lake, MO: Naiad Press.

Hoagland, Sarah Lucia, and Julia Penelope. 1988. *For Lesbians Only*. London: Onlywomen Press.

Jay, Karla. 1999. *Tales of the Lavender Menace: A Memoir of Liberation*. New York: Basic.

Martin, Del, and Phyllis Lyon. 1972. *Lesbian Woman*. New York: Bantam.

Web Sites

Lesbian Feminism Miscelanea. November 5, 2001. National Capital Freenet Services. Accessed June 7, 2005. http://www.ncfca/freeport/sigs/life/gay/lez/menu. Current discussions and positions on lesbian feminism and lesbian youth.

Lesbian History Project. March 2005. Accessed June 7, 2005. http://www-lib.usc.edu/~retter/main.html. Includes historical materials, links, and scholarship, including lesbians of color.

Lesbian Youth

James T. Sears

The word "lesbian" originated from the mythic Isle of Lesbos. Although women who prefer emotional and sexual relations with other women have been described by various terms, generally it has been as an appendage to male homosexuality or **gay youth**. From research studies to criminal statutes, the lesbian has generally been invisible in most societies. Consequently, there has been relatively little attention to lesbian youth within social or educational institutions. For example, **HIV education** and **research** on lesbian youth is less common than for gay youth, and availability of lesbian images in the media or lesbian-based Web sites is far more limited than for gay males. With the "second wave" of the **women's movement**—corresponding to the later quarter of the twentieth century—interest and commitment to lesbian issues have grown. **Lesbian–feminism,** in particular, has provided both the theoretical and political frameworks for invigorating study into lesbian youth and for providing services to these young people. Nevertheless, there is scant research on or support for—or even visibility of—lesbian youth of color, such as **Asian American, Latina,** and **African American** youth.

Early research into lesbian youth paralleled that of gay youth, especially with respect to **identity development** models. Using some version of a linear stage theory, these models posited that youth—gay or lesbian—proceeded through specific stages of identity development, culminating in "coming out" to themselves, friends, family, and the society. If these models did not correspond well to gay youth, then their correspondence to lesbian youth was even weaker. For instance, lesbians are more likely to report same-gender feelings and to identify as a lesbian prior to sexual activity. Moreover, sexual activity is much more likely to begin as heterosexual. For example, Australian researchers have found that these sexual relationships are generally with friends and are more likely to involve heterosexual sex (Hillier et al. 1998). Heterosexual relationships also often include **sexual abuse and assault**. In fact, one-quarter of lesbian and bisexual girls report attempted sexual violence compared to 6 percent of their heterosexual counterparts (Bontempo and D'Augelli 2002; Fineran 2001). This is even worse for lesbians with developmental **disabilities**, which one research study documents at a rate 1.5 times higher than for gay youth with disabilities; the rate was about twice that of the general population (McCreary Centre 1993).

For adolescent lesbians, demarcated by the age at which the ovaries mature—on average at the age of twelve—youth is generally defined in terms of risks associated

See also Adolescent Sexualities; AIDS; Community LGBT Youth Groups; Compulsory Heterosexuality; Crush; Passing; School Climate, K-12; Sexism; Spirituality; Women's Studies; Youth Culture; Youth At Risk; Youth, Homeless.

with lesbianism. These risks are often differentiated by gender (when studies are large enough to conduct such analyses). For example, the use of **alcohol** among adolescent lesbians has been found to be greater than among gay/bisexual males, whereas the reverse is true among heterosexual males and females (Orenstein 2001; Rosario, Hunter, and Gwadz 1997). One-half of the lesbian youth reported drinking during the previous 30 days compared to one-third of the gay youth—but there were no such gender differences within the heterosexual group.

Lesbian youth have also been found to be at risk for homelessness and **prostitution** (Cochran et al. 2002; Saewyc et al. 1998). Lesbianism, too, has been identified as a risk factor for pregnancy (Rotheram-Borus and Fernandez 1995; Ryan and Futterman 1998). For those who understand **biology** from a heteronormative perspective, this finding would appear nonsensical. But, some lesbian young persons may choose to pass as heterosexual while others seek to experiment or simply to have a child of one's own, proving their femininity and heterosexuality. However, sexual experimentation prior to self-identification as lesbian generally comes at an earlier age than for heterosexual female adolescents, and lesbian youth are less likely to use contraceptives. In one large-scale survey study of Minnesota youth, lesbian (and bisexual) youth were just as likely to engage in heterosexual intercourse and *twice* as likely to experience pregnancies as heterosexual young persons (Saewyc et al. 1999)—a finding that has been confirmed elsewhere (Bridget et al. 2003).

Young lesbians confront challenges worldwide. In research within Zimbabwe, even lesbians who have "come out" may continue to marry and have families, fulfilling their family obligations and ensuring an extended family should there be financial burdens (Epprecht 1998). Similarly, in **Japan**, many lesbians understand that heterosexual marriage preserves their families' reputation while insuring economic stability, in a country where careers for women are still severely limited.

Lesbians also face bullying and harassment—due to their gender and their **sexual orientation**. Despite a general leniency to **gender role** transgression in **childhood**—the **tomboy stereotype**—there is less tolerance for mannish behaviors or engaging in masculine-related activities during adolescence, with epithets like "dyke," often hurled at them. In **physical education**, adolescent girls, who have put away their dolls of childhood, often distance themselves from their physical education teachers who display such cross-gender behaviors, or do not engage in those sports that require any degree of physical stamina (with the exception of cheer leading) due to its association with masculinity (Cockburn and Clarke 2002). And, in sports, lesbian athletes have had to adopt a variety of passing strategies in order to be successful both as athletes and as women athletes on all-female teams (Griffin 1998).

The rates of victimization of lesbian youth are noteworthy. In one study, one out of ten lesbians (or bisexual women) reported being victimized compared to only 1 percent of their heterosexual peers (Bontempo and D'Augelli 2002;

"Dyke" Doll was displayed on a blanket by Marge "Clearwater," one of the pseudonymous leaders of an early lesbian group in Norfolk, as hundreds of thousands gathered for the first march on Washington on a chilly Sunday in 1979. Button to the left reads: "National March for Lesbian & Gay Rights, October 14." Courtesy of Marge "Clearwater" Reed.

Fineran 2001). However, there is somewhat more toleration for sexual behavior among lesbian than for gay youth, in part due to the invisibility of lesbianism in some societies, the assumption that women are simply less sexual, or the titillation that lesbianism holds for some heterosexual men. In **Latino** culture, for instance, girls and women develop close emotional relations, and physical relations may become part of this. In China, frequently young women can express same-sex intimacy and relationships in school settings without significant problems (Li 1998). Nigerian girls can engage in activities which could be construed as "lesbian," but since sex is culturally defined as heterosexual intercourse, these same-sex behaviors are merely considered "playing," and may well extend into adulthood, resulting in same-sex coupling (Emecheta 1989).

The invisibility of lesbianism coupled with the marginality of women is evidenced and reinforced in schools. For example, although greater emphasis has been placed on **women's history** and equal access through legislation, such as Title IX in the United States and The Sex Discrimination Act in the United Kingdom, the curriculum—particularly the sciences and sexuality education—remains firmly male-centered and heterosexual. An evaluation of a **sexuality education** program in the Australian state of Victoria, for example, found meager knowledge coverage or student knowledge of homosexuality, particularly lesbianism, and—as in many other studies—a focus on heterosexual reproduction and a male-centered approach (Harrison 2000). Similar findings are reported in the **United Kingdom** (YWCA 2004). The groundbreaking scholarship of Emily Martin (1991), for example, that found depiction of the egg as a passive object eagerly awaiting reception by sperm, is often cited in the literature and remains prevalent in textbooks and pedagogy.

Not only is most **curriculum** and pedagogy male-centered and heterosexist, but research on queer youth, including lesbians, is focused squarely on a deficit model wherein risks associated with lesbianism cloud the strengths and resilience that young women bring to their lives despite living in a society contoured by patriarchy, misogyny, and **homophobia**. In one survey of **urban** school districts, however, 48 percent of the girls enrolled were lesbian-identified (Friedrichs 1995). Research on **resiliency** among lesbian youth is nearly absent. Also, few studies have been done on leadership roles that lesbian youth play in organizations. Sororities, long a bastion of heterosexual desire and marital grooming, has been a site for such leadership with the founding of Lambda Delta Lambda at the University of California at Los Angeles in 1988 (http://userwww.sfsu.edu/~ldlbeta). Despite problems of discrimination and homophobia, women associated with this sorority, as well as lesbian youth leaders in mainstream **sororities,** have found a site both to express their talents and to support their own development (Windmeyer and Freeman 2000).

Support for all queer youth remains lacking both in schools and in the larger society. For lesbians, however, it is difficult to find positive images in the media (*The L Word*, for instance, features no regular character in contrast to *Queer as Folk*, which has several gay youth characters), and there are relatively few **Internet** sites exclusively for lesbian youth. In **popular culture**, aside from a few coded television shows like *Xena, Warrior Princess*, and *Laverne and Shirley*, or cancelled ones once the main character comes out, such as *Ellen*, lesbian youth find cultural images mostly outside the mainstream. These include **queer zines** like the *Grrrlzine Network* (http://grrrlzines.net) and the **comics** of Alison Bechdel (*Dykes to Watch Out For*), the punk rock music of San Francisco's dyke background Tribe 8, and well-received but poorly distributed **films** like *Heavenly Creatures* (New Zealand

1994), *If These Walls Could Talk 2* (USA 2000) and *The Truth about Jane* (USA 2001). More extensive materials can be found in **literature**, including young adult novels such as Jacqueline Woodson's multiracial story *House You Pass on the Way* (1997), Lois-Ann Yamanaka's *Name Me Nobody* (1999), *Keeping You a Secret* (Peter 2003), and *What Happened to Lani Garver* (Plum-Ucci 2002). Yet, this genre focuses much more on gay or bisexual youth, is essentialistic in its orientation, and generally features urban settings with Caucasian characters.

Similarly, youth groups truly inclusive of young lesbians or solely for them are still difficult to find. In **Japan**, the Bilitis Lesbian and Bi-Women Resource Center give attention to the needs of young lesbian and bisexual women, but there is no single lesbian youth group in the country. In Europe, lesbian youth can find solace in *Diva*, which has some youth focus, or more general youth publications such as *Bliss*, but there is no publication explicitly for lesbian youth in Europe.

Bibliography

Bridget, Jan, Angela Hodgson, Andy Mullen, and Peter Smith. 2003. "Sexual Health." In: *Calderdale Lesbian and Gay Health Action Plan*. Accessed December 6, 2004. http:// www.lesbianinformationservice.org/sexual3.rtf.

Bontempo, Daniel E., and Anthony R. D'Augelli. 2002. "Effects of At-School Victimization and Sexual Orientation on Lesbian, Gay, or Bisexual Youths' Health Risk Behavior." *Journal of Adolescent Health* 30: 364–374.

Cochran, Bryan N., Angela J. Stewart, Joshua A. Ginzler, and Ana Mari Cauce. 2002. "Challenges Faced by Homeless Sexual Minorities: Comparison of Gay, Lesbian, Bisexual, and Transgender Homeless Adolescents with Their Heterosexual Counterparts." *American Journal of Public Health* 92: 773–777.

Cockburn, Claudia, and Gill Clarke. 2002. "'Everybody's Looking at You!' Girls Negotiating the 'Femininity Deficit' They Incur in Physical Education." *Women's Studies International Forum* 25, no. 6: 651–665.

D'Augelli, Anthony. 1998. "Lesbian and Gay Male Development: Steps Toward an Analysis of Lesbians' and Gay Men's Lives." Pp. 118–132 in *Lesbian and Gay Psychology: Theory, Research, and Clinical Applications. Psychological Perspectives on Lesbian and Gay Issues, Vol. 1*. Edited by Beverley Greene and Gregory Herek. Thousand Oaks, CA: Sage.

Emecheta, Buchi. 1989. "Natural Gestures." *New Internationalist*. Accessed July 14, 2004. http://www.newint.org/issue201/gestures.htm.

Epprecht, Marc. 1998. "The 'Unsaying' of Indigenous Homosexualities in Zimbabwe: Mapping a Blindspot in an African Masculinity." *Journal of Southern African Studies* 24, no. 4: 631–651.

Fineran, Susan. 2001. "Sexual Minority Students and Peer Sexual Harassment in High School." *Journal of School Social Work* 11, no. 2: 50–69.

Friedrichs, Terence P. 1995. "Gifted and Gay—Reasons to Help." *The Association for the Gifted (TAG) Newsletter* 17, no. 1: 4–5.

Griffin, Pat. 1998. *Strong Women, Deep Closets: Lesbians and Homophobia in Sport*. Champaign, IL: Human Kinetics.

Harrison, Lyn. 2000. "Gender Relations and the Production of Difference in School-based Sexuality and HIV/AIDS Education in Australia." *Gender and Education* 12, no. 1: 5–19.

Heron, Ann, ed. 1995. *Two Teenagers in Twenty: Writings by Gay & Lesbian Youth*. Los Angeles: Alyson Publications, Inc.

Hillier, Lynne, Deborah Dempsey, Lyn Harrison, Lisa Beale, Lesley Matthews, and Doreen Rosenthal. 1998. *Writing Themselves In: A National Report on the Sexuality, Health and Well-Being of Same-Sex Attracted Young People*, Carlton South: Australian Research Centre in Sex, Health and Society, La Trobe University.

Li Yinhe. 1998. *Tongxinglian Ya Wehua.* (The Homosexual Subculture). Beijing: China Today Publishing House.

Martin, Emily. 1991. "The Egg and the Sperm: How Science Has Constructed a Romance Based on Stereotypical Male-Female Roles." *Signs: Journal of Women in Culture and Society* 16: 485–501.

The McCreary Centre Society. 1993. *Sexual Abuse and Young People with Disabilities Project*: *Results and Recommendations*. Vancouver, BC: Author.

Orenstein, Alan. 2001. "Substance Use among Gay and Lesbian Adolescents." *Journal of Homosexuality* 41, no. 2: 1–15.

Raymond, Diane. 1994. "Homophobia, Identity, and the Meanings of Desire: Reflections on the Cultural Construction of Gay and Lesbian Adolescent Sexuality." Pp. 115–150 in *Sexual Cultures and the Construction of Adolescent Identities*. Edited by Janice M. Irvine. Philadelphia: Temple University Press.

Rosario, Margaret, Joyce Hunter, and Marya Gwadz. 1997. "Exploration of Substance Use among Lesbian, Gay, and Bisexual Youth: Prevalence and Correlates." *Journal of Adolescent Research* 12: 454–476.

Rotheram-Borus, Mary Jane, and M. Isabel Fernandez. 1995. "Sexual Orientation and Developmental Challenges Experienced by Gay and Lesbian Youths." *Suicide and Life-Threatening Behavior* 25(Supplement): 26–34.

Rotheram-Borus, Mary Jane, and Kris A. Langabeer. 2001. "Developmental Trajectories of Gay, Lesbian, and Bisexual Youth." Pp. 97–128 in *Lesbian, Gay, and Bisexual Identities and Youth: Psychological Perspectives*. Edited by Anthony R. D'Augelli and Charlotte J. Patterson. New York: Oxford.

Ryan, Caitlin, and Donna Futterman. 1998. *Lesbian & Gay Youth: Care & Counseling*. New York: Columbia University Press.

Saewyc, Elizabeth M., Linda H. Bearinger, Patricia A. Heinz, Robert W. Blum and Michael D. Resnick. 1998. "Gender Differences in Health and Risk Behaviors among Bisexual and Homosexual Adolescents." *Journal of Adolescent Health* 23, no. 3: 181–188.

———. 1999. "Sexual Intercourse, Abuse and Pregnancy among Adolescent Women: Does Sexual Orientation Make a Difference?" *Family Planning Perspectives* 31, no. 3: 127–131.

Windmeyer, Shane L., and Pamela W. Freeman, eds. 2000. *Secret Sisters: Stories of Being Lesbian and Bisexual in a College Sorority*. Los Angeles: Alyson.

YWCA. 2004. "Pride Not Prejudice: Young Lesbian and Bisexual Women." *Briefings* 11: 1–8.

LGBT Studies

Todd K. Herriott, Jeremy P. Hayes, and *Penny J. Rice*

Lesbian, Gay, Bisexual and Transgender (LGBT) Studies is an umbrella term used to describe a growing field of research and scholarship around the experiences, understanding, and theoretical underpinnings of queer lives and culture. This field of study has many strands, including lesbian studies, gay studies, lesbian and gay studies,

See also Antibias Curriculum; College Campus Programming; Feminism; Men's Studies; Poststructuralism; Professional Educational Organizations.

sexuality studies, gender studies, and **queer studies**. Each of these named subsets typically shows the scholar's attempt to associate with a particular aspect or stance within the broader scope of LGBT-related studies. The names chosen often reflect the current **school climate** of a particular campus culture and the degree to which the **curriculum** is based within **critical social theory** and pedagogy. Typically, lesbian studies is seen as an outgrowth of **women's studies**—so, too, is gender studies, though it tends to be more encompassing of the experiences of men and others who do not identify as women. Queer studies is often the most political in nature, based within the critical postmodernist theory that calls for a deconstruction of the labels and terms used by society to define one's **sexual orientation**, gender, or **sexual identity**. Additionally, this branch of study proclaims that sexual behaviors and identities vary in each culture and historical context; it requires the reader to see sexuality and gender as constructed forms specific to that cultural context and not as the basis for an essentialized identity.

The terms lesbian, gay, bisexual, and transgender are relatively new—coined within the last century and a half. The naming of these individuals, based primarily on a definition predicated by sexual behavior or gender expression, created a new community while ignoring the vast variance within this population. Members of this community, who were then being thought of and treated as a collective group, began to see the ways in which they were considered distinct from the majority heterosexually-defined culture. This distinct difference promoted some of the early exploration into same-sex behavior and sexual identity such as the works of early sexologists **Magnus Hirschfeld** and Havelock Ellis and the later work of **Alfred Kinsey** and Evelyn Hooker. Carried forward by the **women's movement** and birth of **women's studies**, theorists began serious inquiry into the lives and experiences of LGBT people as well as those of historic figures now viewed through a lens of sexual orientation. As the sexual revolution of the late 1960s and 1970s came into being, larger numbers of lesbian and gay individuals were **coming out** openly. This visibility was accompanied by a corresponding increase in intellectual and academic interest in LGBT populations as a specific cultural and sociological group (Jagose 1996).

The earliest contemporary form of LGBT studies sprang out of gay and lesbian academicians. In late 1973, the Gay Academic Union (GAU), comprised of homosexual academicians, sponsored their first national conference at John Jay College under the theme of "Scholarship and the Gay Academic Experience." Among the 325 activist-minded people in attendance were Julia Penelope Stanley, presenting on "coming out" with an interest on language and lesbianism; Jonathan Katz and Lillian Faderman, focusing on gay and lesbian history; and Dennis Altman, analyzing gay political life in the United States. LGBT studies began to be formally introduced early in the women's studies movement under the title of "lesbian studies." This introduction was indicative of a gender split across both academic and organizational issues, which was evident at the first GAU conference with the formation of the lesbian caucus. Nevertheless, there was a growing momentum in academic inquiry—both in discussions and in print. One early edited volume, *The Gay Academic* (Crew 1978), for example, offers both exemplary scholarship in history, library sciences, literature, linguistics, philosophy, psychology, science, sociology, political science, and religion, and a section devoted to "general academic issues." This early period also saw the formation of the landmark *Journal of Homosexuality*, which was one of the first journals based upon an LGBT model.

The early works mirrored many of the predominate social issues in society, such as **gender roles** and women's rights, as did the LGBT writing of the 1980s. The image of white gay men dominated society's view of the "gay community," which, in turn, prompted further reactions by LGB people of color and women. Issues of **race** and intersecting oppressions, gender differences, pornography and erotica, and certainly the **AIDS** epidemic proved fertile ground for LGBT studies. Sarah Lucia Hoagland and Julia Penelope's *For Lesbians Only: A Separatist Anthology* (1988), Denis Altman's *AIDS in the Mind of America* (1986), Anita Cornwell's *Black Lesbian in White America* (1983), and the numerous writings of African American gay authors such as Essex Hemphill, E. Lynn Harris, and James Earl Hardy all served as examples of the ever widening breadth of LGBT studies.

During the 1990s, LGBT studies grew as an increasing number of scholars contributed to the body of literature. As another generation of scholars began to take interest in this subject matter, some critiqued the accepted curriculum and proposed new methods of integrating this growing field of **research** into higher education. Henry Minton (1992), for example, provided one of the first collections of educational strategies and approaches with which to develop gay and lesbian studies in Europe and North America, while Linda Garber (1994) provided a discourse on classroom pedagogy and curriculum from a theoretical perspective. **Queer theory** and **queer studies** also emerged, rejecting the essentialist quality of LGBT studies, providing a postmodern theoretical framework or epistemology in which to "queer" the world, and drawing on the work of European scholars, most notably **Michel Foucault** and Jacques Derrida (Butler 1990; Sedgwick 1990).

The largely essentialist field of LGBT studies, however, continued to produce an enormous volume of research and scholarship as well as some controversy. Yale historian John Boswell, for instance, created controversy over his studies on Christianity as did neuroscience writer Simon LeVay, who examined the biological origins of human sexual behavior by looking at the development, structure, and function of the brain circuits that produce sexual behavior and feelings. Both typified this essentialist direction using the lens of "established" fields of study.

The bisexual and transgender communities, which previously had either been dismissed or further marginalized by the larger "gay" community, began to move center stage in the LGBT studies movement. *The Bisexual Option* (Klein 1993), *Bisexualities and AIDS* (Aggleton 1996), and *Vice Versa: Bisexuality and Eroticism in Everyday Life* (Garber 1995) are illuminative of this scholarship as is the *Journal of Bisexuality*, founded in 1999 to promote scholarly inquiry. Similar advances have been made in the area of transgender studies with publications such as *Sex Changes: The Politics of Transgenderism* (Califia 1997) and *Current Concepts in Transgender Identity* (Denny 1998).

LGBT studies expanded, in part, due to the emergence of scholarly caucuses or special interest groups within diverse academic organizations from the American Historical Association and the American Psychological Association to the American Educational Research Association and the American College Personnel Association. By the early 1990s, research regarding LGBT youth, particularly within an educational context, was advancing, mostly in line with the essentialist nature of LGBT studies—seen by proponents of queer studies as attempts to normalize and assimilate the LGBT experience (Tierney and Dilley 1998).

Europe and North America also witnessed the first successful developments of gay and lesbian studies programs at institutions such as Concordia University in

Montreal, San Francisco City College, City University of New York, University of Amsterdam, and several other institutions in the Netherlands and Europe. Several hundred LGBT studies programs, departments, centers, and courses are offered across North America alone. Institutions such as William and Hobart Smith College in upstate New York, however, are one of the few programs to offer both an undergraduate minor and a major. Other institutions offer certificate programs or cross-disciplinary degrees. Institutions such as University of Chicago, University of Minnesota, and City University of New York have gone beyond the creation of an academic department to the creation of a full research center. These programs are often aligned either with the essentialist LGBT studies approach, such as the program at the University of Maryland at College Park, or with the interdisciplinary approach of queer studies as is the case with Duke University's program.

Irrespective of their ideological leanings, LGBT studies programs typically include some form of an introductory course in which the basic concepts, definitions, and historical background of homosexuality is explored. This foundational course then is used as the entrée into a wide range of possible courses, each linked to the core course through its focus on LGBT issues and concepts. Beyond a basic introductory course, the composition of LGBT studies at any given institution varies widely. Initially, LGBT studies maintained a basic disciplinary and essentialism focus, especially in comparison to women's studies or queer studies. Even so, LGBT studies programs now draw from multiple disciplines with approved courses taught in a variety of disciplines including English, **history, psychology, geography**, linguistics, **political science, art,** film, sociology, and journalism.

There is not only a wide variation in the curriculum of LGBT studies but also in the manner in which it is presented on the college level. Institutional culture, focus, history, and affiliation all play a role in determining to what extent LGBT studies are expressed. In many situations, LGBT studies programs have started as an offshoot of an already established women's studies program or department. In some cases, LGBT studies programs have split off to become distinct and autonomous entities and, in others, the two programs have combined to create new departments or programs of gender and/or sexuality studies. It is rare outside of the more liberal institutions for programs to include the word **"queer"** in the title due to the political implications and historic connotations. Similar again to the path of women's studies, LGBT studies has in many situations chosen to remain a program rather than become a full department due to the institutional structures that come with departmental status. Program status often offers the "third space" discussed recently in feminist literature, referring to the benefits of being a less defined, less constrained institutional entity.

The United States has not been the only country to see an increase in the spread and establishment of LGBT studies within higher education. According to Jeffrey Weeks, "serious study of homosocial and homosexual life is now undertaken in all Western, and many non-Western countries, though often it lacks academic respectability" (2000, 1). The lack of academic respectability has not hampered the establishment of many renowned programs such as the Sexual Diversity Studies program at the University of Toronto or the Gay and Lesbian Studies programs at the University of Utrecht and the University of Amsterdam. Students have the opportunity to study abroad through the School for International Training's (SIT) first-ever undergraduate lesbian, gay, and bisexual study abroad program in the Netherlands. This emergence of LGBT studies has meant that there has been an increased demand for resources and information regarding LGBT issues from a wide range of fields, including psychology, anthropology, **dance**, art history, religion, **poetry**, philosophy, **literature**, economics, and even in conducting marketing and teaching **English as a second language**. Such European and international dialogue has further broadened our understandings of LGBT people. Research by Sheena Asthana and Robert Oostvogels (2001) on the social construction of male homosexuality in **India**, for example, has given greater insight as to how to provide appropriate health care interventions in a non-Western country, as has Kevin Moss' (1995) study of sexual minorities' experiences in Eastern Europe.

Along with this growth in the establishment of LGBT studies in various forms across academia, there has been a corresponding growth of LGBT studies information in scholarly journals. The *Journal of Bisexuality, Journal of Gay and Lesbian Issues in Education, Journal of Lesbian Studies*, and *GLQ: A Journal of Lesbian and Gay Studies* illustrate how this field has become institutionalized and legitimized. In addition to the variety of journals, several collections of scholarly works on current topics related to LGBT studies have been developed. A number of volumes of LGBT studies readers have been compiled (Abelove, Barale, and Halpernin 1993; Duberman 1997; Medhurst and Mundt 1997), each exhibiting the wide range of LGBT scholarship. University and for-profit publishers, such as the University of Chicago Press, Rowman and Littlefield, and Haworth Press, also have specific book series devoted to LGBT topics.

There has been relatively little integration of LGBT issues below the level of higher education as most efforts have gone into **school safety** and **counseling** initiatives like **Project 10, antidiscrimination** and **bullying** policies, and cocurricular groups such as **gay–straight alliances**. There are a number of organizations that have formed with the intent of reshaping curriculum into something more LGBT friendly and inclusive. The PERSON Project (Public Education Regarding Sexual Orientation Nationally), GLSEN (**Gay Lesbian Straight Education Network**), and **GLBT Educational Equity** (GLEE) are examples of an activist network advocating for LGBT inclusive curricular policies in K-12 education.

Bibliography

Abelove, Henry, Michele Barale, and David Halpernin, eds. 1993. *The Lesbian and Gay Studies Reader*. New York: Routledge.

Aggleton, Peter, ed. 1996. *Bisexualities and AIDS: International Perspectives*. London: Taylor and Francis.

Altman, Dennis. 1986. *AIDS in the Mind of America*. Garden City, New York: Doubleday.

Asthana, Sheena, and Robert Oostvogels. 2001. "The Social Construction of Male Homosexuality in India: Implications for HIV Transmission and Prevention." *Social Science & Medicine* 52: 707–721.

Boswell, John. 1994. *Same-Sex Unions in Premodern Europe*. New York: Random House.

Butler, Judith. 1990. *Gender Trouble*. New York: Routledge.

Califia, Pat. 1997. *Sex Changes: The Politics of Transgenderism*. San Francisco: Cleis Press.

Collins, Jack. 1992. "Matters of Fact: Establishing a Gay and Lesbian Studies Department." Pp. 125–136 in *Gay and Lesbian Studies*. Edited by Henry L. Minton. Binghamton, NY: Harrington Park Press.

Cornwell, Anita. 1983. *Black Lesbian in White America*. Tallahassee: Naiad Press.

Crew, Louie, ed. 1978. *The Gay Academic*. Palm Springs, CA: ETC Publications.

Denny, Dallas, ed. 1998. *Current Concepts in Transgender Identity*. New York: Garland.

Duberman, Martin, ed. 1997. *Queer Representations: Reading Lives, Reading Cultures.* New York: New York University Press.

Garber, Linda, ed. 1994. *Tilting the Tower: Lesbians, Teaching, Queer Subjects.* New York: Routledge.

Garber, Marjorie. 1995. *Vice Versa: Bisexuality and Eroticism in Everyday Life.* New York: Simon and Schuster.

Haggery, George E., and Bonnie Zimmerman, eds. 1995. *Professions of Desire: Lesbian and Gay Studies in Literature.* New York: Modern Language Association of America.

Hoagland, Sarah Lucia, and Julia Penelope. 1988. *For Lesbians Only: A Separatist Anthology.* London: Onlywomen Press.

Jagose, Annamarie. 1996. *Queer Theory: An Introduction.* New York: New York University Press.

Klein, Fred. 1993. *The Bisexual Option / Fritz Klein.* Binghamton, NY: Haworth Press.

Medhurst, Andy, and Sally R. Munt, eds. 1997. *Lesbian and Gay Studies: A Critical Introduction.* London: Cassell.

Minton, Henry, ed. 1992. *Gay and Lesbian Studies.* Binghamton, NY: Haworth Press.

Moss, Kevin. 1995. "The Underground Closet: Political and Sexual Dissidence in Eastern Europe." Pp. 229–251 in *Genders 22: Postcommunism and the Body Politic.* Edited by Ellen E. Berry. New York: New York University Press.

Poulsen, Rachel E. 2000. "Queer Studies." Pp. 488–491 in *Readers Guide to Lesbian and Gay Studies.* Edited by Timothy F. Murphy. Chicago: Fitzroy Dearborn.

Sedgwick, Eve. 1990. *Epistemology of the Closet.* Berkeley: University of California Press.

Tierney, William, and Patrick Dilley. 1998 "Constructing Knowledge: Educational Research and Gay and Lesbian Studies." Pp. 49–71 in *Queer Theory in Education.* Edited by William F. Pinar. Mahwah, NJ: Lawrence Erlbaum.

Weeks, Jeffrey. 2000. "The Challenge of Lesbian and Gay Studies." Pp. 1–13 in *Lesbian and Gay Studies: An Introductory Interdisciplinary Approach.* Edited by Theo Sandfort, Judith Schuyf, Jan Willem Duyvendak, and Jeffrey Weeks. London: Sage.

Wilton, Tamsin. 1995. *Lesbian Studies: Setting and Agenda.* London: Routledge.

Web Site

University LGBT/Queer Programs: Lesbian, Gay, Bisexual, Transgender, Transsexual Queer Studies in the USA and Canada. February 2005. John Younger. Accessed June 9, 2005. http://www.people.ku.edu/~jyounger/lgbtqprogs.html. A comprehensive listing of current LGBT/Queer Studies programs and LGBT courses taught on United States and Canadian campuses. Listing includes other LGBT resources available at each site. The Web site is listed alphabetically by state.

Licensure

Catherine A. Lugg

A license is the certificate granted by a state department of education or other state entity certifying that the holder is competent to work in a given profession or trade. For teachers and **administrators**, licensure became a requirement to work in public schools beginning in the early twentieth century. Over the course of that century and up until today, states have added requirements for potential candidates in

See also Activism, LGBT Teachers; Educational Policies; Johns Committee; Passing; Teachers, LGBT and History.

education. Additionally, many states require private school educators also to hold the appropriate licenses. Furthermore, both professional and trade licenses contain certain restrictions that include banning convicted criminals and those deemed "morally unfit" from holding licensure. However, since licensure is granted and regulated by individual states (in the United States), these requirements, restrictions, and classifications can vary. Nevertheless, the threat of licensure revocation historically has forced many LGBT public school workers (as well as other professional and trades people) to hide their identities. The loss of a professional license would bar that person from working in public schools, and in many cases, private schools as well.

Prior to the late 1960s and early 1970s, any sexuality that deviated from heterosexuality was criminalized, and status was equated with potential criminality. Consequently, LGBT school workers who refused to hide their **sexual orientation**, who were "outed," or who were suspected of being homosexual faced immediate dismissal from their positions and the possible revocation of their licenses. Those individuals who were arrested for solicitation (asking someone if they would be interested in having sex), for frequenting a gay bar (disorderly conduct), or for having public sex (typically in restrooms or other public areas), also faced criminal charges. Generally their names, home addresses, places of employment, and sometimes photographs appeared in local newspapers.

At the height of the Cold War, when communism and homosexuality were repeatedly and erroneously linked, purges of suspected "**queer**" educators swept across states and local school districts. At the time, it was believed that homosexuality was literally contagious; furthermore, LGBT people were seen as potential child molesters. "Queers," particularly those working with young people, were portrayed by various media organizations and politicians as a dire threat to the physical and moral well-being of children. Mere suspicion was enough for many LGBT educators to resign, lose their positions—and sometimes their licenses. Purges of suspected queer educators happened in Boise, Idaho (1950s) and Florida (1956–1965), as well as other places. Well into the 1970s LGBT educators were targets of antigay political activists. In 1978, Oklahoma passed a law banning LGBT educators and any pro-LGBT speech by straight educators. Later that year, a similar proposal—Proposition 6 or the Briggs Initiative—was rejected by California voters. Not surprisingly, LGBT school workers took great pains to hide their sexual identities. Some married, others made sure that they had the proper gender escort for every public event. It was critical that LGBT school workers "pass" as heterosexual if they were to keep their jobs and professional licenses.

With the advent of the modern day gay rights movements arising out of **Stonewall**, there has been a gradual relaxation of the sodomy laws. Restrictions barring "out" LGBT people from holding educational licensure have also been eased in many areas—but not all. For example, the Oklahoma law banning LGBT educators was narrowly invalidated by the U.S. Supreme Court in 1985. In June 2003, the high court, in *Lawrence v. Texas*, struck down the remaining state laws banning consensual sodomy. Nevertheless, these thirteen states have yet to redraft their licensure regulations or repeal their sodomy statutes to comply with this decision.

Additionally, many state regulations regarding licensure insist that holders have "a good moral character," or conform to "community morality standards," which can be either broadly or narrowly construed, depending upon who is enforcing the regulations. Historically, morality clauses have banned behavior such as smoking cigarettes, dancing, consuming of alcoholic beverages, working in taverns, and pregnancy—regardless of marital status. With the exception of those states, municipalities, and school districts that specifically bar **discrimination** on the basis of sexual orientation or **gender identity**, LGBT school workers may still be at risk for licensure revocation (however seemingly improbable) or legal challenge (more likely), particularly in those localities that have a history of LGBT persecution.

Bibliography

Blount, Jackie M. 1998. *Destined to Rule the Schools.* Albany: State University of New York Press.

———. 2003. "Homosexuality and School Superintendents: A Brief History." *Journal of School Leadership* 13: 7–26.

Dayoff, Amy D. 2001. "Sodomy Laws: The Government's Vehicle to Impose the Majority's Social Values." *William Mitchell Law Review* 27: 1863–1894.

Eskridge, William N., Jr. 1999. *Gaylaw: Challenging the Apartheid of the Closet.* Cambridge, MA: Harvard University Press.

Gerassi, John J. 1966. *The Boys of Boise: Furor, Vice and Folly in an American City.* New York: Macmillian.

Harbeck, Karen M. 1997. *Gay and Lesbian Educators: Personal Freedoms, Public Constraints.* Malden, MA: Amethyst Press.

Kissen, Rita. 1996. *The Last Closet: The Real Lives of Lesbian and Gay Teachers.* Portsmouth, ME: Heinemann.

Leslie, Christopher. 2000. "Creating Criminals: The Injury Inflicted by 'Unenforced' Sodomy Laws." *Harvard Civil Rights—Civil Liberties Review* 35: 102–181.

Murdoch, Joyce, and Deb Price. 2001. *Courting Justice: Gay Men and Lesbians v. the Supreme Court.* New York: Basic Books.

Sears, James T. 1997. *Lonely Hunters: An Oral History of Lesbian and Southern Life, 1948–1968.* New York: HarperCollins/Westview.

Web Sites

North Carolina Gay & Lesbian Attorneys. January 2005. Accessed on May 30, 2005. http://www.ncgala.org. Works to support LGBT activists and community members in North Carolina.

Sodomy Laws May 2005. Accessed May 30, 2005. http://www.sodomylaws.org. Tracks legal developments regarding sodomy laws and LGBT people around the world, including legal cases, strategies, research, and advocates.

Literature, College

JF Buckley

A wide variety of literature has long been reflecting, resisting, or rejoicing in, the presence of **lesbian, gay, bisexual,** and **transgender** (LGBT) people in various cultural settings. Hence, literature that encourages college students to explore the complex and often contradictory forces linking culture, sexuality, and identity is

See also Antibias Curriculum; Butler, Judith; College Age Students; Curriculum, Higher Education; Gender Identity; Heteronormativity; Poststructuralism; Queer Pedagogy.

vital to a well-balanced education. Although there is no defining text, date, or author, college-level LGBT literature encourages the in-depth examination of linguistic representation, cultural presentation, and critical perspective by avoiding simplistic depictions of LGBT issues and identities, or by allowing professors to complicate simplistic depictions.

Although not the only approach, events and attitudes in nineteenth-century Germany do provide a useful way to introduce undergraduates to LGBT literature. Sex researchers, such as Karl-Heinrich Ulrichs (1825–1895) and **Magnus Hirschfeld** (1868–1935), associated with the Scientific Humanitarian Committee founded in 1897, wanted to repeal Paragraph 175 banning same-sex relations. In brief, their argument was that same-sex desire was biological, hence natural. In 1864, Ulrichs published the pamphlet, *Inclusa*, in which he defends "men who seek other men as sexual partners," calling them "Urnings," mental hermaphrodites by birth.

In 1869, physician Karl Maria Kertbeny (1824–1882), coined the term "homosexual" for such men—then later came up with "heterosexual" to stand for those expressing the opposite **desire**. Both terms were made public in 1892 when Richard von Krafft-Ebing (1840–1902) used them in *Psychopathia Sexualis*. Thanks, however, to the contemporary thinking of Jacques Derrida, in *Structure, Sign, and Play in the Discourse of the Human Sciences* (1966), college students can "deconstruct" the valuing of heterosexuality over homosexuality in literature and culture, understanding these terms as binary opposites dependent on each other for meaning.

Yet, in general, homosexuality remains socially pejorative, as it was in the nineteenth century. Little wonder that early twentieth-century lesbian writer Radclyffe Hall (1880–1943), who preferred to be called "John" rather than her given name, "Marguerite," considered herself "inverted"—her desire masculine. Little wonder, too, that her novel, *The Well of Loneliness* (1928), presents the wealthy English lesbian, Stephen Gordon, as normal and independent—but willing to give up her lover, Mary, to a man because she "can't give her protection or happiness" (Hall 1990, 433–444). Rather difficult reading for introductory LGBT literature courses, this classic novel encourages students to move beyond pity and **stereotypes** if they approach it through the lens of **Michel Foucault** (1926–1984). In *The History of Sexuality, Vol. I* (1990), he explains desire as a challenge that society controls by redirecting its verbalizations into the cultural "truths" of religion, law, and medicine. Hall's depiction of Stephen might challenge, but does not escape, the discursive power of heterosexual patriarchy.

Many turn-of-the-century LGBT novels address challenges to social class posed by same-sex desire. In E. M. Forster's (1879–1970) *Maurice* (1993/1971), the eponymous hero is a student at Cambridge with no social standing when he meets and loves Clive Durham, who never separates the affair from his Anglicized ideal of Platonic male society. Thus, when Maurice finds romantic and sexual love with working-class Alec Scudder, it becomes obvious how much social standing Maurice will sacrifice for love—and the love Clive sacrificed to retain his social standing.

Yukio Mishima (1925–1970) is less concerned with social image, but he painstakingly examines the nineteenth century view that lesbians and gays are inverts in *Confessions of a Mask* (1958), an autobiographical, coming-of-age tale set in World War II **Japan**. When the narrator discovers "a reproduction of Guid Reni's 'St. Sebastian,'" he also discovers that his desire for men is associated with bloodshed and suffering (Mishima 1958, 38). The narrator, who has no model of, nor outlet for, his sexuality, examines his maturing desires as he attempts to be "normal." He fails. It is painfully ironic when he asserts that his "ignorance had been enlightened by reading the theories of Hirschfeld, who explains inversion as a perfectly simple biological phenomenon" (Mishima 1958, 240). Informed by a brief introduction to Edward Said's *Orientalism* (1978), undergraduates can readily see how the Asian narrator's knowledge of his sexual desire is controlled by outdated Western images exported to the East.

Mishima makes few connections between sexuality and nationality—other than the narrator's acknowledgement that Japan's surrender ends his hope of dying romantically and thereby escaping the reality of his homosexuality. For James Baldwin (1924–1987), however, who was writing at the same time, there exists a complex relationship between sexuality and nationalism. Baldwin was America's first nationally recognized **African American** writer to acknowledge his homosexuality publicly and to address LGBT issues consistently in his writing. As early as 1953, in *Go Tell It on the Mountain*, and as late as *Just Above My Head* (1979), homosexuality and **bisexuality** are constant themes. In *Giovanni's Room* (1988/1956), the American narrator, David, is in Paris while his fiancé, Hella, travels in Spain. Having fled the macho heterosexuality of his country and his father, David falls in love with Giovanni. Filled with homophobic fear of his own sexuality, he rejects Giovanni, who is portrayed as dark, foreign, perverse, and, finally, criminal for killing Guillaume. David, however, is white and able to return to America. The novel all but begs students to consider how sexual and racial repression kill the eroticized nonwhite and doom the white to an uncertain future of dealing with "the closet."

This "closet" takes on geographic overtones in United States' pulp fiction that flourished before the 1969 **Stonewall** Riots. Although these cheap paperbacks gave voice to nearly every desire, it was a genre dominated by lesbian fiction in general, and by Ann Bannon (1932–) in particular. In 1962, she retrospectively, but chronologically, starts the story of Beebo Brinker's move to Greenwich Village and sexual freedom: *Odd Girl Out* (1957), *I Am A Woman* (1959), *Woman in the Shadows* (1959), *Journey to a Woman* (1960), *Beebo Brinker* (2001/1962). Set in the 1950s, the last novel reveals a lesbian identity plagued by self-doubt and self-hatred, especially when outside the Village. For that reason it provides a look into the "**geography**" of the closet before the civil rights movement, before the **women's movement**, before the gay rights movement (Barale 2000). When examined through the lens of cultural geography, Robert McGinnis's painting for the original 1962 Gold Medal cover of *Beebo Brinker* encourages undergraduate and graduate students to see LGBT literature as specifically locating desire.

David Leavitt (1961–), novelist and writer of short fiction, also "maps" LGBT desire within larger, heterosexual society. In *Territory* (1984), Neil returns to his **childhood** home where he introduces his lover, Wayne, to his mother, and struggles to align his **sexual identity** as a sexually active gay man with the realization that his mother is an individual in her own right (*Family Dancing* 1984). This is an excellent piece for undergraduate students to use when examining contemporary cultural "truths" of the traditional family.

Two years earlier Audre Lorde (1934–1992) published *Zami: A New Spelling of My Name* (1982). More accessible than Paula Gunn Allen's (1939–) treatment of Ephanie's Native American vision quest for sexual and racial identity in *The Woman Who Owned the Shadows* (1992), *Zami* is a combination autobiography, political statement, and **coming out** story that poetically weaves together what it means to be black and female—and lesbian—in mid-twentieth century New York City. For Lorde, LGBT space is linguistic, spiritual, and political, as it is with black, lesbian poet, June Jordan (1936–2002): *"I am a reflection of my mother's secret poetry as well as of her hidden anger"* (Lorde 1982, 32). As African American lesbians constructing linguistic history amid racism and **homophobia**, both complicate the feminist-based "lesbian continuum" that Adrienne Rich sees as an extension of women working together.

Edmund White (1940–), prolific author and cofounder of "The Violet Quill," a group of New York City gay writers, locates LGBT persons in society through sexual activity in his autobiographical *A Boy's Own Story* (1982). The narrator, for example, asserts his social presence by seducing his music teacher moments after he has turned him in for **drug use**. Ethan Mordden's (1947–) "Buddy" series tells of a close group of gay men who have lived with humor, honesty, and emotional commitment through disco, Fire Island, and **AIDS**: *I've a Feeling We're Not in Kansas Anymore (1985)*, *Buddies (1986)*, *Everybody Loves You (1988)*, *Some Men Are Lookers* (1997). Juxtaposing the youthful **agency** and social involvement of White's narrator, when he comes of age sexually, with a segregated sexual society, observed from a distance by Mordden's narrator, encourages students to see Foucault's notion of society as both empowering and enervating.

For most gay, white writers in mid-twentieth century America, AIDS emphasized society's heterosexual/homosexual split. Discussing how their characters are forced to live and love as socially stigmatized individuals helps students better understand **Jacques Lacan's** (1901–1981) belief that the highest form of desire is the desire to be desired. Paul Monette (1945–1995) started his career with the comic *Taking Care of Mrs. Carroll* (1978), but, in 1988, he confronted the society that was constraining him and the AIDS that was killing him, in *Borrowed Time*. In 1992, he continued the confrontation with *Becoming a Man: Half a Life Story*, an emotional and political bildungsroman.

In the 1990s, notions of individuality were more and more called into question—especially with authors who addressed sexuality outside **race** and **ethnicity**. In Jeanette Winterson's (1959–) *Written on the Body* (1994) the narrator, who is neither named nor identified sexually, has loved many women and a few men before meeting Louise. While Winterson's humorous and creative play with gender and desire is reason enough to read this postmodern tale, it is her use of biological, literary, and biblical discourses that encourages undergraduates to compare cultural depictions and critiques of desire. An accessible book, it encourages all students to extend Derridian deconstruction beyond the text into their own investment in gender roles and sexual identities. Useful in this effort is Lee Edelman's *Homographesis* (1994), which describes how and why patriarchal culture "delimits" and "describes" LGBT persons, "whose very condition of possibility is [their] relation to writing or textuality," over which they have no control (Edelman 1994, 9).

In anthologies such as *Brother to Brother* (1991), edited by Essex Hemphill (1957–1995) and in Rafael Campo's (1964–) *What the Body Told* (1996), students have an opportunity to engage with LGBT **poetry**, which is missing from the novels above, save *Zami*. Furthermore, in both collections, they come face-to-face with specific LGBT identities and refusals of such identities. For Marlin Riggs in "Tongues Untied," to speak out as proud and queer both establishes and critiques his identity as an African American man (Hemphill and Beam 1991). Students can see identity categories as normalizing structures and as rallying points for contesting such oppression (Butler 1990). *What the Body Told* echoes Campo's collective identity as a gay man, a father, and a physician at Harvard Medical School. In "Asylum," for example, he asks if queers replay the performances of "others" as their performance of identity (Campo 1996, 8). These anthologies encourage students to question binary opposites like masculine/feminine and heterosexual/homosexual. Such questioning can benefit from Eve Sedgwick's description of "**Queer:**" as "undertaking particular, performative acts of experimental self-perception and filiation" (Sedgwick 1993, 9), something necessary when examining LGBT literature at the college level.

Bibliography

Barale, Michele Aina. 2000. "Queer Urbanities: A Walk on the Wild Side." Pp. 204–214 in *Queer Diasporas*. Edited by Cindy Patton and B. Sanchez-Eppler. Durham: Duke University Press.

Butler, Judith. 1990. *Gender Trouble: Feminism and the Subversion of Identity*. New York: Routledge.

Campo, Rafael. 1996. *What the Body Told*. Durham, NC: Duke University Press.

Carbado, Devon, W. Carbado, Dwight A. McBride, and Donald Weise, eds. 2002. *Black Like Us: A Century of Lesbian, Gay, and Bisexual African American Fiction*. San Francisco: Cleis Press.

Derrida, Jacques. 1966. "Structure, Sign, and Play in the Discourse of the Human Sciences." Pp. 247–265 in *The Languages of Criticism and the Sciences of Man: The Structuralist Controversy*. Edited by Richard Macksey and Eugenio Donato. Baltimore: Johns Hopkins. (Original Work presented at "The Languages of Criticism and the Sciences of Man Conference" in 1966 at Johns Hopkins.)

Edelman, Lee. 1994. *Homographesis*. New York: Routledge.

Foucault, Michel. 1990. *The History of Sexuality, Volume I*. Translated by Robert Hurley. New York: Vintage Books. (Original published as *La Volente de savoir* in Paris: Editions Gallimard, 1976).

Haggerty, George E., ed. 2000. *Gay Histories and Cultures: An Encyclopedia*. New York: Garland.

Hemphill, Essex, ed. 1991. *Brother to Brother: New Writings by Black Gay Men*. Boston: Alyson. Malinowski, Sharon, and Christa Brelin. 1995. *The Gay and Lesbian Literary Companion*. Detroit: Visible Ink Press.

Said, Edward W. 1978. *Orientalism*. New York: Pantheon Books.

Sedgwick, Eve Kosofsky. 1993. *Tendencies*. Durham, NC: Duke University Press.

Winterston, Jeanette. 1994. *Written on the Body*. New York: Vintage. (Original work published 1992).

Woods, Gregory. 1998. *A History of Gay Literature: The Male Tradition*. New Haven, CT: Yale University Press.

Zimmerman, Bonnie. 1990. *The Safe Sea of Women: Lesbian Fiction, 1969–1989*. Boston: Beacon Press.

———, ed. 2000. *Lesbian Histories and Cultures: An Encyclopedia*. New York: Garland.

Web Site

GLBTQ: An Encyclopedia of Gay, Lesbian, Bisexual, Transgender, and Queer Culture. 2005. Accessed June 9, 2005. http://www.glbtq.com/. GLBTQ's Web site requires that you become a member; however, it is private, and there is no fee. There are links to art, literature, history, a searchable database, and a discussion board.

Literature, Early Childhood

Vicki Harding

Literature available for children between the ages of zero and eight years consists of fiction and nonfiction picture books, early readers, and simple chapter books. Early childhood literature with lesbian and gay content or characters has become increasingly available and more widely used since the 1980s, as some authors, educators, and parents try to ensure that children's diverse lives are reflected in books. Although transgender or explicit bisexual themes have not been well-integrated, the lesbian and gay content in such titles can be subtle or central to the story, very often including **families** with lesbian or gay parents and increasingly reflecting cultural and ethnic diversity. The introduction of these titles to bookshops and classrooms has not been without controversy, however, and some primary educators have been unwilling to use them in their teaching. But many teachers are increasingly utilizing these resources because they believe that the introduction of lesbian and gay themed resources in early childhood is one way to challenge **homophobia** and **prejudice** in adults of future generations.

Literature also can be a tremendous source of knowledge, strength, and reassurance for those children who will identify as **queer** or who have lesbian, gay, bisexual, and transgender LGBT parents. For these reasons, it is vitally important for books that honestly and creatively reflect the enormous variety and complexity of the world to be available to everyone. Omitting LGBT lives, thoughts, and realities from books, these teachers understand, is a dishonest reflection of the world and a social injustice.

Early **childhood** is (romantically) considered by many to be a time of innocence, and at least some educators and parents believe that keeping sexual information, particularly with LGBT content, away from "innocent" children will be in their best interests. Intimately entwined with this belief is an equation where LGBT lives are reduced to sex, ignoring the complexities of these relationships and communities. Perhaps this explains why literature containing lesbian and gay characters was not produced until relatively recently (the first picture book, *Jenny Lives with Martin and Eric*, was published in 1981). But ignoring gay and lesbian existence is dishonest. It also does little to encourage a strong sense of self-identity in children who have LGBT people in their lives, or who may grow up to be LGBT, to not see their world reflected in the books from which they are being read and which they are learning to read.

Since 1981, the publication of picture books with lesbian and gay content has increased substantially. An Australian bibliography of homosexuality in books for young people, *Out of the Closet and into the Classroom*, was first published in 1992, listing ten books suitable for children up to eight years. The second edition, published in 1996, listed twenty-eight picture books. The unpublished 2004 edition lists an additional twenty-seven relevant titles suitable for young children. While there was one chapter book suitable for eight-year-olds, the overwhelming majority of texts suitable for those eight years and younger are picture books. Although

See also Adoption; Antibias Curriculum; Children of LGBT parents; *Children of the Rainbow* Curriculum; Curriculum, early childhood; Literature, middle school; Literature, secondary school; Parents, LGBT.

there has been a dramatic increase in the number of lesbian and gay inclusive titles for the very young, this number is disproportionately low when compared with the total number of picture books published.

Picture books featured in *Out of the Closet and into the Classroom* (Lobban and Clyde 1996) and another useful bibliography *Lesbian and Gay Voices* (Day 2000) have been included in these bibliographies because of their "homosexual" and "lesbian and gay" content, respectively. Many of these titles also challenge gender **stereotyping**, but, at 2004, no early picture book explicitly deals with transgender issues or **bisexuality**. Increasingly, non-Anglo characters and cultures are being reflected in picture books with lesbian and gay themes such as found in *Best Colors/Los Mejores Colores*. Titles published in the United States are also reflecting an increasing occurrence of the gay population adopting children born outside that country.

Most English language picture books with gay or lesbian themes and references are published in the United States and the United Kingdom, often by special interest or feminist publishers. Sasha Alyson, who founded Alyson Publications in 1980, published many of the early picture books under the imprint of Alyson Wonderland. Two Lives Publishing, "the only English-language publisher dedicated exclusively to creating books for kids with LGBT parents," cites fifty picture books with lesbian and gay content in its 2004 catalog. Children's literature with lesbian and gay themes or characters is also increasingly being published by mainstream publishers.

A very early picture book dealing with the topic of gay fathers was written in Denmark by Susanne Bösche, in 1981. Translated by Louis Mackay from the Danish *Mette bor hos Morten og Erik* to English, *Jenny Lives with Martin and Eric* was published in the United Kingdom by Gay Men's Press and then distributed in the United States by Alyson Publications. This fifty-page picture book, featuring black-and-white photographs and a detailed story about five-year-old Jenny who lives with her father and her father's "lover," is remarkable for its explicitness. We see Jenny's fathers shaving, sleeping, resolving conflict, and answering her questions about homophobia.

The theme of many picture books with lesbian or gay characters has become less explicit and less problem-based over time. While earlier books tackled the issue of homophobia and offered a solution to the audience, contemporary picture books seldom label characters, relationships, problems, or solutions gay and lesbian, in part, because of concern about controversy. Due to its overt themes and candid photographs, *Jenny Lives with Martin and Eric* created significant controversy in England when it was discovered in a teachers' center and reportedly used by primary teachers. The resulting media furor and public debate had far-reaching political repercussions, including a stand taken by the Inner London Education Authority to publicly distance itself from any aspect of sexuality, contributing to the creation of **Section 28** (Harris 1990, 23).

Similarly, *Heather Has Two Mommies*, originally written and self-published by Lesléa Newman (with black-and-white illustrations by Diana Souza) in 1989, is notorious for the debate it caused in the United States during the 1990s. As noted in the afterword of the second (tenth anniversary) Alyson Publications edition, the author was accused of having a militant, political agenda and of being "the most dangerous writer living in America today." After distribution, *Heather Has Two Mommies* seemed to systematically disappear from public and school libraries. Alyson Publications offered replacement copies to the first 500 libraries expressing interest; all 500 copies were claimed immediately.

Lesléa Newman wrote *Heather Has Two Mommies* after a lesbian mother suggested that someone should produce a book that reflected their same-sex parented family. Due to her upbringing in a **Jewish** family and the lack of material that reflected her difference as a child, Newman took up the challenge. *Heather Has Two Mommies* tells the story of a little girl attending childcare and realizing that her family is different from other families. The main message in this story, as *Jenny Lives with Martin and Eric*, is that all sorts of families exist and love is what is important. The family theme is easily the most common theme found in picture books with gay and lesbian content.

A picture book that stands out both for the quality of its illustration and for the unique theme of the story is *King & King*. Originally published in the Netherlands as *Koning & Koning* (2002), it was translated into four languages, including an English edition from a mainstream U.S. publisher, Tricycle Press. Linda de Haan and Stern Nijland collectively wrote and illustrated *King & King*, their first picture book. In this story, the central character is a gay adult–a prince–who needs to get married in order to relieve a pushy queen of the responsibility of ruling the state. Women are paraded before the prince via bright and comical illustration, but he eventually falls in love with another prince. Without any other character batting an eyelid, the princes are wed and live happily ever after. A welcome relief from the serious tone and poor artistry of earlier books, *King & King* may be a sign that early childhood literature with lesbian and gay themes has reached a new level of production and acceptance.

My House (2002), *Going to Fair Day* (2002), *The Rainbow Cubby House* (2005) and *Koalas on Parade* (2005) were written with the explicit intention of distribution to schools and the long-term aim of challenging homophobia and prejudice in adults of future generations. A mother and daughter team, Vicki and Brenna Harding, wrote the books when Brenna was first learning to read. They self-published them under the title *Learn to Include* after receiving feedback from grade one children and focus groups of lesbian mothers. Twelve pages long, with illustrations by Chris Bray-Cotton, these books are easy to read and depict a girl in her daily life with her two mothers. *Going to Fair Day* and *The Rainbow Cubby House* also feature a friend with two fathers. The homosexual theme was subtlety employed so that school officials would have little reason to leave the texts out of the home reading system. These books are often donated to schools by lesbian and gay parents to ensure their children see their families reflected in the classroom. *The Learn to Include series* are four of the very few picture books with lesbian and gay characters published in Australia, certainly the first to be government funded, and possibly the only early readers with homosexual characters published internationally.

Going To Fair Day. From and Courtesy of Vicki Harding. Illustrated and © by Chris Bray-Cotton.

Despite the increasing number of LGBT-themed picture books published, few find their way into public and school libraries and even then may be difficult to locate due to the underuse of appropriate subject headings. Clyde and Lobban (2001, 26) identify a "pressure to censor materials" in school libraries, noting that two picture books with gay or lesbian themes were in the top ten of the *100 Most Frequently Banned Books of the Decade*, released by the American Library Association in 2000. However, well before these classroom resources meet criticism, early childhood teachers "as a result of their own sense of students' prior knowledge and maturity, or in anticipation of parents' possible objections, . . . often manage classroom materials and activities in ways that limit democratic foundations such as free expression and access to information" (Bickmore 1999, 17).

Bibliography

Bickmore, Kathy. 1999. "Why Discuss Sexuality in Elementary School?" Pp. 15–25 in *Queering Elementary Education: Advancing the Dialogue about Sexualities and Schooling*. Edited by William J. Letts, WJ and James T. Sears. Lanham, MD: Rowman and Littlefield.

Clyde, Laurel A., and Marjorie Lobban. 2001. "A Door Half Open: Young People's Access to Fiction Related to Homosexuality." *School Libraries Worldwide* 7, no. 2: 17–30.

Day, Francis Ann. 2000. *Lesbian and Gay Voices: An Annotated Bibliography and Guide to Literature for Children and Young Adults*. Westport: CT: Greenwood.

Harris, Simon. 1990. *Lesbian and Gay Issues in the English Classroom*. Buckingham: Open University Press.

Lobban, Marjorie, and Laurel A. Clyde. 1996. *Out of the Closet and into the Classroom: Homosexuality in Books for Young People*. 2nd ed. Port Melbourne: Thorpe.

Web Sites

Annotated Bibliography of Children's Books with Gay and Lesbian Characters. GLSEN. January 1999. Accessed June 9, 2005. http://www.glsen.org/cgibin/iowa/educator/library/record/27.html. Resources for early childhood educators and parents.

A Complete Resource for LGBT Families. 2005. Two Lives Publishing. Accessed June 9, 2005. http://www.twolives.com. Features an online catalogue of around fifty titles suitable for "children in alternative families."

Literature, Middle School

Mollie Blackburn

Literature that addresses lesbian, gay, bisexual, and transgender (LGBT) topics and concerns in ways that are appropriate for readers in grades six through nine is important for young adolescents to be able to access. These novels and short stories allow LGBT readers to find themselves in literature and for all young readers to gain "insight and empathy by shattering **stereotypes** and humanizing their gay and lesbian peers" (Cart 1997, 8). Literature appropriate for middle school students has evolved in the past thirty-five years, such that now LGBT characters are represented sympathetically and with more complexity. Still, it tends to focus on white gay males, neglecting people of color, females, bisexuals, and transgender people. Some recent literature fills those gaps.

See also Adolescence; Antibias Curriculum; Literature, Early Childhood; Literature, Secondary; Queer Pedagogy; Race and Racism; Sissy Boy.

LGBT-themed middle school literature is often difficult for young adolescents (or their parents) to find. It is not typically on school library shelves or integrated into the standard **curriculum**. Even those teachers who recognize the significance of including novels and short stories that represent diverse populations often fail to include LGBT-themed materials. Therefore, middle school students must search collections in libraries, bookstores, and through the **Internet**—and, in the process, make decisions about being open with their interest.

Sometimes literature for middle school readers is clustered together, but more often it is divided between children's literature, which is intended for younger readers, and young adult literature, which is intended for older readers, making middle school literature even more difficult to locate. The lines are unclear, in part, because reading achievement varies so much among middle school students. Children's literature generally includes adults who are family members, friends, or teachers of young people rather than young people themselves who are LGBT, as if sexual and gender identities were not part of **childhood** experience (Mitchell 2000). In contrast, young adult LGBT literature often explicitly acknowledges the sexual and gender identities of adults and youth. This literature, though, rarely examines intergenerational love (Brogan 1995).

Middle school literature addressing LGBT topics and concerns has evolved considerably since, *I'll Get There: It Better be Worth the Trip*, the first gay-themed young adult novel (Donovan 1969). Young adult novels have gone from having gay and lesbian characters be all but invisible (and when visible, only as deviants), to having just a few exceptional characters who are gay or lesbian, to highlighting the problems associated with being gay or lesbian (Jenkins 1998). Throughout this evolution, these characters have been increasingly portrayed in more sympathetic and complex ways (St. Clair 1995) and as being able to share significant loving relationships (Brogan 1995). Most recently, this body of literature has moved beyond essentialist understandings of sexual and gender identities, whereby a character typically rejects the imposed straight identity and "comes out" to accept a gay identity. The most recent literature, paralleling **queer theory**, portrays a few characters who understand their sexual and gender identities as multiple and variable. For example, in Freymann-Weyr's *My Heartbeat* (2002), one of the main characters engages in romantic and sexual relationships with girls and boys, but instead of identifying as **bisexual**, he simply seems open to the possibility of loving people, not particularly gendered people.

One shortcoming in middle school literature remains inclusion. People of color are typically excluded, although the number of characters of color in this body of literature is slowly increasing. More males are represented than females, although this gap is also narrowing. The characters are more often than not portrayed as conforming to typical **gender roles**; "straight gays" are acceptable while "queer gays" are not. Although this contrasts to the historical mainstream depictions of homosexuals, it still fails to embrace a diversity of gender roles and behaviors. There, too, are very few bisexuals and even fewer **transgender** characters, although this, too, is changing (Jenkins 1998).

The representations of support systems are also lacking. Gay and lesbian adult and young adult characters tend to be segregated by gender. Generally, gay male characters have mostly male friends while lesbian characters often have male and female friends. Further, the relationships between gay and lesbian characters' families of origin and gay and lesbian communities are often antagonistic. For example, the parents or siblings of the gay and lesbian characters some times believe that gay and lesbian communities are comprised of pedophiles, perverts, and those determined to recruit others, like their relatives, to a lifestyle that they perceive as sinful. Furthermore, gay and lesbian characters typically appear as the only gay and lesbian people in a predominantly heterosexual community (Jenkins 1998). They rarely are embedded within a community of gay and lesbian characters, such as a queer youth center, or within a sexually diverse group like a **gay–straight alliance**.

The role of LGBT characters in this literature is also problematic. Initially, these characters were peripheral, but in the early 1980s, they began to take center stage. Since the mid-1980s, however, protagonists are less likely and secondary characters are more likely to identify as **queer** (Cart 1997). Therefore, the literature tends to be narrated from a heterosexual's perspective, which pushes LGBT concerns to the periphery, again failing to support and affirm LGBT readers (Jenkins 1998).

Some middle school literature fills the gaps left by these shortcomings. For example, *Rainbow Boys* by Alex Sanchez (2001) is appropriate for older middle school readers. Three high school students, none of whom identify as straight, narrate the book. Jason is an athlete with a steady girlfriend who struggles with his attraction to other boys and his internalized **homophobia**. Kyle, who is a swimmer, identifies as gay, but has never had a boyfriend and is out to only a few friends. Nelson, an effeminate gay guy, is out to everyone and suffers daily from overt homophobia. The sympathetic portrait of Nelson is a rare example of a "queer gay" who is accepted by his mother, peers in an out-of-school group for **lesbian** and **gay youth**, and even a small social circle at school. Kyle and Nelson are best friends, but they are close friends with a lesbian couple who are also high school students, which is atypical in this body of literature. Another difference is that Kyle and Nelson are characters within a larger gay and lesbian context, the **community LGBT support group**, which Nelson's mother supports.

Despite the **Latino** character names, **ethnicity** is all but ignored, and these characters tend to be disturbingly homophobic. For example, it is José's truck from which a homophobic epithet was yelled and a bottle was "hurled past Kyle's head and smashed into the concrete walk" (p. 108); it was Mr. Espinoza, Jason's father, who responded to Jason's **coming out** by describing him as "disgusting" and punching him. Another troubling aspect of the novel is that **bisexuality** is characterized as little more than a transitional phase.

Bisexuality, in terms of **desire** more than **sexual identity**, is explored better in *Empress of the World* (Ryan 2003). At a summer camp for high school students identified as **gifted**, the protagonist, Nic, falls in love with another girl, Battle, and develops a more intimate group of friends. Nic acknowledges her former attraction to guys and her current attraction to Battle—without assuming a particular sexual identity. Nic evades sexual identity labels entirely, describing the larger group of students as "mostly white, some Asians, a few black kids" (p. 4). Her smaller group of friends includes an Asian boy and a Jewish lad, but still the novel centers around three white girls.

This contrasts with Jacqueline Woodson's books for younger middle school readers that address lesbian themes in the lives of young **African Americans**. *House You Pass on the Way* (1997) features Staggerlee, a biracial girl from **rural** Virginia who is visited by her estranged cousin, Tyler. They become fast friends and eventually share their experiences with same-sex desire. *The Notebooks of Melanin Sun* (1995) is told from the perspective of a thirteen-year-old boy who lives in Brooklyn with his mother. While Melanin's heterosexuality gradually plays a more pronounced role in his life, he learns of his mother's new love: a white woman. Melanin struggles with his racial **prejudice** and homophobia.

Lois-Ann Yamanaka's *Name Me Nobody* (1999) also illustrates a young person's coming to terms with the homosexuality of a person close to her, but rather than a parent, it is a long-time best friend. The protagonist, Emi-Lou, struggles with losing and gaining weight, her emerging heterosexuality, and accepting her best friend as a lesbian. Written in Pidgin, or Hawaii Creole English, Emi-Lou lives in Hawaii with her strong and loving grandmother. She helps Emi-Lou develop confidence and maintain her friendship with Von, who spends increasing amount of time with her girlfriend.

In the Australian novel, *Peter* (Walker 1993), the protagonist questions his heterosexuality as he becomes attracted to his brother's gay friend, David. His questioning is complicated by his social circle in which homophobic slurs are regularly used to define appropriate masculine behavior. Peter is a complicated character who both reinforces some stereotypes about gay men, by dressing well for example, and disrupts such stereotypes, by having interests in the mechanics of dirt bikes, lawnmowers, and cars. Ultimately, he tries to initiate a romantic relationship with David, who offers Peter his friendship instead.

There are very few transgender main characters in literature appropriate for middle school students. One is in the short story "Standing on the Roof Naked" (Lantz 2001), in which Jeannie, a masculine fifteen year-old whose assigned gender is female, questions both her gender and sexual identities. Rather than coming to any conclusions about her identities, she seems open to the possibilities. Jeannie is the narrator of the story, so readers get some insight into her thoughts and feelings. For example, Jeannie explores whether s/he is "a girl, a boy, a lesbo, a fag?" as s/he wanders and wonders through her daily activities.

"Winnie and Tommy" (Block 1994) is another short story that includes transgender characters (male-to-female), positively, but only peripherally. Nevertheless, Francesca Block's writing is stunning, whimsical, and particularly appropriate for reluctant and urban readers. *Weetzie Bat* (Block, 1989), for instance, portrays queer characters as an accepted part of daily life, in which Weetzie is given a lamp from which comes a genie who grants her three wishes, and that is just where the magic begins.

Bibliography

Brogan, Jim. 1995. "Gay Teens in Literature." Pp. 67–78 in *The Gay Teenager: Educational Practice and Theory for Lesbian, Gay, and Bisexual Adolescents*. Edited by Gerald Unks. New York: Routledge.

Cart, Michael. 1997. "Honoring Their Stories, Too: Literature for Gay and Lesbian Teens." *The ALAN Review* 25, no. 1: 40–45. Accessed June 12, 2003. http://scholar.lib.vt.edu/ejournals/ALAN/fall97/cart.html.

Day, Francis Ann. 2000. *Lesbian and Gay Voices: An Annotated Bibliography and Guide to Literature for Children and Young Adults*. Westport, CT: Greenwood.

Jenkins, Christine. 1998. "From Queer to Gay and Back Again: Young Adult Novels with Gay/Lesbian/Queer Content, 1969–1997." *Library Quarterly* 68, no. 3: 298–334.

Lantz, Francess. 2001. "Standing Naked on the Roof." Pp. 89–115 in *On the Fringe*. Edited by Donald R. Gallo. New York: Penguin Putnam.

Lobban, Marjorie, and Laurel A. Clyde. 1996. *Out of the Closet and Into the Classroom: Homosexuality in Books for Young People.* Port Melbourne: Thorpe.

Mitchell, Claudia. 2000. "'What's Out There?' Gay and Lesbian Literature for Children and Young Adults." Pp. 112–130 in *Lesbian and Gay Studies and the Teaching of English: Positions, Pedagogies, and Cultural Politics.* Edited by William J. Spurlin. Urbana, IL: National Council of Teachers of English.

St. Clair, Nancy. 1995. "Outside Looking In: Representations of Gay and Lesbian Experiences in the Young Adult Novel." *The ALAN Review* 23, no. 1: 38–43.

Walling, Donovan R. 2004. "Gay- and Lesbian-Themed Novels for Classrooms Reading." *Journal of Gay and Lesbian Issues in Education* 1, no. 2, 97–108.

Web Site

Gay Lesbian Straight Education Network. June 2005. Accessed June 7, 2005. http://www.glsen.org/cgi-bin/iowa/home.html. This site has a "Booklink" for books of interest to both educators and youth. In the "Primary Students Grades K-6" section, there are approximately twenty-five picture books annotated, and the link to books for "Secondary Students Grades 7–12" includes about fifty novels and collections of short stories.

Literature, Secondary School

Laurel A. Clyde and *Marjorie Lobban*

Adolescents generally are developing an awareness of themselves as sexual beings, and sexuality is a significant theme in literature for young adults. It is important that secondary school students have access to literature which is inclusive, authentic, and varied in its reflection of adolescent sexualities. It is only in the last few decades that a range of nonheterosexual sexualities has been represented in novels specifically written for young adults.

Books published in English specifically for this age group and having homosexual characters or themes, or in which homosexuality is a focus, first appeared in the 1970s with the gradual relaxing of attitudes towards the portrayal of homosexuality and the description of homosexual relationships in adult literature (Lobban and Clyde 1996). Among the early examples in literature for young adults are *Run Softly, Go Fast* (Wersba 1970), *Is That You Miss Blue?* (Kerr 1975), and *In the Tent* (Rees 1979). The 1980s saw a four-fold increase in titles from eighteen (1970s) to seventy-one (1980s) novels. Significant books include *Annie on My Mind* (Garden 1982), *Dance on My Grave* (Chambers 1982), *The Milkman's on His Way* (Rees 1982), *Night Kites* (Kerr 1986), and *What Are Ya?* (Pausaker 1987). During the 1990s, another 101 titles appeared, including *Peter* (Walker 1991), *Out Walked Mel* (Boock 1991), *The Drowning of Stephan Jones* (Greene 1992), the collection *Am I Blue?* (Bauer 1994), and *Jerome* (Taylor 1999). There is every indication that this level of publishing is continuing into the first decade of

See also Adolescence; Antibias Curriculum; Bisexual Youth; Curriculum, Secondary; Disabilities, Physical; Gender Identity; Gender Roles; Literature, Middle School; Literature, College; Mentoring; Prejudice; Sexism; Stereotypes; Transgender Youth.

the twenty-first century, bringing some innovative books such as *Sushi Central* (Duncan 2003) by a young Australian author writing about contemporary **urban** gay teen lifestyles.

Despite the increasing numbers of books published across these three decades, it is only in the last few years that occasional books dealing with **bisexuality, transgender,** and **cross-dressing** have been published. As of 2004, just a few books with bisexual characters had appeared for high school students, including *My Heartbeat* (Freymann-Weyr 2002), *Geography Club* (Hartinger 2003), and *Lucky* (de Oliveira 2004). There are fewer examples of books dealing with transgender or cross-dressing characters. In the anthology *Love & Sex: Ten Stories of Truth*, (Cart 2001), "The Welcome" by Emma Donoghue tells of Luce, a young lesbian living in a women's house, who is attracted to a mysterious older woman in the house. Months later Luce learns that J. J. was biologically a man who was undergoing gender reassignment. In *The Flip Side* (Matthews 2003) fifteen-year-old Robert has to dress up to play Rosalind in Shakespeare's *As You like It*. He is disturbed by how much he enjoys the experience, but goes on to experiment further with the help of a female student who plays the male role opposite him. There are no examples of sexual relationships between young people and adults except in stories that deal primarily with child abuse.

Males predominate as teen and adults characters in these young adult novels (Jenkins 1993). Since the 1970s, the ratio of male to female characters has been consistent at two to one (Clyde and Lobban 2001). Further, although female authors write about homosexual men and boys, male authors seldom write about lesbians. Female writers together have created more male homosexual than lesbian characters. Consequently, **lesbian youth** find fewer characters with whom they can identify (Clyde 2003).

What does the literature tell adolescents about being homosexual? Taken as a whole, secondary school literature supports the idea that "being gay or lesbian" is an innate characteristic rather than an identity that one assumes or constructs. Thus, the **"coming out"** novels are about coming to terms with or accepting one's homosexuality rather than making a choice about it. In *Checkers* (Marsden 1996), for instance, Daniel, a gay teenager, says "I can't help the way I am. I didn't choose to be this way. But this is the way I am, this is me . . . ." Sometimes a source of difficulty lies in the young gay or lesbian not wanting to accept his or her **sexual orientation.** For example, Marco in *Jerome* (Taylor 1999) only confronts his homosexuality when his friend Jerome commits **suicide**—apparently because of his unrequited love for Marco. *Independence Day* (Ecker 1983) revolves around sixteen-year-old Mike's increasing acceptance of his homosexuality, despite the problems. A few books depict **sexual identities** as more fluid or more ambiguous. *My Heartbeat* (Freymann-Wehr 2002) and *Lucky* (de Oliveira 2004), deal with bisexuality. The experience of Robert in *The Flip Side* (Matthews 2003) has already been described; Milena, who plays opposite him in *As You Like It* and takes his cross-dressing in hand, is also portrayed as somewhat sexually ambiguous.

A related and enduring theme is the dread that many teenage characters live with, fearing that their sexuality will be revealed and their lives will be changed for ever. Often it is the real or imagined reactions of friends or family that fill the young gay or lesbian with apprehension. Some novels show this apprehension to be well-founded. In *Keeping You a Secret* (Peter 2003), Holland is thrown out of home when she reveals her relationship with Cece; in *What Happened to Lani Garver*

(Plum-Ucci 2002), Lani is subjected to ridicule and even physical violence. Nevertheless, some authors do not depict homosexuality as a problem to be solved or a difficulty to be overcome. On the dust jacket of *Gravel Queen*, Tea Benduhn (2003) explains that she "wanted to write an uplifting story about teen love that had a positive outcome." The novel's focus is on Aurin, who finds another girl who is special to her and embarks on a relationship that enriches them both. Other books in this category include *Boy Meets Boy* (Levithan 2003), *Lark in the Morning* (Garden 1991), and *Postcards from No Man's Land* (Chambers 1999).

It is common that novels and short stories for teens take an "issue" approach; when the issue is homosexuality or coming out, **race** or **ethnicity** is unimportant and the protagonists are seldom members of racial or ethnic minorities; this has not changed over time. Although there have been other changes in LGBT young adult literature, here no obvious changes have occurred. *Blackbird* (Duplechan 1986) is unusual for its focus on being black and gay. Described on the back cover as "the first black coming-out story," it charts the progress of aspiring actor Johnnie Ray Rousseau through his final year of high school in the United States. Although persuaded to try out for the school play, he recognizes that "no way is a black boy, never mind a gay black boy, going to play Romeo in this high school," especially since Juliet will be played by a white girl. However, this does not stop him from finding ways to achieve his ambition to act. Other novels with prominent **African American** characters are *Ruby* (Guy 1979) and *Lucky in Love* (Sakers 1987). The British novel *The Milkman's on His Way* (Rees 1982) describes a long-term homosexual relationship between a white student and a black student in London, while *Name Me Nobody* (Yamanaka 1999) highlights the racial and ethnic mix of modern Hawaii. Paralleling the overall lack of emphasis on race or ethnicity is the treatment of other visible minorities. There are, for example, no physically challenged young gay protagonists.

If novels and short stories suggest "ways of being" to readers, then generally speaking they provide a conservative picture of being gay and lesbian. The **gay youth** or man is usually a very straight gay, not effeminate, just a regular guy who happens to love other men. Young gays are rarely presented in an outrageous manner, and when they are, they suffer for making themselves too obvious. Nelson in *Rainbow Boys* (Sanchez 2001), for example, refuses to modify his **camp** behavior and suffers constant **harassment** from his peers. Lani, in *What Happened to Lani Garver* (Plum-Ucci 2002), appears as neither male nor female, infuriating male and female adolescents in the small community. *Autobiography of a Family Photo* (Woodson 1995) is a notable exception; Troy prances around in high heels sneaked from his mother's closet, promising himself that, as soon as he can, he will outfit himself in "fly clothes" and make a colorful impact. The picture is equally conservative for young lesbians. Evie, in *Deliver Us From Evie* (Kerr 1994), is almost alone in wearing masculine clothes, although these are consistent with her outdoor work on the family farm. Sometimes, problems faced by adults are not glossed over as in *Annie on My Mind* (Garden 1982) where exposure of the long-term lesbian relationship between two teachers results in their dismissal.

Adults generally play important roles in the lives of people of high school age as parents, relatives, teachers, sports coaches, and role models. In these books a significant number of adult gay and lesbian characters appear. They usually fare much better than their adolescent counterparts. They are often idealized individuals, loving, perceptive, sensitive, and supportive. Lesbians tend to be depicted as warm and nurturing people; Deb in *Out of the Shadows* (Hines 1998) is such a person. Gay men, like Trent in *Breaking Boxes* (Jenkins 1997), are mentors and role models. In two of Sarah Walker's books for teens, *Water Colours* (2000) and *Camphor Laurel* (1998), adult lesbian relationships are examined and compared favorably with the disastrous heterosexual adult relationships; in *Jack* (Homes 1989), the main character comes to appreciate his gay father more after he witnesses the **domestic violence** in his best friend's all-American family. Dusty, in *Learning How to Fall* (Klein 1989), tells his friend, "My mother's gay, and she is about the only adult I know who has a decent relationship with another adult."

AIDS, as a topic in books for young people, is often associated with the theme of homosexuality. During the 1990s, death from AIDS and its effect on other people became a subject for treatment in young adult novels, although not as much as in novels and picture books for younger readers. Even for secondary school readers, novels tended to deal with the death from AIDS of a significant person in the life of a teenage character rather than from the perspective of a young person with AIDS. *Night Kites* (Kerr 1986) was the first such book with an AIDS storyline; seventeen-year-old Erick confronts the reality of the impending death of his older brother Pete. In *The Eagle Kite* (Fox 1995), Liam not only has to come to terms with his father's terminal illness, but also the knowledge of his father's homosexuality. Books in which an adolescent character is diagnosed with HIV or AIDS include *The Mayday Rampage* (Bess 1993), and a story in the anthology *Athletic Shorts* (Crutcher 1992).

The majority of the books for high school students have been published in the United States. However, there are significant contributions from other English-speaking countries, particularly the United Kingdom, Canada, Australia, and New Zealand. Translations of books from languages other than English have appeared in recent years. For example *It's Love We Don't Understand* (Moeyaert 2002) has been translated from the Dutch, as has *Brothers* (van Lieshout 2001), while *Damned Strong Love* (van Dijk 1995) has been translated from the German.

Bibliography

Clyde, Laurel A. 2003. "School Libraries and Social Responsibility: Support for Special Groups and Issues—the Case of Homosexuality." Paper presented at the World Library and Information Congress: 69th IFLA General Conference and Council, 1–9 August, 2003, Berlin.

Clyde, Laurel A., and Marjorie Lobban. 2001. "A Door Half Open: Young People's Access to Fiction Related to Homosexuality." *School Libraries Worldwide* 7, no. 2: 17–30.

Cuseo, Allan A. 1993. *Homosexual Characters in YA Novels, a Literary Analysis, 1969–1982.* Metuchen: Scarecrow Press.

Day, Frances Ann. 2000. *Lesbian and Gay Voices: An Annotated Bibliography and Guide to Literature for Children and Young Adults.* Westport, CT: Greenwood Press.

Jenkins, Christine A. 1993. "Young Adult Novels with Gay/Lesbian Characters and Themes 1969–92: A Historical Reading of Content, Gender and Narrative Distance." *Journal of Youth Services in Libraries* 7, no. 1: 43–55.

———. 1998. "From Queer to Gay and Back Again: Young Adult Novels with Gay/Lesbian/Queer Content, 1969–1997." *Library Quarterly* 68: 298–334.

Lobban, Marjorie, and Laurel A. Clyde. 1996. *Out of the Closet and Into the Classroom: Homosexuality in Books for Young People.* 2nd ed. Port Melbourne: Thorpe.

Webunder, Dave, and Sarah Woodard. 1996. "Homosexuality in Young Adult Fiction and Nonfiction: An Annotated Bibliography." *The ALAN Review* 23, no. 2: 40–43. Available on the Web at http://scholar.lib.vt.edu/ejournals/ALAN/winter96/webunder.html.

Web Sites

Out and About: Teen Zone. June 2002. Day County (USA) Library System. Accessed November 17, 2004. http://www.baycountylibrary.org/TeenPage/glfic.htm. Includes teen fiction and nonfiction related to homosexuality.

Reading Rants!: The Closet Club: Gay Fiction for Teens. January 2004. Jennifer Hubert. Accessed November 17, 2004.This listing is current to 2004. http://tln.lib.mi.us/~amutch/jen/closet.htm. Annotations, targeted at teen readers, are both descriptive and evaluative.

Young Adult Literature. December 2002. Melinda Kanner. Accessed November 17, 2004. http://www.glbtq.com/literature/young_adult_lit.html. Links to related articles, including articles about authors such as Jacqueline Woodson, and a bibliography.

Men's Studies

Yin-Kun Chang

Men's studies is an examination and analysis of the ways biology, culture, and society shape male identities and life experiences. In its conceptualization of sex and gender, men's studies analyzes patriarchal power and **sexual orientation** division by interrogating masculinity, which is a vital and necessary extension of the feminist project insofar as it makes gender visible as a set of power relations. Politically, men's studies is rooted in the profeminist men's movement, taking seriously the feminist challenge that men should locate themselves as men rather than with the pretense of being objective experts in a world where women are outsiders. Moreover, the study of masculinities and male experiences as specific and varying social–historical–cultural formations has direct applications to sexual orientation and queer youth. Men's studies is concerned about the traditional place of homosexual masculinities at the bottom of a gender hierarchy among men. Gayness, in this taxonomy, is the repository of whatever is symbolically expelled from masculinity, in the common sense; thus, gayness is easily assimilated to femininity. As boys, most men are socialized within a conventionally patriarchal household with a repressive attitude toward sexuality, resulting in tension and anxiety. Most receive no **sexuality education** from their parents and, at best, only moralized sex education from their schooling. Consequently, men's studies offers an important avenue for young males, particularly **gay youth**, to share cultural experiences about sex and gender with others and to challenge biases and **stereotypes**.

Rooted in the search for progressive profeminist change in male roles, the issues in men's studies are both theoretical and practical. These issues include the relationship between men's studies and **feminism**, discussion about patriarchy, the formation of masculinity, the division of housework, participation in social movements, and male same-sex **desire**. Such studies situate masculinities as objects of study on par with femininities, focusing on how multiple femininities and masculinities are a central fact about gender and the way its structures are lived. Thus, the ultimate goal is not merely to study forms of masculinity and femininity, but rather to understand the possibilities for a commonly shared humanity not defined in terms of gender.

Men's studies is a continuation of feminist methods in an area of scholarship that is virtually untouched. In the 1960s, feminism assumed a more radical focus, seeking a revolutionary transformation of society. If first-wave feminists were inspired by the abolition movement, their great-granddaughters were swept into feminism by the civil rights movement, the attendant discussion of principles such as equality and justice, and the revolutionary ferment caused by protests against the Vietnam War. Unlike their ancestors, second-wave feminists engaged in extensive theoretical discussion about the origins of women's oppression, the nature of gender, and the role of the family. During the 1980s and 1990s, feminist social theory

See also Identity Politics; Sexism; Sissy Boy; Spirituality; Sports, Gay Men in; Women's Movement; Women's Studies.

was influenced by **poststructuralist** and postmodernist analysis. Following post-modernist emphasis on difference and plurality, feminist theorists argued that tradi-tional feminist analysis tended to reflect the viewpoints of white, middle-class European Americans and European women. Thus, "third-wave feminism" claims to reject a universalistic perspective, and is instead more sensitive to local, diverse voices.

Men's Studies comes from the same historical origins as third-wave feminism. It suggests that we need desperately to critically interrogate masculinity, both to re-veal the dynamics of power and privilege and to find those points of entry for men into the discussion of gender equality. Critical analysis doesn't need to be relent-lessly critical of the men themselves. It also needs to examine the ways in which men are changing and have changed, and to recognize the strategies of resistance to male domination that groups of men have developed.

The key strategy in men's studies is to interrogate hegemonic masculinity, which is always constructed in relation to various subordinated masculinities as well as in relation to women (Connell 1987). For gay youth, the most visible bearers of hege-monic masculinity are not always the most powerful people; instead, it may be ordi-nary people, such as classmates and educators, or even cultural or social configurations in their everyday lives, such as textbooks and school activities. Schools are sites where this masculinity is developed, practiced, and actively pro-duced and reproduced in relation to the cultural repertories and institutional condi-tions of schooling.

The interplay between different forms of masculinity, such as hegemonic and subordinate masculinities, is an important part of how the patriarchal social order works. Thus, we need to distinguish hegemonic masculinity from a generalized male gender role. The public face of hegemonic masculinity is not necessarily what powerful men are, but what sustains their power and what large numbers of men are motivated to support. The main reason for this support is that most men, in-cluding gay and bisexual males, benefit from the subordination of women. Many feminist analyses have documented men's control of governments, corporations, and media; men's better jobs, incomes, and command of wealth; male control of the means of violence; and the entrenched ideologies that pushed women into the home and dismissed their claims for equality. This is the best example of domestic patriarchy being perpetuated by most men, regardless of their sexual orientation.

Hegemonic masculinity, however, operates at a more fundamental and uncon-scious level. It does not maintain itself through repression as an end in itself, but through discourses on identity. Thus, masculinity (for instance, being a heterosexual man) is understood as a fixed, coherent, and singular identity unrelated to **race**, **social class**, and culture. White men's masculinities, however, are constructed not only in relation to white women but also in relation to black men. Similarly, it is impossible to understand the shaping of working-class masculinities without giving full weight to their class as well as their gender politics. An ideal of working-class manliness was constructed in response to class deprivation, and through the same gestures as it was defined against working-class women.

Teaching about hegemonic masculinity, therefore, means critically examining the dominance of male heterosexuality, the ideologies that have supported it by silencing the experience of others, and the power structures and privilege that it disguises. It also means interrogating how hegemonic masculinity subordinates women and gay men, persecutes effeminate men, and underpins the racism of men's colonial legacy. Men's studies programs, in formal or informal educational institutions, are designed to investigate these issues. Emphasizing the history of male oppression, men's studies also explores the spiritual, cultural, social, familial, tonic, political, economic, historical, philosophical, medical, and psychological aspects of hegemonic masculinity. In the process, it strives to empower students and men with the knowledge and capabilities needed to manage the resulting changes in men's roles and responsibilities effectively.

There is not a single men's movement today. In the United States, there are at least five types of men's movements. The mythopoetic men's movement is interested in men's inner work such as recovery, working through grief issues and anger management. Generally open to the idea of different roles for men and women, this movement is tolerant of homosexuality, but gay issues are not central. In contrast, the feminist men's movement is more political, identifying with the more radical wing of feminism and favoring political action in the areas of gay rights, antiwar, antirape, and solidarity with oppressed peoples. Here gender is seen as a social construct and male violence as the result of role-conditioning. Its antipathy to the traditional family generally puts it in opposition to fathers' rights groups. This third type is organized primarily around issues and problems confronting single and divorced fathers, with a growing interest in the social issue of fatherless families. The men's tights movement overlaps with the fathers' rights group, but has a broader spectrum of interests (including the draft, men's treatment in prisons) and an opposition to **gender roles**. Strongly egalitarian, it views gender mostly as a social construct, opposing public policies, such as affirmative action and an all-male draft, that treat men and women differently, while tolerating homosexuality. Finally, the Christian men's movement, primarily evangelicalism and **religious fundamentalism**, favors traditional gender roles, opposes feminism, and disapproves of homosexuality. Like mythopoetic men's movement, its primary focus is on inner work.

These men's movements can be distinguished between those which accept the notion of men as "the oppressor" and those which reject it. Those who accept the oppressor notion believe that women have suffered more than men from sexual **discrimination** and refer to themselves as feminist men. Those who reject this notion of the feminist men have no one label on which they agree. As a result of their emphasis on gender as a social construct, feminist men's movements also largely focus on the issues of boys and young men. Almost all of the men's movement organizations standing by feminism have been sympathetic to such objectives as breaking down sexual stereotypes and passing the Equal Rights Amendment. For instance, the first of these organizations was the Men's Awareness Network, which evolved into Men Allied for Liberation and Equality. Similarly, New York Men Against Sexism is an organization that supports the profeminist men's movement. It is involved in eliminating gender and race discrimination, **homophobia**, and patriarchy.

Although men's studies as well as the men's movements emanated from United States, it has become popular throughout the world. Many male professors offer men's studies classes in different disciplines, and research about men's studies range from men in nontraditional occupations to male feminism. Some of the most striking men's movements are outside the United States, like Canada's famous white ribbon campaign, symbolizing men's opposition to male violence against women. Other formal and informal organizations are emerging worldwide, dealing with issues such as fatherhood, men's rights, false abuse allegations, paternity suits, **sexual harassment**, employment, and child support.

Bibliography

Brod, Harry, ed. 1987. *The Making of Masculinities: The Men's Studies.* Boston: Allen and Unwin.

Christian, Harry. 1994. *The Making of Anti-Sexist Men.* New York: Routledge.

Connell, Robert W. 1987. *Gender and Power: Society, the Person and Sexual Politics.* Stanford, CA: Stanford University Press.

———. 1995. *Maculinities.* Berkeley: University of California Press.

Digby, Tom, ed. 1998. *Men Doing Feminism.* New York: Routledge.

Spender, Dale, ed. 1981. *Men's Studies Modified: The Impact of Feminism on the Academic Disciplines.* New York: Pergamon.

Web Sites

American Men's Studies Association. 2004. Accessed December 3, 2004. http://www. mensstudies.org/. This multidisciplinary forum of men and women promotes critical discussion of issues involving men and masculinities, and disseminates knowledge about men's lives to a broad audience via the *Journal of Men's Studies.*

International Association for Studies of Men. 1999. Accessed December 3, 2004. http://www.rolstad.no/iasom. Promotes international cooperation and development of studies of men, based on profeminist, gay-affirmative and antiracist principles, and seeks to enhance the critical depth, variety and methodological, and theoretical development of this field. Site includes the organization's platform and newsletter archive.

Masculine Virtues. 2004. Accessed December 3, 2004. http://www.masculinevirtues.com/. Access to masculine issues, offering relevant Web sites which embrace a spectrum of men's interests, from the broadly masculine to the feminine-disguised-as-masculine.

Men Teach: A Recruitment for Men in Early and Elementary Education. November 2004. Accessed December 3, 2004. http://www.menteach.org/. Clearinghouse for research, education and advocacy with a commitment to increase the number of men teaching young children in early and elementary education.

Mental Health

Bryan N. Cochran

Youth who identify as lesbian, gay, bisexual, or transgender (LGBT) appear to be at greater risk for mental health problems (defined by meeting criteria for a ***Diagnostic and Statistical Manual*** (DSM) diagnosis that causes significant distress or impairment) than their heterosexual peers; explaining this increased risk, however, requires an understanding of the factors that lead to mental health difficulties.

See also Adolescence; Agency; Behavior Disorders; Counseling; Parents, Responses to Homosexuality; Passing; Religion and Psychological Development; Sexual Health, Lesbian and Bisexual women; Sexual Health, Gay and Bisexual men; Youth, At Risk; Youth, Homeless.

The prevailing view in the field of mental health is that psychological problems arise as a combination of "biopsychosocial" factors. For example, a biological predisposition toward major depressive disorders may be activated by a social stressor, such as ongoing conflict with a parent, and may be influenced by the person's psychological makeup, such as a tendency to blame one's self for the conflict. Obviously, LGBT youth face the same psychological, biological, and social risk factors as youth in the general population, but they also face additional stressors that increase their risk for mental health difficulties.

Stressors faced by LGBT youth include both externally-imposed **discrimination** and the internal turmoil of understanding their sexual identities. One way that this stress impacts the individual is that it shows up in mental health problems. **Research** studies have provided some support for the contention that LGBT youth are at increased risk for mental health problems. For example, **substance use**, suicidal behavior, and depression are more frequently found among LGBT youth than among heterosexual youth (Fergusson, Horwood, and Beautrais 1999; Lock and Steiner 1999). LGBT youth may be at increased risk for **eating disorders**, particularly **gay youth**. **Transgender youth** may receive the diagnosis of **Gender Identity Disorder** if they experience significant distress regarding their cross-gender identification, a likely possibility given that their peers and families may be rejecting or nonempathic. Even among populations already at risk for mental health problems, such as homeless adolescents, LGBT individuals experience more victimization and mental health difficulties than their heterosexual counterparts (Cochran et al. 2002). Longitudinal research studies that follow LGBT youth over time might indicate whether these problems are greatest at a particular time in the individual's life (such as while **coming out**) and what characteristics of LGBT youth contribute to **resiliency**.

There are two primary theories in the field of mental health to explain the increased rate of problems among sexual minority and transgender youth. The first is internalized **homophobia** (Shidlo 1994). From this perspective, LGBT youth are surrounded by negative messages about their sexual and gender identities that they eventually come to believe (consciously or unconsciously) about themselves. Hatred and misunderstanding of LGBT people are so pervasive in society that LGBT youth develop guilt and shame about who they are. These negative feelings turned toward the self may result in reckless or self-destructive actions, such as **drug use** or **suicide**. From the internalized homophobia viewpoint, treatment would involve making the person aware of the internalized negative attitudes while simultaneously affirming a healthy self concept that incorporates one's **sexual identity**.

The other major perspective that explains the increased risk of LGBT individuals for mental health problems is that of minority stress (Meyer 1995). People who are part of an oppressed minority group (based on ethnicity, **social class**, gender, or **sexual orientation**, for example) experience ongoing stressors that others in society do not have to face. Stressful experiences and the ways in which people cope with them are likely contributors to mental health problems (Lazarus and Folkman 1984). The additional stressors of living as an oppressed minority may contribute to an increased rate of disorders among minority group members. For example, a **lesbian youth** who is unable to be out at school may become anxious around others, anticipating sexist or homophobic comments from fellow students. Or, a **bisexual youth** may cope with the rejection of his family by drinking excessively to numb the hurt he feels. Treatment from the minority stress perspective would involve helping the individual learn new ways to cope with the **prejudice** and misunderstanding of others. This perspective encourages a broader movement of societal attitudes toward greater acceptance as well.

Neither the internalized homophobia nor the minority stress theory has been proven to explain why LGBT youth are at-risk for mental health problems. However, the internalized homophobia perspective has received some criticism in recent years (Williamson 2000). Specifically, this approach has been cited as explaining LGBT mental health problems based on characteristics of the LGBT person her/himself (an internalized set of beliefs) as opposed to identifying the cause as a social problem. Opponents of the internalized homophobia view believe that this perspective ultimately "blames the victim" rather than stressing the importance of social change.

Behavioral disorders in youth are typically grouped into either "externalizing disorders" (examples include conduct disorder, **alcoholism**, attention deficit hyperactivity disorder, or other conditions in which distress experienced by the individual is *outwardly* visible to others) or "internalizing disorders" (such as depression and anxiety disorders, in which distress is turned *inward*). Both types of disorders are likely to result from the complex interplay of biopsychosocial factors for each individual. For LGBT youth, it is possible that externalizing problems may arise when youth are dealing with an often hostile, discriminatory, and misunderstanding environment. Internalizing problems may result from the youth's struggle to understand his or her sexual identity. Because LGBT **identity development** is typically not an accepted developmental task for youth (indeed, efforts toward understanding one's sexuality are often met with criticism, judgment, and fear by parents or other authority figures), the consequences of this distress may be less visible to the adult observer. Therefore, it is particularly important that mental health practitioners assess LGBT youth clients for both internalizing and externalizing problems.

Recognition that one is having mental health difficulties is often a very different process than actually taking the steps needed to obtain treatment. Youth are less likely than adults to receive necessary treatment for mental health problems, often because their difficulties are interpreted as developmental processes that "they'll grow out of over time." LGBT youth, in particular, may be even less likely to receive treatment for mental health problems. First, the struggles that they experience with their sexual identities may be invisible to parents or other caregivers. Second, the history of mental health professionals' attitudes toward LGBT individuals is not one of complete tolerance and understanding. Homosexuality, in one form or another, remained a mental health disorder until the diagnostic system was revised in 1973. Even today, some mental health practitioners endorse "**reparative therapy**" to change individuals' sexual orientations, despite ethical guidelines discouraging such practice. Third, finding practitioners who will support LGBT youth in their struggles is a difficult task, especially in **rural** areas where there are few mental health practitioners in general. Even if youth manage to find a LGBT-affirmative practitioner, those who are not yet out must find a way to access care (facing barriers of transportation and cost) without their family's or caregiver's knowledge. An added layer of difficulty is present for LGBT youth from underrepresented minority groups or disadvantaged economic backgrounds. For example, a transgender **Asian American** individual with limited financial resources would be likely to encounter difficulties in finding a provider with cultural competence in working with Asian Americans, paying for psychotherapy services provided, and locating a provider with experience in understanding how transgender issues may intersect with emotional or psychological issues.

Bibliography

Cochran, Bryan N., Angela J. Stewart, Joshua A. Ginzler, and Ana Mari Cauce. 2002. "Challenges Faced by Homeless Sexual Minorities: Comparison of Gay, Lesbian, Bisexual, and Transgender Homeless Adolescents with Their Heterosexual Counterparts." *American Journal of Public Health* 92: 773–777.

Fergusson, David M., L. John Horwood, and Annette L. Beautrais. 1999. "Is Sexual Orientation Related to Mental Health Problems and Suicidality in Young People?" *Archives of General Psychiatry* 56: 876–880.

Lazarus, Richard S., and Susan Folkman. 1984. *Stress, Appraisal, and Coping.* New York: Springer.

Lock, James, and Hans Steiner. 1999. "Gay, Lesbian, and Bisexual Youth Risks for Emotional, Physical, and Social Problems: Results from a Community-Based Survey." *Journal of the American Academy of Child and Adolescent Psychiatry* 38: 297–304.

Meyer, Ilan H. 1995. "Minority Stress and Mental Health in Gay Men." *Journal of Health and Social Behavior* 36: 38–56.

Ryan, Caitlyn, and Donna Futterman. 1998. *Lesbian & Gay Youth: Care & Counseling.* New York: Columbia University Press.

Shidlo, Ariel. 1994. "Internalized Homophobia: Conceptual and Empirical Issues in Measurement." Pp. 176–205 in *Lesbian and Gay Psychology: Theory, Research, and Clinical Applications.* Edited by Beverly Greene, and Gregory M. Herek. Thousand Oaks: Sage.

Williamson, Iain R. 2000. "Internalized Homophobia and Health Issues Affecting Lesbians and Gay Men." *Health Education Research* 15: 97–107.

Web Sites

American Psychological Association. APA. Accessed June 9, 2005. http://www.apa.org/pi/lgbc/facts.pdf. This document, intended for educators in a school setting, discusses issues related to LGBT youth. It is in response to those who favor "conversion therapy" for LGBT youth and provides accurate data about the relationship between LGBT identity and mental health.

Sexuality Information and Education Council of the United States. 2005. SIECUS. Accessed June 9, 2005. http://www.siecus.org/pubs/pubs0004.html. Annotated bibliographies, fact sheets, and other documents about sexuality, youth sexual orientation, and mental health.

Mentoring

Dominique Johnson

Mentoring is a personal, reciprocal, helping relationship that provides emotional and psychological support and direct assistance with career and academic development. Mentors acts as role models, showing greater experience, influence, and

See also Allies; Career Counseling; Community LGBT Youth Groups.

achievement within a particular environment relative to their mentee. **Lesbian, gay, bisexual, transgender,** and questioning (LGBTQ) youth have unique educational contexts that require innovative approaches to ensure their educational equity. An engaging program for LGBTQ youth development, mentoring provides connections with caring peers and adults. Youth **agency,** empowerment, and LGBTQ community-based mentoring are critical considerations given the negative effects of **heterosexism** and **homophobia** on mentoring relationships not based in an LGBTQ or allied community. In heterosexist mentoring programs such as Big Brothers or Big Sisters, LGBTQ youth, whose **gender identity** and/or **sexual orientation** are unaccepted by their mentors, do not participate or under participate. Positive mentoring provides a way for **queer** youth to enter into healthy adulthood.

Because LGBTQ youth are generally not born into an LGBTQ community, the inaccessibility of cultural knowledge about queer communities and the absence or invisibility of role models poses significant challenges through **adolescence.** For example, LGBTQ youth often choose to focus on a single area of life, depending upon whether their mentors or role models are academic, career, cultural, religious, and/or identity-based. Some LGBTQ students might focus solely upon their academic or career pursuits because they do not have the necessary support to negotiate their sexual and/or gender **identity development.** Conversely, other LGBTQ youth who can or do focus on their emerging LGBT identities might be denied crucial academic support. Not given the support to integrate the multiple aspects of their lives, LGBTQ youth often find that they alone cannot effectively address identity development, school responsibilities, career planning, and their roles in cultural communities.

In meeting these challenges, LGBTQ youth are in need of positive adult role models but, paradoxically, LGBT adults who could be the most effective mentors or source of support, particularly **teachers** and school **administrators,** are not often available (Rofes 1997a, 1997b). Not only have these youth been failed by the school system, they have been failed by a community that should be a source of their strength. Bass and Kaufman (1996) attribute the lack of such support in adults to their not wanting to remember the pain of their queer adolescence, as well as the stigmatized fear of being accused of recruitment and/or exploitation. Ageism also engenders adult dismissal of youth and their issues, resulting in the **silencing** of youth (Sonnie 2000).

LGBTQ adult allies who genuinely engage with LGBTQ youth in their academic, career, and cultural communities hold promise for youth empowerment. However, an agenda for mentoring queer youth has yet to be developed by the greater LGBTQ community. "Until activists working toward lesbian and gay liberation make schools a primary site for their social justice **activism,** not only will queer youth continue to experience isolation, invisibility, and very difficult identity management choices, but the gay movement will continue to be marginalized . . ." (Rofes 1997b, pp. xvi–xvii).

LGBTQ and allied community-based mentoring is a viable method for educational support, particularly when in-school support is difficult for youth to find, or to supplement existing educational initiatives and promising school-based programs. Such mentoring contexts can emerge through informal relationships youth have with family members, coaches, religious leaders, doctors, therapists, social workers, neighbors, employers, coworkers, friends, romantic partners, friend's parents, and others.

Characteristics of mentoring programs include those that are individual and/or group-based, peer or adult mentoring, and informal or formal in context. Community centers and youth support services, for instance, offer mentoring programs based on a one-on-one peer interaction. LYRIC (Lavender Youth Recreation and Information Center) of San Francisco offers a mentoring program in its queer youth leadership project (http://www.lyric.org). In these and other community center programs, older queer youth serve as peer mentors, enabling youth agency and empowerment in mentoring opportunities. The one-on-one youth/adult interaction model is also used in youth support services such as Supporting Our Youth of Toronto which provides a comprehensive Housing and Mentoring Project (http://www.soytoronto.org/frame.html).

Both informal and formal mentoring community efforts can address the goals of school retention for students of diversity. Among these goals are: promoting greater student, faculty, and administrator contact, **communication**, and understanding; and, encouraging the use of school resources designed to aid students with traditionally nonacademic issues (Wunsch 1994).

Within the school, mentoring can occur in many different ways. **Gay–straight alliances** (GSAs) can provide a context for both informal and formal peer and faculty–student mentoring in schools. Individual mentoring can occur between a GSA leader and her/his successor while they plan for a transition to a new school year, and a GSA faculty adviser and a GSA member as they plan a fundraising event. Group-based mentoring can occur at different levels between GSA members, leaders, and advisers as they work on, for example, project management or event planning. Peer-mentoring programs in higher education, many of them formal individual peer-mentoring relationships, have been successful (Alford-Keating 2002). Stanford University (http://www.lgbt.stanford.edu?), University of California, Los Angeles (http://www.uclalgbt.com), and the University of Southern California (http://www.usc.edu/org/glbmentoring) have LGBTQ peer-mentoring programs for undergraduate students.

Examples of faculty/student mentoring opportunities are also emerging on United States college campuses. For example, Stanford University offers a resource database of faculty and student affairs staff volunteers who serve as points of contact within their departments or offices for queer students. This database also contains the names, locations, and personal statements of LGBTQ alumni. University of Chicago (http://queer.uchicago.edu) provides mentoring opportunities for LGBTQ undergraduate students with an LGBTQ faculty or staff member, and University of Michigan (http://www.umich.edu/~inqueery) sponsors mentoring for LGBTQ graduate and professional students with faculty by publishing an LGBTQ mentoring directory.

Educators can effectively serve as LGBTQ youth mentors, and the need for queer adult allies as mentors is great. Mentoring might be especially important as a developmental benefit for these youth because not only has the adult LGBTQ community agenda excluded them, but their teachers are all too often unsupportive. These youths' feelings about their teachers often play an important role in explaining their troubles in school (Russell, Seif, and Truong 2001). Educators can be adult **allies** to LGBTQ youth by sponsoring mentoring programs in their schools and communities. They can also act as youth allies by understanding the power of youth agency and respecting the voices of LGBTQ youth in dedicating themselves in working toward the fundamental right to a just education. LGBTQ students who have supportive school faculty or LGBTQ-related resources available to them do better in school and are more likely to plan to attend college (GLSEN 2003).

There are no data or research, however, in this area with particular respect to mentoring LGBTQ youth. Communities of practice, however, demonstrate that through mentoring, collaborative cultures of understanding and support should develop between LGBTQ youth and the meaningful adults in their lives. Among these, communities of understanding include **secondary schools** with an LGBT focus or counseling programs such as **Project 10**, which have proven effective in working with LGBTQ youth.

Bibliography

Alford-Keating, Patricia. 2002. "Mentoring Programs." Pp. 101–106 in *Our Place on Campus: Lesbian, Gay, Bisexual, and Transgender Services and Programs in Higher Education*. Edited by Ronni Sanlo, Sue Rankin, and Robert Schoenberg. Westport, CT: Greenwood Press.

Bass, Ellen, and Kate Kaufman. 1996. *Free Your Mind: The Book for Gay Lesbian, and Bisexual Youth—and Their Allies*. New York: HarperCollins.

GLSEN. 2003. *National School Climate Survey*. Accessed June 9, 2005. http://www.glsen.org/cgi-bin/iowa/all/library/record/1413.html.

Rofes, Eric. 1997a. "Gay Issues, Schools, and the Right-Wing Backlash." *Rethinking Schools* 11, no. 3: 1, 4–6.

———. 1997b. "Schools: The Neglected Site of Queer Activists." Foreword in *School Experiences of Gay and Lesbian Youth*. Edited by Mary B. Harris. Binghamton, NY: Haworth Press.

Russell, Stephen R., Hinda Seif, and Nhan L. Truong. 2001. "School Outcomes of Sexual Minority Youth in the United States: Evidence from a National Study." *Journal of Adolescence* 24: 111–127.

Sonnie, Amy. 2000. *Revolutionary Voices: A Multicultural Queer Youth Anthology*. Los Angeles: Alyson.

Wunsch, Marie A. 1994. "Developing Mentor Programs: Major Themes and Issues." *New Directions for Teaching and Learning* 57: 27–34.

Web Sites

Live Out Loud. May 2004. Accessed December 4, 2004. http://www.liveoutloud.info. Providing LGBT youth the opportunity to speak with accomplished LGBT people, Live Out Loud organizes panel discussions held after school and at high school general assemblies about men and women in the gay community who are passionate and powerful in their life's work, who are making a difference in the community, and who are interested in sharing their story with LGBT youth.

National Youth Advocacy Coalition. Fall 2003. Accessed December 4, 2004. http://www.nyacyouth.org. The National Youth Advocacy Coalition is a social justice organization that advocates for and with young people who are lesbian, gay, bisexual, transgender, or questioning (LGBTQ) through various programs and services such as an online, searchable database of youth organizations and support services.

OutProud. 2004. Accessed December 4, 2004. http://www.outproud.org. OutProud, The National Coalition for Gay, Lesbian, Bisexual & Transgender Youth, serves the needs of these young men and women by providing advocacy, information, resources, and support through online resources such as the Community Role Models archive, created so that queer and questioning youth can become aware of the wonderful contributions so many gay, lesbian, bisexual, and transgender individuals have made throughout history.

Mexico, LGBT Youth and Issues in

Paulina Millán Álvarez

Although **lesbian, gay, bisexual,** and **transgender youth** (LGBT) in Mexico have slowly emerged from invisibility, they urgently require the attention and protection of various social and government institutions. Over the last three decades, the Mexican LGBT population has won many battles against **discrimination** and has supported the inclusion of **antidiscrimination policies,** laws, and campaigns. However, issues such as legal recognition of same-sex couples, rights of **adoption,** and protection of LGBT youth throughout the country have failed to attract legislators' attention. No law protects LGBT minors against discrimination by authorities such as teachers and parents, and the laws prohibiting abuse by policeman are poorly enforced.

Until very recently, support groups in Mexico were only focused on the adult gay and lesbian population, as human rights and gay activists directed all efforts toward necessary legal and political reform. In September 1999, the Legislative Assembly of the Federal District banned discrimination based on **sexual orientation.** This ordinance—the first of its kind in Mexico—modified Article 281 of the Federal District Penal Code to punish those persons who "provoke or incite hatred or violence, refuse to provide an individual with a service . . . offered to the general public, harass or exclude an individual or group, or deny or restrict employment" based on sexual orientation. However, the ordinance applies only to Mexico City: there is a longstanding breach between law and practice in the country. This makes it difficult, especially for minors who fear a disclosure of their sexual orientation, to claim their rights or to accuse any authority or institution of **harassment** or discrimination.

As a mean to give additional protection to LGBT and other vulnerable communities in Mexico, a "Comisión contra la Discriminación" (Commission against Discrimination) was created by the Mexican government. Once a person files a complaint about discrimination, the commission makes a "recommendation" to the discriminatory authorities or institution in order for them to revise their policies and stop any form of discrimination. Absent the funds (the government has reduced its budget by 50 percent) and legal power to prosecute discriminators, the commission exerts little genuine authority. Further, since it doesn't deal with "family" discrimination, the most common site of violence against LGBT youth, its effectiveness is further limited.

Consequently, Mexican LGBT youth are unprotected and segregated. Schools can easily expel students who are gay, lesbian, or bisexual without any legal consequences. Further, minors are considered "property" of their parents who have all legal rights over them. Parents, for example, can send their queer teenage daughters or sons to clandestine institutions where criminals and drug addicts are kept for "rehabilitation," which consists of seclusion and violent punishment. Additionally, many health professionals and other adults who work with adolescents, lack information about **sexual orientation** and **gender identity.**

See also Activism, LGBT Youth; Catholic Education and Youth; College Campus Organizing; Cross-Dressing; Homophobia; Identity Politics; Latinos and Latinas; Legal Issues, Students; Parents, Responses to Homosexuality; Professionalism; Religion and Psychological Development; Secondary Schools, LGBT; Youth, At Risk.

In 2004, an "open" high school, the first in the country for teenagers who have been thrown out of school or denied education, was opened by older members of the LGBT community. Operating in the "Centro de la Diversidad Sexual," it is part of Centro de Atención para Adolescentes y Jóvenes Gays, Lesbianas y Bisexuales de México (CAIPAJ), recently formed by gay activist, Josué Quino.

Until 1988, those adults seeking to support LGBT youth faced a major hurdle. The Federal District Penal Code provided for three to eight years imprisonment and a fine for the corruption of minors, with homosexuality listed as an aggravating factor. If the minor later acquired "corrupt habits," such as "homosexual practices," the penalty increased. Since no definition of "corruption" was included in this law, some authorities imprisoned many homosexuals who were already legally considered as adults (men and women over age eighteen) for establishing relationships (friendly or romantic) with teenagers. This prevented adult support groups from accepting minors into their sessions or the formation of **LGBT community support groups**. Simply providing information about homosexuality could easily be interpreted as a form of corruption. When this law was repealed, many groups accepted members under eighteen years old, and a couple of other groups solely for adolescents and young adults were formed.

Nowadays, LGBT youth can find support in a few groups and institutions, particularly in big cities. Nueva Generación de Jóvenes Lesbianas (New Generation of Young Lesbians) started in 1996 with the objective of creating a space where lesbian youth could express themselves, exchange ideas, and get information. This group has attracted the attention of hundreds of young lesbian and bisexual women. It has published documents and brochures directed to this population and has participated and organized events that support the LGBT community. Recently created groups include: Proyecto de Gays, Lesbianas y Familia por una Comunicación Asertiva, and Centro de Atención Integral para Adolescentes y Jóvenes Gays. Families of gay and lesbian people have also received attention in the last years, and parents who have gay sons or daughters have started support groups for those who are in need of talking to someone or of receiving information (http://mx. geocities.com/padresporladiversidad). Bisexual groups remain scarce, however; the only one, Sentido Bi, operates in Mexico City. Two transgroups operate, Crisálida and TV MEX. The latter is a group opened to transgender, transsexual, and transvestite women, but neither focuses on youth. The only university LGBT group currently operating is Grupo Universitario de Diversidad Sexual, which provides information and support to a small community based at the National Autonomous University of Mexico. Although it is one of the most important state institutions in Mexico, the university hasn't been able to provide adequate support or protection. This group has been attacked by other students attending this university. There is no inclusion of LGBT material or courses at any college or university in Mexico.

Mexican teachers, doctors, and psychologists study in professional schools that follow very specific programs dictated by government institutions such as the Ministry of Public Education. These programs include basic information about sexuality and human reproduction, but they do not analyze topics such as sexual orientation in depth. Some university-based programs inform their students that homosexuality is not considered a disease and that therapies that claim to change people's sexual orientation are not effective or necessary. However, specific resources and strategies are not provided in even these programs. Thus, once they start their professional careers, few are able to meaningfully assist a student, client, or patient who is gay. Teachers are ill-prepared to respond when a student is being harassed by others, and psychologists often offer **reparative therapies** as the first choice for a patient who is having difficulty accepting his or her sexual orientation or identity (bisexuals are most vulnerable since even less is taught about this topic). Because there is no government or official associations that issue licenses to therapists, anyone can provide therapy. Not surprisingly, LGBT persons are reluctant to ask for **counseling** help or to start therapy, and LGBT minors who are sent to therapists by parents are likely to be rejected or questioned by professionals who wish to "change their minds" or convince them that homosexuality or **bisexuality** is wrong.

During the last couple of years, some books have been published in Mexico about sexual orientation, which are helpful to parents and LGBT youth. Affordable in price, their distribution outside of bookstores in a few cities is not efficient. *La Experiencia Homosexual* (*The Homosexual Experience*) was written by a Mexican psychologist to provide information about being gay, LGBT families, and "**coming out**" to gay and bisexual people. Marina Castañeda also wrote the book for heterosexual individuals who want to understand what it means to be sexually diverse in a Latin-American country. Another book directed to LGBT youth and their parents, *Mamá, Papa . . . Soy Gay* (*Mom, Dad . . . I'm Gay*), is an effective guide to communicating and understanding the processes of coming out and the social difficulties that many parents and gay adolescents face.

Research on LGBT youth in Mexico is scarce, as evidenced by the lack of data on suicidality, **substance abuse**, and run-aways. Even on the topic of **AIDS**, studies fail to consider the LGBT population. Although, AIDS is among the leading causes of death in the young adult Mexican population, scientific reports of same-gender sexual behavior and risks for HIV in Spanish-speaking countries are rare (Izazola-Licea et al. 2000). Censida, an organization that is part of the Mexican Ministry of Health, has recently declared that there are between 116,000 and 177,000 people who are HIV positive; six out of every ten are men who have sex with men. However, INEGI, Mexico's official institution for statistic and geographic information, only reports figures on people between ages fifteen and forty or so; no information is provided about LGBT young people or adolescents. Further, there are no official interventions aimed at the LGBT population.

Many NGOs in Mexico are dedicated to AIDS and **HIV education**. Some issue pamphlets or brochures with information and provide legal counseling, such as La Manta de México or Acción Humana por la Comunidad. These groups also offer workshops and lectures as well as assist HIV patients obtain medical support from the government or present formal complaints against the denial of such services by government institutions. Other groups, such as Fundación Mexicana para la Lucha contra el Sida, Albergues de México, or La Casa de la Sal are more involved in the caring of HIV patients who are abandonded by their families or who are unable to purchase medicine or medical care.

Bisexuality in Mexico has barely been in the public eye and seldom researched. One study of the perceptions of bisexuals found this sample of 500 Mexicans equated bisexuality to infidelity, confusion, illness, and indecision (Millán and Gayou 2003). Magazines, newspapers, and television reinforce this negative image, which has also entered the legal framework. For example, in 2002, Toluca (a city near Mexico City), changed its local law to allow wives to divorce those husbands who are bisexual.

Although bisexual characters have not yet been included in **films** or television shows, during the past twenty years female and male homosexuality as well as transgenderism have been topics for the Mexican mass media. Some shows, such as soap operas, have recently included a few gay characters, mostly men. The portrayals of gay and lesbian people vary greatly. In general, the drama genre has included gay-positive characters, people who have feelings, problems, and relationships—and who also happen to be gay. Comedy, on the other hand, has only included highly **stereotyped** gay characters (again, mostly men), who dress and act femininely and who work as hair stylists, designers, and the like. There has been only one gay youth character. His 2004 appearance, in a soap opera targeted at young people, was well-accepted. It included, in a natural and objective way, some problems LGBT youth have to deal with such as coming out and discrimination.

Television has an enormous impact on the opinion and attitudes of a vast majority of Mexican people. The messages from some of these shows are that certain types of gay men are acceptable (those whom you can laugh at), and that it is accepted for gay men to show their sexuality, but only in certain places or jobs. The other characters—the more real ones—seem to be soon forgotten, both by their audiences and by the television executives who created them, realizing that these brought too many complaints from conservatives and contributed to poor ratings.

Less coverage has appeared in Mexican cinema and radio. The film *Mil Nubes de Paz Cercan el Cielo, Amor, Jamás Acabarás de ser Amor* (*A Thousand Clouds of Peace*, Mexico 2004) depicts the life of a young man who discovers he is gay. It appeared in relatively few movie theaters. There is one gay radio show, "Triple G," directed to young gay people and whose hosts are two gay men and a lesbian.

Just as this **popular culture** reflects it, Mexican culture remains very conservative. The majority of the population is educated directly or indirectly by the Catholic Church, which exerts significant influence on many legislators. The presence of the Church extends to the privately-owned media and education. For LGBT youth, the impact of religion is partly offset by the **Internet**. Many LGBT youth find in it a source of information and even the possibility to make friends and find support groups. Nevertheless, access is a privilege that only youth who live in cities and have some money can use. Those from families of the lower **social class** or **rural** communities are very far from the issues and the consideration of LGBT activists.

Larger states like Guadalajara, Monterrey, Puebla, and Mexico City have seen a dramatic growth in places that provide entertainment for the LGBT youth, although none are exclusively for young people. These include cafés, bars, restaurants, and shops that compete fiercely among each other for this population's attention and money. Weeknights and weekends in Zona Rosa (Pink Zone) in Mexico City are one good example. Although there is no official recognition of the place as publicly gay, rainbow flags in shops and the many young same-sex couples who fill the few streets of this rapidly growing neighborhood make it difficult to miss. Gay Pride parades also take place in some cities; Mexico City's is the biggest. In June, the main streets in these cities are closed one Saturday to allow the many participants to walk, followed by trailers decorated with balloons and flags in this mixture of a political rally and carnival-like celebration.

This generation of Mexican LGBT youth is witnessing important changes. With the election of the second openly-gay congresswoman, Enoé Uranga (the first was Patria Jiménez), a bill for the recognition of the rights of same-sex couples was discussed in Congress for the first time. The legislation, which failed to receive support from the majority of lawmakers, would have allowed couples to form "unions of cohabitation," entitling partners to share insurance and property rights. However, no further discussion of this proposed law has occurred.

Bibliography

Amnesty International. 2001. *Crimes of Hate, Conspiracy of Silence. Torture and Ill-Treatment Based on Sexual Identity*. United Kingdom: Alden Press.

Carrier, Joseph M. 1995. *De los Otros: Intimacy and Homosexuality among Mexican Men*. New York: Columbia University Press.

Castañeda, Marina. 1999. *La Experiencia Homosexual (The Homosexual Experience)*. Mexico City: Editorial Paidós.

Izazola-Licea, José A., Steven L. Gortmaker, Kathryn Tolbert, Victor De Gruttola, and Jonathan Mann. 2000. *Prevalence of Same-Gender Sexual Behavior and HIV in a Probability Household Survey in Mexican Men. Journal of Sex Research* 37, no. 1: 37–43.

Lagunes, Francisco Javier, Homero Arriaga, and Rubén Del Valle. 2003. *Referencia de Medios para la Cobertura de las Acciones de Orgullo LGBT (Reference of Media for the Coverage of LGBT Pride Actions)*. Accessed December 3, 2004. http://www.orgullomexico.org/comunicadores/referencia.shtml.

Millán, Paulina, and Juan Luis Álvarez Gayou. 2003. *Bisexuality Seen form the Outside*. Presented at the16th World Congress of Sexology, Habana, Cuba. Accessed December 4, 2004. http://www.imesex.edu.mx.

Reding, Andrew A. 2000. *Question and Answer Series; Mexico: Update and Treatment of Homosexuals*. Washington: INS Resource Information Center.

Riesenfeld, Rinna. 2001. *Mamá, Papa . . . Soy Gay (Mom, Dad . . . I'm Gay)*. Mexico City: Editorial Grijalbo.

Web Sites

Grupo de Padres y Madres por la Diversidad Sexual. Accessed November 6, 2004. http://mx.geocities.com/padresporladiversidad. Information about many LGBT and supportive groups, including one the first groups created by and directed to parents. See also: Proyecto de Gays, Lesbianas y Familia por una Comunicación Asertiva. http://www.jornada.unam.mx/2002/ene02/020103/ls-proyecto.html.

Nueva Generación de Jóvenes Lesbianas. 2003. Martha Cuevas. Accessed November 6, 2004. http://www.generacionlesbica.org. Information about the first group created especially for young lesbians.

Travestis México. 2004. Accessed November 6, 2004. http://www.travestismexico.org. Information about one of the largest transgender groups created especially for women.

Multicultural Education

Cris Mayo

The most recent educational attempt to ensure United States' schooling equitably educates the country's diverse population, multicultural education in its current manifestations grew out of the civil rights movement of the 1950s and 1960s and the ethnic revivals of the 1970s. Parents and children of color organized to demand that schools reform curricula to more accurately represent their cultural backgrounds. Multiculturalism, as a curricular strategy, reminds educators that one

See also Critical Social Theory; Families, LGBT; Films, Youth and Educators in; Identity Politics; Literature, Early Childhood; Literature, Middle School; Literature, Secondary School; Racial Identity; Secondary Schools, LGBT; White Antiracism.

561

method of instruction does not fit all students, nor are all students facing the same risks of exclusion. A multicultural approach to education attempts to understand how a **curriculum** might better address the diversity of students, be aware of cultural biases that may affect their educational experiences, and use their cultural backgrounds as resources to help them do well in school. Following this logic, the relatively high drop out rate and high **suicide** rate ought to be sufficient cause for multiculturalism to include **lesbian, gay, bisexual,** and **transgender** youth. Further, multiculturalism provides a school context for discussions about sexual minority students that are not pathologizing, but part of a fuller understanding of the diversity of the school community. At present the major texts of multiculturalism briefly mention gay rights in a list of other movements indebted to the civil rights movement, but continue to focus largely on **race, ethnicity, social class,** and language. These texts, often used in teacher education, neglect how sexuality may also complicate the educational experience of LGBT youth of color and ignore the pressure of bias on all LGBT youth.

For LGBT students, multiculturalism provides a framework for examining the place of bias within the LGBT community. It reminds all community members of the problematic divisions of racism, ethnocentrism, sexism, able-bodyism, and classism that need to be addressed and continually worked against. LGBT-inclusive multiculturalism include lessons on different family structures, explaining that many children are in families that are not traditional, heterosexual, married couples. LGBT-inclusivity encompasses adoptive families, intergenerational families, and single-parent families. LGBT issues can also be incorporated into the multicultural classroom by examining the different forms sexuality takes in different cultures. In addition, because LGBT issues overlap with gender-related issues, discussions on femininity and masculinity can explore the relationships among **sexism, heterosexism,** and bias against transgender people. Lessons on **prejudice** and bias in multicultural classrooms can detail particular problems facing LGBT people and, in multicultural teacher education, provide ways for educators to prevent these forms of bias.

A few multicultural texts address LGBT issues (Grant and Lei 2001; Grant and Sleeter 2002). Still most multicultural education texts do not address sexuality, though they do provide space for young LGBT people of color, working class background, and/or young women to see parts of themselves reflected more fully in curricula. For LGBT youth of any ethnicity, race, class, or gender, multicultural education may provide the starting place for a consideration of the educational implications of their identities, as well as an understanding of sexual diversity.

Because multiculturalism tends to focus on aspects of identity in the cultural/ethnic model, it has so far largely neglected an examination of how the gay liberation movement and women of color **feminism** complicate the ideas of group membership and internal cultural differences. For instance, women of color feminists have long argued for understanding the interlocking of systems of oppression of racism, ethnocentrism, classism, heterosexism, and sexism (Combahee River Collective 1981) and called for a better account of the queerness of people who do not easily fit within their home cultures because of their sexuality (Anzaldúa 1981).

Versions of culture or group identity, like those often found in multicultural texts, simplify what it means to be a member of a culture or subculture, neglecting the complexity of identity. Though its roots are in the political movements that have grappled with complexity within groups, multicultural education rarely examines diversity within cultural, class, or gender groups.

Multicultural textbooks for teachers have been more successful in describing a variety of approaches to multicultural education. Some texts educate students about their cultural or gender group's history in order to make up for absences in the traditional school curriculum. Another approach is to emphasize intergroup relations and cultural exchange, educating diverse students about one another's cultural background through food fairs, cultural stories, and histories. Some forms of multiculturalism stress the democratic context of the United States and teach all students to understand themselves as part of the national plurality. In contrast, antibias multiculturalism stresses a need to understand the ways that racism, ethnocentricity, classism, and sexism, and in some curricula, able-bodyism, create barriers to equality. More radical, social reconstructionist or "transformative" approaches advocate transforming the curricula, school, and social institutions to ensure that children experiencing cultural, racial, and class bias are educated in culturally sensitive ways to offset their experiences of bias.

Some have argued that the conservative tendency of multiculturalism in public education stems from the general conservatism of public education itself (Weis and Fine 1993). Schools are institutions in a society characterized by inequities, and those inequities are in turn reflected in and perpetuated by schools, even through school-based attempts to address diversity. Schools, textbooks companies, and textbook selection committees all may have a moderating effect on multiculturalism's social transformational impulses. Where the more transformative multiculturalists may advocate social justice, school decision makers may find it more politically neutral to advocate that students understand culture in order to compete in a global marketplace. Multicultural education's concentration on particular definitions of culture may enable it to more easily turn away from more decidedly **antibias curriculum** that raise personal and institutional biases as difficult and contentious issues that must be talked through and acted against. It may be easier, particularly for people who are members of majority groups, to talk about comparative cultural practices, like festivals or cooking, than to discuss the biases that keep certain cultural, racial, class, and gender groups in positions of power (Davis 1996).

The particular definition of "culture" used in multiculturalism also has an effect on how much controversy it generates. For those who advocate assimilation, the call to bring diverse cultures into school curricula signaled an unwillingness to conform to a white, Euro-centric, national culture. In the 1980s and 1990s, multiculturalism was faulted by conservatives for creating and exacerbating social divisions (Schlesinger 1992). They asserted that schools ought to be institutions where diverse cultures are educated into the common bonds of citizenship. In contrast, New York educational reformers argued that curricula neglected to represent the diverse history of the state; because of that neglect, diverse children, especially children of color, were not seeing themselves reflected in important knowledge and were not doing well in school. In response to concern over its culturally biased curriculum, this state revised its social studies curriculum to more centrally include the histories of peoples of color and other minority groups. By representing its culture more accurately in terms of diversity, the revision nonetheless raised the ire of those who contended that minor parts of history were edging out white, male, historically revered figures.

LGBT issues were a central part of the ensuing culture war. One of the most visible of these controversies was over the "Children of the Rainbow," a first grade teacher's guide to implementing a multicultural curriculum introduced in New York

City schools in 1992. Despite the eventual revision of most of the gay-inclusive content and the cancellation of the contract of the schools chancellor who had championed the gay-inclusive multicultural curriculum, this controversy publicized the existence of gay- and lesbian-headed families and sexual minority students in schools. This activism LGBT people of color on behalf of the Children of the Rainbow was later directed on behalf of Harvey Milk High School. In addition, many LGBT activists turned their attention more comprehensively toward a broad array of school issues by working together with parents and students.

While many multicultural curricula and texts continue to neglect LGBT issues (Wallace 2000), multicultural education does provide an opportunity for students and teachers to take their identities seriously as educational issues, examine how curricula addresses or neglects aspects of their identities, and critically analyze inequities in public schooling. Even in schools where multiculturalism does not include sexuality, LGBT students have used the lessons of multiculturalism to structure their requests for curricular revisions, including broadening **educational policies** and curricula to address bisexuals and transgender people, faculty and administrative advocacy, and **gay–straight alliances.**

Bibliography

Anzaldúa, Gloria. 1981. "La Prieta." Pp. 198–209 in *This Bridge Called My Back*. Edited by Cherrie Moraga and Gloria Anzaldúa. Watertown, MA: Persephone Press.

Combahee River Collective. 1981. "A Black Feminist Statement." Pp. 210–218 in *This Bridge Called My Back*. Edited by Cherrie Moraga and Gloria Anzaldúa. Watertown, MA: Persephone Press.

Davis, Angela Y. 1996. "Gender, Class, and Multiculturalism: Rethinking 'Race' Politics." Pp. 40–48 in *Mapping Multiculturalism*. Edited by Avery F. Gordon and Christopher Newfield. Minneapolis: University of Minnesota Press.

Grant, Carl A., and Joy L. Lei. 2001. *Global Construction of Multicultural Education: Theories and Realities*. Mahwah, NJ: Erlbaum.

Grant, Carl A., and Christine E. Sleeter. 2002. *Making Choices for Multicultural Education: Five Approaches to Race, Class, and Gender*. New York: Wiley.

Irvine, Janice M. 1997. "One Generation Post-Stonewall: Political Contests over Lesbian and Gay School Reform." Pp. 572–589 in *A Queer World: The Center for Lesbian and Gay Studies Reader*. Edited by Martin Duberman. New York: New York University Press.

Schlesinger, Arthur M. 1992. *The Disuniting of America*. New York: Norton.

Wallace, Barbara. 2000. "A Call for Change in Multicultural Training at Graduate Schools of Education: Educating to End Oppression and for Social Justice." *Teachers College Record* 102, no. 6: 1093–1111.

Weis, Lois, and Michelle Fine, eds. 1993. *Beyond Silenced Voices: Class, Race, and Gender in United States*. Albany: State University of New York Press.

Web Sites

Advocates for Youth. 2004. Accessed December 7, 2004. http://www.advocatesforyouth.org/glbtq.htm. Advocates for Youth provides links to support groups, Web chats, Web rings, and resources for LGBT youth of all races and ethnicities, including links to Spanish language Web sites and groups.

Gay, Lesbian, and Straight Educators' Network. December 2004. Accessed December 7, 2004. http://www.glsen.org. GLSEN provides diverse LGBT youth contribute articles, organizing strategies (including a Students of Color Organizers' conference), and exchange information about school issues.

Youth of Color. 2005. YouthResource. Accessed June 9, 2005. http://www.youthresource. com/community/youth_of_color/index.htm. YouthResource provides LGBTQ youth of all races and ethnicities with information on health and community building. Links for youth of color include magazines, chat rooms, and organizations, as well as specific information and stories about coming out.

Multiple Genders

Christopher P. Toumey

Multiple genders are culturally legitimate social statuses which give a society a third category beyond male and female. Some young persons realize after puberty that they will not fulfill the usual expectations of becoming men or women in a conventional sense. For these youth, certain creative cultures produce additional categories in which people are genuinely happy in their **gender roles** and **sexual identities**, and are valid members of society, without having to fulfill the roles and norms expected of males or females. When compared with binary schemes of only-male-or-female, these multiple genders reveal that a binary vision of gender is neither universal nor inevitable.

Most of us were raised to believe that gender is binary: There are only two categories, male and female, and they are mutually exclusive in anatomy, feelings, and behavior. But how does binary gender make sense of categories like homosexuals, transvestites, and hermaphrodites? These latter categories are undeniable realities of human experience and anatomy, but binary thinking cannot account for them. They strongly suggest that there is something missing in the primary assumptions of binary gender.

Cultural anthropology reveals that some societies accommodate these realities by generating additional social categories. Most people in these societies conform to well-defined male or female roles. But it can also be acceptable for some members— usually a small percentage—to depart from those roles during or after puberty by entering other categories, that is, multiple genders. These are not merely variations on the theme of binary gender, for example, people who occasionally dress like the other sex, or whose sexual **desire** is same-sex while the rest of their lives is conventionally male or female. Rather, they are separate gender categories which are approximately as distinct as the categories of male and female.

One of the strongest examples of this phenomenon is the case of the hijras in **India,** as presented in Serena Nanda's (1999) ethnography, *Neither Man Nor Woman.* According to a powerful expectation in India, a male ought to become a husband and a father. Most adolescent boys accept this plan and behave accordingly. But during those years of sexual awakening, a few males begin to realize that they will not be able to fulfill the expectations of an adult male. Some understand that they are homosexual, while others are **intersex.** Those features exclude them

See also Africa, LGBT Youth and Issues in; Asia, LGBT Youth and Issues in; Colonialism and Homosexuality; Cross-Dressing; Gender Identity; Heteronormativity; Intersex; Native and Indigenous LGBT Youth; New Zealand, LGBT Issues in; Poststructuralism; Sexual Identity; Sissy Boy; Social Class; Tomboy.

from normative adult male roles, but traditional Indian culture, especially in the **rural** villages, has no category of gay male.

Imagine how a teenage boy in India confronts his predicament if he is homosexual or intersex. He has to fit into society in a clear status which is considered legitimate by the standards of Indian culture. If he lives in a large city, he notices a kind of people, the hijras, who might give him an acceptable status for his situation. This legitimation is based on a certain theory of male procreative energy. Homosexual and intersex males will not marry or have children, but they still possess unused male procreative energy. This can be transferred to other males—bridegrooms and baby boys—by blessing them at their weddings and births. Such a blessing will help the bridegroom become a father, or help the baby boy grow into a good man. This transfer-by-blessing makes good use of male procreative energy, which would otherwise be wasted. That line of reasoning gives cultural legitimacy to the hijras: These people are former males who help other males become better men.

Some intersex and **gay youth** leave their homes and attach themselves to a hijra community where they learn how to perform the blessing-by-transfer rituals, which include singing, dancing, playing musical instruments, and telling bawdy jokes. The hijra household becomes the youngster's new family, modeled on mother–daughter and sister–sister relations. Hijras adopt female names, dress, speech, and other attributes.

As the teenager becomes a young adult among the hijras, a momentous decision looms. Will I become a "true" hijra? This involves undergoing an emasculation ritual to remove the male genitalia. Hijra culture includes several mechanisms which cause new members to postpone this decision for five to ten years. In the ideal model of hijra life, one would make a decent living by conferring blessings at weddings and birth rituals. A large proportion of hijras, however, have to supplement that income by engaging in **prostitution**. Others find happiness by marrying male lovers.

It is important to note that sex between a male and a hijra is not thought of as male–male homosexuality. Sex with a hijra is heterosexual in the sense that a hijra is no longer a man, even if such a person is not a woman either. In effect, the hijras constitute a third gender. They also represent one of the rare instances in which a person can move from one caste to another, since the hijras are a caste apart from those into which they were born. They have their cultural paraphernalia for marking their caste identity, including unique origin myths, a patron goddess, rituals, and taboos. Thus, they constitute a culturally legitimate social status.

The other classic example of a third gender is the HalfMan–HalfWoman of certain Native American societies (more recently known as a Two-Spirit people). Two more statuses that might have been third genders in the past were the kathoey of Thailand and the bakla of the Philippines. Our knowledge of these is clouded by the arrival of Western medical thought which was strictly binary in its thinking. Westerners diagnosed kathoey and bakla as homosexuals, that is, pathological males. A more recent development was the influence of the Western idea of "gay," in the sense that gay describes homosexual males who are unashamed to be themselves. This switched bakla and kathoey from pathological to affirmative, but it retained the view that they were variations on the binary category of male. While it is regrettable that these historical developments obscured or suppressed indigenous thought which accommodated multiple genders, in these cases, notions of gender are vulnerable to change.

People in these multiple genders are appreciated as leaders of rituals and vessels of good fortune. They are so far removed from male and female personalities that they seem to be infused with magic. This is an important element of their social acceptance, and they embody it by virtue of **spirituality** very unlike that of normative males or females.

Anthropologists emphasize that the sexuality of a person in a third gender, as interesting as it is to some observers, is only a fraction of that person's entire life. As with conventional males and females, the interesting social and cultural realities of gender are missed if it is reduced it to the sexual act.

Multiple-gender categories creatively expand the gender schemes of their respective cultures to accommodate young people who will not fit the categories of male or female, but it is important to see that these are not whimsical lifestyle options. The pressures that steer youth into these categories are approximately as powerful as those that require other people in the same societies to conform to the conventions of male or female. Ordinarily, people entering these third genders remain in them for the rest of their lives.

It is difficult to establish cross-cultural statements about multiple genders beyond the above generalizations. Intersex anatomy, homosexual desire, and transvestite taste can arise to some degree in each and every human society, and some societies have creative cultural systems which produce and appreciate third genders. Most, however, restrict themselves to various kinds of binary gender. Furthermore, multiple genders are highly specific to the problems and values of their respective societies and cultures. Therefore, it is easier to say that binary gender is not universal, than to say that multiple genders are or should be universal.

Bibliography

Garcia, Neil C. 1996. *Philippine Gay Culture*. Quezon City: University of the Philippines Press.

Herdt, Gilbert, ed. 1994. *Third Sex/Third Gender: Beyond Sexual Dimorphism in Culture and History*. New York: Zone Books.

Jacobs, Sue-Ellen, Wesley Thomas, and Sabine Lang, eds. 1997. *Two-Spirit People: Native American Gender Identity, Sexuality, and Spirituality*. Urbana: University of Illinois Press.

Morris, R. C. 1994. "Three Sexes and Four Sexualities: Redressing the Discourses on Sexuality and Gender in Thailand." *Positions* 2, no. 1: 15–43.

Nanda, Serena. 1999. *Neither Man nor Woman: The Hijras of India*. 2nd ed. Belmont, CA: Wadsworth.

———. 2000. *Gender Diversity: Crosscultural Variations*. Prospect Heights, IL: Waveland.

Williams, Walter L. 1992. *The Spirit and the Flesh: Sexual Diversity in American Indian Culture*. Boston: Beacon.

Music, Popular

Louis Niebur

Popular music, defined as a category of music intended for commercial mass consumption using forms derived largely from early twentieth-century Tin Pan Alley songs and influenced by **African American** blues and jazz harmonies, has long been

See also Gender Roles; Queer Studies.

one of the primary locations for **gay** and **lesbian youth** to assert their identity. Just as in **popular culture** at large, lesbian and gay youth have consistently used popular music as a method of defining themselves within a specific subculture. Before **Stonewall**, this was primarily realized in an underground system of appropriating popular icons, reading their otherwise mainstream music as somehow "gay" or "lesbian," but in the years since, many more popular musicians have come out with relative mainstream acceptance, providing a direct source of inspiration to **lesbian, gay, bisexual**, and **transgender youth** (LGBT).

During the 1950s and 1960s, singers like Judy Garland and Ethel Merman developed a following among gay men who "read" their music as a combination of heightened sentimentality, often labeled "**camp**," and genuine pathos. Gay men, in this repressed environment, reveled in the artificiality of the "larger than life" performances of these musical icons and sympathized with the struggles of these strong women. For pre-Stonewall lesbians, there were a similar system of iconic images such as Doris Day, in particular her performance of "Secret Love" in the **film** *Calamity Jane* (USA 1953), which seems to capture perfectly the plight many felt in a largely closeted culture.

Among the few relatively open popular musicians in the first half of the twentieth century were blues artists. Capitalizing on their already-marginalized status as black women, openly bisexual blues singers like Gertrude "Ma" Rainey and Bessie Smith often included coded references to homosexuality in their songs. Billy Strayhorn, author of the jazz standards "Take the 'A' Train" and "Lush Life" among many others, was never shy about his sexuality, and his long partnership with heterosexual Duke Ellington remained unstrained throughout their long collaboration.

The emergence of rock and roll in the 1950s coincided with the development of "**youth culture**," a direct appeal by popular musicians (and marketers) for the attention of a teenage audience. One of the immediate effects was the practical elimination of women from popular music-making; as a genre, early rock and roll is almost entirely concerned with masculine posturing. One early rock performer, Johnny Ray, whose histrionic performances of his hit song, *Cry*, made him an instant icon for gay audiences, provides the first example of a popular musician whose relatively open homosexuality destroyed his career when disclosed by a tabloid magazine. A potentially contradictory impulse of rock and roll, however, was the increasing androgyny of many rock performers. Elvis Presley is an obvious example of an artist whose soft features were marketed as desirable, but a much more overt example, and equally as popular, were the falsetto shrieks and mincing dance moves of a heavily made-up Little Richard. With the "English Invasion" of the mid-1960s, bands such as The Beatles, The Rolling Stones, and The Who, with their long hair, accents, and dandyish behavior were labeled effeminate in comparison with contemporary American standards of masculinity. Rock and roll became a symbol of decadent excess (a label which included homosexuality) while largely textually extolling the virtues of heterosexuality.

With the rise of the **women's movement**, in the late 1960s, and lesbian feminism, came an increasing openness in popular music about all aspects of sexuality. Olivia Records, founded in 1972 as a commercial outlet for lesbian artists, built on the success of various women's live music festivals, in particular the annual event in Michigan, and empowered lesbians in local communities who promoted their musicians. Olivia was for years a prolific label with such folk/rock artists as Meg Christian, Holly Near, and Cris Williamson. In a more mainstream way, the emergence of powerful women musicians such as Janis Joplin and Dusty Springfield offered young women alternatives to proscribed **gender role** options.

For black women jazz musicians such as Nina Simone, Sarah Vaughan, and soul singers like Aretha Franklin and Gladys Knight, the late 1960s saw a shift in their output to a more "popular" sound and, consequently, a larger audience. Invariably, in the context of the women's and civil rights movements, this contributed to the perception of greater equality for both African Americans and women, and, by implication, gays and lesbians. For gay men, however, there were very few outlets in a still-predominantly "macho" rock culture. Exceptions include The Velvet Underground's Lou Reed, operating in the rarified art world of Andy Warhol's New York City "Factory." Reed consistently sang openly about his **bisexuality**, dedicating his album "Coney Island Baby" to his **transsexual** girlfriend.

Outside of these relatively insular communities, however, popular music, and in particular, rock and roll, in its most mainstream formulations, remained ambiguous in its attitude toward homosexuality in the 1970s. Early in the decade, David Bowie and Mick Jagger declared their bisexuality (denying it less than ten years later). During the mid-1970s, first proudly "out" gay musicians thrived in the gay discothèques of New York, Philadelphia, and Chicago. This distinctly gay genre developed as a mixture of African American Philly Soul, the relentless mechanical four-on-the-floor beat of European (primarily German and Austrian) electronic music, and the complexity of Latin (mostly Puerto Rican) polyrhythms. As an underground dance phenomenon, disco flourished underground until the blockbuster film *Saturday Night Fever* propelled the genre to the top of the charts. This success had the effect of stifling many of the more overtly gay qualities of the music or the musicians. Freddie Mercury of Queen and the Village People were widely misread due to the purposeful appropriation of stereotypically "masculine" attributes intended as irony. Nevertheless musicians like Sylvester achieved a degree of fame unknown for openly gay performers before this time. His hit "You Make Me Feel (Mighty Real)" achieved the status of gay anthem.

In the context of growing social conservatism, there was a backlash against disco (seen by many as a backlash against the dominance of gay and African American influences in popular music), culminating in the "Disco Sucks" movement. Rock and roll, too, returned to its masculine posturing, with a particular working class emphasis and a return to the prominence of the guitar, articulated successfully by Bruce Springsteen. This movement was encouraged by the mainstream music culture industry, particularly the influential magazine, *Rolling Stone*, which, in an attempt to legitimize rock as a "serious" music on par with classical music, distanced the genre from gender deviance.

Gay and lesbian audiences during the 1980s had to look largely to England for musical inspiration, where the legacy of disco still flourished and sexual androgyny ruled. In the new visual era of MTV, the success of such foreign "synth" groups as Wham!, Culture Club, Pet Shop Boys, and Duran Duran depended largely on their gender-bending looks. Similarly, The Smiths, particularly lead singer Morrissey, although not participating in the electronic, disco sounds, constructed, gender-neutral songs about alienation, unrequited love, and isolation. In the United States, because of more widespread music distribution and the success of late night "underground" video programs, gay and lesbian youth were able to access this "other" music as a way of forming subcultural communities, often in **rural** locations, enabling new "gay" lifestyles, identities, and sensibilities.

For many, disco never really died; it just returned underground. The rapid evolution of disco into house music in the 1980s in **urban**, mostly black, nightclubs exemplifies this. With its pared down rhythms and more forceful beat, house music incorporated aspects of Detroit and Chicago techno music. Like disco, it depended often on strong vocals. By the early 1990s, it was almost always sung by a black woman who delivered inspirational messages to a queer audience. House music was also influenced by the more commercial Hi-NRG and funk movements in the mid-1980s, which attracted a large, primarily young, gay following.

With the emergence of MTV in the early 1980s, the visual image of artists became more important. Although the popular video music show banned overtly "out" musicians like Bronski Beat, American artists who participated in house-related genres like Madonna, Prince, and Cyndi Lauper, broadcast a freer reading of gender. There, too, was the rise of "queercore," an aggressive, punk and grunge influenced, often militant form of rock directly addressing issues of homosexuality, gender, and civil rights. The predominately lesbian (as in Team Dresch and Tribe 8) or gay male (God is My Copilot, Pansy Division) performers can be distinguished from earlier gender-bending acts by the openness of their sexuality in performances and lyrics. Similarly, South African lesbian filmmaker and musician Beverly Ditsie used her art to fight sexual oppression. Other examples of queercore include Feucht Rasiert, an all woman queercore German band, Herbert from the Netherlands, the Polish Homomilitia, and the Noc Walpurgii festival, a biannual music festival in Poland that celebrates feminist and queer music.

The mid- and late 1990s witnessed a greater openness about female performers' sexuality in the United States. The Indigo Girls, Melissa Etheridge and k. d. lang all came out to much public attention without serious damage to their careers—labeled "lesbian chic" by the mass media. Gay or bisexual American male performers, however, remained largely closeted. The B-52s and REM (particularly out lead singer Michael Stipe) did allow for a more nuanced reading of gender, although the only explicit references to homosexuality in American popular music was most notably Hip Hop as exemplified by Eminem.

The Millennium has seen a continuation of this trend; greater openness about lesbian sexuality sits alongside the embargo on American male "alternative" sexualities. The fleeting but worldwide success of Russian faux-lesbian duo tATu—primarily marketed to the heterosexual audience—illustrates this. Their hit "All the Things She Said" tells the story of a sexual relationship between two young women. But, as before Stonewall, there remains an ongoing queer "reading" by a LGBT youth of certain male popular musicians like Ricky Martin, N*Sync, and Robbie Williams.

Bibliography

Bergam, David, ed. 1993. *Camp Grounds: Style and Homosexuality*. Amherst: University of Massachusetts Press.

Crawford, Richard. 1993. *The American Musical Landscape*. Los Angeles: University of California Press.

Fikentscher, Kai. 2000. *"You Better Work!": Underground Dance Music in New York City*. Hanover, NH: Wesleyan University Press.

Garofalo, Reebee. 2002. *Rockin' Out: Popular Music in the USA*. 2nd ed. Upper Saddle River, NJ: Prentice Hall.

Gill, John. 1995. *Queer Noises: Male and Female Homosexuality in Twentieth-Century Music*. London: Cassell.

Hadleigh, Boze. 1991. *The Vinyl Closet: Gays in the Music World.* San Diego: Los Hombres Press.

Hawkins, Stan. 2001. *Settling the Pop Score: Pop Texts and Identity Politics.* Aldershot, England: Ashgate.

Hickey, Dave. 1997. *Air Guitar: Essays on Art and Democracy.* Los Angeles: Art Issues Press.

Web Sites

Guide to Gay and Lesbian Resources: Music. November 2002. Accessed June 7, 2005. http://www.lib.uchicago.edu/e/su/gaylesb/glgxiv-mus.html. A large bibliography on books and articles related to gay and lesbian issues in music, including popular music.

International Queer Hotlist. December 2004. Accessed June 9, 2005. http://www.holytitclamps.com/. Contains links and a database of important international LGBT popular musicians and periodicals dedicated to largely queercore groups.

Music, Teaching of

Louis Niebur

The teaching of music in the United States, as in Europe, has been affected by the evolving contemporary perception that music is gendered female and those men participating in its creation compromise their masculinity. This impacts **lesbian, gay, bisexual,** and **transgender youth** (LGBT) particularly since musical choices like instrument and formal education are usually made in **childhood**. Placing music within the domain of feeling and emotion, hence within the purview of women and homosexual men, has had an impact on its teaching. One result of music's gendering has been a consistent "closeting" of queer musicians and composers by music teachers in an attempt to "redeem" the field. Closely connected to this are deep-seated racial issues. **African Americans**, in general, have for complex reasons been accepted as musicians (in the popular and jazz realms) more readily in mainstream society without the necessary association with homosexuality. Jazz and hip-hop, in particular, have been coded in our society with a specifically black masculinity. Music, though, remains one of the best educational tools for informing both LGBT and heterosexual youth about the issues of sexuality in contemporary society. Particularly in its popular genre, it can convey information about sexuality that might be difficult for educators to discuss, and it can also serve as a conduit for the expression of student's own emotional reactions to the topic (Russell 1997). Further, the association of particular types of music or musical instruments with deviancy has attracted some queer youth who can find in school and community music groups support and safe space.

Until relatively recently, music, at least in Western civilization, has been nearly exclusively written by men for performance by men who were trained by men. The schools that taught music, particularly composition, accepted only men whose teachers emphasized the "masculine" and removed any trace of "aberrant" sexuality. There existed in the nineteenth century a profound contradiction in musical

See also Gender Roles; Mentoring; Sexism; Social Class; Stereotypes.

education. White women of the middle and upper classes were encouraged to learn to perform music, but before a restricted audience. Training beyond an "amateur" level was deemed inappropriate because it threatened to take women into the world of the performing arts, which was believed to be populated by social deviants (homosexuals, prostitutes, nonwhite Europeans). Also, women were discouraged from classical music training since they were thought incapable of expressing anything beyond blatantly sentimental or childish emotions in music. Thus, America and Europe's orchestras (which grew in size and number throughout the century) were staffed exclusively by men.

Formal classical music education was also inaccessible to most working class, African American, and other minority groups before the twentieth century. Musical education was confined to the church and the primary school. Despite such restrictions a few notable exceptions of prominent musicians include the classical black composers William Grant Still and Nathaniel Dett, both of whom achieved great success in what had been a primarily "white" arena.

Even at the amateur level, music making opportunities for men were much more numerous than for women. Men, regardless of **race**, were encouraged to seek the social company of other men. This led to the development of all-male amateur musical organizations in working class communities such as brass bands, choral societies, and the barbershop quartet. Equally popular in white and African American communities, the quartet allowed men with a modest musical education to express their talents and to bond with other men, if not to channel homoerotic **desire** within these all-male settings.

Musical education was relatively informal for African American women, centering around the church. They, along with working class white women, fared better in public performing venues, since they had little to lose from their perceived "lowly" social position. African American women singers, as the twentieth century began, participated in the emergence of a distinctly American musical form, the blues. Two bisexual performers, Bessie Smith, the "Empress of the Blues," and Gertrude "Ma" Rainey directly referenced their sexual experiences in their songs.

As women gained more rights in society, some rose to prominence as classical musicians and composers. But, those participating in this male world were often suspect. To assume the "properness" of a "lady composer," some adopted their husband's name, as in the case of Amy Beach (Mrs. H. H. A. Beach). Other composers wore their supposed deviancy proudly, such as the relatively open lesbian composer Ethel Smyth or the infamously gruff Elisabeth Lutyens.

Gradually, women earned acceptance as musicians. Music schools began accepting women for training, and soon it was unexceptional for a woman to pursue musical ambitions. There, too, was a gradual shift regarding forms of masculinity, directly related to the incursion of women into the performing arts. The image of the "strong silent type" entered popular consciousness to such an extent that the expression of even natural emotions called into question one's masculinity. Following World War II, there was increasing pressure on young people, certainly at the precollege level, to choose **cocurricular activities** that were gender appropriate. For boys, it was contact **sports**, and for girls, music and **dance**. Boys choosing to pursue music were "**sissy**"; individual instruments became gendered as well. The flute shifted its place to the realm of the feminine, as did other perceived "ethereal" instruments like the harp. Brass instruments, given their connection to military music and jazz, became more masculinized.

One of the most strongly affected instruments was the human voice. Lacking the mediation of an instrument, sung music directly appeals to the emotions. Thus, men and boys have become more reticent about expressing themselves through singing, seeing this as betraying a certain emotional vulnerability. Further, the connection of opera to gender "deviance" goes back at least as far as the seventeenth century, which saw the castrati (men who were surgically castrated before puberty to preserve the high range of their singing voices) rise to the top of the musical world, superstars in their day.

One effect of music's gendering has been the closet. The longstanding presence of gay men as operatic performers and audience attests to the power of the voice to express "the inexpressible," particularly in a closeted environment. Further, as musicologist Philip Brett has pointed out, music teachers, often scared of being thought of as gay themselves, have deliberately "butched up" its history. Only composers far enough from the Germanic mainstream or who's biography fits accepted stereotypical associations of homosexuality (such as the erroneous belief that gay Russian composer Tchaikovsky committed suicide in a fit of homosexual pique) have been traditionally discussed. Recently, though, parallel with the development of queer studies at large, musicologists (those studying or teaching music history), have begun to acknowledge the importance of sexuality among many prominent composers like George Frederick Handel and Franz Schubert, which have sparked heated debate.

Teaching music means not only integrating sexuality and LGBT persons into the **curriculum**, but enlarging the field to embrace openly **queer** teachers who can serve as role models for all youth as well as mentors for LGBT musicians. One of the most prominent teachers, with enormous stature as a composer, was Leonard Bernstein. He educated an entire generation about music through the "Young People's Concerts" television series (1958–1973), in addition to his teaching talented young musicians throughout the world. Other twentieth-century composers who have embraced their sexuality openly include Aaron Copland, John Corigliano, Ned Rorem, Benjamin Britten, Lou Harrison, and John Cage.

In addition to creating teaching environments where open LGBT teachers can mentor youth and including LGBT history in the music curriculum, there are other ways in which music can be taught queerly:

- Band directors, while often guilty of perpetuating **heteronormative** thinking, can serve as an important **ally** by defusing **homophobia** and rigid gender definitions and by encouraging students to expand their culturally conditioned beliefs, showing that each instrument (like each student) has a unique contribution to make to the overall group's music making.

- By encouraging singing as a nongendered activity, contemporary educators can show all students that singing is a healthy way to access emotions and feelings not ordinarily public.

- Within musical communities such as choirs, high school and university bands, and the musical theater communities, queer youth have found havens. School and community-based educators can encourage these youths by acknowledging the debt musical culture owes to openly gay and lesbian performers and by assisting them as they integrate their **sexual identity** into their art and lives.

Bibliography

Blackmer, Corinne E., and Patricia Juliana Smith, eds. 1995. *En Travesti: Women, Gender Subversion, Opera*. New York: Columbia University Press.

Brett, Philip, Elizabeth Wood, and Gary C. Thomas. 1994. *Queering the Pitch: The New Gay and Lesbian Musicology*. New York: Routledge.

Cook, Susan C., and Judy S. Tsou, eds. 1994. *Cecilia Reclaimed: Feminist Perspectives on Gender and Music*. Urbana: University of Illinois Press.

Fuller, Sophie, and Lloyd Whitesell, eds. 2003. *Queer Episodes in Music and Modern Identity*. Urbana: University of Illinois Press.

Gill, John. 1995. *Queer Noises: Male and Female Homosexuality in Twentieth Century Music*. Minneapolis: University of Minnesota.

Koestenbaum, Wayne. 2001. *The Queen's Throat: Opera, Homosexuality, and the Mystery of Desire*. New York: Da Capo Press.

Kramer, Lawrence. 1990. *Music as Cultural Practice: 1800–1900*. Berkeley: University of California Press.

McClary, Susan. 1991. *Feminine Endings: Music, Gender, and Sexuality*. Minneapolis: University of Minnesota Press.

Russell, Glenda M. 1997. "Using Music to Reduce Homophobia and Heterosexism." Pp. 155–166 in *Overcoming Heterosexism and Homophobia*. Edited by James T. Sears and Walter L. Williams. New York: Columbia University Press.

Scott, Derek B., ed. 2000. *Music, Culture, and Society*. Oxford: Oxford University Press, 2000.

Walser, Robert. 1993. *Running with the Devil: Power, Gender, and Madness in Heavy Metal Music*. Hanover, NH: Wesleyan University Press.

Muslim Moral Instruction on Homosexuality

Suhraiya Jivraj and *Anisa de Jong*

Most Muslims (and non-Muslims) believe that Islam prohibits any same-sex sexual activity and that homosexuality is irreconcilable with being Muslim. As a result, Muslim **lesbian, gay,** and **bisexual youth** (LGB) often struggle to reconcile their **sexual orientation** with their cultural or religious identities, and the consequences of their "coming out" (or being "found out") can be extremely harsh. In addition, stereotypical ideas of LGB people and Muslims reinforce **prejudices** and misconceptions in both LGB and Muslim communities. This, in turn, contributes to the stigmatization and **discrimination** faced by Muslims, LGB people, and Muslim LGB people alike. Education and dialogue on religion and homosexuality is important in order to encourage a better understanding and mutual respect among individuals and communities as well as to empower Muslim LGB young people to deal with the questions and issues they face.

There is great diversity in how Muslims experience and view Islam. Some talk about "Islam" when referring to a particular culture or certain traditions, others

See also Christian Moral Instruction on Homosexuality; Colonialism and Homosexuality; Feminism; Jewish Moral Instruction on Homosexuality; Parents, Responses to Homosexuality; Religion and Psychological Development; Religious Fundamentalism; Spirituality; Stereotyping.

use the word "Islam" to refer to the practice of religious rituals, *shari'ah* (classical Muslim law), a certain type of spirituality, or a political viewpoint. Therefore, when discussing the topic of homosexuality and Islam it is important to clarify first what is meant by "Islam" by the various participants, and second, to acknowledge that there may be variety in what Muslims consider a correct and acceptable moral instruction.

When speaking of Muslim moral (or legal) instructions, most traditional or conservative Muslims will refer to *shari'ah* (classical Muslim law) as their guidance. However, many modern Muslims choose to base their morality on the Quran itself or on Islam's spiritual message. *Shari'ah* is a body of rules, norms, and laws according to which, from a traditional viewpoint, Muslims (are supposed to) live their lives. The *shari'ah* rules are largely moral or religious, carrying consequences only in the hereafter. However, some *shari'ah* rules are also considered to be punishable in the here and now, although most Muslim scholars agree that these punishments should only be executed in "true Muslim societies" run by "true Muslim governments" and are, therefore, not applicable in modern states.

Shari'ah developed somewhere between the eighth and ninth centuries AD in various Muslim schools of thought where legal and religious rules were derived from the Quran and *hadith*. *Hadith* are recounts of the practices and sayings of the Prophet Muhammad that had been passed on from generation to generation. Although *shari'ah* is presented by some conservative Muslim scholars as a monolithic set of rules, it actually includes a variety of opinions between the original schools of thought and differing opinions of individual scholars. It also reflects regional influences and local customs. The process of understanding and formulating legal and religious rules from the Quran and *hadith* is known as "interpretation" (*ijtihad*). Traditional Muslim scholars believe that somewhere between the tenth and the fourteenth centuries "the gate of *ijtihad*" was closed, preventing new interpretations of the Quran (or *hadith*) being recognised as *shari'ah*. This idea has made it difficult for progressive Muslim scholars to challenge rules and morals of *shari'ah* that were shaped in the social contexts of previous centuries.

Generally, it can be said that according to *shari'ah* sexual relations are only allowed within a heterosexual marriage. Therefore, most sexual relations outside of marriage qualify as adultery or fornication, both of which are sinful and punishable by flogging for unmarried men and women, or death for married men and women. Some traditional Muslim scholars have argued that lesbian or gay sexual relations would always take place outside of a marriage (as recognised by *shari'ah*) and, therefore, the *shari'ah* prohibition of heterosexual adultery and fornication also applies to all same-sex sexual relations. However, most traditional Muslim scholars base their opinion that homosexuality is sinful on the basis of Quranic verses, in particular the story of Lut (similar but not identical to the story of Lot in the Bible) and/or on several *hadith*. As the Quran does not specify any punishment for same-sex sexuality in these verses, some scholars refer back to the *shari'ah* rules on heterosexual adultery or fornication. They therefore argue that anal sex between men, as considered equivalent to heterosexual intercourse, is punishable by one hundred whiplashes for an unmarried man and death by stoning for a married man. Other traditional scholars have ruled that "sodomy" between men is always punishable by death for both partners, whether married or not, based on a *hadith*. The punishment of toppling a wall on two men who practiced "sodomy," which is sometimes reported, particularly in Afghanistan, is based on another *hadith*. Most traditional scholars also hold that sexual contacts, other than anal sex between men, and sexual relations between women are sinful. This is based on analogies to *shari'ah* rules prohibiting illicit heterosexual sexual activities other than full intercourse as well as on *hadith*. Sexual activities between men other than anal sex or sexual activities between women are usually considered punishable by flogging.

Today only few Muslim countries have legal systems that are entirely based on *shari'ah*. Nine countries have laws in place that prescribe the death penalty for same-sex sexual activities: Afghanistan, Arab Emirates, Chechnya, Iran, Mauritania, Pakistan, Saudi Arabia, Sudan, and Yemen. Reports of official executions are rare, although prosecutions and **harassment** of LGB people by the police and authorities does take place regularly, as it does in many non-Muslim countries. Many other countries (Muslim and non-Muslim) use secular laws (often deriving from colonial times) to prosecute LGB people, allowing for punishments such as imprisonment, hard labor and fines.

In **Egypt,** for example, there are no laws specifically prohibiting homosexuality, but since 2001, many gay men have been arrested, charged, and convicted for "the habitual practice of debauchery," which is part of a law on prostitution. These arrests include young people like fifteen-year-old Mahmoud who was apprehended along with fifty-two other men aboard the Queen boat, a Cairo restaurant/discotheque on the Nile, in May 2001. He was forced to undergo a medical examination that proved he had practiced anal sex. The court stated that he had confessed to "practicing homosexuality and being a member of a gay organization," but Mahmoud pleaded innocent at the trial, arguing his confessions were made under duress and torture during interrogation. Initially he was convicted to the maximum penalty of three years imprisonment followed by three years of probation by the Cairo Juvenile Court, but seven months after his arrest, the sentence was reduced on appeal to six months jail and six months probation. Another case involved a nineteen-year-old Egyptian student who was arrested by the Vice Squad as he stood on a Cairo street. He had allegedly arranged a face-to-face encounter with a man he had met on the **Internet,** who turned out to be a police informer. He underwent humiliating medical examinations and ill-treatment while awaiting trial. His initial conviction was eventually overturned.

Although *shari'ah* remains (at least in theory) the moral guidance for traditional and conservative Muslims, many Muslims actually believe that it is each individual's responsibility to live in accordance with *shari'ah*. Moreover, an increasing number of Muslims do not look to *shari'ah* but to the Quran itself or to Islam's spiritual message for their moral guidance. This development, sometimes referred to as "progressive Islam," includes Muslim reformists and feminists who argue that *shari'ah*, unlike the Quran, is merely an understanding of Islam that has been influenced by traditional customs and social values of the historical time in which it was formulated. In addition, feminist scholars have also asserted that the formulation of *shari'ah* was carried out mostly by men, reflecting a male understanding and experience, that led to a gender bias in *shari'ah* that justified (and continues to justify) patriarchal practices.

Feminist Muslim scholars also point out that many of the ideas of male superiority over women in *shari'ah* are largely based on *hadith*, whereas the Quran itself generally affirms women's rights and equality. They question the reliability of these *hadith*, which they believe to have been strongly influenced by patriarchal prejudices. Even among traditional Muslim scholars, there are many differing opinions on which *hadith* are reliable. Most progressive Muslims, therefore, concentrate their studies on the Quran as the only reliable and most important text on which to base Muslim morality.

Having acknowledged *shari'ah* as a historical understanding of Islam and having reduced the importance of *hadith*, progressive Muslim scholars have developed new Muslim ethical frameworks through various methods. For example, feminist Muslim scholars have reinterpreted Quranic verses placing them in their sociohistorical context, demonstrating that Islam actually expanded and enforced women's rights and envisioned equality between men and women. Some progressive Muslim scholars have developed approaches that go beyond the reinterpretation of the Quran. They see the *Quran* as two types of documents within one: the first relating to the socioeconomic issues at the time of the *Quran's* revelation; the second embodying the spiritual or ethical message of Islam. They believe that the spiritual message of Islam and principles of justice underlying the Quran should form the basis of a modern Muslim moral framework. The development of progressive Muslim scholarship has provided a context in which to explore issues in relation to gender and sexuality, including homosexuality.

Some Muslim scholars point out that the Quran and early Muslim scholars actually dealt with (hetero) sexuality quite openly and positively. However, some feminist scholars argue that this "positive approach" to sexuality among classical Muslim scholars, mostly (or only) affirms masculine heterosexual experience. Reformist and feminist Muslim scholars challenge the idea that Islam requires men and women to live in accordance with prescribed **gender roles** or impedes women from controlling their sexuality. Progressive and feminist Muslim scholars have explored issues such as women's rights in family laws, women's control over reproduction, violence against women including honor crimes, and HIV/**AIDS**.

A few Muslim scholars have built upon this work to question the assumption that homosexuality is always an un-Islamic expression of love and sexuality. They have analyzed the Quranic verses that are said to refer to male homosexuality, and have reinterpreted and examined these verses using reformist and feminist techniques of interpretation. According to these scholars, the word "homosexuality" is not mentioned in the Quran, and the interpretation of the words used are reflecting preconceived assumptions about the meaning of the story of Lut and prejudiced views of homosexuality. The words that are mentioned in the Quran include: *fahisha* (7:80 & 27:54—lewdness, indecency, atrocity, gruesome deeds); *khabaidh* (21:74—improper or unseemly things); *munkar* (29:29—that which is reprehensible), and *sayyi'aat* (11:78—bad or evil deeds).

The word *fahisha* is most often quoted as referring to anal sex or homosexuality. Although most scholars reinterpreting these verses acknowledge that this term can possibly be understood to include anal sex or homosexuality, they point out that it does not refer explicitly or only to homosexuality, but actually to illicit sexual behavior in general. Therefore, these progressive scholars argue that the story of Lut is not specifically about homosexuality or same-sex relationships. They believe that the story is about people taking part in widespread unlawful sexual behavior, possibly including anal sex (which can also occur in a heterosexual relationship), but also engaging promiscuity, bestiality, pedophilia, and rape, as well as inhospitality towards guests, abuse of power, and intimidation. In short, these scholars hold that the condemnations of the people of Lut are not about condemning loving and mutually respectful relationships between men or between women.

With regard to lesbian sexuality very little scholarly work has been done by progressive Muslim scholars. Some extend their conclusions regarding what the Quran says about male homosexuality to female homosexuality. The only verse in the Quran that is sometimes cited by traditional scholars to refer to lesbian sexuality is verse 15 of Surah An-Nisa'a. In this verse, reference is made to women committing indecency or lewdness (*fahisha*), but again there is no clear indication of what exactly this indecency is. Most scholars do believe it suggests some form of sexual indiscretion, such as adultery or fornication and possibly lesbian sexuality, but usually the verse is understood to refer to **prostitution**. Therefore, or otherwise, the Quran is said to be silent on sexual relationships between women.

A few progressive Muslim scholars have argued that it may be possible for Muslims to view same-sex relationships positively. They refer, for example, to gender-neutral verses in the Quran affirming the importance of companionship and love between people, not just between a man and a woman. They argue that an affirmation of these relationships through a form of a Muslim "marriage" or "union" could be possible within a progressive Muslim framework.

Although the number of Muslims that would find the latter an acceptable view (or experience) of Islam is still extremely limited, it is empowering for Muslim LGB youth to be aware of the possibilities explored by these Muslim scholars. Discovering and accepting one's own as well as other people's identities can be difficult, but exploring the variations that exist within often stereotyped identities can be a helpful tool. Many Muslim LGB young people find themselves caught between a Muslim community that rejects LGB people and an LGB community that scorns Muslims and Islam. A better understanding and mutual respect within and between these communities are crucial for LGB Muslim youth as well as for Muslims and LGB communities in general. Some ways of working toward this are: acknowledging that "prejudice is prejudice" in whatever form; breaking down stereotypes and acknowledging diversities of opinion, and most of all, respecting each other's beliefs, choices and life experiences—between communities as well as within communities.

Bibliography

Anwar, Ghazala. 2001. *Islam, Homosexuality and Migration*. Paper presented at Yoesuf Foundation Conference on Islam in the West and Homosexuality—Strategies for Action, Utrecht, the Netherlands, 5 & 6 October 2001.

Esack, Farid. 2001. *Islam and Sexual Otherness*. Paper presented at Yoesuf Foundation Conference on Islam in the West and Homosexuality—Strategies for Action, Utrecht, the Netherlands, 5 & 6 October 2001.

Hassan, Riffat. 2003. *Women and Sexuality—Normative Islam versus Muslim Practice*. Paper presented at 2nd International Muslim Leaders Consultation on HIV and AIDS, Kuala Lumpur, Malaysia, 19–23 May 2003.

Jamal, Amreen. 2001. "The Story of Lut and the Quran's Perception of the Morality of Same-Sex Sexuality." *Journal of Homosexuality* 41 no. 1: 10–20.

Kugle, Scott Siraj Haqq, and Omid Safi, eds. 2003. *Progressive Muslims: On Justice, Gender, and Pluralism*. Oxford: Oneworld Publications.

Nahas, Omar. 2001. *Islam en Homoseksualiteit*. Amsterdam/Utrecht. Bullaaq/Yoesuf.

Safra Project. 2002. *Initial Findings—Identifying the difficulties experienced by lesbian, bisexual & transgender Muslim women in accessing social & legal services*. Accessed July 8, 2005. http://www.safraproject.org.

Wadud, Amina. 1999. *Qur'an and Woman—Rereading the Sacred Text from a Woman's Perspective*. Oxford, UK: Oxford University Press.

Web Sites

Al Fatiha Foundation Web site. May 2003. Accessed December 18, 2004. http://www.al-fatiha.net. Based in the United States, this organization is dedicated to Muslims who are lesbian, gay, bisexual, transgender, intersex, questioning, those exploring their sexual orientation or gender identity, and their allies, families, and friends. Al-Fatiha promotes the progressive Islamic notions of peace, equality, and justice.

Queer Sexuality and Identity in The Qur'an and the Hadith. Faris Malik, Accessed December 18, 2004. http://www.well.com/user/aquarius/Qurannotes.htm. Source of information on, and analysis of, Quranic verses and *hadith* relating to homosexuality.

Safra Project Web site. 2004. Accessed December 18, 2004. http://www.safraproject.org/sgi-intro.htm. Resource on issues relating to lesbian, bisexual, transgender, queer, and questioning women who identify as Muslim religiously and/or culturally. It includes a section dealing with progressive and feminist views on "Sexuality, Gender & Islam" and other relevant social and legal information.

N

National Coming Out Day

Jeremy P. Hayes and *Ronni Sanlo*

National Coming Out Day (NCOD) commemorates the 1987 March on Washington for Lesbian and Gay Rights and the first display of the NAMES Project Quilt, remembering those who had died from **AIDS**. On October 11, across the United States and in **Canada**, high schools, colleges, and community organizations host a variety of events to celebrate and encourage the act of **coming out**. Individuals who are honest and open about their sexual orientations and gender identities as well as about their support for and acceptance of **lesbian, gay, bisexual**, and **transgender** (LGBT) people have increasingly been viewed as important to raise public awareness. NCOD is often used as an opportunity to educate the general community about LGBT concerns and the importance of LGBT individuals' coming out.

The 1987 March, the second national political demonstration of its kind, was attended by half a million people. (The first Lesbian and Gay March on Washington occurred in 1979.) Four months after the 1987 March, a group of 100 activists gathered in Manassas, Virginia, and decided that the movement, which at the time focused primarily on gay and lesbian issues, needed to do something other than simply reacting defensively to antigay actions. The idea for a national day to celebrate coming out was developed by Rob Eichberg, founder of a personal growth workshop known as The Experience, and Jean O'Leary, head of the National Gay Rights Advocates (NGRA).

In the first year, NCOD events were held in eighteen states and received national media attention. O'Leary expanded the West Hollywood, California, office of NGRA to provide a headquarters for NCOD. Activist Sean Strub enlisted artist Keith Haring to donate the image of a person dancing out of the closet that has become a symbol for the event. Under the direction of Eichberg and coordinator Pilo Bueno, NCOD expanded to events in twenty-one states. Lynn Shepodd was hired as executive director of NCOD in 1990. Over the next three years, the project continued to grow. Shepodd requested free ad space in the gay press for the Haring coming out image. Over 150 publications eventually agreed, expanding NCOD to all fifty states.

In 1993, NCOD merged with what was then the Human Rights Campaign Fund (HRCF). Wes Combs was named HRCF's project director for NCOD. One of his first innovations was to add

National Coming Out Day. © The Estate of Keith Haring.

See also Activism, LGBT Youth; Activism, LGBT Teachers; College Campus Programming; Day of Silence or Silencing; Identity Politics; Lavender Graduation; Music, Popular; Rainbow Flag and Other Pride Symbols.

celebrities to the project. Actress Amanda Bearse, then the only nationally-known actress open about being a lesbian, agreed to be chairperson for NCOD 1994. Bearse's participation in events across the country drew a new and larger audience. She also appeared in a public service announcement with the message: "I'm not a straight woman, but I play one on TV. And that's where acting belongs—on television or in the movies. Not in real life. That's why I stopped acting and came out." Under the Human Rights Campaign (HRC, formerly the Human Rights Campaign Fund) and its executive director Elizabeth Birch, NCOD grew into a year-round program called the National Coming Out Project.

Candace Gingrich became a spokesperson for the National Coming Out Project, in 1995, along with actor Dan Butler. That year, NCOD was celebrated by a morning news conference with Birch, Gingrich, and Butler at the U.S. Capitol and an evening reception at the Los Angeles Gay and Lesbian Community Center. In 1996, a presidential election year, HRC combined the project's message of honesty and openness with a message of political action with a theme of "You've Got the Power. Register. Vote." More than 1,000 supporters attended a "Come Out Voting" rally in Washington, D.C., which was carried live by C-SPAN and rerun repeatedly. The project's first heterosexual spokesperson was Betty DeGeneres, mother of actress/comedian Ellen DeGeneres, in 1997.

At the tenth anniversary of NCOD, in 1998, Gingrich returned to the National Coming Out Project as Associate Manager and developed a National Coming Out Day Kit as a resource for individuals and organizations. The kits contained event ideas, planning tools, stickers, posters, balloons, and HRC literature. Over 500 kits were distributed, and the kit has become a staple of the project with the number of kits requested growing each year. The 1999 theme, "Come Out to Congress," encouraged people to make themselves known to their representatives. Each NCOD kit included pens, paper, envelopes, and a sample letter to Congress. Nearly 2,000 letters were written to Congress members.

During the 2000 presidential election year, the NCOD campaign again focused on voting. Promotional materials and public service announcements reminded voters that the newly-elected president would likely nominate several U.S. Supreme Court justices. The official NCOD celebration was held at the University of Pennsylvania in conjunction with the kickoff of a capital campaign to build the first stand-alone **college campus resource center** in the United States.

The theme for National Coming Out Project, in 2002, was "Being Out Rocks," celebrating LGBT musicians who had achieved their dreams while living open, honest lives. On October 11, a benefit CD, featuring songs of openly LGBT musicians and straight allies, was released. Artists who donated songs to the album included Cyndi Lauper, Queen, k.d. lang, Jade Esteban Estrada, and Sarah McLachlan. Nineteen openly LGBT artists, including Melissa Etheridge, Ani DiFranco, Michael Stipe, the Indigo Girls, RuPaul, Rufus Wainwright, and The Butchies, appeared on a poster celebrating the theme and declaring: "You may feel like just a face in the crowd, but coming out as gay, lesbian, bisexual, or transgender makes you a star." Family was the focus of 2003's National Coming Out Project with a theme of "It's a Family Affair." In 2004, the theme was "Come Out. Speak Out. Vote." The focus was on encouraging LGBT people to talk with their friends and families about their lives.

By 2003, 65 colleges, universities, high schools and organizations across the country registered events with the National Coming Out Project, ranging from rallies and speakers to plays and film showings. Each organization adapted their

NCOD events to fit with their communities and their organizations' missions. For example, religious and spiritual organizations hosted an interfaith service or encouraged local religious leaders to include coming out topics in their sermons. Dignity USA, an LGBT Catholic organization, developed Solidarity Sunday as an annual event on the Sunday preceding NCOD to raise awareness about anti-LGBT violence.

Colleges and universities frequently celebrate NCOD events as one day to a weeklong collection of educational and social events. These events may include a rally where campus community members come out publicly and share their coming out experiences, guest speakers, sidewalk chalking with educational messages, and dances, parties, or drag shows. Often, the focus of NCOD events is to increase the visibility of LGBT communities. In 1994, the National Coming Out Project of Dallas/Ft. Worth, TX, and the University of California at Los Angeles (UCLA) developed NCOD visibility ads, or OUTLists, where out LGBT individuals and their supporters were named in a local or campus newspapers. Community organizations as well as colleges and universities may also provide information tables, take political action, or simply encourage individuals to come out as part of the NCOD events. NCOD events often occur as collaborative events to support Gay and Lesbian History Month, which is also celebrated each October.

There are currently no studies or research that explores the impact of NCOD-type events on **queer** youth but some anecdotal literature suggests that these celebratory events provide visibility and remind youth that they are not alone.

Web Sites

Dignity USA. November 2004. Accessed December 18, 2004. http://www.dignityusa. org/solidarity/Solidarity Sunday, a faith-based antiviolence initiative, is an annual event related to NCOD and it is held on the Sunday before October 11.

Human Rights Campaign. November 2004. Accessed December 18, 2004. http://www.hrc. org/ncop/. Includes coming out resources as well as history, tools, and resources for the National Coming Out Project.

National Coming Out Project—Dallas/Ft. Worth. December 2004. Accessed December 18, 2004. http://www.comeout.org. One of the longest-running and largest regional NCOD-based organizations. Includes an example of community NCOD visibility advertisements.

Native and Indigenous LGBT Youth

Victor J. Raymond

Native and indigenous lesbian, gay, bisexual, and transgender (LGBT) youth includes adolescent and young adult members of the native cultures indigenous to North and **South America, Australia, New Zealand,** and other parts of the world,

See also Africa, LGBT Youth and Issues in; Colonialism and Homosexuality; Identity Politics; Multiple Genders; Race and Racism; Youth, At Risk.

who would be described in Western European terms as being **lesbian, gay, bisexual** and/or **transgender**. In many cases, these cultures recognize sexual identities and gender identities and expressions that do not match Western European ideas of masculine/feminine duality and heterosexuality as a cultural norm. In the past, native and indigenous cultures experienced the effects of Western European colonization and the imposition of Western cultural norms. More recently, many have slowly gained greater autonomy and (in some cases) sovereignty, allowing for the reemergence of native and indigenous understandings of gender and sexual expression, albeit not without controversy within these cultures and in relation to society at large. Because of this, native and indigenous LGBT youth sometimes encounter increased stress, **drug use**, occurrence of STDs, and other problems as well as growing social acceptance when expressing their sexual and gender identities.

The Western European construction of gender as a "male/female" duality is not shared by many North or South American tribal cultures, or by many Asian and Pacific Islander cultures. Instead, many non-European cultures view gender as having several components or as being along a continuum of gender identity, in which "male" and "female" are not necessarily at polar opposites. Some examples of this include:

- The *māhū* of Hawaiian and Polynesian cultures, or males who traditionally took on respected healer and other roles valued socially but otherwise reserved for women, and who are now often associated with transgender and gay identities (Bopp, Juday, and Charters 2004).

- The *nádleehí* in the Navajo culture, males or females who took on a "third gender" position while having same-sex relationships, and who were traditionally respected and valued (Roscoe 1998).

- The Zapotec *muxeâ* (derived from the Spanish *mujer*) in Oaxaca, **Mexico,** who are considered to be particularly artistic and intellectually gifted, while combining male and female genders. The emergence of a Zapotec movement for political autonomy has coincided with the growth of a homosexual rights movement in Mexico, resulting in greater political activity on the part of many *muxeâ* (Ramsey and Trembley 2004).

This view of gender as being along a continuum and not as a duality is fundamental to understanding the place of LGBT youth in native and indigenous cultures. After several centuries of colonization and cultural domination, many native and indigenous cultures around the world have been experiencing a reawakening during the latter half of the twentieth century and the beginning of the next. This revival is largely coincidental with the emergence of a distinct LGBT civil rights movement and a LGBT subculture in the predominantly white culture of Europe and North America, but is generally independent of it.

Historically, native and indigenous people have lived on reservations or reserves often geographically distant from urban population centers. In contemporary Native society there are an increasing number of native and indigenous people, particularly youth, living in **urban** areas rather than on reservations or reserves. This has led to a greater exposure to other cultures and less cohesion in tribal culture. Urban life has also provided native and indigenous LGBT youth with access to alternatives to traditional native culture, particularly the mostly-white

LGBT community. While some native and indigenous communities have been able to maintain themselves within the framework of mainstream society, many have not, leading to considerable stress on native and indigenous populations on and off reservations and reserves. Among native and indigenous youth, this has led to poor educational attainment, increased drug use, and a variety of other negative outcomes. Native and indigenous LGBT youth have been particularly hard hit, as they often lack support from their families and community for their **sexual orientation** and/or **gender identity**. This has resulted in increased stress, breakdown of family ties, drug use, and a greater risk for sexually-transmitted diseases, including HIV/**AIDS** (Saewyc et al. 1998).

As tribes and native bands work for cultural survival, there is increased recognition of the role once played by tribal members who expressed alternative **gender roles** and sexual orientations. In many cases, such alternative gender roles and sexual orientations were seen as playing a vital and legitimate role within native and indigenous culture, and often connected with important religious and spiritual practices. For native and indigenous LGBT youth, the intersection of resurgent indigenous cultural identity, and the development of a LGBT subculture and civil rights movement presents both opportunities and conflicts, not only between themselves and their native cultures of origin, but also with the largely-white, urbanized LGBT community, and more generally with contemporary European and American culture.

Some native and indigenous LGBT youth have sought validation of their sexual orientation and gender identity within the emergent LGBT communities found in urban areas. However, since these communities are mostly white in their leadership and demographic make-up, there is little recognition of racial and cultural differences; native and indigenous youth are tacitly expected to assimilate to a white LGBT cultural norm. This has contributed to the rise of a new description for native and indigenous LGBT people: "two-spirited"–a modern term created by and for LGBT native people as an "umbrella" term (even though it is not necessarily an exact fit with all tribal definitions of sexual orientation and gender identity). Two-spirited refers to the alternative sexualities, alternative gender presentation and the integral role of Native spirituality among members of tribes, which historically and anthropologically have been mislabeled as "berdaches." Fortunately, the recent development of native and indigenous LGBT leadership and a culturally-specific identification (i.e., two-spirited) has provided an alternative to assimilation within the existing white-dominated LGBT culture.

In the 1970s and 1980s, native and indigenous participation within the LGBT and **women's movement**s led to the creation of organizations for LGBT and two-spirited people. This nascent native and indigenous LGBT community has provided some hope for the future of native and indigenous LGBT youth. Working with other organizations—particularly state, provincial, and national government agencies—educational and community health efforts have been started to help address the needs of these youth.

The experience of the Indigenous People's Task Force (formerly the Minnesota American Indian AIDS Task Force) is illustrative of the positive effects of peer education on HIV risk reduction and sexuality education among native and indigenous youth. The Task Force's group of young native actors, the Ogitchidag Gikinooamaagad Players, educate the American Indian community about AIDS through story telling, drama, **music,** and **dance.** Since the early 1990s, the Ogitchidag Players have performed youth-scripted plays on reservations and in communities in the Upper Midwest United States and in **Canada**, receiving several awards and other recognition for their work. Outside the continental United States, the experience of the Chrysalis program in Hawaii is similarly positive, providing a weekly after-school drop-in group for transgender and questioning youth (who are considered to be *mahu* in Polynesian culture), distinct from existing gay student groups or **gay–straight alliances** (Bopp, Juday, and Charters 2004). There also is a growing awareness of LGBT identity within indigenous Australian culture and the specific needs of native and indigenous LGBT youth. The Anwernekenhe Gatherings, in 1994 and 1998, resulted in a series of specific recommendations on a wide range of issues, including the creation of forums specifically recognizing gay and transgender youth.

Native and indigenous LGBT youth are finding greater acceptance of their gender identity and sexual orientation in many tribes, but may also encounter transphobia, homo- and biphobia, largely as a legacy of colonization and conversion to Christianity. The imposition of European and **Christian** norms regarding gender and sexual orientation led to the suppression and erasure of the existence of two-spirited people and the roles they played in tribal society. Additionally, this legacy has tended to suppress discussion of sexuality in general among many tribes, which is at odds with traditional tribal culture and knowledge. The pressures felt within many tribes to assimilate to the larger "white" culture heighten the tensions created by such discrimination. Political endeavors by many native and indigenous nations in North and Central America, as well as in Australia, New Zealand/Aotearoa, and elsewhere to achieve greater economic and political autonomy have led to efforts to rediscover and strengthen their cultural foundations—but the precise place of native and indigenous LBGT youth is in many cases still in a state of flux.

Native and indigenous LGBT youth also encounter difficulties when dealing with the mainstream predominantly white Euro-American culture. They face multiple challenges in expressing their personal identities, particularly due to differences between native and European-American understandings of sexual orientation and gender identity. Because of these challenges, native and indigenous LGBT youth have been at greater risk for educational failure, **discrimination**, stress, and sexually-transmitted diseases. Recent **research** indicates that efforts to provide positive culturally-appropriate models of sexual and gender identity are critical for the development of native and indigenous LGBT youth, however. What is lacking in almost all countries with native and indigenous cultures is both a general awareness of the critical nature of problems encountered by native and indigenous LGBT youth and the political will to provide the necessary resources to ensure healthy outcomes for youth and their families.

Bibliography

Allen, Paula Gunn. 1986. *The Sacred Hoop: Recovering the Feminine in American Indian Traditions*. Boston: Beacon Press.

Bopp, P. Jayne, Timothy R. Juday, and Cloudia W. Charters. 2004. "A School-Based Program to Improve Life Skills and to Prevent HIV Infection in Multicultural Transgendered Youth in Hawai'i" *Journal of Gay and Lesbian Issues in Education* 1, no. 4: 3–21.

Jackson, Peter A., and Gerard Sullivan, eds. 1999. "Multicultural Queer Australian Narratives." *Journal of Homosexuality* 36, nos. 3/4.

Jacobs, Sue-Ellen, Wesley Thomas, and Sabine Long. 1997. *Two-Spirit People: Native American Gender Identity, Sexuality, and Spirituality*. Urbana: University of Illinois Press.

Ramsay, Richard, and Pierre Tremblay. 2004. Race/Ethnic Minorities: Internet Resources, Part A, 2004. http://fsw.ucalgary.ca/ramsay/gay-lesbian-bisexual/3g-of-color-minority-gay.htm#Aboriginal. Accessed June 10, 2005.

Roscoe, Will. 1988. *Living the Spirit: A Gay American Indian Anthology / compiled by Gay American Indians.* New York: St. Martin's Press.

———. 1998. *Changing Ones: Third and Fourth Genders in Native North America.* New York: St. Martin's Press.

Saewyc, Elizabeth M., Carol L. Skay, Linda H. Bearinger, Robert W. Blum, and Michael D. Resnick. 1998. "Sexual Orientation, Sexual Behaviors and Pregnancy among American Indian Adolescents." *Journal of Adolescent Health* 23, no. 4: 238–247.

Williams, Walter L. 1986. *Spirit and the Flesh: Sexual Diversity in American Indian Culture.* Boston: Beacon Press.

Wilson, Alex. 1996. "How We Find Ourselves: Identity Development and Two-Spirit People." *Harvard Educational Review* 66, no. 2: 303–317.

Web Sites

Indigenous People's Task Force (formerly the Minnesota American Indian AIDS Task Force). 2002. Accessed June 10, 2005. http://www.indigenouspeoplestf.org. HIV information, FAQs, and programs for indigenous youth.

Walking With Honor: Northwest Two-Spirit Society. 2004. Northwest Two-Spirit Society. Accessed June 10, 2005. http://nwtwospiritsociety.org. History, resources, and events related to this tradition.

Youth of Color. 2005. YouthResource: A Project of Advocates for Youth. Accessed June 10, 2005. http://youthresource.com/community/youth_of_color/index.htm. Articles, Web rings, books, message boards and other resources for queer youth of color.

New Zealand, LGBT Issues in

Kim Jewel Elliott

Since the late 1960s and the emergence of "gay liberation" in Aotearoa/New Zealand, **lesbian, gay, bisexual, transgender** (LGBT) communities and issues have largely moved to mainstream visibility. The nation of 4.2 million citizens is lightly sprinkled (mostly in **urban** areas) with **queer** bookshops, nightclubs, festivals, support groups, businesses; and openly LGBT politicians, entertainers, and ministers. However, growing up queer in Aotearoa/New Zealand today, although arguably easier than forty years ago, still encounters copious obstacles. The responses to LGBT communities range from celebration and acceptance to ignorance and misunderstanding, to imposing the label of pathology to antagonistic acts of rejection, ridicule, or violence. Ongoing issues include changing current limiting legislation, the translation of law into practice, invisibility in education, and cultural identities. These overarching issues in turn impinge on the quality of life for contemporary queer youth.

See also Activism, LGBT Youth; Bullying; Cross- Dressing; Educational Policies; Gender Roles; Heterosexism; Mentoring; Multicultural Education; Multiple Genders; Native and Indigenous LGBT Youth; Physical Education, Teaching of; Proms; School Safety and Safe School Zones; Spirituality.

Three major legislative reforms are the cornerstones for the modern gay movement in Aotearoa/New Zealand. The *Homosexual Law Reform Act of 1986* decriminalized homosexuality, the *Bill of Rights Act of 1990* banned **discrimination** for everyone, and the *Human Rights Act of 1993* specifically outlawed discrimination against someone on the basis of **sexual orientation** (transpeople were not included). These acts apply to public schools and tertiary institutions of learning as well as the wider community. A gap remains, however, between the law and everyday practice.

In practice, although same-sex couples are legally recognized for immigration purposes, there are no next-of-kin rights when one partner is ill or has passed away, no parental leave from employment for the nonbiological parent, no spousal insurance benefits, no clear access to in vitro fertilization and embryo transfer, and no legally recognized marriage rights. Civil Union rights were legalized in April 2005 for all people regardless of sex. In schools, although discrimination on the basis of sexual orientation is illegal, the discussion of sexualities and **gender identity** issues in secondary and tertiary education is usually limited to that of heterosexuality and "normal" gender identities (Elliott 2003).

In 2001, the *Human Rights Amendment Act* added a new function to law, advocating the promotion of—by education and publicity—and respect for and observance of all human rights; alongside a requirement to develop a national plan of action, in consultation with interested parties, for the promotion and protection of human rights in New Zealand. This act contributed to the development by the Ministry of Youth Affairs, in 2002, of a social policy called the Youth Development Strategy detailing the government action plan for child and youth development. The strategy noted that:

> LGBT young people face the same health, **mental health** and other challenges as their heterosexual peers with the addition of social and health challenges associated with society often not accepting their identity. Developing a positive sexual identity is crucial to these young people's self-esteem and well-being. (Ministry of Youth Affairs 2002, 42)

As in other social institutions, the challenge is to effectively and consistently put the strategies and theories into practice, so that all youth identities are positively strengthened. Key issues identified in the Strategy for LGBT include: identity issues; discrimination and **harassment** in schools and the **workplace**; and access to support groups and programs.

Identity issues for LGBT youth include the pressure to keep secret their sexual orientation or gender identity for fear of rejection, ridicule, physical or verbal violence, isolation, and loss of friends on **coming out,** and for some the struggle of melding sexual and gender identities with ethnic identities and religious affiliations. Some level of discrimination and harassment in secondary schools, tertiary institutions, and workplaces also is more common than not.

The school system in Aotearoa/New Zealand was decentralized in the early 1990s, and every school has a Board of Trustees. According to the new Health and Physical Education Curriculum (Ministry of Education 2002), the Board of Trustees governing each school has a responsibility to ensure a safe physical and emotional environment for all its students so that all can achieve to their potential. However, there are no national school policies/programs specifically designed to ensure a safe environment for LGBT young people, and the term "gay" is often used by students as a put-down and is intended to mean trivial, feminized, or unimportant. Further, the *Health and Physical Education in the New Zealand Curriculum* (HPENZC) states that, "classroom programmes must be sensitively developed so that they respect the diverse values and beliefs of students and of the community," (Ministry of Education 1999, 39), but makes no mention of respecting students' sexual diversity. The *Sexuality Education: Revised Guide for Principals, Boards of Trustees and Teachers* similarly suggests that "many schools find it useful to develop overarching policies for the . . . **sexuality education** component of the [health education] program. A policy may . . . indicate how programs will recognize, respect, and respond to the diversity of values and beliefs in the school's community" (Ministry of Education 2002, 39). Individual schools have developed antibullying policies, but these, too, are extremely unlikely to focus specifically on safety for LGBT young people. Thus situations involving harassment or victimization in relation to sexual identity are often glossed over in the school setting, leaving the onus for emotional/physical safety of LGBT students to students themselves.

Making LGBT youth and issues visible in the **curriculum** and school functions meets with some opposition, silence, and invisibility. Of all the topics in the curriculum, teachers find sexualities most difficult to teach (Elliott 2003). The heterosexist nature of many schools, peers, families, and traditional religious moralities make it difficult for young LGBT to find positive role models or support systems. There is no material related to LGBT issues integrated into the formal curriculum; what is included is due to a comparatively few committed teachers and schools.

Also, little support is evident in the informal curriculum. The annual school ball is a traditional part of a young person's coming of age experience in Aotearoa/New Zealand. This is the last formal opportunity for the senior high school students to celebrate, dance, dine, and socialize with their partners and peers before entering tertiary education or the workplace. Most schools do not allow or support same-sex partners at this event. On the rare occasion when school officials are confronted about this issue, they generally cite a desire not to "promote homosexuality"—the same reasoning applied to sexuality education and sexual health services in schools, which can be seen to "promote sex" by providing condoms and the like.

The *Human Rights Act 1993* specifically outlawed discrimination of the basis of sexual orientation, but schools exert considerable power and autonomy in day-to-day practice. Particularly where the practice is historical and long-term, considerable effort is required to bring about change—and often at an emotional and visible cost to those seeking change. Schools supporting LGBT youth tend to be located in specific urban areas with largely liberal populations and supportive school staff.

Currently, there are no national requirements with regard to teacher training on LGBT issues. *Sexuality Education: Revised Guide for Principals, Boards of Trustees and Teachers* suggests that teachers need to "respond openly and honestly to students' questions and have enough knowledge either to answer any queries or at least to direct the student toward others who could help, as they would do in any other subject area." (Ministry of Education 2002, 42) This assumes that teachers have the knowledge, self-awareness, and training to respond to any sexualities question, and will be aware of support agencies in the community for referral as appropriate. This is rarely the case and the three-year teacher training programmes currently available offer minimal, if any, education for preservice teachers in this area. A very limited number of institutions such as the Auckland College of Education and organizations like the Family Planning Association offer in-service teacher education on LGBT youth issues. However, these professional development opportunities are taken up at the behest of individual teachers, rather than being a mandatory requirement for all teachers of sexualities education in Aotearoa/ New Zealand.

Despite these challenges, a small number of social support services for LGBT exist throughout Aotearoa/New Zealand. Three examples in Tamaki Makaurau (the largest city also known as Auckland) are The Auckland Pride Centre, Rainbow Youth, and Genderbridge, all located in the central city area The Pride centre provides space for LGBT social support groups to meet and organize local events such as The Coming Out Day and HERO Parades. It also provides access to LGBT books and **literature, community LGBT support groups,** and services.

Rainbow Youth provides support, contact, information, education, and advocacy for LGBT youth. This youth-led organization facilitates regular groups where young persons can meet, socialize, and gain support from others who experience similar issues. It also provides emergency short-term residential care for young people with sexual or gender identity issues. Rainbow Youth also facilitates workshops in schools to increase awareness of LGBT youth and share experiences of coming out. Workshops are designed to fit with the national curriculum, to decrease homophobia, and to create safe, supportive, learning and working environments.

Genderbridge supports transgender people and their friends and family. Started in 1999, it offers regular meetings, social functions, newsletters, and information on transyouth, surgery, **research,** and book and film lists. There are currently no other groups in the country specifically for transyouth.

Unique to the South Pacific are *Fa'afafine*. Fa'afafine is a Samoan word meaning like or in the way of a woman (Wallace 2003). Fa'afafine are biologically male and express female gender identities in a variety of ways. Different terms exist in other Pacific languages such as the Tongan *fakaleitï*, French Polynesian *rae rae* or the Fijian *vakasalewalewa*. Because more Samoans live in Tamaki Makaurau/ Auckland than in Samoa, the city has a special relationship with non-Western forms of transgenderism. Thus, being Fa'afafine is experienced differently in Aotearoa/New Zealand, viewed through Western concepts of gender and sexuality, than in Samoa. Being Fa'afafine in Samoa is grounded in cultural history with strong support from family and society. Gender identity is largely defined by ones' work contribution to the family and community (Wallace 2003). Fa'afafine preference for feminine labor defines gender identity, rather than being associated with sexual practices and dressing like a woman, as is the case in Tamaki Makaurau. Thus, Fa'afafine are subject to both **racism** and homophobia, and invisibility in education curricula. While Pakeha (New Zealanders of European descent) transyouth are invisible in the curriculum through their gender identity, fa'afafine youth are additionally invisible through their cultural identity. There are currently no support groups in Aotearoa/New Zealand for fa'afafine young people.

Unique to Aotearoa/New Zealand is the *takatäpui* identity. Takatäpui, or hoa takatäpui, is a Mäori word meaning intimate companion of the same sex. As the tängata whenua, the indigenous people, Mäori people occupy a unique place in New Zealand society, and about one fifth of Mäori are young people. Mäori LGBT may identify as takatäpui täne (gay Mäori), takatäpui wahine (lesbian Mäori), whakawahine (Maori transwoman), or whakatane (Maori transman). The identification of self as takatāpui or whakawahine/whakatane upholds a specific identity that melds ethnic, sexual, and gender identities. It requires an acceptance of self as both lesbian/gay/transgender, and as Maori.

The state education system does not explicitly provide the opportunity for this exploration of multiple identities, thus requiring young takatāpui or whakawahine/whakatane to seek other sources of education and support. Like tāngata whenua, takatāpui and whakawahine/whakatane are also subject to both racism and homophobia from the wider community. There is an absence of culturally relevant content in the state school curricula and a lack of inclusion, and thus protection, under the *Homosexual Law Reform Act of 1986 and Human Rights Act of* 1993. There, too, is limited support and accessible information for takatāpui or whakawahine/whakatane, whose whanau (family) may believe that a past whanau hara (wrongdoing) has caused them to be takataapui as utu (punishment).

Despite a mandate from the Ministry of Education (2002), there is a wholesale absence of a culturally appropriate sexuality curriculum in schools for Māori. Although the Māori concept of Hauora underpins the Health and Physical Education Curriculum, Hauora is little more than the translation of terms into English into a curriculum document. Hauora is an indigenous holistic view of health and well-being comprising four aspects, Tinana (physical), Wairua (spiritual), Hinengaro (Emotional), and Whanau (Social). It is a concept that teachers sometimes find difficult to incorporate practically into their teaching, such as exploring the spiritual and social roles that takatāpui, whakawahine, and whakatane have played in historical Maori societies.

Bibliography

Elliott, Kim J. 2003. "The Hostile Vagina: Reading Vaginal Discourse in a School Health Text." *Sex Education* 3, no. 2: 133–144.

Ministry of Education. 1999. *Health and Physical Education in the New Zealand Curriculum.* Wellington, NX: Learning Media.

———. 2002. *Sexuality Education: Revised Guide for Principals, Boards of Trustees, and Teachers.* Wellington, NZ: Learning Media.

Ministry of Youth Affairs. 2002. *Youth Development Strategy Aotearoa.* Wellington, NZ: Ministry of Youth Affairs.

Town, Shane. 2002. "Playing with Fire: (Homo)sexuality and Schooling in New Zealand." Pp. 1–15 in *From Here to Diversity: The Social Impact of Lesbian and Gay Issues in Education in Australia and New Zealand.* Edited by Kerry Robinson, Jude Irwin, and Tania Ferfolja. New York: Harrington Press.

Wallace, Lee. 2003. *Sexual Encounters: Pacific Texts, Modern Sexualities.* Ithaca, NY: Cornell University Press.

Web Sites

The Auckland Pride Centre. October 2003. Interpride. Accessed June 10, 2005. http://www.pride.org.nz. The Web site contains links to the sites of over 200 national and international groups and organizations, LGBT history, Queer search engines, and news providers, and outlines the services provided by the Centre.

Genderbridge. May 2005. Rainbow Net. Accessed December 4, 2004. http://www.genderbridge.org. Genderbridge is a national online community and resource network for transpeople, their friends, and families.

Ministry of Youth Affairs. May 2005. New Zealand Ministry of Youth Affairs. Accessed June 10, 2005. http://www.youthaffairs.govt.nz. The Ministry of Youth Affairs Web site is an online resource providing information on the policies, programmes, legislation and services that concern young people in New Zealand.

Rainbow Youth. May 2005. Rainbow Net. Accessed June 10, 2005. http://www.rainbow youth.org.nz. Rainbow Youth provides support, information, and advocacy for young lesbian, gay, bisexual, transgender, takatāpui, and fa'afafine people in New Zealand.

New Zealand, Teaching of Sexualities in

Joseph A. Diorio and *Kim Jewel Elliott*

Teaching about sexualities in Aotearoa/New Zealand is conducted within the health and **physical education** school **curriculum** in schools (Ministry of Education 1999). Topics dealing with sexualities are intended to be presented holistically as part of the integrated development of students' personal and social well-being. In practice, teaching focuses significantly on heterosexuality and the **biology** of reproduction. The health and physical education curriculum explicitly promotes cultural and gender inclusiveness and respect for diversity. Students learn not to discriminate against persons on the basis of differing sexual orientations. The curriculum makes no direct mention of issues affecting lesbian, gay, bisexual, or transgendered people, however. And teaching about sexualities is the only aspect of the compulsory National Curriculum Framework from which parents legally may withdraw their children.

New Zealand—known to Māori, the indigenous people, as Aotearoa—is a parliamentary democracy of 4.2 million people in the South Pacific. The country is centrally governed, with nation-wide educational policies administered by the Ministry of Education. Each school has a Board of Trustees and devises its teaching program, but this must be compatible with the National Curriculum Framework.

Historically, teaching about sexualities has been contentious. Debates during the 1970s and 1980s centred on removing an existing prohibition on **sex education** (as it was then called) in presecondary schooling. Those who sought removal of the prohibition often linked teaching about sexuality to the promotion of stable marital relationships. The government, however, retained the prohibition until 1989, when the Education Act was amended.

Education about sexualities today is included in all schools through *Health and Physical Education in the New Zealand Curriculum* (Ministry of Education 1999). This document incorporates portions of three previously separate subjects: health education, physical education, and aspects of home economics. It defines seven key learning areas: **mental health**, sexuality education, food and nutrition, body care and physical safety, physical activity, sport studies, and outdoor education.

Teaching about sexualities relies heavily on biological understandings of sexual phenomena, and often is conducted by teachers with backgrounds in **science** or physical education. As in many other countries, teaching about sexualities in

See also Adolescent Sexualities; Australia, Sexualities Curriculum in; Coming Out, Teachers; Heteronormativity; Native and Indigenous LGBT Youth; Poststructuralism; Sexism.

New Zealand is driven significantly by concerns about **teenage pregnancy**, sexually transmitted infections, and HIV/**AIDS**. Sexuality commonly is seen as naturally reproductive and heterosexual, and sexual activity is assumed normally to involve heterosexual genital intercourse. A recent Ministry of Education publication, for example, notes that between 10 and 30 percent of young New Zealanders have had sexual intercourse by the time they reach the age of 15, that the median age for the first experience of sexual intercourse is 17 for males and 16 for females, and that there is a higher risk of cervical cancer among women who begin sexual intercourse at an early age (Ministry of Education 2002).

Teaching about puberty also reflects the focus on reproductive sexuality. Puberty is presented as a universal and purely natural experience undergone by "every young person, whatever their gender, **ethnicity**, culture, religion, physical stature, and abilities or **disabilities**" (Ministry of Education 2002, 5). Reproductive heterosexuality is seen as the natural outcome and the primary meaning of pubertal development. School-based sexuality educators commonly teach students that the bodily changes of puberty not only make reproduction possible, but also that they are naturally intended to lead to reproduction and parenthood. Girls, for example, are taught that the onset of menstruation is a source of physical discomfort and of new hygiene needs, which must be endured and dealt with in order to have children (Diorio and Munro 2000).

Teaching about puberty does not consider many of the diverse experiences of puberty that individuals may have such as premature or delayed pubescence or the feelings of students for whom reproduction is not a welcome prospect. Neither does it explore the different meanings puberty may hold within their cultures. One example is the Maori concept of "Te Whare Tapu O Te Tangata," where females at the onset of menarche, are viewed as "the sacred house of the people." Here the womb is the birth house of human kind and as such should be seen as sacred. Thus, their reproductive capabilities denotes more than an individual choice, it is a responsibility to their "iwi" (tribe). Teaching about puberty also omits any consideration of differing experiences or understandings of puberty had by young people who have identified, or who are beginning to identify, as **lesbian, gay, bisexual,** or **transgender youth** (Diorio and Munro 2003).

Despite the emphasis on gender equity, many New Zealand teaching materials reveal a masculinist bias. Puberty is presented to boys as an opportunity for excitement and fun, while the major focus on female puberty concerns not only reproduction but also the stresses associated with menstruation (Elliott 2003). An Australian-made video, widely used in New Zealand schools, for example, tells boys that during puberty there are "wonderful things happening, these are erections, they are a natural instinct. . . . [and] exciting dreams, fantasies about girlfriends" (Mayle 1992 in Diorio and Munro 2000, 15). Girls are not given anything exciting to look forward to except childbirth. Instead, girls are told that they will "have breasts, and breasts are popular—boys like them a lot, and so should you." The message provided to presumed heterosexually-oriented girls is to value the development of their bodies because this will make them more attractive to boys.

Health and Physical Education in the New Zealand Curriculum (HPENZC) says little about the actual content of sexuality teaching. Individual schools are required to consult with their local communities every two years on how they will implement the health education components (Ministry of Education 2002). Four of the seven learning areas in HPENZC, including sexuality education, are identified as relating to health education and hence as requiring consultation. Consultation does not necessarily involve negotiation between the school and its community over the content of the program, nor does it require that the community agree with what that the school ultimately implements. Parents have the right to withdraw their children only from those components of the program that deal with sexuality education. Young people are not usually consulted on program content and it is not necessarily informed by or responsive to their sexual experiences, queries, or uncertainties (Diorio and Munro 2003; Elliott and Lambourn 1999). Once a health education program has been set up in a school, however, HPENZC aims to enable students to "develop the knowledge, skills, attitudes, and motivation [to] . . . contribute to their personal well-being, the well-being of other people, and that of society as a whole" (Ministry of Education 1999, 6).

The concept of "well-being" is presented in terms of the Māori word "hauora," which includes physical, mental, emotional, social, and spiritual well-being. Focus on the idea of hauora is grounded in the special position of Māori people and culture. New Zealand strives toward being a bicultural society constituted by a partnership between Māori people on one hand and all other peoples and cultures on the other. Because of the position of Māori people and since the rest of the population has become culturally diversified, HPENZC emphasises cultural differences and requires schools to develop and teach culturally relevant content inclusive of all groups.

The promotion of cultural inclusiveness, however, stands uneasily alongside the scientific grounding of HPENZC with respect to teaching about sexualities. Students are expected to learn about the "natural processes" of pubertal development, sexual reproduction, avoidance of sexually transmitted infections, and effective contraceptive techniques. Teachers also are directed to enable students to develop sensitivity toward others, to respect others' rights, and to "critically examine the social and cultural influences that shape the ways people learn about and express their sexuality" (Ministry of Education 1999, 38).

Sexuality thus has two separate dimensions within the New Zealand curriculum: one that is scientific and assumed to be independent of culture, and one that is dependent on cultural understandings and expressions. While respecting cultural diversity regarding sexuality, students still are to learn what sexuality "really" is from a scientific point of view. Culture, thus, is acknowledged as influencing the ways people respond to natural sexuality, but not as affecting what sexuality is itself. For example, menstruation for Maori can be viewed as a time of grieving, as the passing of the egg is the passing of that particular child who will not be born. Puberty and sexualities are thus more than an individual experience; these are links to membership in communities.

HPENZC adopts a predominantly essentialist approach to sexuality, which is understood as being determined biologically rather than as constructed socially and culturally. Although teachers are expected both to promote scientific understanding and to support cultural differences, the possibility that cultural approaches to sexuality might conflict with a scientific understanding is not considered. The effect is that sexualities tend to be presented in schools as culturally neutral, with little real attention to the ways in which cultural differences can affect the nature and meaning of sexuality.

There are significant moves underway to broaden teachers' awareness of social constructionist understandings of the topic. Tasker and Aldridge (2000, 1), for example, have developed a resource for teachers of sexuality education that encourages "critical analysis of media portrayal of sexuality and gender" and "assumptions, myths and realities of the sex industry."

The New Zealand Ministry of Education also has informed teachers that **discrimination** on the grounds of **sexual orientation** is illegal, but the absence of LGBT-related content effectively excludes positive consideration of diverse sexualities. Further, teachers inadvertently risk damaging LGBT students by teaching them that the meaning of their bodily development is inherently reproductive and reinforcing among all students the normality of heterosexuality. Once teachers have presented puberty as leading naturally to heterosexuality, it is difficult for heterosexual students, who have been taught to see themselves as biologically "normal," to empathize with LGBT peers. Students are provided with no conceptual framework in which to understand LGBT students as anything other than deviant or pathological.

Because of variations among schools, it is difficult to generalize nationally about sexualities teaching. Some schools have openly LGBT staff and students who work to provide an environment that is free from discrimination. The environment of other schools is such that even LGBT staff chooses not to be "out" at school. Funding by student roll numbers means that schools generally seek to please the majority of parents—"the majority" being defined as those who are most visible and vocal. As a result, teaching about sexuality, as in most countries, focuses significantly on heterosexuality and the biology of reproduction.

Bibliography

Diorio, Joseph, and Jenny Munro. 2000. "Doing Harm in the Name of Protection: Menstruation as a Topic for Sex Education." *Gender and Education* 12, no. 3: 347–365.

———. 2003. "What Does Puberty Mean to Adolescents? Teaching and Learning about Bodily Development." *Sex Education* 3, no. 2: 119–132.

Elliott, Kim J. 2003. "The Hostile Vagina: Reading Vaginal Discourse in a School Health Text." *Sex Education* 3, no 2: 133–144.

Elliott, Kim J., and Andrew J. Lambourn. 1999. "Sex, Drugs and Alcohol: Two Peer Led Approaches in Tamaki Makaurau/Auckland, Aotearoa/New Zealand." *The Journal of Adolescence* 22, no. 4: 503–511.

Ministry of Education. 1999. *Health and Physical Education in the New Zealand Curriculum.* Wellington, NZ: Learning Media.

———. 2002. *Sexuality Education: Revised Guide for Principals, Boards of Trustees, and Teachers.* Wellington, NZ: Learning Media.

Tasker, Gillian, and Lynne Aldridge. 2000. *Social and Ethical Issues in Sexuality Education: A Resource for Health Education Teachers of Year 12 and 13 Students.* Christchurch, NZ: Christchurch College of Education.

Web Site

Ministry of Education. 2004. New Zealand Ministry of Education. Accessed December 4, 2004. http://www.minedu.govt.nz/. Compiled from information obtained from sources commissioned by the Ministry of Education and within the Ministry, this site includes information on topical issues, news and media releases, research and general education.

P

Parents, LGBT

Pat Hulsebosch

There are an estimated six to ten million **lesbian** and **gay** parents in the United States (Lambda Legal 2004); no estimates are available worldwide. Although **research** and writing by and about **bisexual** and **transgender** parents are only now beginning to appear, their numbers are likely to add to reported United States estimates. Lesbian and gay parents first received widespread public attention in the 1970s as lesbian mothers began to fight for custody of their children conceived within heterosexual relationships. Until then, few outside of gay and lesbian communities knew of the existence of lesbian and gay parents. Nowadays the existence of LGBT parents is common knowledge, although not commonly accepted. Family issues are currently at the forefront of the LGBT civil rights movement and have become some of the most hotly contested issues in public debate. In education, however, LGBT parents and their children have been largely ignored, although both face challenges in the schools. Historically, society (including many gay men and lesbians) assumed that being a parent and being gay were incongruent. **Stereotypes** of gay men, lesbians, bisexuals, and transgendered adults as narcissistic and non-nurturing at best, and pathological sexual predators at worst, have often supported beliefs that they could not be trusted to raise children. At times, this myth served a protective function for some gay men, lesbians, and bisexuals who, as parents within a marriage, enjoyed

Lesbian Couple with Quadruplets. © Gigi Kaeser from the book and the touring photo-text exhibit LOVE MAKES A FAMILY: Portraits of Lesbian, Gay, Bisexual, and Transgender People and their Families. For information, visit www. familydiv.org or email info@familydiv.org.

queer relationships beyond the legal structure. The advent of **Stonewall** and changing (albeit slowly) public acceptance has been coupled with an increasing desire among many to be openly gay or lesbian.

While the majority of **children of LGBT parents** are still conceived in heterosexual relationships, a growing numbers of parents choose to have children within queer relationships. Queer families have benefited from a greater availability of reproductive technologies, including donor insemination and surrogacy. However, such expensive options are differentially available according to **social class**.

LGBT parents also create families through **adoption** within the United States and internationally. In the United States, a mounting number of adoption and foster care agencies accept lesbians and gay men as potential parents; almost half of the

See also Childhood; Children of the Rainbow Curriculum; Curriculum, Early Childhood; Curriculum, Primary; Discrimination; Families, LGBT; Literature, Early Childhood; Passing; Prejudice.

states have allowed second-parent adoptions for same-sex couples. If a couple is fortunate enough to live in such a state, then one partner can legally adopt internationally and their partner can later adopt in their home state. International adoption has sometimes been an attractive choice for LGBT adults because of the more liberal "single parent" adoption policies of some countries such as Guatemala, Haiti, and the Ukraine. Although some countries in **Europe** such as the Netherlands, Sweden, Denmark, Iceland, and the **United Kingdom** have granted adoption rights to gay couples within their country, *all* countries offering children for international adoption have taken a negative stance on adoption by same-sex couples beyond their borders. Some of these countries (most notably **China**) now demand a written statement that a single applicant is not a gay male or lesbian.

By their very existence, LGBT parents challenge societal norms. Queer parents call into question assumptions about **gender roles** (Can two mothers raise a boy without a male parent? Can two men nurture a baby?), sexuality (Can queer parents be good parents?), **biology** (Is a mother a "real mother" if her partner gave birth?), **sexual identity**, (Will he grow up to be gay if his parents are queer?), and legality (Should a school share pupil information with both fathers?). Early research on lesbian and gay parents examined many of these assumptions and found no evidence to support them (American Psychological Association 2003; Johnson and O'Connor 2002). However, seldom have these researchers challenged heteronormative and assimilationist assumptions as they documented that LGBT families are "just like" heterosexual families. Few research studies have explored the "interesting differences" that can "in no way be considered deficits" associated with growing up in a queer family (Stacey and Biblarz 2001, 176). Those which have looked at differences in children raised in queer families found these children were more tolerant and less bound to gender role traditions.

LGBT parents also challenge society to consider what it means to be a legal couple. Formal recognition of same-sex unions, including domestic partnership, civil union, and marriage, (both pro and con) is currently on national, state, and local agendas. In the United States, only Massachusetts currently issues a marriage license; five states and the District of Columbia have domestic partnership laws that provide limited rights to same-sex couples. One other state, Vermont, licenses civil unions, which provides all the state-level rights and responsibilities of marriage. None of these state-level provisions, however, provide access to the more than a thousand federal protections available to heterosexual married couples (Human Rights Campaign 2004). Meanwhile, forty states have laws or state constitutional amendments that aim to ban marriage for same-sex couples.

In **Canada**, three provinces and one territory currently issue marriage licenses to same-sex couples. Because these three are the most populace provinces, three out of four Canadians live in a jurisdiction that recognizes same-sex marriage (Human Rights Campaign 2004). The Netherlands and Belgium also grant same-sex couples the right to legally marry, while other countries, such as **Brazil** and Denmark, have legislation recognizing civil unions or domestic partnerships for same-sex couples. However, even where legalization includes some of the rights of heterosexual marriages, other rights (e.g., adoption rights, pensions, medical decisions, and immigration) are considered a separate legal issue.

Educational institutions, with their reliance on legal and bureaucratic frameworks, are confronted with parents who may or may not have legal or even biological ties to their children. Thus, the growing awareness of the existence of LGBT parents challenges educational institutions to reconsider and revise their assumptions about parents and families.

LGBT adults become parents through many different routes: heterosexual marriage or sexual relations; adoption; foster parenting; donor insemination; and surrogacy. Some children are aware that their parents are queer from their earliest understandings, whereas others may not become aware that their parents are LGB or T until their **adolescence** or well into adulthood. Regardless of how their families were created, queer parents live with their children in many different types of family structures, including single parents, blended families, family of origin, or with extended families created with other members from LGBT communities. And, like other parents, the child-rearing practices and community acceptance of LGBT parents are likely to be influenced by cultural background and family of origin (Bernstein and Reimann 2001).

While LGBT parents confront many of the typical joys and challenges of parenting, there are also factors unique to their families. Because of the added obstacles to parenting, lesbian and gay parents tend to do a great deal of reflection about their potential role as parents before undertaking parenthood. Research on LGBT relationships shows positive adjustment even in the face of stressful conditions. LGBT parents, particularly those who choose to have children within already-existing, openly gay and lesbian lives, face decisions about whether to become parents, how to become parents, and how to negotiate the parental roles within the relationship. This may make them more aware of what is required for effective parenting, and better prepared to face the challenges of parenthood.

In addition, heterosexist and homophobic laws and policies affect their parenting and the lives of their families, particularly when they enter educational institutions. A coparent may be prevented from picking up the couple's child at school, requesting progress reports, or participating in educational conferences unless there has been a second parent adoption. And, school district policies may punish students and teachers who attempt to use words like "gay" and "lesbian" in formal class assignments. For LGBT parents, the discrepancies between parents' self-definitions and identity and those of educational institutions create challenges in their lives. Schools, which tend to adhere closely to legal and bureaucratic structures in making decisions, particularly in situations which challenge their assumptions, may ask, "Who's the real parent?" or "Who's the legal parent? Who has custody?" Or, when both parents are not readily identifiable, they simply will not ask, assuming a single parent.

LGBT parents, particularly in **urban** areas, are often able to offset some of these challenges by establishing networks with other LGBT families. This has become easier in recent years for lesbian and gay parents, but remains a challenge for bisexual and transgender parents who are in the earlier stages of community building. Increased visibility for LGBT parents, however, has brought increased resources, including magazines such as *Gay Parent* and *Alternative Family Magazine*, online discussion groups (e.g., SMO Message Board: Surrogacy for Gay Parents), and several U.S.-based national organizations and advocacy groups.

Although LGBT people recognize the impact of social stigma and the possibility of **harassment**, LGBT parents must also take into consideration both the positive and negative impact on their children should they decide to come out. One way that LGBT parents may respond to this is through an emphasis on issues of diversity, equity, and advocacy in the values they teach their children. These values, and the skills and knowledge that accompany them, are then strengths that schools can tap into.

However, schools, with their conservative tendencies, often, either implicitly or explicitly, promote invisibility for LGBT parents and their children. This invisibility ranges from a lack of representation of diverse families in the curriculum, and in forms requesting "mother" and "father" names, to disciplinary action against a child that tells another his mothers are "gay." LGBT parents may, in the preschool years, be open and out. However, they sometimes become more cautious when their children enter public school settings. Some LGBT parents seek out private or public schools that are explicitly antibiased. For example, schools based in the Quaker religious tradition have been at the forefront in developing and including family (and other) diversity in their curricula.

Some LGBT parents take an activist stance with regard to the school. Brill (2001) describes three levels of **activism** or engagement with the school. Level One involvement (silent activism) means becoming visible in the school, attending school functions as partners, and adapting school forms to fit your family. At Level Two, LGBT parents actively educate educators by asking questions about sources of potential bias, brainstorming responses with the teacher, and providing resources. At Level Three, LGBT parents move beyond responses to bias to larger curricular and **educational policy** issues. They may arrange for school-wide speakers on the LGBT civil rights movement, and work to change school and district policy to include antidiscriminatory language related to sexual orientation.

Bibliography

Benkov, Laura. 1994. *Reinventing the Family: The Emerging Story of Lesbian and Gay Parents.* New York: Random House.

Bernstein, Mary, and Renate Reimeann, eds. 2001. *Queer Families, Queer Politics.* New York: Columbia University Press.

Brill, Stephanie A. 2001. *The Queer Parent's Primer: A Lesbian and Gay Families' Guide to Navigating the Straight World.* Oakland: New Harbinger.

Glazer, Deborah F., and Jack Drescher, eds. 2001. *Gay and Lesbian Parenting.* Binghamton, NY: Haworth Press.

Hulsebosch, Pat, Mari E. Koerner, and Daniel P. Ryan. 1999. "Supporting Students/ Responding to Gay and Lesbian Parents." Pp. 183–193 in *Queering Elementary Education.* Edited by Will Letts, IV and James T. Sears. Lanham, MD: Rowman and Littlefield.

Johnson, Suzanne M., and Elizabeth O'Connor. 2002. *The Gay Baby Boom: The Psychology of Gay Parenthood.* New York: New York University Press.

Stacey, Judith, and Timothy Biblarz. 2001. "(How) Does the Sexual Orientation of Parents Matter?" *American Sociological Review* 66 (April): 159–183.

Web Sites

ACLU Fact Sheet: Overview of Lesbian and Gay Parenting, Adoption and Foster Care; American Civil Liberties Union, 1999. Accessed June 17, 2005. http://www.aclu.org/ LesbianGayRights/LesbianGayRights.cfm?ID=9212&c=104 Though not updated with recent information, it provides a good summary of myths vs. facts on lesbian and gay parenting, along with legal, policy, and research overviews on the topic.

APA Online: Public Interest: Lesbian and Gay Parenting; American Psychological Association. 2004. Charlotte J. Patterson. Accessed June 17, 2005. http://www.apa.org/pi/parent.html. Includes a summary of research findings and an annotated bibliography on lesbian and gay parenting.

Human Rights Campaign Foundation: HRC Focus on the Family-Marriage. Accessed March 3, 2005. http://www.hrc.org/Template.cfm?Section=Partners&Template=/ TaggedPage/TaggedPageDisplay.cfm&TPLID=26&ContentID=22127. Site provides up-to-date news releases, as well as links to resources on relevant state laws, legal documents for couples, international and state summaries of marriage equality laws, census data, and HRC pamphlets such as *Answers to Questions About Marriage Equality*.

Lambda Legal. Accessed March 3, 2005. http://www.lambdalegal.org/cgi-bin/iowa/issues/ record?record=5. The "Family" page of Lambda Legal provides a lengthy list of legal and resource documents on issues relevant to LGBT parents and their children including custody, adoption, coming out, and parental rights.

Parents, Responses to Homosexuality

Maria Pallotta-Chiarolli

When same-sex attracted or transgender young people are "**coming out,**" their parents often undergo a process of "coming in." They come in to the reality of their child's nonheterosexual sexuality and diverse gender expression, and any homophobic/gender dualist assumptions and **prejudices** they may hold. Parents also experience their own "coming out" to other family members, friends, local communities, and the wider society as parents of **lesbian, gay, bisexual,** or **transgender** (LGBT) children. These two processes are important for many parents to work through in order to be able to affirm and support their child more effectively. An increasing number of parents are becoming proactive in schools and local communities in resisting and challenging **homophobia.**

Parents often experience one or more of three reactions when their child first comes out (Pallotta-Chiarolli 2005). Some parents "go into the closet," concealing, glossing over, or trivializing their child's sexualities with other family members, friends, and work colleagues (Baker 2002). Evasions become common: "There's no special girl in his life at the moment;" "She isn't thinking about marriage yet;" "He's sharing the apartment with a friend." Parents report that being closeted requires an enormous amount of emotional and mental energy that interferes with personal and professional relationships. Their silence or deception takes its toll. They must be consistent with lies, juggling the different stories different people know, the explanations, edits, and erasures.

Second, some parents find their child's coming out has repercussions in other parts of their lives and other relationships (Griffin, Wirth, and Wirth 1996; Jennings and Shapiro 2003). For example, if parents cannot share the news with their partner or mother or friend or sibling, what is this saying about the kind of marriage, relationship, friendship they have always had that now comes to the fore and troubles them? Does their son's or daughter's coming out raise old grievances and frustrations in other relationships and facets of their lives that have never been resolved? Does it raise buried issues about their sexualities, or guilt about their sense of inadequacies, or failure as parents?

Third, some parents find that as their child lets go of destructive feelings (e.g., shame, guilt, grief, disappointment, self-blame, anger, and despair), these feelings

See also Community LGBT Youth Groups; Educational Policies; Families, LGBT; Gender Identity; Passing; Sexual Orientation.

605

arise in themselves: "I'm ashamed of my child;" "They won't have the life I'd dreamed for them;" "What did I do wrong?;" "This isn't fair, why my family?;" "I hate them for doing this to me;" "How do I hold my head up in the local church/town/community?" (McDougall 1998; Pallotta-Chiarolli 2005). These feelings can lead to further guilt, frustration, and shame as "good" parents are not meant to hold such feelings in response to a child's "coming out." Some parents block or "closet" these reactions rather than working through them. Other parents find that they do not feel guilty or frustrated or ashamed of their negative feelings. They are genuinely ashamed, angry, hateful, and disappointed in their child—and believe they have the right to be. As "good" parents, they deserved "better" from their son or daughter. Indeed, they get angry if other parents, friends, or health workers try to tell them these negative feelings are temporary, or damaging in the long term (Fairchild and Hayward 1998; Pallotta-Chiarolli 2005).

Parents' responses to a child's "coming out" appear to be dependent upon whether their perceptions of gender diversity and sexual diversity are framed by discourses of **heteronormativity** and gendernormativity or challenging and critiquing these discourses (Pallotta-Chiarolli 2005). Parents who perceive and respond to their same-sex attracted or transgender offspring from within such discourse tend to see "the problem" as being their child and themselves as parents. They seek psychological, religious, and other "reasons" for why "this crisis" has occurred in their families such as the explanation provided through a diagnosis of **Gender Identity Disorder**. They also seek medical, psychological, and religious "cures," like **reparative therapy**. They ask questions such as: "What did I do wrong?" "Who influenced my child?" "Was my child sexually abused by a gay pedophile?" "How can my child be cured?" "Is it just a phase?" "How do I save my child from going to hell?" (Baker 2002; Jennings and Shapiro 2003; McDougall 1998; Pallotta-Chiarolli 2005).

An increasing number of parents are not limited by these heteronormative and gendernormative discourses (Griffin, Wirth, and Wirth 1996). Instead, they believe that affirming and celebrating their child's "coming out" is "what all parents should automatically do." They critique and challenge social, political, and cultural myths as well as religious, educational, and media institutions that led them to problematise and pathologise their children (Pallotta-Chiarolli 2005). These parents speak in terms of resistance to the notion of same-sex attracted children and transchildren being "deficits," "sick," and "failures." They refuse to accept homophobic and gendered **harassment** of their son or daughter in any social, religious, and political setting as justifiable and "normal;" they refuse to accept that having a same-sex attracted or transgender child is something to "cope" with, "grieve" over, or "come to terms" with. They insist that adults such as educators, health workers, and local community members do not ignore or deny their responsibility and accountability for the health and well-being of LGBT youth (Baker 2002; Griffin, Wirth, and Wirth 1996; Pallotta-Chiarolli 2005).

So what can parents do to work through the three reactions outlined above? Research shows that parents often undertake one or more of the following four strategies:

- Find and create their support and social networks. These can be formal networks such as Parents and Friends of Lesbians and Gays (PFLAG), and informal networks of other parents, family members, counselors, community workers, trusted teachers, and ministers (Griffin, Wirth, and Wirth 1996).

- Replace ignorance, misinformation, and prejudices with knowledge, awareness, and understanding. Both individually and with support networks, parents challenge the "taken-for-grantedness" and "the unquestionable and unquestioned" social, cultural, political, and religious myths and prejudices about sexual and gender diversity. They gather resources and connect with resource persons to get informed with reliable facts. They become open to a new way of speaking, seeing and experiencing a world that was always there but which they were prevented from seeing and understanding by heteronormative and gendernormative institutions and social forces. For example, some parents get to know the LGBT community by attending forums and festivals, often accompanying their children to these and other events. Parents of transchildren seek out health workers and medical personnel who are affirming and supportive. Often, LGBT young people initiate such processes by giving their parents "homework," taking materials and resources home for their parents to read and talk about (Jennings and Shapiro 2003).

- Work through a range of reactions and feelings such as anger, hurt, frustration, disappointment, shame, blame of self and others. Rather than problematise their children, parents interrogate and are self-reflexive about their reactions and feelings. For example, parents will acknowledge their shame and then move on to ask, "Why am I feeling ashamed? Is it my child's sexuality or the way society makes me feel about my child's sexuality? And what can I do about this feeling so that it doesn't destroy me, my child or our relationship?" (McDougall 1998).

- Script, stage, and manage their outings about being the parents of a sexual minority child. Parents negotiate with their children about who to tell, when, and how. They plan what to say in various situations, respecting and supporting the needs and requests of their child, as well as the safety and well-being of other family members. For example, some LGBT youth will only want certain family members to know at certain points in time. Likewise, if there are younger siblings attending school and likely to be bullied for having a LGBT older sibling or if the family lives in a neighborhood where family members may experience harm, parents may decide not to "come out" to certain community members (Pallotta-Chiarolli 2005).

Parental conservatism is often cited as a major reason why K-12 schools do not challenge homophobia and gendered harassment. Yet, parents of same-sex attracted and transgender children are taking several kinds of supportive actions in schools (Baker 2002; Jennings and Shapiro 2003; Pallotta-Chiarolli 2004).

- Speaking up, letting school **administrators** and student welfare coordinators know that they want the school to undertake sexual diversity teaching and affirmation.

- Rewarding principals and teachers when they do undertake good practice such as writing letters, making phone calls, attending sexual diversity events, acknowledging the school's efforts at local community forums, and publicly stating that they support and appreciate the school's actions.

- Registering of complaints about incidents of homophobic harassment by those parents who are aware of homophobic language used by students and teachers, and pointing out inclusions/exclusions in the **curriculum**.

- Becoming informed of their legal rights as a parent and the school's legal responsibilities toward the children in its care.

- Linking up with each other to present their views and concerns collectively, and becoming a vocal group of parents in support of gender and sexual diversity education and policies. This is significant given the power of a vocal minority of parents in many schools in vetoing sexual diversity education.

- Reassuring any LGBT **teachers** on staff that they have parental support, as well as asking these professionals what can be done to support their work and improve the **workplace**.

Bibliography

Baker, Jean M. 2002. *How Homophobia Hurts Children: Nurturing Diversity at Home, at School, and in the Community*. Binghamton, NY: Harrington Park Press.

Fairchild, Betty, and Nancy Hayward. 1998. *Now That You Know: A Parent's Guide to Understanding Their Gay and Lesbian Children*. San Diego: Harcourt, Brace.

Griffin, Carolyn W., Marian J. Wirth, and Arthur G. Wirth. 1996. *Beyond Acceptance: Parents of Lesbians and Gays Talk About Their Experiences*. New York: St Martin's Griffin.

Jennings, Kevin, with Pat Shapiro. 2003. *Always My Child: A Parent's Guide to Understanding Your Gay, Lesbian, Bisexual, Transgendered or Questioning Son or Daughter*. New York: Fireside.

McDougall, Bryce. 1998. *My Child is Gay: How Parents React When They Hear the News*. Sydney: Allen and Unwin.

Pallotta-Chiarolli, Maria. 2004. *When Our Children Come Out: How to Support Gay, Lesbian, Bisexual and Transgendered Young People*. Sydney: Finch.

Web Sites

My Child is GAY! Now What do I do? March, 2000. Bidstrup, Scott. Accessed June 10, 2005. http://www.bidstrup.com/parents.htm. Provides answers for parents' frequently asked questions. It also suggests strategies on how parents can support their children, as well as how parents can play an important role in community actions to address homophobia. There is also a list of additional Internet resources.

Ten Tips for Parents of a Gay, Lesbian, Bisexual, or Transgender Child. Maurer, Lisa. Accessed June 7, 2005. http://www.advocatesforyouth.org/parents/experts/maurer2.htm. The site's ten detailed sections explain how a parent or other caring adult can support LGBT youth.

Passing

Tania Ferfolja

Passing refers to the various explicit and implicit strategies that many **lesbian, gay, bisexual, transgender**, and questioning youth use to prevent others from recognizing or identifying their sexuality. In educational institutions, as in society more generally, there is frequently an assumption that all people are heterosexual; those who identify differently often experience social marginalization, stigma, **harassment**, and **prejudice**. Such discriminatory attitudes and behaviors not only manifest themselves on an interpersonal level, that is, from an individual or group toward the LGBTQ person, but also through **educational policies**, curricula, and practices that construct heterosexuality as the only "natural and normal" sexuality. Moreover, this apparent "normality" and superiority of heterosexuality—known as **heteronormativity** and **heterosexism**—are constructed, reinforced, and condoned through other dominant social institutions (law, medicine, the media, the church, and the family). Hence, many LGBTQ youth and teachers fear potential hostility if their sexuality becomes known and may endeavor to appear, or "pass" as heterosexual.

Some societies are more open to sexual variance than others. Native American cultures, for example, view androgyny and variances as sacred, and some South Asian societies, such as Thailand, are also open to sexual variance where there is little need to "pass" as heterosexual. However, many modern Western industrial societies have institutionalized **homophobia** and repressed nonheterosexual identities.

Schools inculcate dominant understandings about prevailing social values and norms; they actively produce "acceptable" gender and sexual identities. Schools monitor, regulate, and police heterosexuality through careful scrutinizing of masculinity and femininity. Such regulation often begins in early childhood education. Not conforming to dominant constructions of gender and (hetero)sexuality may result in implicit or explicit harassment or other prejudicial behaviors, which are a form of punishment for transgressing social expectations. Homophobic and heterosexist school cultures are also produced and reinforced through institutional policy, **curriculum**, and pedagogy, perpetuating heteronormativity. Issues pertaining to "homosexuality," for example, are generally ignored through silences and omissions. Formal **sexuality education** curricula focus almost exclusively on heterosexuality, particularly within the framework of family values and procreation. LGBTQ sexualities are most often omitted, discussed as a passing phase, or aligned with illness, such as AIDS. Finally, most schools exclude positive representations of LGBTQ people.

As a result, many LGBTQ students and teachers frequently avoid reference to their sexual preference or actively hide it to avoid stigmatization, **bullying**, and or **discrimination** from others. A recent study, which examined discrimination based on sexual orientation in employment, generally found that LGBTQ identified educators often work in hostile climates (Irwin 2002). Moreover, education was identified as one of the worst professions in terms of experiencing discrimination and

See also Adolescent Sexualities; Agency; Asia, LGBT Youth and Issues in; Children of LGBT Parents; Coming Out, Teachers; Coming Out, Youth; Compulsory Heterosexuality; Families, LGBT; Identity Development; Latinos and Latinas; Pregnancy, Teenage; Workplace Issues; Youth, At Risk.

harassment based on perceived or actual **sexual orientation**. Such discrimination is exacerbated in some regions within the United States and the **United Kingdom**. In **Australia**, legal protections do not exist for "homosexuals" in education in some private religious institutions, and teachers may be dismissed if their sexuality becomes public knowledge. Not surprisingly, studies (Clarke 1996; Kissen 1996) have documented the perceived need of LGBT teachers to attempt to pass as heterosexual. Such prejudices have also resulted in a difficult **school climate** for sexual minority youth. They may leave or skip school; in extreme cases they have been forced out of their educational institution.

Numerous strategies are used by LGBTQ teachers and students to pass in various contexts. Some individuals use strategies to appear as heterosexual by omitting a same-sex partner's gender during discussions. Others reinforce the heterosexual perception through deceit such as making up a partner of the other gender; avoiding specific topics containing LGBTQ issues, and/or identifying themselves with outwardly heterosexual individuals. To avoid "discovery" and to reinforce the heterosexual presumption, some endeavor to pass by establishing heterosexual liaisons with the other gender or partake in heterosexual **dating**. This is particularly true for LGBTQ youth whose peer (and school) cultures construct an expectation for heterosexual relationships. Others withdraw from friendship groups in an effort to avoid being targeted or being forced to disclose their sexuality.

Many LGBTQ youth are compelled to constantly regulate their behaviors, mannerisms, and appearance to avoid being identified as anything other than heterosexual. Witnessing what may potentially happen if one fails to conform to dominant representations of gender and sexuality may even result in active participation in homophobic harassment and vilification in an endeavor to not be perceived as homosexual. As Owens (1998, 27) points out, "By teasing others suspected of similar [homosexual] feelings, a youth hopes to deflect suspicion from herself or himself. In other words, *the best defense is a good offense.*"

Passing as heterosexual for some youth may correspond with avoidance of those activities which are associated with gay or lesbian **stereotypes**. Girls, for example, may not express an interest in mechanical subjects or **sports**, and boys may shun subjects such as **art** or **dance**. Thus the need to appear heterosexual or prove one's heterosexuality—regardless of how one personally identifies—limits and restricts the options of *all* youth. Some LGBTQ youth also assume exaggerated gender forms to deflect any suspicion about their secret sexual identity. A gay youth who possesses attributes reflecting dominant forms of masculinity, such as being a talented and aggressive rugby player, dating heterosexually, or demonstrating bullying behaviors, may not need to adopt other passing strategies. Non-LGBTQ youth also can engage in heterosexual passing as in cases where they are from an LGBT family in which one or more parents is a sexual minority. Not bringing friends home or expressing discomfort with a parent visiting the school are examples of passing strategies.

Passing is a complex phenomenon, as sexuality intersects with other aspects of one's identity such as **race**, gender, **social class, ethnicity**, and religion. For example, those from ethnic backgrounds where there is a strong construction of "machismo" may feel compelled not to defy **gender role** expectations. Similarly, some LGBTQ Asian youth may pass as heterosexual because of traditional values that emphasize family, marriage, and off-spring along with the fear of potential shame imposed on parents and siblings. Additionally, these queer youth may fear losing the support of family in societies that lack strong LGBT communities or where LGBTQ ethnic minorities experience discrimination. Indeed, some LGBTQ youth, having little or no experience of similar individuals in their cultural or ethnic community, may view nonheterosexuality as a "white" and/or "Western" identity. Thus, to maintain their familial ties and cultural standing requires them passing as heterosexual.

Pat Griffin (1991) developed a continuum of passing strategies employed by teachers. On one end of the continuum are those strategies where one's **sexual identity** becomes known to all through the opposite end where certain behaviors ensure absolute secrecy. Between these are gradations of "passing" behaviors from not actively challenging other people's presumptions about one's assumed heterosexuality to self-presenting as heterosexual. Another kind of strategy identified by Griffin, "covering," involves censoring and hiding one's sexual identity without trying to make others believe that one is heterosexual. "Implicitly out" strategies occur when teachers assume that others know of their sexuality but do not explicitly state their sexual preference.

Within educational institutions, using certain aspects of one's identity may help to pass. For example, LGBT teachers who are publicly known to have had a heterosexual relationship, particularly in a married or de facto relationship, or who possess offspring may effectively pass, as can lesbian or bisexual female students who have become pregnant. Similarly, young "single" educators may be positioned by others as just not having found the "right" heterosexual partner, or queer youth may position themselves as too engaged in activities like academics or sports to date or go steady. Unknowing parents also may apply this rationalization to explain their child's disinterest in, or inability to form heterosexual relationships.

Passing however can be problematic because it requires a strict division between one's public and private identity. The constant effort and awareness required to maintain the public façade of heterosexuality may result in numerous **mental health** issues, including but not limited, to stress, anxiety, depression, and feelings of isolation. It may also negatively impact on the formation of friendships as the individual may fear that nurturing a close alliance may necessitate disclosure or may result in the "discovery" of one's sexual secret.

Through passing, however, one can also challenge, question, and deconstruct the apparent naturalness of heterosexuality, by demonstrating that heterosexuality is a type of performance and that its' seeming "normality" is socially constructed rather than innate. Additionally, assuming a heterosexual position may enable LGBTQ people to educate and promote understandings in relation to these issues without being labeled as "pushing their agenda." Thus, even LGBTQ individuals who pass possess and exhibit instances of power.

Bibliography

Centre for the Study of Sexually Transmissible Diseases. 1998. *Transmissive* [special edition] 17. Melbourne, Australia: La Trobe University Press.

Clarke, Gill. 1996. "Conforming and Contesting with (a) Difference: How Lesbian Students and Teachers Manage Their Identities." *International Studies in Sociology of Education* 6, no. 2: 191–209.

Griffin, Pat. 1991. "Identity Management Strategies among Lesbian and Gay Educators." *Qualitative Studies in Education* 4, no. 3: 189–202.

Irwin, Jude. 2002. "Discrimination against Gay Men, Lesbians and Transgender People Working in Education." Pp. 65–78 in *From Here to Diversity. The Social Impact of*

Lesbian and Gay Issues in Education in Australia and New Zealand. Edited by Kerry
H. Robinson, Jude Irwin, and Tania Ferfolja. Binghamton, NY: Harrington Park Press.
Kissen, Rita M. 1996. *The Last Closet. The Real Lives of Lesbian and Gay Teachers.*
Portsmouth, NH: Heinemann.
Owens, Robert E., Jr. 1998. *Queer Kids: The Challenges and Promise for Lesbian, Gay and
Bisexual Youth.* Binghamton, NY: Harrington Park Press.
Plummer, David. 1999. *One of the Boys. Masculinity, Homophobia, and Modern Manhood.*
Binghamton, NY: Harrington Park Press.

Philosophy, Teaching of

Susan Birden

Because philosophy is not a body of doctrine or texts, but a kind of activity, the
teaching of philosophy indicates a need for students to place ideas and values on a
formal and justified footing in order to develop greater intellectual freedom and to
avoid falling victim to the philosophy of others, as well as their own unexamined
thinking. Teachers engage students in exploring ideas and beliefs; unearthing assumptions, meanings, and values; and, developing skill in reasoning and argumentation. Many teachers of philosophy still deem **sexual identity** to be a political
topic, the study of which subverts "pure" philosophical education. Increasingly,
however, philosophy teachers are coming to regard questions of identity, and especially sexual identity, to be one of the major issues of our day, fraught with questions about choice and destiny, nature and nurture, essentialism and social
constructionism, morality and legislation. Philosophy teachers have employed four
major pedagogical approaches that run the gamut from ignoring to embracing discussions of sexual identity: traditional philosophy, **critical social theory**, feminist
philosophy, and postmodern thought.

Traditional approaches to the teaching of philosophy predominate in academic
philosophy departments. This approach advocates the study of classic and mainstream texts that emphasize rationality and argumentation and explore themes like
justice, ethics, and epistemology. Based on the liberal education prescribed by the
Greeks for free males, this pedagogy has focused on development of the mind, leaving little room for considerations of the body and no place for sexuality. However,
reformed liberal philosophers, like Martha Nussbaum (1997) and Susan Moller
Okin (1999), argue that citizens of today's world must acquaint themselves with
issues related to sexual difference.

Alan White and Jo A. Chern (1998) suggest that traditional philosophical pedagogy need not be restricted to historical/philosophical surveys or remedial training
in critical thinking. They organize courses around a single issue, such as the ethics
of abortion, the existence of God, personal identity, and free will, arguing that it
provides a middle ground between the desire for a traditional curriculum while
simultaneously improving students' thinking and writing.

Some teachers have also used this single-issue format for examining basic questions about gender or sexual identity, erotic love, and ethical debates surrounding
pornography and **prostitution**. Almost everyone has an opinion on these topics, so

See also Poststructuralism; Queer Pedagogy; Queer and Queer Theory.

they are particularly advantageous for teachers because they promote lively discussions and offer opportunities for students to evaluate their attitudes and beliefs. Furthermore, a philosophical examination of sexual identity, for instance, can undermine the purely emotive responses it often elicits, revealing ideological foundations for the various positions to which students adhere, and allowing both teacher and peers to point out conceptual confusion, fallacies of reasoning, and the connections with other normative questions.

Other teachers advocate the use of case studies in philosophy. Although this method is not without controversy, it provides a lively and effective means of teaching diverse students because individuals are placed in the position of deciding hard conceptual problems, rather than reviewing others' solutions. Case studies may be drawn from a variety of popular or literary sources, so teachers can easily choose controversial examples like **transgender students** running for **prom** queen, same-sex **adoption**, or the United States' military's "don't ask, don't tell" policy.

Since the 1970s, Matthew Lipman, Ann Margaret Sharp, and Frederick Oscanyan (1985), among others, have introduced philosophy as a feature of the elementary school **curriculum**. They have assembled numerous comprehensive workbooks for teachers to use for leading youngsters in philosophical inquiry by looking for hidden assumptions, defining truth, thinking about ambiguity. Although gender or sexuality are not addressed in their exercises, discussion questions on difference, family, friendship, and numerous other topics can be directed easily to gay friends or nontraditional families without modification.

Liberal philosophy underwent intense critique by "critical theorists" of the Frankfurt School, named for their base in postwar Germany. Theorists Max Horkheimer, Theodor Adorno, Herbert Marcuse, Erich Fromm, and Jürgen Habermas brought together liberal philosophy, Marxist critiques of capitalist exploitation of labor, and social theory with the goal of transforming society and ending all forms of domination. They took aim at noncritical social theories that described social conditions but failed to criticize the practices and beliefs that allowed negative conditions to persist.

Critical social theory was the foundation of the liberatory pedagogy developed by Brazilian educator Paulo Freire whose literacy work with oppressed peoples of South America has been influential among educators. Rather than viewing learners as empty vessels to be filled with the teacher's knowledge, "banking knowledge," Freire (1994) believed that teachers must engage learners in both critical thinking and cocreation of the learning process. Learning content, he argued, should be drawn from the experiences of the learners' lives; learning methods should lead learners into "conscientization," a developmental process by which people who have been submerged in their realities, merely *feeling* their needs, are able to step back and look objectively at the structural significance of the processes that are the *causes* of their needs. Unlike traditional approaches to such learning, however, Freire was adamant that critical consciousness was not merely an intellectual exercise. It must emphasize praxis: free, creative engagement in the world, whereby the individual both transforms the world and is likewise transformed through the experience of working for change.

Although Freire and others following him, like Henry Giroux, Ira Shor, and Peter McLaren, were generally concerned with **social class**, rather than gender or sexual orientation, their conceptualizations of freedom and education have prompted both teachers and activists to apply these same notions to sexuality and **sexual orientation**. Freire, in fact, explicitly stated that the oppressed are human beings who have been forbidden to be what they are, whether the oppression is a result of being a particular class; gender, like women; or social group, like homosexuals.

Teachers of philosophy may employ critical pedagogy in issues of sexual identity. Asking students to interrogate sexual difference in politically transformative ways, encouraging them to exercise self-reflection, usually through the telling of their narratives, and then interpreting these experiences in terms of social categories of difference are some of their techniques. Using this narrative approach makes it possible to invite students to view their lives as part of larger social negotiations with the goal of creating a more democratic society. Students may describe their claimed identities as socially and historically embedded—to articulate the self in history.

Critical social theory has been very influential on feminist philosophy. Yet, feminists charged that while men have slowly enlarged the dialogue of humanity to include nonhegemonic classes and races, their political stances consistently have failed to open that dialogue to women. Simone de Beauvoir (1989), Nancy Hartsock (1996), and Lorraine Code (1991), demonstrated how mainstream philosophers had created universal categories based on stereotypical masculine characteristics and dualistic thought, which then found women lacking by comparison. These feminists and many others reintroduced the body, sexuality, and gendered concerns into philosophy by studying the ways in which gender influences our conceptions of knowledge, the knowing subject, and practices of inquiry and justification, disadvantaging women and other subordinated groups. Like critical theory, **feminism** strives for not only intellectual understanding, but seeks to reform both conceptions and practices so that they serve the interests of women and other marginalized groups.

Feminist pedagogy evolved from consciousness-raising practices from the women's movement of the 1960s, the progressive tradition in education led by John Dewey, and the more general liberatory pedagogy associated with Paulo Freire. Feminist pedagogy suggests that critical pedagogy's emphasis on consensus and the force of the better argument often does not feel empowering at all to women and minorities. Therefore, particularly through **women's studies**, they have brought significant changes to the classroom through providing discursive, supportive, and participatory class environments that seek to connect learning to students' lived experiences. With particular attention to the needs of women students, feminist pedagogy is interactive, integrating students' contributions into the subject matter. Unlike the teacher's push for conscientization and *praxis* in critical pedagogy, feminist philosophical pedagogy proceeds, at least partly, from the questions and political interests of the students themselves. It aims to encourage students to gain an education that is relevant to their concerns, creating their meanings, and finding their voices in relation to the course material.

A feminist pedagogy in philosophy dislodges the central authoritative position of the teacher in the classroom. It also focuses on issues of sex or sexuality in mainstream philosophical texts that are usually ignored or evaded in traditional philosophy. For instance, Jane Roland Martin (1985) suggests that in reading mainstream texts, like Plato's *Republic* or Rousseau's *Emile*, feminist philosophers should ask themselves and their students, "What is the place of women in this education?" and "What happens to educational thought when women are brought into it?" Martin argues that because the just society that the philosopher pictures is peopled by both genders, one cannot evaluate the liberal ideal it holds up for males without knowing its expectations for females. This sort of analysis changes even the questions asked. Martin claims that once teachers and students begin to take women's issues and roles within these texts seriously, the entire meaning of the reading changes. Similarly, when students are asked to focus on, for instance, the centrality of male-to-male sexuality or the denigration of female sexuality in the philosopher's ideal of a just society, discussions lead naturally into weighty questions about essentialism and social constructionism, nature and nurture, choice and destiny.

In the last half of the twentieth century, postmodern philosophers using a "deconstructive" approach have suggested that there are no universal truths, that modernity's conception of individuals as autonomous, rational agents is unjustifiable, and that belief in humanity's progression toward freedom and truth is philosophically and empirically unfounded. Jacques Derrida and **Michel Foucault** have demonstrated that many so-called "truths," which appear to be natural, normal, universal, or given, are constructed through discourse, usually to the detriment of society's weakest citizens, and often tyrannically suppressing, excluding, or marginalizing all otherness and difference. Foucault (1990) suggested that the paradigmatic example of this social construction of "natural" desires and habits is norm-based sexuality. Postmodern feminists **Judith Butler**, Diana Fuss, and Eve Kosofsky Sedgwick posit that identity, including sexual identity, is temporary, unstable, fragile, and contingent.

Teaching philosophy using a postmodern approach must first contend with helping students understand difficult readings and develop strategies for deconstructing texts. It is important to mention, however, that the prominence of sexual identity in postmodern thought means that these works are as likely to be included in gender studies or literature courses as in traditional philosophy classrooms. For instance, Harriet Malinowitz (1995) explores sexual identity in a lesbian and gay-themed writing class in which she asks the "discourse communities" in her classes to confront the ways in which gay and lesbian people function as social metaphors, depending upon the time and place, for sin, sickness, criminality, bourgeois decadence, and the demise of the family. She focuses the class's collective gaze on gay and lesbian identities and acts of identification that traditionally have been marginalized.

Margrit Shildrick's (1997) approach in her philosophy classes, on the other hand, interrogates parts of the self that are concealed when adopting a specific identity. That is, by adopting a lesbian identity one is never *just* a lesbian but an identity that is not only multiple, but constantly changing. Distinctions between male and female, gay and straight, do not cease to be of relevance but, instead of mapping out essentialist differences, they can be seen to represent a spectrum of possibilities from discursive convenience to politically efficacious performances. In this way, students consider fragmentation and multiplicities of difference, which are both so prominent in postmodern thought. She further emphasizes that postmodern pedagogical approaches for teaching philosophy need not mean reading only postmodern **literature**. Challenging notions of neutrality, abstraction, and objectivity can serve to disrupt signifiers in traditional philosophical works. What is at stake in "queering" the discourse is not a turn toward alternative or rival sets of values and concerns, but intervening in ways that show such terms are always permeable and leaky, making productive use of the slides between categories and identities.

Finally, postmodern teaching strategies seek ways to disrupt so-called truths about "normal" and "natural" sexuality in classrooms. One college teacher tells a story about her husband, then asks the class how they felt about her "**coming out**" as heterosexual, which leads to discussions of heterosexual privilege and the critique of **heteronormativity**. Other professors have used a "Gender Performativity Journal" to accompany readings of Butler or Fuss. They ask students to log instances of people around them, including themselves, performing their gender. By focusing on examples of themselves or others announcing their gender or sexuality, students begin to see the possibilities for disrupting such performances, thereby problematizing the attribution of any identity, sexual or otherwise.

Bibliography

Code, Lorraine. 1991. *What Can She Know? Feminist Theory and the Construction of Knowledge*. Ithaca, NY: Cornell University Press.

De Beauvoir, Simone. 1989. *The Second Sex*. Translated by H. M. Parshley. New York: Random House.

Foucault, Michel. 1990. *The History of Sexuality: An Introduction*, volume 1 of 3. Translated by Robert Hurley. New York: Vintage.

Freire, Paulo. 1994, original published 1969. *Education for Critical Consciousness*. Translated by Myra Bergman Ramos. New York: Continuum.

Hartsock, Nancy. 1996. "Postmodernism and Political Change: Issues for Feminist Theory." Pp. 39–55 in *Feminist Interpretations of Michel Foucault*. Edited by Susan J. Hekman. University Park: Pennsylvania State University Press.

Kasachkoff, Tziporah, ed. 1998. *In the Socratic Tradition: Essays on Teaching Philosophy*. Lanham, MD: Rowman and Littlefield.

Lipman, Matthew, Ann Margaret Sharp, and Frederick S. Oscanyan. 1985. *Ethical Inquiry: Instructional Manual to Accompany Lisa*. Lanham, MD: Rowman and Littlefield.

Malinowitz, Harriet. 1995. *Textual Orientations: Lesbian and Gay Students and the Making of Discourse Communities*. Portsmouth, NH: Heinemann.

Martin, Jane Roland. 1985. *Reclaiming a Conversation: The Ideal of the Educated Woman*. New Haven, CT: Yale University Press.

McLaren, Peter. 1995. "Moral Panic, Schooling, and Gay Identity: Critical Pedagogy and the Politics of Resistances." Pp. 105–123 in *The Gay Teenager*. Edited by Gerald Unks. New York: Routledge.

Nussbaum, Martha C. 1997. *Cultivating Humanity: A Classical Defense of Reform in Liberal Education*. Cambridge, MA: Harvard University Press.

Okin, Susan Moller. 1999. *Is Multiculturalism Bad for Women?* Princeton, NJ: Princeton University Press.

Shildrick, Margrit. 1997. "Queering the Master Discourse: Lesbians and Philosophy." Pp. 184–196 in *Straight Studies Modified*. Edited by Gabrielle Griffin and Sonya Andermahr. London: Cassell.

White, Alan, and Jo A. Chern. 1998. "Teaching Introductory Philosophy: A Restricted Topical Approach." Pp. 21–28 in *In the Socratic Tradition: Essays on Teaching Philosophy*. Edited by Tziporah Kasachkoff. Lanham, MD: Rowman and Littlefield.

Web Site

APA Online. May 2003. APA Committee on the Teaching of Philosophy. Accessed June 10, 2005. http://www.apa.udel.edu/apa/governance/committees/teaching/orc. Numerous resources for teachers of philosophy in an academic setting.

Physical Education, Teaching of

Carrie Paechter

Physical education (PE) is educating the body through **sports**, gymnastics, **dance**, weight training, outdoor and adventurous pursuits, and related activities. PE is also a major site for the construction of dominant masculinities. It celebrates the traditional masculine values of toughness, competition, and violence in a context of overt heterosexuality. Boys and young men who do not like or are not skilled at sports, or who take part in feminized activities such as dance, are stigmatized and may be subject to homophobic **harassment** or **bullying**. Dominant forms of femininity, on the other hand, are constructed in opposition to PE. Here the muscular body is seen as unfeminine and girls as "naturally" less skilled than boys in all forms of PE and sport, except for dance and, to a lesser extent, gymnastics. Proficient or enthusiastic sportswomen are thus likely to find their femininity and **sexual orientation** questioned. In order to develop a more inclusive and less homophobic PE, activities must engage a wider range of students, challenging the construction of PE and sports as predominantly masculine areas.

In most cultures, masculinity, bound up with strength, endurance, and physical prowess, is demonstrated through the competent use of a muscular body, particularly in sports. Athletic participation—as either player or viewer—is an important male homosocial activity. Male sporting heroes are objects of reverence for men and women as men's sports dominate the media and those such as soccer, basketball, and football often receive greater school support. Thus when taking part in PE or sports, both boys and girls enter a world in which masculine values are celebrated, encouraged, and inculcated.

In many countries, PE is taught in single-sex groups for reasons of modesty, organization, or tradition. The forms taught to male and female students have significant differences, reflecting traditional notions of masculinity and femininity. In particular, girls are more likely to work on gymnastics, aerobics, dance, and body toning, which emphasize endurance, flexibility, and the "look" of the body. Boys, meanwhile, play more competitive sports and do multigym work based on developing strength and power; when they study gymnastics, they learn competition rather than personal development. Although both genders play a variety of sports, girls are usually taught feminized forms using smaller and lighter balls, adapted rules and versions such as "touch rugby." Aggressive play is not encouraged in girls. Consequently, in many countries, PE lessons for boys and girls are significantly different.

The social arenas in which young men and women learn PE and sports are also distinct. Boys' lessons (as with adult male sports) emphasize the interdependence and camaraderie of the team within a context of hypermasculinity and **homophobia**. Male teachers and coaches may develop good relations with the more sports-oriented male students to the exclusion of their female and less athletic male peers. Boys excluded from the group or rarely chosen as team players may suffer bullying or other forms of humiliation, in which some male PE teachers become complicit. Homophobic taunts, in this context, are used to signify a deficiency of manliness, which is associated with lack of physical or sporting ability. Changing rooms are

See also Antibias Curriculum; Disabilities, Physical; Gender Roles; Mentoring; Sexism; Sissy Boy; Tom Boy.

Pedro Almodóvar's *La Mala Educación* (*Bad Education*) tells, in part, the fictional story of two young boys, Ignacio and Enrique, living in a Catholic orphanage, who discover friendship, love and desire—while encountering the torments of physical education and the abuses of a jealous pedophile priest. Directed by Pedro Almodóvar. Shown: exercise class at the Catholic school. Showtime/Photofest

frequent sites for bullying, and activities involving physical contact provide cover or even legitimation for deliberate violence against individuals. Boys' PE lessons, particularly those focused on competitive sports, thus become arenas of masculinity wherein they learn toughness (e.g., playing despite injury), aggression through formalized violence, and competitiveness, where winning is emphasized over participation. In some cases (such as American and Australian football and rugby), there is a concomitant need to wear gladiator-style protective clothing. This makes it particularly difficult for young men with physical disabilities to be considered fully masculine, perpetuating their marginality.

Physical proficiency is not all that matters in the construction of dominant masculinities within PE and sports. Ballet and dance are considered highly feminine, and young men who practice these may be particularly stigmatized. With few exceptions (such as participants in Cretan dance, expertise at which is an important part of local dominant masculinity), male dancers are seen as wimpish, effeminate, and homosexual. This is despite the extreme strength and fitness required for high level performance. Some young dancers manage to avoid bullying at school by using their physical prowess to excel in sports such as football. The cost of feminizing some physical activities is also paid by high-level performers in other sports, who may resist learning dance or deliberately perform badly, to avoid compulsory dance training.

Sports are so central to the construction of dominant masculinities that, in some communities of young men, obsession with them, rather than expertise, is a key signifier of what it is to be male. This is particularly the case with younger boys, who, as they are more often taught in mixed groups, are aware that their female peers may be as proficient as they are. In these situations, boys avoid challenges to their assumed dominance by refusing to discuss sports with girls, and, when taking part in mixed sports, by excluding girls from the game.

In contrast to dominant masculinities, which are constructed through PE, dominant femininities are constructed in opposition to it. The muscular body is seen as explicitly unfeminine, and thus avoided by many girls through resistance to PE in multiple ways. In claiming and demonstrating their femininity, some young women avoid any activity that involves getting sweaty, messing up their hair, or damaging their nails. Consequently, teenage girls are far less likely than boys to take part in extracurricular physical activity, and many avoid even compulsory PE sessions, by "forgetting" their kit, feigning illness, or refusing to make any effort. In contrast to the majority of young men, who admire and aspire to the skill levels and self-presentation of PE teachers and coaches, most young women use such avoidance tactics to distance themselves from PE staff, who may be perceived as masculine by virtue of their competitiveness or toughness. As a consequence girls who are active in sports or other physical activities may find that they need to demonstrate heterosexual femininity in other ways, such as adopting ultrafeminine dress when not playing sports. Alternatively, girls who value fitness and athleticism may pursue more feminized forms. Dance and ballet are particularly important in this regard.

Although government-led initiatives such as Title IX (1972) in the United States and The Sex Discrimination Act (1972) and National Curriculum for PE (1999) in the United Kingdom have gone some way toward addressing structural issues of female access to PE and sports in schools, these deeper concerns remain.

There are a number of pedagogical approaches teachers can use to address these issues. They should deemphasize competitive games by stressing the cooperative aspects of sports. In outdoor and adventurous activities, for example, the team has to work together not to win, but to survive. The Australian program *Human Race*, developed by the Children's Health Development Foundation for children ages ten to fifteen, is a good model. It is based on improving personal best performance rather than competitiveness and references a wide variety of international sports and activities, as well as providing role models from a range of cultures, including sportspeople with disabilities. Other approaches have also been put forward. Gard (2001, 221), for instance, suggests that

> by virtue of dance's suspect status as a physical pursuit for boys, . . . some dance forms offer a unique setting for explicitly addressing sexist and homophobic norms of bodily practice. . . . Students might discuss, create, enact and reflect upon movement sequences that explicitly challenge heterosexist assumptions about what qualities male and female bodies can exhibit, and who and under what circumstances they can touch.

Teachers and sports coaches must also take explicit steps to combat homophobia and homophobic abuse in PE and sporting arenas. Formal and informal prohibitions on LGB athletes acting as teachers and coaches need to be outlawed through government legislation. Senior LGB athletes must work in solidarity with feminist colleagues to develop a climate in which it is possible for athletes at all levels to be out, providing role models for younger students and participants. Such role models also need to be incorporated into teaching and coaching situations in such a way that their sexual orientation is known but not singled out. In combating homophobic bullying, Hickey and Fitzclarence (1999) suggest unpacking the narratives that lie behind specific incidents of violent and bullying behavior by examining how such incidents are legitimated in the local community in which it takes place.

Physical education teachers and sports coaches must become more gender-aware and conscious of how gender is constructed in and through PE. They need to address gender and sexual **stereotypes** and not, wittingly or unwittingly, encourage or permit the bullying and stigmatization of those who do not fit the masculine ideal. Girls should see fitness and strength as compatible with conventional femininities, even as these are challenged. This can be approached partly through a revaluing of currently subordinated women's sports and through a reorientation of sports clubs to cater to young women's interests. Some national PE and sports associations, particularly those for women in the field, are explicitly addressing these issues.

Teachers and coaches who challenge the **heteronormativity** of PE and sports do so with care. They can make clear to students that athleticism is compatible with conventional femininities, while not rendering invisible or excluding those lesbian and heterosexual women athletes who prefer a more butch self-presentation. Similarly, in encouraging girls to be more physically active, it is essential that activities such as aerobics, which reinforce a culture of femininity, are not simply offered, but instead support girls in challenging stereotypical body images, uses, and forms. To insure that feminist, queer, and antihomophobic athletes, teachers, and coaches are not themselves victims of homophobia or sexist behavior, legislation and **educational policies** protecting their rights to work in such roles without harassment are essential.

Bibliography

Bramham, Peter. 2003. "Boys, Masculinities and PE." *Sport, Education and Society* 8, no. 1: 57–71.

Brown, David, and John Evans. 2004. "Reproducing Gender? Intergenerational Links and the Male PE Teacher as a Cultural Conduit in Teaching Physical Education." *Journal of Teaching in Physical Education* 23, no 1: 48–70.

Burgess, Ian, Allan Edwards, and James Skinner. 2003. "Football Culture in an Australian School Setting: The Construction of Masculine Identity." *Sport, Education and Society* 8, no. 2: 199–212.

Cockburn, Claudia, and Gill Clarke. 2002. "'Everybody's Looking at You!' Girls Negotiating the 'Femininity Deficit' They Incur in Physical Education." *Women's Studies International Forum* 25, no. 6: 651–665.

Gard, Michael. 2001. "Dancing Around the 'Problem' of Boys and Dance." *Discourse* 22, no. 2: 213–225.

Griffin, Pat. 1992. "Changing the Game: Homophobia, Sexism and Lesbians in Sport." *Quest* 44: 251–265.

Hickey, C., and L. Fitzclarence. 1999. "Educating Boys in Sport and Physical Education: Using Narrative Methods to Develop Pedagogies of Responsibility." *Sport, Education and Society* 4, no. 1: 51–62.

Kirk, David, and Richard Tinning. 1990. *Physical Education, Sport and Schooling*, Basingstoke, UK: Falmer.

Martino, Wayne, and Maria Pallotta-Chiarolli. 2003. *So What's a Boy? Addressing Issues in Masculinity and Schooling*. Maidenhead, UK and Philadelphia: Open University Press.

Paechter, Carrie. 2003. "Masculinities, Femininities and Physical Education: Bodily Practices as Reified Markers of Community Membership." Pp. 137–152 in *Social Justice, Education and Identity*. Edited by Carol Vincent. London and New York: Routledge-Falmer.

Parker, Andrew. 1996. "The Construction of Masculinity within Boys' Physical Education." *Gender and Education* 8, no. 2: 141–157.

Shakib, Sohaila, and Michele D. Dunbar. 2002. "The Social Construction of Female and Male High School Basketball Participation: Reproducing the Gender Order through a Two-Tiered Sporting Institution." *Sociological Perspectives* 45, no. 4: 353–378.

Vertinsky, Patricia. 1992. "Reclaiming Space, Revisioning the Body: The Quest for Gender-Sensitive Physical Education." *Quest* 44: 373–396.

Web Sites

The Human Race: Physical Education, Sport and Health for Schools Online. Children's Health Development Foundation. 2000. Accessed June 7, 2005. http://www.human-race.org/. Aimed at teachers and schools, this Australian Web site that introduces a noncompetitive, inclusive, multicultural personal-best physical activity program for ten to fifteen-year-olds.

National Association for Girls and Women in Sport. May 2005. Accessed June 7, 2005. http://www.aahperd.org/nagws/template.cfm?template=main.html. This U.S. Web site links to a range of material including some related to equity issues, particularly the implementation of Title IX.

Pink Triangle

Jerry Rosiek and *John E. Petrovic*

A pink equilateral triangle with one of its corners pointing downward has become one of the world's most recognizable symbols of resistance to **homophobia** and the persecution of **lesbian, gay, bisexual**, and **transgender** (LGBT) persons. The symbol is used by members of the LGBT communities and their **allies** to indicate solidarity with the struggle to end homophobic oppression of sexual minorities.

The pink triangle was originally a symbol of exclusion used by the National Socialist Party in Germany during WWII to mark homosexual men as deviants and enemies of the state. These triangles were part of a larger classification scheme applied to those persecuted by Party members who were known as the Nazis. Jewish people were forced to wear yellow stars of David, two yellow triangles imposed upon one another, one pointing upward, the other downward. They wore these whether or not they were interned in concentration camps. In the camps, this system of marking people was extended to other prisoners. Jehovah's Witnesses were required to wear purple triangles. Common criminals wore green triangles. Political prisoners were given red triangles. Those convicted of asocial behavior, including lesbians, wore black triangles. Persons convicted under Paragraphs 174, 175, and 176 of the Reich Penal Code were forced to wear pink triangles.

See also Identity Politics; Prejudice; Rainbow Flag and Other Pride Symbols.

Treatment of homosexuality as a crime had taken place in Germany since the early Middle Ages. In 1871, this practice became national law with the addition of Paragraph 175 to the Reich Penal Code. (Paragraphs 174 & 176 dealt with incest and pedophilia). As the twentieth century began, signs of a more accepting attitude toward homosexuality could be seen in many European **urban** centers. In Germany, physician **Magnus Hirschfeld** founded the Scientific-Humanitarian Committee, which circulated a petition to repeal Paragraph 175. Although the Reichstag rejected this proposal, this petition started a movement to repeal the law. By the 1920s, Berlin was a place where gay men and lesbians lived relatively open lives amidst an exciting subculture of artists and intellectuals as well as gay organizations and magazines, as depicted in the documentary **film**, *Paragraph 174* (Germany 2000).

Despite the fact that a number of high-level Nazi party members were gay, including Ernst Rohm, commander of the Stormtroopers, this period of relative progressivism came to an abrupt end when the Nazi's consolidated their hold on the German government. Mere days after the 1933 Reichstag Fire (the event leading to the Nazi takeover of government), a crackdown was announced on public indecency, focusing on **prostitution**, pedophilia, and homosexual men. Gay clubs throughout Germany were forced to close. Magazine publishers and offices used in the homosexual liberation movement were shut down. Paragraph 175 was used in the prosecutions associated with this crackdown.

In 1935, Paragraph 175 was strengthened by adding a mandatory prison term. During the Nazi regime, an estimated 100,000 men were arrested as homosexuals. Some 50,000 of those prosecuted under Paragraph 175 were sentenced. Although most of these men spent time in regular prisons, an estimated 5,000 to 15,000 were incarcerated in concentration camps (Plant 1986). It is in the camps that they were forced to wear pink triangles, which marked them as homosexuals and visibly marked homosexuality as a crime. Since Paragraph 175 referred only to men, lesbians, if they were incarcerated in prison camps for their sexuality, were probably labeled asocial and forced to wear the black triangle. Some lesbians and feminists, wishing to develop alternatives to male-dominated gay pride movements that frequently ignore their distinctive experiences, reappropriated the black triangle as a symbol of resistance to oppression of homosexual women.

It was the sudden rise of state sponsored attacks on LGBT persons in an era otherwise characterized by limited progress on issues of sexual freedom that gives the pink triangle its salience today as a symbol of resistance to homophobia. The hope in pre-Nazi Germany had been that an increasingly modern and scientific attitude about human life would bring more open-mindedness about sexuality. Instead, the rhetoric of scientific rationality was employed by Nazis in their persecution of homosexuals. National Socialist ideology grounded German nationalism in the science of eugenics, which justified the incarceration and execution of Jewish persons, disabled persons, and homosexual persons as a means to "purify" the "Aryan" race.

When the concentration camps were liberated in 1945, those wearing the pink triangles were not always freed. Allied soldiers often transferred them to other prisons. Because Paragraph 175 predated Nazism, it remained part of German law after the war. There was never a definitive rejection of state-sponsored persecution of LGBT persons by the Allied Forces, and the statute was not repealed by the German government until 1969.

Although few students learn about the pink triangle in secondary school **curriculum**, the lesson is clear. Widespread and even state-sponsored attacks on sexual minorities are not simply a product of ancient bigotry and superstitions; they survive and can even thrive in secular and scientific societies. Further, state-sponsored homophobia and **heterosexism** are not limited to adherents of Nazism; they continue into modern Western democratic states as evident in the absence of **hate crime** legislation and the controversy over gay marriage in the United States.

The pink triangle began to appear as an emblem of organized gay pride movements in Germany and the United States during the early 1970s. The German group Homosexuelle Aktion Westberlin called upon people to wear it as a sign of solidarity. In 1973, the San Francisco journal *Gay Sunshine* and, a year later, Toronto's *The Body Politic* published articles about the concentration camp prisoners who had worn the pink triangle. Both encouraged readers to use the symbol as a memorial to the victims of homophobia. However, it was not until the struggle to pass a gay rights ordinance in New York City to end **discrimination** in employment, housing, and public accommodation that the pink triangle received widespread attention. Orthodox **Jewish** groups had voiced opposition to the proposed law. In response, gay activists encouraged protestors to wear pink triangle armbands in an effort to remind onlookers that homosexual men had been fellow victims in the Holocaust. In a 1975 *New York Times* editorial, Ira Glasser, executive director of the New York Civil Liberties Union, called upon readers to wear the pink triangle to show support for the pending bill. Although the ordinance was not passed, since then the pink triangle has become an internationally recognized symbol of the gay liberation struggle. It has been used to make personal statements, to rally political support for issues, and to market goods to LGBT communities.

Bibliography

Giles, Geoffrey J. 2002. "The Institutionalization of Homosexual Panic in the Third Reich." Pp. 223–255 in *Social Outsiders in Nazi Germany*. Edited by Robert Gellately and Nathan Stolzfus. Princeton, NJ: Princeton University Press.

Grau, Gunter. 1995. *Hidden Holocaust?* Translated by Patrick Camiller. London: Fitzroy Dearborn Publishers.

Jensen, Erik. 2002. "The Pink Triangle and Political Consciousness: Gays, Lesbians, and the Memory of Nazi Persecution." *Journal of the History of Sexuality* 11: 319–349.

Lautmann, Ruediger. 1990. "Gay Prisoners in Concentration Camps as Compared with Jehovah's Witnesses and Political Prisoners." Pp. 200–206 in *A Mosaic of Victims: Non-Jews Persecuted and Murdered by the Nazis*. Edited by Michael Berenbaum. New York: New York University Press.

Plant, Richard. 1986. *The Pink Triangle*. New York: Henry Holt.

Web Sites

The History of the Gay Male and Lesbian Experience during World War II. Scott Safier. Accessed December 18, 2004. http://www.pink-triangle.org. A multilingual archive of documents and analysis related to the internment of homosexuals in Nazi Germany. Sections include symbols Paragraph 175, lesbians, death toll, and specific concentration camps.

SwadeWorx, Inc. Swade's GLBT Symbols Gallery. November 14, 2003. Susan Wade. Accessed December 18, 2004. http://www.swade.net/gallery/index.html. A gallery of LGBT pride symbols suitable for downloading.

Triangle Roses. March 1999. Collaboratively created by the Mémorial de la déportation homosexuelle. Accessed December 17, 2004. http://www.chez.com/triangles/. A comprehensive collection of archival resources on the Nazi internment of homosexuals as criminals. Many documents are in French.

Poetry, Teaching of

Eric M. Richardson and *Ana Ferreira*

The teaching of poetry provides an ideal opportunity for young people to engage personally and intellectually with lesbian, gay, bisexual, and transgender (LGBT) experiences and concerns. As a genre, poetry offers rich terrain for the exploring of identities and for interrogating the ways in which poetic texts construct and represent social identities. The discourse of poetry can be expressive and highly personal, often inviting emotional engagement from the reader. This can be harnessed for the purpose of designing a LGBT poetry **curriculum** which seeks to develop learners' understandings of **sexual identity**; and to develop their appreciation of the need to challenge **heteronormativity** and to value sexual diversity. There are different ways to develop LGBT poetry curriculum. A teacher seeking to implement such a curriculum should be guided by an understanding of what course of action would be most suitable for the particular school and community context. Clearly, poetry which challenges any form of sexuality-based **discrimination** will be most at home within **multicultural education,** which foregrounds equality and social justice across all social groupings, including **race**, ethnicity, gender, and **social class**.

One relatively nonconfrontational strategy for incorporating LGBT issues into the study of poetry is to include biographical information about the poets under discussion. A well-rounded poetry reading programme includes poets of varying sexual identities, even when the selected poems do not focus on such issues. Specific inclusion of works by well-known LGBT poets in the English **literature** class is a more direct option. Although this raises awareness of diversity and demonstrates inclusivity, there is also something to be said for handling an LGBT poet or poem as something unremarkable. From such a pedagogical framework, the poetry syllabus does not need to be justified beyond the usual, much-debated criterion of literary value that is applied to all literary texts. In either case, bringing in LGBT voices through the medium of poetry increases visibility and challenges the heterosexist bias of the traditional English canon. Most critical, however, is the manner in which the teacher uses the poems since this determines the extent to which students' thinking and attitudes can be meaningfully engaged and potentially shifted.

Instead of simply including the "voices" of LGBT poets, the teacher could use their poems to open up spaces for the active discussion of LGBT experiences and issues. These discussions could be less about the poems themselves and more about contexts in which poetry is written and received. By extending the discussion to include changes in sociohistorical contexts and in their cultural values, a writer's

See also Critical Social Theory; Language Arts, Teaching of; Music, Teaching of; Native and Indigenous LGBT Youth; Poststructuralism; Queer Pedagogy.

position on his/her sexual identity becomes part of a broader exploration of shifting attitudes to sexuality. Many famous poets of bygone eras, who we now know to have been lesbian, gay or bisexual, did not themselves adopt LGBT identities or write LGBT-themed poetry. The fact that the sexual identity of poets does not manifest in their writing could be used to frame an interesting intellectual discussion with more sophisticated secondary school students.

Students could be asked to **"queer"** the distinction between the private and public identities of LGBT poets, and encouraged to speculate about different poets' personal motivations for taking up the positions that they did. Since these discussions would revolve around poets who lived in times that were not only historically but socioculturally different from contemporary societies, students could consider how contemporary LGBT poets may have considerably different factors impinging upon their considerations about making themselves "visible." Teachers, for instance, could contrast the work and contexts of famous poets like Adrienne Rich, Judy Grahn, Walt Whitman, Hart Crane, and Allen Ginsburg, with **African American** and Native American lesbian, gay, and two-spirit poets (Audre Lorde, Cheryl Clarke, Taisha Asanti, Chrystos, Paula Gunn Allen, and Clyde Hall), queer **Chicano** poets (Gloria Anzldua and Cherrie Moraga) and even gay South African poets (Hennie Aucamp, and Ettiene van Heerden). It could also be worth considering how **compulsory heterosexuality**, rather than necessarily diminishing over time, is being policed differently, and what these ways may be, as well as to interrogate the purpose of such policing.

The double-bind here is that "historically silenced or underrepresented groups must choose between invisibility (there are no lesbian parents, no gay teenagers, no bisexual teachers) and surplus visibility (Why do you always have to flaunt your identity? Why must you bring up your issue again and again?)" (Sapon-Shevin 1999, 112). Consequently, students might apply similar questions to non-LGBT poets and consider not only how heterosexual identities are treated (and constructed) differently (e.g. the nonissue of "outing" oneself as a straight person because of heteronormativity) but to examine why this should be so.

More directly addressing LGBT issues within an **antibias curriculum** is selecting poetry which explicitly raises sexual minority concerns. In particular, by discussing poems containing some of the more controversial and political issues, teachers can attempt to disrupt their learners' taken-for-granted ways of knowing. There is much to be gained from a close study of a poem, particularly with regard to exploring the positions taken up in response to the poem. An interesting and well-known poem is W. H. Auden's "Stop All the Clocks," made popular by the mainstream film *Four Weddings and a Funeral*. This poem is most commonly read as an expression of extreme grief at the death of a lover and thus taught as a love poem, but often with a surprisingly heterosexist slant. The same-sex identities of the narrator and the addressee are glossed over, silencing the homosexual nature of the love. In fact, the preferred reading position which this poem sets up is one in which the reader will feel compassion for the narrator and understand his grief in light of his great love for the person who has died. Such texts, in which LGBT characters are presented in a positive light, foster acceptance and encourage gay-affirmative readings, which are often built on notions of identification and emotional engagement. These can be used as starting points for discussions of homosexuality, which "interrupt" dominant heteronormative thinking and interrogate notions of normality, of what counts as "natural," questioning who makes these decisions (Martino 1999).

It is neither necessary nor desirable to limit the teaching of poetry only to the work of famous poets. There is an increasing amount of contemporary LGBT published poetry and there are a great many Web sites with developing bodies of LGBT poetry. Indeed, it is often more effective to use the voices of ordinary people, such as those in *Revolutionary Voices* (Sonnie 2000). These poems, like Antigona's "Straight-Out Pain" describing her church's attempt to exorcise "the demons" of lesbianism, are ideal tools to inspire other LGBT or questioning youth and to raise questions about gender, sexuality, oppression, love, hatred, identity, social change, and poverty. Many of these poems entice the reader to fill in the gaps, make sense of the ambiguities, and experience the writer's world and mood. In addition, because the poems are written by youth, they challenge young readers to make connections with their worlds and future aspirations.

A more radical approach to the poetry teaching could draw on ideas from critical pedagogy. Here the teacher could deliberately select and problematize poetry which silences sexual diversity and perpetuates heteronormative ideologies, in order to develop students' critical reading skills, enabling them to contest the authority of the text by generating alternative readings. Exposing learners to how their reading of a poem emerges from their experiences as socially-constructed individuals can assist them in "imagining difference" by rereading the poem as if it was written from LGBT perspectives. This strategy can often be productively applied to poems which have no overt relevance to LGBT issues. One can always ask: What taken-for-granted assumptions are operating in this poem? How is the reader positioned in relation to the poem? What does the poet want us to believe about his or her world and its people? Who might feel left out in this text and why? Who finds the ideas in this poem clashing with your beliefs/values/experiences? What silences/absences are noticeable and who is excluded? How might the poem be rewritten from an LGBT perspective? Chistopher Marlowe's "The Passionate Shepherd to His Love" could be analyzed using these questions.

At the primary school level, the teacher can introduce young learners to poems by LGBT poets who write about their lives, their hopes, and their fears. These poems can be included in lessons which do not engage formally with poetry analysis techniques but which illustrate themes being dealt with in social studies or guidance lessons. In this way, poetry can be used to reinforce ideas of inclusivity and to challenge heterosexist assumptions.

Of particular relevance in the earlier years of schooling would be poems that address issues of rigid sex-role stereotyping by challenging narrow definitions of **gender identity**. One such poem is Tony Mitten's **"Stereotypes."** The entire poem consists of questions, alternately posed by "Girls" and "Boys" speaking generically who question why gender-specific behavior is expected of them. It begins with girls asking why they have to be pretty, followed by boys asking why they have to be tough. The final two lines are voiced by a now-combined "All" who finally ask, "Why don't we work out our own way/And do what suits us best?" Such a poem can explore why people assume that "feminine" boys are gay and "masculine" girls are lesbian, and how **homophobia** prevents people from recognizing that many masculinities and femininities exist.

Poems which challenge traditional notions of family may be useful in the elementary classroom. There are various playground chants, jump-rope songs, and nursery rhymes, which can raise children's awareness that not everyone lives in a family with a mother and a father; that you are not alone if you live in a "nonstandard" family; and to challenge homophobia, in general (Sapon-Shevin 1999, 122). Song lyrics can be easily integrated into poetry teaching because of their obvious similarity to poetic structure. In fact, the linguistic analysis of popular song lyrics can be most useful when deconstructing representations of gender and the relations between the genders, which could be productively applied to LGBT issues in more advanced reading grades. "Your Funny Uncle," written by Neil Tennant and sung by the Pet Shop Boys, is an example of such a song.

Teachers choosing to integrate LGBT poetry into their classes should consider the level of support or opposition from colleagues, **administrators,** parents, and students. Although token gestures are largely meaningless, overly ambitious aims can create a backlash, which could be counterproductive such as occurred in the **Children of the Rainbow curriculum** controversy in New York City. Furthermore, the teacher's motives and demeanor are of critical importance to the success of any teaching intervention addressing LGBT issues. Before teachers "can work with students on developing broader understandings of love, sexuality, and relationships, they will need to explore their own upbringings, biases, and (mis)understandings about homosexuality and other forms of sexual expression" (Sapon-Shevin 1999, 115). Such self-reflection would, of course, be necessary for any teacher of any sexual identity who embarks on this kind of work and should, therefore, be part of teacher education (Richardson 2004).

Teachers, too, need to be aware of the unpredictable nature of student response, prepared to deal with students' discomfort or resistance, and adept at sensitively managing their discomfort . Some LGBT or questioning students, will also be uneasy. They may perceive that the teaching of LGBT poems and poets shifts them (and the topic, itself) from a relatively invisible position to an uncomfortable level of visibility. Whether or not this discomfort can be avoided or overcome depends largely on how the teacher manages the classroom discussion and the interaction among students. A theoretically sound social justice agenda does not compensate for creating situations in which the very people who should be benefiting from this agenda are left feeling exposed and vulnerable.

Bibliography

Coote, Stephen. 1983. *The Penguin Book of Homosexual Verse*. London: Penguin Books.

Harold, John, ed. 1993. *How Can You Write a Poem When You're Dying of AIDS?* London: Cassell.

Knobel, Michele. 1998. "Critical Literacies in Teacher Education." Pp. 89–111 in *Critical Literacies in the Primary Classroom*. Edited by Michele Knobel and Anna Healy. New South Wales: Primary English Teaching Association.

Martino, Wayne. 1999. "'It's Okay to be Gay:' Interrupting Straight Thinking in the English Classroom." Pp. 137–149 in *Queering Elementary Education: Advancing the Dialogue about Sexualities and Schooling*. Edited by William J. Letts IV and James T. Sears. Lanham, MD: Rowman and Littlefield Publishers.

Richardson, Eric M. 2004. "A Ripple in the Pond: Challenging Homophobia in a Teacher Education Course." *Education as Change* 8, no. 1: 146–163.

Sappon-Shevin, Mara. 1999. "Using Music to Teach Against Homophobia." Pp. 111–124 in *Queering Elementary Education: Advancing the Dialogue about Sexualities and Schooling*. Edited by William J. Letts IV and James T. Sears. Lanham, MD: Rowman and Littlefield Publishers.

Sonnie, Amy, ed. 2000. *Revolutionary Voices: A Multicultural Queer Youth Anthology.* Los Angeles: Alyson.

Wood, Gregory. 1998. *A History of Gay Literature: The Male Tradition.* New Haven, CT: Yale University Press.

Web Sites

GenderTalk. June 2005. Accessed June 10, 2005. http://www.gendertalk.com. Features LGBT poetry.

Isle of Lesbos. 2004. The Small Business Operative. Accessed June 10, 2005. http://www. sappho.com/. Poetry, images of classical art, and numerous links to other sites.

Lodestar Quarterly. Spring 2005. Accessed June 10, 2005. http://www.lodestarquarterly.com. An online journal for lesbian, gay, and queer literature.

Political Science, Teaching of

Stephen Brown

Political science refers to the study of power, including who does or does not have it and how it is wielded. It can entail the study of government legislation on [homo]sexuality, organized attempts to influence public policy on the issue, and the workings of organizations concerned with the rights of **lesbian, gay, bisexual,** and **transgender** (LGBT) youth. These topics are slowly making their way into political science university curricula. In the 1990s, a growing number of political science professors introduced some discussions of LGBT politics into their syllabi and classrooms. By the middle of the first decade of the twenty-first century, following public debates in various parts of the world on issues such as same-sex partnerships and marriage, it was no longer rare for sexuality-related political issues to be discussed in political science classes. Nonetheless, sexuality remains far from being accepted as an important issue for teaching and research in political science.

The control over content by school boards and parents makes teaching of such issues in political science more difficult at the secondary level than in universities. It is generally up to individual teachers to integrate discussion of issues of (homo)sexualities into their classes, often risking censure. Since much of the academic material is too theoretically advanced for high school students, even at upper levels, more appropriate materials would be either well-crafted documentaries (Epstein and Friedman 1999; Epstein and Schmeichen 1984; Kates and Singer 2002; MacDonald 1995) or books that focus on a person such as Bayard Rustin (D'Emilio 2003) or political events like the early response to **AIDS** (Shilts 1987). Framing discussion around political debates of the day could also be a productive way of introducing LGBT themes to high school classrooms.

One of the first in the studies of **sexual orientation** was *Homosexual: Oppression and Liberation* by Australian political scientist Dennis Altman (1971). It was not till the late 1980s and early 1990s that research gained momentum, in part

See also Curriculum, Higher Education; Curriculum, Secondary; LGBT Studies; Pink Triangle; Religious Fundamentalism; Social Class; Women's Studies.

impelled by the AIDS crisis. By the late 1990s, a substantial and still expanding body of literature was available. In 2004, a specialized academic periodical, the *Journal of Gay and Lesbian Politics*, was established in order to provide an outlet specifically geared to political science **research** on sexual minorities.

As in many other topics, academic materials on LGBT people focus mainly on middle-class white men. This is not to say that there are not important works on lesbians (Phelan 1994), LGBT people of color or poor LGBT people—or that these are not used in the classroom. Still, more material on gay men is available than on lesbians, fewer studies focus on bisexuals (Rust 1997) and very few on transgender persons (Currah, Minter, and Juang, forthcoming). Only a handful directly addresses the overlapping of two or more of these identities (Cohen 1999; D'Emilio 2003; Vaid 1996). The United States is by far the most studied country (for instance, Rimmerman 2001), though there is a growing body of literature on **Australia, Canada,** and several Western European countries, especially the **United Kingdom, France,** and the Netherlands. Increasingly, movements in Latin America and other developing regions are also being studied (Adam, Duyvendak, and Krouwel 1999; Drucker 2000).

Why have political scientists taken so long to study LGBT politics? Many consider that the discipline of political science is more conservative than others. Timothy Cook (1999, 680) argues that it is because of a combination of traditional focus on "formal governmental institutions and processes," disincentives to choosing LGBT politics as a research subject (other people's hostility to the topic and concerns about negative effects on the person's academic career), and impediments to carrying out the actual research (lack of funding opportunities, theoretical complexities, methodological problems, and difficulties of obtaining data). Still, LGBT political scientists have long fought for inclusion in their profession. Often, they found more welcoming intellectual homes in interdisciplinary LGBT studies. Likewise, interdisciplinary journals, such as *GLQ* or the *Journal of Homosexuality*, are usually more receptive to publishing research on LGBT politics than actual political science journals.

Few political scientists embrace the feminist slogan, "The personal is political." Indeed, political science has long tended to stay far from the personal, except in some instances how it relates to voting or other narrowly defined forms of political participation. For a long time, the question of sexual orientation was, with very few exceptions, entirely absent from teaching in political science. Increasingly, however, related issues are finding their way onto university syllabi. In a growing number of places, specialized courses on LGBT politics are being offered, frequently by professors who identified as homo- or bisexual themselves. In addition, faculty members of all sexual orientations are including related topics in a variety of courses. This is in a large part aided by the prominent public policy debates since the 1990s on issues such as gays in the military, same-sex partner benefits, nondiscrimination and **hate crimes** legislation, civil unions and same-sex marriage. Issues of sexual orientation are often included in courses on feminist politics or women and politics since there is a natural link between questioning the role of gender in politics and questioning the role of sexual orientation, including silences surrounding both.

There are many entry points for teaching and researching LGBT-related matters in political science or using a political science perspective. One of the most traditional ways is by tracking and analyzing changing public opinion and voter preferences on issues of equal rights and legal protection for homosexuals, such as protection from **discrimination** in housing or employment and the right to serve in the military. This approach focuses not on LGBT people themselves but on general attitudes toward their rights and how this can influence decisions that affect their lives. Those interested in political party behavior study how and when these matters became electoral issues, how and why parties court LGBT voters or, on the contrary, how some right-wing parties demonize LGBT individuals as a method of mobilizing the support of ultraconservative voters, often Christian fundamentalists.

Another approach is through public law and institutions. For instance, in Canada, advances in LGBT rights since the mid-1980s have resulted from legal challenges, usually based on the nondiscrimination clauses of the Canadian Charter of Rights and Freedoms, part of the constitution. Key debates include the role of courts in setting public policy and the relationship between the legislative and judicial branches of government, including the question of who defines and protects of minority rights. For example, should democratically elected legislatures be able to override court decisions on constitutional rights? In many U.S. states, ballot measures are often used to attempt to restrict rights, in the process creating important coalitions to oppose them, as documented in MacDonald's (1995) film on a divisive 1992 voter initiative in Oregon.

Other approaches focus more on LGBT activists themselves. The study of social movements, a concern of both sociology and political science, includes analyses of LGBT-rights movements in various countries, states, provinces, territories and municipalities. Studies attempt to answer a wide range of questions, such as: How do LGBT organizations try to influence legislation or achieve broader social change? How do the various movements define their goals? What strategies do they adopt? What alliances do they form? How do they frame the issues? What explains their success or failure? These are important questions for political science. Rayside (1998), for instance, analyzes the key role of openly gay politicians in Canada, the United Kingdom, and the United States, as well as the intricate dynamics of a specific political battle in each country.

Some studies bridge the two categories outlined above, social movements, and changes in law. For example, Smith (1999) studies lesbian and gay rights movements in Canada and links their evolution to changes in the constitution. The link between AIDS activism and politics likewise bridges these fields (Shilts 1987). Though not strictly speaking an LGBT-specific issue, HIV/AIDS has been central to LGBT movements across the world and a topic of particular interest to LGBT political scientists.

Identity is an important issue in political science and in queer studies. What makes same-sex eroticism (homosexual activity) translate into a specific identity (such as gay or lesbian) or not? In particular, when and how are such identities politicized? How do these identities relate to other identities (such as gender, class, **ethnicity**, or **race**)? Political science grapples with complex answers to these and related questions.

A dilemma of teaching about (homo)sexualities in political science is whether to ghettoize LGBT issues in a separate course or to try to include them in a broad range of other ones. Given that gender is only rarely taught as an integral part of all political science courses, many departments created one or more separate courses on woman and politics or on **feminism**. Since sexual orientation is even less widely integrated, it seems likely that, in the medium term, separate courses will be necessary to ensure presence in the classroom. Some form of LGBT politics course is sometimes created in supportive university departments, when a specific interested professor takes the initiative in developing it. Sometimes, a broader orientation is given, such as "sexual diversity politics," in order to be more inclusive, attract non-LGBT-identified students as well, and, perhaps, avoid controversy. Such a course could study not only LGBT movements but also topics such as the construction of *hetero*sexuality, evangelical Christians' opposition to LGBT rights, the impact of globalization on sexuality, and the limits of **identity politics**.

Still, one must not overstate to what degree LGBT issues are integrated into the political science mainstream—nor underestimate **homophobia** in academia (McNaron 1996). Though decreasingly so, the vast majority of political science courses completely ignore sexual orientation. Significantly, hardly any political science undergraduate textbooks even raise LGBT issues. As long as that remains the case, any LGBT course content will be the result of individual professors' personal interest and not the result of a wider recognition of the place of LGBT politics in the discipline.

Bibliography

Adam, Barry D., Jan Willem Duyvendak, and André Krouwel, eds. 1999. *The Global Emergence of Gay and Lesbian Politics: National Imprints of a Worldwide Movement*. Philadelphia: Temple University Press.

Altman, Dennis. 1971. *Homosexual Oppression and Liberation*. London: Allen Lane.

Cohen, Cathy. 1999. *The Boundaries of Blackness: AIDS and the Breakdown of Black Politics*. Chicago: University of Chicago Press.

Cook, Timothy E. 1999. "The Empirical Study of Lesbian, Gay, and Bisexual Politics: Assessing the First Wave of Research." *American Political Science Review* 93, no. 3: 679–692.

Currah, Paisley, Shannon Minter, and Richard Juang, eds. Forthcoming. *Transgender Rights: History, Politics, and Law*. Minneapolis: University of Minnesota Press.

D'Emilio, John. 2003. *Lost Prophet: Bayard Rustin and the Quest for Peace and Justice in America*. New York: The Free Press.

Drucker, Peter, ed. 2000. *Different Rainbows*. London: Gay Men's Press.

Epstein, Rob, and Jeffrey Friedman (Directors). 1999. *Paragraph 175* [Film]. United Kingdom, Germany & United States: New Yorker Video.

Epstein, Rob (Director), and Richard Schmeichen (Producer). 1984. *The Times of Harvey Milk* [Film]. United States: New Yorker Video.

Kates, Nancy, and Bennett Singer (Producers/Directors). 2002. *Brother Outsider: The Life of Bayard Rustin* [Film]. United States: Bayard Rustin Documentary Film Project.

MacDonald, Heather (Director). 1995. *Ballot Measure 9* [Film]. United States: Fox Lorber.

McNaron, Toni A. H. 1996. *Poisoned Ivy: Lesbian and Gay Academics Confronting Homophobia*. Philadelphia: Temple University Press.

Phelan, Shane. 1994. *Getting Specific: Postmodern Lesbian Politics*. Minneapolis: University of Minnesota Press.

Rayside, David. 1998. *On the Fringe: Gays and Lesbians in Politics*. Ithaca and London: Cornell University Press.

Rimmerman, Craig A. 2001. *From Identity to Politics. The Lesbian and Gay Movements in the United States*. Philadelphia: Temple University Press.

Rust, Paula. 1997. *Bisexual Politics and the Challenge to Lesbian-Feminism*. New York: New York University Press.

Shilts, Randy. 1987. *And the Band Played on: Politics, People, and the AIDS Epidemic*. New York: St. Martin's Press.

Smith, Miriam. 1999. *Lesbian and Gay Rights in Canada: Social Movements and Equality-Seeking, 1971–1995*. Toronto: University of Toronto.

Vaid, Urvashi. 1996. *Virtual Equality: The Mainstreaming of Gay and Lesbian Liberation*. New York: Knopf.

Web Site

Curricular Guide to Gay/Lesbian/Queer Studies. 1999. Committee on the Status of Lesbians and Gays in the Profession of the American Political Science Association. Accessed June 9, 2005. http://falcon.arts.cornell.edu/ams3/cslg.currg.html. Annotated bibliographies organized in some twenty categories.

Popular Culture

Debra Shogan and Gloria Filax

Popular culture in the form of media, **music,** and fashion is central to youth culture and to how individuals identify their desires, beliefs, and values. The diverse ways that **lesbian, gay, bisexual,** and **transgender youth** (LGBT) make sense of their identities is affected by mainstream popular culture, which is often adapted by queer youth to fit personal circumstances. Queer youth also make sense of their identities in the context of an increasingly public queer popular culture that is created by both mainstream and queer cultural producers. The last twenty years have witnessed a mainstreaming of queer people and representations of queer people in popular culture. Supermodel, Rupaul, pop artists, k.d. lang, Melissa Etheridge, Rufus Wainright, the Pet Shop Boys, television series such as *Will and Grace*, **Queer as Folk**, and a *Queer Eye for the Straight Guy*, mainstream films such as *Philadelphia*, and the queer content of MTV are just some examples of popular culture consumed by youth not just in North America but in many places in the world.

In a few cases, queer content is explicitly queer and sexual. *Queer as Folk*, is a television cable gay drama series that celebrates gay lives and relationships, often including explicit sex scenes. Rupaul is the first transgender supermodel to sign a modeling contract with MAC cosmetics, host a talk show, and appear in a number of movies, including the *Brady Brunch Movie*. Country/pop singer, k.d. lang, who has a large mainstream and lesbian following, has recorded with top mainstream male singers, including Roy Orbison and Tony Bennett. Rock and roll star, Melissa Etheridge, came out with her album, *Yes I Am*. Her recent marriage to actress Tammy Lynn Michaels was attended by a number of United States' stars, including Steve Spielberg, Jennifer Aniston, and Sheryl Crow. Also attending was the academy award winning star, Tom Hanks, whose feature role in the film, *Philadelphia*, put the social reality of **AIDS** in front of a mainstream audience.

While the mainstreaming of queer content has put same-sex images and lyrics into mainstream popular culture, the absence of overt sexual content in most of these images and lyrics makes it acceptable within a heterosexual culture. For example, even though the first gay dating television series, *Boy Meets Boy*, would have been unheard of in prime time television in the 1980s, interactions between contestants do not display the overt sexuality found in similar heterosexual shows. When same-sex sexuality in mainstream popular culture does occur, it is performed by people who purport to be straight, such as the infamous Madonna and Britney Spears kiss on MTV's Video Music Awards. World Music Award winners, Russian duo, tATu, two self-proclaimed straight girls who engage sexually with each other on stage, have a large mainstream following, but sexually explicit punk dyke band, Tribe 8 does not.

See also Cartoons; Colonialism and Homosexuality; Stereotypes.

Prior to the 1980s, queer content in popular film, television, novels, and music was represented as negative or farcical. Films, such as *A Florida Enchantment* (USA 1914) and *The Children's Hour* (USA 1961), **literature** like *Well of Loneliness*, *Beebo Brinker Chronicles*, television shows, such as *Marcus Welby, M.D.*, *Taxi*, and *A Question of Love*, and popular songs like "My Girl, Sue" had "queer" content, but it was content that portrayed LGBT people as tragic, deviant, or ridiculous. *The Children's Hour*, a play written by Lillian Hellman in 1934, was the tragic story of a rumored lesbian relationship between two women who operate a school for girls. A 1973 episode of *Marcus Welby, M.D.*, portrayed homosexuality as a serious illness, stereotyping a gay teacher as a child molester, and NBC's 1978 telecast, *A Question of Love*, was a story of a wife and mother whose "dirty secret," a lesbian relationship, is discovered by her husband.

Nevertheless, for LGBT youth, who were otherwise without representations of themselves, this "queer" content and the content of seemingly "straight" texts and images provided a basis for queer readings (Doty 1993). *Laverne and Shirley*, *Star Trek* characters, Barbie, and even Bert and Ernie from *Sesame Street* were reread and reworked for queer purposes. For example, the television show *Laverne and Shirley*, which ran from 1976 to 1983, was about best friends who shared an apartment in Milwaukee and worked in a local brewery. Even though most of the episodes were focused on finding men, the show created a space for viewers to read them as a lesbian couple. Queer readings of muppets, Bert and Ernie, surfaced often enough in popular accounts that the producers of the show, The Children's Television Workshop, issued a statement in 1993 indicating that Bert and Ernie were not a gay couple and that there were no plans for them to be so in the future.

Media corporations produce a large part of youth popular culture, but there is also significant popular culture produced *by* youth subcultures for their uses. Unlike popular culture with queer content produced for mass audiences, the production of queer popular culture for and by queer youth does not target a mainstream audience and is not altered to satisfy straight people. **Queer zine**s, blogs, raves, **comics**, bands, video, and **graffiti** have been produced specifically for the queer consumer. Queer zines are produced all over the world, both in print and on the **Internet**. Some of these include *Androzine* and *Bang Bang* from **France**, *ClitRocket* from Italy, and *Trippers* from Singapore. Creators of slash zines focus on the homoerotic relationships of mainstream media characters. The first slash zines, circulated in hard copy in the late 1960s and 1970s, were about the relationship of Star Trek Captain James Kirk and his first officer, Spock. Most slash zines are about relationships between men, however female slash zines recently have been inspired by *Xena, Warrior Princess* and *Buffy the Vampire Slayer*.

There are a number of comic strips produced for a queer audience, many only available on the Web. Comic strips include *Hot Head Paisan*, *The Chosen Family*, *Dykes to Watch Out For*, *Recipe for Success*, *Chelsea Boys*, *Jake the Rake*, and *Queer Nation*. While *Jake the Rake*, for example, is strictly an online comic that details the adventures of a bisexual guy, *Dykes to Watch Out For* by Alison Bechdel can be found online and in seventy queer and alternative publications, collected in ten books, and translated into a number of languages worldwide. Bechdel's strip is a soap opera with political commentary and chronicles the lives of queer people, including queer youth, and their friends as they live in U.S. consumer culture.

Through music, particularly hip hop, punk, and rap, queer youth have created dynamic queer subcultures. In the United States, hip hop groups include freaky whitechicks, Deadlee, Johnny Dangerous, and God-Des. Bands from **Europe**, include Herbert from the Netherlands and Feucht Rasiert from Germany, Homomilitia from Poland and MaaSen from Sweden. In **Japan**, the band SHAZNA features IZAM, who looks like a woman while acting masculine and presenting as heterosexual. A band that has a large lesbian following, particularly in the United States, is punk-rock, thrash band, Tribe 8, who describe themselves as "San Francisco's own all-dyke, all-out, in-your-face, blade-brandishing, gang castrating, dildo swingin', bull-shit detecting, aurally pornographic, neanderthal-pervert band of patriarchy-smashing snatchlickers" (Wiese 2003). While Tribe 8 has received positive reviews in mainstream publications such as *The Village Voice*, the focus of the group is to fight censorship in both the mainstream and queer music scenes through explicit lyrics, dress, and props.

Despite the prevalence of queer youth popular culture that reflects a unique fusion of values and behaviors particular to the place it was created, the globalization of United States' produced popular culture has led some to argue that there is a global queering of how homosexuality is imagined in the contemporary world. According to Dennis Altman (1996), the ability of the mass media to market imagery of homosexuality from the United States has led to a globalization of a social, political, and commercial homosexual identity based in this country's queer culture. He concedes that homosexual identities and lifestyles will develop differently in non-Western countries but, for now, he claims, United States "books, films, magazines and fashions continue to define contemporary gay and lesbian meanings for the rest of the world" (Altman 1996, 2).

Others point to local queer **youth culture**, produced for a queer audience, as an indication that what makes queer culture queer is that it refuses to be standardized. Queer zines, blogs, raves, comics, bands, video, and graffiti have a specific, local significance and, therefore, cannot be mass-produced. Nor can local queer culture be understood through anything but its own history. For example, the queer significance of the **cross- dressing** boy-band member, IZAM, is to be understood within a Japanese cultural context that conflates homosexuality with cross- dressing and transgenderism (McLelland 2000). Likewise, the significance of the queer punk band, Herbert, in the Netherlands or Pharmacy in Sweden cannot be meaningfully interpreted or replicated outside their locale.

A belief that producers of popular culture control consumers of popular culture neglects the place of these consumers as active producers and manipulators of meaning. "Textual poaching" (Jenkins 1992) uses popular culture in a fashion that serves personal and local interests. As examples from Laverne and Shirley, and Kirk and Spock indicate, queer consumers of popular culture poach seemingly straight representations as well as queer representations produced by mass media in the United States and those produced by queer pop artists for other queer people. Even otherwise straight sites of popular culture can be used for queer purposes. For example, youth rave culture in Atlanta is not only open to queer youth involvement, the participation of a queer youth subculture in these raves has changed and enhanced many of the hallmarks of this rave culture (Walker 2003).

There is, of course, no denying that United States queer imagery is marketed and consumed worldwide. How the imagery is consumed is not predictable, however. As Fran Martin asks, "Are you still a 'global lipstick lesbian' if you live in a Chinese society and identify not as a 'lesbian' nor as a 'femme' but as a *po*, complete with lipstick and k.d. lang CDs as well as a girlfriend who's not butch but *T*?" (1996, 1–2). The Chinese *po* may indeed consume U.S. representations of lesbian culture, but she poaches parts of it and combines these with other poaching from Chinese and other cultures to create an identity that is unique. This poaching by queer people all over the world disrupts the assumption of a global queer culture.

Bibliography

Altman, Dennis. 1996. "On Global Queering." *Australian Humanities Review*. Accessed, December 11, 2004. http://www.lib.latrobe.edu.au/AHR/archive/Issue-July-1996/altman.html.

Burston, Paul, and Colin Richardson, eds. 1995. *A Queer Romance: Lesbians, Gay Men in Popular Culture*. New York and London: Routledge.

Creekmur, Corey K., and Alexander Doty, eds. 1995. *Out in the Culture: Gay, Lesbian, and Queer Essays on Popular Culture*. Durham, NC: Duke University Press.

Doty, Alexander. 1993. *Making Things Perfectly Queer: Interpreting Mass Culture*. Minneapolis: University of Minnesota Press.

Jenkins, Henry. 1992. *Textual Poachers: Television Fans and Participatory Culture*. New York and London: Routledge.

Kenway, Jane, and Elizabeth Bullen. 2001. *Consuming Children: Education-Entertainment-Advertising*. Buckingham, Philadelphia: Open University Press.

Latham, Rob. 2002. *Consuming Youth: Vampires, Cyborgs, & the Culture of Consumption*. Chicago, IL: University of Chicago Press.

Martin, Fran. 1996. "Response to Dennis Altman." *Australian Humanities Review*. Accessed December 11, 2004. http://www.lib.latrobe.edu.au/AHR/emuse/Globalqueering/martin.html.

McLelland, Mark. 2000, January 9. "Male Homosexuality and Popular Culture in Modern Japan." Accessed December 11, 2004. http://wwwsshe.murdoch.edu.au/intersections/issue3/mclelland2.html.

Walker, Michael. 2003. "Gay Male Youth and the Atlanta Rave Scene." Accessed December 11, 2004. http://www.lunarmagazine.com/features/gay_youth.php.

Weise Todd. 2003. "Tribe 8 Interview." Accessed December 11, 2004. http://www.theroc.org/roc-mag/textarch/roc-18/roc18-08.htm.

Web Sites

Gay Hip Hop links. October 2004. Larry-Bob. Accessed June 10, 2005. http://www.io.com/~larrybob/hiphop.html. Site for gay and lesbian hip hop and rap.

Holy titclamps. October 2004. Accessed June 10, 2005. http://www.holytitclamps.com. Includes current event listing and hip hop links and links to queer contacts worldwide.

Poststructuralism

Dennis Carlson

Poststructuralism is a contemporary movement in social theory that has had a significant impact on **research** and scholarship on **sexual identity** since the 1980s. The marker "poststructural" has been used to refer to a broad array of methods and beliefs in literary studies, history, social theory, philosophy, the arts, and the critical study of education. While there are many important poststructural theorists, poststructuralism is

See also Communication; Critical Social Theory; Cross- Dressing; Gender Identity; Identity Politics; Men's Studies; Multicultural Education; Queer Pedagogy; Queer Studies; Queer Zines; Youth Culture.

perhaps most closely associated with the French historian of knowledge, **Michel Foucault,** and the French theorist of language and writing, Jacques Derrida. At the core of poststructural analysis is a concern for language, and how written and spoken language (often called "discourse") organizes our understanding of the world. These discourses include those associated with the early psychiatric movement and **religious fundamentalism.** Instead of positing a fixed, unified structure to society, poststructuralists view social reality as something that is constituted or produced by these various discourses, which is the language we use to "name" the world.

In education, poststructuralism implies focusing on the historic representation of "gayness" and homosexual identity in various cultural texts, from psychiatric texts to popular culture texts such as **films** and novels. It also challenges the commonsense, essentialistic view of sexual identity as naturally given. Instead, poststructuralists examine how categories of sexual identity (as well as gender, **race,** and **social class** identities) have been constructed as binary oppositions. Thus, "gayness" or a homosexual identity is not presumed to have a fixed, given, or essential meaning. Rather, its meaning is to be found in an analysis of the historical discourses that have been involved in producing "the homosexual," or "the homosexual problem." At the same time, poststructuralists argue that oppressed groups, such as homosexuals, can and do engage in the production of counter discourses that are self-affirming and empowering, and that challenge their historic treatment as the abnormal and immoral "Other."

As one of the "post" movements in the academy, poststructuralism may be appreciated as a reaction to, and also an extension of, French structuralism. That latter movement, gaining prominence in the 1950s through 1970s, emphasized the role of language or discourse in the social construction of reality and in the production of the human subject or individual. From the structural standpoint, people inhabit a given structure of language ("langue") that enables them to make any particular speech act or utterance ("parole"). Language or discourse is a set of interrelated "signifiers" used to produce "truth" and "reality" as we know it. This means that individuals not only use language to describe a world "out there," but actually produce the world "out there" as well as their sense of identity or self through the use of language and the practices that accompany language. We can imagine only what we can symbolize through language, speak of only what we have language for, and speak only in the ways our rules of discourse allow us to.

Poststructuralism continues the structuralist concern with language or discourse, but understands language as nonunified and contested, as historically emergent rather than static, and as open to multiple interpretations and new uses. Rather than view discourse as an abstract language system or structure, poststructuralism approaches discourses as inseparable from practice and as actively engaged in organizing and distributing power.

One movement within poststructuralism that addresses issues of sexual identity in particular is "**queer theory.**" According to Eve Sedgwick (1990), one of the early and most influential proponents of queer theory, heterosexual privilege has been maintained in modern culture through an "epistemology of the closet." That is, the dominant culture has sought to make homosexuals invisible and to silence discussion of homosexuality in public contexts, including public schools. So long as homosexuals denied their homosexuality and remained invisible in public, and so long as homosexual love remained the "love that dare not speak its name" (to use Oscar Wilde's phrase), heterosexual privilege and **heteronormativity** are unquestioned.

Thus, being "out" is a form of self-affirmation of a gay identity in public that is radical in the sense that it challenges this epistemology of the closet and these silencing practices. For LGBT youth, the politics attached to being "out" was perhaps best represented by Queer Nation in the 1980s and early 1990s, whose motto was "We're here, we're queer, get used to it." While queer activists and theorists affirm the importance of being "out," and thus affirming a queer identity, they also argue—consistent with poststructuralism—that identity is a social construction without stable or unified meaning, and that it should never be affirmed in an uncritical, unreflective manner. After all, as Foucault (1978) argued, the category "homosexual," was an invention of the modern psychiatric profession and was invented to police, regulate, and treat a group of people defined as "abnormal."

Queer theory seeks to work outside the governing normal/abnormal binaries that have defined sexual identity in the modern era. This means acknowledging greater differences *within* categories of sexual identity, and recognizing that everyone has multiple, overlapping identities. LGBT youth, therefore, cannot be reduced to a single category of identity. In education, this implies, for example, focusing on the different experiences of LGBT youth according to their class, race, gender, and other markers of identity and difference. Indeed, the movement to use the inclusive language of "LGBTQI" youth points to an emerging concern with recognizing differences among youth often positioned in the dominant culture as simply "gay." The greater prominence of transgender youth and **transsexuality** in schools reflects this trend.

The approach to education most associated with poststructuralism is some variation of deconstructionism. The basic method of deconstruction involves revealing the primary binary oppositions that govern the production of "truth" in a text (such as the "truth" about homosexuals or homosexuality). These binaries include: good/bad, virtuous/sinful, mature/immature, sexually "pure"/sexually promiscuous, and so on. Texts not only include books and magazines but any cultural artifact from which one can "read" a message such as film, music, and graphic art.

Allen Drury's 1959 novel, *Advise and Consent*, made into a major Hollywood motion picture in 1962, featured a senator with presidential ambitions who engaged in a homosexual affair while a young man in the Navy. He is blackmailed and, when his secret is revealed, commits suicide. In this example, we might ask: How is "gayness" and homosexuality performed? How is "gayness" or homosexuality represented in ways that associate it with the negatively-valued side of these binaries? Whose interests are served by setting up these binaries? Both the film and the book took for granted the dominant presumption of the era that homosexuality disqualified one from positions of leadership in society (at least partially because homosexuals were presumably open to blackmail), and that homosexuals were sad, neurotic, and suicidal people. By blaming the victim rather than questioning **heterosexism** and **homophobia**, both book and film reinforced a view of homosexuals as the "other."

Since postructuralists do not presume that identity has a stable or authentic core, it is often studied as a kind of performance, albeit a performance that is reiterated so many times that it may seem natural. This is a point most associated with literary theorist **Judith Butler** (1990), whose influence on queer theory has been considerable. Aside from learning how to deconstruct the performance of identity in Hollywood films and television shows as well as everyday life, Butler suggests a form of critical pedagogy aimed at subverting the "normal" performance of identity. Butler looks to "drag," the male performance of heterosexual female identity, as subversive in that it plays with the idea that identity has no fixed "essence." This also implies that it can be performed differently, in ways that challenge the reigning binaries of identity.

Finally, poststructuralists have argued that in the contemporary "postmodern" age, the performance of identity is more closely linked to popular culture style and image. Here, style and image are increasingly used by young people as part of their "identity work," presenting a particular sense of who they are in relation to others at any particular moment. This, of course, raises questions about how important style and image are in the identity work of LGBT youth and how influential commercialized popular culture is in defining "gayness" (Carlson 2001). For example, the popular TV show, *Queer Eye for the Straight Guy*, both represents young gay men as fashion and style-conscious, and also promotes such an image among young gay men.

Much still stands in the way of a broader use of poststructural perspectives in K-12 **sexuality education**, and in multicultural **curriculum** materials and texts that include reference to LGBT people. Part of this resistance to poststructuralist perspective has to do with battles going on within LGBT communities over identity. The LGBT civil rights movement has been heavily invested in an essentialistic view of sexual identity, linked to the political argument that because "**sexual orientation**" is naturally given and thus not a choice, LGBT-identified people cannot be "blamed" for being who they are or denied their rights because some still view them as sinners, criminals, or sick.

Poststructuralism has been associated with a radical challenge to this dominant view of identity. By suggesting that identity is socially constructed and only a performance, poststructuralists appear to some to be undermining the claim that people are born with a sexual identity. Actually, it is consistent with poststructuralism to recognize that sexual preference or orientation may be for the most part given. The point from a poststructural standpoint is that the particular way in which sexual orientation gets performed, represented, and constructed is not naturally given but rather differs from one era to the next, from one culture to another. Poststructuralism opens up the possibility of rerepresenting and reperforming sexual identity in ways that challenge heterosexism and heteronormativity and that are more empowering for LGBT youth.

Bibliography

Biesta, Gert, and Denise Egea-Kuehne. 2001. *Derrida and Education*. New York: Routledge.
Butler, Judith. 1990. *Gender Trouble*. New York: Routledge.
Carlson, Dennis. 2001. "Gay, Queer, Cyborg: The Performance of Identity in a Transglobal Age." *Discourse: Studies in the Cultural Politics of Education* 22, no. 3: 297–309.
Foucault, Michel. 1978. *The History of Sexuality Volume 1: An Introduction*. New York: Pantheon.
Sedgwick, Eve. 1990. *Epistemology of the Closet*. Berkeley: University of California Press.

Pregnancy, Teenage

Michael Reiss

One of the longest-running aims of school **sexuality education** has been to decrease the incidence of teenage pregnancy (Halstead and Reiss 2003), and teenage births in most countries more than halved between 1970 and 2000. In the United States,

See also Adolescent Sexualities; AIDS; Children of LGBT Parents; Mental Health; Parents, LGBT; Parents, Responses to Homosexuality; Sexual Health, Lesbian and Bisexual Women; Social Class; Youth, At Risk; Youth, Homeless.

teen birth rates are now at record low levels. However, the U.S. still has by far the highest teenage birth rate in the developed world (52 out of every 1000 fifteen to nineteen-year-olds in 1998), with the **United Kingdom** having the highest teenage birth rate in Europe (UNICEF 2001). The position of lesbian and bisexual young women is usually overlooked in studies on teenage pregnancy. Yet what data there are suggest that **lesbian** and **bisexual youth** are more likely than their straight peers to have had a pregnancy. Many lesbians are also vulnerable to the same-sexually transmitted infections as heterosexual women. In addition, young lesbians experience higher rates of physical and **sexual abuse** than young heterosexual women.

Why should countries aim to reduce the incidence of teenage births? There are physical health arguments in favour of this aim. Pregnancy in teenage mothers is riskier for the physical health of both mother and baby. Such mothers are more likely to experience anemia, toxemia, eclampsia, hypertension, and prolonged and difficult labor (Social Exclusion Unit 1999). Further, in the United Kingdom, teenage mothers, compared to older mothers:

- usually go to their doctors much later in pregnancy (since three-quarters of them aren't intending to become pregnant)
- often miss out on preconception health measures such as taking folic acid supplements
- are much more likely to smoke during pregnancy
- are 25 percent more likely to have a baby weighing less than 5.5 pounds
- have a 60 percent higher infant mortality rate for the 12 months after birth
- are three times as likely to suffer postnatal depression
- are only half as likely to breastfeed
- have children who are twice as likely to be admitted to hospital as the result of accidents or gastro-enteritis (Social Exclusion Unit 1999).

More careful analysis shows that many of the above correlations are due largely to poverty rather than age, but that teenage pregnancy has an additional, independent effect (Social Exclusion Unit 1999).

However, the major arguments in favor of the reduction of teenage pregnancy are not to do with health (Halstead and Reiss 2003). For a start, young mothers are more likely in almost all rich countries to end up with fewer educational qualifications, to be unemployed or low-waged, to live in poor housing conditions, and to suffer from depression. Their children are more likely to live in poverty, to grow up without a father, "to do less well at school, to become involved in crime, to abuse drugs and alcohol, and eventually to become a teenage parent and begin the cycle all over again" (UNICEF 2001, 3).

In her study of teenage mothers in **Canada** and the United States, Deirdre Kelly (2000) notes that such mothers are scapegoats for social anxieties. They are portrayed in the media and elsewhere as "stupid sluts," as children having children, as teen rebels who flaunt their nonconformity and treat their babies as objects, as vulnerable girls whom nobody loved, as victims of child abuse, as welfare moms, as dropouts, and as neglectful mothers. Kelly found that school-age mothers need flexibility from their schools with regard to such issues as attendance and workload expectations. She also reported that young mothers weren't alone in needing such flexibility: "Some students were living independently, either with social assistance or away from their reserve (reservation). Still others were working long hours, either to supplement their family's income or to care for younger siblings. Still others were sometimes needed by immigrant parents to serve as translators in important matters affecting the family. Some school staff members, although relatively materially advantaged, also found it a struggle to meet family and work obligations around the rigid school timetable" (117).

In a study of pregnancy policies in the education systems of sub-Saharan African countries, Bagele Chilisa (2002) found that in many countries the practice of expelling pregnant girls from schools continues. In some places, the practice is enshrined in law; in others, it is maintained by informal custom. Only a small proportion of girls who drop out of school due to pregnancy reenter the school system. Indeed, given the competition for school places in a number of countries, Chilisa concluded that "expulsion of girl mothers becomes a way of creating spaces for boys" (32).

Teenage pregnancy among lesbians remains underresearched, probably because of an implicit faulty assumption among many that parents are heterosexual. Yet an increasing number of population-based surveys in a number of countries show that lesbian and bisexual young women are around twice as likely to have been pregnant than their heterosexual peers (Bridget et al. 2003). They are also more likely to have engaged in underage sex and **prostitution** and to report having sexual intercourse several times a week (Saewyc et al. 1998). These statistics are partly due to lesbian and bisexual young women being less likely to use birth control than heterosexual young women, and when they do use contraception to their being more likely to use less reliable methods (withdrawal, rhythm method). They are also, in part, related to the finding that sexual abuse, incest, and rape are more common among lesbian and bisexual young women than among heterosexual young women. In addition, prostitution may result from young lesbians being made homeless due to family rejection as a result of their **sexual orientation**. It has also been suggested that some young lesbians may purposely become pregnant to "prove" they aren't lesbians. There is some evidence, too, that gay and bisexual young men are more likely to have caused a pregnancy than heterosexual males (Saewyc et al. 1998; SIECUS 2001).

It is often tacitly assumed by health professionals and others that lesbians are not at risk for sexually transmitted infections, including HIV. However, a high proportion of lesbians, possibly the majority, have had sexual intercourse with men (Bridget et al. 2003). In addition, these male sexual partners are often older than themselves while a small proportion of lesbians have large numbers of sexual partners. Many lesbians of all ages find it difficult or are unable to access appropriate sexual health information and services. When they do discuss their sexual health with doctors or nurses, they typically find that such health professionals assume they are heterosexual.

Although many lesbians want to bear children, access to fertility and artificial insemination services are often difficult for lesbians. This can lead to lesbians using unscreened sperm, since screening for diseases such as HIV infection cannot be done by oneself at home. This can work well—and is, after all, the norm for heterosexual women—but it means that such lesbians miss out on the medical benefits of sperm screening. However, attitudes are changing and, in at least some countries, including the United Kingdom, it is now easier for lesbians than for single heterosexual women to avail themselves of artificial insemination and other fertility services (Lasker 1998).

Bibliography

Bridget, Jan, Angela Hodgson, Andy Mullen, and Peter Smith. 2003. "Sexual Health." In *Calderdale Lesbian and Gay Health Action Plan*. Accessed June 6, 2005. http://www. lesbianinformationservice.org/sexual3.rtf.

Chilisa, Bagele. 2002. "National Policies on Pregnancy in Education Systems in Sub-Saharan Africa: The Case of Botswana." *Gender and Education* 14: 21–35.

Halstead, J. Mark, and Michael J. Reiss. 2003. *Values in Sex Education: From Principles to Practice*. London: RoutledgeFalmer.

Kelly, Deirdre M. 2000. *Pregnant with Meaning: Teen Mothers and the Politics of Inclusive Schooling*. New York: Peter Lang.

Lasker, Judith N. 1998. "The Users of Donor Insemination." Pp. 7–32 in *Donor Insemination: International Social Science Perspectives*. Edited by Ken Daniels and Erica Haimes. Cambridge: Cambridge University Press.

Saewyc, Elizabeth M., Carol L. Skay, Linda H. Bearinger, Robert W. Blum, and Michael D. Resnick. 1998. "Sexual Orientation, Sexual Behaviors, and Pregnancy among American Indian Adolescents." *Journal of Adolescent Health* 23, no. 4: 238–247.

SIECUS. 2001. "Lesbian, Gay, Bisexual, and Transgendered Youth Issues." *SIECUS Report Supplement* 29, no. 4: 1–5.

Social Exclusion Unit. 1999. *Teenage Pregnancy*. London: The Stationary Office.

UNICEF. 2001. "A League Table of Teenage Births in Rich Nations." *Innocenti Report Card* 3. Florence: Innocenti Research Centre. Accessed June 2, 2005. http://www.unicef-icdc. org/cgi-bin/unicef/main.sql?menu=/publications/menu.html&testo=Lunga.sql? ProductID=328.

Web Site

Lesbian Information Service. January 2004. Accessed June 7, 2005. http://www. lesbianinformationservice.org. Established in 1987, Lesbian Information Service has conducted research around young lesbians and gays, alcohol, lesbians and housing, developed a training program which looks at homophobia awareness from a multioppression perspective, and provided training to hundreds of service providers (youth, mental health, health, alcohol, social work, education, housing, clergy, police, and voluntary organizations).

Prejudice

Linda L. Gaither

Prejudice is to have opinions about individual and group differences without knowing the facts, and to hold on to those opinions even after contrary facts are known. Prejudice operates at all levels of social interchange, including educational settings, where distorted opinions based on **race** and **ethnicity**, religion, gender and **sexual orientation** can derail the ideals of inclusion and diversity. Prejudices are often linked to strong and deep-seated emotions, as seen, for example, in the fear, hatred,

See also Allies; Antibias Curriculum; School Safety and Safe School Zones; White Antiracism.

and anger which characterize **homophobia**. Prejudice is transformed into **discrimination** when one social group becomes so powerful and dominant that it is able to control another group and enforce the controlling group's distorted opinions. Racism, **sexism, heterosexism,** anti-Semitism each exemplifies the belief in the superiority of one group at the expense of another. In actuality, educators as well as students may experience the tensions of overlapping memberships in several groups which are ranked by prejudice in a hierarchy of value. For example, an **African American** gay student may experience affirmation in a curricular intervention that promotes the empathic ability to view members of other groups in the context of their history of oppression. Yet, this same student may simultaneously experience some degree of homophobic prejudice in his black community context. On the positive side, the fact that every person is simultaneously a member of many social categories unites people and reduces prejudice.

Educators are challenged to address stereotyping and to reduce prejudice in schools through a range of interventions designed to improve intergroup relations and create a safe place for all students to learn and grow. Programmatic interventions involving younger students (elementary and secondary) have proven to be highly effective (Stephan 1999). But early intervention entails risks for teachers and **administrators.** Despite evidence that prejudice is communicated to children beginning at ages two and three (Letts and Sears 1999), with out-group **harassment** and name-calling a common occurrence on elementary school playgrounds, explicit interventions by teachers, especially when the issue is homophobia, bring censure for saying too much about sex or even acknowledging the existence of gay and lesbian people. This resistance and silencing on behalf of **childhood** innocence involves educators in confronting their interiorized prejudices inculcated through a life-long socialization process. In the case of heterosexism and homophobia, the insidious character of **heteronormativity** may blind administrators, teachers, and counselors to the prejudices that are enshrined in **educational policies** and practices such as the assumption that all children in the school live in "traditional" two-parent heterosexual families. At its worst, such blindness results in verbal and physical assaults against gay and lesbian students.

Social psychologists and other researchers have developed theories that show a variety of explanatory causes of prejudice. Interventions to reduce prejudice in schools and improve intergroup relations use techniques developed on the basis of a range of theories. Pioneering theorists of the 1970s focused on social identity and categorization as primary causal factors in the development of prejudice. **Research** programs demonstrated how basic ingroup–outgroup memberships alone could generate ingroup favoritism. For subjects randomly placed in groups, distinction from the "other" category provided ipso facto a positive identity for one's group. This "minimal group paradigm" suggests that prejudice may be an unavoidable co-efficient of the formation of social identity. As an "other" minority, **lesbian, gay, bisexual,** and **transgender youth** (LGBT) easily become carriers of negative out-group prejudice.

Theorists also focused on the processes of self-stereotyping by group members that make collective action possible. For individuals, different levels of identity become operative in various situations: self as human being, self as group member, self as individual. Identity in terms of group membership involves ingroup–outgroup comparisons; this is the seat of prejudice in identity formation. It is significant that the superordinate level of self as human being offers an inclusive perspective that tempers the prejudice generated at lower levels. Programs and curricula that stress the common hopes and aspirations of LGBT youth that are shared with their heterosexual classmates can reduce prejudice by humanizing the outgroup at the superordinate level. Both social identity and categorization theorists agree that, in order to explain prejudice, an analysis of both collective and individual psychology in complex interaction is necessary.

Social identity theory is applied in classroom approaches, which focus on categorizing and stereotyping. Techniques include: personalizing outgroup members in cooperative learning groups; undoing biased labeling by presenting students with information about outgroups that challenges negative stereotypes; highlighting group similarities, especially common human needs; stressing superordinate categories to which all students belong, such as grade, school, citizenship, humankind; and showing students that every person is simultaneously a member of many social categories, overlapping and uniting people. All of these techniques are appropriately applied beginning at the elementary level. For example, one classroom exercise groups and regroups students on graphs according to various questions: who has brothers in school, sisters, favorite sport. The overlapping groups which emerge illustrate the many ways people are united with each other in common experiences. Such experiential learning has potential to reduce prejudice against LGBT people.

Realistic Intergroup Conflict Theory shifted the focus from relations between individuals to the dynamics between groups as wholes. Muzafer Sherif, the most influential proponent of this approach, maintained that the primary determinant in intergroup relations is material interests. When these coincide, relations are amicable. In an era of pressure on school administrations for diversity awareness, for example, collaboration with groups like Parents and Friends of Lesbians and Gays (PFLAG) can proceed with mutual benefit for the school, the parents, and the students, rather than in an adversarial mode.

Thus intergroup attitudes, perceptions, and images are the result of particular relations between groups, not their original cause. This theory is applied in approaches to develop empathy, usually appropriate for middle, high school, and even **college students**. A history-based, **multicultural education** approach is effective for racial, ethnic, or religious diversity awareness, but is problematic for sex- and gender-related issues since these are often assigned to "health" or **sexuality education** classes and approached in terms of clinical information, not human diversity. Units in **history** and social studies that include sex and gender issues, however, can teach how groups use legitimizing myths, such as innate inferiority, to justify a hierarchy of privileges. The myth of Aryan superiority and its use by the Nazis is one example where students can also learn about the various categorizations of prisoners in concentration camps, including homosexuals who wore the **pink triangle**. In such exercises, teachers undermine prejudice by emphasizing universal values of justice, fairness, dignity, and respect, explored through stories, discussions, and role-playing.

Among the most recent theories on prejudice is the "radial network model," which focuses on four types of threats: realistic threats which challenge a group's existence or economic/political power; symbolic threats, which endanger a group's way of life; intergroup threats, based in the anxiety linked to interacting with outgroups; and negative **stereotypes**. All four of these threats feature in the debate over gay marriage. Some observers see realistic power issues at the heart of the debate; others note the fear of undermining a traditional way of life, often expressed by heterosexuals. There is anxiety of becoming like the outgroup and relating to them as equals; and there is fear that the stereotype of gay promiscuity will corrupt the marriage covenant.

A set of techniques related to the "radial network model" uses intergroup relations skills developed for the Peace Corps and other international programs. This approach highlights tolerating ambiguity, avoiding the use of negative traits to explain the behavior of others, listening and observing carefully, taking on the roles of people in other groups. In a secondary classroom, for example, role playing a marriage ceremony for both heterosexual and LGB couples brings to light for discussion some of the visceral responses that arise.

Since a primary cause of prejudice is fear due to uncertainty about the others' behavior, intergroup relations skills can help students feel comfortable when relating to outgroup members. An important corollary is providing factual information to contradict perceived threats by the outgroup to the ingroup's power or way of life. In a school setting, real or symbolic threats of one group over another can be defused through fair treatment by teachers or administrators. Conflict resolution skills may also be used to teach students about the origins of intergroup conflict and techniques for resolution. Students can learn to respond when they see an injustice taking place if they know school codes for hate speech, **bullying**, acts of discrimination, **sexual harassment**, and so forth.

School climate is a critical element in reducing prejudice on the basis of sexual orientation or **gender identity**. Educational policies stating a zero tolerance for stereotyping and discrimination, and codes of conducts punishing hate speech and harassment are two important areas. Schools can also make use of multicultural **curriculum**, providing exposure to the cultures of all groups, and insure that administrators, teachers, and support personnel model such intergroup relations for the student body as well as mirror its diversity.

Teacher training in the techniques of intervention is also key to improving intergroup relations, beginning with teacher interns and their supervisors and moving through teacher inservice and graduate education. Finally, alliances with heterosexual supporters are often helpful to effect institutional reform, since heterosexuals can influence other heterosexuals in ways that may diffuse the visceral quality of **homophobia**.

Bibliography

Augoustinos, Martha, and Katherine J. Reynolds, eds. 2001. *Understanding Prejudice, Racism, and Social Conflict*. Thousand Oaks, CA: Sage.

Hecht, Michael L., ed. 1998. *Communicating Prejudice*. Thousand Oaks, CA: Sage.

Letts, William J., and James T. Sears, eds. 1999. *Queering Elementary Education: Advancing the Dialogue about Sexualities and Schooling*. Lanham, MD: Rowman and Littlefield.

Stephan, Walter. 1999. *Reducing Prejudice and Stereotyping in Schools*. New York: Teachers College Press.

Walling, Donovan R., ed. 1996. *Open Lives, Safe Schools*. Bloomington, IN: Phi Delta Kappa Educational Foundation.

Web Sites

Teaching for Change: Building Social Justice, Starting in the Classroom. September 2004. Accessed December 7, 2004. http://www.teachingforchange.org. Teaching for Change is a not-for-profit organization based in Washington, D.C., working to provide teachers and parents with the tools to transform schools into socially equitable centers of learning where students become architects of a better future.

Teaching Tolerance. December 2004. The Southern Poverty Law Center. Accessed December 7, 2004. http://www.teachingtolerance.org. A principal online destination for people interested in dismantling prejudice and bigotry, creating communities that value diversity.

Professional Educational Organizations

Kevin C. Franck

Professional organizations for lesbian, gay, bisexual, transgender, and questioning (LGBTQ) educators and many mainstream education groups around the world dedicate significant resources to improving school safety, implementing inclusive curricula, and producing **research**. The United States-based **Gay Lesbian Straight Education Network** (GLSEN) and its European counterpart **GLBT Educational Equity** (GLEE) are the largest and most visible professional organizations specifically dedicated to providing support for queer educators and advocating system-wide school reform. In addition to these organizations, education organizations such as the American Federation of Teachers (AFT), the National Education Association (NEA), and the American Education Research Association (AERA), the British Education Research Association (BERA), the National Unions of Students in Europe (EBIS), and the Australian Association for Research in Education (AARE) have long expressed support for LGBT issues via policy statements, legislative advocacy, research, and professional development programs. In large part, international professional organizations attempt to ease the hardship felt by many queer students and teachers through efforts to confront **bullying** and **harassment**, encouraging LGBT inclusive **curriculum** plans, and promoting research on the effects of **homophobia** and antibias on queer youth. Some notable professional organizations, such as the American School Boards Association and the National Association of State Boards of Education, have been nearly silent on LGBT issues and sometimes hostile to efforts of LGBT education professionals. Additionally, antigay political and religious groups have attacked the LGBTQ-positive work of queer and mainstream education organizations.

From a support group for gay and lesbian private school Boston area teachers, in 1990, GLSEN has grown into a powerful organization, advocating for queer teachers and students in state-wide and national policy discussions. It invests much energy and funding into providing support for **gay–straight alliances**, producing school materials, and conducting research. GLSEN coproduced, with the American Federation of Teachers and the American Psychological Association, *Just the Facts about Sexual Orientation and Youth* (Just the Facts Coalition 2000), perhaps the mostly widely distributed and read pamphlet designed to increase educators' knowledge of LGBT issues. GLEE is the primary professional organization for European LGBTQ educators and their **allies** throughout Europe. This organization empowers teachers to work for social change in their communities, assumes leadership roles in educational administration and policy deliberations, and develops

See also Activism, LGBT Teachers; Japan, LGBT Issues in; Legal Issues, Students; Professionalism; Teachers, LGBT and History.

projects within the European Union. In Japan, the Sexual Minority Teachers Network is the first national organization for LGBT teachers. With its heterosexual allies, "STN21" works on comprehensive **sexuality education**, networks with other educators, and engages in media protests.

Most mainstream alliances of professional educators officially support efforts to improve schools for LGBT teachers and students. In the United States, the two major teacher's trade unions have developed official policy statements and programming to combat **heternormativity** and homophobia. The NEA and the AFT also have supported efforts to ban **reparative therapy** and condemned the discriminatory policies of the **Boy Scouts of America**. Also, the Association for Supervision and Curriculum Development and the American Education Research Association have adopted policy statements against sexual orientation **discrimination** as have the National Unions of Students in Europe, the Australian Association for Research in Education, and the British Education Research Association.

In addition to official policy statements and advocacy, most Western mainstream education organizations support subgroups for their LGBT members and allies. Major research organizations such as the American Education Research Association, the British Education Research Association, and the Australian Association for Research in Education have at least one Special Interest Group (SIG) dedicated to supporting LGBT research and educators. These groups have evolved as has the field of **queer studies** in education. The AERA group, formed in 1987, recently changed its name to the Queer Studies SIG, reflecting its embrace of **queer theory** and **queer pedagogy**. Such groups create room within their umbrella organizations that are designated safe spaces for academics interested in queer issues in education. They also allow members to network via the **Internet**, conferences, and journals to keep in touch with the latest research, test out new ideas in an informal setting, and locate others interested in specific research topics. The *Journal of Gay and Lesbian Issues in Education* emerged, in 2003, as a result of such networking.

Other professional research organizations such as the American Sociological Association, the American Library Association, and the American Psychological Association have similar goals and have formed committees, divisions, or caucuses for their LGBT professors and researchers. The NEA and the AFT have committees or caucuses that help K-12 teachers make professional and personal connections.

The bulk of the work done by professional education organizations on behalf of LGBT students is aimed at making schools safer by increasing legal protection and combating harassment and bullying. In 2004, GLSEN released an inaugural report analyzing and comparing the relative safety of U.S. schools in each of the fifty states and the District of Columbia. The report, *State of the States* (2004), issued a "failing grade" to forty-two states. Only eight states and the District of Columbia offer queer students legal protection from harassment; seven states have laws or policies *prohibiting* positive portrayal of LGBT themes or issues in schools. The American Federation of Teachers offers antibullying workshops as part of their "teacher-to-teacher" series of professional development opportunities. And, in response to findings in *Hostile Hallways: Bullying, Teasing, and Sexual Harassment in School* (AAUW 2001), the NEA teamed up with American Association of University Women teamed to counter the significant harassment that many students face on campus and in school. Similar cross-organization efforts include GLSEN's work with Parents, Friends and Family of Gays and Lesbians, and the American Friends Service Committee to create Safe Schools Coalitions in many parts of the

United States and Canada. In Italy, the Association of Parents and Friends of Homo-sexuals led a successful effort, in 2001, to encourage the Italian Ministry of Education to adopt a policy aimed at protecting LGBT youth in schools, although that **educational policy** has now expired and will not be renewed by the current government (de Pittà and de Santis 2005).

Professional education organizations also work to reform school curricula, removing derogatory and defamatory content and including accurate and friendly portrayals of LGBT topics and people. As part of its Health Information Network, the NEA develops school **curriculum** plans that effectively and honestly help students explore sexuality, sexual health and identity, and HIV/**AIDS**. The NEA offers members and other professional educators resources and training on developing courses that go beyond simple discussions of anatomy or sexual **desire**, instead focusing on the complex set of factors that influence young people's understanding of sexuality. Early in 2004, the NEA bowed to pressure from Parents and Friends of Ex-Gays (PFOX), which forced some schools with GSAs to provide space to "ex-gay" student groups, allowing NEA members to form an "ex-gay" educators' caucus.

The Association for Supervision and Curriculum Development has long held the position that school policies, instructional practices, and curriculum materials should be inclusive of LGBT issues, persons, and issues. Publications such as its large circulation *Educational Leadership* include these topics. In addition to efforts by well-established groups such as GLSEN, which makes resources available to subject-based teachers from **history** and **literature** to **science** and mathematics, there are smaller groups. The P.E.R.S.O.N. Project (www.personproject.org), for example, is a national network of activists who advocate for the presentation of fair, accurate, and unbiased information about sexuality and GLBT people to students. Similarly, non-gay groups such as Teaching Tolerance (http://www.tolerance.org), a project of the Southern Poverty Law Center, also have been inclusive in their materials.

Vital to the ability of professional education organizations to work for **school safety** and to advocate for LGBT inclusive curricula, is the production of research and scholarship on issues facing queer youth in their schools and communities. In addition to the *State of the States* report, GLSEN has conducted a National **School Climate** Survey for several years in order to isolate specific manifestations of homophobia and antiqueer bias and to document the severity of problems facing queer youth. Similarly, the Policy Institute of the National Lesbian and Gay Task Force has produced and funded policy studies related to LGBT youth and educational issues (Holmes and Cahill 2004).

Queer education organizations also make use of research produced by other progressive organizations such as the Human Rights Watch's (2002) documentation of antigay violence. GLEE has made use of a survey of students and teachers attitudes on homosexuality conducted by the Dutch Society for Integration of Homosexuality (COC) to design training programs to help European teachers.

Bibliography

American Association of University Women. 2001. *Hostile Hallways: Bullying, Teasing, and Sexual Harassment in School*. Washington, DC: Author.

de Pittà, Maurizi, and Rita de Santis. 2005. "Rome, Italy: The Lexicon—An Italian Dictionary of Homophobia Spurs Gay Activism." *Journal of Gay and Lesbian Issues in Education* 2, no. 3: 99–105.

Gay, Lesbian, Straight Education Network. 2004. *State of the States: A Policy Analysis of Lesbian, Gay, Bisexual and Transgender (LGBT) Safer Schools Issues*. New York: Author.

Holmes, Sarah E., and Sean Cahill. 2004. "School Experiences of Gay, Lesbian, Bisexual, and Transgender Youth." *Journal of Gay and Lesbian Issues in Education* 1, no. 3: 53–66.

Human Rights Watch. 2002. *Hatred in the Hallways*. New York: Author.

Just the Facts Coalition. 2000. *Just the Facts about Sexual Orientation and Youth: A Primer for Principals, Educators and School Personnel*. Washington, D.C.: American Psychological Association.

Kosciw, Joseph. 2004. *The 2003 National School Climate Survey: The School Related Experiences of Our Nation's Lesbian, Gay, Bisexual and Transgender Youth*. New York: Gay, Lesbian Straight Education Network.

National Education Association. 2004. *Dealing with Legal Matters Surrounding Student' Sexual Orientation and Gender Identity*. Washington, D.C.: Author.

Web Sites

American Psychological Association Committee of Lesbian, Gay Bisexual Concerns. March 2005. American Psychological Association. Accessed June 10, 2005. www.apa.org/ed/hlgb. Links to the organization's committee focusing on LGBT issues.

GLEE. February 2003. Accessed June 10, 2005. http://glee.oulu.fi. Offers resources for GLBT educators and provides virtual space for communication among its members.

The Journal of Lesbian and Gay Issues in Education. May 2005. James T. Sears. Accessed June 10, 2005. www.jtsears.com/jglie.htm Abstracts of articles published in the journal along with links to many professional education organizations working on GLBT issues in education.

National Education Association—Gay, Lesbian, Bisexual, and Transgender Caucus. May 2004. Accessed June 10, 2005. www.nea-glc.org. Official home page for the NEA Caucus representing public education employees concerned with LGBT issues.

National and International Gay and Lesbian Organizations and Publications. June 5, 2004. Alvin Fritz. Accessed June 10, 2005. http://faculty.washington.edu/alvin/gayorg.htm#EDUCAT. Links to professional organizations in a number of disciplines and fields, including education, which work on GLBT issues.

Professionalism

Stacy Otto

The term professional "comes from the roots 'profess' and 'confess' because the original professionals—priests—professed their vows to an authority" (Evans 2002, 129). This view can be seen in the medical and teaching professions, too. In practice, students look at the professionals they see around them in order to consider what social group or groups they seem to belong to. Through these role models they learn the racial and gender structures and expectations of their culture. This narrow definition of professionalism poses a danger for **lesbian, gay, bisexual,** and

See also Activism, LGBT Teachers; Adolescent Sexualities; Childhood; Desire; Psychoanalysis and Education; Sexual Harassment; Teachers, LGBT and History; Women's Colleges.

transgender youth. If a student is never exposed to a social group that he or she can identify with, then one's concept of self is endangered, because "young people pursue only that which they can imagine as possible" (Zirkel 2002, 358). This can have dire consequences for students. For example, a recent **school climate** survey found that 24 percent of LGBT students who did not find supportive teachers within their school report they do not intend to go to college (GLSEN 2003). **Professional education organizations**, such as the 2.7 million member National Education Association (NEA), have adopted positions in support of LGBT students and educators while other professional groups, such as the **Gay, Lesbian, Straight Education Network** (GLSEN) in the United States and **Equality for Gay and Lesbians Everywhere** (EGALE) in **Canada**, study and report on institutional **discrimination** and **homophobia** on a national level and offer professional resources to educators, students, and parents.

In the practice of socializing student teachers, detachment, which means that one must omit the personal parts of their lives as they interact with their students, is nearly synonymous with professionalism. This subjects queer teachers to a similar dilemma as that of their students by insisting on a secreted, silent **sexual identity** in schools. In such a definition of professionalism, there is no place for the personal in the professional practice of the teacher. In the professional lives of **queer** educators, their school or community culture may determine whether they are out, empowered, and activist, or closeted and fearful of discovery. Isolation is a theme within modern-day schools, and it is only amplified by professionalism's insistence on detachment. Queer educators who feel unable to be open with their identity experience a deepened sense of isolation that may pose a threat to their emotional well-being, and result in a split life where the teacher pretends to be heterosexual within the workplace.

Too, some queer educators have reported feeling that they must be exemplary teaching professionals in order to exist above scrutiny or to protect their identity. Some LGBT preservice teachers report feeling as if they are constantly renegotiating polarized aspects of their selves: professional vs. personal, public vs. private, inside vs. outside, safety vs. danger, and neutral vs. political (Evans 2002). And, teachers who are open about their sexual identity may also feel pressure to perform in an exemplary manner while maintaining personal detachment from students.

Viewing the detachment of teachers from their students as right and desirable is manifested in the tradition of British young men's (and, later, women's) boarding schools. The boarding school system is based upon the principles of establishing authority and discipline in the ranks of young men who are largely left by the adult "masters" to a hierarchical system of self-governance. Such detachment is linked to these **single-sex schools**' stereotypical association with same-sex relationships and sexual experimentation. Extreme feelings for an older student or teacher on the part of the student have been documented, but in the late nineteenth and early twentieth centuries were only occasionally labeled deviant (Vicinus 1989).

The practices associated with teachers' professionalism have also occupied the opposite end of the continuum, with some alternative school movements that not just openly encourage, but mandate close but nonsexual relationships with students. Among those are the American Waldorf schools and A.S. Neill's Summerhill in England, which proposed a radical approach to education based upon freedom and derived from the psychoanalytic theories and practices of Sigmund Freud and Homer Lane.

Professional detachment is considered necessary because curiosity in the student/teacher relationship is easily characterized as voyeuristic. Voyeurism, with its roots in the Latin "to see," means literally, "one who lies in wait" and is suspect, partly because it has come to mean a person who spies on another for purposes of sexual gratification. This is part of the concern of queer educators when it comes to the conversation surrounding professionalism. Teachers have reported in qualitative studies (Kissen 1996; Sanlo 1999) that the imagined link between LGBT identity and sexual perversion leads some communities to fear interaction and relationships between queer educators and children. But, all experiences between teachers and students *do* contain an element of sexuality that cannot be removed, for "teaching is not a purely cognitive, informative experience, it is also an emotional, erotic experience" (Felman quoted in Sykes 2003, 10). To deny the sexual discourse of the student/teacher relationship is to (figuratively) mutilate the body of the professionally-detached teacher by insisting that the teacher assumes a manner that is less-than-human (e.g., asexual), and then, in return, that mutilated image of the adult human is revered, held up as a perfect example of professionalism.

One way in which this erotic tension is manifested is in the same-sex or other-sex "**crush**" on the teacher (Sykes 2003). For LGBT youth, these same-sex crushes on teachers are a part of the process of finding a social group that he or she can identify with, along the way to development of their individual concept of self. This attraction, according to the "rules" that student teachers inherit, only goes one way: the student having a crush on the teacher, because "sex and eroticism typically become unthinkable within the material and imaginary space of 'teacher'" (Sykes 2003, 12), even though the student teacher may have had such crushes herself.

Professionalism, at the level of the school and district rather than the individual, has come to be synonymous with teaching standards and "best practices" documents. Many examples such as those formulated by members of the National Education Association, the largest organization of its kind, stress the need to create an equitable environment for all students within schools and, in particular, to offer a safe and hospitable environment to LGBT youth as well as faculty. Members also advocate for students and faculty who are perceived to be LGBT but who do not self-identify as such. The NEA's professional standards task force reports and action plan documents focus upon the mistreatment of LGBT youth and adults within schools, pointing to the risk factors research has identified: **mental health** problems, self-injury and **suicide**. However, in practice, the NEA has been reluctant to discuss sexuality or personal relationships of a nonsexual nature between queer educators and their students, as has GLSEN. Additionally, state regulations regarding **licensure** often create professional barriers within the student/teacher relationships. And even within organizations marketed as "progressive" in their work to unmask discrimination, violence, and **stereotypes** of LGBT individuals of all ages, the student/teacher relationship remains a taboo subject, reinforcing the **educational policy** and practice of professional detachment within schools and in teacher education programs.

Bibliography

Evans, Kate. 2002. *Negotiating the Self: Identity, Sexuality, and Emotion in Learning to Teach*. New York: RoutledgeFalmer.

GLSEN's 2003 National School Climate Survey Key Findings. 2003. Accessed August 4, 2004. http://www.glsen.org/cgi-bin/iowa/all/news/record/1413.html.

Kissen, Rita, ed. 1996. *The Last Closet: The Real Lives of Lesbian and Gay Teachers.* Portsmouth, NH: Heinemann.

Sanlo, Ronni L. 1999. *Unheard Voices: The Effects of Silence on Lesbian and Gay Educators.* Westport, CT: Bergin and Garvey.

Sykes, Heather. 2003. "The Angel's Playground: Same-Sex Desires of Physical Education Teachers." *Journal of Gay & Lesbian Issues in Education* 1, no. 1: 3–31.

Vicinus, Martha. 1989. "Distance and Desire: English Boarding School Friendships, 1870–1920." Pp. 212–229 in *Hidden from History: Reclaiming the Gay & Lesbian Past.* Edited by Martin Duberman, Martha Vicinus, and George Chauncey, Jr. New York: NAL Books.

Zirkel, Sabrina. 2002. "Is There a Place for Me? Role Models and Academic Identity among White Students and Students of Color." *Teachers College Record* 104, no. 2: 357–376.

Web Site

National Education Association. May 2005. Accessed June 3, 2005. http://www.nea.org. See also http://www.nea.org/nr/02taskforce.html. See also http//:www.nea.org/nr/02taskforce.html for a summation of the *Report of the NEA Task Force on Sexual Orientation.* The NEA's focus on professionalism is tied to unionism and to "enhancing the quality" of teaching. The NEA works to protect its members from "arbitrary, abusive treatment" by school districts and advocates for "decent working conditions" for teachers.

Project 10

Lance T. McCready

Project 10 is widely recognized as one of the first organized efforts to provide systematic support and education for **lesbian, gay, bisexual, transgender,** and questioning (LGBTQ) youth in United States' public schools. Originating in 1984 at Fairfax High School of the Los Angeles Unified School District (LAUSD), Project 10 was named after the estimate frequently (though mistakenly) attributed to sexologist Alfred Kinsey that 10 percent of the general population is exclusively homosexual. Virginia Uribe, an earth science teacher who later became a counselor, initiated the program in response to the daily **homophobia** and **harassment** LGBTQ students were experiencing at this high school located in Hollywood. Project 10 has been influential as an important model for the development of support groups and in-school services for LGBTQ youth. However, moving into the new century, supporters of such programs have advocated for greater consideration of **race, ethnicity, social class,** and gender.

Uribe initiated a lunchtime discussion group for LGBTQ students following an incident involving Chris, a black gay male student who transferred to Fairfax in 1984. Chris had been kicked out of his home at age fourteen after telling his parents he was gay. Chris came to Fairfax thinking it was a more tolerant environment for gay students due to its proximity to West Hollywood, a neighborhood known to be affirming of gay, punk, and New Wave subcultures. Despite the surrounding community, Chris was physically abused by his peers and verbally bashed by teachers and

See also Community LGBT Youth Groups; Mental Health; Religious Fundamentalism; Secondary Schools, LGBT; School Safety and Safe School Zones; White Antiracism.

students. Unable to cope with the escalating violence, he dropped out of Fairfax—the fourth high school he had left after **sexual harassment** proved too much.

Chris' plight was hardly unique. Through the discussion group Uribe learned that many academically capable LGBTQ students dropped out of school because of low self-esteem, isolation, and alienation. In some cities, community-based organizations, such as the Hetrick-Martin Institute, had been providing services to LGBTQ youth since the late 1970s. However, school-based services for LGBTQ youth were nonexistent before Uribe, with the support of her principal, used her classroom as the base for Project 10.

Project 10 currently has groups or contact people in the majority of LAUSD's high schools. Over the years it has expanded to include middle and continuation schools. Friends of Project 10, Inc., was formed as a 501c(3) nonprofit organization to seek grants and receive donations to support Project 10-sponsored programs such as The Models Of Pride Conference, Models Of Excellence Scholarship Program, and LGBT Youth **Prom**.

From the outset Uribe emphasized that Project 10 was not an LGBTQ youth program, rather a dropout prevention program *aimed at* LGBTQ youth. Its focus is education, reduction of verbal and physical abuse, **suicide** prevention, and **HIV education**. The work of Project 10 is carried out through workshops for teachers, counselors, and other support personnel, as well as support groups for students dealing with **sexual orientation** issues. The goal of support groups is to improve self-esteem and provide affirmation for students who are stigmatized based on their **sexual identity**. Usually an adult serves as the cofacilitator for the group along with a student. Facilitators are usually school personnel who operate on a volunteer basis. Some of the facilitators are gay, lesbian, bisexual, or transgender, whereas others are **allies**.

Educators throughout the United States and **Canada** have adapted the fluid model of Project 10 to individual school and district needs. For example, in 1988, Cambridge Rindge and Latin photography teacher, Al Ferreira, founded Project 10 East after hearing Uribe speak at Harvard University. Its specific activities include education and outreach in classes, teacher training, field trips, participation in Gay Pride Parade, organizing the Coming Out Day assemblies, movies, group discussions, as well as just hanging out. In recent years, Project 10 East has developed into a nonprofit organization dedicated to creating and sustaining spaces in schools and communities where young people can experience mutual respect with a focus on personal excellence, regardless of **gender identity** or sexual orientation. The specific work of Project 10 East, Inc. includes helping schools develop and sustain **gay–straight alliances** (GSAs), providing support for GSA advisors, and helping Boston area communities hold successful forums on LGBTQ related issues.

An off-site program that builds on the Project 10 model is the Toronto Board of Education's Triangle Program. This is the first program in Canadian history designed for lesbian and gay youth who are at risk of dropping out of high school or who have already done so. It aims to create a "safe" environment in which LGBTQ **youth at-risk** of dropping out can receive instruction in the public system's core **curriculum** until they are able to reenter public schools. Similar to the Hetrick-Martin Institute's Harvey Milk School, the program's main goal is to reinstate students who left school because of homophobia and **heterosexism**, or to keep those students who are considering leaving from dropping out. Besides academic instruction, students attending this off-site alternative school receive **counseling** and support services not available in traditional settings.

Project 10 has received criticism from conservative religious organizations for being a "recruitment" program since from their vantage point homosexuality is a subject that should not be dealt with in school. Almost immediately after its inception, the Traditional Values Coalition and Sen. Jesse Helm's office attacked Project 10. After a day-long hearing in June 1988, at which the school board refused to disband the Project 10 program, threats from the California legislature failed to materialize.

Another criticism of the Project 10 model has been its lack of clarity regarding how homophobia and heterosexism intersect with **racism**, classism, and other forms of oppression that affect the school experiences of LGBTQ youth. Although from Project 10's inception, Uribe recognized that queer youth are a diverse group, it was unclear how the needs of LGBTQ youth of color, who may live within three strongly independent communities—their race/ethnic community, the mainstream, predominantly white LGBTQ community, and their school community—can be addressed within such programs. The de-normalization of whiteness by making a conscious effort to incorporate curriculum, speakers' bureaus, and workshop facilitators that reflect student racial and ethnic diversity is an important challenge for programs such as Project 10.

Bibliography

McCready, Lance. 2004. "Some Challenges Facing Queer Youth Programs in Urban High Schools: Racial Segregation and De-Normalizing Whiteness." *Journal of Gay and Lesbian Issues in Education* 1, no. 3: 37–51.

Uribe, Virginia. 1995. "Project 10: A School-Based Outreach to Gay and Lesbian Youth." Pp. 203–210 in *The Gay Teen*. Edited by Gerald Unks. New York: Routledge.

Uribe, Virginia, and Karen Harbeck. 1992. "Addressing the Needs of Lesbian, Gay, and Bisexual Youth: The Origins of Project 10 and School-Based Intervention. Pp. 9–28 in *Coming Out of the Classroom Closet*. Edited by Karen Harbeck. Binghamton, NY: Haworth Press.

Woog, Dan. 1995. *Schools Out:The Impact of Gay and Lesbian Issues on America's Schools*. Los Angeles: Alyson.

Web Sites

Project 10. Accessed June 10, 2005. "http://www.project10.org. Since 1984 the mission of Project 10 has been to provide education and support for LBGT youth in the Los Angeles Unified School District.

The Project 10 East GSA Handbook. Project 10 East, Inc. Accessed June 10, 2005. http://www.project10east.org. The Handbook includes a glossary of terms and a range of articles addressing questions of parents, teachers, counselors, and students.

Proms

Jeffery P. Dennis

Proms are formal dances held annually in North American high schools, colleges, and elsewhere to celebrate heterosexual romance. Since they also promote **compulsory heterosexuality, lesbian, gay, bisexual** and **transgender** (LGBT) youth are usually

See also Activism, LGBT Youth; Adolescent Sexualities; Dating; Discrimination; Educational Administration; Gender Roles; Heterosexism; Legal Issues, Students; School Climate, K-12; Social Class.

excluded or forced to lie about their sexual or **gender identity**. Recently, however, some have fought for the freedom to attend proms with same-sex dates, and others have established alternative proms for LGBT youth and their friends.

The custom originated in late nineteenth century "promenades" held during the commencement festivities in affluent, progressive high schools in the north-eastern United States. They emphasized the modern freedom for the sexes to intermingle socially and select future spouses, in contrast to the parental control of the **urban** poor, immigrants, and ethnic and religious minorities. However, the presumption that all romantic bonds must derive from heterosexual **desire** helped institutionalize compulsory heterosexuality and marginalize or erase LGBT youth.

During the twentieth century, proms became practically universal in high schools in the United States and **Canada** (but not in other countries), and not only for graduating seniors: Eventually separate proms were established for sophomores, juniors, **college students**, and middle school students. Today it is not uncommon for elementary schools to host proms, and even such nonscholastic venues as summer camps, **scouting** organizations, youth groups, and boys' and girls' clubs sometimes include heavily-promoted proms among their social events. Proms also became extremely complex affairs, requiring a full year of planning. They are nearly as costly as weddings, with each boy–girl couple investing thousands of dollars in prom tickets, a tuxedo, an evening gown, a hair stylist, flowers, gifts, a professional photographer, limousine rental, a preprom dinner, one or more postprom parties—and often a hotel suite.

The ball rooms swirling with boy–girl couples every April or May are not merely celebrations of the end of adolescence and the beginning of adulthood. They represent the culmination of years of careful indoctrination into compulsory heterosexuality on every level of the educational system, from classroom lectures to co**curricular activities** to the content of the school library. Repeatedly, overtly and covertly, students are told that intense, single-minded heterosexual desire is the universal teenage condition, that they and all of their peers, without exception, must devote themselves to the search for the heterosexual partner who will give their life meaning, until prom night when they will celebrate finding him or her. Thus, prom nights are traditional sites for marriage proposals and first heterosexual experiences. Most proms culminate with the crowning of a "king and queen," a boy and a girl, traditionally the champion athlete and head cheerleader, epitomes of stereotypic masculinity and femininity, who must then dance alone as a romantic couple, reenacting the myth of universal heterosexual destiny.

As Amy Best notes (2000), the hysterical importance placed on the prom in high schools across the United States and Canada excludes or marginalizes many types of students: the poor and working-class unable to afford prom night excess; ethnic minorities and interracial couples; Orthodox Jews and Evangelical Christians whose religious beliefs forbid dancing; students who are insufficiently athletic or popular to acquire favorable dates; and those students more focused on academics than heterosexual romance. However, LGBT students are by far the most emphatically excluded and the most severely marginalized, since every aspect of prom night and its year-long preparation ignores their existence. Refusing to attend the most important social event of their high school career can result in severe ostracization for those students who are already negotiating a heterosexist war zone. For many

LGBT youth, staying home is not an option. They must attend, and in a boy–girl pairing.

A history of queer investment in heterosexualized proms (Boyer 2004) reveals that, prior to the 1990s, most LGBT students were yet unaware of their sexuality by the time of prom night, and so they usually attended the prom as part of a boy–girl couple, often going through with the traditional sexual experience or marriage proposal. Those who were aware of their **sexual orientation**, often attended the prom with someone of the other gender (often a close friend), perhaps leaving their real romantic partner behind, or sometimes "double dating" with him or her, masquerading as two boy–girl couples.

Beginning in the 1970s, a student occasionally managed to sneak a same-sex date into a prom, often as a means of **coming out** to classmates, and likely for just a few minutes before being ejected. Official permission to break the boy–girl requirement came in 1980, when Cumberland, Rhode Island, high school senior Aaron Fricke sued to take his boyfriend to the prom. In a case that made national headlines, the victory gained Fricke entry into the prom, spurred him onto the talk show circuit, and resulted in a bestselling book, *Reflections of a Rock Lobster* (1981). Today many LGBT and straight students, with the support of their local **gay–straight alliances** and the American Civil Liberties Union, are challenging boy–girl couples-only policies and fighting for permission to attend proms alone or with same-sex partners. Usually the struggle must extend beyond local school boards and **administrators**, who are often hostile, homophobic, or simply unwilling to believe that LGBT students exist, to the courts. In 2002, Ontario high school senior Matthew Hays sued his principal and school board for $100,000 in damages and a court injunction to allow him to bring his boyfriend to the prom. These cases often have positive outcomes, but the subsequent prom nights under court order and sometimes police escort tend to be the equivalent of **African American** students integrating Southern schools in 1956, tense and dangerous rather than magical and romantic. According to a survey conducted by the **Gay Lesbian Straight Education Network** (GLSEN), less than half of high school students would feel comfortable attending their proms with same-sex dates. "How to Survive Senior Prom If You're Gay" offers sobering advice: Stay in lit and populated areas; inform as many adults as possible about your plans; hang around with other gay-friendly couples (Johnson 2004).

Nevertheless, more administrators are sympathetic to the inclusion of LGBT students and want to fight the heterosexual mandate of traditional prom nights. GLSEN offers several suggestions:

- Eliminate the "boy–girl couples only" rule so that students can attend with anyone they wish: with romantic partners of either sex, with friends, in groups, or alone.
- Eliminate the "boys in tuxedos, girls in evening gowns" rule so that students can attend the prom in any attire of their choice.
- Instead of naming a boy as "prom king" and a girl as "prom queen" and then pairing them as a romantic couple, elect several "kings" and "queens," with both categories open to students of any gender, or else make the awards nongender-specific, such as "best dressed."

Prom King and Queen, 2002, 7th Annual Pride Prom. Courtesy of Triangle Program, Toronto.

- Have students picking up their tickets or entering the prom sign a pledge to create a safe space for all students, regardless of sexual orientation, gender identity, or gender expression.
- Discuss with chaperones and staff the need to treat all students equally, regardless of their sexual orientation, gender identity, or gender expression.

For many LGBT youth, however, alternative proms have become a viable alternative. The first prom organized by and for LGBT youth was held in Boston, in 1981. Today alternative proms are held annually in approximately twenty cities in the United States and Canada. These are usually under the direction of a LGBT organization with sufficient resources to plan city-wide events, and open to all LGBT youth and their friends under the age of twenty-five, allowing those who missed their proms or were forced to pretend that they were heterosexual to experience a gay-friendly prom night. The practice of alternative proms raises cries of marginalization, but high schools proms remain forbidding and dangerous places for all but the luckiest of LGBT students.

Bibliography

Best, Amy L. 2000. *Prom Night: Youth, Schools, and Popular Culture*. New York: Routledge.
Boyer, David. 2004. *Kings and Queens: Queers at the Prom*. New York: Soft Skull Press.
Fricke, Aaron. 1981. *Reflections of a Rock Lobster: A Story about Growing Up Gay*. Boston: Alyson.
Johnson, Ramon. 2005. "How to Survive Senior Prom if You're Gay." Accessed June 7, 2005. http://gaylife.about.com/cs/comingout/ht/prom.htm.
Rotello, Gabriel. 2001. "Shall We Dance?" *The Advocate* no. 841: 72.

Web Site

Kings and Queens: Queers at the Prom. June 2004. David Boyer. Accessed June 10, 2005. http://www.gayprom.com. Offers photos, opportunities to read others' prom stories (dating back to the 1930s) and to add your own, as well as links and news.

Prostitution or Sex Work

Voon Chin Phua

The conventional understanding of trading homosexual services for money or other material gains emphasizes both the stigma of being **queer** and of engaging in sex work. **Lesbian, gay, bisexual,** and **transgender youth** sex work touches on three

See also Agency; Sexual Health, Lesbian and Bisexual Women; Sexual Health, Gay and Bisexual Men; Workplace Issues; Youth, At Risk; Youth, Homeless.

legal issues: homosexuality, sex work, and the age of consent, which varies by country and sometimes within a country. Moral and religious views help to shape these legal issues and the level of tolerance. As such, the politics of LGBT youth sex work as a social concern ranges from effort to save the youth from the sex trade and interests in exploring the relationship between sex work and homosexuality, to attempts at understanding the lives of sex workers and commitment to finding ways to empower sex workers in negotiating a safe work environment.

The legal status of homosexuality varies greatly from one society to another. For example, although homosexual sexual activities are legal in all Scandinavian countries, the same acts can be punishable by death, imprisonment, or fines in most Middle Eastern countries. Similarly, sex work is legal only in some countries, such as in **Canada**, the Netherlands, **Australia**, and **Israel**. In other countries, sex work is tolerated, even though technically it is illegal. Within the United States, sex work is illegal in most states, excepting certain counties in Nevada. Reflecting **heterosexism**, the legal age of sexual consent is often stated only for heterosexuals or is higher for same-sex partners. A fundamental issue is the age at which a person develops the decision-making ability to choose the types of life style, work, and or sexual activity they desire. Historically and at present, some advocate groups have argued against the arbitrary age designation for adulthood and for the rights of youth, including sexual rights, as well as the decriminalization of prostitution (Weitzer 2000). Other groups, including some feminists, have underscored the inherent power relationships involved in sexual relationships between adults and youth or those involving the sex trade.

Given the distinction between the concept of **sexual identity** and engaging in homosexual behavior (West 1993), some sex workers are gay-identified while many identify themselves as heterosexual or bisexual, such as how the majority of Thai male sex workers define themselves (Storer 1999). The gender and sexual identities of sex workers can also be situational, as they adopt a sexual label because of its marketability. For example, some customers seeking same-sex relations might feel safer employing gay-identified sex workers, others **desire** those who identify as straight male, and some prefer men who are transgender or transvestite. The term "gay-for-pay," describing heterosexual-identified male sex workers willing to engage in same-sex sex activities, denotes the critical difference between sexual identity and sexual behavior in the sex trade.

Studies on homosexual prostitution focus on male sex workers (Shaver 2004). The reasons for this are two-fold, and both reflect heterosexist assumptions. First, lesbian or bisexual female sex workers, even if identified, are typically included in heterosexual sex **research** with a focus on the sexual behavior and the male client rather than on sexual identity and the female sex worker. Second, female clients' demands for female sex workers, or even until recently for male sex workers, are considered implausible because of traditional conceptions of female sexuality. Those few studies mentioning lesbian prostitution generally have other foci such as sexual activities among adolescent women (Saewyc et al. 1999). The award winning **film**, *Monster* (2003), tells the story of lesbian prostitute killer Aileen Wournos, reinforcing the negative **stereotypes** of lesbianism and prostitution.

A hierarchy exists among male same-sex workers (Marino, Minichiello, and Disogra 2003). Free-lance street hustlers are on the lowest stratum while high-paid independent callboys and kept boys are at the pinnacle. Those who work for an agency or at bars known to house them fall in between. **Race, social class**, physical appearance, age, and citizenship are factors that determine their point of entry into the sex trade. The latter affects whether they can work for legitimate escort agencies or avail themselves in bars. Street workers are generally the least educated, younger, and with fewer resources, whereas independent callboys generally have more resources to better maintain their appearance and marketability. In reality, these categories need not be mutually exclusive. An independent sex worker may show up at a known hustler bar every now and then. Similarly, a street sex worker may occasionally work for an agency and be on call if he has the right connections.

Another way to categorize sex workers is the image they portray: college boy; rough trade; club kid; muscleman; ethnic type; drag queen. This typology is closely based on access because locations such as bars or "cruising areas" are generally dominated by one image type. Further, the types of sexual behavior in which a worker is willing to engage also intersects with these typologies, ranging from those who are more dominant to those who are submissive.

The **Internet** has made these boundaries more amorphous while further globalizing the sex trade industry. Escort agencies and independent sex workers have customized home pages and are a ubiquitous presence in chat rooms. For example, rentboy.com lists independent sex workers and escort agencies available by city, nation, or worldwide, with cities ranging from São Paulo and Berlin to Kuala Lumpur and Kampala. Internet access breaks spatial boundaries as clients can hire a sex worker through the Internet without leaving the comfort of their home.

Sex workers and their clients' increased mobility, the existence and increased presence of sex tourism as well as advanced in communication technologies have placed LGBT sex work in a global position. Altman (2001) notes that the media references international centers for prostitution such as in cities like Bangkok, Tokyo, Rio de Janeiro, Dubai, and Istanbul. To circumvent some legal issues involving LGBT sex work and often to take advantage of currency exchange rates and differences in economies, clients in countries where prostitution or homosexuality is illegal can travel to another country to indulge themselves.

LGBT youth sex work is generally explained as a survival tactic (Coleman 1989). These researchers argue that LGBT youth sex workers tend to come from abusive families or unwelcoming homes leading them to the streets. Independent yet lacking the appropriate education and skills, these youth turn to sex work and enter a world of exploitation where the realities of street life make exiting difficult. Some **community LGBT support groups**, such as the Larkin Street Shelter in San Francisco, target these youth to help them off the street.

Focusing on those facing difficulties might facilitate the development of better outreach programs but does not provide a complete picture of LBGT youth sex workers. Other researchers posit that the surviving-on-the-streets argument insufficiently explains why some youth *choose* this type of work and remain in this activity (Schifter and Aggleton 1999). Sex work is a viable source of income and professional work for some LGBT youth who reject "legitimate work," lack the skills to secure it, or dislike low wages associated with such jobs. The need for protection, excitement and adventure, easy access to sex partners, and self-validation are other possible motivations to participate in the trade.

While sex work has its attractions, it is also laden with risks (Calhoun and Weaver 1996). The legal status of sex work partly determines the level of police involvement in this trade. Other fears include public exposure (embarrassing family members or friends) and potential violence from the police, clients, fellow sex workers as well as street vigilantes. Further, some sex workers develop a negative self-image associated with the stigma of being a sex worker or feeling trapped in the trade. Researchers have also found a relationship between sex work and **drug use** and **substance abuse** as some sex workers enter the trade to make money for drugs while others become addicted through socializing with peers or as an escape from other troubles (Boles and Elifson 1994).

Another important risk confronting sex workers is contracting sexually-transmitted infections. The relationship between sex workers and AIDS/HIV in different countries is particularly critical as patterns of global movement, particularly sex tourism, partially mark the epidemiological history of **AIDS** (Aggleton 1999). While some people travel to foreign countries for sex, others benefit from immigration to supply potential sex workers. For example, in Germany and **France**, the influx of Eastern European refugees has created a new source of sex workers. However, sex work is not, in itself, a major source of spreading the infection. In fact, in those countries where the sex industry is regulated, such as the Netherlands, practicing safer sex and educating clients is a major factor in reducing the spread of HIV and other infections.

The length of time LBGT youth sex workers stay in the trade varies. Some LGBT youth may treat their involvement as temporary to help them through a difficult financial period, to purchase a particular consumer product, or to engage in work only in those situations where an attractive person makes a proposition. Others may view this work as a career, joining an official sex workers' union such found in New South Wales (Kempadoo 1998). For these youth who view sex work as a profession, their image changes through aging from being a boy-type to being a muscle daddy type. In a study of travesties and gigolos in France, for instance, Laurindo da Silva (1999) posits that transvestites' work life expectancy may last until age forty-five or older but gigolos' working careers end in the early thirties.

Bibliography

Aggleton, Peter, ed. 1999. *Men Who Sell Sex: International Perspectives on Male Prostitution and HIV/AIDS*. Philadelphia: Temple University Press.

Altman, Dennis. 2001. *Global Sex*. Chicago: The University of Chicago Press.

Boles, Jacqueline, and Kirk W. Elifson. 1994. "Sexual Identity and HIV: The Male Prostitute." *The Journal of Sex Research* 31, no. 1: 39–46.

Calhoun, Thomas C., and Greg Weaver. 1996. "Rational Decision-Making among Male Street Sex Workers." *Deviant Behavior* 17: 209–227.

Coleman, Eli. 1989. "The Development of Male Sex Work Activity among Gay and Bisexual Adolescents." *Journal of Homosexuality* 17, no. 1/2: 131–149.

Kempadoo, Kamala. 1998. "Globalizing Sex Workers' Rights." Pp. 1–33 in *Global Sex Workers: Rights, Resistance and Redefinition*. Edited by Kamala Kempadoo and Jo Doezema. New York: Routledge.

Laurindo da Silva, Lindinalva. 1999. "Travesti and Gigolos: Male Sex Work and HIV Prevention in France." Pp. 41–60 in *Men Who Sell Sex: International Perspectives on Male Prostitution and HIV/AIDS*. Edited by Peter Aggleton. Philadelphia: Temple University Press.

Marino, Rodrigo, Victor Minichiello, and Carlos Disogra. 2003. "Male Sex Workers in Cordoba, Argentina: Sociodemographic Characteristics and Sex Work Experiences." *Pan American Journal of Public Health* 13, no. 5: 311–319.

Saewyc, Elizabeth M., Linda H. Bearinger, Robert W. Blum, and Michael D. Resnick. 1999. "Sexual Intercourse, Abuse and Pregnancy among Adolescent Women: Does Sexual Orientation Make a Difference?" *Family Planning Perspectives* 31, no. 3: 127–131.

Savin-Williams, Ritch C. 2001. "A Critique of Research on Sexual-Minority Youths." *Journal of Adolescence* 24, no. 1: 5–13.

Schifter, Jacobo, and Peter Aggleton. 1999. "Cacherismo in a San Jose Brothel–Aspects of Male Sex Work in Costa Rica." Pp. 141–158 in *Men Who Sell Sex: International Perspectives on Male Prostitution and HIV/AIDS*. Edited by Peter Aggleton. Philadelphia: Temple University Press.

Shaver, Frances M. 2004. "Prostitution." *The Canadian Encyclopedia*. Historica Foundation of Canada: Canada. Accessed December 8, 2004. http://www.canadianencyclopedia.ca.

Storer, Graeme. 1999. "Bar Talk: Thai Male Sex Workers and Their Customers." Pp. 223–240 in *Men Who Sell Sex: International Perspectives on Male Prostitution and HIV/AIDS*. Edited by Peter Aggleton. Philadelphia: Temple University Press.

Weizter, Ronald. 2000. "The Politics of Prostitution in America." Pp. 159–180 in *Sex for Sale: Prostitution, Pornography and the Sex Industry*. Edited by Ronald Weitzer. New York: Routledge.

West, Donald J., with Buz de Villiers. 1993. *Male Prostitution*. Binghamton, NY: Harrington Park Press.

Psychoanalysis and Education

Deborah P. Britzman

It is difficult to separate the history of psychoanalysis from the events of education. This is because **childhood** and so education figure prominently in psychoanalysis and, like education, psychoanalysis is interested in the question of learning and not learning. Yet over the course of history in psychoanalysis, **Sigmund Freud** desired to separate the two fields by reasoning that education is didactic, and its processes have an end goal and desired outcomes, whereas the only ethic in psychoanalysis is free association, allowing anything to come to mind for analysis. There is no other goal except that of risking love and work. Another distinction is the prevalent idea that education induces neurosis and discontentment, and psychoanalysis repairs the harm done under the name of education. This lead Freud to name psychoanalysis an "after-education," and argued teachers would significantly benefit from learning about psychoanalysis and undergoing a personal analysis. This personal analysis would entail an exploration of the teacher's sexuality and its relation to pedagogy as both content and dynamic.

However, much as Freud tried to separate these fields, more than once, and for good reasons, he named education as one of the three impossible professions (the other two were governance and medicine). The problems of practice are interminable. Like psychoanalysis, education begins in attempts to influence others, change minds and attitudes, affect behavior and social relations, and help others learn from conflict, suffering, mistakes, hubris, projections, and fantasy life. Significant learning is utterly arduous and slow and subject to undoing and reversals into its opposite. Although learning and refusing to learn go hand-in-hand, humans are not caused by education, though they are susceptible to others and to feelings of helplessness and loss when others do not follow along.

See also Desire; Professionalism; Psychoanalysis and Feminism.

Child analyst Alice Balint noticed another side: education begins too early, before it can depend upon understanding. This leads to the second way in which education becomes an impossible profession. If it cannot depend upon understanding, education must depend upon love. Psychoanalysts view dynamics of love as both the obstacle and as the lynchpin of education. Because educators must depend upon addressing the student's capacity to love both the educator and the education, they must also be prepared for the student's hatred. Otto Fenichel (1954) reduced this battle of persuasion in education to three methods parents' utilize with children: "direct threat, mobilization of the fear of losing love, and the promise of special rewards" (327). This power struggle is also doomed because the educator also must cultivate and address, before it is established, the student's autonomy, independence, and capacity for concern. In more contemporary terms, Adam Phillips' writing addresses the creative refusals made from adult/child conflicts.

When Freud thought about these problems of influence and the ways teachers and analysts depend upon love as the persuasive means for education, he developed the concept of "the transference" to describe how love and admiration for one's parents along with the history of one's emotional responses is transferred onto teachers—new authority figures. From the vantage of the unconscious, it is easy to mistake parents and teachers. Transferred as well are the conflicts with authority. Much later, the libidinal relations between students and teachers would be expressed by Rudolf Ekstein, a psychoanalytic educator, as the conflict made when education tries to encourage the student to move from learning for love, and so pleasing the teacher, to the autonomous position of love of learning, where independence in thinking one's own thoughts structure one's learning practices. Given the role of love in education that psychoanalysis stresses, educators are indeed confronted, not just with students' projections and fantasies of the teacher's self, but with their own fantasies and conflicts about the teacher. Thus, what is impossible is not so much that we learn, but that we make insight into the ways authority and love are encountered along the way to knowledge.

Freud was primarily interested in the question of learning relations, particularly the ways in which adult analysands (patients) repeat the history of their childhood conflicts in the presence of the analyst (and this repetition also includes one's history of learning in compulsory education). Psychoanalysis has offered education important critiques on its methods and institutional arrangements as well as contributed to central learning theories and understanding of the relation between thinking and sexuality.

Psychoanalytic theory also inspired diverse schools such as Anna Freud and August Aichhorn's (1878–1951) after-school programs in Vienna in the 1930s and Anna Freud's Wartime Nursery in London in 1940–1950, Bruno Bettelheim's (1903–1990) Chicago's Orthogenic School in 1950s–1970s, Frieda Fromm-Rieichmann's (1889–1957) Chestnut Lodge in Maryland in the 1940s–1960s, and from the 1960s to the present, A.S. Neil's Summerhill School in the **United Kingdom** and Maud Mannoi's school at Bonneuil in **France**. These special schools, many of which were residential, mixed art, theater, and psychotherapy with pedagogical innovation. They addressed emotional distress in humane ways and offered nonauthoritarian, student-centered education. Anna Freud's work in London illustrates the importance of nonjudgmental acceptance of children's sexual researches. Some schools took an analytic position on their own organization, attending to the school's own group psychology, to how the child and teacher are represented in the school's fantasy, and to the clinical supervision of teachers and administrators.

University teaching and scholarship on pedagogy in most academic disciplines and in interdisciplinary study is influenced by psychoanalytic theory. For example, Shoshana Felman's work on **Jacques Lacan** analyzed learning and the transference, Jeffrey Berman teaches psychoanalytic methods in university writing, Stephen Appel analyzes pathological aspects of educational sociology, Eve Kosofsky Sedgwick analyzes **queer theory**'s paranoid and reparative reading practices from the vantage of Melanie Klein, Jacqueline Rose analyzes the relation between knowledge and aggression with the question, "Why War,?" and Deborah Britzman analyzes controversies in education and psychoanalysis.

Bibliography

Appel, Stephen, ed. 1999. *Psychoanalysis and Pedagogy*. Westport, CT: Bergin and Garvey.

Balint, Alice. 1954. *The Early Years of Life: A Psychoanalytic Study*. New York: Basic Books.

Berman, Jeffrey. 1994. *Diaries to an English Professor: Pain and Growth in the Classroom*. Amherst: University of Massachusetts Press.

Britzman, Deborah P. 1998. *Lost Subjects, Contested Objects: Toward a Psychoanalytic Inquiry of Learning*. Albany: State University of New York Press.

———. 2003. *After-Education: Anna Freud, Melanie Klein and Psychoanalytic Histories of Learning*. Albany: State University of New York.

Felman, Shoshana. 1987. *Jacque Lacan and the Adventures of Insight: Psychoanalysis in Contemporary Culture*. Cambridge, MA: Harvard University Press.

Fenichel, Hanna, and David Rapaport. 1954. "The Means of Education" Pp. 324–334 in *The Collected Papers of Otto Fenichel*, Second Series. New York: Norton.

Freud, Anna. 1992. *The Harvard Lectures*. Edited and annotated by Joseph Sandler. Madison, CT: International Universities Press.

Phillips, Adam. 1993. *On Kissing, Tickling and Being Bored: Psychoanalytic Essays on the Unexamined Life*. Cambridge, MA: Harvard University Press.

Sedgwick, Eve Kosofsky. 1990. *Epistemology of the Closet*. Berkeley: University of California Press.

Psychoanalysis and Feminism

Alice J. Pitt

Feminism and psychoanalysis pose questions about the origins of **gender identity**, sexuality, and the difficulties of relations between men and women. Both struggle with the significance of **biology** and the body for the biography of individuals and for culture. For much of their history, psychoanalysis and feminism have been suspicious of each other. Still they share another feature that has recently permitted fruitful dialogue: both meet up with resistance to their ideas and practices. **Sigmund Freud** was surprised to discover that his patients, many of them women, had no wish to believe his interpretations of their dreams and symptoms. They resisted his efforts to relieve their suffering, which he frequently attributed to the confusing pressures of sexual **desire**. Feminism, for its part, identifies the unequal power relations between men and women as responsible for women's unhappiness. It, too, meets resistance to its political

See also Heteronormativity; Lacan, Jacques; Lesbian Feminism; Poststructuralism; Psychoanalysis and Education; Queer and Queer Theory; Women's Movement; Women's Studies.

demands for women's social equality and freedom, choosing lives not centered on the needs of men and children. The resistance of Freud's patients makes perfect sense to many feminists who see it as form of "feminine protest" against patriarchal power. Recent work in feminist theory, however, turns to psychoanalysis in an effort to explore women's resistance, conscious and unconscious, to becoming ideal feminist subjects. For both feminism and psychoanalysis, definitive answers to our questions about what constitutes gender/**sexual identity** remain elusive. The experiences of queer youth, when viewed from feminist psychoanalytic perspectives, challenge heteronormative assumptions about all of our sexual identities.

Freud is often critiqued for privileging biology as the great determinant of gender and sexuality. However, his interest in the psychical obstacles to "normal" development suggests that biology may count for very little when it comes to achieving a gender/sexual identity. Beginning with a view of innate **bisexuality**, Freud argued that normal male and female sexuality (by which he meant both gender identity and heterosexual object choice) developed in the same way. By taking the boy's development as his model for both sexes, one blind spot is revealed. Another one of particular interest to **LGBT studies** is Freud's insistence on equating *normal* gender development with both biological sex and heterosexual object choice—that is, a male body is to become a man who desires a woman. However, he refused to condemn or subject to treatment those individuals who did not arrive at heterosexuality. On this count, Freud was socially liberal but theoretically conservative.

Freud gradually replaced this view of girls' development with one that describes the specificity of female sexuality. In this version, the little girl must successfully navigate more "turns" along the road to heterosexual femininity than previously believed. First, the girl wishes for a penis. She then becomes dissatisfied with her mother for her own lack of the desired organ and for failing to provide one for her daughter. Finally, in frustration, the little girl turns to her father hoping that he might satisfy her wish for a penis or its substitute, a baby. Freud suspected that feminists would not welcome the news of this theoretical development. He even suggested that feminists would come to critique "penis envy" as an effect of "the 'masculinity complex' of the male . . . designed to justify on theoretical grounds his innate inclination to disparage and suppress women" (1931, 230 n. 1). Freud's female psychoanalytic contemporaries did make some critical interventions even if they did not identify themselves as feminists.

Helene Deutsch (1884–1982), while never straying far from this model, rejected "penis envy," but fell back upon biological explanations for women's passivity and masochism. Karen Horney (1885–1952) strayed further from Freud and also took up the response to his theory that Freud attributed to women. She suggested that it was masculine narcissism that pronounced the female genital as inferior, not women's experience of their bodies. Moreover, if envy were involved, it was masculine envy of women's reproductive capacity. Horney also disputed Freud's assumption that pleasures associated with the clitoris and vagina were inferior to those the penis enjoyed. In her clinical work, she identified social forces at play in women's psychological distress.

Melanie Klein (1882–1960), while insisting upon the specificity of female sexuality, did emphasize innate aspects of sexuality. However, she also explored women's sexual, aggressive, and destructive drives that undermine popular notions of women as naturally caring and self-sacrificing. Klein's emphasis on early infant life and mother/child relations formed the basis for the first avowedly feminist reconception of psychoanalysis. Dorothy Dinnerstein and Nancy Chodorow argued that limiting childrearing to mothers and limiting mothers to childrearing play a large part in perpetuating social inequality between men and women.

The developments within psychoanalysis that contested Freud's tendency to think of women as "the second sex" (de Beauvoir) did little to fend off a wave of feminist critique of psychoanalysis as mired in biological determinism, implicated in upholding a social order oppressive to women, and committed to views of women as both inferior to men and envious of male superiority. This hostility can still be felt today, but a feminist counter movement has also successfully forged new ties with psychoanalytic thought that is capable of revising itself in response to feminist critique. In 1974, Juliet Mitchell, a feminist Marxist, published *Psychoanalysis and Women*. She argued that Freud's views were not prescriptive of what a woman could or should be but that he had developed a theory to account for how women are constructed in a patriarchal society. This reading of Freud gestured toward psychoanalysis as useful to the dismantling of patriarchy. It gained legitimacy, in part, because of Mitchell's credibility within feminism. But it was also because a French psychoanalyst, **Jacques Lacan** (1901–1981), offered a rereading of Freud that also permitted a view of the subject as socially constructed and, hence, as capable of transforming both the self and the social conditions, values, institutional structures, and representational practices that combine to reproduce a sexist, racist, and homophobic society.

Lacan is often thought to have made the most decisive moves away from biological determinism and has, therefore, become the focus of much feminist attention. For this theorist, both sexes come into being by virtue of having given up a state of fusion with the mother's body and then assuming a position within the network of language, laws, and meaning-making systems available to us. Identity itself, both male and female, is an effect of an illusion of wholeness, but masculine and feminine positions within language are not symmetrical. Masculinity is structured by a fantasy of taking possession of the Phallus (a reference to masculinity as a governing social construct, not to be equated with the penis but also difficult to separate from it). In contrast, the feminine has no such reference with which to identify and thus threatens to subvert the social order. The subject of Lacanian theory is made in relation to a system of social structures, not biology. This is important for feminism because of its interest in challenging social structures.

For Luce Iragaray, however, neither Freud nor Lacan has produced a theory able to contemplate the debt we owe to the mother. Both theories remain, in her view, problematically devoted to the Law of the Father. **Judith Butler**, whose political philosophy is familiar to feminism and gay and lesbian studies, finds psychoanalytic theory a useful tool for considering the price we must pay for assuming a singular gender and sexuality. She argues that such singularity is achieved at the cost of repudiating the identity position not occupied, a repudiation that lends itself to social hatred of homosexuality. Yet, she also contends that identity does have the potential to assume a position in a manner less preoccupied with boundary maintenance.

These developments encourage readings of Freud that locate his ideas within his social and historical context, while also identifying aspects of his thought that break from theories of gender and sexuality rooted in biology. They have also provided the grounds for imagining and representing LGBT identities in new, creative and complex ways in all cultural arenas, including the classroom. Many contemporary psychoanalysts identify as feminist, and, while these theorists take an eclectic and nondogmatic approach to their work, incorporating and critiquing Freud,

Lacan, and others, they also call into question the dominant views of gender and sexuality as fully explained by theories of social constructions. However, rather than return to biology, writers such as Nancy Chodorow, Jane Flax, and Jessica Benjamin explore the ways in which we experience our gender/sex identities as imbued by personal psychical and social meanings. Chodorow, for example, argues that, "categories of gender and self are created both culturally, in historicized, socially specific contexts, and at the same time biographically," (1999, 65). For instance, one can adopt the category "lesbian" as a political and/or as a sexual identity. There is resistance to both psychoanalysis and feminism, but dialogues between them suggests the productivity of considering the resistance in all of us to totalizing theories to explain who we are, what we want, and who we love.

Bibliography

Buhle, Mary Jo. 1998. *Feminism and its Discontents: A Century of Struggle with Psychoanalysis*. Cambridge, Massachusetts and London: Harvard University Press.

Butler, Judith. 1993. *Bodies That Matter: On the Discursive Limits of Sex*. New York: Routledge.

Chodorow, Nancy. 1999. *The Power of Feelings*. New Haven and London: Yale University Press.

Freud, Sigmund. 1931. "Female Sexuality." Pp. 225–243 in Vol. 21 *The Standard Edition of the Complete Psychological Works of Sigmund Freud*. Edited and translated by James Strachey in collaboration with Anna Freud. Assisted by Alix Strachey and Alan Tyson. London: Hogarth Press and the Institute for Psychoanalysis.

Mitchell, Juliet. 1974. *Psychoanalysis and Feminism: Freud, Reich, Laing and Women*. New York: Vintage Books.

Pitt, Alice. 2003. *The Play of the Personal: Psychoanalytic Narratives of Feminist Education*. New York: Peter Lang.

Wright, Elizabeth, ed. 1992. *Feminism and Psychoanalysis: A Critical Dictionary*. Oxford and Cambridge, Massachusetts: Basil Blackwell.

Psychology, Teaching of

Bryan N. Cochran and *K. Michelle Peavy*

Teaching courses on human psychology (the scientific study of behavior) may incorporate LGBT-relevant topics such as psychological adjustment and **resiliency**, LGBT **identity development**, promotion of **research** into psychological issues as they pertain to LGBT individuals, specialized courses on understanding the experiences of LGBT individuals, education about LGBT relationships (romantic, parenting, and friendships) or diversity training with regard to **sexual orientation**. From an historical perspective, psychologists have shifted over time from initially viewing LGBT identities as illnesses in need of treatment to currently conceptualizing LGBT identities as normal variants of the human experience. The teaching of psychology, at least ideally, reflects this shift as well. It is not enough, however, to merely incorporate LGBT perspectives into the psychology classroom as one would with any other "new" topic in the field. Providing research-based information about LGBT identities greatly enhances the understanding of this issue. For example, learning

See also Antibias Curriculum; Heteronormativity; LGBT Studies; Psychoanalysis and Education.

about how the aftermath of a hate crime has affected a **transgender youth** can make LGBT issues more salient to students. Examining the stigma and pervasive **stereotypes** that exist in our society is another effective way to explore psychological aspects of LGBT experiences. Students of psychology may, therefore, benefit from inclusion of LGBT perspectives and training in the psychology of **prejudice** and **discrimination**. Due to the popularity of psychology as both an undergraduate major and, increasingly, as a topic studied in secondary schools, including LGBT content in the teaching of psychology has the potential to inform millions of students annually about the challenges and experiences of LGBT individuals. In turn, students of psychology may learn to be more understanding about LGBT issues, and the topics of sexual orientation and **gender identity** will be further legitimized as research topics in the field.

Addressing the history of psychologists' views on sexual orientation is a daunting but necessary task for those who teach psychology. At the start of the discipline's inception, in the late nineteenth century, homosexuality (**bisexuality** and transgender identity were rarely discussed) was viewed as a medical illness in need of treatment. Since this early perspective, much has been made of how different researchers, clinicians, and psychology instructors have viewed homosexuality. **Freud** (1951, 787), for example, wrote the following in a 1935 letter to an American mother, whose son he surmised to be gay:

> Homosexuality is assuredly no advantage, but it is nothing to be ashamed of, no vice, no degradation, it cannot be classified as an illness; we consider it to be a variation of the sexual function, produced by a certain arrest of sexual development . . . It is a great injustice to persecute homosexuality as a crime—and a cruelty, too.

While maintaining this relatively compassionate view of homosexuality for his time, Freud still theorized that gay men experienced a more infantile and underdeveloped sexuality than heterosexuals. Additionally, Freud's negative views of women and his emphasis on male sexuality at the expense of female sexuality (notable in such concepts as "penis envy") make it unlikely that his concept of sexualities would extend favorably to lesbians or transgender individuals.

Alfred Kinsey's (1948; 1953) revolutionary studies of human sexual behavior bear mention here. Although not a psychologist, Kinsey provided the first data indicating that sexual orientation falls on a continuum from exclusively homosexual to exclusively heterosexual. Whereas Kinsey's methods and conclusions have been the subject of much debate, his theories have stood the test of time and continue to be discussed in many introductory psychology textbooks. Kinsey's research influenced psychologists such as Evelyn Hooker (1957), who studied patterns of gay and heterosexual males' responses to psychological tests. She asked experts to select which responses were those of homosexuals, based solely on the test results. The experts' ratings of the gay men's results were indistinguishable from those of heterosexual men, thus indicating that homosexuals were as psychologically well-adjusted as heterosexuals. These results were subsequently replicated, giving further credence to a new conceptualization of homosexuality in psychology as evidence slowly accumulated that being gay or lesbian was not a mental illness.

The work of Hooker and Kinsey propelled the field forward, but the 1950s also brought a new perspective to the forefront of psychology: behaviorism.

The application of principles of learning to shape behavior was in many ways a setback in the history of psychology and sexual orientation. From a behaviorist perspective, any human behavior, such as eating or socializing, could be strengthened or extinguished through principles of reinforcement. In a misguided application of behaviorist principles, some behaviorally-oriented researchers during the 1960s and 1970s employed techniques such as "aversive therapy" in a flawed attempt to change the sexual behavior of **gay** and **lesbian youth** or adults. Such "therapy" might involve pairing images of same-sex attraction with an aversive stimulus, such as a nausea-inducing drug. Currently, all major **mental health** associations denounce "**reparative therapy**" as unethical and counter to the medical principle of "do no harm."

The 1960s, however, also brought about human-affirmative ideas into the discipline of psychology. Namely, Carl Rogers, Abraham Maslow, and others developed a system of humanistic psychology, which focused on self-actualization, health, creativity, intrinsic nature, being, becoming, individuality, and meaning. Although these humanists did not directly address issues of sexuality, their work gave rise to a more accepting science that draws upon the experiences of the individual rather than emphasizing mental illness.

Only a few decades have passed since homosexuality was removed from the list of mental illnesses most widely used by psychologists, the *Diagnostic and Statistical Manual of Mental Disorders*. Since 1973, the number of articles studying LGBT issues in the psychological literature has risen exponentially. Current students of psychology may access a wealth of information to help them understand LGBT perspectives. The likelihood of students being exposed to this information in the classroom, however, depends on the competency of the instructor.

As a subject of study, psychology is linked to the social service and mental health professions, tending to capture students aspiring to this line of work. Because these career options are common among students in U.S. universities, and because psychology subject matter is inherently interesting, psychology is the second most popular undergraduate major. It is estimated that 1.4 million students took an introductory psychology course during each year in the 1990s (Kennesaw State University Department of Psychology 2000). Therefore, teachers of psychology have a unique opportunity to reach a large audience and to provide a knowledge base regarding LGBT issues for future social workers, educators, and mental health clinicians (to name only a few careers).

Those instructors, however, who rely on textbooks for students' content knowledge are unlikely to find suitable coverage in this area. A textual analysis by Simoni (2000) revealed that LGBT content in over half of twenty-four psychology textbooks (introductory, abnormal, social, and developmental) was "poor." Three textbooks had no index citations for sexual orientation; others restricted content related to lesbians and gay men to sections on sexuality. Textbooks with better incorporation of LGBT identities portrayed, for example, a photo of two **Latina** women kissing in a section on kissing as an acquired taste, or statistics on LGB individuals in a chapter discussing diversity in the United States. There, too, are specific texts appropriate for use at the college (Garnets and Kimmel 1993; Patterson and D'Augelli 1998; 2001) and secondary (Bass and Kaufman 1996; Bauer 1994) levels.

When psychology teachers do discuss sexual orientation, the focus is almost always on homosexual sex as a behavior, as opposed to the components of romantic or affectional attraction that also comprise LGB identities, even though these topics necessarily fall under the psychology rubric. Transgender issues receive even less attention; rarely are students taught the distinction between biological sex and socially-ascribed gender. This focus on sexual behavior at the expense of identity issues often shifts discussion toward the topic of what *causes* homosexuality, or why one might choose to homosexual activity over "normal" sex. Although we do know some likely biological determinants of homosexuality (among gay men, in particular), discussion of this topic area is inherently pathologizing: If we discover what might cause a person to be a certain way, a cure for such a condition may be found. This discussion also frequently omits an important parallel question of what causes heterosexuality. Thus, psychology instructors benefit their students most when they go beyond issues of a cause and promote discussion of other topics related to sexual identity and orientation, such as how one copes with being part of a stigmatized group, or issues that LGBT individuals face in coming out to their families of origin.

Some pioneering educators in the field of psychology have proposed methods to explicitly bring LGBT issues into the classroom. In one experiential spaceship exercise, students are asked to pretend that they have landed on another planet where homosexual behavior is the norm and heterosexual behavior is punished by law or by public humiliation. Students discuss how they might adapt to such a situation. Preliminary data suggested that those who participated in this exercise showed more positive attitudes toward gays and lesbians (Hillman and Martin 2002).

Entire courses on the psychology of sexual orientation have been conducted on some university campuses. One proposed format of such a course covers topics from identity development and LGB individuals across the lifespan to stigma management and **coming out** (Bohan 1997). While the question about what "causes" homosexuality was addressed, this was followed by a discussion on "why we care." The latter allowed students to consider deviance as a social construct. Evaluations of this pilot course indicated that heterosexual students appreciated these topics being discussed in an academic setting; they also commented that they felt better able to address LGB issues in many aspects of their lives after completing this course. Also, the class allowed LGB students to better understand their experiences and to integrate their sexual identities into overall life experiences. The likelihood of such courses being accepted into the psychology **curriculum** depends on a university's general encouragement of diversity as well as the presence of out LGBT faculty (Liddle et al. 1998).

At present, LGBT-specific courses are likely to reach a minority of students, mostly at the graduate level. The integration of such content, however, is especially important in lower level survey courses as these educate a general **college age student** population, which typically is not exposed to LGBT issues in an academic setting. Major shifts in the presentation of LGBT issues within large classes such as introduction to psychology courses (at the undergraduate level, but also within high schools) require personal as well as institutional commitment. Before these shifts can occur or prior to embarking on course changes, psychology instructors must first challenge their heterosexist assumptions about the world and the material they teach. "Why am I using an example of a male–female couple to demonstrate how similarity leads to liking?" or "Why does a scale of significant life events include 'death of a spouse' or 'marital separation' but not 'coming out'?" help to overcome the "heterosexual default."

Bibliography

American Psychiatric Association. 1973. *Diagnostic and Statistical Manual of Mental Disorders.* 2nd ed. Washington: Author.

Bohan, Janis S. 1997. "Teaching on the Edge: The Psychology of Sexual Orientation." *Teaching of Psychology* 24: 27–32.

Bohan, Janis S., and Glenda M. Russell. 1999. *Conversations about Psychology and Sexual Orientation.* New York: New York University Press.

Bass, Ellen, and Kate Kaufman. 1996. *Free Your Mind: The Book for Gay, Lesbian, and Bisexual Youth – and Their Allies.* . New York: HarperCollins.

Bauer, Marion Dane, ed. 1994. *Am I Blue?: Coming Out from the Silence.* New York: HarperCollins.

Freud, Sigmund. 1951. "A Letter from Freud." *American Journal of Psychiatry* 107: 786–787.

Garnets, Linda D., and Douglas C. Kimmel, eds. 1993. *Psychological Perspectives on Lesbian and Gay Male Experiences.* New York: Columbia University Press.

Haldeman, Douglas. 1994. "The Practice and Ethics of Sexual Orientation Conversion Therapy." *Journal of Consulting and Clinical Psychology* 62: 221–227.

Hillman, Jennifer, and Renee A. Martin. 2002. "Lessons about Gay and Lesbian Lives: A Spaceship Exercise." *Teaching of Psychology* 29: 308–311.

Hooker, Evelyn. 1957. "The Adjustment of the Male Overt Homosexual." *Journal of Projective Techniques* 21: 18–31.

Kennesaw State University, Department of Psychology. 2000, September. Accessed June 10, 2005. http://www.kennesaw.edu/psychology/pseries2.htm.

Kinsey, Alfred C., Wardell B. Pomeroy, and Clyde E. Martin. 1948. *Sexual Behavior in the Human Male.* Oxford: Saunders.

Kinsey, Alfred C., Wardell B. Pomeroy, Clyde E. Martin, and Paul H. Gebhard. 1953. *Sexual Behavior in the Human Female.* Oxford: Saunders.

Liddle, Becky J., Mark A. Kunkel, Sherri L. Kick, and Anita L. Hauenstein. 1998. "The Gay, Lesbian, and Bisexual Psychology Faculty Experience: A Concept Map." *Teaching of Psychology* 25 no. 1: 19–25.

Patterson, Charlotte J., and Anthony R. D'Augelli. 1998. *Lesbian, Gay, and Bisexual Identities in Families: Psychological Perspectives.* New York: Oxford University Press.

———. 2001. *Lesbian, Gay, and Bisexual Identities in Youth: Psychological Perspectives.* New York: Oxford University Press.

Simoni, Jane M. 2000. "Confronting Heterosexism in the Teaching of Psychology." Pp. 74–90 in *Education, Research, and Practice in Lesbian, Gay, Bisexual, and Transgendered Psychology: A Resource Manual.* Edited by Beverly Greene and Gladys L. Croom. Thousand Oaks: Sage.

Web Sites

American Psychological Association. March 2005. APA. Accessed June 9, 2005. http://www.apa.org/pi/lgbc/. Provides information about current guidelines for practitioners in working with LGBT individuals, policy statements on LGBT mental health issues, and links to groups that focus on LGBT issues in psychology.

Encyclopedia of Psychology. June 2005. Don Walter. Accessed June 9, 2005. http://www.psychology.org/links/Career/. Links to many sites that cover career issues in psychology. It provides information about the various topics studied in psychology as well as practical advice on making psychology a career.

Q

Queer and Queer Theory

William F. Pinar

Adolescence is a time of self-definition, including sexual self-definition. Perhaps that helps explain the appeal of the concept of *queer* to many, not only **lesbian, gay, bisexual,** and **transgender** (LGBT) youth. Previously considered a derogatory term used by heterosexuals, the word *queer* is now considered not only acceptable but preferable to many differently gendered individuals. "Part of queer's semantic clout, part of its political efficacy," Annamarie Jagose (1996, 1) explains, "depends on its resistance to definition and the way in which it refuses to stake its claim." Nor is *queer* a neutral term, even though it aspires to be a term of political coalition among lesbians, transgender, bisexuals, and gay men. And queer theory's range of study does not stop with these three categories; it includes **cross- dressing,** hermaphroditism, gender ambiguity, and gender-corrective surgery.

Stephen Murray (1996, 2) prefers the term "lesbigay," a neologism that constructs queers as a "quasi-ethnic group," although the notion of "sexual minorities" is not self-evident, at least not to radical social constructivists (focused on the inherent instability of identity categories) and to theorists of ethnic minorities, such **African Americans.** Constructed as an ethnic minority rather than a possibility for all, lesbians and gay men become positioned to demand recognition and equal rights within the existing social system. As such, it has been incorporated a curricular element of multiculturalism (Pinar 1998).

Sexual "culture" or **"ethnicity"** has often been construed as "white" (Jagose 1996, 62). Indeed, within various LGBT communities, "queer" has been accused of the effacing specific subject positions with these broad and diverse groups. Other activists (e.g., Boykin 1996) have pointed to the perceived classism, **racism,** and Eurocentrism of the terms "gay" and "lesbian," suggesting that "queer" may need the queer position from which to speak. Others (e.g., Pinar 1998) have employed the notion of queer to examine black **popular culture,** including rap and hip-hop **music.** Queer may not be adequately multicultural, but it is multinational. Queer, then, is a category that resists categorization. Its conceptualization requires "de-conconceptualization" or, even, "reconceptualization." There is mobilization—moments of solidarity—required by those political conditions that demand stable categories of gender and sexuality: **heteronormativity.** "Queer," Jagose (1996, 131) observes, "is always an identity under construction, a site of permanent becoming." And, perhaps, that is its most appealing feature to "straights," namely its simultaneous self-shattering and self-mobilization, its embrace of self-dispersion (even "pere-version") in private and self-assertion (e.g., ACT-UP) in public (Pinar 1998).

Queer has become the chosen term for many who have come to be dissatisfied with what they perceive to be the assimilationist politics associated especially with the terms *gay* and *lesbian* (Sears 2001). Of course, the terms lesbian and gay have hardly outlived their usefulness for those focused on the civil rights struggle for

See also Communication; Critical Social Theory; Curriculum, Higher Education; Identity Politics; Feminism; Lacan, Jacques; LGBT Studies; Men's Studies; Multicultural Education; Poststructuralism; Pscyhoanalysis and Feminism; Queer Studies; White Antiracism.

what is conceptualized as sexual minorities. Nor can they be forgotten given certain nonessential but nonetheless politically significant divisions between men and women. So framed, *queer* may be considered a provisional term of momentary and changing coalitions. Bringing us all into one room may serve important intellectual as well as political and pedagogical purposes (Pinar 1998; Pinar 2001).

But political coalition is only one agenda item of "queer." In queer theory, the key is an assault on essentialized and normalized conceptions of sexuality, especially heterosexuality. Indeed, the **compulsory heterosexuality** of contemporary "disciplinary" society constructs false binaries such as "gay" and "straight," politically structured into inequality and, on occasion, spectacular violence, as in the case of **Matthew Shepard**. Certainly it is the key to understanding the **AIDS** crisis (Pinar 1998). Queer theory enables us to understand how political conservatives imagined the disease as a property of the abject sexualized other, rationalizing their initial inaction and, in fact, welcoming the disease as a version of "ethnic cleansing."

Eve Kosofsky Sedgwick (1990, 1) argues that "an understanding of virtually any aspect of modern Western culture must be, not merely incomplete, but damaged in its central substance to the degree that it does not incorporate a critical analysis of modern homo/heterosexual definition." Focusing on how the latter concept ("heterosexuality" was coined at the end of the nineteenth century) depends upon the invention of the former ("homosexuality" was coined mid-nineteenth-century), queer theory underlines the discontinuities among sex, gender, and **desire**. Insisting on the impossibility of any "natural" or "normal" sexuality, queer theory calls into question even such apparently self-evident terms as "the opposite sex," even "man" and "woman" (Jagose 1996). "Queer theory," Daniel Boyarin (1997, 14) points out, "is theory that recognizes that human desire—that is, even desire for 'straight sex'—is queer, excessive, not teleological or natural, and is that for which the refusal of heteronormativity on the part of gays, lesbians, bisexuals, and others provides a privileged but not exclusive model." Queer theorists, most prominently, **Judith Butler**, have emphasized the "performativity" of all sexual practices (Pinar 2001).

Not only is "straight sex" not "natural," it is historical. Around 1870, and in various medical discourses, the notion of homosexual as an identifiable type of person begins to emerge. Of course, same-sex sex acts were condemned in both religious and civil law before 1870, but they were regarded as temptations to which anyone might succumb, not as expressions of an essential identity (Pinar 2001). As Foucault (1981, 43) put the matter: "The sodomite had been a temporary aberration; the homosexual was now a species." The conflation of sexual practice with (**sexual**) **identity** is, presumably, a twentieth-century phenomenon.

"Heterosexuality" became "compulsory" after its invention near the end of the nineteenth century during, significantly, the so-called "crisis of masculinity" in the United States. Historians name several ingredients to the "perfect (gender) storm," among them shifts in the economy, the political and social gains of African Americans and of white women (including the campaign for suffrage), the disappearance of "romantic friendship," the closing of the American frontier, the mass immigration of Eastern and Southern Europeans, and in the South an ongoing racialization of a defeated white manhood. All contributed to white men in the United States feeling besieged, uncertain, indignant, and frightened. Not committed to working through such changes self-consciously and psychologically, the majority of (white) men resorted to defensive and compensatory distractions, among them obsessions with body building, sexual restraints (especially of adolescent boys), reactionary racial and gender politics (although both the suffrage and the civil rights movements continued), a "muscular" Christianity, and the lynching of black men. Like whiteness, this fantasy of hypermasculinity functioned as a standard to which all men must aspire; it was an ideal few men reached. To be a "man" now required exertion and self-policing and continual demonstrations, even violent; one must *prove* that one was a "man" (Pinar 2001). So understood, heterosexuality, in the United States at least, is an historically constructed, psychologically defensive, and compensatory phenomenon. As an ideology demanding conformity, it is named "heteronormativity."

Challenging "heteronormativity," queer theory has influenced research in various disciplines, among them English, French, anthropology, rhetoric and communications studies, even conservative and intellectually underdeveloped disciplines such as education. Now we have studies of **queer pedagogy**, queer **curriculum**, queer youth, queered elementary education, even educational autobiography as queer (Pinar 1998).

There are those, including the theorist often credited with inaugurating the phrase "queer theory"—Teresa de Lauretis—who assert that "queer politics may, by now, have outlived its political usefulness" (Halperin 1995, 112). Annamarie Jagose (1996, 131) locates these assertions of demise within queer discourse, pointing out that "queer is always an identity under construction, a site of permanent becoming." Not only its definitional instability and expansiveness of its interest, but its very fragility as a concept may be, Jagose (1996, 131) suggests, queer theory's "most enabling characteristic," a capacity "for looking forward without anticipating the future."

Bibliography

Boyarin, Daniel. 1997. *Unheroic Conduct: The Rise of Heterosexuality and the Invention of the Jewish Man*. Berkeley: University of California Press.

Boykin, Keith. 1996. *One More River to Cross: Black and Gay in America*. New York: Anchor.

Foucault, Michel. 1978/1981. *The History of Sexuality, Col. 1, an Introduction*. Translated by Robert Hurley. Harmondsworth: Penguin.

Halperin, David. 1995. *Saint Foucault: Towards a Gay Hagiography*. New York: Oxford University Press.

Jagose, Annamarie. 1996. *Queer Theory: An Introduction*. New York: New York University Press.

de Lauretis, Teresa. 1991. "Queer Theory: Lesbian and Gay Sexualities: An Introduction." *Differences* 3, no. 2: iii–xviii.

Murray, Stephen O. 1996. *American Gay*. Chicago: University of Chicago Press.

Pinar, William F., ed. 1998. *Queer Theory in Education*. Mahwah, NJ: Lawrence Erlbaum.

———. 2001. *The Gender of Racial Politics and Violence in America: Lynching, Prison Rape, and the Crisis of Masculinity*. New York: Peter Lang.

Sears, James T. 2001. *Rebels, Rubyfruit, and Rhinestones: Queering Space in the Stonewall South*. New Brunswick, NJ: Rutgers University Press.

Sedgwick, Eve Kosofsky. 1990. *Epistemology of the Closet*. Berkeley and Los Angeles: University of California Press.

Web Site

Queer Theory. May 2005. Accessed June 10, 2005. www.theory.org.uk. Visual and textual resources for all matters queer.

Queer as Folk

Mary Lou Rasmussen and **Jane Kenway**

Showtime's *Queer as Folk* is the United States' version of the ten-episode British series of the same name, which was commissioned by Channel 4 in the **United Kingdom**. The original UK series first aired in 1999 and is set in Manchester; the U.S. series, aired a year later, is filmed in Toronto and set in Pittsburgh. Showtime's *Queer as Folk* airs in several European countries, as well as the United States, **Australia**, Aoteroa/**New Zealand**, and **Brazil**; it has a cult following in many of these places. The series centers around a group of young, mostly gay friends who hang out in various urban locations, including a fictional gay club, Babylon. Through the character of Justin, a young student featured prominently in the series, *Queer as Folk* speaks directly to school age audiences modeling a strong sense of sexual agency. Indeed, it speaks invitingly to them by challenging the authority of political correctness. Consumer-media culture is very astute in producing the child as an agent via this strategy. The shrewd youthful viewer may participate in a queer reading of *Queer as Folk*; a reading that enables them to recognize and enjoy the sexual aspects of the series, while also being able to read the different "dream-scapes, collective fantasies and facades" that the show makes possible.

Queer as Folk Cast (Showtime) Season 1, 2000-1. Shown: Standing L-R: Peter Paige (as Emmet Honeycutt), Michelle Clunie (as Melanie Marcus), Thea Gill (as Lindsay Peterson), Gale Harold (as Brian Kinney), Randy Harrison (as Justin Taylor), Scott Lowell (as Ted Schmitt); Kneeling: Hal Sparks (as Michael Novotny). Showtime/Photofest

Overall, the *Queer as Folk* phenomenon is a good example of what Kenway and Bullen (2001) call "consumer media-culture," bringing together as it does the branded world of the commodity with the virtual and image based world of the media. The program is interlinked with numerous Web sites dedicated to *Queer as Folk* chat, merchandizing, trivia, pop quizzes, comic books, screen writer and cast interviews, and with expert commentaries. These chats cover a wide range of topics from the cast's fashion choices to the possible health implications for gay men who view the program.

See also Adolescent Sexualities; Colonialism and Homosexuality; Mentoring; Popular Culture; Queer Pedagogy; Sexual Identity; Youth, At Risk; Youth Culture.

Within and beyond the fan community, debates have raged about the program's foci and style. In Australia and the United States, the series has been criticized for its graphic depiction of gay male sexuality, intergenerational sex, and frequent references to recreational **drug use**. This has led to further debates about its broadcasting. In Australia, for example, the United States version is aired on the Special Broadcasting Service, a free-to-air channel. However, as Alan McKee (2002, 235) notes:

> none of Australia's terrestrial channels would play the [UK version of the] programme, fearing that its representation of a fifteen-year-old man having gay sex would be seen as child pornography. When it was eventually shown by Pay TV providers Foxtel, a separate channel had to be created solely for the programme, in order to ensure that no children would accidentally see this tale of queer community.

This anxiety is partially overcome in the Showtime version by the transformation of the fifteen-year-old Nathan into the seventeen-year-old Justin. In the first series Justin loses his virginity, comes out of the closet, at home and at school, successfully navigates the club scene, and forms a **gay–straight alliance** at his high school with the support of a straight girlfriend. Justin's adventures pose a range of political and pedagogical questions for educators—particularly for teachers. The most obvious is how to bring young people both sexual pleasure and critique. A second question, but no less important, is how to interpret the *Queer as Folk* phenomenon itself.

Queer as Folk may be best understood as part of a transnational movement of meanings and imaginings. It is clearly transnational in reach, and, seemingly, appeal—despite the fact that the cast oozes a gay, white, Western, and urban sensibility. *Queer as Folk* delights in transgressions. It articulates a critique of the clean queer who is often held up for the consumption of straight communities and, indeed, for queer youth by "responsible" queer adults. Instead, it promotes a particular brand of gay male sexuality. And, it is this brand of sexuality that attracts particular debate in cyberspace. The brand not only offers a range of modes of sexual behavior, it also provokes contemplation of how young people might care for themselves and others through the construction of sexual practices. Sixteen-year-old Dan writes:

> I found *Queer as Folk* a cool opportunity to check out the life out there that I'll be able to discover—one day! I found the sex anytime/anyplace theme quite scary though and am just hoping that there are some steady relationship type gay blokes out there too! The trouble with *Queer as Folk* was that the sex was what everything revolved around which might seem really cool for some but for the likes of me and definitely the straight audience it just promotes the idea that gay men just shag and shag and shag. ALSO I know Queer as Folk2 did address the issue of coming out to a certain extent—the scenes in Nathan's school which were realistic. BUT Nathan (Justin in the U.S. series) seemed way too confident and arrogant to me where as I think a 16y/old would be a lot more intimidated in his situation. . . . I think *Queer as Folk* missed out on making a really good point about the effect of society on gay youth as they struggle with their sexuality.

This critique of *Queer as Folk* was posted by Dan on an **Internet** site produced by *Outzone*, a youth group for gay and bisexual young men under twenty-six who live in or around London. *Outzone*, is an organization that is likely to concur with Dan's critique of *Queer as Folk*, a critique that is partially embedded in a "wounded identity" (Haver 1997, 278), a term deployed to convey the notion that those who identify as **lesbian, gay, bisexual,** and **transgender youth** may be perceived to be "at risk" by virtue of their sexual or **gender identity**. Dan's opening remarks allude to his eagerness to discover opportunities for sexual interactions. However, he tempers his **desire** with an expression of frustration over what he sees as the overemphasis on sex in the series and its failure to address the struggles that confront many gay youth.

The *Outzone* Web site, which advertises social activities "away from the commercial gay scene," as well as services relating to **sexual health** and **coming out** issues, is one of many which exude sexually respectable/responsible sensibilities. These sensibilities, underlying Dan's critique of *Queer as Folk*, may be learned through the production of numerous stories of "queer" oppression. For instance, Stephen Goldstone (2001), in his Web column in GayHealth,™ notes:

> LGBT youth often turn to alcohol and drugs to fight off self-hate. Like Justin, they may seek out roll models [sic] they desperately need in adult gay clubs. But teens are often too young to handle sexual and emotional relationships with older men and women that develop from these encounters. And the exposure to alcohol and recreational drugs available in many clubs increases their risk for unprotected sex and HIV. A lack of emotional support, appropriate roll [sic] models, and ostracism by their peers fosters depression in LGBT youth. Drugs and alcohol can also potentiate [sic] depression, and left untreated, depression can lead to suicide. Statistics show that gay and lesbian youth are 13.6 times more likely to attempt suicide than their heterosexual counterparts.

It can be inferred from such sites that *Queer as Folk* sets a bad example and offers young gay males negative role models. In contrast, they encourage the young to be safe sexual subjects/citizens. In so doing, they fail to engage the various pleasures that the series evokes and, indeed, the debates the series opens up about appropriate sexual subjects or citizen roles it is appropriate and possible for young people to become.

Queer as Folk steadfastly rebuffs any attempt to provide young people with respectable role models and it refuses to sanitize gay (or straight) life. It endeavors to represent a more complex understanding of gay (and straight) cultures. For example, it suggests that the intergenerational encounters young men may find in clubs can be equally as rewarding or devastating as the relationships in which adults are regularly embroiled. But the sexual pedagogies of the series do not stop there. While *Queer as Folk* may appear to resile from the conformity of the politically correct gay identity, it nonetheless offers a particular branding or stylistics of a transgressive and highly consumptive sexual culture.

Certainly, the *Queer as Folk* brand fails to represent the complexities of everyday queer cultures and the exclusions produced through branding processes, such as those depicted in *Queer as Folk* (some of which were identified by Dan). Nevertheless, through his interaction with this brand, Justin, and potentially other young people who are gay-identified, may be able to develop a sense of their worth and through this style of gay branding-within and outside school space. Equally, young people may find themselves, like Dan, wondering if there is more to life than "shagging."

The question of pride is also writ large in Justin's attempts to develop a gay–straight alliance at his conservative high school. In a *Queer as Folk* forum on the Web, Russell Davies, the creator of the original British series, elaborates on this aspect of the development of Nathan's (Justin's) character:

> Pink Panther: I'd like to know why the programme didn't show any bullying or harrassment of Nathan when in school as I find this part a bit unrealistic, or is it included later on?
>
> Russell Davies: It does show bullying, in episode four. But frankly I'm sick of seeing gay men and gay boys as victims in a permanent states [sic] of passive suffering. To be honest, you can find those plots in soap operas. I'm trying to do something different. Nathan is a survivor, an optimist, and he's the opposite of what you'd expect the gay schoolboy to be. (Curie 2001)

Davies designed Nathan's character to refuse the "wounded identities" often attached to young people who identify as LGBT. The alternative that he offers to the young viewer is the proud, liberated, sexualized gay man. Young people need access to pleasurable discourses about their sexual lives; these provide an antidote to those discourses that present queer youth as wounded and in need of adult assistance. While *Queer as Folk* does tend toward the fetishization of gay sex, it also provides sanction to an important avenue of exploration for youth.

Clearly, *Queer as Folk* teaches "the art of living" in many different ways, ways that include but also exceed the logic of the commodity. And through Justin, *Queer as Folk* speaks directly to school-age audiences, offering them a strong sense of sexual **agency** and challenging the authority of political correctness.

Bibliography

Curie, Aidan. 2001. "Russell T. Davies: Queer As Folk 2." Accessed December 18, 2004. http://pub88.ezboard.com/fqueerasfolk87597frm4.showMessage?topicID=26.topic.

Goldstone, Stephen. 2001. "Queer as Folk: Gay/Straight Student Alliance." *GayHealth*. Accessed December 15, 2004. http://www.gayhealth.com/templates/. 10463226912609171429640001/news?record=510. Commentary on the potential negative consequences of programs such as *QAF* on young people's health.

Haver, William. 1997. "Queer Research; or, How to Practise Invention to the Brink of Intelligibility." Pp. 280–288 in *The Eight Technologies of Otherness*. Edited by S. Golding. New York: Routledge.

Kenway, Jane, and Elizabeth Bullen. 2001. *Consuming Children: Education-Edutainment-Advertising*. Buckingham, UK: Open University Press.

McKee, Alan. 2002. "Interview with Russell T. Davies." *Continuum: Journal of Media and Cultural Studies* 16, no. 2: 235–244.

OUTZONE Dan in the Midlands. Accessed June 17, 2003. http://www.outzone.org/outzone/filmtv/Queer as Folk.htm.

Web Sites

Advocate Commentary. 2000. My So-*Queer* life. Ash Gordon. Accessed December 15, 2004. http://www.advocate.com/html/stories/819/819_soqueerlife.asp. A Canadian teenager talks about his and his family's relationship to the *QAF* series.

Queer as Folk. Showcase. 2004. Accessed December 15, 2004. http://www.showcase.ca/queerasfolk. Official Web site of the American version that includes discussion boards, episode summaries, and feature interviews.

Young Gay America. November 30, 2001. Pittsburgh GLBT Community Center. "Pittsburgh Youth: 'Who's united with us?'" Accessed December 15, 2004. http://www. younggayamerica.com/midwest36.shtml. Article about Pittsburgh's LGBT youth and how their perceptions of the city differ from those presented in *QAF*.

Queer Pedagogy

Kevin C. Franck

Queer pedagogy is less concerned with integrating gay and lesbian content into the **curriculum** than it is with exploring queer understandings by encouraging queer "readings" of various texts (visual, audio as well as written materials), and disrupting normative regimes of truth such as biological notions of **sexual orientation** or gender binaries. Based on **queer theory**, queer pedagogy, like **critical social theory**, is concerned with oppression and justice, resistance to power, and lessening and the authority of universal truth. But queer pedagogues, like many feminists, are focused on sexuality and **sexual identity**. Thus, queer pedagogy can best be understood as an approach to teaching and learning that grows out of the merger of queer theory with progressive pedagogy aimed at creating social change through the interaction of teachers, students, and knowledge in the classroom.

The queering of pedagogy produces a tension between the queer aim of disrupting taken-for-granted knowledge and the pedagogical **desire** to impart certain bodies of knowledge. As a result, queer pedagogy becomes more a method of asking questions then a set of teaching techniques. For example, queer pedagogues ask: Can some sexual knowledge be correct and incorrect at the same time? How could we understand human interaction without the binary categories of male and female? What would classroom learning look like without gender? How is **heternormativity** embedded in our teaching and learning? Queer pedagogy is both an attempt to destabilize pedagogical practice and to develop guidelines for teaching and learning queerly.

Queer pedagogy asks if we can even imagine the process of learning and teaching, the development of curriculum plans, and **educational administration** without relying on the assumption of fixed and stable identity positions: teacher/student; male/female; white/non-white; masculine/feminine; gay/straight. The queer pedagogue makes the point that these conceptions are built upon unexamined assumptions conveyed in Western knowledge found in conventionally taught subjects like mathematics, **history, science, literature**, and the social sciences.

Queer pedagogy does not refer to a specific set of techniques or indicate any specific processes to accomplish its objectives. The queering of pedagogy does result in the development of three main strategies to help inquire, critique, and transform discursive formations that regulate the production of heteronormative ways of knowing and that give authority to official classifications of knowledge. Embracing elements of **poststructuralism** and semiotic analysis, queer pedagogy helps to access alternative meanings in texts. The process of reading queerly begins with an understanding of how the texts maintain straight meaning. A dominant reading of the classic portrait,

See also Antibias Curriculum; Art, Teaching of; Biology, Teaching of; Butler, Judith; Communication; Dance, Teaching of; ESL, Teaching of; Feminism; Foucault, Michel; Geography, Teaching of; LGBT Studies; Lacan, Jacques; Literature, College; Philosophy, Teaching of; Psychology, Teaching of; Queer Studies.

"American Gothic," for example, might give us the impression that the two people shown in front of their farmhouse are husband and wife. Queer pedagogy poses the deceptively simple question: How is it that we understand the painting as a depiction of a "normal" couple? In the process of interrogating the text of the portrait—and students various rereadings of that text—queer pedagogues suspend students' taken-for-granted assumptions to make clearings for new understandings.

In the example mentioned above, a queer pedagogical approach might attempt to disrupt a normal reading of the painting by identifying signs and symbols in the text that can be understood with queer meanings. Is the woman in the painting exhibiting a normal style of femininity? Perhaps her unstylish hair and drab attire make her look a little more masculine—a little "butch"? Is the reading of the "couple's" relationship changed when students are told that the man featured in the painting is actually the artist and the woman his sister? In general, this disruptive approach asks students to contemplate what happens to the dominant meanings of texts when read queerly.

In itself, the term "queer" has a disruptive presence in the academy, as it does in the society at large. It is a term bought at an etymological thrift store, reclaimed from a century's use as invective, and employed to catch the attention of nearly any audience. Along with shock, humor is one of queers' primary tools for disruption. To this end, queer pedagogy often begins discussion by presenting standard formulations of knowledge with a satirical queer twist. The early Queer Nation slogan, "I am Out. Therefore, I am," is a perfectly queer example. This slogan's close resemblance of Descartes' famous philosophical dictum, "I think, therefore I am," grabs attention. In the classic phrase, the presence of self-conscious thought is both a prerequisite and a product of existence. The queer version replaces "I think" with "I am out," thereby using a clever twist of words to argue that the existence of queer folks is inexorably linked to our willingness to be out.

Queer pedagogy also leaves space for a reimagining of knowledge separated from unitary, fixed subject positions. To extend the above example further, a queer pedagogue might ask students to tell a different story about the two individuals pictured in Wood's painting, using the signs and symbols in the painting. Students could imagine how the gender performance, biological sex, or relationship of the two people pictured might differ from what is assumed in a straight reading of the painting. What if it is suggested that the "woman" is only apparently one? Through readings, disruptions and reimaginings, queer pedagogy seeks to make the coherent incoherent, the unitary fragmented and the unknown knowable. In no way are these elements of queer pedagogy a linear set of techniques meant to follow, coincide, or even acknowledge each other.

Bibliography

de Lauretis, Teresa. 1991. "Queer Theory: Lesbian and Gay Sexualities: An Introduction. *Differences* 3, no. 2: iii-xviii.

Letts, William J., and James T. Sears, eds. 1999. *Queering Elementary Education: Advancing the Dialogue about Sexualities and Schooling.* Lanham, MD: Rowman and Littlefield.

Pinar, William F., ed. 1998. *Queer Theory and Education.* Mahwah, NJ: Lawrence Erlbaum.

Sears, James T., ed. 1992. *Sexuality and the Curriculum.* New York: Teachers College Press.

Sedgwick, Eve Kosofsky. 1990. *Epistemology of the Closet.* Berkeley: University of California Press.

Seidman, Steven. 1997. *Difference Troubles: Queering Social Theory and Sexual Politics.* New York: Cambridge University Press.

Queer Studies

Gloria Filax and *Debra Shogan*

Queer studies is an academic discipline, which documents the array of sexual and other differences among people and explores social processes that attempt to make everyone "normal." Queer studies questions the assumptions of a two-sex (female/male), two-gender (masculinity/femininity), one-sexuality (heterosexuality) ordering, which systematically divides humans into a normal category and a deviant category. Queer studies is critical to the study of youth and education since young people are often assumed to be alike with common characteristics, including a common sexuality. Queer studies questions educational practices directed at assisting those young people who are assumed to be normal, as well as those practices used to change behaviors and values of young people who do not meet educational norms.

"Queer" was first used in an academic context at a conference at the University of California, Santa Cruz in February 1990 (de Lauretis 1991). Prior to this, **LGBT studies** focused on what was believed to be stable and even universal identities of straight, lesbian, gay, bisexual, and sometimes transgender people. Queer studies has shown that, by taking for granted that "straight," "lesbian," and "gay" are fixed and constant categories, lesbian and gay studies did not disrupt the notion that there are normal and deviant sexualities. For example, lesbian and gay studies have portrayed the experiences of sexual minority young people in schools almost exclusively in terms of **suicide** rates, depressions, and **substance abuse**. While this work has been very important in making public the difficulties many nonconforming young people face and must be recognized as crucial work along a continuum of understanding sexual diversity, many of these studies have also inadvertently reinforced the notion of healthy "straight" youth and unhealthy, deviant **lesbian** and **gay youth**. Queer studies of young people in schools, while acknowledging the negative effects of **homophobia** and **heterosexism**, is more interested in how these young people create possibilities for their lives, including variations on their sexuality.

Like lesbian and gay studies, which has assumed that "lesbian" and "gay" are permanent categories, traditional youth studies has assumed that "youth" is a stable category of people whose members share common characteristics. Like the notion of "homosexuality," which was coined by psychiatrist, Carl Westphal, in 1870, the category "youth" is a relatively recent age distinction. The notion of youth as a distinct age category emerged from changes in political organization of work, family, kinship, and urbanization in the 1800s. **G. Stanley Hall** was one of the first scholars to research young people in relation to these phenomena. Hall produced "**adolescence**/youth" as an identity category that had previously not been regarded as such.

Along with the category "youth," the "problem of youth" was also created. While "normal" youth were assumed and expected to be economically and emotionally dependent on adult caregivers and spend most of their time in school with people of their age, they were also believed to have a number of problems. They were portrayed as emotionally unstable, as struggling with puberty because of

See also Communication; Curriculum, Higher Education; Geography, Teaching of; Identity Politics; Literature, College; Poststructuralism; Queer Pedagogy; Resiliency; Sexual Orientation; Youth, At Risk.

bodies raging with hormones, as engaging in risky behaviors—including dangerous driving, **drug use** and other substance abuse, sexual activity—as underachievers or school dropouts. These "normal" behaviors did not match the lives of many young people. They particularly did not match the lives of queer young people, who are typically left out of traditional youth studies, except in suicide statistics. Traditional youth studies has regarded young people's behaviors to be deviant in relation to adults, and sexual minority young people have been regarded as deviant in relation to "normal" youth (Filax 2002).

By studying the lives of queer young people, queer studies has demonstrated that the category "youth" is not as stable as it is assumed. The daily circumstances of many queer young people do not fit the descriptions of what counts as a normal youth life. Many queer young people do not live at home; many experience various forms of **harassment**, while others engage in **passing** and experience the silence of the closet; still others live on the periphery of queer adult cultures leading quasi-adult lives; and many more lead lives in which they self identify as emotionally stable and in charge of the demands with which a homophobic world presents them (Filax 2002). Many queer young people, however, also do match closely the **stereotypes** of youth from traditional youth studies. Since queer youth have diverse and varied lives, which also sometimes match that of their straight peers, queer youth studies demonstrates that it is not so easy to decide who is normal and who is deviant. Thus, queer studies also shows that having categories such as normal and deviant is political, designed to change those who are labeled "deviant" to make them more like those who are labeled "normal."

Traditional youth studies take for granted that young people are heterosexual. Traditional youth studies also often reflect what are assumed to be the values of young people who are male, white, middle class, and from the United States. Queer studies, on the other hand, reveals that young people's identifications are informed by sexuality, but also by **ethnicity/race**, culture, gender, as well as histories of **colonialism, racism**, ethnocentrism, and postcolonialism. Studies of young people includes the *tombois* and *lesbi* in West Sumatra, *two-spirited* **native/indigenous** people, the Chinese *po*, and North American drag kings. Queer studies makes clear that understanding the sexuality of queer young people is limited when the focus is on the lives of some young people in North America who identify as lesbian or gay. As well, the fact that there are so many ways young people can identify sexually, demonstrates that it is problematic to assume that there is a single category, "youth," that can account for diversity among young people. The diversity of sexuality also shows that sexuality cannot be neatly divided between those who identify as heterosexual and those who identify as homosexual.

By showing that sexuality is diverse and unstable, queer studies questions beliefs that heterosexuality is normal sexuality and whether to categorize something or someone as "normal" is even helpful or appropriate to understand human behavior. Beliefs about heterosexual normalcy, for example, take for granted that biological sex determines a person's gender, **sexual identity**, sexual **desire**, and sexual practice. The assumed normalcy of heterosexuality is based on the belief that if, say, one is biologically male, one will also be masculine in behavior, be heterosexual, and desire a particular kind of heterosexual genital sex. Queer studies shows that genitalia do not determine whether one will identify as masculine or feminine. Neither do genitalia predict whether someone will have one, several, or no sexual identities. Genitalia also do not establish a person's sexual desire or practice or whether sexual desire or practice is even connected to the gender of the person desired. By showing that it is false to assume that behavior, identity, desire, and sexual practice can be predicted from **biology**, queer studies demonstrates that what counts as "normal" depends on maintaining and often socially regulating a belief that there are necessary connections between biology, behavior, identity, desire, and sexual practice.

Queer studies is interested in how assumptions about the normality of heterosexuality, or **heteronormativity**, structures the organization of everyday life. Queer studies explores how human endeavors such as education, law, religion, psychiatry, family, work, health and wellness, leisure, politics, and economy are based on beliefs of what counts as normal sexuality. For example, laws in most countries—including family, contract, and criminal law—are founded on heterosexuality as the standard from which other sexuality deviates. Consequently, even progressive countries like Denmark and **Canada** must refer to queer people as sexual minorities in relation to the heterosexual norm.

Queer studies is interested in ways in addition to sexuality that people are encouraged and coerced to change their behaviors to match an expectation that we all be alike. Whereas most modern institutions work to "norm the nonstandard" (Davis 1995), queer studies attempts to "queer the nonstandard." For example, queer studies of education is not only interested in showing how education maintains and reinforces standards of the heterosexual, nuclear family, and behaviors associated with assumptions that all young people are or will be heterosexual, these studies show how organization of educational practices works to keep all students compliant and alike. "Queering" education exposes how educational structures and practices also work to normalize nonwhite students and students with disabilities through interventions by experts who assume and produce standards for education based on beliefs that there are normal behaviors, values, and activities to which all students must aspire (Shogan 2002).

Queer studies is interested in opening up categories of identification and by doing so creating other possibilities for human relations. By studying diverse ways of living, queer studies shows that there are many ways that people might live their lives. By studying and communicating how people are different from each other, queer studies creates the opportunity to produce new and different forms of identity, community, and social relations. Queer studies dismantles the notion that there is one true way to express sexuality by documenting that there are many different ways of living in the world. This provides young people, in particular, with a place from which to refuse expectations that they unquestioningly conform to standards with which they may fundamentally disagree, whatever institutions or values these standards reflect, including sexuality and education. Queer studies, then, documents how people live both locally and globally in vastly different ways, including a range of ways of experiencing sexuality. By virtue of these studies, queer studies also creates possibilities for the limits of human experience to be pushed beyond the bounds of "the normal" and, in doing so, shows how contrived the notion of "the normal" is.

Bibliography

Davis, Lenard. 1995. *Enforcing Normalcy: Disability, Deafness and the Body*. London and New York: Versa.

de Lauretis, Teresa. 1991. "Queer Theory: Lesbian and Gay Sexualities: An Introduction." *Differences* 3, no. 2: iii-xviii.

Filax, Gloria. 2002. *Queer Youth and Strange Representations in the Province of the Severely Normal*. Unpublished dissertation. Alberta: University of Alberta.

Jagose, Annamarie. 1996. *Queer Theory: An Introduction*. New York: New York University Press.

Martin, Fran. 1996. "Response to Dennis Altman." *Australian Humanities Review*. Accessed December 3, 2004. http://www.lib.latrobe.edu.au/AHR/emuse/Globalqueering/martin.html.

Pinar, William, ed. 1998. *Queer Theory in Education*. Mahwah, NJ: Lawrence Erlbaum.

Sears, James T. 1997. "Centering Culture: Teaching for Critical Sexual Literacy Using the Sexual Diversity Wheel." *Journal of Moral Education* 26 (September): 273–283.

Shogan, Debra. 2002. "Social Construction of Disability in a Society of Normalization." Pp. 65–74 in *Adapted Physical Activity*. Edited by Robert Steadward, Jane Watkinson, and Garry Wheeler. Edmonton: University of Alberta Press.

Web Sites

Annotated Links to LGBT/Queer Studies. January 2003. Accessed June 10, 2005. http://www.lgbtcampus.org/resources/lgbt_studies.html. This site includes information about U.S. centres, institutes, and university programs devoted to queer studies, as well as resources such as libraries, archives, journals, and researchers.

Australian Centre for Lesbian and Gay Research. 2004. Accessed June 10, 2005. http://www.arts.usyd.edu.au/centres/aclgr/. Includes events, resources, and research related to Australian queer youth.

LGBT/Queer Library Research Guide. December 2001. Susan A. Vega Garcia. Accessed June 10, 2005. http://www.public.iastate.edu/~savega/lesbigay.htm. Includes selected LGBT Web resources useful for academic research and information purposes.

Queer Zines

Barbara Bolt

"Zines" are a hybridized form of publication that has grown out of the tradition of the maga*zine*, rhyming with scene and not sign. Like mainstream magazines, zines are designed to appeal to a select audience but are produced by and address the interests of subcultural groups who lack voice in the mainstream media. Queer zines are for queers. Unlike mass circulation queer magazines, queer zines are primarily a youth phenomenon; they are cheaply produced, small circulation underground publications made by queer youth for queer youth. Queer zines provide a forum where youth can tell queer stories, make queer connections, express queer ideas in word and image, and celebrate queerness without fear of censorship or retribution.

Building on the spirit of do-it-yourself, an ethos that pervades alternative sub-cultures, zinesters (makers of zines) originally handmade their productions, produced the content, mass copied the original, and then distributed the edition by hand to friends and acquaintances or through mail order. A mainstream interest in zines, coupled to advanced photocopy technology and desktop publishing, means

See also Activism, LGBT Youth; Communication; Internet, Gay Men and the; Internet, Lesbians and the; Popular Culture; Youth Culture.

zines are more likely to be bought in retail stores or accessed on the World Wide Web in the form of e-zines and e-mail order. Zines are born of urgency, appear in a flurry, and most disappear into the ether as the need dies, the money runs out, or the energy flags. The zines that survive create strong underground networks. Archives such as *The Queer Zine Archive Project* and *Grrrlzine Network* have begun to develop a history of the queer zine.

Deriving from science-fiction fan magazines called "fanzines," queer zines share a history with other zines, which dates from the invention of small table top printing presses and the mimeograph introduced by Edison in the late nineteenth century. These inventions allowed self-publishing to become a reality. With changes in technology and culture, self-publishing has mutated and proliferated, but what has remained constant is the passion that inspires people to express themselves through self-publishing.

Zines are personal and idiosyncratic offerings, ranging from the artistic, the polemical, and the political through to the religious and the pornographic. Zinesters are obsessed and obsessive. Their productions celebrate subjective and located point of views. Veruska Outlaw, zinester from the queer fanzine *Clit Rocket*, demonstrates the obsessive drive behind being a zinester. In an interview with *Grrrlzine network*, in 2002, Outlaw explained, "I love to feel the sensation across my stomach when I sit to write a zine and I love to feel impatient making it and to know there are people from different parts of the world waiting to read my zine. I love to get tough with new people, share information, stories, stuff, ideas and interview bands and artists I admire so much" (http://grrrlzines.net/interviews/clitrocket. htm). When asked what advice she would give to others wanting to start a zine, she simply replied, "Make it."

Produced and edited by individual zinesters or networks of zinesters, zines are compiled to encompass reviews, editorials, letters, interviews, images, and any other combination of word and image that might appeal to their target audience. Additionally, message boards and contact lists become critical in creating global community networks and fostering collaborations. Although zines can be extraordinary, much of the voluminous production that parades under the banner of the zine lacks quality, in both form and content, due to a lack of editorial process. Nevertheless queer zines are an increasingly potent cultural phenomenon of significant cultural importance. Part of their power is that zines remain small circulation, nonprofessional, noncommercial, independently produced underground productions. The idiosyncratic nature and immediacy of zines enables them to tap into and encompass the zeitgeist of the time. As Outlaw (Zobl 2002) observed, "The most radical aspect is the great underground artistic, political, literature, music revolution we are building" (http://grrrlzines.net/interviews/clitrocket.htm).

So what makes a queer zine queer? **Queer** is a slippery term, and nowhere is this more evident than in the activities of queer zines and queer zinesters. From serious political zines produced by groups such as *Grrrlzine network*; punk zines such as *Le Streghe* from Italy and *Trippers* from Singapore; queer fanzines such as *Androzine* from France, *Clit Rocket* from Italy and *Holy Titclamps* from the United States; to personal and idiosyncratic monologues such a *Fatty Fatty 2×4: Social Commentary by a Queer Fat Chick* and *Satan Heartbreakr Tarts it Up*, queer zines invoke the ordinary and the extraordinary, the political and the apolitical. Queer zines slip between categories to evoke the strange and uncanny world inhabited by queer.

In the shift from the **identity politics** of being (I am a lesbian, I am gay, I am a transsexual, I am bisexual), characteristic of gay liberation and second wave **feminism,** to embrace the fluid notion of becoming, queer is theorized as a mobile field that is in constant formation. Its concerns are with the possibilities of becoming rather than the fixity of being. Queer is not defined in terms of the sexed body or the binary identification of homosexual or heterosexual, but rather as a field of possibilities where the interaction of bodies and pleasures constantly breaks boundaries of what is possible. In this queer world to be mega-queer straight is a possible subjectivity to be explored among the range of subjectivities possible. In a queer life as in a queer zine, the trick is to keep it all moving; to produce intertextuality between word and image that grates, bounces around, contradicts, slips between the pages, and perhaps disappears altogether. To produce queer zines, zinesters need to constantly break out of the habitual logic of the familiar and keep proliferating new words, new concepts, new practices, new writing, and new imaging to keep the face of queer constantly changing. In queer zines, total irreverence for any form—visual or textual—makes the queer zine the wild child of zine.

Given that **queer theory** sets out to problematize identity and fixity, a Web search of e-queer zine reveals that gay, lesbian, feminist, transgender, transsexual, and color identity politics continues to be played out under the sign of queer. Strategically, there remains a political necessity to use queer zines as a vehicle for feminists, lesbians, queers, people of color, and transgender people to express their voices globally without censorship. Access to a global audience through e-zines offers a radical political potential, particularly in countries where censorship laws and restrictions on freedom of press muzzle debate. The range and immediacy of the e-zine can inform the global networks of breaking events and provoke immediate and radical responses to them. Zines, such as *Grrrlzine Network*, have mobilized the radical potential of the e-zine to create global subversive networks that link identified queers. Through mobilizing queer zines, grrrlzine zinesters are able to "share experiences and set up networks of resistance against the patriarchal, colonizing and homophobic forces of globalism" (http://grrrlzines.net). Radical is underground.

Queer Zinesters are bricoleurs. With few resources and little money they make do, "cobbling together" their zines with imagination and what ever else they can scrounge. In "A Student's Guide on What a Zine is and Tips on How to Make One," Matt Holdaway (2004) lays out the tools of the trade for the aspiring zinester. At its most basic level, all that is needed to make a zine is an old typewriter, scissors, old magazines, pens, pencils, a glue stick, passion and imagination, and access to a copier. In an increasingly technological world, a computer, scanner, printer, and layout programs such as Pagemaker are used to create zines. The advent of desktop publishing and photocopying technology, however, has resulted in the loss of much of the original rawness of the look of zine with its "typing errors, grammatical mistakes, misspellings and jumbled pagination" (Row 1997).

Collage, montage, and concrete poetry provide the models that inform the "look" of the zine. These word-image compilations combine text and image in random disorganized ways, breaking all the traditional graphic design principles traditionally associated with magazine production. However, although some zinesters have adopted the potential of sophisticated software to change the "look" of the zine, there is still a tendency to maintain the rawness that was characteristic of the original zines. It is the cut'n'paste zine that is quintessential queer zine.

Bibliography

Angel, Jen, and Jason Kucsma, eds. 2004. *The Zine Yearbook, Volume 8: A Year in the Underground Press.* Toledo: Clamour. Available at http://www.clamormagazine.org/yearbook.

Block, Francesca Lia, and Hilary Carlip. 1998. *Zine Scene. The Do it Yourself Guide to Zines.* San Francisco: Girl Press.

Brent, Bill. 1997. *Make a Zine! A Guide to Self-publishing Disguised as a Book on How to Produce a Zine.* San Francisco: Black Books.

Burston, Paul, and Colin Richardson, eds. 1995. *Queer Romance: Lesbians, Gay Men and Popular Culture.* London: Routledge,

Duncombe, Stephen. 1997. *Notes from Underground: Zines and the Politics of Alternative Culture.* London: Verso.

Farrelly, Liz. 2001. *Zines.* London: Booth-Clibborn.

Friedman, R. Seth. 1997. *The Factsheet Five Zine Reader: Dispatches from the Edge of the Zine Revolution.* New York: Three Rivers Press.

Green, Karen, and Tristan Taormino. 1997. *A Girl's Guide to Taking over the World: Writings from the Girl Zine Revolution.* New York: St. Martin's Press.

Gunderloy, Mike, and Janice Cari Golderberg. 1992. *The World of Zines: A Guide to the Independent Magazine Revolution.* New York: Penguin.

Holdaway, Matt. 2004. "A Student's Guide on What a Zine is and Tips on How to Make One." Accessed October 30, 2004. http://grrrlzines.net/writing/student%20zine%20guide.pdf.

Romanesko, Jim. 1995. "Fanzines Explained." American Journalism Review. Accessed October 18, 2004. http://www.stayfreemagazine.org/ml/readings/zines_article.pdf.

Row, Heath. 1997. "From Fandom to Feminism: An Analysis of the Zine Press." Accessed October 30, 2004. http://www.geocities.com/echozinedistro/history.html.

Rowe, Chip, ed. 1997. *The Book of Zines. Readings from the Fringe.* New York: Henry Holt.

———. 2004. "Whatcha Mean What's a Zine?" Accessed October 30, 2004. Accessed through the link "What's a Zine," http://www.zinebook.com.

Sabin, Roger, and Teal Triggs, eds. 2001. *Below Critical Radar: Fanzines and Alternative Comics from 1976 to Now.* Hove, England: Slab-O-Concrete Publications.

Zobl, Elke. 2002. "Clit Rocket: Queer Revolution! An Interview with Veruska Outlaw." GRRR Zine Network. Accessed June 11, 2005. http://grrrlzines.net/interviews/clitrocket.htm.

Web Sites

Echozinedistro. October 2004. Accessed October 30, 2004. http://www.geocities.com/echozinedistro. This resource and network site offers opportunities for zinesters to submit their zines, provides overviews and personal reviews of published zines and Internet orders.

Grrrlzine network. October 2004. Accessed October 18, 2004. http://www.grrrlzines.net. Provides a rich and varied resource and network site, specifically aimed at grrrl, lady, queer, and transfolk. Offerings range from more academic discussions and essays to interviews, resources, and message boards.

The Queer Zine Archive Project. October 2004. Accessed October 18, 2004. http://www.qzap.org. Caters to the specific needs of queers in providing a searchable archive of past and present queer zines and aims to create a history for queer zine as well as nurture current and emerging zinesters.

Zinebooks. The Zine and E-zine Guide. 2004. Chip Rowe. Accessed October 30, 2004. http://www.zinebook.com. A generalist resource for those who want to write, order, or research zines. The Zine and E-zine Guide is edited by Chip Rowe, one of the experts in this field.

R

Race and Racism

Kevin K. Kumashiro

Race and racism intersect with **sexual orientation** and **heterosexism/homophobia** in multiple and often hidden ways, and can significantly impact the ability of educators to address these issues. What it means for students to be lesbian, gay, bisexual, transgender, or intersexed (LGBTI), as well as heterosexual, can differ depending on their racial background or cultural context. And, how to effectively challenge heterosexism/homophobia in a school can differ depending on how racism is playing out in that school. Creating forms of education that address all students and work toward social justice requires addressing these intersections.

Perhaps the most common way of thinking about the influence of race and racism is to view them as adding another layer of difference or oppression to the lives of LGBTI youth. LGBTI students not only experience heterosexism/homophobia but, in a white-dominated context, they experience racism because their race, culture, and/or skin color differs from the white norm. It is difficult to speak conclusively about the experiences of all LGBTI students of color because of the numerous racial and ethnic groups encapsulated by the term, "of color." Furthermore, little **research**—quantitative or qualitative—has been done on LGBTI students of color (Ryan 2002). Nonetheless, research and theory do suggest that the combination of racial and sexual marginality can put LGBTI students of color at heightened risk of harm from **discrimination** and **harassment**, academic underachievement, lack of social and familial support, low self-esteem, and self-destructive behaviors.

Racism comes to bear on the experiences of LGBTI students of color not only in contexts where whites dominate. In many non-Western countries, as well as in **native/indigenous** populations of North America and the Pacific Islands, heterosexism/homophobia can impact differently depending on the structure of race relations and the construction of racial identities in those countries. For example, in Hawaii, earlier forms of Western **colonialism** and Christian missionary work, as well as contemporary forms of globalization and tourist consumption, have affected how different people view racial hierarchies and sexual normalcy, as when teaching that being "civilized" means being like whites and being "moral" means being heterosexual. Furthermore, in the name of ethnic pride or national unity, especially in the face of Western domination, some countries and cultures, such as Zimbabwe and **Egypt**, have narrowly defined what is normal and desirable regarding sexual relationships and gender appropriateness, and created harsh punishments for those who do not conform. Although many of these cultures have historically accepted and even valued sexual and gender diversity, contemporary manifestations of cultural norms and mores reflect the ongoing impact of heterosexism/homophobia and racism in the lives of youth of color around the world.

Of course, examining the intersections of race and sexuality does not mean examining only LGBTI students of color. White is a race just as heterosexuality is a

See also African American Youth; Antibias Curriculum; Asian American Youth; Latinos and Latinas; Multicultural Education; Racial Identity; School Climate, College; School Climate, K-12; White Antiracism; Youth, At Risk.

sexuality, although these categorizations often get lost in discussions of race and sexuality. In the United States, common understandings of sexuality in the **popular culture** and even in school **curriculum** are already centered on race, namely, the often invisible race of white Americans. While media images are slowly changing as evidenced in television shows such as **Queer as Folk** and *Queer Eye for the Straight Guy*, there remains a **stereotype** that lesbian, gay, and bisexual people are generally white, and that among people of color, same-sex attraction is like a "white disease." Talking about sexuality already involves talking about race. Similarly, common understandings of race are already centered on sexual orientation. Ethnic pride or the celebration of one's racial and cultural heritage often privileges what some consider to be "traditional values," or such values as the heterosexual family unit that are believed to have traditionally held a racial community together. Being virtuous or authentic to one's cultural group often involves performing heterosexuality by getting married and procreating.

When whiteness is valued, normalized, or privileged among LGBTI people, and heterosexuality among people of color, the communities that form do not often include people on the "margins of the margins." This is certainly the case in schools where **gay–straight alliances** are sometimes seen as groups for LGBTI students who are white, or where cultural/ethnic-based extracurricular organizations do not always welcome students of color who are LGBTI. Thus, those youth of color experience not only racism and heterosexism/homophobia in mainstream society, but also racism within LGBTI communities and heterosexism within communities of color. **Coming out** can be especially difficult if a young person's family and ethnic community is homophobic and the LGBTI community is racist.

Schools are not often places that proactively disrupt homophobia, much less its intersection with racism. The limited availability of spaces and communities that embrace their multiple identities can force LGBTI students of color to silence aspects of who they are in order to fit in, find support, and succeed in schools. For example, some may—consciously or not—choose to align themselves with other youth of color while masking their sexual differences and overlooking sexual discrimination. Others may align themselves with other LGBTI students while deemphasizing their racial and cultural differences and overlooking racial discrimination. Or, they may mask their feelings of sexual and racial inferiority by overachieving in academics and **sports** or by aggressively pursuing heterosexual romantic relationships that help them to look like someone in a "normal" relationship. Some LGBTI students of color may even internalize the valuing of only certain sexual and racial identities, and learn to dislike the LGBTI or of-color parts of themselves.

Not all schools are alike. Some schools have successfully created safe and affirming spaces for students who are LGBTI and/or of color. And, just as heterosexism, homophobia, and racism can play out differently in different contexts, so, too, can students respond in a variety of ways, including ways that reveal their **resilience** and savvy. For example, LGBTI youth of color may think strategically about when and how to emphasize or assert their LGBTI or **ethnic identity**. Or, they may form peer groups in which being LGBTI takes on a slightly different meaning, as happens when modeling ways that other cultures, ancestors, or even celebrities and public figures place a different value on fluid sexualities. Autobiographies of LGBTI students of color share stories of **dating**, finding independence, and coming to an empowered sense of self (Sonnie 2000). The lives of LGBTI students of color do not consist only of enduring multiple forms of oppression, but also succeeding in schools, experiencing joys, and looking to the future with optimism.

LGBTI students of color play a role in promoting social change. When in **gay–straight alliances** or cultural organizations, they sometimes insist that these organizations and their members address both racism and heterosexism/homophobia. Or, they form a school- or **community-based support group** that explicitly embraces their multiple identities. Whether in a group or individually, they can produce cultural texts that explore new ways to express their LGBTI-of-color identities and experiences, including **poetry**, rap, autobiography, and **art** through such media as the **Internet**, journals, mass media, **graffiti**, clothing, and speakouts.

Students are not the only ones speaking out. For decades, educators and researchers have pointed to the racism and heterosexism/homophobia that pervade education (Kumashiro 2001). They have suggested many parallels between these in the formal curriculum, as when only certain racial and sexual groups are included and only certain racial and sexual ideologies are perpetuated while other groups and perspectives are excluded or, at best, tokenized. Educators have also suggested many parallels between racism and heterosexism/homophobia in the hidden curriculum of schools, as when discrimination and a hostile school environment target certain racial and sexual groups more than others, and when schools fail to disrupt such actions and conditions. And educators have suggested parallel ways to address these problems, such as by implementing curricula that include more accurate representations of various racial and sexual groups, **educational policies** and staff that prioritize **school safety** and affirmation of various racial and sexual differences, and instructional methods that encourage critiquing the racially and sexually oppressive status quo of society and acting to bring about change.

Such work has not proven easy and many difficulties arise when trying to enact these changes. Different contexts require different approaches, such as in **rural** versus **urban** areas, curriculum at the early childhood, primary, elementary, and higher education levels, and even one national or linguistic context versus another. Although much of the **research** in English on antiracist and antiheterosexist education has focused on the United States, **Canada, Australia**, and the **United Kingdom**, educators in other countries have shed much light on the particular challenges of doing this work in non-Western contexts. For example, recently the first book was published in Japanese on challenging homophobia and gender oppression in **Japan**'s schools, and the difficulties that emerge from religious and cultural norms unique to Japanese identities and histories (Sugiyama et al. 2002). Other research and curriculum projects are currently in development in such countries as **South Africa**, Argentina, and the Philippines.

Difficulties faced by antiracist and antiheterosexist forms of education do not result merely from the contexts in which they are enacted. Difficulties can arise from the limitations of the approaches themselves. Antiracist or antiheterosexist curriculum often fails to challenge the privilege of certain identities even while challenging the privilege of other identities. For example, antiracist curriculum can reinforce heterosexual privilege when ignoring the sexual diversity among people of color, or when implying that the heterosexual family unit is and should be the bedrock of communities of color, or even when suggesting that improving conditions for people of color involves addressing only issues of race (as if issues of gender, sexuality, and other identities do not affect people of color). Similarly, antiheterosexist curriculum can reinforce white privilege when ignoring the racial diversity among LGBTI people, when implying that the authentic LGBTI identity, lifestyle, or culture is reflected in that of white LGBTI people, or even when suggesting that improving conditions for LGBTI people involves addressing only gender and sexual issues (as if race, color, and other markers do not affect LGBTI people). The formation of curriculum, like the formation of community, can continue to marginalize certain groups even while working to empower others. Therefore, while it is important to include LGBTI people in the curriculum, create policies and initiatives that affirm the intersections of racial/sexual difference, and raise critical awareness of racism and heterosexism, it is also important to look to the margins and see who or what remains excluded from the curriculum or educational policies or critical thinking, or more insidiously, who or what is now classified as a difference that does not matter in our movement towards social justice.

Bibliography

Kumashiro, Kevin K., ed. 2001. *Troubling Intersections of Race and Sexuality: Queer Students of Color and Anti-Oppressive Education.* Lanham, MD: Rowman and Littlefield Publishers.

Ryan, Caitlin. 2002. *A Review of the Professional Literature and Research Needs for LGBT Youth of Color.* Washington, D.C.: National Youth Advocacy Coalition.

Sonnie, Amy, ed. 2000. *Revolutionary Voices: A Multicultural Queer Youth Anthology.* Boston, MA: Alyson.

Sugiyama, Takashi, Akihiko Komiya, Daisuke Watanabe, and Masami Tsuzuki, eds. 2002. *Homosexuality and Other Sexualities: How to Teach about Human Rights and Living Together.* Tokyo: Japan Institute for Research in the Education and Culture of Human Sexuality.

Web Sites

International Lesbian and Gay Association. September 2004. Accessed December 20, 2004. http://www.ilga.org. Site contains information on groups in over 80 countries on all continents, many which address issues of education and youth.

National Youth Advocacy Coalition. 2004. Accessed December 20, 2004. http://www.nyacyouth.org. Links to many resources and organizations addressing youth of color.

Racial Identity

Lance T. McCready

Racial identity is a person's sense of belonging to a group based on the perception that he or she shares common heritage with a particular group such as Blacks/ African Americans, Caucasians/Euro-Americans, Latinos/Hispanics, Asian/ Pacific Islanders, and Native Americans/Indigenous Peoples. Understanding racial identity development is increasingly necessary for educators, mental health, and social

See also Adolescence; Asian American Youth; Identity Politics; Prejudice; Stereotypes; White Antiracism.

service professionals to address the complex ways LGBTQ youth interact and involve themselves in schools and LGBTQ programs. In short, racial identity has significant bearing on how LGBTQ youth perceive themselves and thus choose to socialize in educational institutions.

Although the terms *race* and *ethnicity* are often used interchangeably, it is generally understood that *race* refers to perceptions of observable phenotype while *ethnicity* refers to cultural background. At times, it is useful for educators, mental health, and social service professionals to focus on ethnicity; for example, the culturally specific family experiences of first generation Hmong Americans and second generation Chinese Americans may differ. However, youth from the two groups may experience similar racial stereotyping and treatment based on the common denominator of race. Depending on the particular circumstances, it may be more useful to focus on one or the other. Nonetheless, it is important to note that many LGBTQ youth may perceive their racial and ethnic backgrounds as interchangeable, if not identical, and, therefore, they are intricately linked in **identity development**.

Despite its importance, the concept of racial identity has been misunderstood and contested, in part, because its meanings are derived from biological, social, and cultural dimensions. As a biological category, race is derived from an individual's physical characteristics such as skin color, shape of the eyes, size of lips, hair texture. Using these features as distinguishing characteristics, European scholars and politicians grouped people hierarchically by physical ability and moral quality, with Caucasians being the most valued, followed by Asians and Native Americans, and Africans last on the racial ladder. This formed the thinking of American educators such as Edward Thorndike, a leader in measurement and testing, and **G. Stanley Hall**, the founder of the child study movement.

However, looking beyond these characteristics, there are more similarities than differences between racial groups and more differences than similarities within these groups. Although biological notions of race have popular appeal in some arenas (most notably **sports**), most often race is not discussed today in biological terms (which implies a racist perspective), but as a social construction, that refers to a sense of a group or collective identity based on one's perception that he or she shares common heritage with a particular racial group.

Sexual identity is misunderstood in ways similar to racial identity. Like racial identity, its meanings are derived from biological, social, and cultural dimensions. For example, the question of whether or not there is a "gay gene" suggests a tension between the idea that human **sexual orientation** is rooted in biological mechanisms that can be explored by laboratory science and the idea that sexual identity, **desire**, and behavior are outcomes of techniques of social control. The former assumption has led to research comparing the way that gay men's brains function compared to heterosexual men's (LeVay 1993). The latter idea has led to research and writing on the political and social consequences of privileging certain sexual practices and identities while stigmatizing others (Seidman 2003). Overall, whether you operate from a biological essentialist or social constructionist perspective, racial identity and sexual identity are misunderstood in comparable ways. What appears to be at stake is belonging, more specifically, who belongs to what race or sexual orientation, on what basis, and with what consequences.

According to psychologist William Cross (1991), black students go through five stages of racial identity development: preencounter, encounter, immersion/emersion, internalization, and internalization commitment. The first stage assumes that the prototypical African American student has absorbed many of the beliefs and values of the dominant white culture, including the notion that "white is right" and "black is wrong." The next stage is often precipitated by an event that forces the individual to acknowledge the personal impact of racism. In this "encounter" stage, the individual is faced with the reality of the inequality that she/he feels and is forced to focus on her/his identity as a person targeted by this racial inequality. Immersion/Emersion stage is characterized by the simultaneous desire to surround oneself with visible symbols of one's racial identity and an active avoidance of symbols of whiteness.

The fourth stage, "internalization," is when the individual is secure with her/his racial identity and feels less defensive and alienated from whites. During this stage the individual may try to establish meaningful relationships with respectful whites, while maintaining connections with black peers. The final stage moves the person's sense of blackness beyond just personal awareness to a state of commitment to the concerns of African Americans as a group. This "internalization-commitment" stage is stable over time and the individual has a secure sense of racial identity, a point of departure for discovering the universe of ideas, cultures, and experiences beyond blackness in place of mistaking blackness as the universe itself.

Cross' model of racial identity development offers a partial answer to the question which serves as the title to Tatum's book "*Why Are All the Black Kids Sitting Together in the Cafeteria?*" Black students, at a particular stage of their identity development, may prefer the company of racial peers rather than integrating themselves with non-black students. In some cases, if a school's **gay–straight alliance** is predominantly white, students of color who are in the "immersion/emersion" stage of development may stay away from the group because it symbolizes whiteness. Instead, LGBTQ students of color may surround themselves with visible symbols of their racial identity by congregating in groups of students who share this identity. Socializing in racially-defined groups may also reflect the belief that homosexuality is not accepted in broader non-white communities, making support among LGBTQ students of color even more important.

In addition to drawing on Cross' work to explain how racial identity affects the way black students and other students of color interact with their white peers, Tatum uses Janet Helms' (1990; 1994) research on white racial identity development to explain the cross-race behavior of Euro-American students. Tatum (1997) asserts that it is important for white students to understand that their racial identity does not depend on the perceived superiority of one racial group over another.

Tatum's discussion of white racial identity development calls attention to the fact that white LGBTQ adolescents, like LGBTQ youth of color, may go through a process of racial identity development that affects the way peer interaction. In particular, when white LGBTQ adolescents are taught not to recognize their privilege they may inadvertently oppress students of color. As white students interact with more people of color, they move into the "disintegration" stage consciously questioning assumptions about what it means to be white. At this point, white students may "reintegrate" themselves by conforming to the status quo and accepting racism. On the other hand, fear and anger may replace the initial dissonance and guilt associated with this stage. Consequently, privilege and superiority are seen as just due and the belief in the meritocracy of the United States is affirmed. Black students may be avoided or confronted violently. This stage is the easiest for whites to remain in, unless there is some catalyst for further growth that causes them to abandon white supremacy and acknowledge the white role in racism. The final stage in white racial identity formation is "autonomy." A consistent effort to work through and internalize the newly developed positive, nonsupremacist identification as a white person occurs. In this final stage, white students can forge meaningful relationships with students of color.

Whereas LGBTQ youth of color may choose not to participate in predominantly white LGBTQ youth organizations to avoid symbols of whiteness, white LGBTQ youth who participate in these organizations may view the demographics as normal. White students who have been tracked most of their lives may not have had a lot of contact with students of color and, therefore, may view all-white settings as the norm. Moreover, even though, as a group, all LGBTQ youth are likely to experience some form of marginalization and alienation, white LGBTQ youth have greater visibility in the media and LGBTQ youth organizations. This visibility affords white students a degree of privilege in relation to students of color. White students may not understand or recognize the privileged position they hold in relation to students of color. Thus, in situations when LGBTQ students of color participate in **queer** youth organizations, having the opportunity to interact with students of color may precipitate white LGBTQ youth to consciously question assumptions about what it means to be white for the first time in their lives.

Although Beverly Tatum's research on racial identity is focused on black and white adolescents (whose gender and sexual identities are never identified), applying her racial identity framework to the lives of LGBTQ adolescents has the potential to give educators insight into racially-defined patterns of participation in LGBTQ youth organizations. In particular, these models offer a partial explanation for why LGBTQ students of color may choose to avoid LGBTQ youth organizations in which the participants are predominantly white or continue to socialize in racially-defined groups. According to Tatum, some of the environmental cues in schools that trigger an examination of racial identity are tracking and ability grouping. In racially mixed schools, African American and Latino students are much more likely to be in the lower track while white and Asian students (predominantly Japanese, Chinese, and Korean ethnicities) tend to be in the honors or college-bound track. Such apparent sorting along racial lines sends LGBTQ youth a message about what it means to be a person of a particular racial identity.

While some people say there is too much talk about race and racism in the United States, this is certainly not the case in community school-based and **youth LGBTQ support groups**. Educators who work with LGBTQ youth in multiracial settings need to consider multiple dimensions of LGBTQ students' identities and break the silence regarding racism. At the core, speaking up about racism requires that educators confront their fears of being isolated from their peers for speaking about a controversial issue.

Good examples of antiracist/multiracial organizing are efforts of the National Youth Advocacy Coalition (NYAC) in Washington D.C. and the Gay Straight Alliance (GSA) Network in California. The National Youth Advocacy Coalition is a social justice organization that advocates for and with LGBTQ youth. Through its Web site (http://www.nyacyouth.org/index.html), various publications, and conferences, NYAC is creating a space and opportunity for youth to dialogue with, train, and organize one another across racial, ethnic, sexual orientation, gender, ability, and socioeconomic lines. Its Youth of Color Report is an important resource for understanding the racial identities of LGBTQ youth of color. In an effort to assist young leaders in their antidiscrimination efforts, NYAC has also developed a Racial and Economic Justice (REJ) Initiative focused on developing youth leadership through youth-led civic action activities. The GSA Network (http://www.gsanetwork.org.) is a youth-led organization that connects school-based gay–straight alliances (GSAs) to each other and community resources. Its work with students focuses on leadership development and activism that prioritizes building alliances not only across sexual orientation and gender identity lines, but also across race, ethnicity, and class lines. In particular, it offers resources on how to build an antiracist GSA.

Bibliography

Arias, Russell A. 1998. *The Identity Development, Psychosocial Stressors, and Coping Strategies of Latino Gay/Bisexual Youth: A Qualitative Analysis.* Ann Arbor, MI: University Microfilms.

Carter, Robert T., and A. Lin Goodwin. 1994. "Racial Identity and Education." Pp. 291 in *Review of Research in Education*. Edited by Linda Darling-Hammond. Washington, DC: American Educational Research Association.

Cross, William E. 1991. *Shades of Black: Diversity in African American Identity.* Philadelphia: Temple University Press.

Helms, Janet E. 1990. "Toward a Model of White Racial Identity Development." Pp. 49–66 in *Black and White Racial Identity: Theory, Research, and Practice*. Edited by Janet E. Helms. Westport, CT: Greenwood.

———. 1994. "Racial Identity and 'Racial' Constructs." Pp. 285–311 in *Human Diversity: Perspectives on People in Context*. Edited by Edison J. Trickett, Roderick J. Watts, and Dina Birman. San Francisco: Jossey-Bass.

Kumashiro, Kevin K., ed. 2001. *Troubling Intersections of Race and Sexuality: Queer Students of Color and Anti-Oppressive Education.* Lanham, MD: Rowman and Littlefield.

LeVay, Simon. 1993. *The Sexual Brain.* Boston: MIT Press.

McCready, Lance T. 2004. "Understanding the Marginalization of Gay and Gender Non-Conforming Black Male Students." *Theory Into Practice* 43, no. 2: 136–143.

Merighi, Joseph R. 1996. *Coming Out in Black and White: An Exploratory Analysis of African American and Caucasian Gay Male Youth.* Ann Arbor, MI: University Microfilms.

Phinney, Jean S. 1991. "Ethnic Identity in Adolescents and Adults: Review of Research." *Psychological Bulletin* 108, no. 3: 499–514.

Seidman, Steven. 2003. *Social Construction of Sexuality.* New York: Norton.

Suarez-Orozco, Carola, and Marcelo Suarez-Orozco. 2001. *Children of Immigration.* Cambridge, MA: Harvard University Press.

Tatum, Beverly Daniel. 1997. *"Why Are All the Black Kids Sitting Together in the Cafeteria?" and Other Conversations about Race.* New York: Basic.

Web Sites

Center for Anti-Oppressive Education (CAOE). May 2005. Accessed, June 11, 2005. http://www.antioppressiveeducation.org/index.html. Through its projects on research, curriculum, professional development, and local advocacy, CAOE develops and provides resources for educators, leaders, students, and advocates who are interested in creating and engaging in antioppressive forms of education.

Expose Racism and Advance School Excellence. 2004. Accessed, June 20, 2004. http://www.arc.org/erase/. A national program, coordinated by the Applied Research Center, that challenges racism in public schools and promotes racial justice and academic excellence for all students.

Rainbow Flag and Other Pride Symbols

Jerry Rosiek

A six-striped rainbow flag triangle has become one of the most recognizable symbols of resistance to **homophobia** and the persecution of **lesbian, gay, bisexual,** and **transgender** (LGBT) persons. The symbol is used by members of LGBT communities and their **allies** to indicate solidarity with the struggle to end homophobic oppression of sexual minorities. It is placed on cars, in offices or classrooms, or on documents and Web pages, to signal that it is safe to speak frankly about **sexual identity** issues with the person(s) displaying the symbol.

A rainbow striped flag has been used as a symbol by many groups and for many purposes. Most notably, the rainbow flag was used as a symbol of an international peace movement throughout the twentieth century. This use of the rainbow as a symbol of peace movements continues in **Europe**, where the rainbow flag was used during the 2003 protests against war on Iraq. The most common variety of the rainbow peace flag has seven colors rather than six, and often includes the Italian word *pace*, "peace," in its center. The rainbow flag was also used in the United States by "The Rainbow Coalition," which was founded in the 1990s by the Reverend Jesse Jackson as part of his campaign for the U.S. presidency. He and his supporters used it to symbolize the diversity and inclusiveness of their coalition. It has been used as a symbol of the cooperative movement (commercial entities owned by their customers or residents), in Peru as a symbol of the pre-Columbian Inca empire, and in the Middle East as a symbol of some Druze communities.

Since the late 1970s, however, the rainbow flag has become known in the United States, and to a lesser extent in the rest of the world, as a symbol of LGBT rights and liberation. The first Rainbow Flag used for this purpose was designed, in 1978, by Gilbert Baker, a San Francisco artist, who constructed a rainbow flag in response to a local gay rights activist's call for a community symbol. Baker designed a flag with eight stripes: pink, red, orange, yellow, green, blue, indigo, and violet. According to Baker, those colors represented, respectively: sexuality, life, healing, sun, nature, art, harmony, and spirit.

Baker hand-dyed the first flag made. When he began receiving requests from people wanting to purchase copies of the flag, he approached San Francisco's Paramount Flag Company about mass producing this "gay rights flag." At the time, the pink color he used was not commercially available, so mass production of his eight-striped version became impossible. The flag was thus reduced to seven stripes.

In November 1978, San Francisco's gay community was shocked when the city's first openly gay supervisor, Harvey Milk, was assassinated. Wishing to

See also Bisexuality; Cross- Dressing; Identity Politics; Lesbian Feminism; National Coming Out Day; Transsexuality.

demonstrate the gay community's strength and solidarity in the aftermath of this tragedy, the 1979 Pride Parade Committee chose to use Baker's flag. The committee eliminated the turquoise stripe so they could divide the colors evenly along the parade route: three colors on one side of the street and three on the other. Soon these six colors were incorporated into a six-striped version that became widely popular.

In 1989, this six-striped rainbow flag received nationwide attention when a landlord in West Hollywood tried to force resident John Stout to stop displaying the flag from his apartment balcony. Stout sued his landlord and won his case. Today, this six-striped version is recognized by the International Congress of Flag Makers.

The LGBT movement has had numerous symbols of pride and solidarity. The **Pink Triangle** is the most widely known but other symbols include the following:

The Lambda. In 1970, New York City's Gay Activists Alliance (GAA) selected the Greek letter lambda as its symbol. The GAA was a group which broke away from the larger Gay Liberation Front (GLF) at the end of 1969, only six months after GLF was founded in response to the **Stonewall** riots. While the GLF wanted to work with the black and women's liberation movements for justice, the GAA wanted to focus their efforts more concisely on only gay and lesbian issues. The symbol quickly became popular, less for its militant associations than for the fact that its significance is often unrecognized by the uninitiated. In 1974, the Lambda was adopted by the International Gay Rights Congress held in Edinburgh, Scotland. It has also been used by organizations such as Lambda Legal Defense and Education Fund, as a way of identifying with LGBT rights movements.

Many explanations are in circulation about why the letter lambda was chosen as a gay rights symbol. These include: the Greek letter "L" stands for "liberation;" the Greek Spartans believed that the lambda represented unity; the Romans took it as meaning "the light of knowledge shining into the darkness of ignorance;" the charged energy of the gay movement. This stems from the lambda's use in chemistry and physics to denote energy in equations. Most likely, it is some combination of these reasons that have given the lambda its longevity as a symbol of gay pride and liberation. As Joseph Goodwin (1989, 26) declaims, "Thus the lambda, with all its meanings, is an especially apt symbol for the gay liberation movement, which energetically seeks a balance in society and which strives through enlightenment to secure equal rights for homosexual people."

Often the rainbow symbol will be mixed with other symbols, such as the triangle, the lambda, or the flag of the United States:

 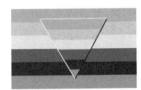 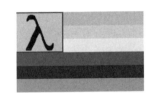

Other pride symbols that denote the needs, interests, and struggles of particular subsets of the LGBT community include:

The Labrys. This image of the double-bladed ax is drawn from the weapon/scepter allegedly held by the goddess Demeter (Artemis). Legend has it that this same weapon was originally used in battle by Scythian Amazon warriors. Today, the labrys has become a symbol of lesbian and feminist strength and self-sufficiency.

The Bisexual Pride Flag. The pink color at the top represents sexual attraction to the same sex only (gay and lesbian), the blue at the bottom represents sexual attraction to the opposite sex only (straight) and the resultant overlap color purple represents sexual attraction to both sexes (bi).

The Bear Pride Flag. A "bear" is a homosexual man that has an abundance of hair on their face, chest, and body. The diagonally-striped bear flag shown was first displayed on June 18, 1995, at Spags, a Seattle bear bar. The colors of the flag represent the earth and the different bears that live between the sky and the ground: white for polar bears; black for black bears; brown for brown bears. The Golden yellow paw shaped sun represents the spirit and brotherhood of all bears. The blue stripe (upper left corner) represents the sky and green (lower right corner) stands for the Earth. The second bear flag shown is the International Bear Brotherhood Flag.

Leather Pride Flag. Created by Tony DeBlase and first displayed in Chicago in 1989 at the Mr. Leather Contest, the Leather Pride Flag, gained quick, universal recognition as a symbol of those with leather, S M B D, uniform, latex, western, and other fetishes.

Victory Over AIDS Flag. In the 1990s, some **AIDS** activists added a black stripe to the bottom of the rainbow flag to commemorate all of those lost to the AIDS epidemic. Sgt. Leonard Matlovich, a decorated Vietnam War veteran dying of AIDS, proposed that when a cure for AIDS was found, all of the black stripes should be removed from these flags and ceremoniously burned in Washington, D.C.

The Transgender Symbol. The International Foundation for Gender Education (IFGE) has adopted this symbol for its logo. It has become a widely recognized symbol for or cross-dressers, transvestites, transsexuals, and transgenderists.

Despite the wide variety of flags and symbols representing LGBT identity, a common purpose underlies them. Each is part of a struggle for positive visibility for LGBT populations in societies that encourage and sometimes enforce invisibility. Even in the most homophobic contexts, these symbols are displayed by LGBT persons and their allies as a sign of solidarity. They are used in educational settings to let students and teachers know that here all sexual identities are safe and welcome. Knowing what these symbols are, their history, and their meaning can help LGBT youth and their allies recognize one another and work together in the struggle for LGBT rights and freedom.

Bibliography

The Alyson Almanac: A Treasury of Information for the Gay and Lesbian Community.
    1993. 3rd ed. Boston: Alyson Publications.
Goodwin, Joseph. 1989. *More Man Than You'll Ever Be: Gay Folklore and Acculturation in Middle America.* Bloomington: Indiana University Press.

Web Sites

Gay Lesbian Bisexual Transgender Alliance Pride Symbols. November 2004. The 10% Society, University of South Dakota. http://www.usd.edu/student-life/orgs/glba/pride.html.
Gay, Lesbian, Bisexual, & Transgender Symbols. October 2001. Charles Edward Riffenburg IV. LΛMBDA GLBT Community Services. http://www.lambda.org/.Rainbow Icon Archive. November 2004. Jase P. Wells. Enqueue Design. http://www.enqueue.com/ria/.
SwadePages. November 2004. Susan Wade. Accessed November 23, 2004. http://www.swade.net/gallery/
Symbols of Pride. February 2002. J. Daniel Pierce and Gary Edwards. SUNY Potsdam. http://www2.potsdam.edu/clubs/LGBA/pages/other/NewSymbols.html.

Religion and Psychological Development

Geoffrey L. Ream

Religion refers to identification and involvement with organizations and institutions that facilitate **spirituality** and meaning-making through engagement with the supernatural. Although voluntary religious involvement is generally understood to be a source of **resiliency** and positive contribution to the development of youth, this is not necessarily true for all youth, particularly sexual-minority youth. Sexual prejudice is often a component of religious belief systems, and internalized sexual prejudice can complicate already difficult developmental tasks for sexual minorities, including self-labeling and **coming out**. Additionally, conservative religious and political ideology acts on sexual-minority youths' environments to make their lives more difficult. Nevertheless, many sexual-minority individuals draw strength from religious faith and connections with religious organizations.

Religion is complex, multifaceted, and hard to define. Religion is an attachment process between individuals and higher powers and/or religious organizations, but it is more than that. Religion is also a belief system which individuals synthesize from religious ideas they have learned. Consideration of multiple facets of religious experience—socially mediated and personal, emotional and cognitive, and many others besides—is necessary for understanding how youth choose their religious paths and how environmental religious influences affect them. For instance, while individuals who grew up in families characterized by secure attachments are likely to internalize the religiousness or non-religiousness of their parents, individuals who grew up with insecure attachments are likely to either abandon their parents' religion or choose a religious path that compensates for the security and stability they never had as children (Kirkpatrick and Shaver 1990).

Attachment to religious organizations and adherence to religious belief systems, which generally prohibit risky or immoral behaviors and encourage positive values toward family and community, are negatively correlated with **substance use**, sexual activity, and delinquency (Donahue 1995). Religion's effects on behavior are most pronounced in "moral communities" where religious attendance is high and religious

See also Adolescence; Identity Development; Jewish Moral Instruction on Homosexuality; Parents, Responses to Homosexuality; Religious Fundamentalism; Reparative Therapy; Youth, At Risk.

values assert strong social control (Stark 1996). In addition to forestalling maladaptive behavior, religious organizations provide needed social services to youth, foster social connections, create opportunities for youth–adult partnerships, encourage community service, and facilitate the development of higher meaning and purpose in life and connections with things greater than the self (Ream and Witt 2003).

Although sexual-minority youths' experiences with religion are not necessarily less positive than those of heterosexual youth, these are often complicated by religion-based sexual **prejudice**. Most major American religious denominations and Evangelical Christian ministry and media organizations teach that same-sex sexual activity is an offense against God with dire health consequences, that same-sex attractions are a symptom of a psychological disorder, that "practicing homosexuals" have disregarded the harm they can cause to themselves and others and selfishly given in to their disordered and destructive desires, and that to self-identify as lesbian or gay is to align oneself with a political "gay agenda" that seeks to co-opt and destroy the institution of the heterosexual, two-parent, father-headed family that they allege is crucial to the survival of society. In a 1999 statement, Roman Catholic Cardinal Joseph Ratzinger, currently Pope Benedict XVI, asserted that same-sex attractions are "intrinsically disordered." Evangelical media ministry organizations such as Focus on the Family, in their fundraising letters, consistently speak of the need to defend society against the threat posed by efforts to achieve equal rights for LGB individuals. The audience for these viewpoints is not an extremist minority. It includes the 41 percent of Americans who identify as "born-again" or "Evangelical" and the roughly one-in-four Americans who identify as Catholic (Gallup Brain 2003).

Individuals internalize the anti-gay values of their religion. Several studies have found intrinsic religiousness, a psychological measure of internally-motivated religious belief, to be strongly correlated with antigay attitudes in mostly-**Christian** or all-Christian samples. It is counterintuitive that, although intrinsic religiousness has historically been known to be negatively associated with racial prejudice, it is positively associated with anti-gay prejudice (Herek 1987). A study measuring the association between intrinsic religiousness and **homophobia** while controlling for two other strongly correlated constructs—fundamentalism, which is belief in the absolute truth of a single religion; and Christian orthodoxy, which is adherence to specific doctrines—found that the independent effect of intrinsic religion was negative (Fulton, Gorsuch, and Maynard 1999; Kirkpatrick 1993). Although this finding does point out the complexity of individual religious belief systems and the location of sexual prejudice within them, it also reinforces the fact that intrinsic religion, fundamentalism, orthodoxy, and homophobia are likely to be found within the same individuals. It further implies that **gay youth** facing conflict over religion looking for someone to trust will have difficulty finding someone both religious and gay-friendly.

Religion-based homophobia interferes with and sometimes reverses adaptive functions of religion and spirituality for sexual-minority youth, both through internalized homophobia and by contributing to an intolerant, socially toxic environment. Families ascribing to traditional family values are less tolerant of homosexuality and can complicate the task of coming out (Newman and Muzzonigro 1993). Conservative activists oppose anti-bullying programs in schools that mention sexual orientation as an inappropriate motivation for victimizing other students (Tomsho, 2002). Evangelical media organizations, such as James Dobson's Focus on the Family, promulgate misinformation about homosexuality through radio, print, and electronic media. They teach parents that early gender nonconformity is not merely correlated with, but actually causes, homosexuality, and that homosexuality can be treated or even prevented if caught early enough. Using this information, parents, teachers, and other concerned adults, believing that they are doing the right thing, prevent accurate information about homosexuality (and sexual health in general) from reaching their youth and scrutinize children for any sign of difference, such as introversion or an unusually high or low interest in athletics, that may predict later homosexuality (Ream & Savin-Williams, 2004).

Despite the current pervasive influence of conservative ideology, there remain several religious ideologies, organizations, branches, and movements that are tolerant and affirming (Ream 2003). Acceptance of sexual minorities varies between and within denominations as well as within regions and between nations. In the United States, the Metropolitan Community Church, Reform Judaism, and Wicca are gay and lesbian friendly. In other countries, the religious landscape is different and the same denomination may not have the same position from one country to the next. The Episcopal Church, the branch of the Anglican Communion in America, has ordained gay priests in certain dioceses for years recently appointed a gay bishop. Some parishes, particularly in the Southern states, have rejected this position, as have staunchly anti-gay Anglican churches in Singapore and Africa. Buddhist organizations in America tend to be gay-friendly, but are not always so in Southeast Asian and other countries where Buddhism, although not an inherently patriarchal belief system, upholds a patriarchal social system (Gross 1993). Although no major branch of Islam is gay-tolerant, the Al-Fatiha Foundation advocates for sexual-minority **Muslim** issues. It is fair to say that there is no major religion or religious denomination without a gay-friendly sect, movement, or advocacy group.

Factors regarding sexual-minority youths' decision whether to remain involved in religion are many of the same factors which govern religious change in general (Sherkat 2001): They seek to hold onto what is important and helpful to them, leave behind what they find hypocritical or inauthentic, and preserve and advance their integrity and sense of self. If they value religion, they will seek to give up as little religious human capital as they can while moving to a more gay-friendly space. For example, sexual-minority Catholics, upon deciding to switch, are likely to join the Episcopal Church or become involved in Santería in order to continue practicing the liturgy with which they are comfortable. A sexual-minority Orthodox Jew is more likely to become a Reform Jew or join an Orthodox gay organization than to leave Judaism. Evangelicals and Charismatics may move to the Metropolitan Community Church in order to stay with their accustomed worship style. Many do not move at all, perhaps hoping to change their institution from within. Adults concerned about helping sexual-minority youth with conflicts with religion can best serve them by protecting them from religion-based homophobia and supporting their choices and their right to choose.

Bibliography

Diamond, Sara. 1998. *Not by Politics Alone: The Enduring Influence of the Christian Right.* New York: Guilford Press.

Donahue, Michael J. 1995. "Religion and the Well-Being of Adolescents." *Journal of Social Issues* 51, no. 2: 145–160.

Fulton, Aubyn S., Richard L. Gorsuch, and Elizabeth A. Maynard. 1999. "Religious Orientation, Antihomosexual Sentiment, and Fundamentalism among Christians." *Journal for the Scientific Study of Religion* 38, no. 1: 14–35.

Gross, Rita M. 1993. *Buddhism after Patriarchy: A Feminist History, Analysis, and Reconstruction of Buddhism.* Albany: State University of New York Press.

Herek, Gregory M. 1987. "Religious Orientation and Prejudice: A Comparison of Racial and Sexual Attitudes." *Personality and Social Psychology Bulletin* 13, no.1: 34–44.

Kirkpatrick, Lee A. 1993. "Fundamentalism, Christian Orthodoxy, and Intrinsic Religious Orientation as Predictors of Discriminatory Attitudes." *Journal for the Scientific Study of Religion* 32, no. 3: 256–268.

Kirkpatrick, Lee A., and Phillip R. Shaver. 1990. "Attachment Theory and Religion: Childhood Attachments, Religious Beliefs, and Conversion." *Journal for the Scientific Study of Religion* 29, no. 3: 315–334.

Newman, Bernie S., and Peter G. Muzzonigro. 1993. "The Effects of Traditional Family Values on the Coming Out Process of Gay Male Adolescents." *Adolescence* 28, no. 109: 213–226.

Ream, Geoffrey L. 2003. "Religion and Sexual Orientation in America." Pp. 608–613 in *Encyclopedia of Human Ecology*, Vol. 2: I–Z. Edited by Judith R. Miller, Richard M. Lerner, Lawrence B. Schiamberg, and Pamela M. Anderson. Santa Barbara, CA: ABC-Clio.

Ream, Geoffrey L., and Ritch C. Savin-Williams. 2004. "Religion and the Educational Experiences of Adolescents." Pp. 255–286 in *Educating Adolescents: Challenges and Strategies.* Edited by Tim Urdan & Frank Pajares. Greenwich, CT: Information Age Publishing.

Ream, Geoffrey L., and Peter A. Witt. 2003. "Organizations Serving All Ages." Pp. 49–74 in *Handbook of Youth Development.* Edited by Stephen F. Hamilton and Mary Agnes Hamilton. Thousand Oaks, CA: Sage.

Sherkat, Darren E. 2001. "Tracking the Restructuring of American Religion: Religious Affiliation and Patterns of Religious Mobility, 1973–1998." *Social Forces* 79, no. 4: 1459–1493.

Stark, Rodney. 1996. "Religion as Context: Hellfire and Delinquency One More Time." *Sociology of Religion* 57, no. 2: 163–173.

Tomsho, Robert. 2002. Schools' Efforts to Protect Gays Face Opposition. *Wall Street Journal* (February 20): B1.

Web Sites

Al-Fatiha Foundation, Inc. 2003. Al-Fatiha Foundation. Accessed December 8, 2004. http://www.al-fatiha.org. Resources for sexual-minority Muslims.

Focus on the Family. 2004. Homosexuality in Schools. Accessed December 8, 2004. http://www.family.org/cforum/topics/a0018824.cfm. Position paper from a Christian Right media conglomerate.

Gallup Brain. 2003. Poll Topic & Trend—Religion. The Gallup Organization. Accessed January 12, 2004. http://www.gallup.com/poll/topics/religion2.asp. Statistics of membership in various Christian denominations and profession of various Christian beliefs. Gallup's figures are updated continually. These are only available to account holders.

GayTeenChristians. Accessed December 8, 2004. http://www.gaychristian.net/. Old but still interesting Web site with original stories and essays written by gay Christian youth.

Religious Fundamentalism

Susan Birden

Religious fundamentalism claims authority over a sacred tradition and seeks to re-vitalize that tradition as an antidote for a society that has strayed from its cultural moorings. It refutes the split between sacred and secular that characterizes mod-ernist and humanist thinking. Many religious scholars argue that the term "funda-mentalism" is so rooted in a particular form of Protestant Christianity that it poses difficulties when used to characterize other religions. However, Martin Marty, whose five-volume Fundamentalism Project brought together numerous scholars from different religious traditions, argues that even though fundamentalisms cer-tainly differ among religions, there are striking resemblances. Marty maintains that fundamentalists across religions see themselves as a righteous minority involved in a cosmic struggle, stress selective parts of their tradition and heritage, and act con-frontationally toward both secularists and wayward religious followers. Because fundamentalists view homosexuality as one of the indications of cultural decline, they uniformly denounce it, believing that the faithful should oppose homosexual practices and discipline not only believers, but societies that support or tolerate homosexuality. Consequently, religious fundamentalism, in religious and secular so-cieties, poses serious issues for many sexual minority youth, who are already at risk for **suicide, harassment, substance abuse,** homelessness.

The term "fundamentalism" has its origin in a series of pamphlets, "The Fun-damentals: A Testimony to the Truth," published between 1910 and 1915. Milton and Lyman Steward "freely circulated three million copies" among clergymen and seminarians to counter the loss of influence of traditional revivalism, the liberaliz-ing trends of German Biblical criticism, and the encroachment of Darwin's theories of evolution. Today, "fundamentalist," when used to describe Christians, is associ-ated primarily with conservative Protestants, but early fundamentalists were both Protestant and Catholic.

Hierarchies in the Roman **Catholic** and orthodox **Christian** traditions such as the Greek and Russian Orthodox Church, adhere to views on homosexuality that are consistent with Protestant fundamentalists, understanding the primary purpose of human sexuality to be for procreation and development of the human species—a social good that establishes and promotes a stable family. These traditions teach that homosexual orientation is not itself morally evil, but that all such behavior is morally wrong (as is all sexual behavior outside of marriage). They counsel believers to avoid such behavior through celibacy.

Fundamentalist Protestants, on the other hand, particularly in the United States, have been influenced by a Reformed approach to the scope of Biblical authority. This interpretive strategy adheres to two main suppositions: because the Bible is the high-est religious authority, every directive contained therein is applicable at all times to all people; and the meaning of the biblical text is directly accessible to commonsense literal interpretation. The proscription against homosexual behavior is based on four

See also Children of the Rainbow Curriculum; Educational Policies; Jewish Moral Instruc-tion on Homosexuality; Muslim Moral Instruction on Homosexuality; Parents, Responses to Homosexuality; Religion and Psychological Development; Spirituality; Youth, At Risk; Youth, Homeless.

main passages from the Bible, through which fundamentalists assert the sinfulness of homoerotic behavior: "You shall not lie with a male as with a woman; it is an abomination" (Leviticus 18:22); "If a male lies with a male as with a woman, both of them have committed an abomination; they shall be put to death; their blood is upon them" (Leviticus 20:13); "Their women exchanged natural intercourse for unnatural, and in the same way also the men, giving up natural intercourse with women, were consumed with passion for one another" (Romans 1:26–27); "Fornicators, idolaters, adulterers, male prostitutes, sodomites, thieves, the greedy, drunkards, revilers, robbers—none of these will inherit the kingdom of God" (I Corinthians 6:9–10).

Although fundamentalist and liberal Protestant scholars agree that the Scriptures are negative with respect to homosexual behavior, they disagree about what these passages mean for godly social relations. Scholars using a historical–critical interpretive approach, for instance, seek to understand the prohibitions against homosexual practice within their original cultural and historical context, drawing a contrast between the homoerotic practices prohibited in the text and committed gay and lesbian relationships in contemporary society. Fundamentalists maintain that in light of the plain meaning of the Scriptural text, it is unreasonable and revisionist to challenge the proscription of homosexuality on a Biblical basis.

Conversely, theologians practicing historical–critical scholarship seek to situate the prohibitions against homosexuality in the cited texts in their original cultural and historical context. The purpose is to draw a contrast between the actual homoerotic practices prohibited in the text and those forms of committed lesbian and gay relationships for which religious and social sanction are being sought today. A key presupposition of this tactic asserts that "homosexual" is a social construction related to form of life. An example of this strategy, with respect to Leviticus prohibitions, begins by discriminating between the criminal and cultic law codes of ancient Israel (Birden, Gaither, and Laird 1999). There is no condemnation of homosexuality in the civil and criminal laws, but in liturgical laws of Leviticus the prohibition is tied with the word to'ebah, "abomination," which also implies idolatry. To'ebah, in Hebrew scriptures, designates idolatrous actions associated with the fertility cults and religious prostitution of the nations surrounding Israel. Thus, historical–critical scholars believe that the cultic prohibitions of Leviticus, when understood in their historical context, have nothing to do with contemporary social relations. Emphasizing the distance between an ancient text and any contemporary reader, historical–critical theologians believe that Christians cannot ignore a growing body of secular, scientific knowledge surrounding human sexuality and the social construction of gender.

Regardless of interpretation, each of these religious leaders teaches that homosexuals should be accorded pastoral care and confidential medical and psychiatric services. Some Protestant fundamentalists have also advocated psychological "conversion" or reparative therapy that seeks to reorient persons toward heterosexuality.

Orthodox Judaism, like fundamentalist Christianity, points to the passages from Leviticus. However, rabbinic exegesis of the Torah finds several other homosexual references in the Scriptural narratives. According to midrashic, an approach to reading and interpreting Scripture, Jewish scholars claim that the generation of Noah was condemned to eradication by the Flood because they had sunk so low morally that they were writing out formal marriage contracts for sodomites.

The rabbis of the Talmud, Jewish commentaries and interpretations on Scripture, elaborated four general rationales for the scriptural prohibitions on homosexuality: 1) A primary function of sexuality is reproduction, which is frustrated by

Youth, Education, and Sexualities

homosexuality; 2) Interpretation of homosexuality as "going astray" suggests the danger of a married man with homosexual tendencies disrupting his family life; 3) The unnaturalness of the homosexual liaison defies the very structure of the anatomy of the sexes; and 4) the Biblical characterization of homosexual relations as an "abomination" need not be further defined or explained.

Jewish scholars argue, however, that even passing moral judgment does not mean that in the name of Judaism one should demand the harshest possible punishment. The singling out of homosexuals as the victims of society's righteous indignation is patently unfair, they assert, since such crusades are often marked by cruelty, destruction, and bigotry. Orthodox Judaism allows for no compromise in its abhorrence of sodomy, but encourages compassion toward homosexuals and efforts at rehabilitation.

Conversely, many Reform and Reconstructionist synagogues welcome openly lesbian and gay couples into their congregations. These movements within Judaism have official policies of nondiscrimination on the basis of **sexual orientation** in all aspects of synagogue life. Reform and Reconstructionist rabbis perform same-sex unions at their discretion.

The *sharī'a*, or traditional law of Islam, is based on the Quran, which was revealed to the Prophet Muhammad by God, and on the *hadīth*, or traditions, which are sayings attributed to the Prophet. Deemed to be the word of God, the Quran condemns male and female homosexuality as "transgressing beyond bounds." The Quran has seven references to the story of Lot or Lot's people, the Sodomites, that fundamentalists interpret as condemnation of sexual relations between persons of the same sex. They consider the destruction of Sodom to be explicitly associated with their sexual practices: "And they indeed sought to shame his guest (by asking to commit sodomy with them). So We blinded their eyes (saying), 'Then taste you My Torment and My Warnings'" (al-Qamar 54:37). "So when Our Commandment came, We turned (the towns of Sodom in Palestine) upside down, and rained on them stones of baked clay, in a well-arranged manner one after another; Marked from your Lord" (Hood 11:82–83).

Islamic fundamentalists argue that modern society's characterization of homosexual tendencies as inborn are ploys of the devil to convince people that they cannot escape sinful behavior. Contending that people are free agents, Islamic clerics believe that through prayer and exercise of free will, individuals can avoid the sin of homosexuality.

All the Islamic legal schools regard sex between males as unlawful, but they differ over the severity of the punishment. Many clerics have urged imprisonment for homosexuality. Others, such as Sheik Shadi, an Islamic cleric in **Australia**, have called for an Islamic court to be given the legal right to stone gay men and lesbians to death. Even moderate Islamic leaders denounce the evil of homosexuality. However, in Islam, as in Christianity and Judaism, some religious scholars take a historical–critical approach to textual interpretation that seeks to understand these passages in the context of the time and to develop more compassionate responses to gay and lesbian Muslims. In fact, in 2003, a group of leading Muslim clerics in the **United Kingdom** joined with other faith leaders for the first time to condemn the growing tide of **homophobia** in Islam.

Given the unequivocal condemnation of homosexuality in these three major fundamentalist traditions, it is not surprising that LGBT youth who have undergone years of religious training about the sinfulness and sickness of homosexuality often experience confusion, guilt, shame, depression, and low self-esteem. Feelings of isolation are common since these youth often know no other sexual minority people and feel like outsiders even in their families of origin. All of these factors contribute to this group's increased risk of substance abuse, suicide, and **mental health** problems. Risks are also great if these gay and lesbian youth choose to reveal their same-sex orientation to their families. Many suffer physical abuse and are forced out of the home. Lacking familial financial support, these homeless youth often turn to **prostitution** and other risky behaviors to support themselves (Blaker 2003).

Even in countries that purport separation of church and state, like the United States and **France**, popular ethics and opinion remain grounded in religious values. **Research** also indicates that persons with more fundamentalist religious attitudes also evince more negative attitudes toward LGBT persons and civil rights (Sears 1997). Lobbyists, backed by fundamentalist groups, negatively influence governmental policies on such critical issues as AIDS research and treatment. Additionally, these groups have lobbied state and local school districts to prevent comprehensive **sexuality education, counseling** programs for LGBT youth, inclusive **curriculum**, and formation of **gay–straight alliances**.

Bibliography

Birden, Susan, Linda L. Gaither, and Susan Laird. 2000. "The Struggle Over the Text: Compulsory Heterosexuality and Educational Policy." *Educational Policy* 14, no. 5: 638–663.

Blaker, Kimberly, ed. 2003. *The Fundamentals of Extremism*. Boston: New Boston Books.

Countryman, William L. 1994. *Biblical Authority or Biblical Tyranny? Scripture and the Christian Pilgrimage*. Cambridge: Cowley.

Kellner, Menachem Marc, ed. 1978. *Contemporary Jewish Ethics*. New York: Sanhedrin Press.

Lawrence, Bruce B. 1990. *Defenders of God: The Fundamentalist Revolt against the Modern Age*. London: Tauris.

Marty, Martin, and R. Scott Appleby, eds. 1994. *Accounting for Fundamentalisms: The Dynamic Character of Movements* (The Fundamentalism Project, Vol. 4). Chicago: University of Chicago Press.

Murray, Stephen O., and Will Roscoe. 1997. *Islamic Homosexualities: Culture, History, and Literature*. New York: New York University Press.

Olyan, Saul M., and Martha C. Nussbaum, eds. 1998. *Sexual Orientation and Human Rights in American Religious Discourse*. New York and Oxford: Oxford University Press.

Remafadi, Gary, ed. 1994. *Death by Denial: Studies of Suicide in Gay and Lesbian Teenagers*. Boston: Alyson.

Sears, James T. 1997. "Thinking Critically/Intervening Effectively About Homophobia and Heterosexism. Pp. 13–48 in *Overcoming Heterosexism and Homophobia*. Edited by James T. Sears and Walter L. Williams. New York: Columbia University Press.

The Surgeon General's Call to Action to Prevent Suicide. 1999. United States Department of Health and Human Services. Last Accessed September 15, 2004. http://www.surgeongeneral.gov/library/calltoaction/fact3.htm.

Web Site

Religious Movements Homepage. May 2005. University of Virginia. Accessed June 11, 2005. http://religiousmovements.lib.virginia.edu. Gives an overview of many religious movements, including extensive information on fundamentalism.

Reparative Therapy

Gerald Walton

Reparative therapy (also known as conversion therapy) is a controversial and profitable practice in **psychology** that seeks to change one's homosexual orientation to heterosexual. Since the early 1900s, attempts have included psychotherapy, aversion therapy (nausea-inducing drugs), castration, electric shock, and brain surgery. These harmful and ineffective methods were mostly abandoned, in North America at least, during the 1970s (Besen 2003). Current therapies include one-on-one **counseling**, group therapy, and avoidance strategies (such as interrupting one's homosexual fantasies and avoiding potential homosexual encounters). For **lesbian, gay, bisexual**, and **transgender youth** (LGBT), reparative therapy signifies that being LGBT is inferior to being heterosexual, and for some young men and women marks a traumatic experience. The American Psychological Association (APA) does not support the theories, methods, and ethics of this approach. On youth sexuality, the APA (1997) asserts that many LGBT youth are at risk for "self-injurious behaviors," not because of their **sexual orientation**, but from "society's attitudes, behaviors, and tendency to render lesbian, gay and bisexual persons invisible [in] all societal institutions including the family and school system." LGBT youth of color, of physical and/or mental **disabilities**, and of lower socioeconomic status may face additional social prejudice (APA 1997). Undergraduate psychology textbooks provide overviews on issues related to LGBT youth, but tend not to delve into the controversies of reparative therapy specifically.

Homosexuality was removed, in 1973, as a category of mental illness from the *Diagnostic and Statistical Manual of Mental Disorders* (DSM). However, some psychologists and social workers, including those who work with youth, continue to practice as if homosexuality is, per se, an illness (Morrison and L'Heureux 2001). Joseph Nicolosi and Charles Socarides, for example, were instrumental in forming the National Association for Research and Therapy of Homosexuality (NARTH) in 1992, which associates homosexuality with "maladaptive behaviours" in adulthood and claims that these can be prevented and treated. NARTH proponents allege that the APA prohibits discussion in public schools about sexual reorientation. "Respect for diversity . . . requires teaching about all principled positions," they assert on their Web site, adding that, "[t]olerance must also be extended to those people who take the principled, scientifically supportable view that homosexuality works against our human nature." NARTH psychologists say little about bisexual and transgender individuals.

While reparative therapy psychologists posit homosexuality as a mental illness, proponents of "ex-gay" ministries classify homosexuality as unnatural, abnormal, deviant, and ungodly. The most prominent ex-gay ministry, Exodus International, is based in the United States. The mandate of Exodus Youth, a subministry of the larger organization, is to spread their message to youth that "freedom" from homosexuality is possible. These Christian ministries claim to achieve high "success"

See also Compulsory Heterosexuality; Gender Identity Disorder; Homophobia; Mental Health; Parents, Responses to Homosexuality; Religious Fundamentalism; Social Class; Social Work; Suicide.

rates among the participants, yet have not produced reliable data (Besen 2003). Even ex-gay leaders fail to demonstrate strict adherence to heterosexuality, in spite of their testimonials and lifestyle choices such as heterosexual marriage.

Reparative therapy as a scientific method is methodologically problematic. A study of 200 participants conducted by Spitzer (2003), for example, appears to validate reparative therapy. However, the study suffers from lack of scientific rigor as its sample is not representative of a diverse LGBT population but skewed toward a religious, white, Protestant, middle-aged, and middle class population (Carlson 2003). Further, 76 percent of the men and 47 percent of the women were married when they participated in the study. Thus, respondents were severely conflicted about their homosexuality and had significant religious and marital motivation to conform to **heteronormativity** and to oppose homosexuality. Many of the participants of such **research** are actually bisexual rather than homosexual (Haldeman 1999, 3).

Another important question to consider is not *if* sexual orientation can change, but *why* it should be changed. Even if homosexuality can be changed (notwithstanding methodological quandaries about how "change" is measured or why it is necessary), it remains unclear why self-assured gays and lesbians should consequently be denied social and legal justice.

Pressure to be heterosexual is especially pronounced and widespread among youth (Thurlow 2001). LGBT youth are often convinced, if not coerced, by their parents into participating in sexual reorientation programs even though reparative therapy, at its best, merely changes behavior, not orientation (Haldeman 1999). Parents, Families, and Friends of Lesbians and Gays (PFLAG) affirm the well-being of LGBT youth and reject proponents of reparative therapy. According to the PFLAG (2003) Web site, "[m]any PFLAG parents have seen firsthand how damaging this 'therapy' has been to their children."

Some religious-based organizations also target youth in their ex-gay campaigns. Focus on the Family, for example, holds conferences entitled *Love Won Out*, in which they purport to provide the "truth that homosexuality is preventable and treatable" (Focus on the Family 2003). According to its Web site, attendees will, "learn how to respond to the misinformation in the public school system" from experts on homosexuality.

The fundamental message of reparative therapy is that homosexuality signifies mental illness. Such a misrepresentation is one of several myths perpetuating the social alienation, **prejudice, discrimination**, and emotional and physical violence routinely encountered by LGBT youth in school environments. Stigmatization of homosexuality, often manifested as homophobic verbal **harassment**, increases the likelihood of suicidal ideation for youth (Morrison and L'Heureux 2001). According to Besen (2003), reparative therapy and ex-gay ministries confound the **coming out** processes of adolescents, in part, by presenting **queer** "lifestyles" as unhappy, lonely, and morally corrupt. Besen also documents how such programs have targeted youth through the use of CDs, **comics**, and MTV-style videos.

Reparative therapy has been featured in **films** such as *Going Straight, But I'm a Cheerleader*, and *Far From Heaven*; in the television series *Will and Grace, Law and Order: Special Victims Unit*, and **Queer as Folk** as well as various daytime talk shows. In all of these programs, reparative therapy is presented as a questionable choice that self-denigrating homosexuals or youth who feel pressure from family might make.

Bibliography

American Psychological Association. August 1997. Accessed July 16, 2005. http://www.apa.org/pi/lgbc/policy/youths.html.

Besen, Wayne. 2003. *Anything but Straight: Unmasking the Scandals and Lies Behind the Ex-Gay Myth*. Binghamton, NY: Harrington Park Press.

Carlson, Helena M. 2003. "A Methodological Critique of Spitzer's Research on Reparative Therapy." *Archives of Sexual Behaviour* 32: 425–427.

Haldeman, Douglas C. 1999. "The Pseudo-Science of Sexual Orientation Conversion Therapy. *Angles: The Policy Journal of the Institute for Gay and Lesbian Strategic Studies* 4, no. 1: 1–4.

LeVay, Simon. 1996. *Queer Science: The Use and Abuse of Research into Homosexuality*. Cambridge. MA: MIT Press.

Morrison, Linda L., and Jeff L'Heureux. 2001. "Suicide and Gay/Lesbian/Bisexual Youth: Implications for Clinicians." *Journal of Adolescence* 24, no. 1: 39–49.

Spitzer, Robert L. 2003. "Can Some Gay Men and Lesbians Change Their Sexual Orientation? 200 Participants Reporting a Change from Homosexual to Heterosexual Orientation." *Archives of Sexual Behaviour* 32: 403–417.

Thurlow, Crispin. 2001. "Naming the 'Outsider Within:' Homophobic Pejoratives and the Verbal Abuse of Lesbian, Gay, and Bisexual High-School Pupils. *Journal of Adolescence* 24, no. 1 : 25–38.

Web Sites

"Ex-Gay" Ministries and "Reparative Therapy." 2003. Parents, Families, and Friends of Lesbians and Gays. Accessed June 1, 2005. http://www.pflag.org/education/index.php?id=280. Useful summary of problems with reparative therapy.

Exodus Youth. 2003. Accessed June 1, 2005. http://exodusyouth.net/youth/index.html. The youth-oriented Web site of Exodus International.

Focus on the Family. 2003. Accessed June 1, 2005. http://www.lovewonout.com. Love Won Out is a conference for youth that endorses treatment to prevent homosexuality.

National Association for Research and Therapy of Homosexuality. November 2002. Accessed June 1, 2005. http://www.narth.com/menus/statement.html. Using the language of science, NARTH endorses sexual orientation conversion through reparative therapy, including for youth.

Research, Qualitative

Laura A. Szalacha

Doing qualitative research with **lesbian, gay, bisexual, transgender, queer,** questioning, and **intersex** (LGBTQQI) youth—those who self-identify with the social categories of lesbian, gay, bisexual, transgender, queer, questioning or intersex or whose emerging sexual attractions or behavior are directed toward same-sex partners—involves the collection and interpretation of various forms of narrative data (interviews, focus groups, ethnographies, life histories, case studies) to understand the situated meanings constructed about their lives and experiences in schools from their perspectives. This interdisciplinary, transdisciplinary research methodology crosscuts

See also Australia, Research on Sexual Identities; Gender Roles; Mentoring; Youth, At Risk.

the social sciences, humanities, and education. Qualitative inquiry is properly con-ceptualized as a participatory, collaborative project and, as such, well-suited to the examination of the worlds of LGBTQQI students and teachers. Just as the qualita-tive research paradigm differs from quantitative paradigm, qualitative research with LGBTQQI youth must differ from that conducted with heterosexual youth.

Quantitative research is rooted in a logical positivist paradigm, using deductive logic and known valid and reliable instruments to test a priori hypotheses. In con-trast, qualitative research uses a naturalistic constructivist framework, employing inductive logic and varying narrative and observational techniques to build knowl-edge that is situationally and historically specific to a given social context. Qualita-tive research acknowledges the interplay between the knowledge seeker and the informant by openly recognizing that the social locations of each (such as **race/ethnicity**, gender, **sexual orientation**, age, and/or **social class**) will inevitably influ-ence what the informant shares and reveals and what the researcher observes and hears. Quantitative research seeks causal determination and generalization of findings, whereas qualitative research seeks in-depth understanding and, perhaps, extrapola-tion to similar contexts.

There has been an ongoing debate about the advantages and disadvantages, as well as appropriate research paradigms and misnomers such as "hard" and "soft" sciences, dating back to the seventeenth century BCE. The challenges of increas-ingly complex social realities of LGBTQQI lives, however, demands that those who wish to understand queer lives, must use and rely on both quantitative and qualita-tive methods (Tolman and Szalacha 1999).

During the 1990s, the United States and the **United Kingdom** witnessed a bur-geoning of discourse on queer youth. This can be broadly cataloged into two types of "story" texts: personal narratives and qualitative studies. The personal narra-tives, reminiscent of the 1980s adult "coming out stories," began primarily as retro-spective life histories of adults which then progressively included poignant interviews with LGBTQQI youth describing their "coming of age" (Chandler 1995; Due 1995); their experiences in scholastic settings (Rogers 1994) and the experi-ences and lives of LGBTQ educators (Jennings 1994). These texts brought many unheard voices to the fore, challenged and broadened contemporary understand-ings, and paved the way for the development of qualitative research centered on the experiences of LGBTQQI students and educators in schools.

Rather than simply compiling narratives, qualitative researchers conduct inter-views, focus groups and ethnographies and then analyze the transcripts at a theo-retical level, exploring the various intersections of identities of gender, race and ethnicity, sexuality, and social class. Sears (1991) study in the American South is illustrative. Another of these first such studies was Uribe and Harbeck's (1992) inter-views of fifty self-identified "homosexual" secondary school students in Los Angeles. Along with the findings from a student survey, they documented that school-based **homophobia** was associated with lower self-esteem and increased likelihood of self-destructive behavior. Its results provided the rationale for devel-oping **Project 10**, the first U.S. school-based intervention for LGBTQQI youth. Soon afterwards, Khayatt (1995) explored the experiences of lesbian students in several secondary schools of Toronto. Through her interviews and observations of various aspects of the schools, she determined that the practices, curricula, and even disciplinary procedures of schools reproduce and maintain a social organiza-tion of schooling that promotes **compulsory heterosexuality**.

This construction of theory, grounded in the meanings made of the lived experiences of LGBTQQI youth, was echoed in qualitative studies of LGB teachers, counselors, librarians, and administrative staff members in the United States (Kissen 1996) and lesbian teachers in Canada (Khayatt 1992). These studies of teachers and professional staff members underscore the many dangers the educators feared in acknowledging a minority **sexual identity**; often forcing a reconsideration of the entire profession of education and the pleasures in serving as a role model and mentor of queer youth.

Similar studies in the United Kingdom (Epstein 1994; Epstein 1997), not only examined individual LGBTQQI lives and experiences, but these researchers broadened the implications of the construction of sexual identities in scholastic environments to identify and analyze varying issues of **educational policies**, such as which physical or verbal acts constitute **sexual harassment**; the expansion and reevaluation of **curriculum**, such as the inclusion of all sexualities and examining the curriculum for instances of **heterosexism**; and the philosophies of pedagogies as a whole.

Another qualitative method, ethnography, emerged during the same decade for studies of queer youth. Researchers working with adolescents at Horizons, a social program for LGBTQQI youth in Chicago, produced one of the first comprehensive studies of the psychological development of multiracial gay and lesbian youth. In contrast to many commonly held beliefs at the time, Herdt and Boxer (1993, 166) described the continual "**coming out**" processes, the "death and rebirth of a new self," while often commencing in adolescence, can begin as early as nine years old and is lifelong.

In an ethnographic study of boy's experiences of education in a central London high school, Epstein (1997) identified schools as the primary sites of **identity development** (of which gender and sexuality are central elements) where dominant forms of masculinity are markedly misogynistic and homophobic. She observed that **sexism** and homophobia were reproduced in the behaviors and interactions of students and teachers, as well as within the curriculum and through the pedagogical strategies that teachers routinely employ. These range from verbal instructions that boys not be "Nancy-boys" and that girls be "ladylike," to the playing out of a "mock wedding" in "it's traditional (white, British) form with 'an imaginary aisle and . . . confetti'" with the girls dressed in brides dresses while the boys remained in their ordinary clothing and the distress of one white "bride" who was paired with a black "groom" (Epstein 1997, 107). Key to her findings was the intersections between race, gender, and sexuality. Similarly, the ethnography of Kehily and Nayak (1997) examined the role of humor in the cultures of young men in secondary schools. Game-playing, such as punch-n-run, and ritualized insulting, especially verbal attacks on an opponent's mother, reinforced **stereotypes** of heterosexual masculine identities.

While the field of qualitative research with LGBTQQI youth is only two decades old, there has been remarkable development in terms of both methodological sophistication and conceptual clarity. For example, one of the most difficult issues with which early studies had to grapple was recruiting a sample of participants from this "hidden population." Today, the issue of sampling for qualitative studies includes the recruitment of subpopulations in terms of race/ethnicity, socioeconomic status, and, as Elze (2003) has discussed, even organizational and developmental variation, such as those youth not associated with school-based or **community support groups** or youth at varying stages of sexual identity development.

A second critical issue inherent to qualitative research is that of viewpoint. There are advantages and limitations of having either an "insider" or an "outsider" perspective. On the one hand, queer investigators studying LGBTQQI issues may bring special knowledge and understandings to their research, which can facilitate sampling, data collection, and analysis. On the other hand, there remains the risk that "inside" researchers might incorrectly assume common cultural understandings or write "over" their participants' unique perceptions (LaSala 2003). Moreover, as in any research related to social injustice, there is the possibility of "social desirability effects": individuals responding to convey a particular self-image or to provide the researchers' anticipated findings. Paradoxically, failing to attend to these possibilities can compromise the validity of the data, result in a misinterpretation of the findings, and, ultimately, reify the injustices that the research was meant to address.

Finally, a concern unique to studying LGBTQQI youth is that of the standard of ethics. Research with queer youth, a marginalized population which is often at risk for experiencing violence and **discrimination**, may involve greater potential for exploitation or harm to study participants (Meezan and Martin 2003). Some of the protections ordinarily employed when conducting research with youth, such as parental permission, may represent greater harm to the LGBTQQI subjects. It is incumbent on the researchers to use different or additional measures to ensure the safety of research participants.

Bibliography

Chandler, Kurt. 1995. *Passages of Pride: Lesbian and Gay Youth Come of Age*. New York: Random House.

D'Augelli, Anthony T. 2003. "Foreword: Toward the Future of Research on Lesbian, Gay, Bisexual and Transgender Populations." Pp. xix–xxii in *Research Methods with Gay, Lesbian, Bisexual, and Transgender Populations*. Edited by William Meezan and James Martin. Binghamton, NY: Harrington Park Press.

Due, Lorna. 1995. *Joining the Tribe: Growing Up Gay and in the '90s*. New York: Anchor.

Elze, Diane. 2003. "8,000 Miles and Still Counting . . . Reaching Gay, Lesbian and Bisexual Adolescents for Research." Pp. 127–138 in *Research Methods with Gay, Lesbian, Bisexual, and Transgender Populations*. Edited by William Meezan and James Martin. Binghamton, NY: Harrington Park Press.

Epstein, Debbie. 1994. *Challenging Lesbian and Gay Inequalities in Education*. Buckingham, England: Open University Press.

———. 1997. "Boyz Own Stories: Masculinities and Sexualities in Schools." *Gender and Education* 9, no. 1: 105–115.

Herdt, Gil, and Andrew Boxer. 1993. *Children of Horizons: How Gay and Lesbian Teens are Leading a New Way Out of the Closet*. Boston: Beacon Press.

Jennings, Kevin. 1994. *One Teacher in 10: Gay and Lesbian Educators Tell Their Stories*. Boston: Alyson.

Kehily, Mary Jane, and Anoop Nayak. 1997. "'Lads and Laughter:' Humour and the Production of Heterosexual Hierarchies." *Gender and Education* 9, no. 1: 69–87.

Khayatt, Madiha Didi. 1992. *Lesbian Teachers: An Invisible Presence*. Albany: State University of New York Press.

———. 1995. "Compulsory Heterosexuality: School and Lesbian Students." Pp. 149–163 in *Knowledge, Experience and Ruling Relations: Studies in the Social Organization of Knowledge*. Edited by Anne Manicom and Campbell, Marie. Toronto: University of Toronto Press.

Kissen, Rita M. 1996. *The Last Closet: The Real Lives of Lesbian and Gay Teachers*. Portsmouth, NH: Heinemann.

LaSala, Michael C. 2003. "When Interviewing 'Family:' Maximising the Insider Advantage in the Qualitative Study of Lesbians and Gay Men." Pp. 15–30 in *Research Methods with Gay, Lesbian, Bisexual, and Transgender Populations*. Edited by William Meezan and James Martin. Binghamton, NY: Harrington Park Press.

Meezan, William, and James Martin. 2003. "Exploring Current Themes in Research on Gay, Lesbian, Bisexual and Transgender Populations." Pp.1–44 in *Research Methods with Gay, Lesbian, Bisexual, and Transgender Populations*. Edited by William Meezan and James Martin. Binghamton, NY: Harrington Park Press.

Rogers, Marigold. 1994. "Growing up Lesbian: The Role of School" Pp. 31–48 in *Challenging Lesbian and Gay Inequalities in Education*. Edited by Debbie Epstein. Buckingham, England: Open University Press.

Sears, James T. 1991. *Growing Up Gay in the South: Race, Gender and Journeys of the Spirit*. Binghamton, NY: Haworth Press.

Tolman, Deborah L., and Laura A. Szalacha. 1999. "Dimensions of Desire: Bridging Qualitative and Quantitative Methods in a Study of Female Adolescent Sexuality." *Psychology of Women Quarterly* 23, no. 1: 7–39.

Uribe, Virginia, and Karen M. Harbeck. 1992. "Addressing the Needs of Lesbian, Gay and Bisexual Youth: The Origins of Project 10 and School-Based Intervention." Pp. 9–28 in *Coming out of the Classroom Closet: Gay and Lesbian Students, Teachers and Curricula*. Edited by Karen M. Harbeck. Binghamton, NY: Haworth Press.

Research, Quantitative

Laura A. Szalacha

Quantitative research with **lesbian, gay, bisexual, transgender, queer**, questioning, and **intersex** (LGBTQQI) youth—those who self-identify with the social categories of lesbian, gay, bisexual, transgender, queer, questioning, or intersex or whose emerging sexual attractions or behavior are directed toward same-sex partners—youth involves the collection and analysis of numerical data to measure constructs. Its purpose is to determine the relationships between one or more variables (independent or predictor variables) and others (dependent or outcome variables) in a sample drawn from a given population. The social science and educational research on LGBTQQI individuals and issues is quite broad. It includes studies of **sexual orientation**, sexual identities, **"coming out,"** school climates, the victimization of LGBTQQI students in schools, and challenges for LGBTQ educators. These statistical studies are almost exclusively descriptive, such as surveys, examining the relationships among variables or processes rather than experiments which center on causality. Substantively, adolescent LGBTQQI quantitative research has progressed from an overemphasis on psychological pathologies and vulnerabilities to larger developmental concerns such as the social construction of sexual identities, the developmental interactions among sexual, ethnic or racial, national, and gender identities, as well as issues of **resilience**. Methodologically, LGBTQQI research has

See also Alcoholism; Australia, Research on Sexual Identities; Drug Use; Ethnic Identity; Racial Identity; School Safety and Safe School Zones; Sexual Abuse and Assault; Sexual Harassment; Youth, At Risk.

become more sophisticated as large scale data sets, such as the **Youth Risk Behavior Surveys,** have become available, and now incorporates rigorous sampling methods and more complex statistical techniques such as multilevel and structural equation modeling.

In spite of the ground-breaking research of psychologist Evelyn Hooker (1957), the "homosexual adolescent" wasn't noted again in social science research until an empirical quantitative study (Roesler and Deisher 1972). By the 1980s, there was a small body of empirical research, mostly conducted by social scientists. The vast majority (75 percent) of LGBTQQI research in education conducted from the late 1980s until 2001 was quantitative (mostly using survey research with only a few quasi-experimental studies) and focused on **college age youth** (Sears 2002). This research was conducted predominantly in the United States with a disproportionate representation of Euro-American subjects (and a virtual exclusion of transgender and bisexual youth). **Sexual identity,** coming out, and **suicide** have been the predominant areas of research focus.

From a conceptual viewpoint, the major assumption underlying virtually all of the earliest quantitative research with LGBTQQI youth was that homosexuality was fraught with psychological and, subsequently, social difficulties. The foci were the poor **mental health** and self-destructive behaviors, such as alcohol, tobacco and **substance abuse,** and suicidality of one subpopulation of queer youth while failing to study the normative development of the majority of LGBTQQI adolescents. This emphasis on negative behaviors was often used to "pathologize" these youth. Concomitantly, numerous studies have documented the persistent victimization of LGBTQQI students or those youth who appeared to be LGBTQQI in the forms of physical or verbal threats and attacks at or on the way to schools.

In the **United Kingdom,** researchers in England and Wales documented the use of homophobic pejoratives among secondary students providing evidence of the increasingly well-documented daily assault on the psychological health of young LGBTQQI students (Thurlow 2001). These findings were corroborated by studies of deeply embedded **heterosexism** and **homophobia** in secondary schools of Scotland (Buston and Hart 2001). In a survey of **"hate crimes"** against lesbians and gay men, of those respondents age 18 and under, 79 percent reported they had been subject to homophobic verbal **bullying,** 24 percent had been subject to homophobic physical bullying, and 19 percent had been subject to severe homophobic physical bullying (Mason and Palmer 1996).

In **Australia,** researchers examining the general health and well-being of same-sex attracted young people found that schools were the site of 70 percent of the homophobic abuse disclosed, making the school as unsafe as living on the streets for a number of participants (Hillier et al. 1998). In some cases, this abuse occurred with the knowledge of teachers and other school authorities. In response, some students appropriated arguments against **racism** to use as arguments against heterosexism and challenged a range of discriminatory practices which existed in schools such as the failure to honor basic human rights and the selective granting of privileges based on gender and sexuality.

In the United States, the research in the last two decades has grown from an overemphasis on internal psychological processes, suicidality, and victimization to attention paid to larger developmental concerns regarding sexual orientation (Diamond 1998), the social contexts, for example, neighborhoods and schools, in which LGBTQQI adolescents live, grow, and interact with others, as well as factors that contribute to resilience among queer youth. In spite of this expansion, there remains very little quantitative research on LGBTQQI youth of color, lesbian youth, and virtually no studies of transgender or intersex youth in schools.

One primary arena for almost all adolescent development in Western societies is secondary education. Schools themselves vary widely in the degree to which they foster positive development and healthy behavior among the youth they serve, just as individual adolescents differ in their experiences within any given school. LGBTQQI youth appear to be one subset of young people who are at especially high risk of negative outcomes from their interactions within school contexts. Secondary schools may be hostile places for many LGBTQQI students, but they are likely to be more dangerous for some queer adolescents than for others. D'Augelli, Pilkington, and Hershberger (2002) found **gay** and bisexual male youth to be more frequently harassed or assaulted in schools than their female counterparts, though Fineran (2001) found that lesbian and bisexual females were most likely to be the targets of in-school sexual **harassment**.

The only state-wide evaluation of a mandated school intervention program in the United States to date is Szalacha's (2003) study of the Massachusetts Safe Schools Program for Gay and Lesbian Students. The surveys of 1,700 students and 700 faculty and staff at 35 secondary schools in Massachusetts documented a statistically significant, positive, "sexual diversity climate" in schools with "higher levels of implementation of the Safe Schools Program." More specifically, students in schools that had implemented staff training, nondiscrimination policies, and/or **gay–straight alliances** reported significantly less homophobic school climates and higher levels of personal safety for LGBTQQI students.

A recent critical addition to these quantitative studies are secondary analyses concerned with the experiences of LGBTQQI youth in secondary schools as documented in large, representative data sets. In the United States, one such dataset is the National Longitudinal Survey of Adolescent Health (Add Health). Russell, Seif, and Truong (2001), in examining school outcomes, found that girls who reported being romantically attracted to other females reported less positive attitudes about school, lower GPAs, and more school troubles (especially so for girls reporting bisexual attractions). Only bisexual-attracted boys experienced school troubles and lower GPAs. Boys reporting exclusively same-sex attractions did not differ from their peers on school outcomes. A key finding for U.S. schools was that relationships with teachers were critical in explaining the school troubles experienced by those students reporting bisexual attractions. Szalacha's (2000) analyses of the Add Health data found that girls who reported being romantically attracted to other females reported smoking, drinking, using illegal drugs, and contemplating suicide significantly more often than did the heterosexual girls. However, bisexual and lesbian-attracted girls also reported significantly higher rates of unwanted and coerced sexual encounters (by boys/men), and lower parental support. Thus, external stressors play a significant role in these girls placing themselves at risk. Corroborating Russell's relational findings, Szalacha found that social support, school connectedness, and a good relationship with one's mother mitigated the negative effects of "bisexual and lesbian-attracted status," but not those of forced sexual intimacy.

Some states, such as Massachusetts and Vermont, augment the Center for Disease Control's biannual **Youth Risk Behavior Surveys** (YRBS) in the United States by including questions about sexual orientation and sexual activity. Here researchers have matched the YRBS data with school-level data collected from principals about programs and school policies and teachers about **AIDS/HIV** instruction (Blake et al. 2001; Goodenow and Szalacha in press). Consistent with previous research, these studies demonstrated that LGB adolescents in Massachusetts were significantly more likely than heterosexual youths to engage in substance use, sexual risk behaviors, and suicide attempts and to experience threats to personal safety. LGB youths were less likely than heterosexuals to report having received HIV instruction or instruction related to condom use. However, in schools where gay-sensitive HIV instruction was provided, LGB youths reported lower sexual risk behaviors. Moreover, the presence of a gay–straight alliance or support group for LGBTQQI youth was significantly associated with lowered probabilities of queer adolescents being threatened or injured with a weapon at school, skipping school because they felt unsafe, experiencing **dating** violence, or making multiple past-year suicide attempts (Goodenow and Szalacha in press).

Finally, the most recent expansion in conducting quantitative research regarding LGBTQQI youth and issues in education is the use of the **Internet**, both to gather information and to assist others in collecting data. Continuous data collection is maintained by organizations such as **Gay, Lesbian and Straight Education Network** (GLSEN) and others that host surveys on school climate available for LGBTQQI youth to respond to anonymously. Others, such as the Gay–Straight Alliance Network, provide basic questionnaires and encourage GSA members to conduct surveys in their schools. While there are still difficulties with GLSEN's self-selected sample and the reliability and validity of studies conducted by high school students, they serve as creative avenues for both researchers and youth to come to understand others and themselves.

Bibliography

Blake, Susan, Rebecca Ledsky, Thomas Lehman, Carol Goodenow, Richard Sawyer, and Tim Hack. 2001. "Preventing Sexual Risk Behaviors among Gay, Lesbian, and Bisexual Adolescents: The Benefits of Gay-Sensitive HIV Instruction in Schools." *American Journal of Public Health* 91: 940–946.

Buston, Karen, and Graham Hart. 2001. "Heterosexism and Homophobia in Scottish School Sex Education: Exploring the Nature of the Problem." *Journal of Adolescence* 24, no. 1: 95–109.

D'Augelli, Anthony, Neil Pilkington, and Scott Hershberger. 2002. "Incidence and Mental Health Impact of Sexual Orientation Victimization of Lesbian, Gay, and Bisexual Youths in High School." *School Psychology Quarterly* 17, no. 2: 148–167.

Diamond, Lisa. 1998. "Development of Sexual Orientation among Adolescent and Young Adult Women." *Developmental Psychology* 34: 1085–1095.

Fineran, Susan. 2001. "Sexual Minority Students and Peer Sexual Harassment in High School." *Journal of School Social Work* 11, no. 2: 50–69.

Goodenow, Carol, and Laura Szalacha. In press. "School Support Groups and the Safety of Sexual Minority Adolescents" *School Psychology Quarterly.*

Hillier, Lynne, Deborah Dempsey, Lyn Harrison, Lisa Beale, Lesley Matthews, and Doreen Rosenthal. 1998. *Writing Themselves In: A National Report on the Sexuality, Health and Well-Being of Same-Sex Attracted Young People.* Melbourne, AU: National Centre in HIV Social Research.

Hooker, Evelyn. 1957. "The Adjustment of the Male Overt Homosexual." *Journal of Projective Techniques*, 21, 18–31.

Mason, Angela, and Anya Palmer. 1996.*Queer Bashing: A National Survey of Hate Crimes Against Lesbians and Gay Men.* London: Stonewall.

Roesler, T., and R. Deisher. 1972. "Youthful Male Homosexuality: Homosexual Experience and the Process of Developing Homosexual Identity in Males Aged 16 to 22 Years." *Journal of the American Medical Association* 219: 1018–1123.

Russell, Stephen, Hinda Seif, and Nhan Truong. 2001. "School Experiences of Sexual Minority Youth in the United States: Evidence from a National Study." *Journal of Adolescence* 24, no. 1: 111–127.

Sears, James T. 2002. *Fifteen Years Later: The Draft Summary Report on the State of the Field of Lesbian, Gay, Bisexual and Transgender Issues in K-16 and Professional Education, A Research Review (1987–2001).* Paper presented at the Annual meeting of the American Educational Research Association at Seattle, WA, April.

Szalacha, Laura A. 2000. *Sexual Minority Adolescent Girls: A Population at Risk? A Secondary Analysis of the National Longitudinal Study of Adolescent Health.* Paper presented at the American Public Health Association Conference, Boston, MA, November.

Szalacha, Laura A. 2003. "Safer Sexual Diversity Climates: Lessons Learned from an Evaluation of Massachusetts' Safe Schools Program for Gay and Lesbian Students." *American Journal of Education* 110, no. 1: 58–88.

Thurlow, Crispin. 2001. "Naming the 'Outsider Within:' Homophobic Pejoratives and the Verbal Abuse of Lesbian, Gay and Bisexual High-School Pupils." *Journal of Adolescence* 24, no. 1: 25–38.

Residence Life in College

Nancy J. Evans

Living in a college residence hall is an important part of the collegiate experience for many students, including those who identify as **lesbian, gay, bisexual,** or **transgender** (LGBT). **Research** has demonstrated that on-campus living provides opportunities for students to make independent decisions, become clearer about their values, interact with individuals from different backgrounds, and assume leadership positions (Brooks 2002). For LGBT students, living in a residence hall away from their families of origin is often an impetus to more fully explore who they are as sexual, social, and/or gendered beings and to become more open with others about their identity. Depending on their staff, policies, and programming, residence hall environments can range from hostile and unwelcoming to supportive of such exploration. Although structured residence hall programming is well developed in the United States and to a lesser extent in Canada, it generally does not exist in other countries.

A review of recent research and a recent study of students' experiences in college residence halls suggest that the climate of residence halls for LGBT students is frequently negative (Evans 2001). LGBT students reported experiencing **harassment** in the form of direct threats, verbal taunts, derogatory statements on message boards, threats left on phone answering machines, and defacement of LGBT-related materials posted on bulletin boards or doors. In addition, many incidents of indirect

See also Antidiscrimination Policy; College Age Students; College Campus Programming; Coming Out, Youth; School Climate, College; Passing; Pride Symbols; School Safety and Safe School Zones.

harassment were also reported, including generalized homophobic comments, use of derogatory language, **graffiti**, and minimization of concerns raised by LGBT students. Lesbian and bisexual women perceived women to be less physically violent than men; they felt that women were "more emotionally violent," as one participant put it (Evans and Broido 2002, 34). **Homophobia** was usually not openly evident, but women in this study felt that it would not be wise to be open about their **sexual identity.**

Some students did report positive experiences in residence halls, including receiving support from residence life staff, roommates, and other students on the floor (Evans 2001). These supportive individuals attended LGBT events, became involved in student organizations for **allies**, presented programming on LGBT issues, and stood up for LGBT students when negative comments were made. In addition to receiving direct support, students reported that seeing information posted about LGBT services and events, being treated in a friendly manner, and experiencing a lack of harassment helped to create a welcoming residence hall climate.

The most prevalent perception that LGB students often have of their experience in residence halls is being invisible. In this study (Evans 2001), they reported that LGBT issues were not addressed in programming, that there was a lack of awareness of issues among staff and students, and that there were few opportunities for social interaction with other LGBT students. LGBT students' experiences in residence halls have a significant impact on their **identity development** (Evans and Broido 1999). The extent to which students choose to identify as lesbian, gay, bisexual, or transgender is greatly influenced by whether they find a supportive environment in which to do so and how their self-identification is accepted by the individuals to whom they first come out. Students who believe that they must hide their sexual identity to be safe often experience anxiety and guilt as well as loneliness and isolation. These feelings can lead to thoughts of **suicide**, self-doubt, and self-hatred. On the other hand, students who are open about their sexual identity experience a sense of relief, pride in their identity, enhanced self-concept, and feelings of being more honest. Disadvantages of being out include an increased likelihood of harassment, distress about being labeled, fear of hurting family and friends, and the need to be more careful to avoid unsafe situations.

The research just discussed underscores the importance of enhancing the residence hall climate for LGBT students. **Educational policies** and procedures, staff selection and training, programming, and alternative housing options can all contribute to a positive environment.

Policies make a difference in the type of climate that develops in a residence hall (Evans and Broido 2002). Establishing a policy at the beginning of the school year about appropriate behavior and the procedures that will be taken if the policy is violated sends a message that all students are expected to treat others with respect and that those who discriminate against or harass others will be held accountable. It is not enough, however, to just establish a policy. Quick action must be taken when violations occur. If roommate situations become uncomfortable for LGBT students, residence life staff should assist them in finding better alternatives. Likewise, if LGBT students experience harassment or name calling in the halls or bathrooms, students involved in the **bullying** should be confronted.

Residence life must also address the specific concerns of transgender youth living on campus. Policies must be in place to insure that safe and comfortable living arrangements are available for transgender students, particularly for individuals who are transitioning. Gender inclusive restrooms are especially important since many transgender individuals have been harassed in this setting.

Residence hall staff must provide active support for LGBT students by being a sounding board for students, by letting them know of resources that are available to them, and by modeling what it means to be an ally. Resident assistants—students who are hired to assist students on residence hall floors—play an important role in establishing a sense of community in a residence hall (Evans, Reason, and Broido 2001). LGBT students are more accepted in halls where students get to know each other as individuals, spend time together, and participate in floor activities. Resident assistants have a responsibility to personally support LGBT students on their floor as well as to create an open and accepting atmosphere.

If they are to create a positive environment for LGBT students in their halls, residence life staff, including resident assistants, must be carefully selected and thoroughly trained to understand the issues that LGBT students face. They must also be aware of resources available on campus and in the community that would be of interest to LGBT students. Advertising of residence life positions, questions asked on applications, and interview procedures should make clear that the ability to work effectively with LGBT individuals is a requisite qualification for being hired. Residence life divisions should also actively seek and hire LGBT staff who can be role models for LGBT students and who can break down **stereotypes** which heterosexual students may have about LGBT people.

Once hired, residence life staff should complete training to prepare them to address issues faced by LGBT students and to educate heterosexual students about LGBT concerns. Having classes that expose potential resident assistants to these issues is important. Training should include opportunities to interact with LGBT individuals. Having panels of LBGT students talk about their experiences in residence halls is a good way of introducing the topic. Encouraging residence life staff to attend LGBT events and student organization meetings is another way of facilitating learning through direct interaction. Training should also include opportunities for staff to explore their beliefs and feelings. Just reading or hearing about issues LGBT students face is not enough to bring about attitude change. Role-playing and experiential activities in which individuals must put themselves in the position of an LGBT person can also help residence life staff become more aware of what it is like to be LGBT.

To overcome the invisibility that LGBT students feel in their residence halls, LGBT topics must be included in campus programming initiatives. Unfortunately, many students who would benefit from attending programs on LGBT topics do not attend. Passive programming can be used to introduce LGBT topics in a more subtle way. Passive initiatives include display cases on LGBT topics, postings of LGBT resource materials, and symbols of support for the LGBT community such as Safe Space stickers.

A few colleges and universities, like the University of Massachusetts at Amherst, have created special interest houses or floors that provide space for LGBT students and their allies to live together (Herbst and Malaney 1999). Such housing can help LGBT students to feel more comfortable on campus, although some **administrators** argue that it isolates these students from others and hinders the mission of educating the broader student population about LGBT concerns. Employing LGBT and ally staff to work in these halls and developing programming designed to build community are keys to their success.

Since students spend a considerable amount of time during their college years in their living environments, residence life is an important consideration when selecting a college. Students should actively explore the level of support provided to LGBT individuals in residence halls. Students should look for visible signs of recognition and they should examine written policies and residence hall student handbooks to determine if nondiscrimination clauses and antiharassment statements exist. Students can use the **Internet** to investigate campus and residence life Web sites, determining if there is information about LGBT student organizations, social activities readily available, and staff knowledgeable in this area. A final strategy for determining the climate of campus residence halls is to contact LGBT students who currently attend the college (usually student organizations have an e-mail address or Web site with contact information).

Bibliography

Beemyn, Brett. 2003. "Serving the Needs of Transgender College Students." *Journal of Gay & Lesbian Issues in Education* 1, no. 1: 33–50.

Brooks, Shawn-Eric. 2002. *A Critical Pedagogy of Residential Education: Toward Empowering Representation of Lesbian, Gay, and Bisexual Identity*. Doctoral dissertation, University of California, Los Angeles.

Evans, Nancy J. 2001. "The Experiences of Lesbian, Gay, and Bisexual Youths in University Communities." Pp. 181–198 in *Lesbian, Gay, and Bisexual Identities and Youth: Psychological Perspectives*. Edited by Anthony R. D'Augelli and Charlotte J. Patterson. New York: Oxford University Press.

Evans, Nancy J., and Ellen M. Broido. 1999. "Coming Out in College Residence Halls: Negotiation, Meaning Making, Challenges, Supports." *Journal of College Student Development* 40: 658–668.

———. 2002. "The Experiences of Lesbian and Bisexual Women in College Residence Halls: Implications for Addressing Homophobia and Heterosexism." *Journal of Lesbian Studies* 6, no. 3/4: 29–42.

Evans, Nancy J., Robert D. Reason, and Ellen M. Broido. 2001. "Lesbian, Gay, and Bisexual Students' Perceptions of Resident Assistants: Implications for Resident Assistant Selection and Training." *College Student Affairs Journal*, 21: 82–91.

Herbst, Sandra, and Gary D. Malaney. 1999. "Perceived Value of a Special Interest Residential Program for Gay, Lesbian, Bisexual, and Transgender Students." *NASPA Journal* 36: 106–119.

Sousa, Lydia A. 2002. "Updating College and University Campus Policies: Meeting the Needs of Trans Students, Staff, and Faculty." *Journal of Lesbian Studies* 6, no. 3/4: 43–55.

Web Sites

National Association of Directors of Lesbian, Gay, Bisexual, and Transgender Resources in Higher Education. March 28, 2005. TigerTech. Accessed June 1, 2005. http://www.lgbtcampus.org. Assistance for individuals interested in creating higher education environments in which lesbian, gay, bisexual, and transgender students, faculty, staff, administrators, and alumni have equity in every respect.

ResLife.net. 2005. Accessed June 1, 2005. http://www.reslife.net. Provides information on college and university residence life and housing, for housing professionals, the resident assistant, and students and parents.

Standing Committee for Lesbian, Gay, Bisexual, and Transgender Awareness of the American College Personnel Association. March 9, 2005. Jared Tuberty. Accessed June 1, 2005. http://www.sclgbta.org. The site focuses on education and advocacy on behalf of LGBT students and staff on college and university campuses.

Resiliency

Geoffrey L. Ream and *Ritch C. Savin-Williams*

Resiliency, when applied to youth, refers to the achievement of better developmental outcomes than would be expected given the levels of risk factors the individual faces. Resiliency of **lesbian, gay,** and **bisexual,** and **transgender youth** (LGBT) refers both to their overall resiliency and to their development of a positive sense of self in spite of experiences of **heterosexism, homophobia,** and intolerance of variations in gender expression. Although most societies can fairly be called sexist and heterosexist, some LGBT youth are fortunate to grow up in accepting and affirming environments and do not personally experience **discrimination**. Because youth must, by definition, be at risk before they can be resilient, it is important in considering resiliency to evaluate not only outcomes but risk factors, protective factors, and developmental assets. Research on LGBT youth, following trends in the mainstream study of **adolescence**, has only recently broadened its focus from risk factors and at-risk youth to consider resiliency and positive development.

Resiliency depends on *protective factors* and *developmental assets*. There is significant overlap between what these two concepts describe. To the extent that there is a distinction, protective factors are generally thought of as environmental or innate characteristics that are difficult to change. These include a well-functioning family system, good schools, physical and social attractiveness, and high intelligence. In contrast, developmental assets can be imparted through socialization and development. Youth–adult partnerships and mentorship, strong sense of life goals, and connection with **spirituality** or religion are examples of these. Protective factors and developmental assets balance against risk factors—such as poverty, crime in the neighborhood, racial and sexual prejudice, disease, and victimization—to determine outcomes.

LGBT youth face several risk factors related to social intolerance of variance from established sexuality and gender norms. Parents, teachers and peers, if they respond to religious and secular pressures to believe homosexuality is necessarily connected with social decay and gender-nonconformity with developing homosexuality, vigilantly stigmatize any atypicality in youth, including shyness, introversion, atypical interest in sports, and off-brand clothing. The most telling sign of developing homosexuality is, of course, gender-atypicality. This arguably puts transgender youth in a particularly awkward position, as they must either compromise their authenticity by "**passing**" as conventional or face the stigma of acting out who they believe themselves to be. In addition to the stress of inauthentic self-presentation, all LGBT youth are at risk for developing internalized homophobia/ transphobia if they believe society's negative **stereotypes** and apply them to themselves personally.

Similarly to risk factors, sources of resiliency compound for greater effect. Protective factors and developmental assets reinforce other protective factors and developmental assets. A supportive family, for example, can advocate for change in, or remove a young person from, a problematic school. A supportive school can help a young person cope with a problematic family and also ensure that sexuality

See also Agency; Coming Out, Youth; Community LGBT Youth Groups; Identity Development; Mental Health; Mentoring; Religion and Psychological Development; School Climate, College; Social Class; Youth, At Risk.

education curricula contain information specific to the needs of same-sex sexually active students. Individual characteristics such as intelligence, social grace, expertise with the **Internet**, and access to money and transportation can help sexual-minority youth find information, referral, and supportive peers in community centers, bookstores, youth groups, Web sites, and electronic chat rooms.

In the best case scenario, young people are in charge of where and how they seek support, belonging, and sense of self. LGBT youth-oriented contexts, such as **gay–straight alliances** in high schools and **Project 10** programs in Los Angeles and Boston, may offer the best chance of meeting supportive peers. Although concerned adults may be tempted to steer youth away from religious involvement, **sports, fraternity/sorority** membership, and nightclubs, conventional wisdom that these are always problematic is not necessarily correct. Gay-positive religious organizations which support LGBT people who do not want to give up religion in favor of positive LGBT identity exist on many campuses and even in many modest-sized towns. Nightclubs also may be worth the risk if they are an expedient means to meet supportive peers, particularly in smaller towns where bars function as community centers and youth groups are not available. LGBT communities often foster contexts that non-normative gender presentation such as gay men's choruses, lesbian sports teams, and drag queen/king events.

For many LGBT youth, risk factors are sufficiently absent and/or protective factors and developmental assets are sufficiently present to create positive developmental outcomes. However, problem-free is not necessarily fully prepared for adulthood. Even for youth who do not face significant harassment and victimization, there must be opportunities to develop a positive LGBT identity, learn about sexual-minority culture and history (particularly that of the LGBT subculture within their ethnic group), access health and sexuality information specifically for same-sex active people, and form friendships with supportive others.

Discussion of resiliency of LGBT youth requires some qualification of the usual use of the concept of resiliency. Resiliency is usually held to characterize youth and families who "beat the odds" against poverty and racial discrimination. Certain members of a population are said to be resilient if the population as a whole shares risk factors and is definably at risk, e.g., residents of a high-crime neighborhood, children of families with incomes below the poverty level, students at failing elementary and middle schools. The population of LGBT youth is not definably at risk because, although all are in a context within which there is potential for anti-LGBT bias to affect them, not all are equally exposed to homophobia and heterosexism. Thus, they share a risk context, but not necessarily a risk factor. Some who have tolerant parents, live in tolerant communities, and attend tolerant schools and places of worship are not definably at risk. Earlier research on LGBT youth often treated this population as definably at risk. This may have been a safe assumption given the social climate of intolerance during the late 1970s and 1980s, the need to call attention to this neglected population, and the fact that participants in these early studies were usually recruited from support groups, community centers, and dedicated facilities for at risk LGBT youth, such as the Hetrick-Martin Institute. Those using these services needed support to cope with antigay discrimination, harassment, and victimization. Because they had these stressors in common, they were definably at risk.

In part because of those earlier studies, society is changing toward greater recognition, toleration, and affirmation of LGBT youth. This is particularly true on college campuses where in-depth interviews with college youth have made different populations of LGBT youth visible to researchers and educators. A college sample presumably has more protective factors present than a community sample of LGBT youth. College students are also more intelligent and have higher socioeconomic status and family income than the general population. College campuses are also far more likely to have resources like LGBT support groups and resource centers, campus programming and curricula, and openly LGBT and **ally** faculty and staff. Additionally, findings that many **college age youth** report having waited until their college years to come out to their parents indicate that these youth controlled their disclosure, coming out on their own terms and not being "outed" in high school before they were ready. College LGBT youth are not all at risk.

Additionally, there are new research methods, such as secondary analysis of national longitudinal data sets. Large-scale studies such as the National Longitudinal Survey of Adolescent Health ("Add Health") and the Centers for Disease Control's **Youth Risk Behavior Survey** (YRBS) recruit general populations of youth in sufficient numbers to include several same-sex attracted, same-sex sexually active, or LGBT-identified youth without having to specifically target that population. Most of these studies recruit youth from schools, and do not include those who are absent, truant, dropouts, incarcerated, or attending special schools (such as the Harvey Milk School). In contrast to work with support group samples, their sexual-minority samples likely contain a *lower* proportion of at-risk youth than exists in the general population. LGBT who participate in large panel studies are not all at risk.

Therefore, discussion of LGBT youth resiliency must always include the caveat that LGBT youth are not all at risk. Resiliency is not necessarily evident in a sample of college-age youth or a sample culled from a school-based survey just because they report better outcomes than are found in support group and urban community center populations. These are distinct groups who have different levels of risk factors, protective factors, and developmental assets. The label "resilient" is best reserved for those youth who have fared well despite problems with homophobia, heterosexism, and other risk factors.

Bibliography

Bass, Ellen, and Kate Kaufman. 1996. *Free Your Mind*. New York: HarperCollins.

Hetrick, Emery S., and A. Damien Martin. 1987. "Developmental Issues and Their Resolution for Gay and Lesbian Adolescents." *Journal of Homosexuality* 14, no. 1–2: 25–43.

Masten, Ann S. 2001. "Ordinary Magic: Resilience Processes in Development." *American Psychologist* 56, no. 3: 227–238.

Savin-Williams, Ritch C. 2001. "A Critique of Research on Sexual-Minority Youths." *Journal of Adolescence* 24, no. 1: 5–13.

Savin-Williams, Ritch C., and Geoffrey L. Ream. 2003. "Suicide Attempts Among Sexual-Minority Male Youth." *Journal of Clinical Child and Adolescent Psychology* 32, no. 4: 509–522.

Scales, Peter C., and Nancy Leffert. 1999. *Developmental Assets: A Synthesis of the Scientific Research on Adolescent Development*. Minneapolis: Search Institute.

Web Sites

Hetrick-Martin Institute. 2003. The Hetrick-Martin Institute, home of the Harvey Milk School. Accessed December 8, 2004. http://www.hmi.org. A description of the services, organizational structure, and mission of the Hetrick-Martin Institute.

Masten, Ann S. October 2002. Ordinary Magic: A Resilience Framework for Policy, Practice, and Prevention. Accessed December 8, 2004. http://www.cce.umn.edu/nrrc/resource.shtml. A conference paper outlining current understandings of youth risk and resiliency.

Young Gay America. December 2004. Young Gay America–Gay and Lesbian Youth Resource. Accessed December 8, 2004. http://www.younggayamerica.com. Online news, health information, and popular media magazine for gay youth with links to several youth-serving agencies and groups.

Rural Youth and Schools

Gerald Walton

Existing outside of incorporated **urban** areas, rural communities can be roughly described as having fewer than 1,000 people and as socially conservative in character. Thus, such communities usually lack community and educational support for **lesbian, gay, bisexual**, and **transgender youth** (LGBT) and educators. Many people leave rural communities for professional and economic opportunities in cities, as well as to find organizations, resources, and social opportunities that specifically meet the needs of sexual minorities. However, unlike adults, rural queer youth are less able to travel or move to cities in search of supportive communities. Although resources for queer youth have proliferated in LGBT communities and in some urban schools, most rural LGBT youth continue to lack adequate social, community, and educational support. Rural LGBT and LGBT-friendly educators, too, usually lack administrative and community support to participate in or launch professional development programs on LGBT educational issues. Not surprisingly, some youth consider their small communities a "hell" from which "escape" is essential (Gray 1999).

Research on LGBT youth that specifically explores rural contexts and issues, especially of non-Western nations and societies, is generally scarce. Like their Western counterparts, rural LGBT youth in non-Western nations are usually raised in conservative community and family environments. In **South Africa**, for example, traditions of the extended family are paramount within rural social mores. Most South Africans live in rural settlements. Becoming socially acceptable men and women in this community context leaves no opportunities for recognizing genders and sexualities that lie outside of conventional norms. LGBT youth, particularly those living in rural areas, risk losing familial, community, and cultural ties, even though the South African constitution provides legal protections. In **China**, too, traditional expectations of marriage, which do not provide flexibility for same-sex relationships, steer many LGBT youth into culturally-sanctioned gender and sexual roles.

Among Western nations, **Australia** has produced much of the research on rural LGBT youth. One study (Hillier, Warr, and Haste 1996) of same-sex attracted youth (SSAY) reported a greater sense of isolation and lack of access to information and resources compared with their urban counterparts. Social isolation, self-abusing behaviors, loneliness, and negative self-image tend to be dominant themes in research on rural LGBT youth in Australia and elsewhere (Morton 2003). Although

See also Activism, LGBT Teachers; Africa, LGBT Youth and Issues in; Bullying; Legal Issues, Students; Mental Health; Native and Indigenous LGBT Youth; Passing; Professional Educational Organizations; Secondary Schools, LGBT; Sissy Boy.

rural LGBT youth encounter these issues on a daily basis, their **resilience** is often not highlighted by researchers. In the southern United States, however, Sears (1991) focused on the strengths of rural youth, describing them as "sexual rebels" whose gender and sexuality identities confound the boundaries of respectability. Similarly, Kinder (1998) describes the strengths of a young high school lesbian in rural Wisconsin who survived through **literature**, literacy, and her **poetry**, as well as by breaking the rules of gendered social convention. Such resilience exemplifies the ways in which the LGBT youth in these studies endure social isolation and emotional despair to become self-assured in their **sexual orientation** and **gender identities.**

Rural communities and schools tend to be characterized by tight-knit social groups with common beliefs where "everybody knows everybody's business" (Hillier, Warr, and Haste 1996, 11). Being **queer** defies conformity to rural expectations on heterosexuality and family. Lack of privacy in rural communities combined with the stigmatization of homosexuality further pressure rural LGBT youth to hide their **sexual identity.** Possibly due to the association of male homosexuality with predatory behavior and compromised manhood, boys tend to be especially disturbed by the idea that one among them might be gay, particularly if he is gender nonconforming (Hillier, Warr, and Haste 1996).

Friendships, socializing, and **dating** become problematic in the lives of rural LGBT youth. Fear of disclosing their sexual orientation renders rural LGBT youth as more isolated and less likely to have access to helping resources, such as **community LGBT support groups, counseling** services, community resources, and their families. Lack of meeting places to socialize with other LGBT youth as well as dependence on others for transport to events that are usually held outside their community exacerbates rural isolation (Morton 2003). Further, **sexuality education** in rural schools tends to focus on the mechanics of, and safety and health issues related to, heterosexual sex (Hillier, Warr, and Haste 1996). Concerns about privacy, community attitudes, and social stigma are also significant obstacles to the provision of **HIV education** and services in rural areas (Buchanan 2003), leaving queer youth ill-informed about safer sex practices. For this reason, school nurses in rural areas play a vital role in HIV prevention education and in supporting students who may be struggling with issues of sexual orientation (Yoder and Preston 1997).

For those who have skills, financial resources, and safe access, the **Internet** can be a vital source of education and information for and about LGBT rural youth (Gray 1999), especially in communities that tend to be conservative and traditional. In Australia, the Human Rights and Equal Opportunity Commission launched, in 1999, a project called Outlink to bring rural LGBT youth and youth service agencies together to share resources and information, to promote increased inclusion through community education, and to establish a national LGBT youth network. Some organizations offer Web-based information on LGBT resources specifically for prairie regions, such as the Prairie Open and Affirming Sexual Orientation Support (Prairie OASOS 2003) in the U.S. areas of Minnesota, the Dakotas, the Red River Valley, and the Midwest.

The quarterly magazine for rural gay men, *RFD*. Winter 1988–89. Courtesy of RFD, www.rfdmag.org

The specific needs of rural LGBT youth are not directly served through organizations such as the **Gay, Lesbian, and Straight Education Network** (GLSEN) and the Gay and Lesbian Educators of British Columbia (GALE BC) or through educational programs such as Toronto's Triangle Program and New York's Harvey Milk School. Addressing such needs requires increased resources for community education to counter intolerance and **homophobia** (Morton 2003). Such education might include: displaying posters with positive messages about LGBT issues prominently throughout the community; providing training and awareness programs for teachers and youth service providers; organizing school educational programs such as "Sexuality Awareness Week;" and supporting **gay–straight alliances.**

Teachers have an important role in providing affirming resources for LGBT youth, in responding to LGBT students supportively, in referring youth to other resources, and in confronting homophobic slurs in schools. As one queer youth, raised in a "redneck town," puts it: "Teachers have to know how to accept students for being gay or being different, because different is good" (Gray 1999, 157). Unfortunately, educators who initiate or participate in educational programs and resources for LGBT students, especially in rural communities, risk their jobs and their professional and personal reputations (Yoakam 1997).

In Saskatchewan, a mostly rural province in **Canada**, the specific needs of rural LGBT youth and educators are the focus of an annual conference sponsored by the College of Education at the University of Saskatchewan. Appropriately called *Breaking the Silence*, it fosters discussion on LGBT issues in schools, such as: the political and ethical issues on being an "out" LGBT teacher in rural communities; **curriculum** as a venue for inclusion/exclusion; policies on resource materials for LGBT youth and educators; and dilemmas related to LGBT issues faced by school counselors, teachers, resource librarians, and **administrators**. Although rural LGBT educators might be reluctant to attend for fears of being involuntarily "outed," the conference has stimulated the Saskatchewan Teachers' Federation to provide resource support for teachers across the entire province. In addition, a spin-off conference is now held at the University of Alberta.

For LGBT students who do not receive adequate protections and resources in their schools, litigation is emerging as a viable option. Rural LGBT students have launched some of the more high-profile court cases. In a small town in Ontario in 2001, for example, Marc Hall successfully challenged his public Catholic school board for attempting to prevent him from taking his boyfriend to his high school **prom**. In 1996, Jamie Nabozny was awarded over $900,000 in damages after a high-profile lawsuit against school officials for not protecting him against homophobic **harassment** from peers in his rural Wisconsin high school. Also, a 2003 ruling by the U.S. Supreme Court in *Lawrence v. Texas* overturned sodomy laws across the United States. The ruling will eventually benefit LGBT youth, particularly those who live in rural states where sodomy had been criminalized. Such laws had been used routinely to thwart efforts to address LGBT issues in schools and provide programs and resources that serve LGBT youth (Cahill and Cianciotto 2004).

Bibliography

Buchanan, Robert J., Bonnie J. Chakravorty, Miguel A. Zuniga, and Jane N. Bolin. 2003. "HIV Education, Prevention, and Outreach Programs in Rural Texas." *The Health Education Monograph Series* 20, no. 2: 19–25.

Cahill, Sean, and Jason Cianciotto. 2004. "Policy Interventions That Can Make Schools Safer." *Journal of Gay and Lesbian Issues in Education* 2, no. 1: 3–17.

Epp, Roger, and Dave Whitson. 2001. *Writing Off the Rural West: Globalization, Governments, and the Transformation of Rural Communities.* Edmonton: University of Alberta Press.

Gray, Mary L. 1999. *In Your Face: Stories from the Lives of Queer Youth.* Binghamton, NY: Haworth Press.

Hillier, Lynne, Deborah Warr, and Ben Haste. 1996. *The Rural Mural: Sexuality and Diversity in Rural Youth.* Melbourne: Australian Research Centre in Sex, Health, and Society.

Kinder, Deborah Jean. 1998. "To Follow Your Heart: Coming Out Through Literacy." *English Journal* 88, no. 2: 63–69.

Morton, Mavis. 2003. "Growing up Gay in Rural Ontario: The Needs and Issues Facing Rural Gay, Lesbian, Bisexual, and Transgendered Rural Youth." *Our Schools/Our Selves* 12, no. 4: 107–118.

Sears, James T. 1991. *Growing up Gay in the South: Race, Gender, and Journeys of the Spirit.* Binghamton, NY: Haworth Press.

Yoakam, John. 1997. "Making the Invisible Visible: Organizing Resources for Gay, Lesbian, Bisexual, and Transgender Youth in School and Communities." Pp. 91–105 in *Gay/Lesbian/Bisexual/Transgender Public Policy Issues.* Edited by Wallace K. Swan. Binghamton, NY: Haworth Press.

Yoder, Ruth E., and Deborah Bray Preston. 1997. "Rural School Nurses' Attitudes about AIDS and Homosexuality." *Journal of School Health* 67: 341–348.

Web Sites

Breaking the Silence: Gays and Lesbians in Our Schools. 2004. Accessed June 1, 2005. http://www.usask.ca/education/edfdt/breaksilence.htm. Web site for an annual conference in Saskatchewan, a mostly rural province in Canada, for educators to discuss a wide range of topics related to LGBT educators and youth in schools.

Outlink. 2004. Accessed June 1, 2005. http://outlink.trump.net.au/index.htm. Initiated by the Australian Human Rights and Equal Opportunity Commission to bring together young lesbian, gay, and bisexual rural people, and the people who work with them. Site includes research reports, updates, and bulletins.

Prairie Open and Affirming Sexual Orientation Support. January 2005. Accessed June 7, 2005. http://www.geocities.com/prairieoasos. Provides information on LGBT resources in Minnesota, North Dakota, South Dakota, Red River Valley, Midwest, and Canada.

Russia, LGBT Youth and Issues in

Sharon G. Horne and *Heidi Levitt*

Lesbian, gay, bisexual, and transgender youth (LGBT) in Russia face numerous and unique challenges in comparison to their Western counterparts; their lives, too, are drastically different from LGBT Russians only a generation ago. LGBT sexual expression is no longer punished by imprisonment in Siberian labor camps, jails, or psychiatric hospitals. The Russian government decriminalized male homosexuality in 1993, which had been punishable for up to five years in prison, and homosexuality

See also Coming Out, Youth; Discrimination; Europe, LGBT Youth and Issues in; Passing; Rural Youth and Schools; Sexism.

was removed as an official **mental disorder** by the Ministry of Health in 1999. However, many social norms, expectations, and beliefs are in flux as a result of transition from communism to capitalism. Igor Kon (1993, 402), the leading scholar on gay issues in Russia, described his country's youth as formed "not by the nascent new social order but by the decomposition of the old one." For these youth, the changing social structures and the shifting understanding of sexuality significantly impact their experience of being queer.

Despite rapid social changes in Russia, negative attitudes toward homosexuality dominate, and, according to **research** data, homosexuals remain the most stigmatized of all social groups (Kon 2002). Prior to becoming the current Russian nation, a communist Soviet system operated from 1917 until 1991. Under this system, dissent and nonconformity were censured severely. Not surprisingly, in a poll conducted by All-Union Public Opinion Centre (VTsIOM), in 1989, with a representative sample of people throughout Russia, 33 percent favored "liquidation" and 30 percent endorsed isolation of homosexuals. Only 10 percent favored "leaving them alone," and 6 percent endorsed helping them (Kon and Riordan 1993).

Public opinion about homosexuality has been reshaped following the fall of communism. In a 1994 replication study, the endorsement of liquidation of homosexuals had fallen to 18 percent, isolation had fallen to 23 percent, and the percentages for leaving them alone and wishing to help had risen to 29 and 8 percent, respectively (Kon 1998). Four years later, in a survey of the general population, only 17.5 percent and 14.7 percent of respondents in a survey of the general population endorsed liquidation and isolation, respectively; 40.8 percent favored leaving homosexuals to themselves (VTsIOM poll 1998, as cited in Kon 1998). Despite this attitudinal change, these opinions do not address the inequities that Russian LGBT peoples face. For example, one-third considered homosexuality an illness or a result of psychic trauma, and another third viewed it as a depravity or a bad habit; only 18 percent considered it to be a valid **sexual orientation** with the right to exist. The attitudes of Russian youth, as in most cultures, are more accepting of LGBT individuals that those of older generations. Russian youth were found to have more positive or neutral opinions about homosexuality than negative ones, with Russian young women endorsing greater tolerance than young men (Chervyakov, Kon, and Shapiro 1993).

During the Soviet era, the most dangerous identity was that of the dissident. It was difficult, however, to define dissidence; any difference made one suspect. In a country where people were jailed for years as punishment for being a few minutes late for work, any difference in behavior or identity that could be construed as being anti-Soviet was unsafe. Those whose sexual orientation or **gender identity** could place them at risk of jail sentences, many of which were tantamount to death sentences when served in northern Siberian work camps, were silent (Applebaum 2003).

Today, this tendency toward privacy persists, with few LGBT individuals being open about their sexual orientation at work and with family (Healey 2001). LGBT youth still experience social and family pressure to marry, sometimes the only means to privileges such as residency access to major cities and visas to visit and work abroad. And, given the drastic lack of affordable housing due to the transitional economy, queer youth experience difficulties in finding places to meet and in setting up households. Forced to gather in public spaces they are vulnerable to attacks and threats. Further, given the housing shortage, many LGBT youth continue to live with their parents well into adulthood, where they may be vulnerable to maltreatment or abuse and are likely to remain closeted.

Paradoxically, there are ways in which this silencing and invisibility has been an advantage. Because sexuality was considered hedonistic and anti-Soviet, there was a lack of discourse on any aspect of sexuality, serving as protective shield for LGBT people. Absent sexual discourse, few heard pejorative remarks about their sexual orientation, grew up in an explicit atmosphere of **homophobia** that many Westerners experienced, or witnessed gender atypical traits socially policed. Similarly, since religion was repressed during the communist era, generally LGBT Russians did not encounter the topic of homosexuality as an instance of sin or as inherently immoral behavior. Although in both Western countries and the Soviet countries, LGBT people remained closeted about their relationships, the reasons for this behavior and the meaning of being LGBT were starkly different.

As the economic system in Russia underwent transition, so did the social system. As capitalism was imported, so was the economic restructuring of gender norms, which was unlike the communist system in which almost all men and women had been employed. Documented changes in the social conditions include an accompanying rise in **prostitution** and an unemployment problem that has been particularly severe for women (Gal and Kligman 2000), leaving lesbians at a particular economic disadvantage because they do not have access to either comparable wage opportunities or income from male partners. As Russia integrates the values of the West, homosexuality has been characterized as an imported Western phenomenon, corrupting social norms and youth. Recent political efforts have attempted to reinstate the criminality of same-sex male behavior and in political circles there has been concern about Western homosexual conspiracies (Kon 1998). Further, with the revival of Russian Orthodoxy and the influx of Western religious traditions, religious censure of homosexuality appears to be increasing.

In Russia, sexuality has entered the public arena and along with it the appearance of same-sex attraction. Depictions of homosexuality are not presented in the same way as heterosexuality, however. Although images of LGBT people are beginning to appear in the mainstream media, they tend to be of women depicted as sexually indiscriminate. Lesbian images are used to sell products to men, as lesbians are portrayed as impulsive or as having few moral or sexual inhibitions. For instance, beer advertisements lining Moscow's main streets depict two women's lips touching with text that promises consumers "a cocktail without inhibitions."

As sexuality has become more public, information on LGBT people has become more accessible. Russian youth are at the forefront of progressive attitudes toward LGBT individuals, perhaps due to the information revolution and the increased access to global media. Discussion of same-sex love and **desire** has become fashionable in newspapers, magazines, and television shows. For example, the rock group, tATu, which plays with same-sex love between two women, was popular on Russian television before it became an international sensation.

At the same time, the LGBT community is shaping its culture by developing media and establishing organizations to serve the diverse needs of LGBT communities. For example, The Russia National GLBT Center "Together" serves the LGBT community and strives for equality for LGBT concerns by maintaining a Web site http://www.Gayru.com and running health and support programs. Labris is a St. Petersburg lesbian organization, working for greater visibility and rights for lesbian women. There, too, are approximately a dozen gay magazines and newspapers published such as KVIR (Queer) for Russian gay men and Ostrov (Island), a literary journal for lesbians.

Some prominent Russia **arts** figures are publicly out, such as the popular theater director, Roman Viktyuk, and classical dancer, Valery Mikhailovsky, and interviews and writings make these aspects of their lives public. tATu rode to fame in part because of its symbolic play on lesbian **desire**, and the transgender singer Verka Serdyuchka is popular among mainstream youth. Even the lives of LGBT people outside of major cities are now being brought to light, such as in Sonja Franeta's (2004) masterful exploration of LGBT lifestories. Her collection of Serbian narratives has challenged the myth that homosexuality is a Western import and does not exist outside of the major cities of Moscow and St. Petersburg.

Although homosexuality was removed as a psychiatric disorder in 1999, the perception of it as such persists. Even the director of the leading National Research Center for Psychiatry, in Moscow, disputes the removal of homosexuality as a diagnosis. Fears about hospitalization remain among LGBT youth, whose parents can make the decision to have them treated. LGBT identities tend to be viewed within the framework of mental disorder. Although this pathologizing may be read by some as propaganda, the fear of being committed may keep many young people closeted, despite changes in their culture. In addition, gay **hate crimes** appear to be the norm, particularly in nonurban areas (Kon 1995).

There are few resources for queer youth since LGBT organizations have had difficulty obtaining recognition as nongovernmental organizations, which allows them to receive funds and function officially. Currently, the main youth organization, Gayser, located in Moscow, is in its fourth round of applications for consideration but expects to be approved according to its president, Mikhail Syromolotov. This group provides legal advice, which is particularly important for those LGBT youth whose parents are attempting to commit them to asylums. Gayser assists youth starting at the age of consent: 14.5. Although other groups are not specifically focused on youth, there is an openness to provide resources to any LGBT person. The Moscow Lesbian Archives, for instance, is available to those who are interested.

Young people today report being more able to experiment with individuality and to risk standing out. Although youth desire same-sex rights, they live in a culture where grassroots civil rights movements are hard to conceptualize. Even access to the **Internet** or to several nightclubs in each of the major cities requires financial resources.

Bibliography

Applebaum, Anne. 2003. *Gulag: A History*. New York: Random House.

Chervyakov, Victor, Igor Kon, and V. D. Shapiro. 1993. "Teenagers and Sex: Lost Illusions." *Ogonyok* 2: 22–25.

Franeta, Sonja. 2004. *The Pink Flamingo: Ten Siberian Interviews*. Tver, Russia: Ganimed Press.

Gal, Susan, and Gail Kligman. 2000. *The Politics of Gender after Socialism*. Princeton, NJ: Princeton University Press.

Healey, Daniel. 2001. *Homosexual Desire in Revolutionary Russia*. Chicago: University of Chicago Press.

Horne, Sharon G., Heidi Levitt, and Sonja Franeta. Unpublished data.

Kon, Igor. 1993. "Identity Crisis and Postcommunist Psychology." *Symbolic Interaction* 16: 395–405.

———. 1995. *The Sexual Revolution in Russia: From the Age of the Czars to Today*. New York: The Free Press.

Kon, Igor. 1998. *Moonlight Love: Changing Public Opinion.* Accessed April 24, 2004. http://sexology.narod.ru/english/.

———. 2002. *Moonlight at Dawn: Faces and Masks of Same-Sex Love.* Moskva: Olimp.

Kon, Igor, and James Riordan, eds. 1993. *Sex and Russian Society.* Bloomington: Indiana University Press.

Web Sites

Gay Russia. January 2005. Accessed June 7, 2005. http://www.gay.ru. The ultimate online resource for LGBT individuals in Russia (with an English version). In existence for seven years, it provides resources, historical information, arranges guided tours, and provides news updates about LGBT issues in Russia.

Gayser. June 2005. Accessed June 7, 2005. http://www.gayser.org. A national online community serving Russia's LGBT youth, providing legal and psychological consultation to Russian LGBT youth and their families. In addition, it sponsors events on safe sex, provides information about meeting spaces for LGBT youth, and serves as a general resource for youth.

S

School Climate, College

Susan R. Rankin

Sexual minority students on college/university campuses encounter unique challenges because of how they are perceived and treated as a result of their **sexual orientation, gender identity,** or gender expression. The challenges faced by **lesbian, gay, bisexual,** and **transgender** (LGBT) **college age students** may prevent them from achieving their full academic potential or participating fully in the campus community. Similarly, other campus community members, including LGBT teachers, staff, and **administrators,** may also suffer as a result of the same **prejudices,** limiting their ability to achieve their career goals and in **mentoring** or supporting students. What are the specific challenges facing LGBT people on campus and how are institutions of higher education addressing these challenges?

The hostile environment that LGBT students, faculty, staff, and administrators often experience has been documented in numerous studies since the mid-1980s (Rankin 1998). Many LGBT campus members find that they must hide significant parts of their identity from peers and others, thereby isolating themselves socially or emotionally. Those who do not to hide their sexual orientation or gender identity have a range of experiences including **discrimination,** verbal or physical **harassment,** and subtle or outright silencing of their **sexual identities**. Although higher education provides a variety of opportunities for students and others, these are greatly limited for those who fear for their safety when they walk on campus, or feel they must censor themselves in the classroom, or are so distracted by harassing remarks that they are unable to concentrate on their studies or are fearful every time they walk into a public restroom that they will be told to leave.

More recent **research** (Rankin 2003) reveals that the campus community is not an empowering place for LGBT people and that anti-LGBT intolerance and harassment are prevalent. A climate of **heterosexism** inhibits the acknowledgment and expression of LGBT perspectives. It also limits curricular initiatives and research efforts, as seen in the lack of LGBT content in university course offerings. Furthermore, the contributions and concerns of LGBT people have often remained unrecognized. The research findings indicate that:

- More than one-third (36 percent) of LGBT undergraduate students have experienced harassment within the past year.
- Derogatory remarks were the most common form of harassment (89 percent).
- Seventy-nine percent of those harassed identified students as the source of the harassment.
- Twenty percent of the respondents feared for their physical safety because of their sexual orientation/gender identity, and 51 percent concealed their sexual orientation/gender identity to avoid intimidation.
- Respondents felt that LGBT people were likely to be harassed on campus. Seventy-one percent felt that transgender people were likely to

See also College Campus Programming; Passing.

suffer harassment, and 61 percent felt that gay men and lesbians were likely to be harassed.

- Forty-three percent of the respondents rated the overall campus climate as homophobic.
- Forty-one percent of the respondents stated that their college/university was not addressing issues related to sexual orientation/gender identity.
- Forty-three percent of the participants felt that the **curriculum** did not represent the contributions of LGBT people.

The research further suggests that LGBT people of color were more likely than white LGBT people to conceal their sexual orientation or gender identity to avoid harassment. Many respondents said they did not feel comfortable being out in predominantly straight people of color venues, but felt out of place at predominantly white LGBT settings. Additionally, while the same proportion of nontransgender LGB men and women (28 percent) reported experiencing harassment, a significantly higher proportion of transgender respondents (41 percent) reported experiences of harassment.

Several colleges and universities, aware of the challenges facing LGBT members of their communities and understanding their responsibility to provide a safe educational environment for all community members, initiated structural changes. Some created LGBT **college campus resource centers** and **LGBT studies** programs. Others developed or revised LGBT-inclusive administrative policies, such as domestic partner benefits and nondiscrimination policies.

A shift of basic assumptions and beliefs is necessary to address successfully the challenges facing LGBT people on campus. In this transformed institution, heterosexist assumptions are replaced by assumptions of diverse sexualities and relationships; these new assumptions govern the design and implementation of any institutional activity, program, or service. New approaches to learning, teaching, decision-making, and working are implemented by a leadership committed to both policy and goal articulation. Addressing the challenges faced by LGBT people on campus, then, is the catalyst for change. It moves beyond analysis of difference to praxis (the organizational activities and actions that challenge dominance, critique the status quo, and have social justice as a central core value) that informs the strategic approach that runs through the fabric of an organization.

The first step in transforming the campus climate is to conduct a climate assessment to determine the challenges facing LGBT people. Rankin (2003) proposes one paradigm that takes into account five main aspects of campus culture (access and retention, research and scholarship, intergroup and intragroup relations, curriculum and pedagogy, and university commitment/service), and is designed to assist the campus community in maximizing LGBT equity through the use of assessment tools and specific intervention strategies.

In contrast, some argue that rather than focusing exclusively on "surface level issues"—for example, faculty appointments, an inclusive curriculum, an LGBT-friendly environment, etc.—that "structures need to be disrupted" (Tierney and Dilley 1996). Some suggested methods of disrupting structures include: creating centers for interdisciplinary study and cross-cultural teaching and learning—inclusive of LGBT issues—that extend education in areas not included within existing departments; supporting active, collaborative learning enabling students to address their realities; reconfiguring the curriculum by encouraging students to assist in developing or changing the syllabus during the semester.

The articulation by participants of institutional actions that they feel would improve campus climate for LGBT people follow. While not an exhaustive list, these recommendations are a starting point for policy makers and program planners to maximize LGBT equity on campus. A written plan inclusive of the recommended actions should be created including timelines, resources (both human and fiscal), persons responsible for the implementation of the recommendations, and a system of accountability.

Policies that explicitly welcome LGBT employees and students powerfully express the commitment of a college or university to building a diverse and pluralistic community. Individuals will be more likely to be open about their sexual orientation or gender identity knowing that the institution is supportive.

- Provide services to potential employees to assist their same-sex partners in securing employment.
- Include sexual orientation and gender identity or expression in the institution's nondiscrimination clause.
- Extend employee spousal benefits to domestic partners (health insurance, tuition remission, sick and bereavement leave, use of campus facilities, child care services, comparable retirement plans).
- Provide single stall gender-neutral restroom facilities.
- Provide housing for same-sex partners.

Integrating LGBT concerns into all aspects of the institution's administration and policies acknowledges the existence of sexual minorities. Because of the high rate of harassment experienced by LGBT people, policies that directly respond to acts of intolerance, including harassment and violence, are especially needed.

- Integrate LGBT concerns into university documents/publications (grievance procedure, housing guidelines, application materials).
- Create a documentation form in police services for reporting **hate crimes** committed against LGBT people.
- Form a standing advisory committee on LGBT issues similar to other university standing committees (e.g. **race** and ethnicity, disability) that advise the administration on constituent group issues and concerns.
- Provide a clear, safe, visible means of reporting acts of intolerance.
- Respond visibly and expeditiously to acts of intolerance directed at LGBT members of the community.

Acknowledging the contributions of LGBT individuals to all arenas of scholarship, in addition to creating the space for LGBT-specific studies, is important in order to fully integrate LGBT concerns and experiences into the academic community (for one example of this integration see Fletcher and Russell 2001).

- Create an LGBT studies center or department.
- Expand LGBT-related library holdings.

- Integrate LGBT issues into existing courses, where appropriate.
- Promote the use of inclusive language in the classroom (for example, create a pamphlet with examples of heterosexist assumptions and language with suggested alternatives).

As both LGBT and non-LGBT individuals are socialized into a homophobic and heterosexist society, campus community members need *the safe space and educational programming* to question and examine unfounded attitudes and beliefs that they may have otherwise taken for granted.

- Include sexual orientation and gender identity issues in new student orientation programs.
- Create an office for LGBT concerns.
- Create LGBT groups for underrepresented populations (LGBT people with **physical** or **mental disabilities**, LGBT people of color, LGBT international people, transgender youth, bisexuals, etc.).

Bibliography

Evans, Nancy, and Susan Rankin. 1998. "Heterosexism and Campus Violence." Pp. 72–81 in *Violence on Campus: Defining the Problems, Strategies For Action*. Edited by A. Hoffman, J. Schuh, and R. Fenske. Gathersburg, CO: Aspen Publishers.

Fletcher, Anne C., and Stephen T. Russell. 2001. "Incorporating Issues of Sexual Orientation in the College Classroom: Challenges and solutions." *Family Relations* 50: 34–40.

Rankin and Associates, Consulting. 2004, June. Accessed July 16, 2005. http://www.rankin-consulting.com.

Rankin, Susan. 1998. "Campus Climate for Lesbian, Gay, Bisexual, and Transgender Students, Faculty, and Staff: Assessment and Strategies for Change." Pp. 277–284 in *Working with Lesbian, Gay, and Bisexual College Students: A Guide for Administrators and Faculty*. Edited by Ronni Sanlo. Westport, CT: Greenwood.

———. 2003. *Campus Climate for Lesbian, Gay, Bisexual and Transgender People: A National Perspective*. New York: National Gay and Lesbian Task Force Policy Institute.

Tierney, William G., and Patrick Dilley. 1996. "Constructing Knowledge: Educational Research and Gay and Lesbian Studies." Pp. 24–32. *Queer Theory in Education*. Edited by William Pinar. Mahwah, NJ: Lawrence Erlbaum.

Web Sites

Campus PrideNet. 2004. Accessed December 20, 2004. http://campuspride.net. Campus PrideNet is a national online community and resource network committed to student leaders and campus organizations working to create a safer campus environment free of homophobia, biphobia, transphobia, heterosexism, and genderism at colleges and universities.

National Consortium of Directors of Lesbian Gay Bisexual and Transgender Resources in Higher Education. December 2004. Accessed December 20, 2004. http://www.lgbtcampus.org/. The combined vision and mission on the Consortium is to achieve higher education environments in which lesbian, gay, bisexual, and transgender students, faculty, staff, administrators, and alumni have equity in every respect.

National Transgender Advocacy Coalition. December 2004. Accessed December 20, 2004. http://www.ntac.org. The National Transgender Advocacy Coalition works proactively to reform societal attitudes and the law to achieve equal rights for the transgender and other gender diverse individuals.

School Climate, K-12

Stephen T. Russell and *Susan R. Rankin*

The school environment is one of the most important development contexts for children and adolescents, not only for the development of academic and occupational skills, but also for the development of the personal and social skills that shape the first twenty years of life. Studies of **lesbian, gay,** and **bisexual** youth (LGB) show them to be at risk for some of the greatest difficulties experienced by adolescents. Several of those problems pertain directly to education and schooling, such as poor academic performance, negative school attitudes, or victimization at school. In addition, recent research has begun to link the negative **mental health** and risk behaviors of LGB youth to challenges that they face in school, including **harassment** and **discrimination**. These challenges impede not only the students' academic performance, but also their general emotional and social development.

In many high schools, verbal abuse, **graffiti,** and other antigay activities permeate everyday relations among students. In a recent survey of over 900 junior high and high school students, 57 percent reported hearing homophobic remarks at school, and nearly three-fourths reporting hearing the comment "that's so gay" frequently. Sixty-nine percent of LGB youth in grades seven through twelve reported feeling unsafe in their schools, and one-third reported that they missed at least one day of school in the past month because they felt unsafe (Kosciw and Cullen 2003). This pervasive homophobia in the school setting is often expressed not only by fellow students but, at times, by teachers as well (Human Rights Watch 2001). Such school-based harassment is a primary antecedent of many of the risks that characterize the lives of LGB youth, and has been linked with compromised emotional health that lasts into adulthood, including depression and thinking about **suicide** (Rivers 2001).

For LGB youth, peers may be the first people to whom they "come out," and peers may also be the people from whom they receive the most harassment or victimization. Because the threat of further victimization often acts as a barrier to reporting LGB bias incidents, the numbers of actual incidents of violence and harassment to LGB youth are probably much higher than those reported. Thus, negative school climates not only enable intolerance but reinforce the invisibility of LGB issues and people (Rivers 2001).

Many schools, **administrators,** and teachers are proactive in assuring that the school environment is free from harassment and discrimination; many more have limited awareness of or are not prepared to understand and manage issues of same-sex identity or sexuality. School personnel often do not take sexuality-motivated harassment or victimization seriously, even for students for whom harassment and victimization experiences are pervasive. Some even express the belief that victims "cause" their harassment and thereby do not support victimized youth (Human Rights Watch 2001).

There is little **research** on effective prevention and intervention strategies related to issues of **sexual orientation** and **gender identity** (McCarn and Fassinger

See also Activism, LGBT Teachers; Antidiscrimination Policy; Coming Out, Teachers; Coming Out, Youth; Legal Issues, Students; Project 10; Rural Youth and Schools; School Climate, College; School Safety and Safe School Zones; Secondary Schools, LGBT; Urban Youth and Schools; Youth, At-Risk.

1996). Further research is critically needed to provide schools with the tools necessary to create supportive educational environments for all students. However, a recent national study indicates that teachers play an essential role in creating supportive school environments where all youth can grow and learn; among seventh through twelfth graders, sexual minority youth with positive feelings about their teachers were significantly less likely than their peers to experience school troubles (Russell, Seif, and Truong 2001). A second study—the first to document the importance of teacher education and sensitivity in the **curriculum** for LGB students—showed that, in schools with gay-sensitive **HIV education**, gay students reported lower sexual health risks (Blake et al. 2001). Comprehensive education on sexual orientation and gender identity is essential for educators and school personnel to prepare them to be supportive of all students.

There is no known empirical research on the school climate for LGBT students in elementary schools. An edited volume by Letts and Sears (1999) provides a collection of essays by elementary teachers that describe strategies for addressing homosexuality in the classroom. The well-known film "It's Elementary" (Women's Educational Media 1996) considers the issue of incorporating issues about LGBT people in the elementary school context.

During the past ten years (and particularly in the last five years), schools have been developing programs and policies aimed at promoting more tolerant school climates for sexual minority youth. These efforts have included the development and implementation of:

- nondiscrimination and harassment **educational policies** that specifically include actual or perceived sexual orientation or identity;
- training for school personnel (including administrators, teachers, custodial, and security staff) on identifying and responding to victimization and harassment, at times including specific attention to issues of sexual identity and orientation;
- programs designed to increase the understanding and awareness of nondiscrimination and harassment policies by school personnel and students; and
- programs and activities that actively promote a supportive school environment for sexual minority youth, including attention to such issues in the curriculum and the creation of **gay–straight alliances** (Perrotti and Westheimer 2001).

Bibliography

Blake, Susan M, Rebecca Ledsky, T. Lehman, Carol Goodenow, Richard Sawyer, and T. Hack. 2001. "Preventing Sexual Risk Behaviors among Gay, Lesbian, and Bisexual Adolescents: The Benefits of Gay-Sensitive HIV Instruction in Schools." *American Journal of Public Health* 91: 940–946.

Human Rights Watch. 2001. *Hatred in the Hallways: Violence and Discrimination Against Lesbian, Gay, Bisexual, and Transgender Students in U.S. Schools*. New York: Human Rights Watch.

Kosciw, Joseph, and M. K. Cullen. 2003. *The GLSEN 2001 National School Climate Survey: The School-Related Experiences of Our Nation's Lesbian, Gay, Bisexual, and Transgender Youth*. New York: Gay, Lesbian, and Straight Education Network.

Letts, William J., and James T. Sears, eds. 1999. *Queering Elementary Education: Advancing the Dialogue about Sexualities and Schooling.* Lanham, MD: Rowman and Littlefield.

McCarn, S. R., and Ruth Fassinger. 1996. "Revisioning Sexual Minority Identity Formation: A New Model of Lesbian Identity and its Implications for Counseling and Research." *The Counseling Psychologist* 24: 508–534.

Perrotti, Jeff, and Kim Westheimer. 2001. *When the Drama Club is Not Enough.* Boston: Beacon Press.

Rivers, Ian. 2001. "The Bullying of Sexual Minorities at School: Its Nature and Long-Term Correlates." *Educational & Child Psychology* 18: 32–46.

Russell, Stephen T., Hinda M. Seif, and Nhan L. Truong. 2001. "School Outcomes of Sexual Minority Youth in the United States: Evidence from a National Study." *Journal of Adolescence* 24: 111–127.

Women's Educational Media. [Videotape.] 1996. *It's Elementary: Talking about Gay Issues.* San Francisco.

Web Site

Gay–Straight Alliance Network. 2004. GSA Network. Accessed December 5, 2004. http://www.gsanetwork.org. This youth-led organization connects school-based Gay–Straight Alliances (GSAs) to each other and community resources. Through peer support, leadership development, and training, it supports young people in starting, strengthening, and sustaining GSAs and builds the capacity of GSAs.

School Safety and Safe School Zones

Dominique Johnson

Appearing in the early 1990s, safe school zones identify, educate, and sustain **lesbian, gay, bisexual, transgender**, and questioning students who often have negative experiences at school, encountering **harassment** and **discrimination** on the part of peers and on occasion from school personnel (Human Rights Watch, 2001; Russell, Seif, and Truong 2001). Current concerns of school safety include violence, an unwelcome or hostile **school climate**, identity-based harassment and **discrimination**, gang membership, delinquency, **bullying**, and truancy. According to a comprehensive statewide 2004 **Gay, Lesbian, and Straight Education Network** (GLSEN) report, a large majority of United States students attend schools in states with no legal protections against anti-LGBT bullying and harassment. LGBTQ students are twice as likely as others to feel unsafe or afraid at school and are approximately two to seven times more likely than their peers to report skipping school because of feeling unsafe (Safe Schools Coalition 1997; 1999). Some LGBTQ youth, particularly students of color, choose not to attend school (GLSEN 2003). A lack of institutional support and protection for LGBTQ and allied educators also contributes to a diminished sense of safety for students who are lacking role

See also Antibias Curriculum; Mentoring; Project 10; Residence Life in Colleges; Youth, At-Risk.

743

models and accompanying sources of encouragement (GLSEN 2003; Schwartz 1994).

Emerging safe schools projects in secondary schools and colleges provide concrete, practical strategies that enhance school safety for LGBTQ youth. These programs, ranging from **gay–straight alliances** (GSAs) and **college campus resource centers** to **counseling** services and LGBT faculty advisors, increase visibility, support, and awareness of LGBTQ people, their experiences, and the issues they face on school campuses (Sanlo, Rankin, and Schoenberg 2002). Safe zone stickers, posters, or other markers can be posted in classrooms, hallways, and offices. While school-based harassment and assault are a troubling reality of LGBTQ youth, safe school zones established and maintained by LGBT teachers, students, **administrators**, and **allies** contribute to student retention and academic opportunity.

Schools that have policies about violence, bias, and harassment against LGBTQ students, conduct faculty workshops on **sexual orientation** and **gender identity/ expression**, and provide safe zones such as GSAs create an increased sense of safety (GLSEN 2003; Perotti and Westheimer 2001). The eventual involvement of the entire school in making school climate safe for LGBTQ students (and therefore all students) is necessary in order to achieve this goal. There are several key elements that contribute to an effective and lasting school safety program: the establishment and implementation of statewide legal mandates, **educational policies**, and programs; the involvement of and support from key school administrators and adult leaders; participation of the community, particularly among LGBTQ members; engagement of student leadership (Griffin and Ouellett 2002).

One strategy that has been employed to launch safe schools programs is to bring the **legal** liability to the attention of school districts and provide them with skills and resources to promote a safe school climate of tolerance and acceptance. Landmark court cases, such as *Nabozny v. Podlesny*, resulting in significant financial damages to school districts for failing to protect LGBT students from harassment, has created a supportive climate for such programs. School districts and administrations have implemented any or all of the following initiatives to create a safer education for all students: include gays and lesbians in **antidiscrimination policies** and expressions of **homophobia** on the list of prohibited behaviors in the school policy manual; offer support and protection for teachers who come out so LGBTQ students can have role models and a source of support; support organizations of LGBTQ students, giving them the same privileges as other student groups; allow or encourage same-sex couples to attend events such as **proms**; create an educational climate where students can reject stereotypical **gender roles** such as hypermasculinity; provide antibias and violence prevention training that includes self-protection strategies; and, include fiction and nonfiction **literature** on homosexuality in the library (Schwartz 1994).

School safety initiatives have also extended to separate programs and **secondary schools** for LGBTQ youth. These range from the public Harvey Milk High School in New York City to the privately operated Walt Whitman Community School in Dallas, to special interest residential houses or floors that provide space for LGBT **college students** and their allies such as the University of Massachusetts at Amherst, to the school-supported Triangle Project in Toronto and the nationwide antibullying policies instituted in the **United Kingdom**. All are intervention models that encourage a safe and successful educational experience and promote **resilience** among LGBTQ students and educators.

Bibliography

Evans, Nancy J. 2002. "The Impact of an LGBT Safe Zone Project on Campus Climate." *Journal of College Student Development* 43: 522–539.

GLSEN. 2003. *National School Climate Survey*. http://www.glsen.org. Accessed July 16, 2005.

———. 2004. *State of the States 2004: A Policy Analysis of Lesbian, Gay, Bisexual, and Transgender LGBT Safer Schools Issues*. Accessed July 16, 2005. http://www.glsen.org/cgi-bin/iowa/educator/library/record/1687.html.

Griffin, Pat, and Mathew L. Ouellett. 2002. "Going Beyond Gay–Straight Alliances to Make Schools Safe for Lesbian, Gay, Bisexual, and Transgender Students." *The Policy Journal of the Institute for Gay and Lesbian Strategic Studies* 6, no. 1. Accessed July 16, 2005. http://www.iglss.org./media/files/Angles_61.pdf.

Human Rights Watch. 2001. *Hatred in the Hallways: Violence and Discrimination Against Lesbian, Gay, Bisexual, and Transgender Students in U.S. Schools*. New York: Author.

National Youth Advocacy Coalition. 2003. *Materials & Training*. Accessed July 16, 2005. http://www.nyacyouth.org/nyac/materials_training.html.

Perotti, Jeff, and Kim Westheimer. 2001. *When the Drama Club is Not Enough: Lessons from the Safe Schools Program for Gay and Lesbian Students*. Boston: Beacon Press.

Russell, Stephen R., Hinda Seif, and Nhan L. Truong. 2001. "School Outcomes of Sexual Minority Youth in the United States: Evidence from a National Study." *Journal of Adolescence* 24: 111–127.

Safe Schools Coalition. 1997. *Safe Schools Report from Washington State*. Accessed July 16, 2005. http://www.safeschoolscoalition.org/blackboard-washington.html.

———. 1999. *Eighty-Three Thousand Youth: Selected Findings of Eight Population-Based Studies*. http://www.safeschoolscoalition.org/83000youth.pdf.

Sanlo, Ronni, Sue Rankin, and Robert Schoenberg. 2002. "Safe Zones and Allies Programs." Pp. 95–100 in *Our Place on Campus: Lesbian, Gay, Bisexual, and Transgender Services and Programs in Higher Education*. Edited by Ronni Sanlo, Sue Rankin, and Robert Schoenberg. Westport, CT: Greenwood Press.

Schwartz, Wendy. 1994. "Improving the School Experience for Gay, Lesbian, and Bisexual Students." ERIC Document No. ED377 257.

Woog, Dan. 1995. *School's Out: The Impact of Gay and Lesbian Issues on America's Schools*. Los Angeles: Alyson.

Web Sites

American Civil Liberties Union (ACLU) Get Busy, Get Equal Safe Schools Project. November 2004. Accessed January 4, 2005. http://www.aclu.org/getequal/scho/index.html. Gives students, educators, parents, and community members the tools to make school a safer space for LGBT students, including information on how to get a safe schools policy, start a gay–straight alliance, get a safe schools training, and other LGBT school issues.

Gay, Lesbian, Straight Education Network (GLSEN). June 2004. Accessed December 3, 2004. http://www.glsen.org/cgi-bin/iowa/educator/library/record/1687.html. Creating safe K-12 schools for all lesbian, gay, bisexual and transgender people, its 2004 state-by-state report of safe school policies provides a comprehensive analysis.

Safe Schools Coalition. 2004. Accessed December 3, 2004. http://www.safeschoolscoalition.org. Includes key resources on legal and policy issues and extensive resources for educators, parents, and students.

School Survival Guide. 2003. Accessed December 4, 2004. http://www.centeryes.org/SIGNS/ A project of the Youth Enrichment Services (YES) Program of the Lesbian and Gay Community Services Center (the Center) in New York City, this is a group of student leaders working to end hate and homophobia in schools, which includes specific strategies on creating safer schools.

Science, Teaching of

Will Letts

Science education has traditionally focused on skills and content related to the physical, geological, and biological sciences. Science education reform efforts internationally have worked to broaden the portrayal of school science and to challenge educators to think in diverse ways about how to teach science. These reformers have examined the curricula, pedagogies, and policies of science education and advocated a move away from only focusing on traditional content and skills. To this end, there has been an abrupt movement away from science teaching as transmission of facts and skills to a focus on teaching about the nature and process of science, doing science, and on the attendant pedagogies that would facilitate this type of learning about an expanded sense of science. These "critical pedagogies of science education" shift the concern from the most effective way to transmit large volumes of science content to an interest in issues of language, identities, and sense-making. This shift in thinking about the teaching of science in schools is a particularly important for **lesbian, gay, bisexual**, and **transgender youth** (LGBT), for it destabilizes dualities (such as male/female, nature/culture, and heterosexual/homosexual), (re)presents science in a social and environmental justice framework, and emphasizes the coconstruction of knowledge and understanding between teacher and learners. These moves upend decades of normalizing science instruction in favor of strategies that start from the lives of young people to connect them to science.

Debates have raged about the nature of science, focusing not only on the content of science, but also on social and cultural perspectives of science and, in turn, on the most engaging and situated pedagogies for teaching science. Starting with the feminist critiques of science, "traditional science" has been interrogated from a variety of theoretical positions including antiracist, postcolonial, multicultural, and queer critiques. For example, feminist critiques of science have revealed how many of the metaphors and even theories used to describe scientific phenomena are masculinist and sexist; queer critiques have shown how traditional science is predicated on unspoken but pervasive norms of heterosexuality. This phenomenon is illustrated in such groundbreaking work as Emily Martin's (1991) discussion of how accounts of fertilization read like the tale of a damsel in distress (egg) being reached by a valiant prince (sperm), and in Ruth Hubbard's (1990, 87) work that demonstrates that Darwinian evolutionary theory "has wide areas of congruence with the social and political ideology of nineteenth-century Britain and with Victorian precepts of morality, particularly as regards the relationships between the sexes."

Science is covered with the fingerprints of the societies that have shaped it (Figueroa and Harding 2003). But the myths about science and scientists—including its alleged value-free nature, its objectivity, and its appeal to a universal Truth—are pervasive and still enjoy some cultural prevalence today, perpetuating its misrepresentation through science teaching (Hodson 1998). Karen Barad (1995), for instance, describes how students studying quantum physics are taught concepts like the uncertainty principle completely stripped from their historical and cultural contexts and presented as the result of probing a pure and unadulterated

See also Biology, Teaching of; Critical Social Theory; Feminism; Heterosexism; Poststructuralism; Queer and Queer Theory.

nature. Thus, "It is as if we are all to believe that the scientific method serves as a giant distillation column, removing all biases, allowing patient practitioners to collect the pure distillate of truth. There is no agent in this view of theory construction: Knower and known are distinct—nature has spoken" (66). Contrary to this idealized picture of "objective" science, Barad notes that recent critiques of science have revealed the "various ways in which the sciences are marked by the cultural and ideological specificities of their creators" (70).

The science pedagogies that flow out from the critiques of this "traditional" science are consistent with a more democratic and inclusive science. Here, teaching strategies focus on the importance of individual students and their coconstruction of scientific knowledge rather than relying on "objective" and value-free truths about the student (Roth and Barton 2004). Thus, teaching science, like other subjects, requires attention to students' identities and the ways these identities allow them (or hinder them) to make sense in and of science. These strategies for teaching science now offer students resources for **identity development**, and teach a more socially and culturally situated view of school science.

An example of a group traditionally disenfranchised from science is sexual minority youth. In the past, issues of sexualities have been perceived as largely irrelevant to science **curriculum** and teaching. Heterosexuality was taken as the norm that guided knowledge production in science (as it was in most other disciplines) as traditional science teaching strategies and techniques reflected this heteronormative and masculinist norm.

Letts (1999; 2001), for instance, describes the ways in which elementary school science pedagogies take heterosexuality as the "natural," unremarkable starting point and are thus "heteronormative." In one pedagogical episode, the teacher assumes that boys and girls must not be in the same groups for an activity that involves feeling one another's limbs to try to discern bone structure. The teacher mistakenly assumes that it is "unsafe" for young boys and girls to touch each others' limbs, and forces children into same-sex groups. This reasoning (hetero)sexualizes the actions and motives of young children, unwittingly reinforcing powerful messages about what is and is not acceptable in science—and in gendered relations.

At the secondary or tertiary level, biology teachers often uncritically generalize an evolutionary drive for members of species to reproduce to perpetuate their genes to humans, ignoring human **agency** and the choices that humans are free to make. Further, it renders as "not normal" those who don't strive for and attain heterosexual reproductively active partnerships. Not only is sex relegated to procreation, but the variety of technologies and choices available to people to craft families of choice is marginalized. Thus, teaching about seemingly straight-forward science content actually involves issues of identity and a sense of one's place in science. Many students are excluded by science that renders their families (or themselves) invisible, as abnormal. Close and critical examination of teaching science demonstrates how underlying **heteronormativity** translates into poor pedagogical decision-making, lost opportunities for learning, and even in student alienation from science.

During the course of one's entire science education, hidden messages are unmistakable and have a cumulative impact, ranging from the mostly male and white scientists to the very Westernized understanding of science as a method for understanding, prediction, and control of the natural world. Some people are acceptable to and accepted in science, and others are not; some issues are "in bounds" within science, and others are not. Traditional science lessons are also marked by the

747

teacher-dominated monologue that signals an anxiety to "cover" as much content as possible; therefore, students occasionally engage in predictable experiments rather than understanding the constructed and experimental nature of the scientific enterprise itself. Traditional teacher education offers teachers little by way of reconceptualizing both *who* they teach and *how* they teach them.

An antidote to such a hidden curriculum in science teaching is to adopt a critical pedagogy of science education. Taken collectively, the following characteristics promise a more democratic future, including one for LGBT youth:

- *A focus on dialogue in the classroom rather than domination by teacher talk, to allow for negotiated understandings and acknowledge scientific knowledge as problematic rather than simply as given.* This might be accomplished by making classes more issue-based and discussion-centred, enabling students to see the sometimes competing interests that inform scientific issues and problems, and to express their beliefs and understandings about those issues. Students could explore, for example, the evidence in the nature–nurture debates about sexuality, noting which parties have what to gain by advocating particular views on the issue.

- *A related shift to a pedagogy that centers around hands-on experiences to immerse students in the science rather than teaching strategies that merely "transmit facts."* This might be accomplished by using relevant practical experiences as stimuli for discussions about science concepts, as well as more traditional laboratory or practical experiences. Here, student interviews of one another or with family and community members about sex and **gender roles** is a basis for an exploration of the "naturalness" of the constructs of sex and gender.

- *Teaching that acknowledges students' agency and even resistance in the science classrooms, and attempts to engage this rather than ignore it.* This might be accomplished by asking students periodically to reflect on their sense of self in science, or "science selves" to scrutinize their relationship with and even sense of "fit" with science, focusing on whose identities are represented within and are congruent with science, whose are not, and exploring why this might be so.

- *"Dangerous teaching"* (Osborne 1998; Roth and Barton 2004) *that explicitly acknowledges teaching science as a sociopolitical act in order to build a more just society.* This might be accomplished by engaging students in rich, relevant issues, such as water quality, pollution, pharmaceutical prices, rates of illness in certain parts of town, or more generally, science's history as a heterosexist (among other biases) enterprise.

- *It engenders in students a care for and about what they are learning, which in turn gives a purpose and commitment to what they are doing* (Appelbaum 2001). This might involve taking an emergent approach to science curriculum, drawing on students' interests and tapping into their strengths. Human sexuality, therefore, might be taught in a way that exceeds "the mechanics" of human reproduction, to encompass issues of **desire**, pleasure, consent, and agency.

- *A multifocal (rather than singular) view of knowledges and knowledge production* (Weinstein 2001), *where scientists' voices are not privileged over those of their participants or subjects*. This could be enacted by valuing the contributions of students and acknowledging what they bring "to the table" to make sense of science by marshalling evidence to explain their understandings. Such an approach would also welcome cross-curricular work, troubling what seem like firm boundaries between different subjects. Learning about families might entail some work with family trees and genetic inheritance, but would also recognize the broad range of family configurations that transcend the "biological" family.

- *Simultaneously challenging one's own role as teacher as you envision and enact science education practices that challenge the purposes and goals of science education* (Roth and Barton 2004). This might be accomplished by involving the students in curricular decision-making, and by asking them to reflect on your practice as a teacher as well as their own performances as students. The reflection could exceed a focus on science content and ask students to offer feedback about how you as a teacher are nurturing their science selves and the place they see for themselves with/in science.

Bibliography

Appelbaum, Peter. 2001. "Pastiche Science: Bringing Cultural Studies of Science to Education and Education to Cultural Studies of Science." Pp. 111–127 in *(Post) Modern Science (Education): Propositions and Alternative Paths*. Edited by John Weaver, Marla Morris, and Peter Appelbaum. New York: Peter Lang.

Barad, Karen. 1995. "A Feminist Approach to Teaching Quantum Physics." Pp. 43–75 in *Teaching the Majority: Breaking the Gender Barrier in Science, Mathematics, and Engineering*. Edited by Sue V. Rosser. New York: Teachers College Press.

Figueroa, Robert, and Sandra Harding, eds. 2003. *Science and Other Cultures: Issues in Philosophies of Science and Technology*. New York: Routledge.

Hodson, Derek. 1998. "Science Fiction: The Continuing Misrepresentation of Science in the School Curriculum." *Curriculum Studies* 6, no. 2: 191–216.

Hubbard, Ruth. 1990. *The Politics of Women's Biology*. New Brunswick, NJ: Rutgers University Press.

Letts, William J. 1999. "How to Make 'Boys' and 'Girls' in the Classroom: The Heteronormative Nature of Elementary School Science." Pp. 97–110 in *Queering Elementary Education: Advancing the Dialogue about Sexualities and Schooling*. Edited by William J. Letts and James T. Sears. Lanham, MD: Rowman and Littlefield.

———. 2001. "When Science is Strangely Alluring: Interrogating the Masculinist and Heteronormative Nature of Primary School Science." *Gender & Education* 13, no. 3: 261–274.

Martin, Emily. 1991. "The Egg and the Sperm: How Science has Constructed a Romance Based on Stereotypical Male-Female Roles." *Signs* 16, no. 3: 485–501.

Osborne, Margery. 1998. "Responsive Science Pedagogy in a Democracy: Dangerous Teaching." *Theory into Practice* 37, no. 4: 289–296.

Roth, Wolff-Michael, and Angela Calabrese Barton. 2004. *Rethinking Scientific Literacy*. New York:Routledge-Falmer.

Weinstein, Matthew. 2001. "Science Education through Situated Knowledge." Pp. 129–145 in *(Post) Modern Science (Education): Propositions and Alternative Paths*. Edited by John Weaver, Marla Morris, and Peter Appelbaum. New York: Peter Lang.

Web Sites

Critical Pedagogy. June 2005. Martin Ryder. Accessed June 17, 2005. http://carbon. cudenver.edu/~mryder/itc_data/crit_ped.html. Although not solely focused on science teaching, this includes a detailed selection of readings from prominent scholars on critical pedagogy and a list of resources to help think about what critical pedagogy might look like in your classroom.

National Science Teachers Association. June 2005. Accessed June 17, 2005. http://www. nsta.org. Sponsored by the USA's NSTA, it includes links to journal articles, discussion boards, upcoming events, numerous resources, and science news digests. It is an invaluable reference point for science teachers from early childhood through to tertiary settings. Teachers may find the organization's statement about gender equity (at http://www.nsta.org/positionstatement&psid=37) particularly helpful.

Social Action and Critical Pedagogy. 2000. Abby Wolk. Accessed June 17, 2005. http:// www.allkidsgrieve.org/Classroom/class4.html#top. Includes information about critical pedagogy in the context of both social and environmental action, linking the key tenants of critical pedagogy to strategies to engage students in "real world" issues. It has links to other Web sites that develop similar notions of linking theory to action.

Scouting

James Anthony Whitson

The international Scouting movement began with the establishment of the first national organization of Boy Scouts in England in 1908, followed by a proliferation of national Boy Scout, Girl Scout or Girl Guide, and Camp Fire organizations around the world. Opportunities provided by these organizations have been enjoyed by young people over the past century, including youth of diverse sexual orientations as well as diverse ethnic, racial, and religious backgrounds. The role of Scouting in the lives of sexual minorities, in the past, may have been to some extent the same as for heterosexual youth; but in recent decades, the Boy Scouts of America (BSA) has adopted a policy of excluding gays and lesbians. Even when **discrimination** against sexual minorities was not an issue, however, the Boy Scout movement has from its beginning been devoted to the formation of young men according to ideals of masculine normality.

On February 6, 2002, the Executive Board of the Boy Scouts of America adopted an official resolution declaring that "conduct of both Scouts and [adult] Scouters must be in compliance with the Scout Oath and Law," and that "homosexual conduct is inconsistent with the traditional values espoused in the Scout Oath and Law" (Boy Scouts of America 2002). Critics have argued that there is no record of such exclusionary policies being part of the historical mission of Scouting. Dissenting from the majority opinion in *Boy Scouts of America v. Dale* (2000), for example, Justice Stevens noted the argument that the Boy Scouts' stance in that case was contradicted by declared policies of inclusiveness, including the BSA's description of itself as "having a 'representative membership,' which it defines as 'boy membership [that] reflects proportionately the characteristics of the boy population of its service area'" (666).

See also Mentoring; Professional Educational Organizations; Psychoanalysis and Education.

In an exceptionally informative synopsis of the history, and discussion of recent developments, Soskis (2001) observes that

> . . . despite the BSA's conservative defenders' claim that they are upholding scouting tradition, the organization's real tradition bears no more resemblance to contemporary Christian-right ideology than it does to contemporary liberal ideology. In fact, from its earliest days, in an effort to create good citizens and good men from a diverse pool of boys, the Boy Scouts sidestepped precisely this kind of partisan tug-of-war with a genuinely pluralistic ideal.

The association's history does show a genuine and energetic commitment to extend the Scouting experience to all boys, notably including racial minorities (Murray 1937). The history also shows, however, that values and character formation—and not just hiking and camping—have always been at the heart of the association's mission (Macleod 1983). In this, the BSA reflects its origins in the Boy Scout movement in Great Britain, where its aspiration was to build the kind of character in young men that would prepare them to maintain the world-wide British Empire (MacDonald 1993; Rosenthal 1986).

While hiking and camping have an obvious relation to the military maintenance of empire, it may be less obvious how sexuality is related to this mission. In his biography of the founder of the English (and international) Boy Scout movement, Jeal (1990, 87–88) describes Baden-Powell's "idea of the Scout Movement [as] a safe haven for boys and young men," in which "hiking, camping, cheery singsongs and other 'safe' activities" would serve to counteract the dangers of the adult world. For him, these dangers included sex, but mainly the dangers arising from sexual interest in females or of "self-abuse" (Rosenthal 1986).

Certainly Baden-Powell would condemn Scoutmasters for sexually abusing boys, and Jeal (1990, 95) concludes that "his hatred of paederasty was genuine:" it appears that he did not regard a homoerotic interest in the boys as a disqualification to serve as Scoutmaster—provided that the Scoutmaster did not act on such "sentiments" (94–96). Other Scout leaders at that time did not share Baden-Powell's ambivalence with regard to homosexual Scoutmasters, and they would not have shared "his idea that a man could be a suitable Scoutmaster if he needed to make constant efforts to do so" (Jeal 1990, 95).

Critics of the BSA's policies today are not advocating tolerance of sexual conduct between men and boys in any case, so those issues are not on point with the controversy now. The BSA itself labels as a "fiction" the idea that "fear of pedophilia" is the reason for its policy of "exclude[ing] homosexuals from the ranks of its members and leaders," explaining that its actual reason is what it considers the inappropriateness of homosexuals as "role models for Scouting youth" (BSA 2003). According to Soskis (2001), "even in 1986, when the Boy Scouts, citing a study of convicted child molesters, admitted that avowed homosexuals were no more dangerous than heterosexuals, they still rejected gays, pointing to the threat they posed to the traditional family."

Nancy Lesko (2001) recounts how Scouting has functioned as an institution dedicated to the normalizing regulation of boys' life, especially the life of working-class boys and in their time spent outside of other normalizing institutions such as schools. Locating this historically with respect to sexuality, Lesko notes a "sea change in relationships [that] occurred after the Oscar Wilde trials, a time when the easy blurring of homosocial and homosexual was halted in Britain as in the United States" (71).

Lesko calls attention to the role of Scouting and related movements in normalization through the regulation of play and of youth activity outside of home and school. In this light, we may consider Jay Mechling's (2001) account of life in a Boy Scout camp after joining one troop in camp for a number of summers from 1976 to 1999. Mechling contends that "One of the main 'projects' . . . of the Boy Scout camp is the creation of the heterosexual male" (195). His explanation of that statement is informed by anthropological and psychoanalytic theory. It also draws from the experiences related throughout his book, which includes a discussion of reasons why he believes that the BSA should change its policy, and what he sees as the prospects for such change after **Boy Scouts of America v. Dale** (2000), in which the Supreme Court ruled that the organization has a constitutional right to exclude homosexuals from adult leadership positions.

The Boy Scout experience that Mechling portrays may be contrasted with the experiences in Girl Scouting discussed by thirty-three lesbian writers in a collection edited by Nancy Manahan (1997). While the experiences they relate were not uniformly positive, they portray life in the Girl Scouts as generally far more open, accepting, supportive, and conducive to the happiness, well-being, and growth of its members—gay or straight. Manahan supplements these first-person reflections with her views on the association's policies, including an appendix listing Girl Scout area councils that had adopted **antidiscrimination policies** at the time of her writing.

The Girl Scouts and the Camp Fire Boys and Girls differ from the BSA in that, while the U.S. Supreme Court doctrine would recognize these organizations as having the same constitutional right to determine membership policies, these groups have chosen very different policies as explained in a statement released after the *Dale* decision:

> The Girl Scout organization does not discriminate. We do not permit the advocacy or promotion of a personal lifestyle or sexual orientation. These are private matters for girls and their families to address. Girl Scout membership is open to all girls who accept the Girl Scout Law and makes [sic] the Girl Scout Promise. (as quoted in Gustafson 2000).

The home page of the Camp Fire Boys and Girls proclaims, "For nearly a century: integrity, responsibility, tolerance;" and the "all about us" page on its Web site continues:

Camp Fire USA takes pride in its long-standing commitment to providing fun programs and services to all children and families in America. We are inclusive, open to every person in the communities we serve, welcoming children, youth and adults regardless of race, religion, socioeconomic status, disability, sexual orientation or other aspect of diversity. (Camp Fire USA 2004)

Steven Cozza, Cofounder Scouting for All. Courtesy of Scouting for All

Since the *Dale* decision, diverse efforts have continued trying to either get the Boy Scouts to change their policy or else to withdraw forms of public support that are not generally provided for the kinds of organizations that are free to discriminate because they are truly private associations. These efforts are notably spearheaded by a group called "Scouting for All," which was founded by two heterosexuals, then ages twelve and sixty-nine, who were both kicked out of the Boy Scouts for opposing its policies (Shepard 2001).

Bibliography

Boy Scouts of America, et al., v. James Dale, 530 U.S. 640. 2000.

Boy Scouts of America, National Council. 2002. *Resolution*. February 6. Accessed December 21, 2004. http://www.scouting.org/media/press/020206/resolution.html/.

———. 2003. *Fiction vs. Fact*. 2003. Accessed December 1, 2003. http://www.scouting.org/media/values/fact.html.

Buckler, Helen. 1980. *Wo-He-Lo: The Camp Fire History*. Kansas City, MO: Camp Fire, Inc.

Denniston, Lyle. 2003, September 14. "Embattled Scouts Struggle To Maintain Funding, Ideology." Boston *Globe*: A12.

Fudge, Helen. 1939. *Girls' Clubs of National Organization in the United States—Their Development and Present Status*. Philadelphia: Westminster Press.

Gustafson, Mary. 2000, October 1. "Scouting and Discrimination." *Knot Magazine*. Accessed December 21, 2004. http://www.knotmag.com/?article=139.

Jeal, Tim. 1990. *The Boy-Man: The Life of Lord Baden-Powell*. New York: Morrow.

Lesko, Nancy. 2001. *Act Your Age!: A Cultural Construction of Adolescence*. New York: Routledge/Falmer.

MacDonald, Robert H. 1993. *Sons of the Empire: The Frontier and the Boy Scout Movement, 1890–1918*. Toronto and Buffalo: University of Toronto Press.

Macleod, David I. 1983. *Building Character in the American Boy: The Boy Scouts, YMCA, and Their Forerunners, 1870–1920*. Madison: University of Wisconsin Press.

Manahan, Nancy. 1997. *On My Honor: Lesbians Reflect on Their Scouting Experience*. Northboro, MA: Madwoman Press.

Mechling, Jay. 2001. *On My Honor: Boy Scouts and The Making of American Youth*. Chicago: University of Chicago Press.

Murray, William D. 1937. *The History of the Boy Scouts of America*. New York: Boy Scouts of America.

Rosenthal, Michael. 1986. *The Character Factory: Baden-Powell and the Origins of the Boy Scout Movement*. 1st ed. New York: Pantheon Books.

Shepard, Tom. 2001. *Scout's Honor*. San Francisco, CA: New Day Films. Available from http://www.scouts-honor.com/. Accessed December 21, 2004.

Soskis, Benjamin. 2001, September 17. "Big Tent: Saving The Boy Scouts From Its Supporters." *The New Republic*. Available to subscribers at http://www.tnr.com/091701/soskis091701.html; publicly available at http://www.scoutingforall.org/aaic/092002.shtml. Accessed June 22, 2005.

Web Sites

Boy Scouts of America. November 2004. BSA National Council. Accessed November 30, 2004. http://www.scouting.org. The homepage links to a media center, fact sheets, and research reports. There are also links for membership in various programs within the organization (Cub Scouts, Boy Scouts, Venturing, etc.)

Camp Fire USA. 2004. Accessed November 30, 2004. http://www.campfire.org. The "All About Us" page links to information about the organization's history, mission, programs, core values, and demographics. The site also has a Press Room and pages for alumni and for teens.

Girl Scouts of the USA. November 2004. Accessed November 30, 2004. http://www. girlscouts.org/. The "About Girl Scouts of the USA" page links to information about the program, history, resources, and International Girl Scouting as well as pages for news and pages "Just for Girls" and on "Adults in Girl Scouting."

Scouting for All. November 2004. Accessed November 30, 2004. http://www. scoutingforall.org/. The single most complete source of continually updated information about developments concerning scouting opportunities for all youth, regardless of sexual orientation, gender, or religious belief or nonbelief. The site provides a wealth of information and links to information and resources on scouting around the world, as well as information on how to join and support its ongoing efforts and a photo gallery.

Secondary Schools, LGBT

Mary M. Clare and *Steven E. James*

Secondary schools provide one of the most challenging social settings for **lesbian, gay, bisexual,** and **transgender youth** (LGBT). Because of the confluence of physical, emotional, and sexual developmental changes in adolescence and the ever-widening social pressures and opportunities, many LGBT youth find middle and high school among the most difficult years in their journeys to self-discovery and self-acceptance. There is an alarming incidence of **harassment** and other violence toward these youth alongside related increases in underachievement, unsafe behavior, and dropping out (Kosciw 2004; Rivers 2000). Three programmatic approaches have emerged to address the needs of these youth and their families. Within primary and secondary schools are internal support programs such as **gay–straight alliances** and **counseling** programs like **Project 10.** There are also **community LGBT support groups** for youth. Most recently, secondary schools or classrooms have been established specifically to serve sexual minority youth.

Adolescence is a time when most youth develop their sexual identities and related sexual self concept. In fact, the development of one's **sexual identity** can be seen as a primary developmental task of adolescence. When a young person has the experience of understanding herself or himself as having sexual feelings and attractions that are other than those represented by the dominant culture, the already complex experience of **identity development** becomes significantly more challenging. In addition, it is during middle and high school years that the importance of identity and social affiliation becomes most exaggerated. Cliques form and are often aggressively defended.

In the urgency to establish identity, students can express their fragile and fledgling senses of belonging in ways that disrespect and even harm others outside a given group. The collision of ways of understanding self and group identity makes middle and high schools tinder boxes of conflict and potential violence. LGBT youth are significantly affected by this **school climate.** They do not feel safe at

See also Activism, LGBT Teachers; Adolescence; Mexico, LGBT Youth and Issues in; South America, LGBT Youth and Issues in; Youth, At-Risk.

schools due to verbal and physical harassment, they often hear homophobic remarks not only from peers but from faculty and school staff, and **curriculum** as well as **cocurricular activities** are seldom inclusive. Consequently, LGBT teens drop out of school at a rate that is three times the national average (Rivers 2000).

Recent research has underscored the necessity for alternative secondary school settings for LGBT youth, as **coming out** is occurring at earlier ages. The mean age of awareness of same-sex sexual orientation is ten; 9 percent of high school students identify as gay, lesbian, bisexual, or questioning (Futterman and Ryan 1998). Most schools, however, continue to be places where LGBT youth are at risk. Forty-two states have failed to provide safety for queer youth in public middle and high schools (Lamont 2004). When high school-based counselors, psychologists, **social workers**, and nurses were surveyed, 89 percent indicated that school staff members retain negative attitudes toward LGBT people (Smith 2001). Half of the respondents reported a lack of support from **administrators** for LGBT youth. More than four out of five of these school professionals described a general lack of training, knowledge, skills, and materials in their schools regarding LGBT issues. These respondents indicated this lack of information, combined with negative staff attitudes and students' fears of disclosure, created the greatest obstruction to providing service to LGBT learners. Finally, few respondents reported receiving training themselves in the graduate work preparing them to provide services for sexual minority youth; most who received some training reported it was inadequate (Smith 2001). These findings parallel other studies finding negative attitudes held by school staff and those entering the profession. For example, 52 percent of prospective teachers report feeling uncomfortable working with an openly lesbian or gay colleague (Sears 1991).

The evidence for what supports the learning of queer youth is growing. LGBT students who can identify supportive faculty members in their schools obtain grade point averages 10 percent higher than those who cannot. When surveyed, about one-in-three LGBT high school students who were unaware of antiharassment policies in their school reported skipping school in the past month because they felt unsafe compared to one-quarter of LGBT high school youth who were aware of some sort of antiharassment policy (Kosciw 2004).

These and related understandings have resulted in several programmatic strategies. From the 1970s onward, there have been LGBT community-based programs for sexual minority youth. Programs such as the Larkin Street Center in San Francisco, the Horizons youth group in Chicago, the Hetrick-Martin Institute in New York City, and the Sexual Minority Youth Assistance League in Washington have served different populations of queer youth (Cohen 2004; Herdt and Boxer 1993). Counseling programs, most notably Project 10, established in 1984, and student-led gay–straight alliances, which emerged in the 1990s, were the first school-based initiatives. More recently, LGBT-based secondary schools or classrooms have been established. These programs tend to be established in **urban** communities where the number of LGBT youth and the pressures on them have risen to levels that require separate, safe learning environments. In New York City, the Hetrick-Martin Institute established the Harvey Milk School. In Dallas, the Walt Whitman Community School enrolled students from 1997 to 2004. And the Toronto school district established the Triangle Program a classroom for LGBT students in 1995.

The Harvey Milk School (HMS) opened as a public school in New York City in the fall of 2003. Named for the first openly gay supervisor in San Francisco, who was assassinated in 1978, the school's explicit purpose is to serve LGBT youth in a safe and academically supportive environment. HMS was originally established 1985 as an alternative school program provided by the Hetrick-Martin Institute. Emery S. Hetrick, a psychiatrist, and A. Damien Martin, a New York University professor, founded the Institute when they became aware of the beating and sexual assault of a fifteen-year-old boy. The youth, who was living in a group home, had been subsequently discharged and then accused by staff members of causing the incident by being gay. Given the obvious gap in social services for LGBT youth, Hetrick and Martin established the Institute for the Protection of Lesbian and Gay Youth in 1979; it was later renamed in honor of the two men after their deaths.

HMS received international attention when the Hetrick-Martin Institute and the New York City Department of Education collaborated to transform it into an accredited four-year public high school, providing significant renovation and school expansion. One hundred students enrolled during its inaugural year. Along with its goals of providing a safe environment and a community of independent learners, HMS offers an academically challenging curriculum. In addition to mandatory English and math programs articulated by the school district, there are courses in computer technology, the arts, and culinary arts. Low teacher–student ratio, college and **career counseling**, tutoring, and **mentoring**, constant availability of the Hetrick-Martin Institute's counseling and case management staff, and the comprehensive after-school recreation opportunities (hot meals, entertainment, and social events) support a total educational community. HMS nurtures the learning success reflected in the school's graduation statistics. On average, 95 percent graduate, and the college acceptance rate is 60 percent.

The Walt Whitman Community School (WWCS) was established in Dallas, in 1998, as a first private alternative school specifically to serve LGBT youth. Because of its unique mission and its location in a southern city, considered nationally to represent conservative social values, the opening of WWCS drew international media attention. In its first year, the school year began with nine students: one identifying as transgender, two identifying as bisexual, four as gay and two as straight. Both straight youth lived with lesbian mothers. The group also included students from ethnic minority groups. Only two of the nine students were seniors—an indicator of the earlier age at which youth are becoming aware of their **sexual orientation** and identity. By the end of the school year, enrollment had increased to fourteen.

The founders of the school, teachers, and concerned community members, committed to establishing WWCS based on growing evidence that LGBT youth were suffering in Dallas' public school setting. The concept of the school grew as the founders review of psychological and public health data on the incidence of depression, addiction, and **suicide** among LGBT youth, and closely studied experimental school programs in New York City (HMS, in particular) and Project 10 in Los Angeles. They also spoke with the youth themselves to learn that, in spite of the harassment they had experienced and the low self-esteem and expectation of school failure they had developed, these youth remained articulate and curious about the world.

For five years, WWCS provided a college preparatory curriculum at the Metropolitan Community Church/Cathedral of Hope's youth center, which had been renovated to serve as classrooms. Annual tuition was originally set at $7,000, but students attending the first year were provided financial aid from the Dallas gay community and fundraising activities, such as the GAYla Prom, sponsored by the Walt Whitman Community School Foundation.

With this support, WWCS kept a steady enrollment during its first five years, but was unable to move toward its goal of enrolling thirty students. In recent years, its financial survival was dependent on partnerships with other schools. The school abruptly closed its doors just prior to the 2004–2005 school year when Winfree Academy Charter Schools, a partner that school officials had understood to be committed to WWCS, unexpectedly withdrew its support.

The Toronto District School Board responded to the pressures facing LGBT youth by developing the Triangle Program in 1995. This program emerged from ten years of growing concerns and activism on the part of citizens and school officials, which followed the brutal 1985 assault and murder of a gay school librarian by high school students in a Toronto park. Following this incident, serious questions arose about why these students would be involved in a **hate crime** and the link, if any, to what they were learning in schools. In response, the school board issued a formal statement that **discrimination** and harassment should not be tolerated, and they supported curricula and programs to increase students and faculty understanding of human rights. In spite of these efforts, LGBT students continued experiencing unsafe learning environments. Employing principles of antiracist education adopted by **Canada** and by the Toronto Board of Education in the mid-1980s and linking them to anti-homophobia education and **school safety**, educators and activists succeeded in establishing the Triangle Program.

Triangle Program Classroom and Students Getting Ready for Solstice Party. Courtesy of Triangle Program, Toronto and Vanessa Russell

The Triangle Program, one of several programs comprising the Oasis Alternative Secondary School, is Canada's only classroom for queer and questioning youth in grades nine through twelve. Its mission is to provide "a classroom where Lesbian, Gay, Bisexual and Transgender (LGBT) youth can learn and earn credits in a safe, harassment-free, equity-based environment," and to develop/implement "curriculum which includes and celebrates LGBT literature, history, persons and issues." (http://schools.tdsb.on.ca/triangle/mission.html). Triangle students have experienced oppressive school settings and require the safety and encouragement within this one-room school house for students, ages fourteen to twenty-five. The students in the program vary in their living circumstances, some in supportive families, some living in shelters or on their own, some on welfare, and some with relative economic privilege.

Like the other two schools, Triangle follows a traditional academic program. The program also supports the development of social skills and self confidence sufficient for students to transition back into other alternative schools, work, or higher education. Since its establishment, there has been an emphasis on presenting the work and accomplishments of LGBT people. Health and **sexuality education** relevant to queer youth have been integrated into the curriculum. In recent years, these practices have come under attack as being too explicit. This and other conservative public policy shifts are seen by some Triangle staff as threatening the program's continuation (Russell In Press).

Even amidst such controversy, the Triangle Program maintains a social atmosphere supporting and celebrating the identity of LGBT youth. In particular, the social gatherings sponsored throughout the year and the annual **proms** for LGBT youth help to provide for the larger climate of acceptance and celebration. The link between this kind of social support and academic success in consistent and is clearly supported by the success the Triangle Program has had in graduating students who otherwise would have left school prior to graduation (Barclay and Walker 2002).

These three programs represent efforts to provide positive educational experiences for LGBT youth. Controversy about the need for such schools and school programs continues as evident in the closing of the Walt Whitman Community School and, more recently, in challenges to the inclusion of the Harvey Milk School in New York City's public school system or to the scope of the Triangle Program's curriculum. Detractors and supporters offer important questions to be considered as these students' rights to learn continues to be pursued. The most common challenge from those who question the appropriateness of separate schools or classrooms is to ask for evidence that LGBT youth learn differently and, therefore, warrant delivery of different curricula. The primary assertion of those who support separate school programs is that though learning is not different, it is significantly hindered by the negative conditions experienced by so many LGBT youth in secondary schools. Supporters of separate programs, however, lament the circumstances requiring such separation and look for a day when all learners may peacefully, respectfully, and collaboratively attend schools together.

Bibliography

Barclay, Patty, and Jim Walker. 2002. *Triangle Program Annual Report*. Toronto: Toronto District School Board.

Cohen, Stephen. 2004. "Liberationists, Clients, Activists: Queer Youth Organizing, 1966–2003." *Journal of Gay and Lesbian Issues in Education* 2, no. 3: 67–86

Futterman, Donna, and Caitlin Ryan. 1998. *Lesbian & Gay Youth: Care & Counseling*. New York: Columbia University Press.

Herdt, Gilbert, and Andrew Boxer. 1993. *Children of Horizons*. Boston: Beacon Press.

Kosciw, Joseph. 2004. *The 2003 National School Climate Survey*. New York: Gay, Lesbian and Straight Education Network. Available at http://www.glsen.org/binary-data/GLSEN_ATTACHMENTS/file/300-3.PDF. Accessed June 22, 2005.

Lamont, Joshua. 2004, June 28. "42 States Receive Failing Grades in Inaugural Safe Schools Report." Available at http://www.geocities.com/sacglsen/040712enews.html. Accessed June 22, 2005.

Russell, Vanessa. In Press. "Equity Undone: The Impact of the Conservative Government's Education Reforms on the Triangle Program, Canada's Schoolhouse for Queer Youth." *Journal of Gay and Lesbian Issues in Education* 3, no. 1.

Rivers, Ian. 2000. "Social Exclusion, Absenteeism and Sexual Minority Youth." *Support for Learning* 15, no. 1: 12–18.

Sears, James T. 1991. "Educators, Homosexuality and Homosexual Students: Are Personal Feelings Related to Professional Beliefs?" *Journal of Homosexuality* 22, nos. 3–4: 29–71.

Smith, Deborah. 2001. "Assessing the Needs of Lesbian, Gay and Bisexual Youth." *American Psychological Association Monitor* 32, no. 8. Available at http://www.apa.org/monitor/sep01/lgbneeds.html. Accessed June 22, 2005.

Snider, Kathryn. 1996. "Race and Sexual Orientation: The (Im)Possibility of These Inter-sections in Educational Policy." *Harvard Educational Review* 66: 294–302.

Web Sites

To Be Gay, and Happy, at School. 1997. Tim Martin. College Site Student.Com. Accessed November 4, 2004. http://articles.student.com/article/gayschool. Describes the opening of the Walt Whitman Community School.

The Harvey Milk School. 2004. The Hetrick-Martin Institute. Accessed November 10, 2004. http://gaylife.about.com/gi/dynamic/offsite.htm?zi=1/XJ&sdn=gaylife&zu=http% 3A%2F%2Fwww.hmi.org%2F. Photographs, program information, FAQs, and resources on the school.

Triangle Program. 2004. Toronto District School Board. Accessed November 10, 2004. http://schools.tdsb.on.ca/triangle/index.html. Examples of student work, program information, mission statement, teacher resources, and photographs of the school and its students.

Walt Whitman Community School. March 2004. WWCS Foundation Board of Directors. Accessed November 10, 2004. http://www.waltwhitmanschool.org. Home page for the Walt Whitman Community School.

Sexism

Karen Lovaas

Sexism is one of a number of interconnected systems that privileges the members of one group of people over other classes of people; specifically, sexism privileges men over women. Sexism reflects the ideology of male supremacy and supports the larger structure of male dominance known as patriarchy. Other systems of oppression include **racism**, classism, **heterosexism**, ageism, and ableism. Like all "isms," sexism is a complex, intricate system involving symbols, beliefs, practices, and institutions. It is not always accompanied by misogyny, or hatred of women; some sexism is, in fact, justified as a form of benevolence in which women and girls are believed to be in a variety of ways weaker than men and boys and, therefore, in need of their protection. Sexism affects **lesbian, gay, bisexual**, and **transgender youth** (LGBT) in a variety of subtle and not so subtle ways, from enforcement of rigid **gender role** expectations to the subservice of lesbians and their interests to gay men during different historical periods.

Because males are viewed and treated as superior within patriarchal societies, people, concepts, and objects deemed more masculine are similarly accorded higher status; defined in opposition, females and femininity are regarded as inferior and, therefore accorded lower status. When this is combined with a belief that members of one gender should only **desire** the other, same-gender desires and homosexual identities pose a threat to the patriarchal order. Individuals acknowledging or assumed to desire others of the same sex are likely to suffer social stigmatizing. For

See also Antibias Curriculum; Compulsory Heterosexuality; Educational Policies; Feminism; Gender Roles; Literature, Early Childhood; Lesbian Feminism; Men's Studies; Spirituality; Sexual Health, Lesbian and Bisexual Women; Stereotypes; Women's Studies.

example, as a female, a lesbian youth has lower social status in most cultures and may simultaneously be disparaged for not making herself sexually available to men; and a gay youth may be perceived as "acting like a girl" and relinquishing his male privilege, for which he is likely to experience ridicule, **discrimination**, and **harassment**. Thus, male supremacy tends to produce both sexism and heterosexism.

The term sexism came into usage in the mid-1960s, becoming widely used as a result of the women's liberation movements of the late 1960s and 1970s, especially in the United States and **Europe**. These movements succeeded in bringing issues of sexism to public consciousness. Sexism is perpetuated by formal and informal social institutions such as the family, religion, media, education, and the law as well as by individuals. In scores of cultures, property rights and nationality have been traditionally passed down through the male line. It was not until the twentieth century that women gained voting and property rights in many countries. As of 2005, women still cannot vote in Saudi Arabia. Sex discrimination is against the law in many countries. Nevertheless, some laws may still grant preferential treatment to one gender. Overall, the legal status of women has been lower than that of men, and human rights issues continue to be the focus of campaigns against sexism in many parts of the world.

Sexism has all too often been found in gay movements and communities, from the early homophile movement in Europe and North America to the gay liberation movements of the 1970s and 1980s. Even though the discrimination gays and lesbians face in relation to their sexuality may be parallel, gay men have often enjoyed unexamined male privilege. Lesbians felt unwelcome due to the sexism of many gay men and formed separate organizations, from the Daughters of Bilitis to Old Women Lesbians, focusing more on the issues most important to them as women-loving-women. Lesbians face the same manifestations of sexism as do straight girls and women, but fewer of the remedies developed to address sexism are tailored to the lives lesbians, for example, lesbian mothers lead.

People who are bisexual or transgender have rarely had the same access to positions of power within queer movements as gays and lesbians, especially white gay males. Girls and women who identify themselves as bisexual have long faced suspicion from both lesbians and straight women. From lesbians, the concern may be that a girl who calls herself bisexual is avoiding taking a strong political stand in solidarity with lesbians. More recently, it has been common to regard **bisexuality** as a trend with which one is superficially experimenting in order to be seen as fashionable. Transgender individuals, as Kate Bornstein has said, "call into question the construct of gender itself" (1994, 121), don't fit readily into the binary categories of sex, gender, and sexuality and may make gays, lesbians, and heterosexuals equally uncomfortable. If a male friend transitions from male to female, how will her gay and straight male friends adjust to her new identity as female? Will she experience the internalized sexism that most girls and women do to some degree?

Powerful evidence of sexism is in the gross disparities between the wealth held by men and by women. It is still the case that the bulk of the wealth in the world is owned by men. Women hold the majority of low-paid jobs and even with comparable qualifications, and when doing the same or comparable work, are frequently paid less than men. Women predominate in seasonal and temporary, as opposed to permanent, jobs. Women still perform the bulk of the domestic labor, whether in their domiciles for no pay or in the homes of others for low wages. Most large institutions, including governments and corporations, are controlled by men. Women are not allowed to assume leadership roles in most major religions. Around the world, girls are far more likely than boys to be denied the opportunity to learn to read. Unfortunately, what is available to be read, according to much feminist analysis, frequently is housed in languages that are themselves sexist, coming from a male perspective and conveying conventional and biased ideas about women and men.

Girls and women's bodies and images of their bodies are marketed for sexual consumption in much of the world. Representations of gender and sexuality in mainstream media tend to be in line with stereotypical visions of a narrow range of sex-typed roles and heterosexual relationships. Too often, the materials found in classrooms are not much better and there is a growing body of critiques of sexism in education. There has been a concerted effort in the last couple of decades, however, to create children's books and textbooks that are nonsexist, more ethnically inclusive, and that portray a wider range of family structures, including single parents and same-sex couples with children. More support groups for **queer** youth, such as **gay–straight alliances** can also be found at public schools (Cahill and Cianciotto 2004).

Another arena that may suggest reason both for concern and for cautious optimism is **sports** and athletics. In the United States, Title IX legislation, passed by the federal government in 1972, requires that girls be provided opportunities in athletics that are equal to those of boys. As a result, there have been increases in the numbers of girls and young women participating in a variety of sports, including some traditionally considered strictly for boys and young men such as football. However, sexism and **homophobia** are rampant in academic and professional sports, so that prejudiced language and behaviors confront female athletes, who will be closely scrutinized for evidence that they are insufficiently feminine, as well as male athletes, who must perform a potent brand of masculinity to disguise their sexuality if they happen to be gay or to appear so to others.

Feminism is widely perceived as one of the most, if not the most, significant social movements of the twentieth century, resulting in attitudinal and societal changes that support greater equality between males and females across a number of cultures. Many gay and straight men support efforts to create gender equality and justice and identify themselves as feminist or profeminist. Some profeminist men's groups in Europe, the United States, **Australia**, and **Canada** are active in activities such as antiviolence education in schools, communities, and **workplace**s. Similarly, gay men's groups, such as the "radical faeries" have challenged stereotypical gender roles, adopting androgynous lifestyles and embracing the feminine within themselves.

However, sexism continues to be a pervasive dynamic in many societies. The enduring presence of sexism has been explained in a variety of ways. Similar to other forms of prejudice, it may be viewed in terms of individual psychology and psychopathology as well as linked to family structures and social, economic, political, and religious ideologies. How one analyzes the major forces contributing to sexism shapes the type of solutions one will advance to eliminate it. For example, Marxist and many radical feminist theorists see connections between sexism and the uneven distribution of wealth in capitalism. Increasingly, activists and theorists recognize that sexism, heterosexism, and other systems of oppression interlock with one another and cannot be well understood or addressed in isolation. At the same time, what is perceived as sexist in one cultural context may be experienced as liberating in another. For example, the wearing of the hijab or head scarf by a Muslim woman may be interpreted by some as representative of her inferior status within a sexist cultural or religious community. However, many women who wear the hijab report that, on the contrary, it is emblematic of the respect and dignity with which they are treated.

Bibliography

Bornstein, Kate. 1994. *Gender Outlaw: On Men, Women, and the Rest of Us*. New York: Vintage Books.

Bourdieu, Pierre. 2001. *Masculine Domination*. Translated by R. Nice Stanford, CA: Stanford University Press.

Cahill, Sean, and Jason Cianciotto. 2004. U.S. Policy Interventions That Can Make Schools Safer. *Journal of Gay & Lesbian Issues in Education* 2, no. 1: 3–17.

Cameron, Deborah, ed. 1998. *The Feminist Critique of Language: A Reader*. 2nd ed. London and New York: Routledge.

Götz, Ignacio L. 1999. *The Culture of Sexism*. Westport, CT: Praeger.

Herbst, Philip H. 2001. *Wimmin, Wimps & Wallflowers: An Encyclopaedic Dictionary of Gender and Sexual Orientation Bias in the United States*. Yarmouth, ME: Intercultural Press.

Lerner, Gerda. 1986. *The Creation of Patriarchy*. New and Oxford: Oxford University Press.

Lovaas, Karen E., Lina Baroudi, and S. M. Collins. 2002. "*Transcending Heteronormativity in the Classroom: Using Queer and Critical Pedagogies to Alleviate Trans-Anxieties*." Pp. 177–189 in *Addressing Homophobia and Heterosexism on College Campuses*. Edited by Elizabeth P. Cramer. Binghamton, NY: The Haworth Press.

Pharr, Suzanne. 1988. *Homophobia: A Weapon of Sexism*. Inverness, CA: Chardon Press.

Rhode, Deborah L. 1997. *Speaking of Sex: The Denial of Gender Inequality*. Cambridge, MA: Harvard University Press.

Ronai, Carol R., Barbara A. Zsembik, and Joe R. Feagin, eds. 1997. *Everyday Sexism in the Third Millennium*. New York: Routledge.

Sattel, Sue, Melissa Keyes, and Pat Tupper. 1997. "Sexual Harassment and Sexual Orientation: The Coaches' Corner." Pp. 233–246 in *Overcoming Heterosexism and Homophobia: Strategies that Work*. Edited by James T. Sears and Walter Williams. New York: Columbia University Press.

Web Sites

FAIR's Women's Desk. March 2005. Accessed June 10, 2005. http://www.fair.org/womens-desk.html. Analyzes media coverage for racist, sexist, and homophobic bias.

The National Organization for Men Against Sexism. 2004. Accessed June 10, 2005. http://www.nomas.org/sys-tmpl/door/. Site includes history of the organization, resources and publications, chapters and conference schedule.

QueerTheory.com. January 2005. Accessed June 10, 2005. http://www.queertheory.com/theories/gender/sexism.htm. Links to a variety of online resources related to understanding and ending sexism.

Understanding Prejudice.org. 2004. Accessed June 10, 2005. http://www.understandingprejudice.org/links/sexism.htm. A page of links to other Web sites with information regarding sexism and related topics. Also includes teachers' corner, directory of experts, multimedia center, and reading room.

Sexual Abuse/Assault

Peggy Lorah

Sexual assault is defined as sexual intercourse—oral, vaginal, and/or anal—that occurs without consent; rape is sexual intercourse that occurs by force or with the threat of force. Sexual assault becomes rape if the perpetrator of the crime gets the victim drunk or high for the purpose of making the victim incapable of giving consent. Both sexual assault and rape are crimes that affect many **lesbian, gay, bisexual,** and **transgender youth** (LGBT). In the few studies of small groups that have been done, the range of responses from LGBT participants who have been sexually assaulted has been from 11 percent (Rivers and D'Augelli 2001) to 50 percent. Youth, particularly those identifying as transgender, are most at risk (Wingspan 1998). Male-to-female young persons appear to be in increased danger because of their new-found sexual objectification by men (Carroll and Gilroy 2002). In most cases, LGBT youth who are victims of sexual assault know their attacker. Sometimes sexual assault occurs in the context of a relationship or happens expressly because the victim is LGBT.

For the general population, one-in-four women will be the victim of an attempted sexual assault and one-in-eight women will experience a completed sexual assault. For the general population, in about 95 percent of the incidents, women are the victims of male assailants; the remainder occurs with either men as victims and women as assailants or as same-sex sexual assaults (National Sexual Violence Resource Center 2003). With the exception of the studies cited above, virtually all of the research on sexual assault has been conducted with the heterosexual population, so it is difficult to estimate the prevalence for LGBT individuals. Further, LGBT victims rarely report incidents of sexual assault and rape. Distrust of law enforcement, fear of medical providers, and the stigma that comes from **homophobia** combine to silence these individuals. For victims who are persons of color and/or for whom there are **social class** concerns, another layer of reasons to be concerned about reporting or receiving care is added. For example, a poor LGBT person of color might expect to be treated poorly because of social class, **sexual orientation/ gender identity**, and **race/ethnicity**. Any one of these reasons causes a problem; added together, they can feel insurmountable.

Sexual harassment and sexual assault have some dynamics in common, but they are in different places on a spectrum of abusive behaviors. Both are expressions of power over someone with the goal to debase the victim. Sexual harassment is typically expressed in sexually-charged speech and actions, whereas sexual assault involves the acting out of those behaviors, culminating in intercourse. Sexual assault can happen under many circumstances, but it often occurs within the **dating** context. Many sexual assaults are both planned and purposeful.

There are two types of sexual assault that are particular to LGBT victims. The first is as a bias-related or **hate crime** in which the victim is chosen and attacked explicitly because she or he is a sexual minority. When this is the case, the assailant is typically a heterosexual man; the victim can be a lesbian woman, a gay man, a bisexual woman or man, or a transgender individual. Hate speech can accompany

See also Domestic and Relationship Violence; Youth, At-Risk.

this sexual violence, and the victim is certain that the attack was motivated by the assailant's bias against sexual orientation or gender identity. In the second type of sexual assault the assailant is also LGBT. These often happen in the context of a social event. The event may be a party or a meeting in a bar where the assailant is clear that the victim is LGBT. In both of these types of assaults, the perpetrator assumes that the victim will not report the crime because of the stigma and shame that come from identifying oneself as LGBT and as a victim. The assailant may tell the victim that there is no help available for her or him because of sexual orientation or gender identity.

Victims of sexual assault are not responsible for the crime that is committed against them, and they cannot prevent an assault from occurring. Only the assailant can prevent an assault. However, there are some steps that a potential victim can take to reduce the risk of an assault. It is important for an individual to make responsible choices about drinking and using other drugs, because alcohol and other drugs can impair both the ability to communicate a sense of what he or she does and does not want to do, and the ability to recognize and deal with potentially dangerous situations. Bars have served as "safe" meeting places for many LGBT individuals, and they have afforded places to get away from the homophobia and **heterosexism** of the dominant culture. Potential assailants who frequent such bars may make incorrect assumptions about the willingness of other patrons to be sexual. Therefore, for those in such social situations, it is important to think about sexual limits and to be prepared to state them clearly. Because the lack of consent is an element of sexual assault, it is important to know that it is okay to say "no" to any sexual activity in which one is not interested. Saying "no" can be done in verbal and nonverbal ways.

LGBT individuals who have been victims of sexual assault should go to a safe place as soon as possible and contact a trusted friend. Because of feeling guilt, responsibility, disgust, and self-hatred, most victims never tell anyone; when they do, it is usually a friend. The best help a friend can provide is to support the choices the victim makes and to offer assistance in seeking resources. Victims should seek medical attention to deal with any physical injuries, to obtain medication to prevent sexually transmitted infections, and in cases of lesbian women having been assaulted by men, to obtain emergency contraception.

LGBT victims may be reluctant to seek assistance from health care providers, law enforcement officials, or even advocates and counselors from rape crisis hotline programs. Their reluctance may be justified, because even individuals trained to deal with sexual assaults and rapes may not be sensitive to the special circumstances and needs of LGBT victims. In order to access LGBT-sensitive services, victims can call their local service providers by looking in the blue pages of their phone book under "Sexual Assault," "Abuse," or "Rape." The call is anonymous unless the victim chooses otherwise. When contacting the counselor or advocate, ask what special training she or he has had in dealing with LGBT victims. Rape crisis programs across the country routinely seek out opportunities to become more sensitive to LGBT concerns, and the person answering the phone should be able to address any issues the caller has. Victims can also access anonymous hotlines on the **Internet**.

In communities where there are organized and publicized resources for LGBT individuals, victims can often find help in community centers and in **community LGBT support groups**. Victims who are in high school can talk to a trusted teacher, guidance counselor, **gay–straight alliance** advisor, or member of a student assistance team. Since school personnel are mandated to report violent, abusive, or assault events, sexual assault information may not be able to remain confidential. In college settings, victims can talk with student affairs staff members, most of whom have diversity training that enables them to be LGBT-affirming. Many campuses also have women's centers that deal with sexual assault and rape for women and men students and that are LGBT-affirming. College **counseling** centers often have designated therapists who are trained to deal with sexual assault issues, including those who victims are LGBT. Campus health care providers are also likely to employ staff trained to provide information and support. Some have either **college campus resource centers** for LGBT students or multicultural centers with LGBT offices, and these centers and offices also typically employ individuals who can deal with sexual assault and rape, either themselves or by referral to appropriate organizations.

Bibliography

Carroll, Lynne, and Paula J. Gilroy. 2002. "Transgender Issues in Counseling." *Counselor Education and Supervision* 41: 233–242.

Gartner, Richard B. 1999. "Sexual Victimization of Boys by Men: Meanings and Consequences." *Journal of Gay and Lesbian Psychotherapy* 3: 1–33.

Girshick, Lori B. 2002. *Woman-to-Woman Sexual Violence*. Boston: Northeastern University Press.

National Sexual Violence Resource Center. 2003. Newsletters. http://www.nsvrc.org/publications/newsletters.html. Accessed June 22, 2005.

Ottens, Allen J. 2001. "The Scope of Sexual Violence on Campus." Pp. 1–29 in *Sexual Violence on Campus: Policies, Programs, and Perspectives*. Edited by Allen J. Ottens and Kathy Hotelling. New York: Springer.

Rivers, Ian, and Anthony D'Augelli. 2001. "The Victimization of Lesbian, Gay, and Bisexual Youths." Pp. 199–223 in *Lesbian, Gay, and Bisexual Identities and Youth*. Edited by Anthony R. D'Augelli and Charlotte J. Patterson. New York: Oxford University Press.

Ryan, Caitlin. 2001. "Counseling Lesbian, Gay, and Bisexual Youth." Pp. 224–250 in *Lesbian, Gay, and Bisexual Identities and Youth*. Edited by Anthony R. D'Augelli and Charlotte J. Patterson. New York: Oxford University Press.

Schiefelbein, Virginia L. 2002. "Rape and Sexual Assault." Pp. 359–392 in *Handbook of Crisis Counseling, Intervention, and Prevention in the Schools*. 2nd ed. Edited by Jonathan Sandoval. Mahwah, NJ: Lawrence Erlbaum.

Tuel, Beverly. 2001. "Sexual Assault When Victims Are Gay, Lesbian, or Bisexual Students." Pp. 190–217 in *Sexual Violence on Campus: Policies, Programs, and Perspectives*. Edited by Allen J. Ottens and Kathy Hotelling. New York: Springer.

Wingspan Domestic Violence Project. 1998. *Abuse and Violence in Same-Gender Relationships: A Resource for the Lesbian, Gay, Bisexual and Transgender Communities*. Tucson, AZ: Author.

Web Sites

National Coalition Against Domestic Violence. October 2004. Accessed December 8, 2004. http://www.ncadv.org. Links to programs that deal with sexual assault as well. Programs listed will have had special training in dealing with LGBT victims.

Pennsylvania Coalition Against Rape. September 2004. Accessed December 8, 2004. http://www.pcar.org. Web site incorporates lesbian and gay information with a thorough general overview of facts about sexual assault. It further provides access to hotline numbers and sites across the United States.

RAINN. September 2004. Accessed December 8, 2004. http://www.rainn.org. Provides a comprehensive list of definitions and facts about sexual assault and rape. It offers links to many resources. Although it focuses primarily on heterosexual sexual assault, it addresses LGBT issues.

Sexual Harassment

Kerry H. Robinson

Sexual harassment is primarily an expression of power, which involves any physical, verbal, or visual behaviors of a sexist or sexual nature that are directed at a person making them feel a range of possible feelings, including being uncomfortable, embarrassed, frightened, hurt, degraded, humiliated, or compromised. This behavior generally results in diminishing a person's power and confidence at particular times and in various contexts. The inclusion of sexist practices and comments in this definition highlights how sexual harassment is intimately linked with constructions of heterosexual gendered identities. That is, some of this practice is not directly sexual in nature, but is directed at controlling "appropriate" masculine and feminine behavior within the context of **compulsory heterosexuality**. Although sexual harassment is commonly understood in heterosexual terms, it affects **lesbian**, **gay**, **bisexual**, **transgender**, and questioning youth who are harassed for being different or pressured to conform to traditional **gender roles**. Recently, the term has significantly broadened to include sexual harassment that is based on real or perceived homosexuality or cross-gender behaviors.

The most common forms of sexual harassment experienced, both in the **workplace** and in educational contexts, are nonphysical forms of the behavior, mainly verbal and visual in nature. These commonly include abusive language of a sexist and sexually derogatory nature (e.g., poofter, fag, slut, leso, dyke), gender jokes, calling boys "girls," teasing or comments about one's body, appearance, or sex appeal, staring sexual looks, invading one's personal space, cat-calls, whistles, licking one's lips or making sucking noises in a sexual manner, being teased about one's sexual activities, being the target of sexual rumors or sexual and sexist **graffiti**, and being pressured to have sex. Much "sexual banter" is normalized in everyday interactions; whether such behavior is sexual harassment is determined by the person experiencing the behavior.

Physical forms of sexual harassment can include a range of behaviors such as being brushed past in a sexualized manner, having one's clothes pulled at in a sexual way, being pinched or touched on the bottom, breasts or genitals, being forced

See also Asia, LGBT Youth and Issues in; Feminism; Legal Issues, Students; Mental Health; Sexism; Sexual Abuse and Assault; School Safety and Safe School Zones; South America, LGBT Youth and Issues in; Youth, At-Risk.

to kiss or embrace someone against one's will, or being forced to do some other sexualized act (e.g., touching someone's genitals or being forced to have sex). The impact of these behaviors on individuals can vary, but there can be a range of short- and long-term impacts such as anger, depression, fear, guilt, loss of confidence and self-esteem. **Harassment** can also result in restricting an individual's choices, dropping out of school, or leaving one's employment, especially if that person feels he or she has no support in dealing with the harassment.

Sexual harassment, as a culturally constituted phenomenon, has long existed, yet it has a relatively short history. The term was not coined until the late 1970s and early 1980s as a result of the efforts of individual feminists and the broader **women's movement** in Western countries such as the United States, **Canada, United Kingdom**, and **Australia**. Sexual harassment acknowledged working women's experiences of harassment from men, particularly those who had the authority and power to force compliance with their demands for sexual favors. Thus, traditional views of sexual harassment consider this behavior as principally a result of patriarchal heterosexual relations where male power, status, and privilege are institutionalized and women are positioned as subordinate to men in their everyday lives. In this context, sexual harassment is part of a continuum of violence against women and a powerful means of social control, particularly in those societies where females challenge male power, compete with them in the workplace, and step outside traditional ways of being female.

This traditional perspective of sexual harassment premised on patriarchal male/female relations has tended to exclude recognition of this behavior in male-to-male and female-to-female contexts. Sexual harassment can be experienced in any relationship; a gay or lesbian person can be sexually harassed by a straight person or they can sexually harass a heterosexual, or other gays and lesbians. Those people who identify as transgender can also experience sexual harassment based on their gender, gender expression, or **sexual orientation**, and are often more at risk than lesbians, gays, and bisexuals.

There has also been a disturbing silence around how sexual harassment is experienced by women of color and by those women from non-Western cultures. Greater awareness of the widespread nature and complexity of this practice across a range of sociocultural contexts, including non-Western perspectives, has deepened understandings of the multiple ways that sexual harassment is perpetrated and experienced. Sexual orientation, **ethnicity, race, social class**, and other sites of difference intersect with power and gender either within the context of the perpetrator's motivations or the "victim's" experiences. For example, in terms of lesbian identities, harassment can be experienced in terms of both their female gender and also in relation to their sexual orientation. Sexual harassment can be increased, in some instances, as their lesbian sexuality can be titillating for some men or considered as a site requiring regulation through sexually harassing behaviors. Prevailing myths such as "all lesbian women need is a good man to put them on the right track" can underpin sexual harassment. The intersections of sexual harassment with gender, power, race, and/or ethnicity are also strong. For many women of color, issues of race and gender cannot be separated in their experiences of sexual harassment, thus creating a racialized form of sexual harassment. Wen-Chu Chen (1997) highlights that although **Asian American** women have similar experiences to **African American** women in terms of racialized sexual harassment, they also have distinct experiences. Some factors contributing to these distinct experiences are Asian female racial **stereotypes**, patriarchal cultural traditions, immigration status, and institutional barriers. In Malaysia, sexual harassment, reinforced by religious ideology, may be used as a tool to control some women's sexuality, dress, and behavior (Ng and Othman 2002).

Some boys and men can experience sexual harassment from both male and female perpetrators, but in comparatively smaller numbers and often with differing effects and consequences from those experienced by females. For example, the same level of fear and threat is generally not experienced by males if they encounter this behavior from females, in comparison to many girls' and women's experiences of sexual harassment from boys and men. Femininity does not carry the same association with aggression, threat, and violence as does some forms of masculinity. However, when boys experience sexual harassment, it is largely from other male peers and is couched in homophobic sentiment (American Association of University Women 1993; Robinson 2005). The lower number of official reports of male-to-male sexual harassment may be largely due to the homophobia that is inherent in these cases. Since this behavior is often viewed in terms of **bullying** behavior among boys, sexual harassment has been traditionally underplayed or not recognized. Bullying has been seen largely in terms of individual boys' personalities and antisocial behaviors. In comparison, there has been less focus on female-to-female sexual harassment, with girls tending to be the "victims" of this behavior from males. However, girls can and do sexually harass other females, but this tends to be verbal in nature such as being called names like "slut," "whore," "dyke," "dog," and "leso." Alluding to their actual or perceived sexual activities and sexual orientations is also common in schools.

Recent **research** into sexual harassment highlights how it is manifested through everyday heteronormative practices and linked to constructions of **gender identity** (Epstein 1997; Larkin 1994; Robinson 2000). Sexual harassment, for example, is integral to the performance of "doing" hegemonic masculinity (the form of masculinity considered to be the norm (Robinson 2005). Some adolescent males demonstrate their heterosexualized masculinity, particularly in front of their peers. It is considered to be part of doing their masculinity correctly, which intersects with race, sexuality, ethnicity, class, and other aspects of their identity. For example, some adolescent males from "machismo" cultures, who take up hegemonic masculine identities, may engage in public sexual harassment of females as an expected expression and confirmation of their culturally sanctioned masculinity, heterosexuality, and traditional gendered power relationships.

Sexual harassment located in **homophobia** is part of this gendered performance, which is directed at other males whose behaviors are outside the boundaries of regulatory gendered norms in society. Some homophobic adolescent males may publicly harass gays or those perceived to be gay to validate and affirm their masculinity and heterosexuality—particularly in front of other males, who operate to police the performance of a "correct" masculinity.

There are many misconceptions about sexual harassment. Of particular importance is the belief that it is inherent in male **biology**. Within this context, sexual harassment is explained in terms of "boys will be boys," "harmless fun," men's and boys' clumsy attempts at courtship, and boys needing to "sow their wild oats." However, this explanation does not take into account the many different ways that sexual harassment is experienced and played out, including male-to-male and female-to-female experiences. Another misconception is that harassers have personality and /or psychological problems. This explains the occurrence of a small number of sexual harassment cases and not its widespread social practice.

What constitutes sexual harassment has been a contentious legal issue, and there is not a universal accepted definition. Legal definitions of sexual harassment vary from country to country and within countries across states and provinces. How these definitions are applied in educational policy also vary. In some definitions, particularly legal ones, sexist comments tend not to be included, but rather they focus solely on more sexually explicit behaviors, such as being forced to give sexual favors, or unwelcome and uninvited physical contact. In some parts of Australia, the term sex-based harassment is officially used in schools to encompass harassment of both a sexist and sexual nature. This is similar to the way the term gender-based harassment is used in the United States. Definitions today tend to utilize gender-neutral terms to allow for a variety of experiences. Since the mid-1980s, sex discrimination legislation has been developed in various countries and has resulted in sexual harassment policies within educational, government, and nongovernment organizations. For example, in Australia, in order to meet the requirements of such sex discrimination legislation, schools, government, and nongovernment organizations must develop sexual harassment policies and procedures. However, due to the various manifestations of power that operate around sexual harassment, including fears of further harassment or not being believed, most experiences are never reported.

Bibliography

American Association of University Women. 1993. *Hostile Hallways: The AAUW Survey on Sexual Harassment in America's Schools*. Washington D.C.: Author.

Buchanan, Nicloe T., and Alayne J. Ormerod. 2002. "Racialized Sexual Harassment in the Lives of African American Women." *Women & Therapy* 25, nos. 3–4: 107–124.

Epstein, Debbie. 1997. "Keeping Them in Their Place: Hetero/sexist Harassment, Gender and the Enforcement of Heterosexuality." Pp. 154–171 in *Sexual Harassment: Contemporary Feminist Perspectives*. Edited by Celia Kitzinger and Alison M. Thomas. London: Open University Press.

Larkin, June. 1994. *Sexual Harassment: High School Girls Speak Out*. Toronto: Second Story Press.

Robinson, Kerry H. 2000. "'Great Tits Miss!' The Sexual Harassment of Female Teachers in Secondary Schools. Issues of Gendered Authority." *Discourse: Studies in the Cultural Politics of Education* 21, no.1: 75–90.

———. 2005. "Reinforcing Hegemonic Masculinities through Sexual Harassment: Issues of Identity, Power and Popularity in Secondary Schools." *Gender and Education* 17, no. 1: 19–37.

Ng, Cecilia, and Jamilah Othman. 2002. "Unwanted and Unwelcome: Sexual Harassment in the Malaysian Workplace." *Gender, Technology & Development* 6, no.3: 389–407.

Wen-chu chen, Edith. 1997. "Sexual Harassment From the Perspective of Asian-American Women." Pp. 51–62 in *Everyday Sexism in the Third Millennium*. Edited by Carol R. Ronai, Barbara A. Zsembik, and Joe R. Feagin. New York: Routledge.

Web Sites

Bullying. No Way! 2004. Accessed December 4, 2004. http://www.bullyingnoway.com.au. This Australian based Web site deals with a range of issues relating to harassment and violence in schools. It not only covers sexual harassment/sex-based harassment, but provides an overview of other forms of harassment including those based on sexuality, religious diversity, and socioeconomic status.

Conflict Research Consortium. Accessed December 4, 2004. http://www.conflictresearch. com. Provides useful links and valuable information around legal and social issues pertaining to sexual harassment. The links address sexual harassment issues in schooling, college, and workforce U.S. contexts.

Sexual Health, Gay and Bisexual

James T. Sears

Sexual health includes not only physiological issues but psychological as well. Historically gay young men of European descent have been the most researched of sexual minority adolescents; therefore, it is not surprising that during the past two decades considerable amount of **qualitative** and **quantitative research** has emerged. Generally, **gay youth** have been found to be at significantly higher risk than their heterosexual counterparts for sexually transmitted infections (STI) and **AIDS, substance abuse, suicide, mental health,** and certain types of **eating disorders.** Although efforts have been extended in nonformal education, particularly in **community LGBT support groups,** to provide health information and engage these youth in intervention strategies, the concerns (and even visibility) of gay youth—as other sexual minorities—within traditional health and **sexuality education** courses within school remain unmet. In contrast, there is little research related to physiological or psychological issues facing bisexual youth. Until recently, most studies aggregated bisexuals with gay youth despite obvious differences between homosexuality and **bisexuality.** There are emerging data suggesting that bisexual youth are at different risks than gay youth in some areas. Additionally, issues of **social class, race,** and **racism** as well as **rural** living further complicate the delivery and quality of sexual health care provided to gay and bisexual youth.

The earliest research studies related to sexual health of gay youth used, by necessity, small nonrepresentative samples, notably college students (mostly Euro-American). As community-based LGBT groups emerged, largely in response to STI and HIV infections, this nonrepresentative pool of respondents broadened, at least in terms of education level, race, and ethnicity. These studies provide additional insight into problems confronting gay and bisexual youth, which directly or indirectly impact sexual health. For example, in studies of gay youth groups in New York City, three out of four males reported regular use of alcohol with no differences found between gay and bisexual youth (Rosario, Hunter, and Gwadz 1997; Rotheram-Borus et al. 1994; Rotheram-Borus et al. 1995). The more recent use of **The Youth Risk Behavior Surveys'** data has provided more statistically reliable data. However, even within these relatively large data sets it is difficult to analyze differences between bisexual and homosexually-inclined youth controlling for gender (Faulkner and Cranston 1998).

Collectively, these studies document challenges facing gay and bisexual youth with respect to sexual identity development, complicated by homophobia and

See also Adolescent Sexualities; Coming Out, Youth; Sexual Identity; Sexual Orientation; Youth, At-Risk; Youth, Homeless.

heterosexism. For example, their greater vulnerability for substance abuse and eating disorders not only impacts psychosexual development, but places them at greater physiological risk. The abuse of drugs and alcohol—both of which find gay and bisexual youth at higher risk than heterosexual youth (Rosario, Hunter, and Gwadz 1997)—reduces the likelihood of engaging in safer sex behaviors, just as poor self-esteem increases the likelihood of engaging in sexually risky behaviors. Raves, clubs, and traditional gay bar scenes provide alcohol and drug contexts coupled to heightened eroticism.

Young men who have sex with other men are at greater risk for HIV infection and other sexually transmitted infections such as chlamydia and gonorrhea. For instance, the Centre for Infectious Disease Prevention and Control has found that in the twenty and older age bracket, nearly one-half of zero-positive conversions were due to same-sex behavior (Health Canada 2004). Similarly, the Centers for Disease Control and Prevention reported, in 2000, that youth who engage in same-sex behavior now account for one-third of new AIDS cases within the thirteen to twenty-four age range; particularly at-risk are sexually active **African American** and **Latino** youth. A similarly higher rate of HIV infection was found for multiracial and African American youth compared to Euro-American youth who engage in homosexual behavior (Valleroy et al. 2000). There is also some research to document the higher level of at-risk sexual behaviors engaged by male bisexual youth, including unprotected sex, drug use, and multiple sexual partners (Goodenow, Netherland, and Szalacha 2002).

As HIV enters its third decade, the level of knowledge and interest among today's gay and bisexual youth is considerably less than their older generation. In Ireland, only one-in-three gay youth, ages sixteen to nineteen surveyed, have chosen to be tested, and this age cohort is demonstratively less knowledgeable about HIV-risks and more willing to engage in unprotected sex than older cohorts (Carrol et al. 2001).

Gay and bisexual youth, too, are disproportionately represented as sex workers. They confront health risks ranging from STI and HIV infection to drug addiction and abuse—either sexually or physically (Boles and Elifson 1994). Given that many of these are street youth, health-related problems associated with homelessness are also a concern (Cochran et al. 2002). However, **prostitution** per se is not necessarily a vehicle for impairing sexual health if properly regulated by the state. Rather than adopted as a tactic of survival, some gay and bisexual youth freely enter the sexual **workplace** (Calhoun and Weaver 1996). Here, religious proscription, **social work** bias, police and judicial activism, and cultural convention can increase the risk encountered by these youth sex workers.

Gay and bisexual youth—like heterosexual young men—may confront psychological and physiological problems associated with **sexual abuse**. This can range from **sexual harassment** and **bullying** to incest and rape (Gartner 1999; Savin-Williams and Cohen 1996). Although long associated with male–female relationships, the scandals within the **Catholic** Church have stirred public discussion of this problem.

Additionally, a **biology** and sexuality educational curriculum of **heteronormativity** silences gay and bisexual issues in content and pedagogy (Reiss 1998). This is even more acute when these youth have **disabilities**, as adults (teachers and parents) view discussion of sexuality, and especially nonheterosexuality, as inappropriate (Brantlinger 1992). Consequently, this subpopulation is at great sexual risk including sexual abuse, STI and HIV infection, and internalized homophobia (Allen 2003).

The emergence of openly gay communities in urban areas and the infusion of private and public monies to support HIV education and outreach, have resulted in the development, staffing, and support for community-based youth groups. Most of these groups provide sexual health information through brochures, workshops, and peer-counseling. Some, such as London's *Outzone* (http://www.outzone. org/outzone/safersex/axis.htm), offer health clinics for gay and bisexual youth. Based on a grass roots and self-empowerment model of health care, best exemplified by the Gay Men's Health Crisis, youth health services for gay and bisexual youth, notably the MPowerment Project (Hays, Rebchook, and Kegeles 2003) and the Sexual Stories Project (Mutchler, Ayala, and Neith 2005) bring these young men together to assume responsibility for their safer sex education and practice. Similarly, youth organizers of go-com provide educational outreach at a gay community center in heart of the Tokyo's gay district. Paradoxically, even in countries which have provided little freedom for sexual minorities, such as China, the development of youth-operated HIV programs, such as the Shanghai Hotline (Gu 2005), have resulted in empowerment of a new generation of gay youth and the development of leadership and communication networks within and between cities that significantly contour **identity politics.**

Sexual health for rural gay and bisexual youth is often compromised due to the relative lack of medical facilities compared to those found in urban centers, the increased homophobia in these regions along with the concomitant absence of LGBT support services (Buchanan et al. 2003; Frere, Jukes, and Crowhurst, 2001). This is beginning to change in some regions of the world. For instance, in Canada, the AIDS Committee of Newfoundland and Labrador's *Reaching Out to Young Gay Men* and, in Onatrio, GaBaLoT (http://gabalot.ca) target rural queer youth.

Both urban and rural youth who are under the legal age for emancipation, confront issues related to sexual health privacy. The legal requirement or desire of medical professionals to inform parents complicate access to health care services and lessen the willingness of gay and bisexual youth to disclose sexually-related issues or problems. This is a special concern in countries such as **Mexico**, where a largely ill-informed group of health professionals, ranging from medical doctors to mental health counselors, coupled to laws which given parents property-like custody of their children, make any disclosure by gay or bisexual youth dangerous.

The Internet has created greater opportunities for queer youth to be informed about sexual health issues as well as to network with other gay and bisexual persons to discuss health-related issues and, conversely, to meet online for later sexual rendezvous—sometimes resulting in health-related problems. Nevertheless, the growing use of software to filter "objectionable" sites and government-imposed restrictions, such as found in many U.S. public schools as well as in more authoritarian Middle Eastern countries, have made it more difficult for gay and bisexual youth to access accurate sexual health information.

Bibliography

Allen, John. 2003. *Gay, Lesbian, Bisexual and Transgender People with Developmental Disabilities and Mental Retardation.* Binghamton, NY: Harrington Park Press.

Ayala, George, and Rafael Diaz. 2001. "Racism, Poverty and Other Truths about Sex: Race, Class, and HIV Risk Among Latino Gay Men." *Revista Interamerica de Psicologia* 35, no. 2: 59–77.

Boles, Jacqueline, and Kirk W. Elifson. 1994. "Sexual Identity and HIV: The Male Prosti-tute." *The Journal of Sex Research* 31, no. 1: 39–46.

Brantlinger, Ellen. 1992. "Sexuality Education in the Secondary Special Education Curri-culum: Teachers' Perceptions and Concerns." *Teacher Education and Special Education* 15, no.1: 32–40.

Buchanan, Robert J., Bonnie J. Chakravorty, Miguel A. Zuniga, and Jane N. Bolin. 2003. "HIV Education, Prevention, and Outreach Programs in Rural Texas." *The Health Education Monograph Series* 20, no. 2: 19–25.

Calhoun, Thomas C., and Greg Weaver. 1996. "Rational Decision-Making among Male Street Sex Workers." *Deviant Behavior* 17: 209–227.

Carrol, Davis, Bill Foley, Brian Sheenan, Mick Quinlan, and Ronan Watters, eds. 2001. *Vital Statistics 2000: An All Ireland Gay Men's Sex Survey.* Dublin: East Coast Area Health Board Publishing.

Centers for Disease Control and Prevention. 2000, October. *Youth and HIV/AIDS 2000. A New American Agenda.* Accessed February 15, 2005. http://www.thebody.com/ whitehouse/youthreport/problem.html.

Cochran, Bryan N., Angela J. Stewart, Joshua A. Ginzler, and Ana Mari Cauce. 2002. "Challenges Faced by Homeless Sexual Minorities: Comparison of Gay, Lesbian, Bisex-ual, and Transgender Homeless Adolescents with Their Heterosexual Counterparts." *American Journal of Public Health* 92: 773–777.

Faulkner, Anne H., and Kevin Cranston. 1998. "Correlates of Same-Sex Sexual Behavior in a Random Sample of Massachusetts High School Students." *American Journal of Public Health* 88, no. 2: 262–266.

Frere, Marion, Janet Jukes, and Michael Crowhurst. 2001. *Our Town: Working with Same-Sex Attracted Young People in Rural Communities. Key Learnings from the Sexual Diversity Grants Scheme.* Carlton South: Vichealth.

Gartner, Richard B. 1999. "Sexual Victimization of Boys by Men: Meanings and Conse-quences." *Journal of Gay and Lesbian Psychotherapy* 3: 1–33.

Goodenow, Carol, Julie Netherland, and Laura Szalacha. 2002. "AIDS-Related Risk Among Adolescent Males Who Have Sex With Males, Females or Both: Evidence from a Statewide Survey." *American Journal of Public Health* 92, no. 2: 203–210.

Gu, Stephen. 2005. "Shanghai, China: Hotline for Sexual Minorities." *Journal of Gay and Lesbian Issues in Education* 2, no. 3: 95–98.

Hays, Robert B., Gregory M. Rebchook, and Susan M. Kegeles. 2003. "The Mpowerment Project: Community-Building with Young Gay and Bisexual Men to Prevent HIV1." *American Journal of Psychology* 31, nos. 3–4: 301–312.

Health Canada: AIDS. 2004. http://www.hc-sc.gc.ca/english/diseases/aids.html. Accessed November 16, 2004.

Mutchler, Matt G., George Ayala, and Katie L. Neith. 2005. "Safer Sex Stories Told by Young Gay Men: Building on Resiliency Through Gay-Boy Talk." *Journal of Gay and Lesbian Issues in Education* 2, no. 3: 37–50.

Reiss, Michael J. 1998. "The Representation of Human Sexuality in Some Science Textbooks for 14–16 Year-Olds." *Research in Science & Technological Education* 16: 137–149.

Rosario, Margaret, Joyce Hunter, and Marya Gwadz. 1997. "Exploration of Substance Use among Lesbian, Gay, and Bisexual Youth: Prevalence and Correlates." *Journal of Adolescent Research* 12: 454–476.

Rotheram-Borus, Mary Jane, Margaret Rosario, Heino F. L. Meyer-Bahlburg, Cheryl Koopman, Steven C. Dopkins, and Mark Davies. 1994. "Sexual and Substance Use Acts of Gay and Bisexual Male Adolescents in New York City." *Journal of Sex Research* 31: 47–57.

Rotheram-Borus, Mary Jane, Margaret Rosario, Ronan Van Rossem, Helen Reid, and Roy Gillis. 1995. "Prevalence, Course, and Predictors of Multiple Problem Behaviors among Gay and Bisexual Male Adolescents." *Developmental Psychology* 31: 75–85.

Russell, Stephen T., Anne K. Driscoll, and Nhan Truong. 2002. "Adolescent Same-Sex Romantic Attractions and Relationships: Implications for Substance Use and Abuse." *American Journal of Public Health* 92, no. 2: 198–202.

Savin-Williams, Ritch C., and Kenneth M. Cohen. 1996. "Psychosocial Outcomes of Verbal and Physical Abuse Among Lesbian, Gay, and Bisexual Youths." Pp. 181–200 in *The Lives of Lesbians, Gays, and Bisexuals*. Edited by Ritch C. Savin-Williams and Kenneth M. Cohen. Fort Worth: Harcourt Brace College.

Valleroy, L. A., D. A. MacKellar, J. M. Karon, D. H. Rosen, W. McFarland, D. A. Shehan, S. R. Stoyanoff, M. LaLota, D. D. Celentano, B. A. Koblin, H. Thiede, M. H. Katz, L. V. Torian, and R. S. Janssen. 2000. "HIV Prevalence and Associated Risks in Young Men who Have Sex with Men." *Journal of the American Medical Association* 284, no. 2: 198–204.

Web Sites

Ambiente Joven. February 2005. Accessed February 15, 2005. <http://www.ambientejoven.org>. A Spanish site for Latino youth who have sex with other men.

Gay Boy Support. January 2005. Accessed February 15, 2005. http://www.gayboysupport.nl/gbs/00-en-start.html. Detailed Netherlands-based site providing specific information for gay and bisexual youth ranging from masturbation to dating.

Guy's Health. 2005. Sex,etc: A Web site by Teens for Teens. Network for Family Life Education, Rutgers University. http://www.sxetc.org/index.php?topic=Guys+Health Topics range from body image to penis size with material also directly related to LGBTQ youth.

Health Issues for Gay Teens. 2004. Charles Downey. Swedish Medical Center. Accessed February 15, 2005. http://www.swedish.org/15269.cfm. Brief but detailed overview of some health-related concerns for gay youth.

Teen Health. February 2005. About.Com. Accessed February 15, 2005. http://menshealth.about.com/od/teenhealth. Site for males, both gay and not, including visuals and useful clearly written information on health-related issues facing youth.

Scarleteen. Sex Education for the Real World. February 2005. Heather Corinna. Accessed February 15, 2005. http://www.scarleteen.com/about.html. Established in 1998, this site provides frank and jargon-free information about sexuality of all types to youth in a nonjudgmental manner.

Youth Resources. February 2005. Advocates for Youth. Accessed February 15, 2005. http://www.youthresource.com. Created by LGBT youth, the site includes peer-to-peer education on issues of sexual health.

Sexual Health, Lesbian and Bisexual

Denise Tse Shang Tang

Sexual health for lesbian and bisexual women encompasses physical, social, and mental well-being. A healthy and positive approach to sexual health includes accurate information about sexually transmitted infections (STI) and HIV, support services for victims of sexual violence and those with unwanted pregnancies, and

See also Adolescent Sexualities; Coming Out, Youth; Compulsory Heterosexuality; Domestic and Relationship Violence; Intersex; Sexism; Sexual Harassment; Sexual Identity; Transsexuality; Youth, At-Risk; Youth, Homeless.

access to culturally competent and affordable health care services sensitive to the needs of lesbian and bisexual young women. Social stigmatization of homosexuality and **sexism** contributes to a lack of understanding among health practitioners and educators on the physical and **mental health** concerns of lesbian and bisexual young women. In general, **research** on adult lesbian health focus on the correlation between lesbians and various health conditions: cancer, cardiovascular disease, STIs, HIV/**AIDS**, mental health, and **substance abuse**. The experiences of young lesbians and bisexual women have not always been included in research studies on lesbian health. As a result, there is very limited analysis on how young lesbians and bisexual women view sexual health risks, the choices they make to ensure well-being, and the barriers they face in accessing health care services.

Bisexual and **lesbian youth,** like their male counterparts, encounter **discrimination** in school and community settings, ranging from social isolation and verbal **harassment** to sexual abuse and physical violence. **Coming out** may not be an option due to the risks of being thrown out by their families and being isolated by peers. Dropping out of school and running away from home is a familiar coping mechanism and survival strategy. Homeless lesbian and bisexual teenagers are more at risk of entering **prostitution** as a means for survival (6 percent compared to 1 percent among adolescents who were heterosexual and unsure (Saewyc et al. 1998).

The prevalence of **pregnancy** among young homeless women is high according to studies on homeless youth in Canada and the United States. Contrary to popular assumptions, many lesbians have had heterosexual relationships during sometime in their life. Youth often question their sexualities during adolescence. A lesbian and bisexual teenager may engage in heterosexual behavior prior to identifying as lesbian or bisexual. By being in heterosexual relationships, lesbian and bisexual teenagers can negotiate the differences between homosexuality and heterosexuality. There, too, have been cases where adolescents engage in heterosexual behavior in order to hide their same-sex **desire** or where an adolescent may chose pregnancy to prove that she is not a lesbian (Rotheram-Borus and Fernandez 1995).

According to one survey conducted among lesbians on lesbians' sexual history with men, seventy-seven had one or more male sexual partners in the course of their lives (Diamant et al. 1999). In another study, three-fourths of young lesbians have had heterosexual intercourse with mostly young gay men as well as with young women (Hunter, Rosario, and Rotheram-Borus 1993). In another study of 3,816 Minnesota public school students, ages twelve to nineteen, researchers compared heterosexual behavior, pregnancy histories, and related risk factors among those who identify as lesbian, bisexual, questioning, and heterosexual (Saewyc et al. 1999). Here, lesbian and bisexual survey respondents were as likely to engage in heterosexual intercourse as heterosexual young women, and 12 percent of bisexual and lesbian adolescents experienced pregnancy compared to only 5 to 6 percent in other groups. Despite these findings and, perhaps, due to popular assumptions, there has been little study on how lesbian and bisexual adolescents face teen pregnancies and related risk factors. Pregnancies often result in miscarriages and abortions.

Unintended pregnancies are sometimes the consequence of **sexual abuse and assault**. In the Minnesota study, the prevalence of pregnancy and physical or sexual abuse was much higher among lesbian and bisexual teenagers compared to heterosexual adolescents (Saewyc et al. 1999). Nineteen percent of bisexual and lesbian respondents reported physical abuse (compared to 11 to 12 percent among heterosexual and questioning adolescents), and nearly one-quarter disclosed sexual abuse

(13 to 15 percent in other groups). Adolescent girls aged fourteen and younger were four times more likely to have a history of sexual abuse than young boys in the same range (Saewyc et al. 1998). Girls between fifteen and seventeen were twice as likely as boys to report sexual abuse (30.7 to 16.7 percent). Almost half of the girls and boys who have experienced sexual abuse did not tell anyone.

Dating violence is another critical issue for lesbian and bisexual young women. A 1999 **Youth Risk Behavioral Survey** conducted by the Massachusetts Department of Education has shown that adolescents reporting **dating** violence were two to five times more prone to harmful consequences than other adolescents. These consequences include rape, taking higher risks in sexual behaviors, **eating disorders**, teen pregnancy, substance use, and being suicidal. Young lesbians and bisexual teenagers face additional barriers in experiencing and reporting dating violence. They were often threatened by male dates or partners to reveal their **sexual orientation** to others, and they are less likely to disclose sexual violence to friends or adults.

Childhood sexual abuse can be linked with many negative health outcomes such as substance use, **suicide**, and mental health issues. The rates for sexual abuse among lesbians and heterosexual women were similar in most studies. A 1990 study on lesbians in a substance abuse treatment center showed that 70 percent of them had a history of sexual abuse (Neisen and Sandall 1990). Another study on substance abuse patterns, based on interviews with twenty-two lesbian and bisexual women between the ages of seventeen and sixty-three, found that **alcoholism** is linked with traumatic life histories such as childhood sexual and physical abuse, depression, incest, and alcoholism within the family. Poor self-esteem, discrimination, and social isolation are also factors that contribute to substance abuse (Camlin 1994).

Young lesbians and bisexual women of color, facing ethnic and racial discrimination, can experience a higher incidence of substance use and unsafe sexual behaviors. The prevalence of alcohol and **drug use**, mental illness, and HIV infection is high among young LGBT **Native American**s: 75 percent of all reported gonorrhea cases in 2002 affected youth of color with 114 per 100,000 population affecting Native Americans compared to 29 among non-Hispanic whites (Pagliaro and Gipson 2000). Similarly, **African American** and **Latina** young lesbians are more likely to become pregnant or be infected with sexually transmitted infections, partly as a result of the strong cultural values in motherhood and childbearing among African American and Hispanic communities (Centers for Disease Control and Prevention 2000). **Asian American** and Pacific Islander queer youth have challenges in obtaining adequate health-related services due to language difficulties and the "model minority" stereotype (Center for AIDS Prevention Studies 1998). HIV/ AIDS has become an emerging issue for these young women: 10 percent have contracted HIV, and 31 percent living with AIDS are under the age of 25 (Centers for Disease Control and Prevention 2002).

Complicating these problems is the quality of the interactions between health care practitioners and lesbians, who have found providers to show hostility and unease toward the treatment of lesbians (Stevens 1992; Stevens 1996). Trust is a significant factor for lesbian and bisexual teenagers seeking physical and mental health services. A qualitative study on the accessibility of health care for this population has shown that lesbian and **bisexual youth** encounter multiple barriers to health care (Scherzer 2000). **Prejudice** among health care providers reinforces the notion of distrust that already exists among those seeking medical care. As a result of **homophobia** and **heterosexism**, young lesbian and bisexual women were hesitant to voice their medical needs. Bad experiences with health care providers left them with "physical and emotional trauma," as well as "anger at the provider's ignorance, disrespect, and/or abuse" (Scherzer 2000, 97). On the other hand, positive experiences encouraged them to take better care of themselves and to include regular physical and gynecological examinations as part of their goal of better health and well-being. Pelvic examinations and blood tests can be frightening for some and shameful for others. This is a particularly sensitive issue for **transgender youth**, where few health care professionals have adequate knowledge about **gender identity**. Teenagers seldom return to their family doctors for advice on such matters due to fear of disclosure to other family members or friends in the community.

Bibliography

Camlin, Carol S. 1994. "An Exploration of Patterns of Substance Abuse among Lesbians and Bisexual Women in Central North Carolina." Accessed June 22, 2005. http://www.glma.org/programs/lhf/abstracts/camlin.shtml.

Center for AIDS Prevention Studies, University of California at San Francisco. 1998. *What are Asian and Pacific Islander HIV Prevention Needs?* San Francisco: Author.

Centers for Disease Control and Prevention. 2000. *Young People at Risk: HIV/AIDS among America's Youth*. Atlanta: Author.

———. 2002. *HIV/AIDS Surveillance Summaries 2002*. 13, no. 2: 1–44.

Diamant, Allison L., Mark A. Schuster, Kimberly McGuigan, and Janet Lever. 1999. "Lesbians' Sexual History with Men: Implications for Taking a Sexual History." *Archives of Internal Medicine* 159: 2730–2736.

Freedner, Naomi, Lorraine H. Freed, Y. Wendy Yang, and S. Bryn Austin. 2002. "Dating Violence among Gay, Lesbian, and Bisexual Adolescents: Results from a Community Survey." *Journal of Adolescent Health* 31, no. 6: 469–474.

Hunter, Joyce, Margaret Rosario, and Mary Jane Rotheram-Borus. 1993. "Sexual and Substance Abuse Acts that Place Adolescent Lesbians at Risk for HIV." Poster presentation at the Ninth International Conference of AIDS/Fourth STD World Congress, Berlin.

Jackson, Kayla. 2002. "Meeting the Special Needs of GLBTQ Youth of Color." *Transitions* 14, no. 4: 10.

Leach, Charlene A. 2002. "Transgender Youth and the Role of Service Providers." *Transitions* 14, no. 4: 12.

Leung, Man Chui. 2004. "Asian and Pacific Islander Youth: Diverse Voices, Common Challenges." *Transitions* 15, no. 3: 10.

Massachusetts Department of Education. 2000. *Massachusetts 1999 Youth Risk Behavior Survey Results*. Malden, MA: Author.

Neisen Joseph H., and Hilary Sandall. 1990. "Alcohol and Other Drug Abuse in Gay/Lesbian Populations: Related to Victimization?" *Journal of Psychology and Human Sexuality* 3, no. 1: 151–168.

Pagliaro, Susan, and Michael Gipson. 2000. *Effective HIV/STD and Teen Pregnancy Prevention Programs for Young Women of Color*. Washington, DC: Advocates for Youth.

Rotheram-Borus, Mary Jane, and M. Isabel Fernandez. 1995. "Sexual Orientation and Developmental Challenges Experienced by Gay and Lesbian Youths." *Suicide and Life-Threatening Behavior* 25 (Supplement): 26–34.

Saewyc, Elizabeth M., Linda H. Bearinger, Patricia A. Heinz, Robert W. Blum, and Michael D. Resnick. 1998. "Gender Differences in Health and Risk Behaviors among Bisexual and Homosexual Adolescents." *Journal of Adolescent Health* 23, no. 3: 181–188.

———. 1999. "Sexual Intercourse, Abuse and Pregnancy among Adolescent Women: Does Sexual Orientation Make a Difference?" *Family Planning Perspectives* 31, no. 3: 127–131.

Scherzer, Teresa. 2000. "Negotiating Health Care: the Experiences of Young Lesbian and Bisexual Women." *Culture, Health & Sexuality* 2, no. 1: 87–102.

Solarz, Andrea L., ed. 1999. *Lesbian Health: Current Assessment and Directions for the Future.* Washington, DC: National Academy Press.

Stevens, Patricia E. 1992. "Lesbian Health Care Research: A Review of the Literature from 1970 to 1990." *Health Care for Women International* 13: 91–120.

———. 1996. "Lesbians and Doctors: Experiences of Solidarity and Domination in Health Care Settings." *Gender & Society* 10, no. 1: 24–41.

Web Site

Lesbian Health Research Center. 2004. Institute on Health & Aging, University of California at San Francisco. Accessed June 22, 2005. http://www.lesbianhealthinfo.org. A public service for lesbians and their practitioners about health-related topics specific to lesbians.

Sexual Identity

Ray Misson

Sexual identity is the conception that we have of ourselves (or that others have of us) as sexual beings with particular desires, propensities, and orientations. Whereas the debate can rage on **sexual orientation** over whether (homo)sexuality is biologically, psychologically, or culturally determined, such a debate is, at one level, meaningless in terms of defining sexual identity. What matters is how our sexual lives are subjectively or externally perceived to be configured. On another level, since identity is usually discussed in terms of culture rather than of **biology** or **psychology**, sexual identity is generally seen as a cultural phenomenon. We set up categories by which we classify people, including how they "do sex" (or would like to do it); we believe that these categories are constitutive of what a person "really" is. These days the most basic sexual categorization is in terms of whether one predominantly desires a person of the same sex or not (homosexual/heterosexual), but there are many other parameters on which the categorization might be made, including age of desired partner, autoeroticism versus alloeroticism (i.e., masturbators or not), propensity to genital or oral pleasures. Whatever the categorization, our sexual identity is fundamental to our self-perceptions; we establish and confirm it by taking on behavior from the repertoire of ways of inhabiting a particular sexual identity available in the culture. The concept of sexual identity is particularly important for young people, since youth is the site for establishing the basics of an identity

See also Australia, Research on Sexual Identities; Communication; Critical Social Theory; Day of Silence or Silencing; Ethnic Identity; Identity Development; Identity Politics; Poststructuralism; Queer Pedagogy; Queer Studies; Racial Identity.

that is likely to persist through adult life. Education as the source of many of our cultural understandings, perceptions, and attitudes plays a crucial role for **lesbian, gay, bisexual,** and **transgender youth** (LGBT). It can be positive in providing affirmation of alternative ways of being; it can have a negative effect by driving certain possibilities into silence.

The noun "identity" is related to the verb "identify," and fundamental to identity is an act of self-identification. We identify with, or recognize ourselves in, a particular category or a particular image of what people might be. The major current theorization of how this happens has been provided by **Michel Foucault** with his notion of "the discursive construction of subjectivity."

Foucault used the term "discourse" to refer to the commonly-accepted ways of speaking that characterize a particular field of interest or a particular range of people. If you hear people scattering words like "yo" and "dude" in their conversation, you realize that these are likely to be people of a certain age and from a certain background. If you are reading a text with words like "genital" and "alloeroticism" in it, you realize that there is not only a particular field of interest, but a particular framework in which that subject is viewed. Each discourse, whether it is the discourse of a social group or the discourse of a particular field, brings with it certain ways of seeing the world, certain values, and certain beliefs. It also brings silences and blind spots, matters that cannot be discussed or known about in that discourse. Discourse is not just a matter of verbal language; visual images and design can be part of a discourse. Look at virtually any advertisement and you will see that these marketing images are created to be read in certain ways. We all participate in many different discourses: It's perfectly possible for students to take part in a "yo, dude" conversation as they walk to the library to write an essay on genital alloeroticism.

It might seem that we use these discourses at will, returning to a general, neutral position in between. But it can be argued that there is no neutral position, that we can only conceive the world through discourses. More than that, we don't just use discourses. Discourses construct our ways of seeing and thinking about the world; they construct what we are subjectively. Hence, Foucault's phrase: "discursive construction of subjectivity." We are all the time becoming the kind of person who speaks the sort of discourse we are currently using. We are also all the time becoming the kind of person who is assumed in and responds to the kind of discourse with which we are being addressed. If we become part of a particular club scene, with its own insider way of talking, then it affects our behavior, our self-perception, and our ways of thinking. To give a different kind of example, **HIV education** has to use language and images at times that create those it is addressing as responsible for their own health and well-being.

Thus, involving ourselves in discourse brings with it a mind set, a way of being; this is what constitutes our identity. We identify with visual and verbal representations of sexuality; we understand our sexual selves through the representations of sexuality that address us (whether it be in the press, through our friends' casual talk, in **popular music**, in advertisements) and feel ourselves to be that kind of person.

If identity is so bound up with discourse, then, of course, silence is a major problem. If a boy or girl feels sexually attracted to a person of the same gender, and there is no way to conceive of this in the discourses available to them, then they will feel that their urges—and they themselves—are quite literally, unspeakable: it will truly be "the love that dare not speak its name." They will have nothing but the silence with which to identify, and the result is almost inevitably anxiety and a sense of severe dislocation. It is not surprising, therefore, that **suicide** rates for young gay and lesbian people are high: There seems to be no discursive space for their existence, no identity; they might as well be dead. Thus, if for no other reason than duty of care, **curriculum** and **literature** should be properly inclusive, presenting a range of positive representations of sexual diversity with which students might productively identify.

Silence is perhaps not such a major problem today as it once was since, in the Western world at least, homosexuality is increasingly public. The main problem for many may be discourses in which homosexuality is named, but negatively. The use of slang like "poofter," "leso," or "**queer**" as abuse, or "gay" for anything that is stupid or dysfunctional, is perhaps not much better than the silence. "Hey, poofter!" is called out behind you on the way to school. Whether you turn around or don't turn around, if you are feeling same-sex-attracted, the identification with the despised naming is made. Turning around is acknowledging that you are the object of derision; not turning around enhances the cowardly private shame of what you are.

Building on Foucault's work, **Judith Butler** adds the important element of the body. She argues that we become gendered by performing gender. It is a matter of our whole way of being in the body. Acting like a male or a female and performing in socially appropriate masculine and feminine ways, we experience our gender and our **gender identity** is established. Butler would argue by extension that we experience our sexuality by performing sexuality (this is not "performing sex"). One may perform sexuality without ever performing sex as in the case of a young woman, for example, who feels her way of being in her body proclaims her as lesbian, even though she has never had sex with anyone). Our ways of being heterosexual or homosexual are socially generated. We establish our sexual identity by enacting it, whether it is through dancing passionately to techno music or by wearing Calvin Klein underwear (or probably both).

That is, of course, a **stereotype**, and it underlines the need for public institutions (such as schools and the media) to acknowledge a range of possible images LGBT youth might identify with. If a young woman, for example, is not automotively inclined, the image of "Dykes on Bikes" leading off the local Pride March may not be a reassuring spectacle, just as not every gay boy feels that he finds his true self in sequined shorts or transgender youth by participating in a drag contest. Even more problematic can be the cross-gendered image of homosexual people, the notion that lesbians act in a masculinized way and that gay men are feminized. It is important to separate out sexual identity from gender identity and, indeed, from biological sex. Gender identity is about how we perceive ourselves as feminine or masculine, and how we perform what that means as we go about our daily lives. Sexual identity is about our sexual preferences. The mainstream belief is that feminine gender goes along with female biological sex, masculine gender aligns with male biology, and the natural order is that the feminine/female and the masculine/male desire each other exclusively for purposes of sex. Needless to say, life is not so simple: A "feminized" male, for example, may be rampantly heterosexual; a female who delights in being thoroughly feminine may love only equally feminine women.

Identity is constantly shifting and constantly being altered by our participation in social practices and related discourses. We are also called on to perform our identity very differently at different times, to the extent that there might seem to be little coherence underlying it all: A lesbian student teacher will enact her sexuality differently on teaching practice in a religious school, at a Gay Pride meeting at university, and at a Saturday night dance party. People lead discontinuous lives, shifting between different aspects of their identity in different contexts, but it is probably true that the discontinuity is greater for young LGBT people than for their peers, as queer youth negotiate their often very disparate, conflicting worlds. The very fact that there are likely to be aspects of their lives in which their sexuality is hidden, and revealing it might be dangerous (as can be the case in school or even the family), means that the different selves making up their identity are more likely to be radically dissociated.

The sociocultural processes that establish our identity are enormously powerful, and we are often unconscious of their influence. Our sexual identity appears (and feels) natural to us: It is just the way we are. We might modify our walk or way of talking, or dress in a particular way to give the world a message about how we would like to be seen, but in most cases this is just embroidering around the edges: The fundamental establishment of sexual identity has already happened and is constantly happening, generally without our awareness or influence.

The seeming naturalness, the invisibility of this process presents a challenge to educators, one that is taken up particularly by those interested in critical pedagogy. Critical pedagogy is concerned to make visible the ways in which society constructs our seemingly natural ways of being; it is concerned about developing an awareness of how our ways of thinking are shaped so that beliefs that are profoundly ideological and contestable (e.g., heterosexuality is the natural order; gender barriers are impermeable) seem to go without saying. However, this critical agenda is not as widely taken up as one might wish since schools, as social institutions, are as likely to be complicit in confirming the (un)natural order as contesting it.

Identity looks two ways: It is defined by both exclusion and inclusion. People define themselves by excluding others, by defining themselves against what they would not want to be. If we happen to be the excluded Other, this can be very isolating and damaging. Identity, on the other hand, is inclusive: It can make us feel part of a community, even if the community is a minority one. Since a feeling of belonging seems in general to be fundamental to human well-being, a strong sense of sexual identity can be a great support to queer youth. It is the feeling of isolation, of being the only one that is particularly damaging. By being genuinely open and inclusive, communities as well as schools can support the establishment of a positive identity for LGBT people.

Bibliography

Butler, Judith. 1990. *Gender Trouble: Feminism and the Subversion of Identity*. New York: Routledge.

Foucault, Michel. 1981. *The History of Sexuality: Volume 1: An Introduction*. Harmondsworth: Penguin.

Mansfield, Nick. 2000. *Subjectivity: Theories of the Self from Freud to Haraway*. St. Leonards: Allen and Unwin.

Sedgwick, Eve Kosofsky. 1990. *Epistemology of the Closet*. Berkeley: University of California Press.

Sexual Orientation

Joseph A. Diorio

Sexual orientation refers to whether individuals are sexually attracted toward, and/or engage in sexual activities with, persons of the same sex as themselves (homosexuals/gays/lesbians), the other sex (heterosexuals/straights), or both (bisexuals). Debate surrounds whether sexual orientations arise from personal choice, environmental influences, or the effects of genes and hormones (Stein 1999), which has significant implications for teaching about **lesbian, gay,** and **bisexual** (LGB) issues and working with sexual minority youth.

An individual may be attracted to people of one or the other sex, but may not always engage in sexual activity with that kind of people. Some heterosexual people engage sexually with persons of the same sex when they live in **single-sex schools** or prisons. Homosexual people may also engage in sexual activity with heterosexual marriage partners. Young persons often engage in same-sex behavior although most will identify themselves as heterosexual adults. Observing people's sexual behavior thus does not necessarily reveal their sexual orientation. Some researchers have sought to assess sexual desires independently of behavior (Bancroft 1989). One way to do this is to ask people what desires they feel, but this can be unreliable since LGB individuals generally suffer public disapproval.

Researchers have applied ideas of "latency" and "falsity" to sexual orientation (Marmor and Green 1977). Persons might be latent homosexuals if, despite engaging exclusively in heterosexual behaviors, they possess unexpressed same-sex desires which ultimately may come to the fore. The notion of latency can destabilize everyone's sexual orientation and can threaten their sense of **sexual identity**. The notion of falsity, or pseudohomosexuality, refers to people who think they are homosexual despite underlying heterosexual desires. Such people might fear heterosexual encounters or, like some feminist women who identify themselves as lesbians, they might call themselves homosexual because of political commitments. The notions of latency and falsity presuppose that individuals always have a real underlying sexual orientation.

Individuals clearly can choose to engage in sexual activities with types of people who are not the objects of their underlying **desire**. During the 1960s, the idea that sexual desires were a matter of choice or personal preference became popular. This idea fit well with the so-called "sexual revolution," which opposed restrictive social attitudes and beliefs about sexuality, and encouraged individuals to decide for themselves what kinds of sexual activities they wanted to perform. In the 1970s, "bisexual chic" became popularized through cultural icons like David Bowie and the "bisexual liberation" movement.

Advocates of personal choice in sexuality believed that established attitudes could be changed because they were socially produced. While the general population did not necessarily share this liberationist agenda, respondents in the United States to a 1977 Gallup poll said that sexual orientation resulted from changeable social influences such as family upbringing, rather than from genetics, by a four-to-one

See also Adolescent Sexualities; Biology, Teaching of; Gender Identity; Identity Development; Identity Politics; Intersex; Lesbian Feminism; Multiple Genders; Sissy Boy; Transsexuality.

ratio. While sexual revolutionaries in the United States promoted the view that sexual orientation was socially generated and hence changeable, they failed to get a majority to accept nonheterosexual orientations as legitimate. Although many states had decriminalized homosexuality and some municipalities had prohibited **discrimination** on the basis of sexual orientation by the mid-1970s, only 38 percent of people in 1977 believed homosexuality was an acceptable lifestyle (Dahir 2001).

Many gay and lesbian advocates today have abandoned appeals to individual rights to *choose* sexual orientations, and have adopted claims that sexual orientations are biologically based. This is because choice has been used against nonheterosexual persons by disapproving conservatives, who argue that rights and benefits should not be granted to persons who deliberately live sinfully or fail to improve themselves in the face of negative influences. Many gay activists now argue that if sexual orientations are biologically caused, individuals should not be blamed for their differing orientations anymore than people should be blamed for being right- or left-handed. In contrast, many gay scholars have embraced **queer theory**, arguing against sexual categorization and the inherent destablization of such categories.

Today's biological **research** on sexual orientation reflects work done in Europe in the nineteenth and early twentieth centuries by writers such as **Magnus Hirschfeld**. Contemporary research draws theoretically on what is called the organizational hypothesis or model, which holds that organisms normally are coherent packages of morphologies and behaviors—that is, combinations of bodily shapes and capacities on one hand, and patterns of activity on the other: Birds have wings and fly; fish have gills and fins and swim. Members of sexually reproducing species, including humans, possess one of two partially different bodily designs—male or female. Each organism develops a consistent array of internal and external reproductive organs, along with a tendency to use these organs to reproduce: Males produce sperm and inseminate the vaginas of females with their penises; females accept insemination to fertilize their eggs. Men and women are attracted to each other and commonly behave differently but complementarily during sexual intercourse. Different movements characterize male and female sexual behavior, and organisms mostly stick to the behaviors which typify their sex. The patterns of bodily differentiation, heterosexual attraction, and genital copulation are claimed to be too common and too significant for reproduction to have resulted from individual choices or social influences.

Biologists often equate sexual behavior with reproductive behavior. Male sexual behavior involves impregnating women; female sexual behavior involves facilitating impregnation. There are two forms of sexual behavior, but organisms of one sex can behave in ways appropriate for the other: Men can behave like women, and women like men, as in the case of the Hjiras of **India** or the Fa'afafine in Samoa. Sexual behavior is linked to gender. Men and women are dimorphic with regard not only to their sexual anatomies, orientations, and behaviors, but also to their overall behavior in gender-differentiated societies. Heterosexuals are taken as models of gender-typical behavior generally, and biologists often present gay males as persons who behave in ways atypical not only for their sexual anatomy but also for the broader **gender roles** attributed to their sex. The sexual orientations of many boys and men have been questioned because they were not aggressive, lacked interest in rough play and **sports**, and enjoyed artistic pursuits and parental activities.

The ultimate source of this dimorphic package supposedly is the sex chromosomes. Most humans have two sex chromosomes: either two X chromosomes, which makes them female; or an X and a Y chromosome, which makes them male.

Everyone obtains one sex chromosome from each parent, including an X chromosome from their mother; sex is determined by whether the person obtains an X or Y chromosome from their father. A human fetus initially possesses undifferentiated reproductive proto-organs which can develop into either testes or ovaries. Once the sex of the reproductive organs is established by the presence or absence of a Y chromosome, the sexual differentiation of the organism is driven largely by hormones secreted by the ovaries or testes. To explain why women are attracted to men, and men to women, biologists have assumed that sexual differentiation includes the brain—men and women have different sexual desires because their brains are differentiated through the effects of different sex chromosomes. Some persons are born with unusual combinations of sex chromosomes: either a single chromosome (always an X), or multiple combinations such as XXY or XYY. These unusual combinations can affect the hormonal secretions of the body, and arguably can influence sexual orientation.

Differences in sex chromosomes *may* explain differences in sexual orientations, desires, and behaviors between heterosexual men and heterosexual women. They do not explain differences between heterosexuals and homosexuals of the same sex, however, who should have similar desires if they have similar brains. Such an explanation is offered by "gay gene" researchers.

Both gay and heterosexual males have an X and a Y chromosome, and both possess the same reproductive morphology. If the X and Y chromosomes govern a common heterosexual pattern of brain development, what then differentiates the sexual orientations of gay and heterosexual men? According to Dean Hamer, the answer lies in "gay" genes located on the X chromosome. Genes are small parts of chromosomes, and while all men inherit an X chromosome from their mothers, Hamer (Hamer and Copeland 1994) claims only some X chromosomes carry gay genes. This claim is supported in three ways. First, the identical twin brothers of gay males have an increased likelihood also of being gay (identical twins develop from a single egg and, therefore, have the same X chromosome). Gay males also have been found to have maternal uncles who are more likely to be gay than paternal uncles, supporting the view that gay genes are maternally transmitted. Finally, Hamer conducted DNA blood tests on gay men and their relatives, finding a similar genetic marker on their X chromosomes known as Xq28. He concluded that different maternally-inherited genes distinguish gay males from heterosexual males.

This research in itself does not explain how the chromosomal differences of gay and heterosexual men translate into different sexual desires. Simon LeVay (1993) examined the brains of deceased men and women, including gay men. He found that part of the hypothalamus—a part of the brain—was smaller in women than in men, and also smaller in gay men than in heterosexual men. By linking this part of the brain to sexual desire and behavior, and by combining LeVay's work with Hamer's, it can be argued that the genetic differences of gay males lead them, through the developmental effects of resulting hormones, to have brains that are similar to women and therefore to be sexually attracted—like women—to men.

There are many criticisms of the gay gene research. Attempts to replicate some of the studies involved have failed, questioning their generalizability. It is doubtful that the gay gene explanation can be applied to lesbian women. Evidence for a chromosomal difference between lesbian and heterosexual women has not been found, and it is unclear whether sexual desire is the same for men and women. The gay gene research explains the sexual interests of only some gay men (e.g., not every gay twin has a gay brother), and it offers no insight into **bisexuality**. Finally, there are fears that this research will lead to further pathologization of homosexuals as biological abnormalities. This might promote a search for genetic cures for homosexuality, and may encourage prospective parents to use genetic testing to identify and abort homosexual fetuses.

Transsexualism and transgenderism suggest that sexual orientation can be independent of sex and gender. Individuals can maintain their sexual orientation through changes of sex and gender, and they may change their sex and gender to accommodate their sense of sexual attraction. Male-to-female transsexuals may seek to function as females in sexual interactions with males, and similarly for female-to-male transsexuals who seek a male role in heterosexual interactions. Persons who change their sex also may interact homosexually with persons who share their new sex, or they may behave bisexually.

Bibliography

Brookey, Robert Alan. 2002. *Reinventing the Male Homosexual.* Bloomington: Indiana University Press.

Bancroft, John. 1989. *Human Sexuality and Its Problems.* 2nd ed. Edinburgh: Churchill Livingstone.

Dahir, Mubarak. 2001. "Why Are We Gay?" *Advocate* 842 (July 17): 30–39.

Hamer, Dean, and Peter Copeland. 1994. *The Science of Desire.* New York: Simon & Schuster.

LeVay, Simon. 1993. *The Sexual Brain.* Cambridge, MA: MIT Press.

Marmor, Judd, and Richard Green. 1977. "Homosexual Behavior." Pp. 1051–1068 in *Handbook of Sexology.* Edited by John Money and H. Musaph. Amsterdam: Excerpta Medica.

Money, John. 1988. *Gay, Straight, and In-Between.* New York & Oxford: Oxford University Press.

Pillard, Richard C., and J. Michael Bailey. 1998. "Human Sexual Orientation Has a Heritable Component." *Human Biology* 70, no. 2: 347–365.

Stein, Edward. 1999. *The Mismeasure of Desire.* Oxford: Oxford University Press.

Vilain, Eric. 2000. "Genetics of Sexual Development." *Annual Review of Sex Research* 11: 1–25.

Web Site

Women's Issues Web Sites: Sexuality. May 13, 2004. Joan Korenman. Accessed December 12, 2004. http://www-unix.umbc.edu/~korenman/wmst/links_sex. Provides extensive links to gay and lesbian issues and related issues in sexuality and gender.

Sexuality Education

John P. Elia

Sexuality education refers to a lifelong educational process that " . . . encompasses sexual development, reproductive health, interpersonal relationships, affection, intimacy, body image and **gender roles**. Sexuality education addresses the biological,

See also Adolescent Sexualities; Australia, Sexualities Curriculum in; Biology, Teaching of; Critical Social Theory; Feminism; HIV Education; New Zealand, Teaching of Sexualities in; Pregnancy, Teenage; Queer Pedagogy; Sexual Health, Gay and Bisexual Men; Sexual Health, Lesbian and Bisexual Women.

sociocultural, psychological, and spiritual dimensions of sexuality . . . " (SIECUS 1996, 3). While this definition is derived from the Sexuality Information Education Council of the United States to capture the main features of comprehensive sexuality education, school-based sexuality education has taken a variety of forms over the past century. However, most instruction on sexual matters originally focused on the physical hygiene aspects of sexual functioning beginning in the early 1900s and initiated, in part, by the educational theorist, **G. Stanley Hall**. A contemporary of G. Stanley Hall, **Magnus Hirschfeld**, a medical doctor and a social scientist in Germany, founded a sexual institute and published widely in sexology. A sexual liberationist, in terms of studying sexual minority issues and presenting them in a positive light, Hirschfeld's views were shared only by a few of his contemporaries studying human sexuality; this is not surprising given relative sexual prudery as a holdover from the Victorian age. Accordingly, school-based sexuality education has been traditionally taught in the biological science and health education curricula, with distinct foci on reproductive anatomy, physiology, and the prevention of sexually-transmitted diseases. It has usually been taught from a sex negative perspective, reflecting **heterosexism** and biological essentialism (Sears 1992). In recent years, more comprehensive sexuality education efforts have been almost entirely supplanted with abstinence-only sexuality education, which requires that students be taught to abstain from sexual interaction until married and that prior sexual activity is likely to result in psychological and physical harm. This **heteronormative** approach to sexuality education renders LGBT youth invisible, negatively impacting their self-esteem and sexual knowledge while fostering heterosexism, **homophobia**, and sexual **prejudice** among their heterosexual peers.

There are over a billion young persons, ages ten through nineteen, in the world (SIECUS 2003). Sexual misinformation, sexual ignorance, tremendously high rates of unplanned pregnancies, not to mention the persisting and alarmingly high rates of HIV/AIDS affect many of these youth, including sexual minorities. In 1993, SIECUS began assisting various agencies worldwide to provide comprehensive sexuality education to youngsters. Countries such as Canada, France, Great Britain, Nigeria, Thailand, and Uganda that have, for the most part, lacked comprehensive sexuality education are beginning to educate youth about sexual matters. Other countries, notably Sweden, which has long promoted comprehensive sexuality education, is often cited for having comparatively fewer unintended pregnancies, incidences of sexually-transmitted infections, sexual assaults, and **hate crimes** based on sexual preference when compared to other industrialized nations (Francoeur and Noonan 2004). Sweden's sexuality education includes age-appropriate information about LGBT issues as a regular part of educating its youth. Its treatment of sexual minority issues is done in a nonjudgmental fashion within a "normal" and healthy sexual lifestyle. For instance, various nonheterosexual sexual behaviors and lifestyles are viewed by educators as just as viable and valuable as heterosexuality. Sweden's laws and **educational policies** reflect this progressive approach.

Comprehensive sexuality education, which has been fading in the United States since the 1980s, is an inclusive form of education covering such topics as sexual anatomy and physiology, contraception, sexual communication, relationship development and maintenance, sexual victimization, sexual values, sexual minority issues, sexual prejudice, and abstinence as a choice. It examines both the problematic and positive (even pleasurable) aspects of human sexual expression (Campos 2002).

Because of its historically strong reproductive and anatomical focus coupled to the current emphasis on abstinence-only approach to which millions of U.S. federal dollars are devoted, sexuality education is extremely heterosexist and reinforces the pervasive heteronormativity. The abstinence-only approach includes lessons about the "plumbing," the mechanics of conception, and the "facts" about heterosexual intercourse. Youngsters are taught and motivated to wait to engage in sexual intercourse until married, learning about the ills that sexual contact can create outside of wedlock such as sexually transmitted infections, depression, shame, guilt, loss of long-term committed relationships. The message of the hidden curriculum is that nonheterosexuals are seen as sexual *others* and viewed as deviant.

Such content and pedagogical practices fail to address the complexities and diversities of sexualities and are potentially injurious to sexual minority youth. Gay, lesbian, bisexual, and transgender students are silenced, pathologized, and systematically erased. Such treatment in schools may perpetuate hate crimes against these youth, including but not limited to being teased, bullied, beaten up, and verbally harassed. Heteronormative sexuality education also hurts straight youth by forcing them to conform to traditional gender roles while understanding heterosexuality from a narrow perspective, thus limiting creativity and self-expression. Additionally, heteronormative sexuality education negatively impacts these youth's relationships with both nonheterosexually-oriented peers as well as those heterosexual peers who are transgressive in terms of gender expression, sexual reputation, and in other ways that depart from social norms.

Race, social class, sexuality, and gender—and their intersections—have not been covered or infused within much of sexuality education. As comprehensive as the Sexuality Education Information Council of the United States has been, in terms of developing and advocating comprehensive school-based sexuality education programs, its published guidelines and curricula approach is from a "color blind" and "class blind" perspective. Given the heterogeneity of the United States and other nations, it is important to offer a truly **multicultural education** experience that is sensitive to the particular cultural backgrounds of youth. Given the plethora of sexual identities, expressions, and relationships, not to mention the vastness of cultural differences, a monolithic approach to sexuality education does not meet the needs of many youth—whether bisexual, heterosexual, homosexual, queer, or questioning.

In the United States, there continues to be a struggle to include LGBT issues in sexuality education as well as in the general curriculum. In some cases, these struggles have been successful in terms of advocating for LGBT youth. Massachusetts, for instance, has been a model for affording LGBT youth respect and protection. Among the advances are school policies that protect LGBT students from **harassment,** teacher training in diversity and crisis intervention, support groups for LGBT students, family education and speakers' bureaus and other structural changes to enhance the lives and well being of LGBT youth (Lipkin 1999). Other states, like South Carolina, however, forbid teachers from even uttering the word "homosexual" or, if instruction on homosexuality is given, requiring it be framed along negative, homophobic, or heterosexist lines (Earls, Fraser & Sumpter, 1992).

The most recent iteration of sexuality education in the United States occurred in the late 1990s following the passage of the Welfare Reform Act of 1996. As part of this federal legislation, millions of federal dollars were poured into abstinence-only sexuality education. For schools to receive federal funding for sexuality education, they must teach that sexual abstinence before marriage and faithful monogamy during marriage are expected standards and the only sure way of protecting against contracting sexual diseases and avoiding potential harmful emotional and physical consequences. To reinforce abstinence-only sexuality education and provide a curricular template for it, the Medical Institute for Sexual Health (MISH) published National Guidelines for Sexuality and Character Education, in the late 1990s. The authors of this document were ". . . almost exclusively from organizations that promote fear-based, abstinence-only programs, including Focus on the Family, Project Reality, the Education Guidance Institute, and Teen-Aid, Inc. . . . The MISH Guidelines include almost no information about **sexual orientation**; none of the developmental messages address this topic" (Mayer 1997, 14, 16).

These abstinence-based and fear-based sexuality education programs include such mottos as ". . . Control your urgin'–be a virgin, Don't be a louse—wait for your spouse, Do the right thing—wait for the ring, or Pet your dog– not your date" (Carroll and Wolpe 1996, 648). Many such programs have found their way into mainstream sexuality education efforts in the public schools (McKay 1998). An extremely popular abstinence-based program for junior high and middle schools, Sex Respect, has the overall message ". . . DON'T DO IT, and this message is strongly enforced. Teachers who use these materials are forbidden to discuss controversial issues, such as masturbation, homosexuality, birth control, or abortion" (Carroll and Wolpe 1996, 650).

As a corrective to this approach, more democratic educational measures are being proposed to reconceptualize sexuality education. Designed to be inclusive and more representative of the adolescent population as well as to challenge biological essentialism, which has dominated sexuality education since its inception, these approaches include critical pedagogies, feminist analysis, and **queer theory**.

Critical pedagogy not only challenges how topics are taught and what is taught, but explores the hegemonic representations and forms of knowledge. Such an approach interrogates, for instance, the white, middle-class, and heterosexual foundation of sexual knowledge. A feminist analysis challenges the often taken for granted **sexism** in sexuality education, particularly regarding the abstinence-only approach, which perpetuates traditional and confining gender roles. Feminist educators challenge the **stereotypes** about female sexual **desire** and sexual behavior, confront the longstanding culturally-based beliefs about women's sexuality, and advocate for women's reproductive rights. In the sexual sense, queer theory has challenged the static nature of **sexual identities** and highlights the complexity and ever-shifting nature of sexual and gender diversity. Queer theory makes it possible—as a theoretical and pedagogical tool—to ". . . deconstruct these sexual and gender binaries (deployed and reified through social text and grammar) that are the linchpins of heteronormativity" (Sears 1999, 6).

Bibliography

Campos, David. 2002. *Sex, Youth, and Sex Education: A Reference Handbook*. Santa Barbara, CA: ABC Clio.

Carroll, Janell L., and Paul R.Wolpe. 1996. *Sexuality and Gender in Society*. New York: HarperCollins.

Earls, Ruth, Joane Fraser, and Bambi Sumpter. 1992. "Sexuality Education: In Whose Interests?" In Pp. 300–327 *Sexuality and the Curriculum: The Politics and Practices of Sexuality Education*. Edited by James T. Sears. New York: Teachers College Press.

Francoeur, Robert T., and R. J. Noonan, eds. 2004. *International Encyclopedia of Sexuality*. New York & London: Continuum.

Haffner, Debra W. 1997. "What's Wrong with Abstinence-Only Sexuality Education Programs?" *SIECUS Report* 25, no. 4: 9–13.

Irvine, Janice M. 1995. *Sexuality Education across Cultures: Working with Differences*. San Francisco: Jossey-Bass.

Levine, Judith M. 2002. *Talk about Sex: The Battles Over Sex Education in the United States*. Berkeley: University of California Press.

Lipkin, Arthur. 1999. *Understanding Homosexuality, Changing Schools: A Text for Teachers, Counselors, and Administrators*. Boulder: Westview Press.

Mayer, Ruth. 1997. "MISH Publishes New Framework for Fear-Based, Abstinence-Only Education. *SIECUS Report* 25, no. 4: 14–17.

McKay, Alexander. 1998. *Sexual Ideology and Schooling: Towards Democratic Sexuality Education*. Albany: State University of New York Press.

Sears, James T., ed. 1992. *Sexuality and the Curriculum: The Politics and Practices of Sexuality Education*. New York: Teachers College Press.

———. 1997. "Centering Culture: Teaching for Critical Sexual Literacy Using the Sexual Diversity Wheel." *Journal of Moral Education* 26: 273–283.

———. 1999. "Teaching Queerly: Some Elementary Propositions." Pp. 3–14 in *Queering Elementary Education: Advancing Dialogue about Sexualities and Schooling*. Edited by William J. Letts and James T. Sears. Lanham, MD: Rowman and Littlefield.

Sexuality Information Education Council of the United States (SIECUS). 1996. *Guidelines for Comprehensive Sexuality Education: Kindergarten - 12th Grade*. 2nd. ed. New York: Author.

———. 2003, July 21. International Sexuality News & Resource Update 2, no. 13. Accessed November 24, 2004. http://www.siecus.org/inter/news/news0028.html.

Web Sites

Alan Guttmacher Institute. June 2005. Accessed June 22, 2005. http://www.agi-usa.org. Major nonprofit organization conducting policy analyses and research on sexuality issues. This site has an extensive publication list and article archives.

Sexuality Information Education Council of the United States. June 2005. Accessed June 22, 2005. http://www.siecus.org. Clearinghouse of information and an advocacy organization for comprehensive sexuality education.

Shepard, Matthew (1976–1998)

Amy K. Kilgard

Matthew Shepard was not an activist, but a queer-identified youth who was the victim of homophobic violence. In 1998, the horrific death of Shepard, who was tortured and killed by two other young men, sparked reactions throughout communities in Wyoming, around the United States, and throughout the world. The lasting reactions, from both young people and adults, have made his life and death a subject of historical significance. Shepard's murder became a focal point for activists advocating tolerance and an end to overt homophobic violence. Reactions in the media and in performance communities included efforts to educate and intervene,

See also Religious Fundamentalism.

particularly in the lives of students dealing with issues of sexuality, gender, and social identity. The play and Home Box Office (HBO) film, *The Laramie Project*, is an ongoing instance of this intervention. One extremist Christian minister used Shepard's life and death as platforms for his campaign of antigay speech and action. For many others, Shepard's life and death serve as focal points for understanding and reflecting upon the complexities of social **activism** in education. The Matthew Shepard Foundation promotes awareness of hate **crimes**, **discrimination**, **suicide**, HIV/**AIDS**, and other issues relevant to youth.

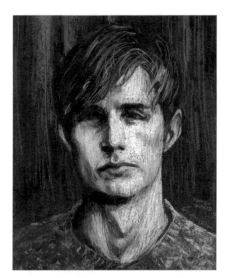

Matthew Shepard Portrait, Stephen J. Bertrand. © 2005 Stephen J. Bertrand, http://www. stephenbertrand.com

Matthew Shepard was born and raised in Casper, Wyoming. He spent his last high school years at a boarding school in Switzerland, learning Arabic and German, and developing a sense of himself as a world citizen. Shepard's parents knew that he was gay before his death and respected his honest but reserved approach to talking about his sexuality.

Shepard attended the University of Wyoming, studying foreign language with the hope of being a diplomat. He was open about his sexuality, attending a meeting of the university's Lesbian, Gay, Bisexual, and Transgender Association on the night of October 6. After the meeting, Shepard went to a bar where he met two young local men. They left together, drove him to a deserted place outside of town, robbed him, brutally beat him, tied him to a fence, and left him bleeding and barely breathing in the freezing cold, alone. Shepard was found by a bicyclist the next evening and was taken to a hospital where he never regained consciousness. He died a week later, on October 12, 1998. His two attackers were convicted of several counts including felony murder and sentenced to life in prison. Importantly, they were not convicted of a hate crime because no such statute existed in Wyoming at the time, nor does it yet.

After their son's death, Shepard's parents responded publicly by forming a charitable organization called The Matthew Shepard Foundation. Judy Shepard has become an active spokesperson, focusing on the importance of tolerance, acceptance, and open discussion about sexual diversity. The Matthew Shepard Foundation, devoted to issues relevant to youth such as the decision to "come out" and violence, provides information and resources for educators and students, including specific activities designed to foster conversation among young people about sexuality, **gender identity**, and social relationships.

Educators can use the events of Shepard's murder and Judy Shepard's call as starting points for small group discussions about students' personal experiences of **discrimination**. Teachers can also ask students to create projects, performances, or papers that explore their own and others' experiences, requiring more advanced students to link these experiences with larger social issues such as **homophobia**, hate crime legislation, or diversity. These educational practices are meaningful not only to **lesbian, gay, bisexual**, and **transgender youth** (LGBT) youth, but for all students.

In the wake of Shepard's death, hordes of media personnel and activists of many different perspectives descended upon Laramie and the surrounding communities.

The events of the murder, Shepard's funeral, the arraignments, protests, vigils, and eventually trials were reported globally. LGBT activists rallied around this terrible incident—many invoking his murder as a symbol of bigotry and hatred. People gathered in many cities calling for legislative reform—for the addition of hate crime legislation and for the end of homophobic violence.

Shepard's murder resulted in concrete resources for others to use in teaching and learning about diversity, **homophobia**, and violence. Perhaps the most widely-known artistic response is Moisés Kaufman's and the Tectonic Theater Project's play *The Laramie Project*. To develop this project, Kaufman and members of his theater company conducted several hundred interviews with Laramie residents about their experiences surrounding the murder. They then constructed a performance that showed some of the complexities of the issues involved and that reflected some hope for societal change. The play has been performed around the United States and is particularly popular on college campuses. *The Laramie Project* was made into a film produced by HBO, in 2002, which reached broader geographic and demographic audiences.

Several other artistic and scholarly responses are especially noteworthy. *Blood and Tears: Poems for Matthew Shepard* is a moving collection of poems published shortly after Shepard's death. Poets in this collection, including those who did not personally know Shepard, found inspiration and hope in writing about his life and death. *Losing Matt Shepard: Life and Politics in the Aftermath of Anti-Gay Murder* is an accessible scholarly account of the complexity of responses to Shepard's murder and to life in Wyoming afterward. Another scholarly volume whose contributors seek to make sense of and learn from these events is *From Hate Crimes to Human Rights: A Tribute to Matthew Shepard*. Essayists explore issues explicitly relating to hate crimes, human rights, and sexuality.

In addition to activists supporting hate crime legislation, tolerance, and acceptance, there was another vocal response to the events surrounding Matthew Shepard's murder. Extremist Christian minister Fred Phelps led rallies and protests in Laramie on several occasions, including during the funeral. During these events, he railed against LGBT people and their sexual practices. His speech, which many decried as hateful, often reached violent peaks. In the fall of 2003, Phelps again entered the spotlight when he insisted that he be allowed to erect a monument in a public park to Matthew Shepard in Shepard's hometown. He explained that the words, "Matthew Shepard, Entered Hell October 12, 1998, in Defiance of God's Warning: 'Thou shalt not lie with mankind as with womankind; it is abomination. Leviticus 18:22,'" were to be inscribed on the monument. Phelps claimed that the statue must be allowed as an example of free religious expression alongside the Laramie's monument proclaiming the Biblical Ten Commandments. The town successfully fought his claim by relocating the commandments to private property.

Bibliography

Gibson, Scott, ed. 1999. *Blood and Tears: Poems for Matthew Shepard*. New York: Painted Leaf Press.

Kaufman, Moisés. 2001. *The Laramie Project*. New York: Vintage Press.

Loffreda, Beth. 2000. *Losing Matt Shepard: Life and Politics in the Aftermath of Anti-Gay Murder*. New York: Columbia University Press.

Swigonski, Mary E., Robin Sakina Mama, and Kelly Ward, eds. 2001. *From Hate Crimes to Human Rights: A Tribute to Matthew Shepard*. Binghamton, NY: Harrington Park Press.

Web Sites

Matthew Shepard Foundation. November 2004. Accessed December 19, 2004. http://www.matthewshepard.org. Provides extensive information about LGBT issues including a resource guide which could be useful for educators.

The New York Times on the Web. The Laramie Project Archives. 2002. Accessed December 19, 2004. http://www.nytimes.com/ads/marketing/laramie/index.html. Republishes some of the important newspaper accounts about the events surrounding Shepard's death.

Tolerance.org. The Laramie Project. 2004. Accessed December 19, 2004. http://www.tolerance.org/laramie. Describes many successful programs that deal with diversity and tolerance. This is a useful resource for educators because it provides concrete activities and suggestions for incorporating diversity into curricula.

Single-Sex Schools

Michael J. Maher

Single-sex school is an educational institution, usually at the secondary or college levels, only for boys (or young men) or only for girls (or young women). However, in countries where girls have often been denied formal education such as part of the Middle East and Africa, schools have sometimes been *de facto* all-male schools. The most common justifications for single-sex education have been the preparation for the different social roles men and women play and the distraction that the other gender could have in a school setting. More recently, advocates of all-female schools have argued that these schools present young women with a wider range of female role models. In Western societies, single-sex schools have become almost a rarity, but there have been efforts to return to single-sex secondary schools in the U.S. public educational systems. Single-sex schooling seems to produce opposite environments in all male-schools and all-female schools in terms of being welcoming and safe spaces for queer youth and young adults; all-female schools tend to be welcoming places for **lesbian youth**, whereas all-male schools tend to be unwelcoming and even dangerous places for **gay youth**.

One form of single-sex schooling has been the boarding school, usually reserved for the elite—young people destined to play some special future role in society, as warriors, priests, or members of the upper **social class**. Some have observed that the correlation between single-sex education and elite status has the effect of promoting socially conservative values and places a high priority on conformity, contributing to a strong pressure for LGBT students to remain in the closet (Maher 2001). However, some boarding schools do have **educational policies** protecting LGBT students and teachers. Ironically, boarding schools have also been used as a tool to control and reform children who were viewed as unruly and dangerous. Recent study has shown the prevalence of institutions for "troubled" girls in **Ireland** (although hardly schools), depicted in the 2002 film *The Magdalene Sisters*, and the export of similar institutions to **Australia**.

See also Adolescent Sexualities; Bullying; Crush; Films, Youth and Educators in; Mentoring; School Safety and Safe School Zones; United Kingdom, LGBT Youth and Issues in; Women's Colleges.

Single-sex boarding schools have a long history. In the sixth century BCE, Sappho founded her school for young women on the Greek Island of Lesbos, from which the word "lesbian" is derived. Ancient Greeks also promoted single-sex boarding schools for boys, where homosexual activity among students and between students and teachers was celebrated. In medieval Europe, education for the social elite and for those preparing for religious life was conducted often in monasteries and convents, where homosexuality among students was also common. Interesting depictions of this life can be seen in the 1986 U.S. film *The Name of the Rose* (1986) and the *The Devils* (UK 1971). In medieval **Japan**, Samurai culture involved the education of boys in monasteries and in warrior dwellings, which also involved sexual activity between boys and men (Boswell 1980; Duberman, Vicinus, and Chauncey 1989).

Tom Brown's Schooldays, the story of a seventeenth-century boy at Rugby School in England, describes close, deep boyhood friendships. It also describes older boys dominating younger boys, calling them "faggots." Some believed that these relationships of dominance included sexual dominance, and it is from this context that the term "faggot" began being applied to gay men. Studies of boys' diaries from this period demonstrate that sexual activity was common and tolerated as long as it was discrete. Set in the 1930s, the 1984 UK film, *Another Country*, depicted life at a British boys' boarding school where discrete homosexual activity was commonplace. British boarding schools for girls and young women from this period display a similar history; close friendships among teachers, between teachers and pupils, and among students were celebrated; the accusation of lesbianism was common (Edwards 1995). Such an accusation at a Scottish girls school, in 1810, was the basis for Lillian Hellman's 1930s stage play, *The Children's Hour*, made first into the 1936 film *These Three* and then, in 1961, under the original

Another Country (1984). Directed by Marek Kanievska. Shown: Rupert Everett (as Guy Bennett), Colin Firth (as Tommy Judd). Showtime/Photofest

title. Oscar Wilde wrote of homosexuality in his secondary boarding school, and Stephen Fry, the actor who portrayed him in *Wilde* (UK 1997), also described his British boarding school experiences in *Moab Is My Washpot*.

The **Catholic** seminary is a particular form of boarding school where young men are trained to become priests, which has dealt with special issues around homosexuality. Evidence indicates as many as 50 percent or more of Catholic seminarians and priests are gay (Maher 2002). The Church has had some difficulty dealing with this although it dates back centuries. Until recent decades, Catholic seminaries had extremely strict rules forbidding students from forming close friendships, ever being alone with another student or being publicly nude even when bathing. With changes in the 1960s and 1970s, these rules were thrown out for the most part. The result seemed to be frequent sexual relationships among seminarians and concerns about **sexual abuse** by Catholic priests.

In Western countries today, single-sex schools are often religiously affiliated schools, mostly Catholic schools. Orthodox Jews and Muslims often also prefer single-sex schools as well. Recent journalistic accounts of Middle Eastern schooling, which is often exclusively for boys, has revealed that homosexual relationships among boys and between boys and men are common. In a comparison between recent graduates of Catholic coeducational secondary schools and Catholic single-sex secondary schools in the United States, graduates of single-sex schools (both male and female) expressed more homophobic attitudes than graduates of coeducational schools. Single-sex school graduates were more likely to view homosexuality as a disorder and immoral as well as less deserving of justice, respect, and friendship. They also were less likely to view gay-bashing, verbal abuse, and violence as unacceptable or to believe that the Church had any responsibility to welcome and protect LGBT people (Maher 2001).

Twentieth century educational theorists, notably **G. Stanley Hall**, argued that boys and girls were essentially different. And because of this natural phenomenon, educators would educate boys and girls differently and separately. In the case of boys, this meant harnessing their more aggressive tendencies and fostering a **school climate** of extreme masculinity. At the same time, a homosexual stigma has grown around all-male schools. The result is often a culture of **homophobia** in which students prove their heterosexuality by publicly demonstrating heterosexual **desire**, engaging in aggressively brutal **sports** such as rugby, and disdaining anything or anyone gay. GBT students in these schools, often fearing exclusion, **harassment**, or violence, may engage in these same activities (Maher 2001; Walker 1988). From a study conducted in Australia, British sociologist David Plummer (1999) has argued that gay-bashing serves as a type of initiation into manhood for adolescent males. Its cinematic equivalent is most aptly set in the American South. The 1957 U.S. film, *The Strange One*, depicts the interplay of dominance and homophobia within a young men's military academy.

Various proponents of all-female secondary schools and colleges argue that the environment and culture of these schools promote greater academic success for girls and young women, allowing them to act out of traditional gender roles or to achieve liberation from sexism (Lee, Marks, and Byrd 1994). Interestingly, the **Women's Movement** of the 1970s did not produce a growth in all-female schooling despite these arguments. In fact, when many elite all-male colleges and universities began to enroll women, the focus for "liberated" young women became enrolling in elite colleges and universities that had been all-male rather than continuing to support elite all-female colleges and universities, which began to be identified as archaic reminders of past sexist segregation. The same trend happened at the level of secondary education in the 1990s. Lesbian youth who have attended all-female schools tend to see them as more welcoming environments for all the reasons mentioned above and because they allow girls and young women to build friendships more easily than at coeducational schools. Professional staff at all-female schools often believes that the environment is more welcoming to lesbian girls and young women because they integrate liberation issues into the **curriculum**. While some lesbian women who attended all-female schools have reported a stigma associated with the schools—that there are many lesbian students—this seems not to have a strong effect on the students enrolled in those schools.

Bibliography

Boswell, John. 1980. *Christianity, Social Tolerance, and Homosexuality: Gay People in Western Europe from the Beginning of the Christian Era to the Fourteenth Century.* Chicago: University of Chicago Press.

Brutsaert, Herman. 1999. "Coeducation and Gender Identity Formation: A Comparative Analysis of Secondary Schools in Belgium." *British Journal of Sociology of Education* 20, no. 3: 343–355.

Duberman, Martin B., Mary Vicinus, and George Chauncey, eds. 1989. *Hidden from History: Reclaiming Our Gay and Lesbian Past.* New York: Meridian.

Edwards, Elizabeth. 1995. "Homoerotic Friendship and College Principals, 1880–1960." *Women's History Review* 4, no. 2: 149–163.

Hickson, Alisdare. 1995. *The Poisoned Bowl: Sex Repression and the Public School System.* London: Constable.

Lee, Valerie E., Helen M. Marks, and Tina Byrd. 1994. "Sexism in Single-Sex and Coeducational Independent Secondary School Classrooms." *Sociology of Education* 67, no. 2: 92–120.

Maher, Michael J. 2001. *Being Gay and Lesbian in a Catholic High School: Beyond the Uniform.* Binghamton, NY: Haworth Press.

———. 2002. "Openly Addressing the Reality: Homosexuality and Catholic Seminary Policies." *Religion & Education* 29, no. 2: 49–68.

Plummer, David. 1999. *One of the Boys: Masculinity, Homophobia, and Modern Manhood.* Binghamton, NY: Haworth Press.

Walker, J. C. 1988. "The Way Men Act: Dominant and Subordinate Male Cultures in an Inner-City School." *British Journal of Sociology of Education* 9, no. 1: 3–18.

Web Sites

Boarding School Review. June 2005. Accessed June 16, 2005. http://www.boardingschool review.com. Rates the quality of U.S. boarding schools with searching available by various criteria.

The Girls' Schools Association. 2005. Accessed June 16, 2005. http://www.gsa.uk.com. Information on UK all-female secondary schools, including a search engine for easy access and teacher vacancies.

International Boys' Schools Coalition. 2005. Hammock Publishing. Accessed June 16, 2005. http://www.boysschoolscoalition.org. Promotes the advantages of all-male primary and secondary schools with this site that features conference information and publications.

The National Coalition of Girls' Schools. June 2005. Accessed June 16, 2005. http://www.ncgs.org/ The Information exchange and advocate for U.S. all-female secondary schools.

Women's College Coalition. 2004. Accessed June 16, 2005. http://www.womenscolleges.org. Acts as an information exchange and advocate for all-female colleges in the United States and Canada.

Sissy Boy

Will Letts

In the eyes of society, sissy boys are gender nonconforming. Even if these boys don't perceive themselves in that way, they do not fit the dominant (hegemonic) configurations of **gender identities**. Sissy boys embody qualities that societies label as feminine and childlike: timidity, reticence, dependence. Their portrayal or enactment of

See also Asia, LGBT Youth and Issues in; Dance, Teaching of; Literature, Early Childhood; Men's Studies; Multiple Genders; Physical Education, Teaching of; Popular Culture; Sports, Gay men in; Tong-Zhi; Transgender.

masculinity is often read by others as nonmasculine, effeminate, and in violation of narrowly prescribed configurations of how boys are meant to act. This failure to enact proper, accepted forms of masculinity has resulted in a societal disavowal of "sissified" gender performances. This is a particularly Western construction of acceptable masculinity, for different cultures value different attributes and behaviors in men and boys. Situated at the intersection of misogyny (hatred of women) and **homophobia** (irrational fear of homosexuality), the sissy boy is an identity that breaks the rules. Because of this, it is subjected to relentless surveillance in order to enforce the "proper" expression of a boy's gender—namely, **compulsory heterosexuality** and an appropriate portrayal of masculinity (Bergling 2001; Steinberg, Epstein, and Johnson 1997; Thorne 1994). And although the enactment of these "rule-breaking" identities has consequences throughout society, they are particularly subjected to policing and reprisals in schools, making schools difficult and often intolerable places for sissy boys to be.

We are all familiar with the requisite vocabulary—mincing, fag, prance, girl, poof, wimp, sashaying, float, **queer**, flaming, swish, pansy, flamboyant, fairy, nancy-boy, flit—used to describe the actions and embodiment of the sissy boy. We have childhood memories of boys like this (or maybe we were one), and public talk about sissies still abounds. We are also well-versed in its popular cultural manifestations in adult characters: Big Gay Al on *South Park*, Smithers on *The Simpsons*, Jack on *Will & Grace*, Emmitt on *Queer as Folk*, and all of the "boys" on *Queer Eye for the Straight Guy*. But the identity category of "sissy" is much more complex than this stereotyped list of words implies, and more diverse (and contested) than these television images of caricatured out and closeted gay men might suggest. And cultural representations of sissies as children and young adults are far less prevalent, particularly sympathetic or positive representations. A few notable exceptions are young Ludovic in the **film** *Ma Vie en Rose* (France 1997), Tobias Wolff's *This Boy's Life: A Memoir* (USA 1993) and Augusten Burrough's *Running With Scissors: A Memoir* (USA 2002). Rarely have our feelings about this image of (non)masculinity been interrogated. Rarely have we examined where societal angst about such a prevalent but vexed identity formation comes from and why it persists.

Societal understandings of sissies are far from coherent. A continuum exists from sissy as slightly effeminate boy to sissy as male who completely rejects his birth sex in favor of living as a female (Green 1987). In 1980, the American Psychiatric Association removed homosexuality from its *Diagnostic and Statistics Manual of Mental Disorders* (DSM III) and replaced it with **Gender Identity Disorder** in childhood, or what was commonly called the sissy boy syndrome. The syndrome has two components: strong and persistent cross-gender identification and an ongoing discomfort with one's sex and accompanying gender role expectations. Critics of the inclusion of this "syndrome" in the DSM III argue that it is a thinly veiled antigay attempt to "straighten up" boys who don't enact the societal norms of masculinity (Sedgwick 1993).

In more colloquial usage, sissy can be a synonym for a "cry-baby," a "scaredy-cat," or a "mama's boy" in the young. This is meant to emphasize (feminine) qualities of weakness, vulnerability, and passivity, expressing scorn for them. Some attribute an inability of boys to separate from their mothers as contributing to the production of sissies, while others simply view their behavior as falling outside of what society will tolerate in enactments of masculinity. As Barrie Thorne (1994, 111)

Running Water (NC), circa 1982, was one of the earliest "fairy" communal retreats for gay and bisexual men who embraced their feminity and sought spiritual connections through rural living. Courtesy of Ron Lambe

notes, "The **tomboy** and the sissy stand at and help define the symbolic margins of dichotomous and asymmetric gender difference; the label 'sissy' suggests that a boy has ventured too far into the contaminating 'feminine'." But unlike its counterpart tomboy, however, sissy is imbued with unremittingly negative connotations. Still, as indicated above, sissies are enjoying some popularity in popular culture, even if many of these are stereotypical portrayals.

Many gay men report living childhoods as sissies. But this is far from determining a direct, causal link between being a sissy and growing up gay, despite the extended analysis of Richard Green (1987). In fact, because the label sissy is applied so widely to any boy who does not embody traditional norms of masculinity, which includes being straight, it is no surprise that many gay men can recall the sting of being labeled a sissy. The label was used to publicly mark their difference in a disapproving way.

Sissies are often the recipients of **bullying** and other forms of violence, and can even sometimes be thought to invite the bullying because of their transgression of gender norms (Gordon 1994; Human Rights Watch 2001; Rofes 1995). They become the lightening rods for the anxieties of others (and sometimes even themselves) around issues of transgressing gender norms or not behaving properly, like a "real" boy should. In her research, Barrie Thorne (1994, 117) found that, "a boy who seems 'girlish,' for example, because he plays girls' games and/or likes to be with girls in a way that is not flirtatious or teasing, may be called 'fag' or 'faggot,' as well as 'sissy'." Their gendered selves incite resentment because of the disdain and even mocking of masculinity that their effeminacy represents (or is seen to represent). The stinging shame of being labeled or called a sissy lingers long after the event that evokes such a label (Bergling 2001).

Starting in early **childhood** and primary education, teachers and parents can open up the topic of **gender role** expectations and expressions by using a storybook as a stimulus. Several picture books tackle the topic in familiar and accessible ways. These books include de Paola's *Oliver Button is a Sissy*, van Emst's *Herbie Dances*, Zolotow's *William's Doll*, and Caple's *The Wimp*. These books use different scenarios as entry points into discussions about what boys are expected to be and ways that peers attempt to enforce those expectations. All four also offer strategies for boys to safely exert their masculinity, whatever form it takes, and suggest ways that adults and other children can play a role. As with any text, it is important to remember that even books such as these can unwittingly serve to reinforce **stereotypes** if not read critically. For example, Bronwyn Davies (1989) found that an uncritical reading of *Oliver Button is a Sissy* enabled children to strengthen their rigid sense of appropriate gender roles rather than challenge them. Thus, these texts aren't benign, but rather must be read with a critical eye toward affirming difference and challenging stereotypes.

These children's books also create the possibility of another line of intervention around these issues: discussion about bullying and antibullying programs. These programs include frank discussions with children about difference, and why bullies are so threatened and annoyed by peers who are different, and what can be done to help bullies to stop bullying.

Rofes (1995) challenges schools to reexamine the hidden and explicit ways in which they cultivate and praise certain kinds of traditionally masculine achievement in boys and willfully ignore other kinds of achievement that are not seen as sufficiently masculine. The valorization that star athletes receive and the relative invisibility afforded the artistic, musical, and dramatic achievements of other boys evidence this phenomenon. Boys are meant to be athletes, not cheerleaders. And when their participation in the arts is encouraged, they are still restricted in how it is able to manifest itself. Boys play brass instruments and drums, not flutes and harps; boys express their creativity through metal work, not through cooking or sewing; boys play dashing, heterosexualized lead roles, not girly comical characters, unless they do it with the appropriate dose of limp-wristed, hypereffeminate self-mocking. Educators and parents, however, can challenge and broaden the mores that determine who children can be to accommodate and affirm the range of roles that boys—and girls—embody and enact.

Bibliography

Bergling, Tim. 2001. *Sissyphobia: Gay Men and Effeminate Behaviour*. Binghamton, NY: Harrington Park Press.

Caple, Kathy. 1994. *The Wimp*. Boston: Houghton Mifflin.

Davies, Bronwyn. 1989. *Frogs and Snails and Feminist Tales*. Sydney: Allen and Unwin.

Gordon, Lenore. 1994. "What Do We Say When We Hear 'Faggot'?" Pp. 86–87 in *Rethinking our Classrooms: Teaching for Equity and Justice*. Edited by Bill Bigelow, Linda Christensen, Stan Karp, Barbara Miner, and Bob Peterson. Milwaukee: Rethinking Schools.

Green, Richard. 1987. *The "Sissy Boy" Syndrome and the Development of Homosexuality*. New Haven, CT: Yale University Press.

Rofes, Eric. 1995. "Making Our Schools Safe for Sissies." Pp. 79–84 in *The Gay Teen: Educational Practice and Theory for Lesbian, Gay, and Bisexual Adolescents*. Edited by Gerald Unks. New York: Routledge.

Rottnek, Matthew, ed. 1999. *Sissies and Tomboys: Gender Nonconformity and Homosexual Childhoo*d. New York: New York University.

Sedgwick, Eve Kosofsky. 1993. "How to Bring Your Kids Up Gay: The War on Effeminate Boys." Pp. 154–166 in *Tendencies*. Durham, NC: Duke University Press.

Steinberg, Deborah L., Debbie Epstein, and Richard Johnson, eds. 1997. *Border Patrols: Policing the Boundaries of Heterosexuality*. London: Cassell.

Thorne, Barrie. 1994. *Gender Play: Girls and Boys in School*. New Brunswick, NJ: Rutgers University Press.

Van Emst, Charlotte. 2000. *Herbie Dances*. London: Red Fox.

Zolotow, Charlotte. 1972. *William's Doll*. New York: HarperCollins Publishers.

Web Sites

Anti-Bullying Network. June 2005. Accessed June 22, 2005. http://www.antibullying.net/index.html. Based at the University of Edinburgh, this site was created so that teachers, parents, and young people can share ideas about how bullying should be tackled. Includes sections for young people, parents and families, and school staff, with discussion papers, advice, and reading lists.

Human Rights Watch. 2001. Hatred in the Hallways. Accessed June 22, 2005. http://www.hrw.org/reports/2001/uslgbt. Report documents incidents of violence and discrimination against LGBT students in U.S. schools (many of whom would be labelled sissies), but it also makes extensive recommendations for change to stakeholder groups including the federal government, local governments, school districts, and individual schools.

New South Wales Department of Education and Training. 2004. Bullying—who needs it? Accessed June 22, 2005. http://www.det.nsw.edu.au/antibullying/. This site, hosted by the southern hemisphere's largest school employer, contains useful information including possible intervention strategies, examples of programs being run in schools to confront and combat bullying, and links to other programs in Australia, New Zealand, and Europe.

Social Class

Ray Misson

Social class is the grouping of people according to their wealth and/or their power in society. Social class determines, to a large extent, how we are able to live, because it means that we have a certain amount of buying power, and, thus, we are presented with a particular range of life choices. There are also different expectations placed on how we will play out our lives depending on our social class. Our ways of thinking are shaped by these expectations and can limit what we are actually able to achieve. This is as true with regard to sexuality as in any other area of life. The treatment of young people identifying as lesbian, gay, bisexual, or transgender will vary depending on how these sexualities are conceived in their social setting. In playing out alternative sexualities, affluence can bring comfortable

See also Critical Social Theory; Identity Politics; Music, Teaching of; Workplace Issues; Youth Culture.

private spaces, from the residential college to the tropical gay resort, that are denied to young people struggling to make enough money to live on or who are unemployed. Most positive media images of gay life, in particular, are based on affluent lifestyles: The greater visibility and acceptance of homosexuality we are currently enjoying is undoubtedly, at least in part, economically motivated.

Although the word was used well before Karl Marx to denote the social status of different groups, the way we understand social class these days is inevitably colored by his theorization. In Marx's thinking, class (as virtually everything in society) was economic in its origins. People were disposed in classes in terms of their relation to the means of production (the land, the mines, the factories); at its simplest, there were those who owned them (the upper class) and those who had to live by selling their labor to the owners (the working class).

Crucial to Marx was the idea that where one was placed in the social system determined how one saw the world. In the words of his famous statement from the Preface to *A Contribution to the Critique of Political Economy*, "It is not the consciousness of men that determines their being, but on the contrary, their social being that determines their consciousness" (Marx and Engels 1968, 182). The determination of consciousness is the work of ideology, manifested through social institutions, such as religion, media, family, and (very powerfully) education, built above the economic base in what Marx calls the superstructure of society. The purpose of these institutions is to produce a way of thinking, an ideology, that makes the social order seem only right and natural, allowing the economic workings of society to continue. As the economic base evolves, new relations of production come into place; the class structure will change and the ideology of society will change (either through evolution or through revolution) to validate the changes. Thus, as societies move from an industrial age, with its emphasis on production, to the information age and beyond, with its emphasis on consumption, there has been a corresponding ideological shift from a concern with hard work and responsibility to a concern with self-fulfilment and personal well-being. This transformation has had a profound impact on the social positioning of homosexuality and LGBT youth.

Among the four major "identity" areas—gender, class, ethnicity, and sexuality—social class remains surprisingly unexamined. Nevertheless, it is basic and closely articulated with the other three. This can be at the very simple level of co-occurrence: nondominant ethnicity is likely to go along with economic disadvantage, for example. More subtly, it can be at the level of an aspect of identity being conceived and played out differently, depending on class positioning: A **lesbian youth** who works in a supermarket is likely to perform her sexuality in a different way than one who joins a law firm.

Thus, **sexual identity** is constructed differently for different classes. There are two aspects worth considering. First, social positioning very powerfully determines how attraction to the same gender can be played out. If a young person is living in a **rural** community in a strictly traditional family structure, the arena for expressing same-sex attraction is severely limited. Homosexual encounters are usually furtive and fraught with danger: The notion of "being gay," as we think of it in twenty-first century **urban** terms, is impossible. If one aspires to this ideal of the gay life, then the only possibility is to move out. However, the success with which that can be done is also determined economically. Most LGBT youth moving to the city do not readily get jobs that sustain a glamorously gay lifestyle, and they often find they surprisingly miss family and community relationships, however problematic.

The second aspect is that different classes are likely to have different views of what a homosexual, bisexual, or transgender person is. Since sexuality is so closely related to gender, different gender ideals in themselves can produce very different conceptions of sexuality. If a lesbian couple fall into the butch/femme pairing, they will play out their sexuality differently if the model is of protective male and needy woman, or of dominant male and submissive wife.

It might also be that homosexuality is seen differently because it violates specific class norms. For a **gay youth** from a lower socioeconomic group, for example, male homosexuality could be violating a particular vision of physically assertive masculinity, whereas for those from the middle-income suburbs, the primary violation could be of the norm of the respectable heterosexual family. In contrast, maintaining one's upper-class position may require heterosexual marriage, but also allow for discrete same-gender relations. Whereas homosexuality and **bisexuality** may find zones of toleration in various social class groups, individuals who cross genders are more likely to be treated with discomfort, since they resist the seemingly natural attribution to a particular gender. So much of our social interaction is based on assumptions arising from the gender of those with whom we are interacting that the ambiguity of the **transgender youth** makes for unease, which tends to be resolved either in mockery or rejection.

These differences across social classes have implications for educational programs aimed at countering **discrimination** against sexual minorities. If students from different socioeconomic backgrounds are constructing their sexual attitudes in terms of different images that LGBT people offend, successful programs need to address this. If the major transgression is seen to be against family values, for example, then a program targeting tolerance of deviation from gender norms is not likely to produce the desired shift in attitudes.

The particular complexities of the relationship between social class and sexuality is due, in large part, to the fact that lesbian and gay people can so easily "pass," that is, be read as heterosexual. This means that a person who is **passing** can, insofar as one does not allow the minority sexuality to show, simply take all the particular social class benefits or disadvantages. The price, however, is the negative effect of constant and vigilant repression, and/or the double life of seeking out ways to perform one's sexuality in secret, often at society's edges. From E. M. Forster's *Maurice* to Tony Kushner's *Angels in America,* many such stories have been told through **literature**.

It is perhaps the clandestine, even criminal, nature of homosexuality historically that can give the impression that it exists outside considerations of class. However, wealth brings greater geographical mobility and, perhaps, greater discretionary latitude, as exemplified in the youthful Lord Alfred Douglas, the one-time lover of Oscar Wilde. It also brings greater ability to recompense for sexual favors, which historically the male homosexual upper class has taken advantage of. In the twenty-first century, the flip side of the closeted businessperson seeking casual sex is the plight of the significant underclass of young people, often driven out of home by a situation made intolerable because of their homosexuality, who can only survive through **sex work**, be it for money or shelter.

It is extraordinarily difficult for us to understand current economic and ideological shifts, Marx believed, because we are so much part of them and their very nature is hidden. It is only retrospectively that we can understand the full significance of these shifts and so any contemporary discussion of class is tentative. One reason we tend to view social class as less important these days is that class boundaries have become so fluid. There is greater individual mobility between class groupings. A hundred years ago, it might have made some sense to talk about lower, middle, and upper classes, but, at least in **urban** Western societies, the distinction has become less and less meaningful. This is not because we are living in a classless society—far from it—but because class alignments are now so complex.

Social class depends on economic capital but, even more today, on cultural capital: the kind of school one attends, along with the different curricula, pedagogies, and classmates one is likely to encounter; the type of job one gets, such as glamour jobs in advertising or computing, that carry prestige often beyond the salaries they pay. Such jobs imply a certain lifestyle, too, and the notion of lifestyle choice complicates the notion of class, although maybe it could be said that one of the major class divisions these days is between those who can afford to choose their lifestyles and those who cannot.

In terms of Marx's theorization of the economic basis of social positioning, the greater visibility and acceptance of homosexuality at the beginning of the twenty-first century deserves some contemplation. Even though these advances are welcomed and celebrated, we might ask what economic purposes they serve. If we think of some of the shifts in late capitalism, it is not hard to see the advantage of allowing homosexuals a respectable economic place. The major shift over the last few decades in westernized capitalist economies has been from an emphasis on production to one on consumption. Goods are produced more easily and plentifully, and the service industries, such as hospitality and tourism have burgeoned and become central to the economy. It is a commodity culture. Nuclear families with limited budgets, producing children who will become workers, are needed less than are avid consumers—and homosexual people are considered or constructed as spectacular consumers. Advertisements, particularly for luxury items such as high-end liquor and clothing, will often be open to a gay reading, or there will be lesbian and/or gay versions of ads developed specifically for the gay press. Gay tourism is a major industry, as a glance at any of the gay travel guides will show. Many restaurants are kept afloat by a gay clientele. The expensive business of house renovation and interior decoration are encouraged as gay pastimes and glamorized in television shows, as are dance parties for which one needs a supply of designer drugs. All this depends on money. Gay men and lesbians are in some ways more likely to be affluent than the heterosexual community (as long as they are not economically discriminated against) because they are less likely to have the expenses that come with children and family, although there is the increasing phenomenon of LGBT **parents**: the so-called "gaby boom." But even this might be seen as a promoted lifestyle choice, opening up a new range of products for gay consumption.

LGBT people are also tending to congregate in particular areas. We see frequent references, even in the mainstream press, to the "gay community" and the "gay lifestyle;" a money-spending community with a lifestyle based on consumption of high-priced commodities. The homogenization of lesbian and gay people implied by these terms makes invisible a great deal of difference, especially in social class. Many people from sexual minorities work in low-paid jobs or are unemployed and their sexuality is lived out rather differently, probably less openly and certainly less comfortably.

Teaching against **discrimination** and supporting the visibility of sexual diversity, while doing a great deal of good for queer youth, also helps create the conditions for the economy to exploit the commodification of gay life by increasing tolerance so that LGBT people can be more openly targeted as a consumer market. Teachers interested in critical pedagogy may feel uncomfortable at the thought that they are complicit with the economic status quo. In some ways it is inevitable, but it highlights the importance of elevating an awareness of class in the classroom. To discuss sexuality (or gender or ethnicity) without considering the shaping power of class is to simplify the complexities enormously. A simple exercise asking students to rewrite a story about an LGBT character, placing the character in different socio-economic circumstances and then analyzing the changes will show a great deal about both homosexuality and class—and the relationship between them.

On the positive side, the economic significance of the current visibility of LGBT people means that any conservative backlash against the freeing-up of attitudes is not likely to be successful: economically too much would be lost.

Bibliography

Day, Gary. 2001. *Class*. London/New York: Routledge.
Gluckman, Amy, and Betsy Reed, eds. 1997. *Homo Economics: Capitalism, Community and Lesbian and Gay Life*. New York and London: Routledge.
Mac an Ghaill, Mairtin. 1994. *The Making of Men: Masculinities, Sexualities and Schooling*. Buckingham: Open University Press.
Marx, Karl, and Frederick Engels. 1968. *Selected Works*. London: Lawrence Wishart.
Sinfield, Alan. 1998. *Gay and After*. London: Serpent's Tail.

Social Work

Brent E. Cagle

The profession of social work is involved in the entire spectrum of services to youth and families at various systems levels including individual, family, group, community, and organization; thus, social workers potentially have a major impact on the lives of **lesbian, gay, bisexual**, and **transgender** (LGBT)—or **queer**—youth. Social workers serve in diverse settings such as schools, child welfare agencies, mental health centers, juvenile justice programs, for-profit and nonprofit human service organizations, government agencies, and private practices. They interact with queer youth and educators both directly as service providers and indirectly as **administrators**, consultants, community organizers, and policymakers. As defined by the International Federation of Social Workers (IFSW), the social work profession promotes social change, problem solving in human relationships, and the empowerment and liberation of people to enhance well-being. Using theories of human behavior and social systems, social work intervenes at the points where people interact with their environment. Principles of human rights and social justice are fundamental to the profession.

Professional social workers are regulated by licensing and certification requirements and by nationally and internationally recognized "codes of ethics." The ethical

See also Community LGBT Youth Groups; Homophobia; Licensure; Professional Educational Organizations; Professionalism; Secondary Schools, LGBT; Youth, At-Risk.

code of the IFSW states that **sexual orientation** is an unacceptable basis for **discrimination** and one that social workers should act to prevent and eliminate. Similar statements appear in the codes of various national organizations including the National Association of Social Workers in the United States, the British Association of Social Workers in the United Kingdom, the Australian Association of Social Workers, and the Canadian Association of Social Workers, among others. Many national and international social work organizations also address appropriate forms of therapy for use with queer people, stating that social workers should not engage in reparative or conversion therapies aimed at "changing" the sexual orientation of queer people because the therapies may be harmful and do not withstand empirical validation.

Within the educational system, social workers interact with school personnel, including educators, counselors, and administrators, as well as with queer youth and families. Some school systems employ social workers at every school. In other places, through arrangements with mental health or other community programs, social workers are on-site or regularly visit schools. Roles of school-based social workers may include: educating school personnel, families, and youth about queer youth issues; providing information, referrals, and direct therapeutic intervention for queer youth and their families; conducting group work focusing on topics of interest to queer youth such as positive self-image and violence prevention; and advocating for and with queer youth within the school setting, the family, and the community for inclusive **educational policies** and programs such as antiharassment initiatives, curricular inclusion of queer issues, and **gay–straight alliances**.

Child welfare is another system where educators, queer youth, and social work intersect. Educators are mandated reporters of child abuse and neglect and may interact with social workers who practice in the child welfare system as investigators of abuse and neglect, or who work with families to improve conditions after substantiations of abuse and neglect are made. Social workers work with queer youth in out-of-home care, including foster families, group homes, and shelters, and as adoption workers in the child welfare system, as well. Social workers may serve as advocates for queer youth and queer youth issues within the child welfare system, providing education and information on queer youth issues to other service providers, individuals and families, and the family court system.

In the mental health and juvenile justice systems, social workers serve in a number of positions such as administrators, court counselors, therapists, in-home workers, and case managers. They work with queer youth individually, with families, and in youth group settings. They, too, are involved in administrative positions that impact queer youth through programming and policymaking. Social workers often work on multidisciplinary teams that include educators and other professionals to better serve the needs of queer youth and their families.

In the past few decades, social workers have been involved in the founding and maintaining of community-based organizations with programs and services specifically designed for queer youth. One of the oldest and largest organizations is the Hetrick-Martin Institute in New York City, founded in 1979, which provides services to meet basic needs of queer youth, including shelter, food, and clothing; as well as case management services, health and wellness programs, street outreach, counseling, after school programs, and job readiness preparation. The Harvey Milk High School, which serves nearly 200 at-risk youth each school year, emerged from the Institute. Community-based queer youth organizations, founded or maintained by social workers, have grown exponentially and exist in cities as diverse as Seattle, Indianapolis, and Charlotte.

Not everyone who has the title of social worker is a professionally trained social worker with a social work degree. Without proper training, workers may not be exposed to the theory, knowledge, and skills that distinguish social work as a profession. In the United States, baccalaureate and master's programs in social work are accredited by the Council on Social Work Education (CSWE), which publishes a document called *Educational Policy and Accreditation Standards* (EPAS). Professional social workers are educated in undergraduate and graduate social work programs at colleges and universities around the world.

Social work is unique among the helping professions in its emphasis on both person and environment in assessment, intervention, and advocacy; its focus on vulnerable and oppressed populations; its strengths-based approach to practice which recognizes human worth, dignity, and self-determination; and its commitment to promoting social justice so that resources and opportunities are made available for all members of society.

The International Association of Schools of Social Work (IASS), an international association of institutions of social work education, supports social work curricula which fosters appreciation and respect for diversity, including sexual orientation. It calls for nondiscrimination policies affecting students, staff, and faculty of schools of social work, analysis of gender and sexuality as part of the **curriculum** of social work education, and aspires for diversity in social work education programs worldwide.

Research studies conducted among social work students document that exposure to course content about queer people, class discussion, and speaker panels decrease homophobic attitudes (Dongvillo and Ligon 2001; Gray, Poynter, and Zimmerman 1999). As in similar studies of preservice teachers and other students, factors such as religiosity and beliefs about **gender roles** impact attitudes about queers, and females are more likely than males to have tolerant or accepting attitudes (Maney and Cain 1997).

The present state of social work education in the United States serves as an example of how political and social backlash against gains made by LGBT activists impacts social work programs. While previous curricular policies and accreditation standards included queer content across the curriculum and spoke more strongly against antigay discrimination, the current EPAS neither mandates queer content in social work programs nor does it take a clear stand against discrimination, only calling for programs to provide a nondiscriminatory "learning context" (CSWE 2001).

Partly due to these unclear messages, the experiences of LGBT students, faculty, and staff, and the curricular content regarding queer people in accredited social work education programs in the United States varies considerably. New social workers may or may not be exposed to theory, knowledge, and skills directly related to practice with queer youth. Similarly, although there is widespread inclusion of queer youth issues in continuing education made available to social workers already in practice, the exposure of each social worker to such education varies and is gained primarily through self-direction. Because terms such as "lesbian and gay" and "sexual orientation" are almost always the ones used in social work codes of ethics and educational policies and standards, bisexual and transgender persons have yet to be adequately recognized within and by the profession.

Bibliography

Council on Social Work Education. 2001. *Educational Policy and Accreditation Standards.* Alexandria, VA: Author.

Dongvillo, Jeff, and Jan Ligon. 2001. "Exploring the Effectiveness of Teaching Techniques with Lesbian and Gay Content in the Social Work Curriculum." *Journal of Baccalaureate Social Work* 6: 15–124.

Gray, Judith, K. Poynter, and Jay Zimmerman. 1999. "Developing a Speaker Panel Program to Provide Curriculum Content on GLB People." *Journal of Baccalaureate Social Work* 4: 121–132.

Hunter, Ski, and Jane C. Hickerson. 2003. *Affirmative Practice: Understanding and Working with Lesbian, Gay, Bisexual, and Transgender persons.* Washington, D.C.: NASW Press.

Mallon, Gerald P. 1992. "Gay and No Place to Go: Assessing the Needs of Gay and Lesbian Adolescents in Out-of-Home Settings." *Child Welfare* 71: 547–556.

———. 1998. "Lesbian, Gay, and Bisexual Orientation in Childhood and Adolescence." Pp. 123–144 in *Not Just a Passing Phase: Social Work with Gay, Lesbian, and Bisexual People.* Edited by George Alan Appleby, and Jeane W. Anastas. New York: Columbia University Press.

Maney, Delores W., and Richard E. Cain. 1997. "Preservice Elementary Teachers' Attitudes Toward Gay and Lesbian Parenting." *Journal of School Health* 67: 236–242.

Van Wormer, Katherine, Joel Well, and Mary Boes. 2000. *Social Work with Lesbians, Gays, and Bisexuals: A Strengths Perspective.* Boston: Allyn and Bacon.

Web Sites

Council on Social Work Education. April 2005. Accessed June 22, 2005. http://www.cswe.org. This national association preserves and enhances the quality of social work education for practice that promotes the goals of individual and community well-being and social justice.

International Association of Schools of Social Work. November 2004. Accessed November 22, 2004. http://www.iassw.soton.ac.uk/Generic/welcome.asp?lang=en. An international association, founded in 1928, with a Web site that includes news, publications, links, and discussion forums.

International Federation of Social Workers. November 2004. Accessed November 22, 2004. http://www.ifsw.org. Promotes the development of social work best practices and international cooperation between social workers and their member organizations.

National Association of Social Workers. November 2004. Accessed November 22, 2004. http://www.naswdc.org. This is the largest membership organization of professional social workers in the world. Its Web site includes multiple NASW news articles on gay youth and education, searchable through its database.

Sororities

Nancy J. Evans

Sororities, which are identified by two or three Greek letters, consist of groups of women at colleges and universities who join together for social, academic, and service-related purposes. Since women were first allowed to enroll in higher education

See also Antidiscrimination Policy; Cocurricular Activities; College Campus Programming; Coming Out, Youth; Compulsory Heterosexuality; Mental Health; Passing; Residence Life in Colleges; School Climate, College; Single-Sex Schools; Women's Colleges.

institutions in the latter part of the nineteenth century, close female friendships have been an important part of college life. Today's college women often look for close friendships and a sense of independence in college sororities. Most sororities are national organizations with chapters on numerous college campuses; however, local sororities that are found only on a specific campus also exist. Sororities are largely a United States' phenomenon, although twenty-five Canadian campuses now have Greek chapters. In Canada, however, universities do not recognize or control Greek life as they do in the United States.

For lesbian and **bisexual youth**, becoming a member of a sorority offers challenges since attitudes of sorority women can be quite homophobic. For example, no national sorority has yet adopted a nondiscrimination policy that includes **sexual orientation**. Sororities also tend to be quite traditional with regard to **gender roles** and activities, making involvement difficult for bisexual and **lesbian youth**. For example, heterosexual **dating** is generally expected for dances and parties. Lesbian and bisexual members can have a positive impact on the attitudes and behaviors of their organizations, however, and sororities can provide a supportive environment for some lesbian and bisexual women. Intentional programming initiatives are needed to raise awareness among sorority members.

In the nineteenth century, romantic friendships, which were referred to as "**crush**es," "smashes," "spoons," or "chumming," helped college women to establish an independent life separate from the traditional domestic roles they were expected to assume. Around the same time, the first "women's fraternities," as sororities are officially called, were established. In addition to fulfilling the social needs of women, sororities often owned their houses in which their members resided while attending college. This tradition continues.

When sororities and fraternities were first established, many students found their secret nature appealing because it provided a vehicle for challenging the near absolute control and authority that college **administrators** had over college students. The popularity of Greek letter organizations continued until the 1960s when traditional student activities became less popular in light of the antiestablishment philosophy of many **college age students** of that time. As involvement in activist social movements increased, membership in Greek letter social organizations decreased. While maintaining their strong social orientation, sororities of today also stress the development of leadership skills, community service, and academic achievement.

Sororities tend to appeal to a certain type of woman. **Research** suggests that many women who join sororities are affluent, conformist, dependent on their families, and more concerned with social life than academics (Baier and Whipple 1990). They provide a safe environment for women who have not yet set a clear direction for their lives and who wish to interact with other women from similar backgrounds who share common values.

A review of research on sorority life indicates that it has both positive and negative outcomes. Women who are members of Greek social organizations are more involved in all aspects of campus life than nonmembers. They report being more satisfied with their social development, and they tend to be more active in their communities after graduation from college. Recent research suggests that sorority women make gains in intellectual development because of their involvement (Pike 2000) and are more engaged in academic pursuits and community service activities (Hayek et al. 2002). On the negative side, sorority members drink more than nonmembers, are more likely to exhibit **eating disorders**, and report more sexually coercive experiences.

Sorority membership is by invitation; women go through a process known as "rush" to learn about sorority life, become acquainted with current members, and indicate their interest in joining a particular organization. Current members vote on whether to issue invitations to young women who have expressed an interest in joining. If accepted for membership, women complete a "pledge" process during which they learn the rituals and traditions of the particular sorority they wish to join. If they successfully complete this process, pledges are initiated into full sorority membership. This system of selecting members perpetuates the lack of diversity that pervades the Greek system. Although there are several **African American** and **Latina** sororities, historically white sororities are very homogeneous with regard to **race**, **ethnicity**, **social class**, and values. Emphasis is placed on finding new members who "fit in," and members are allowed to "blackball" rushees without stating their reasons.

To provide the opportunity for lesbian and bisexual women to be involved in an inclusive sorority open to women of any sexual orientation, Lambda Delta Lambda was founded at the University of California at Los Angeles in 1988. Other chapters of this organization were established at San Francisco State University and the University of Nevada-Las Vegas. None of these chapters remain active. Although the exact reasons for their dissolution are unknown, prevailing **homophobia** and lack of university support are likely contributing factors.

Given the press for conformity and adherence to traditional **gender roles** in established sororities, why would a lesbian or bisexual woman join such an organization? Statements from sexual minority women who are members of sororities indicate that they join for reasons similar to those of heterosexual women: friendship, social involvement, support, and a sense of belonging. Others may not yet recognize that they are not heterosexual or may deny their suspicions by joining an organization that reinforces traditional gender roles. Still other women decide to join because of their friendship with or attraction to a current member.

The experiences of lesbian and bisexual women in sororities are mixed. In a survey of LGBT individuals who were or had been members of Greek organizations (Case 1998), women reported that their organizations were homophobic and there was **discrimination** against LGBT individuals. Heterosexual sorority members were reported to have blackballed prospective members or pledges who were perceived to be lesbian. A majority of sorority members did not reveal their sexual orientation while they were active members, although there was a trend for women who were more recently in college to have come out to their "sisters" (other members of the sorority).

Case's (1998) data and the stories of sorority women that appear in the book, *Secret Sisters*, provide evidence that when initiated lesbian and bisexual women do come out to their sisters, most receive a supportive response. However, some lesbian and bisexual women are ostracized from their organizations or choose to leave voluntarily because of the stress experienced in trying to be authentic while they are expected to participate in heterosexually-oriented activities such as date parties, socials with fraternities, and dances. Many sororities with openly lesbian or bisexual members fear homophobic reactions from other sororities and fraternities as well as from prospective members and may pressure lesbian or bisexual members to hide their identities. There are regional differences with regard to the support that lesbian and bisexual women receive in sororities, with sororities in western states being more accepting and those in southern states being less tolerant.

Having a member openly identify herself as lesbian or bisexual can have a powerful effect on a sorority. Awareness levels of members are often raised as they hear about and observe a person they know well experience **harassment** and discrimination. As a result of the impact of having a lesbian or bisexual sister, many sorority members have become actively involved as **allies** in addressing injustices on their campuses.

Clearly, more work needs to be done to change the attitudes of sorority members and to educate them about the issues that face LGBT individuals. National officers and staff of women's fraternities, however, have resisted providing such education. For instance, several national women's fraternities actively opposed efforts to secure stories about the experiences of lesbian and bisexual women in sororities, later published in *Secret Sisters*. College and university Greek affairs advisors are more willing to undertake the responsibility to offer educational programs on LGBT topics to members and volunteer alumni advisors of sororities.

Educational sessions are generally required for members and pledges. An educational strategy that may be effective is to include LGBT information in sessions on diversity. In today's changing society, students recognize that learning to work with individuals who come from diverse backgrounds is important. Programs that involve peer facilitators to whom participants are more likely to listen are generally more effective than bringing in an older "authority" to speak in an abstract manner about LGBT issues. Panel discussions that provide opportunities for sorority members to hear directly from lesbian and bisexual women about their experiences can be very helpful in putting a "real face" on LGBT concerns. If a panelist is a current or former sorority member it can be very powerful. If lesbian and bisexual students are not available to speak with sorority members, having participants discuss real life case studies presenting issues that could happen in sorority settings can be useful. Role reversal exercises in which participants are asked to imagine what it would be like to be lesbian or bisexual in certain situations also give participants a clearer sense of the experiences that nonheterosexual woman face in their daily lives. Another option is having a program that brings together members of the LGBT student community and members of the Greek community to talk about and work through **stereotypes** that each group has about the other. As Case (1998, 78) pointed out in concluding his discussion of LGBT issues in the Greek community, "educational programming . . . can help to change the homophobic and heterosexual culture of college . . . sororities. In the process, the organizations can come closer to fulfilling the ideal of sisterhood."

Bibliography

Baier, John L., and Edward G. Whipple. 1990. "Greek Values and Attitudes: A Comparison with Independents." *NASPA Journal* 28: 43–53.

Case, Douglas N. 1998. "Lesbian, Gay, and Bisexual Issues within the Greek Community." Pp. 67–78 in *Working with Lesbian, Gay, Bisexual, and Transgender College Students*. Edited by Ronni L. Sanlo. Westport, CT: Greenwood.

Evans, Nancy J. 2000. "Introduction: Challenging the Image of Sororities." Pp. xxvii–xlii in *Secret Sisters: Stories of Being Lesbian and Bisexual in a College Sorority*. Edited by Shane L. Windemeyer and Pamela W. Freeman. Los Angeles: Alyson.

Faderman, Lillian. 1991. *Odd Girls and Twilight Lovers: A History of Lesbian Life in Twentieth-Century America.* New York: Penguin.

Hayek, John C., Robert M. Carini, Patrick T. O'Day, and George D. Kuh. 2002. "Triumph or Tragedy: Comparing Student Engagement Levels of Members of Greek-Letter Organizations and Other Students." *Journal of College Student Development* 43: 643–663.

Moser, Bob. 2002. "Greek Active." *Out.* September: 69–76.

Pike, Gary R. 2000. "The Influence of Fraternity and Sorority Membership on Students' Experiences and Cognitive Development." *Research in Higher Education* 41: 117–139.

Whipple, Edward G. 1996. "Student Activities." Pp. 298–333 in *Student Affairs Practice in Higher Education.* 2nd ed. Edited by Audrey L. Rentz. Springfield, IL: Thomas.

Windmeyer, Shane L., and Pamela W. Freeman, eds. 2000. *Secret Sisters: Stories of Being Lesbian and Bisexual in a College Sorority.* Los Angeles: Alyson.

Web Sites

Lambda Delta Lambda. Accessed June 10, 2005. http://userwww.sfsu.edu/~ldlbeta. A lesbian sorority which provided an opportunity for women to share their experiences and create a network of women who held similar ideals. Their goal was to create a safe, alternative, social environment, eliminate minority oppression, and raise lesbian and gay issue awareness on campus and in the community.

The Lambda10 Project. 2005. Accessed June 10, 2005. http://www.lambda10.org. An online community for gay, lesbian, and bisexual fraternity issues.

National Panhellenic Conference. 2005. Accessed June 10, 2005. http://www.npcwomen.org. An umbrella organization for twenty-six inter/national women's fraternities and sororities that supports its members by promoting values, education, leadership, friendships, cooperation, and citizenship.

South Africa, LGBT Issues in

Allister H. Butler and *Gaynor Astbury*

South Africa has undergone significant sociopolitical transformation in the last six decades, from the "legal" adoption of apartheid in 1948 to the first democratic election in 1994, and a new constitution two years later. The lesbian, gay, bisexual, and transgender (LGBT) community in South Africa is at the forefront of constitutional and sociopolitical reform. Numerous issues are currently facing the South African LGBT community. While significant strides have been made toward racial equality, there is still disparity in accessing health and social services between the white and historically disadvantaged LGBT communities. Furthermore, the LGBT social activist movements have to maintain vigilance in ensuring that the progressive Constitution becomes a reality for LGBT people. Issues such as equal access to antiretroviral HIV/**AIDS** medication, protection of LGBT people against homophobic **hate crimes**, homophobic abuse and **bullying** in secondary education, protection of same-sex domestic partnership rights, equity and removal of discrimination in the **workplace**, and decriminalization of same-sex conduct are primary areas that LGBT advocacy and lobbying groups are placing on the national agenda.

See also Activism, LGBT Youth; Africa, LGBT Youth and Issues in; Community LGBT Youth Groups; South Africa, LGBT Youth in; Legal Issues, Students; Parents, LGBT.

There are three historical markers that kindled and gave impetus to the gay and lesbian struggle in a South African context. The "Raid in Forest Town," a suburb north of Johannesburg, took place in 1966 (three years before **Stonewall** in the United States). Police raided and arrested nine men for "masquerading as women." This was followed by a parliamentary threat to widen antihomosexual legislation. The result, in opposition to this threat, was the instigation of the Homosexual Law Reform movement (1968), the sole aim of which was to prevent the proposed anti-gay bill from becoming law. This movement consisted of gay professionals, led by a prominent gay advocate, whose task was to raise funds needed to retain a firm of attorneys to prepare evidence and lead the case against the proposed antihomo-sexual **discrimination**. In the late 1970s, the second important marker occurred when Johannesburg police raided New Mandy's bar. This was South Africa's "Stonewall," as patrons fought back and demanded their civil rights be protected (Gevisser and Cameron 1994). The final marker was the adoption of the new Constitution, in 1996, which was the first in the world to recognize gay rights.

Today, in postapartheid South Africa, homophobic behaviors and attitudes are anticonstitutional; **sexual orientation** is a basic human right. Despite these guarantees and although other disadvantaged groups such as black South Africans and women have had their human rights upheld and legal discrimination removed, social, legal, and religious discrimination against homosexuals—adult and youth alike—continues. Numerous instances of discrimination range from employment opportunities and serving in the military to the rights of gay and lesbian parents and sexual minority students in secondary and tertiary educational systems.

The case of a high school gay youth expelled from a high school in Port Elizabeth (1999) based solely on his sexual orientation aptly reflects this discrimination in the educational system. This **gay youth** was expelled because he "dressed in drag," entered, and then won his high school's Miss Beauty competition. This was the first publicized demonstration of the gap between the 1996 Constitution and the reality of **homophobia**, which still exists in South African high schools.

Gay and lesbian couples also have long been denied equal status to their heterosexual colleagues. This was highlighted in the case of *JL Langemat vs the Minister of Safety and Security*. Langemat sued the South African Police Services in order to gain equality-based domestic partnership benefits for herself and her partner. In a landmark decision, the judge of the South Africa High Court ruled favourably:

> The stability and permanence of same-sex relationships is no different from the many married couples I know. Both types of unions are deserving of respect and protection. If our law does not accord protection to this type of union then I suggest it is time to do so. (NCGLE legal database 1999, 4–5)

In 2003, the South African Constitutional Court decided that same-sex couples may jointly adopt children. The court, therefore, found the constitutional provision against discrimination on the grounds of sexual orientation to be of more weight than provisions of the Child Care Act banning gay couples from adopting children. Nevertheless, gay and lesbian couples were still barred from legal marriage. A significant setback occurred in October 2003 where the Pretoria High Court dismissed the legalization of marriage between a same-sex couple based on the preexisting (and outdated) definition of marriage. This decision is in direct contradiction to the legal right for lesbian and gay couples to adopt children. Paradoxes like these are at the forefront of the current struggle. In December 2004, however, South Africa's Supreme Court of Appeal ruled that the marriage ban directly conflicted with the Constitution and has left it to the Parliament to reform the Marriage Act.

The Employment Equity Act 55 of 1998 deals primarily with elimination of unfair discrimination in the workplace. LGBT people are thus protected from discrimination in the workplace. However, discrimination of LGBT people is common in the workplace (Vimba 2003). For example, recently lesbian judge Kathleen Satchwell sued her employer and, in turn, won the right for her partner to enjoy the same workplace benefits as spouses of heterosexual employees. In a similar vein, LGBT people are legally permitted to serve in the military and are protected from discrimination and abuse by the Constitution. However, the Lesbian and Gay Equality Project is currently investigating numerous cases of abuse experienced by LGBT military personnel.

Despite such political and legal progress, overt homophobic behaviors exist at all institutional levels of South African society. Antigay sentiment is compounded by a strong patriarchal **Christian** ethic that views same-sex sexual encounters as sinful and wrong. In this context, reaction against homosexual rights is seen, for many, as upholding religious beliefs and, therefore, something to be proud of and actively encouraged. The cultural context is also critical as the concept of "sexual orientation" is unfamiliar in many African cultures. It is clear that homosexual *conduct* has always existed throughout Africa, yet homosexual *identity*, and the concept of sexual orientation, has not (Murray and Roscoe 1998).

Education also has carried a conservative legacy, which has typically been discriminatory toward minority groups. Currently, "conscious attempts to transform South African education" are largely driven by "the legislative flagship"of the 1996 South African Schools Act (Deacon, Morrell, and Prinsloo 1999, 164). Schools are now viewed as inclusive with a strong emphasis on national unity while recognizing cultural diversity and the individual rights of each student. Nevertheless, South African gay and **lesbian youth** still report homophobic attitudes and actions perpetrated by students and their teachers.

There is a gap between legislative reform and the social transformation. "Gay activists have been successful in influencing policy-makers to enshrine their rights in law" (Deacon, Morrell, and Prinsloo 1999, 169), yet "homophobia and discrimination against gays have been and remain unquestioned features of African and white schooling." And, while the experiences of gay and lesbian people in South Africa have improved, in **Africa** as a whole: "Virulent homophobia, incubated in the right-wing movements of the imperialist metropoles and also an outgrowth of Africa's own indigenous patriarchal systems, is finding a home in the political agendas of desperate African leaders" (Brock, Walls, and Campbell 2001, 4).

Key organizations address LGBT issues in South Africa, through international, national, and regional frameworks. Internationally, South Africa is one of the eighty countries affiliated with the International Lesbian and Gay Association. This affiliation has granted South Africa's LGBT movement international recognition, as well as an impetus to furthering its sociopolitical and constitutional reform. The Lesbian and Gay Equality project (formerly known as the National Coalition on Gay and Lesbian Equality), established in 1999, serves as the national agency representing the needs of the LGBT community in South Africa. This nongovernmental organization works toward achieving full legal and social equality for lesbian, gay, **bisexual, transgender,** and **intersex** South Africans. Their endeavors are achieved through advocacy, public policy, education and legal reform, strategic/impact litigation and the provision of access to justice.

Three organizations address the needs of the LGBT community at a regional level. OUT, in Gauteng province, provides health and mental health services to the LGBT community, primarily in the Tshwana and Mamelodi townships. The Durban Lesbian and Gay Community and Health Centre, located in the province of Kwazulu Natal, empowers LGBT community by providing services and training. For example, the HIV/AIDS and Care Outreach Volunteer Trainers coordinate forum discussions regarding sexual practices among lesbian, bisexual, and transgender women. Finally, in the Western Cape province, the Triangle Project serves the LGBT community through health and social development programs that promote individual and community well-being and pride, as well as building individual and community capacity. Here, community outreach teams access new communities to network organizations and individuals in surrounding communities.

The development of these national and regional initiatives has significantly addressed the changing needs of the LGBT communities in South Africa. However, these organizations are primarily based in large **urban** cities (Cape Town, Durban, Johannesburg, and Pretoria). There is, however, a significant absence of organizational infrastructure in the large **rural** areas where the many LGBT youth live and whose communities are historically disadvantaged, socially deprived, and marginalized. Increasing rates of lesbian **sexual assault** in the townships, lack of affordable access to social activities and service providers in the urban centers, as well as a lack of safe meeting places (recreational or support groups) for LGBT people are only a few issues facing this rural population.

Bibliography

Brock, Lisa, Hamaid Walls, and Horace Campbell. 2001. *African Leaders Hide Political Woes Behind Homophobia*. Accessed June 16, 2005. http://www.monthlyreview.org/0401brc2.htm

The Constitution of the Republic of South Africa. 1996. *Act 108 of 1996*. Pretoria: Government Publishers.

Deacon, Roger, Robert Morrell, and Jeanne Prinsloo. 1999. "Discipline and Homophobia in South African Schools." Pp. 164–180 in *A Dangerous Knowing: Sexuality, Pedagogy and Popular Culture*. Edited by Debbie Epstein and James T. Sears. London: Cassel.

The Employment Equity Act of South Africa. 1998. *Act 55 of 1998*. Pretoria: Government Publishers.

Gevisser, Mark, and Edwin Cameron. 1994. *Defiant Desire: Gay and Lesbian Lives in South Africa*. Johannesburg: Ravan Press.

Human Rights Watch and the International Gay and Lesbian Human Rights Commission. 2002. Accessed December 4, 2004. http://www.hrw.org/reports/2003/safrica/safriglhrc0303.pdf.

Murray, Stephen, and Will Roscoe. 1990. *Boy-Wives and Female Husbands: Studies in African Homosexualities*. New York: Palgrave.

National Coalition for Gay and Lesbian Equality. 1997. *Draft Submission*. Johannesburg: Author.

———. 1999. *Legal Database*. Johannesburg: Author.

Plummer, Kenneth. 1989. "Lesbian and Gay Youth in England." *Journal of Homosexuality* 17: 195–223.

Vimba, Mkhuseli. 2005, February. Recognising Same Sex Marriages. Accessed June 16, 2005. http://www.equality.org.za/features/20030204ssmar.php.

Web Sites

Behind the Mask. December 2004. Accessed December 4, 2004. http://www.mask.org. za/index2.htm. A Web site magazine on lesbian and gay affairs in Africa.

Durban Lesbian and Gay Community and Health Centre. June 2005. Accessed June 16, 2005. http://www.gaycentre.org.za. Provides updated list of community activities and forum discussions, news and political issues facing the LGBT community along with the role of volunteers in delivering their various projects.

Gay and Lesbian Archives for South Africa. May 2005. Accessed June 16, 2005. http://www.wits.ac.za/gala. Carries all the South African gay and lesbian archives, and current research being conducted out by the University of Witwatersrand, South Africa.

Lesbian and Gay Equality Project. December 2004. Accessed December 5, 2004. http://www.equality.org.za. Details "The Equality Project," a nonprofit, nongovernmental organization that works toward achieving full legal and social equality for LGBTI South Africans.

OUT. September 2004. Accessed December 4, 2004. http://www.out.org.za. Provides information regarding various health and metal health services provided in local communities, as well as work being done in building local expertise and making this available to mainstream sectors.

Triangle Project, Cape Town, South Africa. 2004. Accessed December 4, 2004. http://www. triangle.org.za. Provides online discussion forums, updated fact sheets (e.g. HIV and AIDS, steps in the coming out process), and an overview of all of their services.

South Africa, LGBT Youth in

Allister H. Butler and *Gaynor Astbury*

Despite political, legal, and educational reforms, South African **lesbian, gay, bisexual**, and **transgender youth** (LGBT) continue to battle against **homophobia** in their daily lives. Although problems confronting these youth are similar to those faced by those within other countries, it would be a disservice to characterize LGBT youth experiences as generic. South African demography, family and cultural support, access to peer support, **curriculum** development and homophobia in education, lobbying efforts, access to accurate literature and information, as well as **mental health** provisions within a new democratic society create unique challenges for these youth. Further, according to the 2001 Census, within a population of nearly forty-five million there are eleven official languages, with the most commonly spoken being Zulu, Xhosa, English, and Afrikaans. Although **urban** centers are well-developed, disadvantaged **rural** settlements are in the majority, with cultural norms and mores strongly influenced by conservative traditionalism. There is no formal method of determining the numbers of LGBT young people, as the 2001 Census did not include LGBT lifestyles despite protests from gay civil rights leaders.

Many rural groups still adhere to the extended family tradition, with strong adherence to African male patriarchy. Even within urban settings, old tribal dictates such as coming of age rituals hold sway. For those from a tribal culture, the

See also Africa, LGBT Youth and Issues in; Bullying; Educational Policies; Mental Health; Race and Racism; Religious Fundamentalism; Sexual Abuse and Assault; Social Class; South Africa, LGBT Issues in; Youth, At-Risk.

extended family plays a role in decision-making and nurturance until such time as the young person undergoes a ritual or symbolic transition to being socially accepted as an adult man or woman. There is no leeway for queer youth to sidestep this cultural transition in order to allow constitutionally sanctioned recognition as LGBT citizens. This conservatism is also found in traditional Afrikaans families, which strongly emphasize **Christian** norms and support for mainstream lifestyles.

Traditional beliefs combined with homophobic **stereotypes** have resulted in traumatic experiences for lesbian and gay youth in South Africa. Young lesbians have been raped by older males "teaching" them to be real women or "curing" them of lesbianism. Young gay men are beaten by other males in order to make them "real men." Further, ignorance, stereotypes, and lack of medical resources in impoverished communities have compounded the problems of **HIV education** and **AIDS**.

Three-quarters of South Africans are black. Due to residual effects of apartheid, those most socioeconomically disadvantaged are within the black population. The legacy of apartheid restrictions mean that many black young people reside in what were formally known as "townships"—black settlement areas on the outskirts of urban centers. This significantly impacts LGBT youth as public transport services remain underdeveloped. Many young people must rely on trains and expensive taxi services, hindering their ability to become involved with LGBT groups predominantly found in urban centers.

Isolation is thus a key issue confronting many LGBT youth, resulting in mental health ramifications such as internalized homophobia, suicidal ideation, and lowered self-esteem. The National Youth Commission has been slow to recognize the vulnerability of LGBT youth within the South African context. The Lesbian and Gay Equality Project (formerly the National Coalition on Gay and Lesbian Equality) has been instrumental in allowing the voices of LGBT young people to be heard, but the sheer size of South Africa and isolated rural areas hamper efforts to network these youth. International organizations such as Gay Rights Watch seek to network adult and youth activists, using the **Internet** and media sources to disseminate relevant information to policy makers, educators, and social service providers.

In South Africa, adolescents spend five years in high school, roughly from ages thirteen to eighteen. However, due to educational injustices in the past, historically disadvantaged students may be considerably older by the time they leave high school. At the 50th General Meeting of the African National Congress (held in Mafeking, December 1997), a commitment was made to LGBT youth to ensure their protection from **discrimination** at home, at school, on the streets, and in the media. Yet, feedback from South African young people indicates that they are not protected in their everyday environments (Human Rights Watch 2003). LGBT youth experience deeply entrenched homophobia within their school contexts, reporting both staff and students are responsible for name calling (e.g., "*moffie*"–an Afrikaans, derogatory term, denoting overtly feminine characteristics), exclusion, and physical and emotional abuse (Butler, Alpaslan, Strümpher, and Astbury 2003; Human Rights Watch 2003). Resultant feelings experienced by LGBT youth include guilt, sinfulness, fear, internal turmoil, helplessness, degradation, and humiliation. For many LGBT young people it is safer to remain invisible.

The National Ministry of Education has invested enormous resources in outcomes based education methods and the development of a life skills training approach, which allow for the protection of cultural identity and minority group self-actualization. Life skills training briefly discusses homosexuality. Curriculum 2005 seeks to actively redress **prejudice**, focusing on racial and gender equality. However, this does not explicitly address LGBT issues or the particular needs of queer youth.

Curriculum content and the provision of accurate and ethical LGBT information to young people is a gap which is felt acutely by South African youth (Butler 2000; Human Rights Watch 2003). These efforts are hindered by the residual inequalities of apartheid and the lobbying of conservative religious groups. The publication of *The Pink Agenda* (McCafferty and Hammon 2001), for example, condemns the inclusion of homosexuality in school curriculum and assists young people "trapped" in a homosexual lifestyle. Church groups have campaigned to place it in every high school library. However, LGBT activists have succeeded in a government ban of this work for those under the age of eighteen. Accurate and positive material on LGBT issues remains difficult to access. In urban centers, popular magazines like *Outright* and *Exit* are available. These are effectively out of reach for LGBT youth who are poor, live in rural areas, or cannot read English. A similar language problem exists with the provision of suitably themed **literature** for LGBT youth. Literature written by and for black LGBT youth in the black languages of South Africa and set in contexts to which the disadvantaged can relate does not exist.

The Internet is another source for mostly privileged LGBT youth. The majority of historically disadvantaged schools in South Africa do not have Internet facilities and rural or poor youth lack the family financial resources to access the Web. Further, in schools with such facilities, parental and religious groups exert pressure to restrict access to LGBT content.

Having recourse to knowledgeable and supportive school counselors or guidance teachers is another problem facing most LGBT students. There are four types of schools in South Africa: independent, government, Christian, and home schooling. While independent schools may have better educated counselors, few are trained in working with LGBT youth. In the majority of state schools, the lack of funding is the major barrier. Historically disadvantaged schools still require large-scale development and investment to provide even the basic essentials of education such as adequate buildings, school books, and desks. These schools typically have no formally prepared guidance teachers or counselors, relying instead on teaching staff not trained in **counseling** or knowledgeable about LGBT issues. Finally, there is no interest within Christian schools or in home schooling in addressing the needs of LGBT youth; these youth are silenced and remain invisible.

Bibliography

Butler, Allister. 2000. *The Coming Out Process of South African Gay and Lesbian Youth*. Unpublished Doctoral Manuscript, University of Port Elizabeth, South Africa.

Butler, Allister, Nicky Alpaslan, Juanita Strümpher, and Gaynor Astbury. 2002. "Gay and Lesbian Youth Experiences of Homophobia in South African Secondary Education." *Journal of Gay and Lesbian Issues in Education* 1, no. 2: 3–28.

The Constitution of the Republic of South Africa. 1996. *Act 108 of 1996*. Pretoria: Government Publishers.

Human Rights Watch. 2003. *State Sponsored Homophobia and its Consequences in Southern Africa*. New York: Author.

McCafferty, Christine, and Peter Hammon. 2001. *The Pink Agenda, Sexual Revolution in South Africa, and the Ruin of the Family*. Pretoria: Africa Christian Action.

Web Sites

Behind the Mask. December 2004. Accessed December 2, 2004. http://www.mask.org.za/
SECTIONS/AfricaPerCountry/ABC/south%20africa/south%20africa_index.html. A
Web site on gay and lesbian affairs in Africa, examining constitutional changes, topical
issues, and ongoing debates. This contains links to other South African LGBT sites.

Home School Legal Defence Association. A Critique on South Africa's New National
Curriculum Proposal. February 2002. Accessed December 2, 2004. http://www.hslda.
org/hs/international/SouthAfrica/200202110.asp. A critique of South African schools'
inclusion of LGBT issues.

The Revised National Curriculum. Accessed December 2, 2004. http://education.pwv.gov.
za/DoE_Sites/Curriculum/New_2005/overview-doc.pdf. Outlines the background to the
development and contents of Curriculum 2005.

South African National Youth Commission. November 2004. Accessed December 2, 2004.
http://www.nyc.gov.za. Provides a useful overview regarding general youth issues in
South Africa and includes a search function to identify issues pertinent to LGBT young
people.

South America, LGBT Youth and Issues in

Henrique Caetano Nardi and *Fernando Altair Pocahy*

The cultural, political, and historical contexts of South American societies create
specific problems for **lesbian, gay, bisexual,** and **transgender youth** (LGBT) in developing a positive **sexual identity**. These youth often face **homophobia**, invisibility,
isolation, poverty, **AIDS**, and the lack of specific social programs. Four distinctive
factors affect South American LGBT youth in their formal and nonformal education. The Roman **Catholic** Church's conservative dogma regarding human sexuality
has an important impact on private and public education systems as well as the
family (Mott 2000). The valorization of the "macho" figure in Latin cultural heritage
and its relations to gender and sexual oppression is particularly visible in schools
due to restricted **gender roles**. The long periods of dictatorships, too, have often silenced social movements, including those for LGBT rights, and contributed to the
invisibility of these issues in the school system. Finally, significant social and economic inequalities impact access to education, the quality of information about
LGBT culture and rights, and youth's vulnerability to HIV and AIDS. There also
are major differences between and within South American countries related to social class, gender, and ethnicity, which affect the education, legal rights, and mental
health of LGBT youth.

Catholic and Protestant Pentecostal churches in South America impact public
and religious education. Sex is understood as exclusively for procreation purposes
performed between heterosexually married couples, and homosexuality is taught to be
"sinful" **desire**. Reproductive and **sexuality education** programs are rare in South
American public schools; when present, the health and biological aspects of the

See also Adolescent Sexualities; Coming Out, Youth; Community LGBT Youth Groups;
Educational Policies; Harassment; Identity Politics; Music, Popular; Secondary Schools,
LGBT; Social Class; Youth, At-Risk.

education are seldom included. **Sexual orientation** is still a taboo for most teachers. Only recently, and mainly in Argentina and **Brazil**, do programs include sexual diversity issues. This symbolic relationship between homoerotic desire and sin is also reinforced outside the formal **curriculum**. In Chile, where Opus Dei, an ultra conservative Catholic organization tried to prohibit the circulation of *Opus Gay* (an LGBT journal), a Catholic high school principal expelled two lesbian girls for kissing. Although denounced by Movilh (the most important Chilean LGBT group) and not allowed to return to school, they were offered early graduation.

Rigid gender roles constructed within a patriarchal social structure evidences "machismo" associated to gender expectations and performances imposed in school. In **physical education** classes, for instance, boys are expected to choose **sports** requiring physical strength such as soccer while girls choose more delicate activities. Homosexual behavior also is learned as a gender role dichotomy. For boys, active penetration is identified with the male heterosexual role, penetrating the feminized "fag/fairy" (*bicha, veado, maricon, marica*) figure (Parker 1999). For girls, this more aggressive behavior corresponds to the "butch" stereotype. This reproduction of gender role binaries in same-sex relationships both contributes to

South American Couple. Photo by Pecoits, F. Nuances Group, 2004

and results from the lack of visibly diverse LGBT role models.

Recently, in **urban** areas there has been more visibility for LGBT youth issues and a less polarized and more diverse behavior. This can be seen in major South American cities in rave parties, gay parades (Santiago, Buenos Aires, Lima, São Paulo, Rio de Janeiro, and Porto Alegre), dancing clubs, as well as in fashion and cultural fairs and festivals, such as the Mix Brasil Festival and the LGBT film festival of Buenos Aires. Nevertheless, **homophobia** is pervasive throughout South America. Recent **research** published by UNESCO (2004) shows that 34.9 percent of Brazilian high school students would not want a homosexual classmate; this rejection of homosexuality is stronger among young men than young women.

Widespread **prejudice** against sexual minorities is associated with the delay of the LGBT rights movement in South America and in implementation of educational programs that fight homophobia. In South American countries such as Uruguay, Paraguay, Peru, Chile, Brazil, and Argentina, the last period of dictatorships—at the end of the 1960s and the 1970s—delayed the discussion of human rights and sexuality, creating a gap between the gains obtained by LGBT movements in **Europe** and North America and the emergence of this movements in South America. The Argentina-based Nuestro Mundo (Our World) was the first such organization, formed in 1967 (Opusgay 2004). Four years later, in order to resist the authoritarian regime, members of Nuestro Mundo, together with other groups, created the Frente de Liberación Homosexual (Homosexual Liberation Front), which was closed in 1976. With the end of the Brazilian military regime worst period of repression, Somos (We Are) was organized in 1979, as was the Homosexual Movement of Lima in 1980. The first groups created specifically by and for the LGBT youth was organized in 2000. E-jovem.com, a Brazilian group that was born as an Internet site (http://www.e-jovem.com), became a nongovernmental organization (NGO), based in Campinas, São Paulo. Another is Contestação, a group formed by students from a public high school, Escola Estadual Júlio de Castilhos, in Porto Alegre, Brazil.

At the beginning of the twenty-first century, there were 137 LGBT organizations in South America (Fundación Ecuatoriana de Acción y Educación para la Promoción de la Salud, 2000). Many of these were formed at the end of the 1980s, receiving financial support from funds such as UNESCO, World Health Organization (WHO), Pan-American Health Organization, Ford Foundation, MacArthur Foundation, and USAID as **HIV education** projects.

In South America, youth is considered the most vulnerable group to the **AIDS** epidemic (UNAIDS 2004). Vulnerability is increased by poverty and worsened by poor education. Despite the effort of the LGBT movements and the governments, recent data indicates an increase in HIV infection among youth, due mainly to non-protected sex and drug use (UNAIDS 2004). A study in Ecuador, for example, with 870 high school students, found that 70 percent of the sexually active responders did not wear a condom in their last sexual intercourse, and, though the research did not specify the differences between heterosexual and LGBT adolescents, widespread unprotected sex may explain why the government estimates that 59 percent of the HIV infections were associated to men having sex with men (UNAIDS 2004).

Despite the increased visibility of the LGBT movement in large South American cities, there are only a few projects specifically directed at LGBT youth within formal education in Argentina, Brazil, Chile and Colombia. With the exception of Brasil sem Homofobia (Brazil without Homophobia), these are usually isolated projects proposed by an LGBT organization, not government initiatives. Although the Brazilian government announced a program to fight homophobia in 2004, there are only a few such projects in the metropolitan areas of Rio de Janeiro, Porto Alegre, and São Paulo. This program works with teachers in order to prevent homophobia and other forms of **discrimination** through seminars and discussions about the major issues concerning LGBT discrimination. Usually, schools or the city's education department invite LGBT group members as well as academic specialists to help create strategies and increase awareness in order to fight homophobia in the school environment.

In Chile, the LGBT organization Movilh, in a partnership with the Ministry of Labor, founded Escuela para Homosexuales y Personas Viviendo con VIH/SIDA (School for Homosexuals and People Living with HIV/AIDS), which provides technical and professional education for youth who drop out of the formal educational system (Movilh 2004). The first group of eighty students graduated in 2004. This initiative is important because LGBT youth, especially transgender, are often expelled from their families, suffer discrimination and violence in the formal education system, and engage in **prostitution** as the only way to survive.

These projects, as confirmed at the First International LGBT Forum organized by Education International and Public Services International in Porto Alegre, are not representative of the ensemble of the political educational programs in South America, and there is a lot to be done in this area. The letter of Porto Alegre (Education International 2004), issued at this world gathering, proposed a political agenda. Participants recommended that the governments ensure the widest and earliest possible access to quality public education, which is free of prejudice, empowers people, especially women and girls, to make their choices, and ensures that sex education, health care materials, and services include information relating to LGBT youth and their needs.

Social inequality and poverty challenge LGBT youth. The urge to work in order to survive limits formal schooling and, in **rural** areas, sexual orientation constitutes an important motive for urban migration. **Queer** youth are more isolated in these regions, which embrace conservative political and religious values and lack public space for them to socialize or organize. **Internet** access, too, is restricted due to geographic availability and poverty.

For more affluent or less isolated queer youth, Internet sites are important portals for contact with other same-sex attracted youth to share experiences, break isolation, and find peer support. Also, it is an important educational resource about queer culture, HIV/AIDS and sexually transmitted infections, and LGBT rights. Two Web sites directed exclusively to LGBT youth provide comic strips, resources, opportunities to participate in surveys and media projects, timely information, and extensive links (http://www.ambientejoven.org and http://www.e-jovem.com).

As in other regions in the world, lesbian and transgender issues were the last ones included in the LGTB agenda. The male-centeredness of the movement (and society), the channeling of AIDS education money to finance mainly the gay organizations, and the greater invisibility of lesbian and transgender people and issues have contributed to their marginalization. Additionally, transgender issues, traditionally viewed as a health problem or subordinated to HIV/AIDS prevention and prostitution, have only recently entered the political debate in terms of human rights. In fact, the first South American **transsexual**, the Argentinean Susana Panelo, gained the right to change her birth name only in 2004. Among the groups providing assistance on transgender issues are Igualdade (Equality) in Brazil and Asociación de Lucha por la Identidad Travesti Transexual (ALITT, Transsexual and Transvestite Identity Association) in Argentina.

There, too, is very little scholarship or research related to the intersection of LGBT youth and education in South America. Most academic inquiry relates to HIV/AIDS prevention and a few academic centers have conducted some research on the theme, but mostly associated to health prevention studies.

LGBT issues and youth have gained greater visibility in the mass media and **popular culture** throughout South America. Many television soap operas in Brazil have dealt with these subjects. The first was *Vale Tudo* (*Everything is Possible*), in 1985; the most recent is *Senhora do Destino* (*Destiny Master*). In Argentina, also in 2004, the soap opera *Los Roldón* (*The Roldons*) featured a transvestite (Florencia de la V) as the main character. Many singers, too, are openly gay and lesbian. Cássia Eller and Renato Russo two Brazilian rock stars that recently died, became important symbols for LGBT youth; Celeste Carballo and Andrés Lewin are popular singers in Argentina. In Peru, the **film** *El Destino no Tiene Favoritos* (*Destiny has No Favorites*, 2003), with a gay subject, represented the country in many international festivals.

Bibliography

Education International. 2004, September. EI-IE. Accessed September 30, 2004. http://www. ei-ie.org/eipsiglbt.htm.

Fundación Ecuatoriana de Acción y Education para la Promoción de la Salud (Ecuadorian Foundation for Action and Education in Health Promotion). 2000. *Directorio de Organizaciones GLBT, America Latina y Caribe*. Ecuador: Author.

Mott, Luis. 2000. "Ethno-Histoire de l'Homosexualité en Amérique Latine" (Latin American's Homosexuality Ethno-History). Pp. 285–303 in *Pour l'histoire du Brésil (For a Brazilian History)*. Edited by François Crouzet. Paris: L'Harmattan.

Movilh. 2004, September. "80 Alumnos se Graduaron de la Primera Escuela para Homosexuales y Personas Viviendo con Vih/Sida de América Latina." Accessed June 10, 2005. http://www.movilh.org/modules.php?name=News&file=article&sid=238.

OpusGay. 2004, October. OpusGay. Accessed June 10, 2005. http://www.opusgay.cl/1264/article-27222.html.

Parker, Richard. 1999. *Beneath the Equator: Cultures of Desire, Male Homosexuality and Emerging Gay Communities in Brazil*. New York: Routledge.

Tielman, Rob, Aart Hendricks, and Evert van der Veen. 1993. *The Third Pink Book: A Global View of Lesbian and Gay Liberation and Oppression*. Buffalo, NY: Prometheus Books.

UNAIDS. 2004, October. UNAIDS. Accessed October, 25, 2004. http://www.unaids.org.

UNESCO. 2004, September. *Sexualidade dos jovens do Distrito Federal é pesquisada pela UNESCO (Youth Sexuality in Brasília is Researched by UNESCO)*. Accessed September 29, 2004. http//www.unesco.org.br/noticias/releases/sex_jovens/mostra_documento.

Web Sites

ADITAL: Agencia de Informacion Fray Tito para American Latina. June 2005. Accessed June 10, 2005. http://www.adital.org.br/. Fray Tito Information agency for Latin America is associated with human rights social movements and is maintained by professional journalists and militants. Useful access tool to information on human rights and sexuality in South America.

CIUDADANIA SEXUAL: Sexuality, Health and Human Rights in Latin America. 2005. Accessed June 10, 2005. http://www.ciudadaniasexual.org. Helpful research tool maintained by the *Universidad Peruana Cayteano Heredia* and sponsored by the Ford Foundation.

E-jovem. June 2005. Accessed June 10, 2005. http://www.e-jovem.com. Brazilian Web site maintained by and directed to LGBT youth. Provides information and hosts chats/forums about sexuality, health, family, education, and rights.

Education International. November 2004. Accessed June 13, 2005. http://www.ei-ie.org/glbtforum. International Gay Lesbian Bisexual Transgender Forum associated to Education International (the largest global teacher organization representing 29 million education personnel in 165 countries) hosts the first International Gay Lesbian Bisexual Transgender Forum.

Special Education, LGBT Youth in

Terence P. Friedrichs

Lesbian, gay, bisexual, and transgender youth and special education students are both groups with socially-ascribed negative connotations. To be a "special education" student (i.e., one with a "disability"), at least in United States school systems, this youth must fit one or more federal disability categories: mild disabilities (learning disabilities, emotional/behavioral disorders, and speech/language impairments), sensory handicaps (including hearing and visual impairments), physical disabilities

See also Behavioral Disorders; Discrimination; Educational Policies; Prejudice.

(including orthopedic and health impairments), and mental retardation (also called "mental disabilities"). Students who receive both the "LGBT" and "disability" labels may experience greater social bias than youth falling within just one of these categories. Certainly, if students with disabilities are affected by name-calling, physical abuse, isolation, and dropping out of school, then LGBT youth with **disabilities** very clearly may be at risk for these by-products of bias (Rahamin, Dupont, and DuBeau 1996). Even closeted LGBT students with disabilities may suffer from overt antigay bias, due to the fear and sometimes the self-loathing that goes with closeted status.

Special education can be narrowly regarded as instruction in school-based special education programs or can be more broadly defined, in deconstructionist fashion, as learning in in-school or out-of-school activities which address special education characteristics. With a fairly consistent 10 to 12 percent of the United States public-school K-12 population in programs for students with disabilities in recent years (Hallahan and Kauffman 1994; National Center for Education Statistics 2002), there are about six million youth today in public school special education programs. If one adds other students who have been assisted by outside experts in the assessment, labeling, and service of disabilities, then the number is higher (Skrtic 1995). Individual out-of-school practitioners may assess students with significant disabilities, using more flexible (either narrower or more sweeping) definitions of disability than the standard ones employed by personnel in school establishments. For example, some diagnosticians with a broad view of the term "disability" may use a "learning disability" (LD) definition that encompasses just a student's slight letter reversals when reading, rather than a more school-based LD definition that requires additional, severe, internally-based memory or organizational problems in reading.

LGBT students may be particularly susceptible to misdiagnosis or misplacement during the assessment of mild disabilities. An LD student, for instance, is supposed to demonstrate a gap between average-range potential and actual achievement, due to "innate" perceptual, memory, or organizational difficulties (Hallahan and Kauffman 1994). However, a LGBT student labeled LD actually may underachieve due to external factors, such as gay-related **bullying**. This taunting may result in reduced attendance and scattered in-class attention, which, in turn, might lead to the student's poor organization and memory. Similarly, an emotionally/behaviorally disordered (EBD) student, by definition, should display, for an extended period, affect or behavior substantially outside most children's developmental norm (Hallahan and Kauffman 1994). In reality, however, a LGBT youth labeled EBD may develop drastic behaviors in response to school- or neighborhood-based **homophobia**, which many other children may not confront.

Mislabeling is more likely to occur with some LGBT students from racial-minority groups, since **African American** and Hispanic Americans, as general populations, have been assessed too frequently as "special needs" students, due to biases in assessment processes (Hallahan and Kauffman 1994). Because many standardized academic achievement measures produce higher scores for European than for African Americans, for example, there may be an inappropriately large number of African American gay youth who are labeled as learning disabled.

Whatever the exceptionality, LGBT youth who fit "special education" assessment criteria should have instruction that takes into account their special needs *and* their sexual-minority status (Rahamin, Dupont, and DuBeau 1996). All LGBT students benefit, to some degree, from teacher intervention to stop the **harassment** they all too commonly face. Many of these students also can benefit from **sexuality education** that includes discussion of homosexuality (Blanchett 2002). Whether in sex education or in other subjects, most students with disabilities can benefit from engagement in a personally relevant **curriculum**, encouragement to use strong learning modalities, explicit enough instruction to compensate for weak learning modalities, development of personal learning strengths, step-by-step instruction and repetition in weak areas, and practice with necessary skills in the broader environment (particularly with peers and mentors) (Hallahan and Kauffman 1994).

LGBT students in special education also benefit from specialized help, in teaching and **counseling**, depending on their specific mild, sensory, physical, or intellectual disabilities (Dworkin and Gutierrez 1992). LGBT–LD students, for example, can profit from personally meaningful curricular references to gay, as well straight, **history, literature**, and health. In the same spirit, LGBT–EBD students, when necessary, can be kept out of homophobic classroom settings (including special-needs settings) and can be provided LGBT-supportive counseling.

In defending an LGBT special education student against harassment and exclusion, educators can advocate for appropriately sensitive guidance for this pupil. In doing so, they can invoke special education law on the student's right to individualized counseling and related services. Further, teachers can ask their school districts for age-appropriate curriculum with LGBT-sensitive content as well as for in-services and readings on how to implement helpful activities, such as objectives on a child's Individual Education Plan (IEP). For example, health teachers of LGBT–LD youth can request health or family life curricula that deal directly and sensitively with the place of LGBT people in traditional and nontraditional families. Similarly, they can ask for advice on how to integrate this material into the adolescent's transitional IEP section (the part that addresses learning steps needed for him or her to become a broadly-functioning "real world" adult). In addition, history teachers of a LGBT–LD youth might provide class commentary or handouts on some similarities and differences between civil rights struggles in the LGBT and other underrepresented communities.

Parents who have openly LGBT children with special needs can lay out for educators their children's learning and emotional pressures (and joys) that are specific to **sexual orientation**. They also can mention past teaching strategies that have worked and have not worked to affirm these youth. Teachers who have openly-LGBT special needs students can ask parents for their advice on workable educational strategies and can keep parents updated on approaches that are being implemented to support these students in the classroom, school, district, and community.

Bibliography

Blanchett, Wanda. 2002. "Voices from a TASH Forum on Meeting the Needs of Gay, Lesbian and Bisexual Adolescents and Adults with Severe Disabilities." *Research and Practice for Persons with Severe Disabilities* 27, no. 1: 82–86.

Dworkin, Sari H., and Fernando J. Gutierrez, eds. 1992. *Counseling Gay Men and Lesbians: Journey to the End of the Rainbow.* Alexandria, VA. American Association for Counseling and Development.

Hallahan, Daniel P., and James M. Kauffman. 1994. *Exceptional Children: Introduction to Special Education.* Needham Heights, MA: Allyn-Bacon.

National Center for Education Statistics. 2002. *Digest of Education Statistics*. Washington, DC: U.S. Department of Education.

Rahamin, Robert, Phillipe J. Dupont, and Tania DuBeau. 1996. "Considerations in Working with Adolescents who are Gay, Lesbian, or Bisexual." Pp. 28–31 in *Understanding Individual Differences: Highlights from the National Symposium on What Educators Should Know about Adolescents who are Gay, Lesbian, or Bisexual*. Edited by Lyndal M. Bullock, Robert A. Gable, and Joseph R. Ridky. Reston, VA: Council for Exceptional Children.

Skrtic, Thomas M., ed. 1995. *Disability and Democracy: Reconstructing (Special) Education for Postmodernity*. New York: Teachers College Press.

Web Site

Council for Exceptional Children. November 2004. Accessed December 4, 2004. http://www.cec.org. Mentions CEC's policy statements and purchasable readings related to equitable treatment for exceptional LGBT students.

Spirituality

Sharon G. Horne and *Wendy J. Biss*

Spirituality is a sense of personal connection to the sacred and, although it often overlaps with religion, it does not require formal expression of faith through participation in a religious community. Spirituality can exist within the context of organized religion or separately, and appears to be very important for LGBT youth, as evidenced by the participation of LGBT youth in nontraditional faiths such as the Radical Faeries, Pagan, and Wiccan communities. **Lesbian, gay, bisexual**, and **transgender** (LGBT) youth often are brought up with religious faiths that deny or overtly denounce their sexual or **gender identity**. Increasingly, these youth are drawn to spiritual faiths that honor and support their whole selves. Nontraditional spiritual communities, located in urban and rural areas, have evolved to meet the needs of LGBT individuals, structured around affirming practices rather than mainstream religious doctrine or teachings. In many cities, LGBT youth may also find help in the form of support groups within mainstream denominations, which assist youth in finding LGBT-positive perspectives and theologies, as well as inclusive religious groups like the Metropolitan Community Church and the Unitarian Universalists.

Generally, youth appear to have decreased their participation with traditional Judeo–Christian faiths such as Catholic, Methodist, Jewish, and Lutheran faiths, and young adults continue to make up the highest proportion of those endorsing Buddhist spirituality (Kosmin, Mayer, and Kayser 2004). Similarly, LGBT youth may also be turning to nontraditional spiritualities and faiths because many religious leaders interpret traditional Scripture in ways that condemn homosexuality.

Both spirituality and religious choices appear to develop over time for most people; their search for spirituality occurs in a variety of ways. For example,

See also Christian Moral Instruction on Homosexuality; India, LGBT Youth and Issues in; Jewish Moral Instruction on Homosexuality; Lesbian Feminism; Religion and Psychological Development.

an individual may retain a personal belief in God or celebrate a larger connection between people or nature. Most youth, including queer youth, are typically introduced to a particular faith within their family of origin. Children rarely choose the congregational services they attend. Thus, many LGBT youth attend religious services rooted in a homophobic theology, often placing them at risk. For instance, attending nonaffirming religious services exacerbated a group of Mormon adults' internal struggles with their developing sexual identities and contributed to internalized **homophobia**, believing their sexual identities were immoral or unacceptable (Beckstead and Morrow 2004). LGBT youth may be even more susceptible to negative teachings, given they have not had exposure to alternate viewpoints on religion and spirituality.

LGBT youth and adults adapt to religious homophobia in a number of ways. Many simply leave the congregations of their **childhood**, choosing not to join any other organized religion (Schuck and Little 2003). Others maintain their familial religions, but switch to denominations such as United Church of Christ, in which leaders interpret Scripture in a more LGBT-supportive fashion. For those who remain in their familial religions, becoming active in official or unofficial support groups is a viable option. Integrity for Episcopalians (http://www.integrityusa.org), Dignity for Catholics (http://www.dignityusa.org), and Affirmation for Mormons (http://www.affirmation.org) are three options as are support groups for other religions.

Some who leave their institutionalized religion maintain spirituality as a central guiding factor within their lives, whereas others join nontraditional faiths supportive of LGBT people. These include earth-spirited faiths like Paganism, which encompasses all of pre-Christian, polytheistic religions, such as Wicca, Santeria, and Shamanism. Paganism itself is not a religion. Although these religions and spiritualities are varied and unique, typically they celebrate communion with nature and belief in more than one god or deity (Penczak 2000).

One Pagan religion that has had tremendous appeal to LGBT individuals is Wicca, a contemporary religion grounded in ancient beliefs. Initiated by Gerald Gardner (1954), Wiccans believe that divinity is expressed through each living being in nature, and they have a reverence for multiple goddesses and gods. Believers in reincarnation and practitioners of "magick" (an expression of energy and will to make changes in the world) many join covens, which are groups of followers meeting regularly to engage in ritual. Some covens are women-focused, considering their groups a revival of female spirituality lost in the witch burning of the Middle Ages (Barrett 2003).

It appears that more lesbians than gay men belong to Wiccan religions. The growing appeal of Wicca can be seen in the attraction of lesbian and bisexual women to the practice of "Dianic" Wicca or Feminist Wicca, which has also been associated with lesbian separatism. The reemergence of Dianic Wiccanism has been related to the origins of **feminism**. "Dianic" Wicca can take many forms although it most often involves worshipping the "Goddess" as well as the power and empowerment of women. Practitioners of Dianic Wicca form covens consisting only of women, are often very politically active, and form support networks.

A Pagan spiritual path practiced primarily by gay men is the Radical Faeries (http://www.geocities.com/WestHollywood/Heights/5347/radfae.html). Initiated as a radical response to the denigration of gay and transgender men and the oppressiveness of urban life, the faerie circle was formed in the late 1970s on the principles of

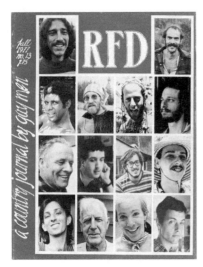

The Radical Faeries Quarterly Magazine, *RFD*, 1977. Courtesy of RFD, www.rfdmag.org

ecology, gay and youth liberation, feminism, anti-racism, and anarchism (Roscoe 1996; Sears 2001). In practice, Radical Faeries create sacred space by casting a circle, in which energy is fostered through dancing and chanting (e.g., the Kali fire that serves to discard that which is no longer needed or desired). They often pass a talisman that signals who within the group speaks. The Radical Faeries publish the quarterly magazine *RFD* (http://www.rfdmag.org), and Faerie communities exist throughout North America, from Short Mountain in Tennessee and Wolf Creek, Oregon, to Northern Rivers in Australia.

During the last decade, there has been growth in the number of adults reporting earth-spirited faiths as their primary form of worship, currently accounting for nearly 3 percent of the overall faiths practiced (Kosmin, Mayer, and Kayser 2002). Among 1,257 LGBT adults surveyed in an international study, 14 percent affiliated with one of these earth-spirited faiths (Smith and Horne In Press). It is more difficult to gauge the number of LGBT youth currently practicing earth-spirited faiths, but by all popular measures, LGBT youth are drawn to earth-spirited faiths as evident in the popularity of television shows with positive witch themes and the increasing number of youth-focused Pagan and Wiccan Web sites. The use of the **Internet** by queer youth to explore difficult and sensitive issues has resulted in some youth finding earth-spirited faiths for the first time while searching online (Praskievicz 2001) or actively using the Internet to reach out to other Pagan practitioners (Chestnut 2001). In Witchvox, one of the most comprehensive Web sites on Pagan information, one can find LGBT affirming messages on every Web page, as well as Pagan communities devoted to LGBT youth. LGBT youth are encouraged to contribute as equals to the Web community and many contribute regular articles about their experiences integrating their sexual identities with their spiritual paths.

Participating in both the Pagan communities and the LGBT communities allows queer youth a place to learn how to negotiate difficult, nonmainstream identities within a larger culture that devalues both their sexual and spiritual identities (Chestnut 2001; Praskievicz 2001). Furthermore, Pagan communities also provide a place for young people to seek further affirmation for their sexual identities and political struggles. In one study, those who affiliated initially with earth-spirited faiths before coming out experienced less religious conflict than those who left traditional religions and later became earth-spirited (Smith and Horne 2004).

Some practitioners of earth-spirited faiths have compiled information that link aspects of LGBT sexuality with spirituality, providing affirmation to individuals who search for a place where both their **sexual identity** and their spirituality are integrated and where masculine and feminine energies are blended (Connor 1997; Penczak 2004). Spiritual writers have described the importance of celebrating and appreciating LGBT eroticism for its spiritual connectedness (Connor 1997). The prizing of LGBT sexuality is reflected in Hindu Tantra communities, which support the integration of LGBT sexuality and spirituality (http://www.gaytantra.org/pages/519899/index.htm). Tantra refers to the practice of harnessing sexual energy to propel spiritual development through breathing techniques, meditation, sexual awareness, and creation of sacred space for spiritual and sexual communion.

Other queer youth find spiritual connection through meditation and mindfulness practice in connection with Buddhism. Sanghas are spiritual communities that practice the five precepts and the eightfold path to enlightenment. Although teachings vary on the interpretation of homosexuality within Buddhism, most Western-influenced teachings are LGBT affirming and offer a sanctuary to practice relaxation and mindfulness meditation. The Dalai Lama, the spiritual leader of Tibet, and largely considered the most important Buddhist spiritual guide, has denounced **discrimination** and violence against LGBT individuals, supporting human rights for all regardless of **sexual orientation**. Such leadership is expanding the appeal of Buddhism as practiced by queer youth.

Bibliography

Barrett, Robert. 2003. "Lesbian Rituals and Dianic Tradition." *Journal of Lesbian Studies* 7, no. 2: 15–28.

Beckstead, Lee, and Sue Morrow. 2004. "Mormon Clients' Experiences of Conversion Therapy: The Need for a New Treatment Approach." *The Counseling Psychologist* 32: 651–690.

Cain, Joey. Undated e-mail posting. Accessed June 16, 2005. http://www.hipfaerie.net/faerieinf.html.

Chestnut. 2001, January. "Finding the Craft." Accessed June 16, 2005. http://www.witchvox.com/teen/teen_2001/teen_finding_craft8.html.

Connor, Randy. 1997. *Cassell's Encyclopedia of Queer Myth, Symbol, and Spirit: Gay, Lesbian, Bisexual, and Transgender Lore*. Los Angeles: Cassell.

Gardner, Gary. 1954. *Witchcraft Today*. Thame, England: I-H-O Books.

Kolodny, Debra, ed. 2000. *Blessed Bi Spirit: Bisexual People of Faith*. New York: Continuum.

Kosmin, Barry A., Egon Mayer, and Ariela Kayser. 2002. "American Religious Identification Survey." Accessed June 16, 2005. http://www.gc.cuny.edu/studies/key_findings.htm.

Lanphear, Roger G., ed. 1990. *Gay Spirituality*. San Diego: Unified.

Penczak, Christopher. 2000, August. "Coming Out of the Broom Closet." Accessed September 1, 2004. http://www.witchvox.com/gay/bcloset2.html.

Praskievicz, Sarah. 2001, July. "Pagan Pride." Accessed June 16, 2005. http://www.witchvox.com/teen/teen_2001/teen_accept5.html.

Roscoe, Will, ed. 1996. *Radically Gay: Gay Liberation in the Words of its Founder*. Boston: Beacon Press.

Schuck, Kelly, and Becky Liddle. 2001. "Religious Conflicts Experienced by Lesbian, Gay, and Bisexual Individuals." *Journal of Gay and Lesbian Psychotherapy* 5, no. 2: 63–82.

Sears, James T. 2001. *Rebels, Rubyfruit, and Rhinestones: Queering the Stonewall South*. New Brunswick, NJ: Rutgers University Press.

Smith, Brandy, and Sharon G. Horne. In Press. "Gay, Lesbian, Bisexual (GLBT) Experiences with Earth-Spirited Faiths." *Journal of Homosexuality*.

Thompson, Mark. 1987. *Gay Spirit: Myth and Meaning*. New York: St. Martin's Press.

Witchvox. 1999. *Smack Upside the Head: A Wake-Up Call from the Queen of the Underworld*. Carlin. Accessed June 16, 2005. http://www.witchvox.com/teen/teen_1999/teen_smack.html. Use key word search "Carlin."

Web Sites

Gay Men's Buddhist Sangha. 2004. Accessed June 16, 2005. http://www.gaysangha.org/cover.html. A Web site community of gay men exploring Buddhist teachings and practices.

Gay Spirituality and Culture. November 2004. Accessed June 16, 2005. http://gay spirituality.typepad.com/blog/queer_youth. This "super blog" of independent writers routinely includes material by and about queer youth.

Hipfaerie: Sacred Space for Hip Youth. June 2005. Accessed June 16, 2005. http://www. hipfaerie.net/spirit.html. LGB youth, their mentors, and allies with common interests join in modern hip culture. Information about contemporary radical faerie youth culture.

Magical Activism. June 2005. Accessed June 16, 2005. http://www.magicalactivism.org. Organized around political action through neo-Pagan spirit, this site provides community organizing around such issues as spells for same-sex marriage.

Radical Faery. June 2005. Accessed June 16, 2005. http://www.combose.com/Society/ Religion_and_Spirituality/Pagan/Wicca/Traditions/Faery/Radical_Faery. This is the official site for the Radical Faeries, which lists community Web pages and links for Radical Faery communities in North America.

White Crane Journal. 2004. Accessed June 16, 2005. http://www.whitecranejournal. com/list.asp. Extensive annotated list of LGBT spiritual resources.

Witchvox: The Witches' Voice. 2004. Accessed June 16, 2005. http://www.witchvox.com. Comprehensive site and community devoted to Wiccanism and Paganism, including voices of LGBT youth and a full glossary of terms associated with and information about earth-spirited faiths.

Women in Conscious Creative. 2004. Norma Joyce. Action Accessed June 16, 2005. http://www.wiccawomen.com. A faith organization that offers support, retreats, and information related to the practice of Dianic Wicca.

Sport, Gay Men in

Judy Davidson

As the ultimate expression of straight male power and privilege, men's athletics can be a difficult place for **gay youth**. Men's sport is a single-sexed social space (that is, men-only space) where classic ideals of masculinity (power, aggression, physicality, brutality, dominance, and strength) are played out and lauded. However, same-sex attraction is not tolerated. Male sport, therefore, is classically heterosexist and homophobic, disciplining all players so that they are seen to be solidly heterosexual. Coaches and teammates in aggressive sports such as American football, rugby, and hockey, often invoke homophobic slurs to push players to work harder and endure more pain. Relatively very few elite or professional male athletes have come out publicly. Recently, two exceptional high school athletes have come out—Cory Johnson (a football player) and Dan Bozzuto (track and cross country)—with great success and support from coaches, teachers, and school communities.

Expressions of **desire** are concentrated in the sporting contest—the desire to win, to achieve, to be the hero, to push one's physicality to the limit, and to identify intensely with an athlete or team as a fan. Because men's sport is single-sexed, Pronger (2000) suggests these desires are a form of homoeroticism. While Pronger is very clear that *not* all men who participate in sport are homosexual, he does

See also Activism, LGBT Youth; Cocurricular Activities; Dance, Teaching of; Gender Roles; Heterosexism; Resiliency; Sissy Boy.

explore how that homoeroticism is disguised in other, more socially acceptable forms of attachment and longing. Pronger's argument works in the following manner. Traditional masculinity is heavily invested in a heterosexual assumption and imperative. Sport is also site of traditional masculinity, emphasizing the masculine values of power, strength, and dominance, and it celebrates close affinity among men. This paradoxical experience of assumed desire for women and intense connection with men produces the blatant **homophobia** in sport. This intense site of complicated desires has to be managed by the players within it. Unfortunately, one of the most entrenched management strategies is to deny and then denigrate anything remotely linked to the eroticism implied in the male-only space of sport. To maintain the masculinist hegemony of heterosexist sport, homophobic actions, speech, and threat are commonplace in policing behaviors and participation by men in sporting contexts.

There are huge social costs associated with this homoerotic paradox in men's sport. Those athletes who may be gay are forced to live in secret and must cut off very important parts of their lives if they choose to continue participating in sport. Otherwise they risk severe abuse and censure if they do come out while still actively participating in sport. The tolerance, let alone acceptance, of gay men in sport is completely dependent upon the whims of a professional sport entertainment marketplace or the uneven efforts of progressive people within relevant organizations that provide noncommercial sporting opportunities such as intercollegiate, intramural, community, or recreational contexts (Pronger 2000). How do boys and men learn such entrenched homophobia through sporting cultures?

One of the basic assumptions of conventional masculinity in Western cultures is that to be a man is to be solidly heterosexual. Any kind of homosexual desire is dangerous and weak, requiring immediate eradication. In athletics, this homophobic discourse is relentlessly reproduced such as in locker room talk about fags being sick, perverse, and disgusting. To keep boys in line, references to homosexual men and/or women, (fag/got, girl, fairy, etc.) are used pejoratively to mock, insult, or aggravate a teammate. Homophobia is also used as a motivational device. By playing on the threat of being labeled "gay," players not conforming to team discipline will be shamed through the invocation of acting or being a homosexual. Often these displays are public, humiliating, and dehumanizing. Male players may exhibit gay-hating or even gay-bashing behaviors in an attempt to secure their heterosexual credentials.

Another tactic to prove one's heterosexuality is to play "manly" sports. Violent sports such as football, hockey, and rugby are considered more virile than gymnastics, diving, or figure skating. Consistent with heterosexist masculinity, male athletes in "feminized" sports are often represented as, and perhaps are even expected "to be," homosexuals. Men's figure skating is the classic **stereotype**. This representation is affirmed when considering media coverage of the HIV-positive status of certain elite athletes. For example, basketball player Magic Johnson was constructed as hyper(hetero)sexual, whereas diver Greg Louganis was assumed to be homosexual. Or, as one gay male athlete suggested: "Swimming is not a butch enough sport to discredit accusations that you're queer" (Pronger 1990, 32).

It is into this very hostile environment that some brave prominent athletes have come out. Examples of out male athletes include: David Kopay, Jerry Smith, Roy Simmons, and Esera Tuaolo of the National Football League (NFL); Greg Louganis and Bruce Hayes in aquatics; Glenn Burke, Billy and Dave Pallone in Major League

Baseball; Justin Fashanu in English soccer (who tragically committed suicide); Olympic decathlete and founder of the Gay Games, Tom Waddell; and Matthew Hall and Rudy Galindo in men's figure skating (Messner and Sabo 1994; Miller 2001). These men are powerful role models and beacons of hope for young, gay male athletes.

Positive media coverage of gay athletes is important. Esera Tuaolo graced the front cover of the United States-based lesbian and gay newsmagazine, *The Advocate*, in November 2002. A nine-year veteran lineman in the National Football League, Tuaolo was a leading tackle throughout his whole career. He was carefully closeted throughout his NFL career—at great personal cost—and only the third NFL player ever to come out. Waiting to come out until retirement, Tuaolo did not think the league was ready to handle an out player, and he knew his career would have been cut short, that fans wouldn't have handled it, and that it likely would have been dangerous for him (Steele 2002). Thus, homophobia in sport forces those who are different to "act normally," often to personal detriment. Biographies by Dave Kopay and Greg Louganis also offer testimonial stories by prominent gay sportsmen.

Depending on what kind of "normal" is foregrounded, today's professional men's team sports can, at times, contain a homosexual athlete. Ian Roberts is an example of how an out gay man managed, to some extent, to maintain his professional rugby career in **Australia** and his popularity and still be an out as a gay man. This may be due to the fact that Roberts does not rock conventional notions of masculinity. In the mid-1990s, Roberts, who was a prop forward, publicly declared his homosexuality. The position that Roberts plays in rugby is a "tough" position—tackling other big forwards, running with the ball, and passing. Prop forwards take bone-crunching hits and have to be fit and hard according to expert commentators. Because Roberts is an aggressive, at times, violent rugby star, he does not evoke the stereotype of a limp-wristed effeminate homosexual. Perhaps, in certain contexts, it is not "being" gay that is troublesome, but the disruption of heteronormative gender discourse. Ian Roberts, for instance, does not threaten the very basis of rugby or rugby culture as he maintains the sport norms of brute strength and physical violence.

Dealing with one's homosexuality in **adolescence** is difficult, and if one is involved in athletics, it can complicate the situation even further. Adolescent gay athletes talk about focusing on sport to distract them from directly acknowledging their homosexuality. Feeling isolated and alone in their sport is a major deterrent in full acceptance of their **sexual identity**. Sharing athletic **coming out** stories is crucial. At the turn of the twenty-first century, two exceptional high school athletes have overcome fears and demonstrated great courage to come out to their coaches, teachers, teammates, and school communities. Both of these resilient young men stand as powerful role models for other young gay athletes to come out.

In 1999, Cory Johnson, cocaptain of a Massachusetts high school football team, was likely the first high school athlete to come out publicly while enjoying high levels of teammate and school support. Although Johnson's coming out was highly successful, it was preceded by months of anxiety, depression, and concern. After telling select teachers, family, and friends, Johnson wanted to come out to his entire team. Admitting his homosexuality surprised many as he does not embody the stereotype of a gay man; Johnson's coach described him as one of his toughest players. Like Ian Roberts, this conventional masculinity may have helped foster acceptance. Another important factor, cited by Johnson's coach, was the ground-work done at the high school by the **gay–straight alliance** and the Massachusetts Safe Schools program (Cassels 2000).

In 2002, Connecticut track athlete Dan Bozzuto used an annual speaking event to come out to over 1,000 fellow high school student students. In his opening words, he said he was "just another student who happens to be gay." Bozzuto is identified as a powerful student leader, excelling academically and athletically. However, he outlined the difficulties (including considering suicide) he had in coming to terms with his sexuality, but "if I can help one or two people who have been going through the same thing that I did, then it will be worth it." Support from members of the track team increased and peers now hold Bozzuto in awe for his poised and courageous statements (Personal Torment 2002).

Coaches play a pivotal role in creating team climates where healthy respect for differences across sexualities is practiced. Coaches have both a responsibility and an opportunity to educate athletes about fairness and social justice for all. As powerful role models, coaches who engage in actions which support and respect gay athletes, directly address antigay or homophobic speech, and educate adults about gay issues promote fairness, respect, and nondiscrimination in the sporting context (Griffin et al. 2002).

Bibliography

Cassels, Peter. 2000. "A Brave Athlete, Supportive School." *Bay Windows Magazine.*

Griffin, Pat, Jeff Perrotti, Laurie Priest, and Mike Muska. 2002. *It Takes a Team! Making Sports Safe for Lesbian, Gay, Bisexual, and Transgender Athletes and Coaches.* East Meadow, NY: Women's Sports Foundation.

Kopay, David, and Perry D. Young. 1988. *David Kopay Story: An Extraordinary Self-Revelation.* New York: Fine.

Louganis, Greg, and Eric Marcus. 1995. *Breaking the Surface.* New York: Random House.

Messner, Michael A., and Donald F. Sabo. 1994. *Sex, Violence, and Power in Sports: Rethinking Masculinity.* Freedom, CA: Crossing Press.

Miller, Toby. 2001. *Sportsex.* Philadelphia: Temple University Press.

Personal Torment Set Aside. 2002, June 11. *Waterbury Republican-American.*

Pronger, Brian. 1990. *The Arena of Masculinity: Sports, Homosexuality, and the Meaning of Sex.* Toronto: University of Toronto.

———. 2000. "Homosexuality and Sport: Who's Winning?" Pp. 222–244 in *Masculinities, Gender Relations, and Sport.* Edited by Jim McKay, Michael Messner, and Donald. Sabo. Thousand Oaks, CA: Sage.

Steele, Bruce. C. 2002, November 2. "Tackling Football's Closet." *The Advocate*: 30–39.

Web Sites

Federation of Gay Games. November 2004. Accessed December 18, 2004. http://www.gaygames.com. Information source for the quadrennial international lesbian and gay sporting and cultural festival.

Gay.Sport.Info. December 2004. European Gay and Lesbian Sports Federation. Accessed December 18, 2004. http://www.gaysport.org. Mandate is to promote gay and lesbian sport without fear of discrimination based on sexual orientation.

OutSports. December 2004. Accessed December 18, 2004. http://www.outsports.com. Site for gay male sports fans and athletes, which includes many testimonials from out gay athletes.

Project to Eliminate Homophobia in Sports. September 2004. Accessed December 18, 2004. http://homophobiainsports.com. Includes a link to the document "It Takes a Team," an important resource for coaches, athletes, and athletic directors.

Sport, Lesbians in

Judy Davidson

Adolescent lesbians may find a lesbian athletic community in sport and/or **lesbian youth** may be dissuaded from **coming out** at all in the very closeted and homophobic world of women's sport. In Western societies, teenage girls and women are caught in the heteronormative squeeze of masculinist sport. Women's participation in sport disrupts sport as a male preserve of power and prestige. Because conventional athletics require aggression, dominance, and physicality, (typically masculine behaviors), athletic women are caught in the bind of appearing masculine while being athletic. The early sexology **stereotype** of a "man caught in a woman's body" otherwise known as the "mannish lesbian," functions to discipline women in athletics to appear strictly heterosexual. The highly physical nature of women's athletics draws attention to how passive, heterosexualized femininity cannot be maintained in such sporting contexts without the stereotype of the mannish lesbian being invoked.

The stereotype functions by labeling those women who are good at sport (esp. nonfeminine sports) by presuming them to be lesbian and masculine. Historically, this stereotype is fixed from one of the earliest theories of sexologists such as **Magnus Hirschfield** at the turn of the twentieth century. This is the notion of the gender invert. Homosexuals were presumed to be men trapped in women's bodies or women trapped in men's bodies. Hence the "mannish lesbian" and the "effeminate fag," which are two stereotypes that are still alive and well in homophobic sporting circles.

The stereotype of the mannish lesbian produces a difficult paradox for women in sport. In our heteropatriarchal culture, women are not to be masculine. Sport often demands bodily performances which involve demonstration of aggression, strength, and competition. When female-identified bodies perform these skills, they run the risk of acting manly and, therefore, being marginalized as "mannish lesbians." Women's behavior and actions are thus carefully circumscribed on and off the court, field, or arena to secure their heterosexual credentials as "real" women. Makeup, hairstyles, and the parading out of husbands and boyfriends all belie this need to heterosexualize female athletes.

Susan Cahn (1994) claims this damning stereotype of the mannish lesbian actually functioned as a way for athletic women who wanted to find lesbian community to do that in the 1930s, 40s, and 50s. The very thing that was supposed to scare the "deviants" or the "perverted Other" away, was, in fact, one of the ways in which lesbians were able to form a kind of athletic community—albeit a community that is still, to this day, a very closeted and careful community. Many lesbians new to a

See also Cocurricular Activities; Gender Roles; Heterosexism; Passing; Queer and Queer Theory; Resiliency; Sexism; Tomboy.

city would congregate at women's softball and fastball games in an effort to locate the local lesbian community.

The influence of McCarthyism, with its outright witch hunt for homosexuals and celebration of patriarchal power in sport, made overt community organizing for lesbians (both within and outside the athletic context) difficult and dangerous. This is part of the reason women's athletic communities, and the lesbians in these communities, were very careful. However, sport provided an outlet for all women, lesbian or not, to escape or at least to stretch the constraints imposed by conventional 1950s and 60s femininity. The presence of women's softball, fastball, and basketball (among others) in major cities in North America provided these outlets.

The reference to the "mannish lesbian" stereotype in the early twenty-first century may seem out of date. However, professional women's tennis, in the late 1990s, exemplifies that the stereotype is alive and well and is an interesting context in which to consider how the mannish lesbian stereotype continues to function. Women's tennis is one of the few sports where women players can earn the huge sums of money often reserved for their male counterparts. It is also a sport in which there have been several public lesbians who have been very successful at their game.

Billie Jean King, the "founding mother" of professional women's tennis and a lesbian, revolutionized the game in concert with the **women's movement** of the 1970s. Along with demands for equal pay for equal work, King was able to get women's tennis professional tournaments. Even still, the Women's Tennis Association (WTA) insisted throughout the 1970s and 1980s that the sport maintain its properly traditional image. There was to be no sponsorship from manufacturers of feminine hygiene products and players were encouraged to disclose about their heterosexual personal lives to the media. This construction of a private self away from the court kept women in the traditionally feminine private realm and out of the public, masculine world.

Chris Evert was the hallmark of this media change. The white American darling chose her earrings and makeup to attract corporate sponsors. She repeatedly suggested that "there was no point that is worth falling down for" (Miller 2001, 108), and references to male lovers kept her orthodox femininity intact. Many other female players have followed the corporate media discipline regime to this day—Gabriela Sabatini, Jennfier Capriati, Monica Seles, and perhaps the crowning achievement, Anna Kournikova. This packaging of players allowed a humanizing element but also commodified the tennis athlete. Rita Mae Brown, novelist and former partner of Martina Navratilova, suggested "that players were packaged and marketed, if not as latter-day Shirley Temples, then as retro-women" (Miller 2001, 113).

The out lesbian, tennis champion Martina Navratilova never had shots of her girlfriend in the stands shown on television. Instead this new commodification of the personalized female tennis star ushered in a new wave of "dyke-bashing." In 1981, Avon (a longtime supporter) cancelled its sponsorship of the women's tennis tour in the wake of Billie Jean King's galimony suit and Navratilova's public relationship with Rita Mae Brown. In 1990, Margaret Smith Court, an Australian champion of the 1960s, set off another moral panic when she held a press conference claiming women's tennis was full of predatory lesbians who seduced and recruited young women to the "lifestyle." Players at the time concurred with her. Gabriela Sabatini summed it up: "I don't even like to take my clothes off in the dressing room" (Miller 2001, 114). The mannish lesbian stereotype was in full force at this time. Near the end of Navratilova's reign, she was pejoratively described as having "had developed unnatural masculine strength through weight training" and that she "must have a chromosomic screw loose somewhere" (Miller 2001, 114).

In 1999, when Amelie Mauresmo defeated number one ranked Lindsay Davenport in the semifinal of the Australian Open, Mauresmo leapt into the arms of her (then) girlfriend Sylvie Bourdon. Mauresmo came out to the media during the Open. After losing the match, Davenport claimed, "A couple of times, I mean, I thought I was playing a guy, the girl was hitting so hard, so strong. . . . I mean she hits the ball not like any other girl. . . . Women's tennis isn't usually played like that" (Miller 2001, 104). Ironically, Davenport, a 6' 2" woman, plays a power game suited to her physical stature. Even though Mauresmo is five inches shorter, she was subjected to a barrage of homophobic statements, which pulled her into the media spotlight. At the same tournament in Australia, Amelie Mauresmo played Martina Hingis (ironically named for the lesbian superstar) in the final. Hingis repeated the stereotype. She told reporters before their match "She came to Melbourne with her girlfriend; I think she's half a man" (Miller 2001, 104). The questioning of Mauresmo's gender, casting doubt on her femaleness, fits perfectly with the stereotype of the mannish lesbian and how it is used to discipline especially sexuality differences in women's sport.

Senior women in tennis counseled against this kind of talk. Hingis was asked to temper the homophobic comments. Steffi Graf spoke out against it. Nonetheless, Mauresmo has become a hero in various lesbian communities. She was the first French athlete to ever come out, and has become vaunted and idolized much like Martina Navratilova. While the homophobia in women's sport persists, there are still lesbians who play and some who are unapologetic about their sexual identities.

Pat Griffin (1998) has characterized five identity management strategies used by lesbian athletes. These are particularly to lesbians in high school and college where peer expectations are strong.

1. Antigay/Denying. Involves female athletes who are sexually attracted to other women but are terrified by those feelings. Fearing they may be suspected of being lesbians, women in this category often speak and act in ways hostile to lesbian teammates, make homophobic comments, and generally express antigay sentiments. This strategy involves dating men, talking about (fictitious) boyfriends, and creating a heterosexual persona to hide a secret relationship with or desire for a woman.

2. *Special Friends/Ashamed and Self-Hating.* Women who are in sexual relationships with other women but who do not identify as gay, let alone lesbian. Perceiving the word lesbian to have political connotations, these women shy away from identifying as lesbian and refer to their "special friend" instead. Their intimate relationships are very secretive and closeted, using a language of "being" with someone or being "that way." The shame and ambivalence of being in a relationship with another woman keeps these athletes deeply in the closet.

3. *Members of a Secret "Club."* Some lesbian athletes, while remaining primarily closeted, manage to expand their social network to include

other lesbians, typically other athletic lesbians, who are also generally very secret and quiet about their sexual identities. The basis of the secret club is shame and fear of being "outed." These women collectively gather at homes or particular clubs, discourage being out or open about their lesbian identities, and generally operate within an athletic context. The "secret" club provides confidentiality while also being an outlet for friendship, a certain form of social support, and a context for sex and/or partnership. In the hostile athletic environment, these "clubs" can be an important oasis of support.

4. *Prudent and Proud.* Women in this category have come to develop a sense of self-acceptance as a lesbian, often come out to teammates and coaches, and generally refuse to tolerate homophobic comments or actions. However, these lesbian athletes respect the secrecy needs of their more closeted colleagues, and won't publicly identify so as to "protect" their team from overt lesbian stigma. There is a fear of politicizing the team as lesbian, with resulting negative consequences.

5. *Out and Proud.* Out and proud athletes are unapologetic about their lesbian sexual identity in all arenas of their life—athletic and otherwise. They may be actively engaged in gay and lesbian organizations, will not tolerate unfair discriminatory treatment, and may work with sympathetic coaches and administrators to educate other athletes about the problems of heterosexism and homophobia.

More and more lesbians in sport are choosing to be out. Changing norms about sexuality among contemporary youth, the success of the gay and lesbian rights movement, and more and more elite athletes coming out as lesbians have produced a somewhat safer climate for lesbian in athletics.

Bibliography

Cahn, Susan K. 1994. *Coming on Strong: Gender and Sexuality in Twentieth-Century Women's Sport.* New York: Free Press.

Griffin, Pat. 1998. *Strong Women, Deep Closets: Lesbians and Homophobia in Sport.* Champaign, IL: Human Kinetics.

Lenskyj, Helen Jefferson. 2003. *Out on the Field: Gender, Sport and Sexualities.* Toronto: Women's Press.

Miller, Toby. 2001. *Sportsex.* Philadelphia: Temple University Press.

Roxxie, ed. 1998. *Girljock: The Book.* New York: St. Martin's Press.

Web Sites

Federation of Gay Games. November 2004. Accessed December 18, 2004. http://www.gaygames.com. Information source for the quadrennial international lesbian and gay sporting and cultural festival.

Gay.Sport.Info. December 2004. European Gay and Lesbian Sports Federation. Accessed December 18, 2004. http://www.gaysport.org. Mandate is to promote gay and lesbian sport without fear of discrimination based on sexual orientation.

Project to Eliminate Homophobia in Sports. September 2004. Accessed December 18, 2004. http://homophobiainsports.com. Includes a link to the document "It Takes a Team," an important resource for coaches, athletes and athletic directors.

Stereotypes

Ray Misson

A stereotype is a simplified image of a particular type of person. The simplification always has an ideological impact. It can highlight good qualities (the nurturing mother, the wise patriarch) but, more powerfully, it can obscure whatever might be good and focus on what is considered unacceptable (the polyamorous bisexual, the hairy dyke). Stereotypes always come with a valuation implicit: They embody myths about particular types of people, and so they are basic fodder for **prejudice** and **discrimination**. They either provide the ideal measure against which other people are found to be wanting, or they provide the readily available reason why a person is to be rejected and despised. Nevertheless, they are a basic form of social thinking. As a mental representation of the (supposed) features that define a particular group, they categorize people and create expectations that there will be a particular configuration of attitudes and attributes: A drag queen will be superficial; a gay boy will be effeminate. This can be insultingly limiting but, in one sense, we couldn't operate without stereotypes since a stereotype is a compression of social information about likely combinations of features. We also create ourselves through stereotypes: We use them to define ourselves, asserting that we are a particular kind of person. This can be particularly important for **lesbian, gay, bisexual,** and **transgender youth** (LGBT) who are searching for an identity. Since (homo)sexuality is largely invisible, **queer** youth may often be driven to inhabiting a stereotype that announces her or his identity to the world (or even just to a potential lover) by evincing an interest in Barbra Streisand or getting a close-cropped haircut. A young gay male may take on effeminate characteristics or start molding the body through strenuous workouts.

Since stereotypes are often negative, identifying with them can be damaging and create an ambivalence about the self, even self-hatred. The young lesbian may see herself as inevitably unattractively butch in keeping with the mainstream stereotype, or the gay teen may view himself as a likely casualty to **suicide** or **AIDS**. Stereotypes are simplifications and for that reason unacceptable as images of ourselves. It is unlikely anyone has ever said—and meant it: "I'm a stereotype." A stereotype is always seen from outside. We credit ourselves with a complexity and individuality that shifts us out of the category of stereotype, even though we may acknowledge we have stereotypical features. As soon as we appropriate a stereotype to represent ourselves, we no longer consider it a stereotype but a feature of our individuality: Our fastidious concern with appearance is not stereotypical, but just the rather attractive way we are.

On the other hand, even negative stereotypes can be appropriated and turned into a positive affirmation of oneself and where one belongs in the world. Stereotypes have a complex relationship with actuality; they may be simplifications, but they are not necessarily false. Indeed the fact that we can define ourselves through them suggests this. At the very least, they become "real" as people inhabit them to identify openly as a member of a particular group.

See also Identity Development; Queer and Queer Theory; Race and Racism; Sexism; Sexual Identity; Sissy Boy; Tomboy.

A stereotype is never neutral but comes with implicit evaluations. The whole point of a stereotype is that it summarizes how a particular group is seen by another usually more dominant group. We are always positioned or position ourselves in relation to a stereotype. Since the stereotype is inherently an image of the Other, we can be positioned with an insider group to which the stereotype is the outsider, and in this case we feel ourselves superior: Disparaging references within a gay group to heterosexuals as "breeders" or to all straight men as homophobes would operate in this way. If we are the excluded outsider, at the most positive, we see the stereotype as an unsatisfactory simplification of what we are, or we reject it as an insultingly false image being imposed.

One sure sign of the deep implication of stereotypes in ideology is that they often come in binary oppositional pairs: gay men, for example, can be stereotyped as either comically and harmlessly unmasculine or as voracious sexual predators; bisexuals can be either sexually indiscriminate or sexually confused. The function of such a range of stereotypes is to map out possible manifestations and to affirm the superior value of the heterosexual norm and the lesser worth of the "deviant." Such stereotypes are strategic: They permit different kinds of discrimination. The **camp** man, for example, can't be taken seriously and so can be treated as less than a proper human being, whereas the sexually voracious man is dangerous and deserves to be beaten up.

Stereotypes are also the stuff of fantasy, both positive and negative. Advertisers use attractive fantasies: the gym-fit body in the Calvin Klein underwear, the lesbian chic couple with their designer jeans. We spend a fortune trying to attain the fantasy because these are stereotypes we have been trained to want to embody. However, when the stereotype is of the despised Other, the deviant from the norm, then it feeds fantasies of heterosexual superiority and rightness. These images, too, can be found in **popular culture**. Stereotypes, such as the gay man as sexual predator in the **film** *Cruising* (USA 1980) and the gay teacher as pedophile in the infamous "Marcus Welby, MD" episode, have fed many fantasies of power and righteous violence, just as the *Basic Instinct* (USA 1992) image of the lesbian as man-hating and ruthless has undoubtedly retarded many a business career. Similarly, racist and sexist stereotypes are commonly found in erotic magazines and films—both gay and straight.

It is worth saying that, when one is thinking of any social group, it is almost impossible to get outside of stereotypes, because of their social function in providing conceptual categories. One might well ask, can we conceive of a neutral middle ground of sexual minorities. The answer is probably "no," because as soon as we think in terms of generalities rather than individualities, we reach for stereotypes. We can acknowledge their inadequacy, we can pile up the various, often contradictory stereotypes to get a more complex image of the range, but we find it very difficult to think outside the types we have been given by society. Our conception of the homosexual person, in general, is fragmented into these different images. Queer youth can be seen as psychologically disturbed victims of an unsympathetic straight society or as confident members of a sexually open generation. They can be seen as sexually innocent or as sexually powerful exerting their desirability. Of course, they may well be all these at different moments or even simultaneously.

Searching for stereotypes is a staple in many media classes, English classes, and elsewhere in schools. The usual strategy is to identify the stereotype and assert how bad it is, because it simplifies and suggests a false universality. This draws on a

Queer Eye for the Straight Guy, first broadcast on Bravo cable network in summer 2003, was a surprise hit. The specific areas of expertise for each of the gay experts and their titles amusingly fit stereotypes of gay men, as did some of their apparel and mannerisms. Shown: Ted Allen (Food & Wine Connoisseur), Jai Rodriguez (Culture Vulture), Carson Kressley (Fashion Savant), Thom Filicia (Design Doctor), Kyan Douglas (Grooming Guru). Showtime/Photofest

simple stereotype/individual opposition. There is sometimes a push to consider what members of the stereotyped group are "really" like. A real live gay or lesbian person (less likely a transgender person) might be invited to the class to display their individual humanity. Providing alternative images of the outsider group is beneficial, but one can doubt whether it manages to undercut the stereotype and the underlying prejudice.

The problem with searching for stereotypes is that once they are identified, it is felt that nothing more needs to be said. However, it is much more productive to raise consciousness of what stereotypes are doing, both positively and negatively, than dismissing them out of hand as false and reprehensible. In the end, one cannot get outside of stereotypes to a neutral and complete image of any group of people, so the stereotype can never actually be dismissed. Thus, teaching about stereotypes needs to be focused on precisely what the stereotype is doing ideologically, how it is functioning within the particular text, or socially. If a text is presenting a gay man as an effeminate interior designer, one can look at how it is being used to police the bounds of **gender identity**. If we have a lesbian kiss in a television series or advertisement, we might analyze how it is represented so as to be a sign of the trendily alternative, rather than of the immorally disgusting. Stereotypes can even be useful in class as the basis of satire. There are many stereotypes of conservative, narrow-minded people that students know and enjoy, and that can be deployed for purposes of caricature. Perhaps working off a newspaper report about some antigay crusader, they could write a comedy sketch that makes her/him a figure of fun. In doing so, they position themselves, at least momentarily, away from the conservative attitudes, and see that there are always other ways of seeing any situation.

Bibliography

Dyer, Richard. 1993. *The Matter of Images: Essays on Representations*. London and New York: Routledge.

Epstein, Debbie, and James T. Sears, eds. 1999. *A Dangerous Knowing: Sexuality, Pedagogy and Popular Culture*. London and New York: Cassell.

Perkins, T. E. 1979. "Rethinking Stereotypes." Pp. 135–139 in *Ideology and Cultural Production*. Edited by Michele Barrett, Philip Corrigan, Annette Kuhn, and Janet Wolff. London: Croom Helm.

Pickering, Michael. 2001. *Stereotyping: The Politics of Representation*. Basingstoke: Palgrave Macmillan.

Stonewall

Jesse G. Monteagudo

In the summer of 1969, a police raid on the Stonewall Inn, a gay bar in New York City's Greenwich Village, led to several days of rioting by the bar's patrons and much of the Village's lesbian, gay, bisexual, and transgender (LGBT) population. Though the uprising of June 27–July 2, 1969 was not the first time that LGBT people stood up against police raids, that fact that it took place in the United States' largest gay neighborhood at the end of the politically-active 1960s helped make it an important and influential event in the history of the struggle for the rights of sexual and gender minorities. Historian David Carter (2004, 267) called the riots "the critical turning point in the movement for the rights of gay men and lesbians as well as for bisexual and transgender people." It inspired a new generation of activists and inaugurated a new, more radical phase in the movement for LGBT rights that was different from the more conservative homophile movement of the 1950s and 1960s. "Post-Stonewall" activist groups like the Gay Liberation Front (GLF) and the Gay Activists Alliance (GAA) were formed by youthful activists who took part in, or were inspired by, the Stonewall riots. Around the world, the June 27th anniversary is observed as Pride Day; many LGBT organizations have named themselves in honor of the Stonewall Inn.

See also College Campus Organizing; History, Teaching of; LGBT Studies; Rainbow Flag and Other Pride Symbols; Youth, Homeless.

Though the Stonewall riots are one of the most influential events in LGBT history, this uprising was not the beginning of the civil rights movement for gay, lesbian, bisexual, and transgender people in the United States. Groups like the Mattachine Society, ONE, Daughters of Bilitis, Tangents, the Society for Individual Rights, and the West Side Discussion Group had been working for LGBT rights and equality long before Stonewall. It was the New York Mattachine Society which, in 1966, successfully challenged the New York City law that made it illegal for bars to serve liquor to admitted homosexuals. In California, activists rioted when local police raided San Francisco's Compton's Cafeteria (1966) and Los Angeles's Black Cat and New Faces bars (1967). Historian John Loughery (1998) places Stonewall at the *end* of a "maelstrom year" of gay resistance and **activism**.

Like any symbolic event, the truth about the Stonewall riots lies hidden in myth and legend. To this day, the uprising has been attributed to a variety of causes, from the full moon on the first night of the riots to the death of gay icon Judy Garland (she was buried the day of the riots). Even the names and the number of the participants are in dispute. For example, major histories of Stonewall by Martin Duberman (1993) and David Carter (2004) disagree as to the presence of **transgender** activist Sylvia Rivera in the Uprising; Duberman gives her a major role, and Carter leaves her out.

The Stonewall Inn, located at 53 Christopher Street in the Village, was a Mafia-owned tavern that operated without a liquor license. Though the Stonewall was repeatedly raided, Stonewall veterans remember the place as being "the only sizable place where gay men could express their sexuality freely and openly for sustained periods of time" (Carter 2004, 87). While "the presence of drag queens at the Stonewall Inn has been much exaggerated over the years," (Carter 2004, 75), the bar attracted effeminate "scare queens" or "flame queens" as well as **gay youth** and other dispossessed queer minorities who had few other places to go. Carter gives "special credit" for the riots "to gay homeless youth, to transgender men, and to the lesbians who fought the police," especially Jackie Hormona, Marsha Johnson, and Zazu Nova. These, "the most marginal members of the gay community . . . felt a special loyalty to the club; because of their anger, their age, and their alienation, these gay homeless youths were ideal candidates to fight in a riot" (261).

The catalyst that sparked the Stonewall riots took place after 1 a.m. on Friday, June 27, when Deputy Inspector Seymour Pine and a squad of eight police officers (not counting two female undercover officers who were already inside the bar) arrived with a warrant charging the management with serving liquor without a license. Police closed the inn, arrested the staff and a few of the patrons, and ejected the other customers. Meanwhile, a crowd gathered outside, cheering the patrons as they exited the bar. The mob's mood turned angry when the cops pushed their prisoners into a nearby paddy wagon. Resistance on the part of one of the prisoners led to a full-scale uprising as the crowd began to throw stones and toss coins at the cops. This melee allowed the prisoners to escape while the police fled inside the Stonewall for protection. The first night riot, lasting no more than forty-five minutes, ended when members of New York City's Tactical Police Force arrived to rescue their colleagues.

Though the Stonewall Inn reopened as a "free store" (still without a liquor license) on Saturday night, rioting resumed outside the bar. Thousands of activists and partygoers gathered on Christopher Street and nearby Sheridan Square, shouting their intent to "Liberate Christopher Street!" (Teal 1971, 22). Once again the

Tactical Patrol Force was called to deal with the rioters, though it took the Force until 3:30 a.m. to disperse the crowd. Riots and demonstrations continued in the Village through Wednesday, though these later riots have been ignored or downplayed by some Stonewall chroniclers.

The Stonewall riots were now history. But their influence was just beginning. By the end of July, many rioters joined other activists to form the first post-Stonewall gay organization, the Gay Liberation Front, inaugurating years of activism (1969–1973) that historians have labeled the "heroic age" of gay liberation. Chapters of GLF and Gay Activists Alliance (a group formed in 1970 by activists dissatisfied with GLF's more radical methods and philosophy) were founded in major cities and university towns across the United States, publicizing the riots and spreading their influence. Activist Craig Rodwell (1940–1993), owner of the Village's Oscar Wilde Memorial Bookshop and a veteran of Stonewall, suggested that the anniversary of the Stonewall Uprising be commemorated as a national holiday for gay, lesbian, bisexual, and transgender people. The first "Christopher Street Liberation Day Parade" was held in New York City on Sunday, June 28, 1970.

Eventually, the Stonewall riots accomplished their desired effect, as the New York Police ceased routine raids on gay bars. But Stonewall's greatest impact was on the hearts and minds of generations of lesbian, gay, bisexual, and transgender people. "Gay Pride" is a fact of life for many LGBT people in much of North America, Western **Europe, Australia,** and **New Zealand.** The gay Beat poet Allen Ginsberg expressed this sentiment well when he visited the Stonewall Inn the morning after the second night's riot: "Gay power! Isn't that great! . . . We're one of the largest minorities in the country—10 percent, you know. It's about time we did something to assert ourselves" (Teal 1971, 23).

Although Stonewall is perhaps the most celebrated and influential event in LGBT history, many young people have been born, grown up, and come of age without any direct knowledge of it. Many do not understand its significance or know the reason why so many LGBT groups are named after it. The event is generally not included in secondary school **curriculum** and even some "gay studies" courses fail to teach about this historical milestone, perhaps because some instructors fear that the rioters' are a poor example for their students.

As a narrative, the Stonewall riots make an exciting story, with obvious "heroes" and "villains" and even a "happy ending." The fact that most of the rioters were youth should make this history especially appealing to students. Properly taught, Stonewall is an inspirational tale for all young people.

In his historical primer, *Becoming Visible: A Reader in Gay & Lesbian History for High School & College Students*, gay educator and activist Kevin Jennings (1994) discusses the ways that educators can teach about Stonewall. This includes a reading from Duberman's history, followed by a series of "questions and activities" that might be the basis of a classroom discussion. Though Duberman's approach to Stonewall is controversial, his unique combination of history and biography makes this story enjoyable from a literary, though not necessarily from a historical, point of view. Teachers who wish to update their facts should supplement Duberman's account with selections from Carter's *Stonewall*, Neil Miller's (1995) *Out of the Past*, as well as one or more documentaries such as *Before Stonewall* (USA 1984) and *After Stonewall* (USA 1999).

One method of discussing Stonewall is for the students to assume various roles (rioters, police, or "innocent" bystanders). Using role play to explore the Stonewall riots and the context of them from particular points of view allows students to become engaged emotionally as well as intellectually. Another good topic for discussion would be to compare and contrast the different methods and philosophies used and expressed by the Stonewall rioters, pre-Stonewall homophile leaders, post-Stonewall activists, and today's LGBT advocates. Instructors may wish to conclude their discussion of the Stonewall riots with a brief history of the "heroic age" and the LGBT groups that emerged during that era: the Gay Liberation Front, Gay Activists Alliance, Radicalesbians, and STAR (Street Transvestite Action Revolutionaries). Teal's history, *The Gay Militants*, is useful in this regard, although his sometimes excessive use of period newsletters and speeches—though useful to historians—might make his book a bit tedious for some students.

Bibliography

Carter, David. 2004. *Stonewall: The Riots That Sparked the Gay Revolution*. New York: St. Martin's Press.

Duberman, Martin. 1993. *Stonewall*. New York: Dutton.

Jennings, Kevin, ed. 1994. *Becoming Visible: A Reader in Gay & Lesbian History for High School & College Students*. Los Angeles: Alyson.

Leitsch, Dick. 1909. "Police Raid on N.Y. Club Sets Off First Gay Riot." Pp. 11–15 in *Witness to Revolution: The Advocate Reports on Gay and Lesbian Politics, 1967–1999*. Edited by Chris Bull. Los Angeles: Alyson. (Originally published in 1969 in the *New York Mattachine Newsletter*.)

Loughery, John. 1998. *The Other Side of Silence, Men's Lives and Gay Identities: A Twentieth-Century History*. New York: Henry Holt and Company.

Miller, Neil. 1995. *Out of the Past: Gay and Lesbian History from 1869 to the Present*. New York: Vintage Books.

Teal, Donn. 1971. *The Gay Militants*. New York: Stein and Day.

Web Sites

Lisker, Jerry. 1969. "Homo Nest Raided, Queen Bees Are Stinging Mad." December 2004. Accessed December 18, 2004. http://www.trikkx.com/history2.html. Originally published in the *New York Daily News* for July 6, 1969, Lisker's article is typical of the New York City press's coverage of the Stonewall Riots.

Marotta, Toby. 2004. "Revisiting Stonewall: A Digital Exhibition." 2004. Accessed December 18, 2004. http://www.tobymarotta.com. This historian's Web site is a valuable collection of historic documents and ephemera from the Stonewall era, including explanatory notes and commentary about each document.

Substance Abuse and Use

Connie R. Matthews

Lesbian, gay, bisexual, and transgender youth (LGBT) are using chemical substances at rates that are consistently higher than the general adolescent population and are experiencing problems as a result. Chemicals are often used as a means for

See also Adolescent Sexualities; African American Youth; Alcoholism; Latinos and Latinas; Prostitution or Sex Work; Youth, At-Risk; Youth, Homeless; Youth Risk Behavior Surveys.

coping with the stress of living as a stigmatized minority or as a means of connecting with the adult LGBT community. Young lesbians appear to be at particular risk for substance abuse, although it cuts across genders as well as racial and ethnic groups. In addition to recreational **drug use**, transgender youth often inject hormones acquired illegally and without medical supervision. Access to healthy role models is critical for LGBT youth, as is support in their sexual **identity development** to avoid the trappings of using chemicals to self-medicate or find connection.

Rosario, Hunter, and Gwadz (1997) asked LGB teens if they had experienced specific situations that would be indicators of substance abuse (e.g., felt dependent on substances; too high or hung over to attend school or work). Affirmative responses to these items ranged from 8 to 24 percent for males and 20 to 41 percent for females. Orenstein (2001) found similar results, with 20 percent of the sample worried about their use of chemicals "often" or "always." General samples of LGB youth report 8 to 16 percent having a history of substance abuse treatment, with rates among females higher than among males (Orenstein 2001; Rosario Hunter, and Gwadz 1997). Among homeless LGB youth, drug abuse treatment rates are much higher—one-quarter of males; one-third of females—(Noell and Ochs 2001). Despite the number of gay, lesbian, and bisexual youth receiving substance abuse treatment, there remains a serious gap in treatment programs that either target or are specifically prepared to address the needs of this population (Gay and Lesbian Medical Association 2001).

Rosario, Hunter, and Gwadz (1997) found that at least three-fourths of the gay, lesbian, and bisexual New York City youth they studied had used cigarettes, beginning at about age thirteen, and/or alcohol (88 percent of females; 78 percent of males), beginning at about age fourteen. About two-thirds had used at least one illicit drug, beginning at about age fifteen. Forty-three percent of the females and 30 percent of the males had used at least two illicit drugs, whereas 25 percent of the females and 17 percent of the males had used at least three illicit drugs. Marijuana was the illicit drug used most by both females and males, with 62 percent of the females and 50 percent of the males reporting usage. Hallucinogens were the next most used substance, followed by inhalants and then cocaine.

Rotheram-Borus and colleagues (1994) studied gay and bisexual male adolescents who were predominantly black and Hispanic. They reported rates of use comparable to those described above, with alcohol (76 percent lifetime use) and marijuana (42 percent lifetime use) the most used substances. Although studies about substance abuse among transgender youth are scarce, limited research with adults suggests it is a serious problem (Kammerer et al. 2001). A drug-related concern of particular relevance to transgender individuals is the use of hormones obtained on the street. These are often cheaper or more accessible than those obtained medically, but the safety risks can be quite high.

Several researchers have compared the patterns of substance use for LGB and heterosexual youth. In one study (Orenstein 2001), substance use patterns of gay and lesbian high school students were consistently higher, with the gap widening as the substance became "harder." The percentage of gay and lesbian students using marijuana was twice that of heterosexual students (48 percent versus 24 percent); the difference in cocaine use was much more dramatic (27 percent for gay and lesbian youth compared to 2 percent for heterosexual students). Garofalo and colleagues (1998) also found greater percentages of LGB adolescents to be involved with a variety of chemical substances than their heterosexual counterparts. In addition, initiation of use of alcohol, marijuana, and cocaine before the age of thirteen was significantly and positively associated with being gay, lesbian, or bisexual. In their study of homeless youth, Noell and Ochs (2001) found that lesbian and bisexual females were significantly more likely to report lifetime use of marijuana, LSD, amphetamines, and injection drugs than heterosexual females; there were no differences in lifetime drug use for gay and bisexual males compared to heterosexual males. When considering recent drug use, there was a greater likelihood of amphetamine and injection drug use for both lesbian/bisexual females and gay/bisexual males, but gay and bisexual males were less likely to use marijuana. Although the rate of involvement with substance abuse treatment was similar for gay/bisexual and heterosexual males, lesbian/bisexual females were almost twice as likely to report treatment than their heterosexual counterparts.

Despite these differences, it is important to keep in mind that substance use and abuse is not unique to gay, lesbian, and bisexual students. Gay and lesbian youth show a number of patterns similar to general populations of youth, including the use of cigarettes and alcohol as gateway drugs. Marijuana tends to be the first illicit drug used for those who use multiple illicit substances, although the use of marijuana does not necessarily move the individual on to other drugs. This suggests that prevention programs aimed at reducing or delaying the onset of use of these substances are not only appropriate for gay, lesbian, and bisexual youth as they are for all young people, but are of critical necessity.

At the same time, there are some aspects of use that are more specific to LGB youth that need to be addressed in efforts geared toward this population. Initiating substance used to cope with psychological issues related to **sexual orientation** can be predictive of the number substances ever used as well as symptoms of substance abuse among LGB youth (Rosario Hunter, and Gwadz 1997). Rotheram-Borus et al. (1994) found that frequency of alcohol and other drug use was associated with number of sexual partners, bartering sex for drugs, engaging in oral or anal sex, and failing to use condoms among gay and bisexual male adolescents. In addition to being problems themselves, all of these factors also increase the risk for HIV infection.

Sexual orientation does not cause substance abuse. The difficulties faced in schools and families create additional stress on LGB youth who resort to substance use as a coping mechanism resulting from the need to hide their **sexual identity** and fear of the consequences should that identity be revealed (Olson 2000). The higher rates of substance use among males with multiple male sexual partners when compared to those with multiple female sexual partners could be self-medication to cope with the increased rates of threats, **harassment**, physical violence, property damage, and general fear of being in school that they experienced (DuRant, Krowchuk, and Sinal 1998).

It is also important to recognize gender differences in substance use and abuse among this population. Recall that Rosario Hunter, and Gwadz (1997) found higher percentages of females than males using every substance—and often multiple substances. Similarly, lesbian/bisexual females are more likely to report lifetime use of several drugs than heterosexual females; this was not the case between gay/bisexual and heterosexual males (Noell and Ochs 2001). These gendered patterns are consistent with research on primarily gay, lesbian, and bisexual adults (Bux 1996). These differences have been attributed to the increased health emphasis within the gay male community as a result of the **HIV/AIDS** crisis and the stigma associated with a lesbian/bisexual identity among females who are socialized to avoid conflict

(Bux 1996; Rosario, Hunter, and Gwadz 1997). Girls also may face a double stigma, experiencing the effects of **sexism** as well as **heterosexism**.

There are also aspects of the gay, lesbian, and bisexual community that seem to invite substance use and abuse. Being marginalized can create among gay, lesbian, and bisexual adolescents a sense of being outsiders living on the edge of society Olson (2000). This can encourage some adolescents to engage in drug use and other risky behaviors that are consistent with such an identity. Among adults, the historical importance of the gay bar as gathering place and the current involvement with "circuit parties," or weekend long gatherings that center around the extensive use of amphetamines and sexual liaisons, are further evidence of this. Although these activities are mixed with pride and celebration, easily accessible healthier alternatives for LGB youth are needed to reduce the risk of perceiving such activities as the only avenue into the community and the only means out of isolation (Gay and Lesbian Medical Association 2001).

Bibliography

Bux, Donald A., Jr., 1996. "The Epidemiology of Problem Drinking in Gay Men and Lesbians: A Critical Review." *Clinical Psychology Review* 16: 277–298.

DuRant, Robert H., Daniel P. Krowchuk, and Sara H. Sinal. 1998. "Victimization, Use of Violence, and Drug Use at School among Male Adolescents Who Engage in Same-Sex Sexual Behavior." *Journal of Pediatrics* 133: 113–118.

Garofalo, Robert, Cameron Wolf, Shari Kessel, Judith Palfrey, and Robert DuRant. 1998. "The Association between Health Risk Behaviors and Sexual Orientation among a School-Based Sample of Adolescents." *Pediatrics* 101: 895–901.

Gay and Lesbian Medical Association and LGBT Health Experts. 2001. *Healthy People 2010: Companion Document for Lesbian, Gay, Bisexual, and Transgender (LGBT) Health.* San Francisco, CA: Author.

Kammerer, Nina, Theresa Mason, Margaret Connors, and Rebecca Durkee. 2001. "Transgenders, HIV/AIDS and Substance Abuse: From Risk Group to Group Prevention." Pp. 13–38 in *Transgender and HIV: Risks, Prevention, and Care.* Edited by Walter Bockting and Sheila Kirk. Binghamton, NY: Haworth Press.

Noell, John W., and Linda M. Ochs. 2001. "Relationship of Sexual Orientation to Substance Use, Suicidal Ideation, Suicide Attempts, and Other Factors in a Population of Homeless Adolescents." *Journal of Adolescent Health* 29: 31–36.

Olson, Eva D. 2000. "Gay Teens and Substance Use Disorders: Assessment and Treatment." Pp. 69–80 in *Addiction in the Gay and Lesbian Community.* Edited by Jeffrey R. Gus and Jack Drescher. Binghamton, NY: Haworth Press.

Orenstein, Alan. 2001. "Substance Use among Gay and Lesbian Adolescents." *Journal of Homosexuality* 41, no. 2: 1–15.

Rosario, Margaret, Joyce Hunter, and Marya Gwadz. 1997. "Exploration of Substance Use among Lesbian, Gay, and Bisexual Youth: Prevalence and Correlates." *Journal of Adolescent Research* 12: 454–476.

Rotheram-Borus, Mary Jane, Margaret Rosario, Heino F. L. Meyer-Bahlburg, Cheryl Koopman, Steven C. Dopkins, and Mark Davies. 1994. "Sexual and Substance Use Acts of Gay and Bisexual Male Adolescents in New York City." *Journal of Sex Research* 31: 47–57.

Web Sites

Gay and Lesbian Medical Association (GLMA). 2004. Accessed December 7, 2004. http://www.glma.org. Works to address a variety of health issues for LGBT people, including substance alcoholism, providing education and information, advocacy, and referrals to LGBT affirmative health care providers. Site includes publications, public policy resolutions, and news.

National Association of Lesbian and Gay Addiction Counselors (NALGAP). 2004. Accessed December 7, 2004. http://www.nalgap.org. Provides information, training, advocacy, networking, facilities, and support for individuals in recovery and addiction professionals and this site includes information on conferences and LGBT resources.

Suicide

Stephen T. Russell

Sexual minority youth are at high risk for experiencing suicidal thoughts and plans, and for attempting suicide (Russell 2003). Numerous studies during the past thirty years have consistently reported elevated suicide risk among youth who identify as gay or lesbian, or who report same-sex romantic attractions or sexual partners. As a critical context for youth development, educational environments have been an important focus for understanding the risk for suicide among sexual minorities. Recent **research** indicates that hostile **school climate**s place sexual minorities at risk for suicide, and schools can take positive steps to alleviate hostility and create support. Further, interventions in nonformal educational settings show promise for alleviating suicide risk among sexual minorities; there are no research studies of school-based interventions.

In the social and behavioral sciences, suicide was one of the first issues in the lives of sexual minority youth to be investigated and remains one of the small set of facts about sexual minority youth that has become common knowledge. The earliest studies, first reporting on young gay males in the early 1970s, were characterized by the many methodological challenges inherent in studies of youth, of gay populations, and of suicidality: opportunistic, nonrepresentative samples of self-identified **lesbian, gay,** and **bisexual youth** (LGB), and no comparison or control groups (Russell 2003). In 1989, the United States Department of Health and Human Services *Report of the Secretary's Task Force on Youth Suicide* included a chapter on "Gay Male and Lesbian Youth Suicide" (Gibson 1989) which included the statistics that "gay youth are two to three times more likely to attempt suicide than other young people," and that they "may comprise up to 30 percent of completed youth suicides annually" (p. 110). These statistics are often quoted and generalized to the broad population of sexual minority youth; these statements are misleading because of the limitations of and variability in the methods of research in this field.

From the late 1970s through the mid-1990s, multiple studies primarily conducted in the United States (with a few notable exceptions including a 1988 Italian study by Bertozzo) continued to provide evidence that these youth were at disproportionate risk for suicide. Then, in the late 1990s, a new generation of studies began to appear. These included the first published studies of large-scale samples of adolescents that were representative at the community, state, or national levels in

See also Community LGBT Youth Groups; Educational Policies; Ethnic Identity; Homophobia; Identity Development; Mental Health; Racial Identity; Mentoring; School Safety and Safe School Zones; Secondary Schools, LGBT; Substance Use and Abuse; Youth, At-Risk.

the United States, and prospective studies from **New Zealand** (Fergusson, Horwood, and Beautrais 1999) and Norway (Wichstrøm and Hegna 2003). These studies confirmed the prior twenty years of research, documenting a strong link between adolescent sexual minority status and suicidality.

Studies of suicide risk have used various measures of sexual minority status, including same-sex identity (as LGB), same-sex behavior, or same-sex attraction or **desire**. While same-sex behaviors and attractions have been linked to suicide risk, the best existing evidence indicates that self-identified gay male youth are among those most at risk for suicide attempts (Russell 2003). There exists only limited prior research that allows for careful comparison of suicide risk based on gender or ethnicity. However, in a recent national study, same-sex attraction was not associated with suicidal thoughts for **Latino** youth, but **African American** same-sex attracted youth were more than twice as likely as heterosexual African American youth to report suicidal thoughts. The same study showed that same-sex attraction is a risk factor for white youth, and that white same-sex attracted females in particular were at highest risk for suicidal thoughts (Consolacion, Russell, and Sue 2004).

Bullying and **harassment** on the basis of **sexual orientation** and gender nonconformity are pervasive in contemporary schools, and this victimization has been argued to be strongly linked to suicide risk for sexual minority youth. Respondents to the 1997 Wisconsin **Youth Risk Behavior Survey** (YRBS) who were harassed because someone thought they were gay were four times more likely to report suicide attempts. Similar results were found in the 1995 Seattle YRBS. In addition to the question about being harassed "because someone thought you were gay," that survey included self-reported **sexual identity**. Results indicate that both sexual minority and heterosexual youth who had experienced gay-based harassment were at risk for suicide attempts (Reis and Saewyc 1999). A recently published study combined the 1995 YRBS data from LGB-identified youth (Massachusetts) and youth engaging in same-sex sexual behavior (Vermont). These analyses show that victimization at school strongly predicts suicidal attempts. Further, the frequency of reported suicide attempts was higher among sexual minority youth who experienced high levels of victimization (Bontempo and D'Augelli 2002).

Finally, analyses of the 2001–2002 California Health Kids Survey indicate that students who experience sexual orientation-related harassment are more than twice as likely to report depression or to use amphetamines, more than three times as likely to carry a weapon to school or to be a victim of relationship violence, and more likely to report low grades, binge drinking, marijuana use, and smoking than other students (California Safe Schools Coalition and 4-H Center for Youth Development 2004). Students harassed because of sexual orientation are more likely to miss school than their peers because they feel unsafe. They are three times as likely to report missing school in the last thirty days because they felt unsafe. These harassed students are more than twice as likely to report seriously considering suicide and making a plan for suicide. In sum, this body of research indicates that the school environment is often hostile for sexual minority youth, that sexual orientation-based harassment is common, and that this harassment is linked with adolescent suicidality as well as many of the key risk factors for adolescent suicide such as substance abuse and depression (Russell 2003).

At this time, there is no known published research on the effectiveness of suicide prevention for sexual minority youth populations and no studies of school-based interventions. The few published studies of prevention efforts for sexual minorities focus on HIV/**AIDS** and sexual risk, and show that strategies involving gay-sensitive health care access and peer support and education networks promote self-esteem and **sexual health** (Wright et al. 1998). Related research indicates that unsatisfying relationships with sexual minority peers is a risk factor for suicidality (van Heeringen and Vincke 2000), and that social support from LGB peers has been linked to positive self-esteem (Anderson 1998). This small body of research suggests that prevention efforts that include well-trained and sensitive staff and a peer component and that focus on coping with stress and stigma should be most effective when working with sexual minority youth who may be at risk for suicide.

Intervention and prevention efforts with these characteristics could be developed both for school as well as nonformal educational settings. School and youth program settings are critical for the development and maintenance of peer friendships; they are also important contexts for developing the resources and skills to manage emotional stress and stigma. Because most young people rarely hear teachers or other adults talk openly about sexual minority status, a first step is integrating basic attention to same-sex sexuality in existing prevention and intervention efforts. Teachers and other youth professionals play an important role in creating supportive learning environments for LGBT youth. Specifically, sexual minority youth fare better in schools where teachers are sensitive to sexual minority issues. A recent study based on the 1995 Massachusetts YRBS documented that LGB youth who attend schools with gay-sensitive **HIV education** (teacher-rated confidence, adequacy, and appropriateness of HIV instruction for LGB students) score lower on multiple indicators of health risk (Blake et al. 2001).

The statistics on suicide risk and the school climate for sexual minority youth, combined with the lack of published evaluations of prevention efforts, are sobering. However, research on sexual minority youth, schools, and health risk is finally being tempered by emerging studies that investigate the possibilities for improving school climates. These studies parallel the shifting paradigm in research on sexual minority youth, from the historically exclusive focus on risk, to considering developmental pathways characterized by **resiliency**. New studies identify promising practices and policies that improve the health and well-being of sexual minority youth at school. A recent study of over 600 California high school students shows that schools can make a difference (California Safe Schools Coalition and 4-H Center for Youth Development 2004). Five school characteristics associated with a positive school environment emerged, including:

1. student awareness of a school policy that prohibits discrimination based on sexual orientation and gender identity;
2. student awareness of information and resources at the school related to sexual orientation;
3. student participation in a **gay–straight alliance;**
4. teacher intervention in stopping harassment; and
5. integration of LGBT issues in school **curriculum.**

Students reporting these factors in their schools also reported safer and more positive overall school climates for sexual minority students, lower rates of harassment based on sexual orientation and **gender identity,** and stronger student resilience (that is, feelings of connection to teachers and the school).

Bibliography

Anderson, Andrew L. 1998. "Strengths of Gay Male Youth: An Untold Story." *Child and Adolescent Social Work Journal* 15, no. 1: 55–71.

Bertozzo, Graziella. 1998. "From the Internet the Voice of 'Quella Ragazza, Quel Ragazzo' (That Girl, That Boy)." *Finisterrae* 1: 5–11.

Blake, Susan M., Rebecca Ledsky, Thomas Lehman, Carol Goodenow, Richard Sawyer, and Tim Hack. 2001. "Preventing Sexual Risk Behaviors among Gay, Lesbian, and Bisexual Adolescents: The Benefits of Gay-Sensitive HIV Instruction in Schools." *American Journal of Public Health* 91: 940–946.

Bontempo, Daniel E., and Anthony R. D'Augelli. 2002. "Effects of At-School Victimization and Sexual Orientation on Lesbian, Gay, or Bisexual Youths' Health Risk Behavior." *Journal of Adolescent Health* 30: 364–374.

California Safe Schools Coalition and 4-H Center for Youth Development. 2004. *Safe Place to Learn: Consequences of Harassment Based on Actual or Perceived Sexual Orientation and Gender Nonconformity and Steps for Making Schools Safer.* Accessed June 22, 2005. http://www.casafeschools.org/SafePlacetoLearnLow.pdf.

Consolacion, Theodora B., Stephen T. Russell, and Stanley Sue. 2004. "Sex, Race/Ethnicity, and Romantic Attractions: Multiple Minority Status Adolescents and Mental Health." *Cultural Diversity and Ethnic Minority Psychology* 10: 200–214.

Fergusson, David M., L. John Horwood, and Annette L. Beautrais. 1999. "Is Sexual Orientation Related to Mental Health Problems and Suicidality in Young People?" *Archives of General Psychiatry* 56: 879–880.

Gibson, Paul. 1989. "Gay Male and Lesbian Youth Suicide." Pp. 110–142 in *Report of the Secretary's Task Force on Youth Suicide, Vol. 3.* Washington D.C.: Department of Health and Human Services, DHHS Pub. No. (ADM) 89–1623.

Reis, Beth, and Elizabeth Saewyc. 1999. *Eighty-Three Thousand Youth: Selected Findings of Eight Population-Based Studies as they Pertain to Anti-Gay Harassment and the Safety and Well-Being of Sexual Minority Students.* Seattle: Safe Schools Coalition of Washington.

Russell, Stephen T. 2003. "Sexual Minority Youth and Suicide Risk." *American Behavioral Scientist* 46: 1241–1257.

van Heeringen, C., and J. Vincke. 2000. "Suicidal Acts and Ideation in Homosexual and Bisexual Young People: A Study of Prevalence and Risk Factors." *Social Psychiatry and Psychiatric Epidemiology* 35: 494–499.

Wichstrøm, Lars, and Kristinn Hegna. 2003. "Sexual Orientation and Suicide Attempt: A Longitudinal Study of the General Norwegian Adolescent Population." *Journal of Abnormal Psychology* 112: 144–151.

Wright, Eric R., Christopher Gonzales, Jeffrey N. Werner, Steven Thad Laughner, and Michael Wallace. 1998. "Indiana Youth Access Project: A Model for Responding to the HIV Risk Behaviors of Gay, Lesbian, and Bisexual Youths in the Heartland." *Journal of Adolescent Health* 23: 83–95.

T

Teachers, LGBT and History

Jackie M. Blount

From Plato and Socrates to contemporary teachers, persons who **desire** others of the same sex or manifest unconventional gender identities/presentation have long been members of the teaching profession. They have served as role models for **lesbian, gay, bisexual**, and **transgender youth** (LGBT) and exemplified the richness of human diversity for all their students. The measure of respect accorded such teachers, however, has varied substantially with changing historical contexts. While some ancient Greek teachers extolled the virtues of same-sex love, teachers during the Cold War lost their jobs for suspected homosexuality. Currently, growing numbers of teachers claim LGBT identities openly while retaining their jobs, although the overwhelming majority still fears employment reprisals.

Like the noted Greek philosophers, numerous teachers throughout history have desired others of the same-sex or defied gender conventions of the time. During the nineteenth century, John Addington Symonds became Professor of Latin and Fellow at Trinity College in Cambridge. In the United States, Walt Whitman, Margaret Fuller, Elizabeth Peabody, Ralph Waldo Emerson and many other prominent writers served as teachers early in their careers and also maintained passionate relationships with others of the same sex at some point during their lives. Several noted leaders and founders of colleges maintained devoted same-sex partnerships, including Mary Woolley and Jeannette Marks of Mount Holyoke, M. Carey Thomas of Bryn Mawr, and Sophia Packard and Harriet Giles of Spelman College.

Many of the early teachers in the United States had studied in single-sex institutions such as boarding schools and colleges. During the 1800s and early 1900s, such institutions faced public accusations that they tolerated, or even promoted, sexual activity among students. In boys' schools, the supposedly rampant "secret vice," or even "mutual masturbation," as such encounters were called, often involved an older boy and a younger admirer. Reformers pressed vigorously for strict monitoring of boys' behavior, strenuous physical activity intended to wear them out, and discouraging most physical demonstrativeness among them. By the late 1800s girls' schools also had developed the reputation for allowing, if not fostering, passionate relationships among students. British sex researcher, Havelock Ellis noted that in female boarding schools and colleges, "ardent attachments" developed between students, often including sexual activity. In the homosocial worlds of these **single-sex schools**, not surprisingly, some teachers desired others of the same sex. And some graduates of these institutions eventually became teachers themselves.

From the mid- to late-1800s as common schooling and then compulsory attendance laws spread, teaching shifted dramatically from work done primarily by men to that done almost exclusively by women. Communities preferred hiring single, rather than married women teachers, which prevented conflicts in women's supposed primary allegiances. Eventually, so many unmarried women taught that the

See also Adolescent Sexualities; Coming Out, Teachers; Crush; Discrimination; Gay, Lesbian, and Straight Education Network; Licensure; Professional Educational Organizations; Professionalism; Sexism; Women's Colleges; Workplace Issues.

word "teacher" came to connote a single woman just as the word "spinster" typically meant a teacher. By the early 1900s, unmarried women teachers often lived with each other in shared housing such as teacherages, which were built to accommodate two or more female teachers. Later studies revealed that some of these women experienced sexual attraction to other women, engaged in homosexual activities, and/or maintained long-term, same-sex primary relationships (Davis 1929). However, as women generally gained greater social and political power in the wake of national suffrage, as they experienced expanded educational opportunities, and as marriage and childbearing rates declined while divorce rates soared, the public became aware that some women might be lesbians. Suspicion particularly surrounded teaching because of the presence of so many unmarried women. By the 1950s, spinster teachers had become so stigmatized as a class that their representation in the classroom plummeted while that of married women rose sharply—even above the rate for married women in the general workforce.

During the Cold War, suspicion of unmarried teachers changed to hostility. The growing visibility of homosexual communities in **urban** areas around the country, combined with public awareness of the prevalence of homosexual behavior in the population inspired by **Alfred Kinsey**, eventually met with a virulent backlash movement. The military and federal government instituted well-publicized purges of suspected homosexuals. Schools summarily followed. A California law required law enforcement officers to notify school officials of teachers charged with "morals" violations and, in Florida, the **Johns Committee**, as it came to be known, later published reports on the supposed cleansing of the state's teaching ranks. The vigorous hunt for lesbian and gay teachers in California created a climate in which mere rumor provided grounds for dismissal. The major motion **film**, *The Children's Hour* (USA 1961), depicted the devastating impact of rumors about suspected teachers' lesbianism.

By the late 1960s, however, self-described homosexuals had experienced so much frustration with social sanctions that passivity and self-destruction eventually gave way to resistance, as symbolized by the 1969 **Stonewall** rebellion. In the wake of this three-day event, a powerful grass-roots gay liberation movement emerged. Individually and collectively, LGBT teachers began fighting back. Teachers such as Peggy Burton (Oregon), John Gish (New Jersey), Joseph Acanfora (Maryland), and James Gaylord (Washington) engaged in protracted court battles when they were fired on account of their **sexual orientation** (Harbeck 1997). Though these teachers could not regain their positions, their cases established legal precedent making such dismissals more difficult.

The growing strength of the grassroots gay liberation movement became stunningly clear in 1974 when the ABC television network planned to air an episode of the then-popular show, *Marcus Welby, MD*, in which a young male student was sexually assaulted by a male teacher. As word of the broadcast spread, gay activist groups around the country mobilized to boycott episode advertisers, wage protests outside local television affiliates, mount letter-writing campaigns, and gain the support of prominent allied organizations such as the American Federation of Teachers. Advertisers withdrew their planned commercials and several local affiliates pulled the episode in response to the outcry, compelling the president of the National Gay Task Force to claim: "I think it has to be viewed as really the first great concerted national effort by gay groups around the country" ("Network Squirms" 1974, 2, 30).

In 1977, Anita Bryant argued that LGBT teachers wanted to molest or corrupt students. After Miami-Dade County had passed a nondiscrimination ordinance that included sexual orientation, Bryant, invoking the specter of dress-wearing male teachers and homosexual child predators, launched her "Save Our Children" campaign to strike down the ordinance. Some gay activists failed to take seriously enough the threat that Bryant's movement posed to newly-won gay rights. However, the issue of lesbian and gay teachers quickly proved politically explosive and central to her larger efforts. On June 7, 1977, Bryant's campaign defeated the nondiscrimination ordinance in a public vote (Blount 2004; Harbeck 1997; Sears 2001).

One week later, Bryant flew to California to assist state Senator John Briggs in initiating a public referendum specifically to rid the schools of LGBT teachers. Briggs wished to tap powerful public sentiment against LGBT teachers to fuel his bid for governor. After initial missteps, Briggs filed a half-million signatures, effectively placing his referendum, officially known as Proposition 6, on the November 1978 ballot. His early momentum gradually eroded, however, as grass-roots lesbian and gay activists forged coalitions with a wide variety of groups. Eventually, **activism** to defeat Proposition 6 earned the support of the state superintendent of schools, the National Education Association, the American Federation of Teachers, Ronald Reagan, San Francisco Mayor Willie Brown, the archbishop of San Francisco, the Los Angeles Board of Education, and entertainers such as Cher, Jane Fonda, and John Travolta. Consequently, Proposition 6 suffered a major defeat.

By the early 1980s, however, activism among LGBT persons necessarily turned to the growing **AIDS** pandemic. Public attention shifted away from LGBT teachers and toward such issues as whether persons with AIDS should be allowed on school property and whether all teachers and students should be tested for the virus. Fearing the toll that AIDS might exact on sexually active, yet uninformed students, some educators offered curricula promoting safe sex. Then, in 1988, the National Education Association narrowly passed a resolution favoring the development and implementation of school **counseling** that supported the unique needs of LGBT and questioning students—as opposed to more traditional counseling that strictly urged heterosexual conformity.

In the early 1990s, the Gay, Lesbian, Straight Teachers Network that Kevin Jennings had organized, grew rapidly as LGBT and allied teachers increasingly recognized a need to work together, to address the needs of LGBT students and their **allies**, and generally to improve the **school climate** for all, regardless of sexuality or gender presentation. Then in 1993, because of ongoing LGBT activism, Massachusetts passed an unprecedented law protecting LGBT students from discrimination in schools as well as providing resources in support of their unique needs. Since this time one of the most important developments concerning LGBT teachers has been the rapid proliferation of **gay–straight alliances**.

Bibliography

Blount, Jackie. 2004. *Fit to Teach: Same-Sex Desire, Gender, and School Work in the Twentieth Century*. Albany: State University of New York Press.

Davis, Katherine Bement. 1929, repr. 1972. *Factors in the Sex Life of Twenty-Two Hundred Women*. New York: Arno Press and The New York Times.

Faderman, Lillian. 1999. *To Believe in Women*. New York: Houghton Miflin.

Harbeck, Karen M. 1997. *Gay and Lesbian Educators: Personal Freedoms, Public Constraints*. Maulden, MA: Amethyst.

"How Sweet It Is!" 1979. *Lesbian Tide.* (January/February): 10–12.

Jennings, Kevin. 1994. *One Teacher in 10.* Boston: Alyson.

"Network Squirms as Sponsors Flee 'Welby' Episode." 1974. *The Advocate* (October 23): 2, 30.

Rofes, Eric. 1985. *Plato, Socrates, and Guys Like Me.* Boston: Alyson.

Rubin, Marc. 1978. "History of the Gay Teachers Association." *Gay Teachers Association Newsletter* (January): 1–4.

Sears, James T. 2001. *Rebels, Rubyfruit and Rhinestones: Queering Space in the Stonewall South.* New Brunswick, NJ: Rutgers University Press.

Web Site

Lambda Legal: Issues: Youth and Schools. June 2005. Accessed June 22, 2005. http://www.lambdalegal.org. This organization, which has brought numerous highly successful lawsuits on behalf of the rights of LGBT persons, maintains an extensive library of online resources about LGBT educators and students.

Theater, Teaching of

Amy K. Kilgard

Theater educators are uniquely situated to raise awareness about lesbian, gay, bisexual, and transgender (LGBT) issues, to improve staged representations of LGBT people, and to create safe spaces for LGBT performers and audience members. Theater has traditionally been a space where many LGBT people have found a haven. Consequently, theater practitioners, especially those in educational settings and those working with youth, have demonstrated a particular responsiveness to the LGBT community. Text selection is one important way many directors and producers work to include LGBT issues and performers. From selecting scripts that deliberately include LGBT characters to picking those that explore sexual identity as foundational to the narrative, many educational theater practitioners are attentive to the needs of LGBT members of their communities as performers and as audience members. Cross-gender casting is another strategy that may make even traditional, heteronormative scripts more inclusive of LGBT experiences. Theater in educational settings is often used in the service of social justice. From Augusto Boal's "Theatre of the Oppressed," to "Playback Theatre," to local initiatives that present short plays to raise audience awareness about such issues as **racism**, homophobic violence, and **hate crimes,** many groups are working to use theater as a strategy for reimagining social relationships. These initiatives enable theater practitioners working with young people to create safe spaces for youth and to encourage discussions about sexuality.

Safe spaces develop both within schools, particularly drama courses and theater productions, and in other community organizations such as theater groups, religious institutions, after-school programs, and neighborhood centers. Performance activities may be formally structured or more spontaneous. Because it is common in theater and rehearsal processes to set aside time for discussion of the script and the issues it raises, choosing a script that incorporates LGBT themes legitimates the frequently taboo practice of discussing sexuality with young people. For example, if a character in a play is struggling with her or his sexuality, members of the cast,

See also Agency; Cocurricular Activities; Cross-Dressing; Heteronormativity; School Safety and Safe School Zones

especially the person playing that role, will research and discuss that character's history, feelings, and expectations—not just the explicit experiences depicted in the play. Because the discussion will be focused on characters and their experiences, **lesbian, gay, bisexual, transgender** and questioning youth may feel less threatened to fully engage in the conversation. They may be able to participate without feeling pressured to out themselves or make their experiences the focal point for group scrutiny. Avoiding this potential pitfall, a facilitator or director can draw on collectively generated themes, images, or experiences. Heterosexually identified participants benefit from this discussion by confronting **sexual** and **gender identity** questions that they may otherwise overlook because of their unexamined privilege.

There are several ways for practitioners to find scripts that deal with LGBT issues, which are appropriate for work with youth of a variety of ages and experience levels. It is most practical with young children (elementary and middle school levels) to develop original compositions or short performances that address the value of open-mindedness, empathy, questioning, and supportive social relationships. One example of a theater group working with these issues is Fringe Benefits. This Los Angeles-based educational theater company has collected and published some of their scripts in *Cootie Shots: Theatrical Inoculations Against Bigotry for Kids, Parents, and Teachers* (Bowles and Rosenthal 2001). When working with high school or **college age students** and performers, facilitators may use similar approaches or search for texts that already exist. One strategy for finding such texts is to search current anthologies of plays. Two collections that deal explicitly with LGBT themes are *The Actor's Book of Gay and Lesbian Plays* and *Staging Gay Lives*. General anthologies may also contain appropriate work. *Angels in America*, by Tony Kushner, and *The Laramie Project*, by Moisés Kaufman, are two texts that have been very popular and successful with mature young adults.

It is important when choosing a script that a director or facilitator considers several factors. One is the level of sexual explicitness and/or violence represented in the script. Another is her or his level of knowledge and ability to discuss the themes and issues raised in a nonthreatening and respectful manner. For example, it would be a mistake to assume that young adults are emotionally capable of performing the roles of aggressor or victim of homophobic violence on stage without discussion and support from adults and peers. However, a facilitator should respect young adults' ability to negotiate complex characters with emotional depth and understanding, and thus should not select scripts that trivialize or simplify gender and sexuality. Instructors might include research assignments and small group discussions as part of a rehearsal process.

Another source of material for play selection is theater history. There are many traditional plays that incorporate LGBT issues in a less direct but still apparent way. Plays such as Oscar Wilde's *The Importance of Being Earnest* and Lillian Hellman's *The Children's Hour* are two often-cited examples. Alan Sinfield discusses these and other British and American plays in *Out On Stage: Lesbian and Gay Theatre in the Twentieth Century*. Other possible resources are new or local playwrights and local LGBT writers and activists. Interested practitioners might contact college theater departments or community writing groups to inquire about new scripts that deal with significant LGBT themes.

In addition to finding scripts that explicitly incorporate LGBT characters or themes, practitioners may incorporate these characters and themes in other ways. One common practice is cross-gender casting—assigning roles to performers of different genders than the characters they will be portraying. This has been a common practice throughout theater history. In European theater, men historically played all the roles. It was considered inappropriate for women to perform on the stage. Also, in the Japanese theater traditions of Noh and Kabuki, men were the only ones allowed to train and thus perform. Today, it has become more common for directors to deliberately cast across traditional gender categories. This may be as simple as casting women or girls in male roles and vice versa or as complicated as making characters' gender representations ambiguous on stage. A director might choose to cast people of multiple genders in the same role to challenge the idea of a character having only one stable gender identity. Another practice calls for performers to pay attention to and challenge the default heteronormative assumptions in some texts. For example, if a script calls for a couple in an ensemble scene, that is a potential location for incorporating a same-gender couple. Being more inclusive of multiple sexual identities requires specific attention to practices of staged representations, particularly of gender and sexuality.

Some of the most exciting current theater initiatives are those dedicated to working toward social justice. There are a number of well-established practices that foster such work and that are especially meaningful and practical in work with youth. Augusto Boal, a Brazilian theater practitioner, has gained international attention and support for his system called "Theatre of the Oppressed" (TO). Using this approach, practitioners work with local communities to find ways to solve problems through doing performances. They create short plays about the problems most important to community members and invite audience members—who Boal calls "spect–actors"—to come on stage where they assume the protagonist's role to try to solve the problem.

TO practitioners use this technique—"a rehearsal of revolution" (Boal 1985)—to help communities address problems such as racism and homophobic violence. Because it provides a technique that privileges everyday knowledge and action instead of language and articulation, it is frequently used in schools—not just in theater classes, but in other classes with a social focus—and outside schools with groups of young people. Participants do not have to have specialized knowledge to propose a solution. Rather, they must rely on their lived experience to help them solve problems. No single solution is offered as the correct one. Instead, participants can see that there are multiple possible ways to improve problematic situations.

Regular classroom teachers of students at all age levels may incorporate performance and theater techniques into their teaching and **curriculum** for the purpose of ending **homophobia** and promoting acceptance of LGBT youth and adults. Image work, in which students explore the embodied core or foundation of a negative or positive event or emotion through the development of physical, nonverbal poses, can help participants understand connections between seemingly unrelated experiences such as peer pressure and punishment. For example, a teacher might ask students in small groups to create a tableau of one person being ridiculed because of her or his sexual identity. They might also create images of the victimized person being accepted by others, or standing against such ridicule.

Another effective technique for incorporating performance into classrooms is based on the composition work of theater director Anne Bogart. Instructors may have students create small performances from ideas generated by the entire class. It is particularly useful for facilitators to provide a list of rules or constraints for students, stating specifically what they must include in their performances and giving a short time limit for creating the performances. This provides a structure for the activity, and allows for great variety and freedom within the form. For example, an instructor might suggest that every group must include five still poses, ten seconds of silence, two lines of poetry, and the title "Out of the Closet."

TO practice usually addresses problems that arise from a community. However, there are other techniques to address problems that a community does not want to acknowledge or of which it is unaware. Some theater companies travel to local schools and other institutions that serve young people with short productions about important issues such as racism, **bullying**, and hate speech. Some companies, including the International Playback Theatre Network and Stage Left Productions, conduct workshops with students to teach them appropriate, safe, and compassionate responses to violent situations.

Bibliography

Boal, Augusto. 1985. *Theatre of the Oppressed*. Translated by Charles A. McBride and Maria-Odilia Leal McBride. New York: Theatre Communications Group.

Bowles, Norma, and Mark E. Rosenthal, eds. 2001. *Cootie Shots: Theatrical Inoculations Against Bigotry for Kids, Parents, and Teachers*. New York: Theatre Communications Group.

Clum, John M., ed. 1996. *Staging Gay Lives: An Anthology of Contemporary Gay Theater*. Boulder, CO: Westview Press.

Lane, Eric, and Nina Shengold, eds. 1995. *The Actor's Book of Gay and Lesbian Plays*. New York: Penguin Books.

Sinfield, Alan. 1999. *Out On Stage: Lesbian and Gay Theatre in the Twentieth Century*. New Haven, CT: Yale University Press.

Web Sites

Bay Area Video Coalition. June 2005. Accessed June 22, 2005. http://www.playback.org. Resources for educators as well as links to practitioners of the International Playback Theatre Network.

Pedagogy and Theatre of the Oppressed. 2005. Accessed June 22, 2005. http://www.ptoweb.org/. Contact information for some groups working with TO techniques. It also contains resources for interested educators as well as information about conferences and workshops.

Stage Left Productions. June 2005. Accessed June 22, 2005. http://www.stage-left.org/main.htm. Provides useful resources for educators interested in learning more about performance-based initiatives for addressing social issues. There are many links to productions, activities, and initiatives promoting tolerance and acceptance.

Tomboy

Carrie Paechter

A tomboy is usually a girl who does not conform to the social expectations of femininity within a particular social world. In general, tomboys are seen as preferring activity to passivity, outdoor sporting pursuits to quieter indoor ones, and as rejecting domestic play, particularly with dolls. **Research** on tomboys is limited in extent and

See also Cross-Dressing; Israel, LGBT Issues in; Israel, LGBT Youth in; Physical Education, Teaching of; Sissy Boy; Social Class; Stereotypes.

diverse in focus; studies of adolescent tomboys are particularly sparse. Most studies are retrospective, considering adult memories of tomboyism. Psychological approaches are generally concerned either with potential causes or with the relationship between **childhood** and adolescent tomboyism and adult butch behavior, lesbianism and/or **transsexuality**. There is some evidence of a link between tomboy childhood and adult lesbian identity, though many heterosexual women also recall being tomboys. Outside of psychology, some writers consider tomboyism as a form of childhood female masculinity. Others have suggested that tomboyism is a more fluid and contested category, developed in relation to dominant masculinities and femininities in specific social situations. In particular, being a tomboy, and what this means for both behavior/performance and in the construction of the self, are raced, classed, and locational. There is also some debate about the extent to which being a tomboy is a form of resistance to dominant patterns of gender construction, with some writers claiming a resistant **queer** identity and others arguing that it confirms gender hierarchies by valuing masculine behavior and so fails to challenge the assumption of male superiority within the peer group. Generally, tomboys are not stigmatized at school, and, indeed, are considered leaders by their peers. However, there is some evidence that tomboyism in **adolescence** is more problematic, with young women who continue to play **sports** experiencing teasing.

Recent research on tomboys stems, with few exceptions, from two main fields. Most empirical studies on non**intersex** tomboys have been carried out by psychologists. These are mainly concerned with the later implications (in terms of future sports participation, lesbianism, and **Gender Identity Disorder**) of childhood tomboyism, or with questions relating to childhood or adult androgyny. With a few exceptions, most of these studies (the exceptions are those in which tomboyism is understood as a form of childhood Gender Identity Disorder) see tomboyism as a frequent aspect of normal childhood, being reported retrospectively in over 50 percent of adult women in several United States' studies. Nonempirical accounts come mainly from literature and cultural studies, largely based on fictional and autobiographical writing. These studies, by contrast, treat tomboyism as a rare occurrence related to forms of female masculinity that border on Gender Identity Disorder, and which, while not pathological, bring long-term outsider status (Halberstam 1998).

The research on child tomboys, from whatever tradition, is limited in a number of ways. Most is based in the United States, though the few studies carried out elsewhere suggest cultural variations in definition and frequency of occurrence (Gottschalk 2003; Safir, Rosenmann, and Kloner 2003). Second, this research is almost all retrospective in focus, looking at adult memories of childhood with the problems of selective recall and the desire for narrative consistency of our past lives (Bailey and Zucker 1995; Gottschalk 2003; Safir, Rosenmann, and Kloner 2003). There is also some evidence that "tomboy" is used more often by adults remembering their childhood than by children (Reay 2001; Thorne 1993), suggesting that for some it may be a stigmatized identity at the time, but not retrospectively.

A third concern is that the main foci of research are **gender identity** (particularly child gender identity disorder and adult transsexuality) and its relation to tomboy roles, as well as the relationship between tomboy childhood behavior and a variety of features of adulthood, such as adult lesbianism, transsexualism, sports participation, career confidence and androgyny.

Psychological studies of tomboyism generally suggest that there is a link between childhood tomboyism and later lesbianism (Bailey and Zucker 1995; Safir,

Rosenmann, and Kloner 2003), though this is contested by some writers, who note in particular that many heterosexual women also recall tomboy childhoods (Gottschalk 2003). In any case, early cross-gender behavior seems to be substantially more predictive of later homosexuality in men than in women (Bailey and Zucker 1995). Being a tomboy is not, however, generally a predictor of later transsexualism, although female-to-male transsexuals have been found to report previous tomboy identities (Lee 2001).

Part of the difficulty of dealing with these at times conflicting studies arises from significant variation in the definition of a tomboy. Most studies use stereotypically masculine activities as the defining feature. Morgan (1998), for example, found that three different generational cohorts of adults, reporting tomboy behavior when children, saw their childhood participation in masculine-labeled sports (football, baseball, fishing), rough and tumble play (climbing trees, getting dirty, taking part in war games), and playing with masculine-labeled toys (trucks, bicycles and action figures) as the overwhelming definers of tomboy experience. Others consider mainly or exclusively male companionship and/or wanting to be a boy as important (Halberstam 1998; Rottnek, 1999). These scholars regard tomboyism as female masculinity rather than androgyny, treating the tomboy as an unusual and marginalized challenge to gender norms.

Variations in cultural assumptions about "normal" childhood can strongly impact who is defined as tomboy. British girls living in the countryside, for example, are consistently (and positively) labeled as tomboys (Jones 1999). This is related to their mother's childhood tomboyism and to parental desires for their children to live healthy outdoor lives in an idealized **rural** setting. Similarly, the lower frequency of tomboy childhoods among Israeli women (compared to the United States) reflects the greater prevalence and encouragement of outdoor activities for both sexes (Safir, Rosenmann, and Kloner 2003). There is also some evidence that even within a particular country, there are ethnic differences in the prevalence and extent of tomboyism. For example, **African American** girls seem to have more scope for assertiveness and active play than their Euro-American peers (McGuffey and Rich 1999; Thorne 1993).

There is little research into what it is actually like to be a tomboy, how tomboys relate to their peer group, or how tomboyism changes as adolescence approaches (several writers claim that a tomboy identity is harder to sustain in adolescence). One of the few studies to focus on tomboys as children found that classmates regard them as popular, cooperative, helpful, supportive of others, and leaders (Hemmer and Kleiber 1981). A more recent study also suggests that preadolescent girls who transgress gender boundaries are not stigmatized by other girls (McGuffey and Rich 1999), supporting the suggestion that tomboyism is a frequently occurring and unproblematic aspect of female childhood.

Although tomboy behaviors are generally accepted and sometimes valued before puberty, they are seen as problematic in adolescence, according to retrospective autobiographical accounts (Rottnek 1999). Many tomboys develop conventional femininities at this stage, but others retain their masculinity into adolescence and adulthood, often bringing them into conflict with parents, peers, and the wider society. Here "tomboy" can be used as a term of **harassment**, particularly for teenage girls who play sports (Cockburn and Clarke 2002).

Although some authors (Morgan 1998) argue that tomboys expand their repertoire to embrace both masculine and feminine pursuits, most research into tomboy childhood suggests that some forms of tomboyism are very similar to dominant masculinity. That is, a tomboy often assumes masculine attributes while rejecting the feminine. Here, rather than being transgressive of gender roles (Halberstam 1998), tomboyism, particularly in its more extreme forms, confirms the prevailing gender order (Reay 2001; Thorne 1993). More extreme tomboys, conforming to local norms of masculine behavior, demonstrate the higher value they give to masculinity.

Bibliography

Bailey, J. Michael, and Kenneth J. Zucker. 1995. "Childhood Sex-Typed Behavior and Sexual Orientation: A Conceptual Analysis and Quantitative Review." *Developmental Psychology* 31, no. 1: 43–55.

Cockburn, Claudia, and Gill Clarke. 2002. "'Everybody's Looking at You!' Girls Negotiating the 'Femininity Deficit' They Incur in Physical Education." *Women's Studies International Forum* 25, no. 6: 651–665.

Gottschalk, Lorene. 2003. "Same-Sex Sexuality and Childhood Gender Non-Conformity: A Spurious Connection." *Journal of Gender Studies* 12, no. 1: 35–50.

Halberstam, Judith. 1998. *Female Masculinity*. Durham, NC: Duke University Press.

Hemmer, Joan D., and Douglas A. Kleiber. 1981. "Tomboys and Sissies: Androgynous Children?" *Sex Roles* 7, no. 2: 1205–1212.

Jones, Owain. 1999. "Tomboy Tales: The Rural, Nature and the Gender of Childhood." *Gender, Place and Culture* 6, no. 2: 117–136.

Lee, Tracey. 2001. "Trans(re)lations: Lesbian and Female to Male Transsexual Accounts of Identity." *Women's Studies International Forum* 24, no 3/4: 347–357.

McGuffey, C. Shawn, and B. Lindsay Rich. 1999. "Playing in the Gender Transgression Zone: Race, Class and Hegemonic Masculinity in Middle Childhood." *Gender and Society* 13, no. 5: 608–627.

Morgan, Betsy L. 1998. "A Three Generational Study of Tomboy Behavior." *Sex Roles* 39, nos. 9/10: 787–800.

Reay, Diane. 2001. "'Spice Girls', 'Nice Girls', 'Girlies' and 'Tomboys': Gender Discourses, Girls' Cultures and Femininities in the Primary Classroom." *Gender and Education* 13, no. 2: 153–166.

Rottnek, Matthew, ed. 1999. *Sissies and Tomboys: Gender Nonconformity and Homosexual Childhood*. New York: New York University Press.

Safir, Marilyn P., Amir Rosenmann, and Orly Kloner. 2003. "Tomboyism, Sexual Orientation, and Adult Gender Roles among Israeli Women." *Sex Roles* 48, nos. 9/10: 401–410.

Thorne, Barrie. 1993. *Gender Play: Girls and Boys in School*. Buckingham, UK: Open University Press.

Tong-zhi

Qiuxi Fann

As a commonly used Mandarin word in mainland **China**, "Tong-zhi" (comrade) is also the nickname of a homosexual person in the Chinese-speaking gay community. In most Chinese dictionaries, Tong-zhi has been primarily defined as people who dedicate themselves to the same cause, especially the party members, and is used as

See also Asia, LGBT Youth and Issues in; Asian American Youth; Colonialism and Homosexuality; Communication; Identity Politics; Literature, College; Sexual Identity.

a prefix similar to the English "Mr." or "Ms." The Chinese word for homo(sexual) is *Tong*, meaning "same/homo" while *Zhi* can be variously translated as "goal, spirit, or orientation." Appearing first in a Hong Kong entertainment magazine in the mid-1980s, Tong-zhi has now entered daily language. Applying a word regularly used in a political context, the term avoids pejorative words such as "*tong-xing-lian*," a Chinese term similar to "homo" labeling gay men to indicate their disapproval, or "*niang-niang-qiang*" (sissy boy) and "*jia-ya-tou*" (fake girl), which are regular nicknames targeted at gay teenagers.

"Tong-zhi" was first orally used by Hong Kong lesbians in San Francisco in the late 1970s, and resurfaced in a magazine titled "*Hao Wai*" (*Extra*) when Edward Lam, a Hong Kong playwright and novelist, critiqued the first American **film** about **AIDS**, *An Early Frost* (USA 1985). In the early 1990s, Lam inaugurated the Tong-Zhi Film Festival. This word was used for two reasons. First, he argued that gay people should make a greater effort to get equal rights, quoting Dr. Sun Yat-sen, the father of modern China: "The Revolution has not yet succeeded. Tong-Zhi, you must carry on." Secondly, he hoped it would broaden the discussion from simple homosexuality to any other gender issues such as **bisexuality** and **transsexuality**.

Tong-zhi, as a high-profile political word, evades the "frivolous, indecent" tone implied in the term *Tong xing lian* (homo). "There is no 'sex' in the word itself, thus helping to counteract the pervasive vulgarization of *tong-xing-lian* (homosexuality) in the mainstream society" (Chou 2000, 3). Since Edward Lam's use of the term, then, it has become a popular nickname for gay people in Hong Kong and Taiwan, traveling back to the mainland with a new meaning. It is now widely accepted within the gay community "for its positive cultural references, gender neutrality, desexualization of the stigma of homosexuality, politics beyond the homo–hetero duality, and use as an indigenous cultural identity for integrating the sexual into the social" (Chou 2000, 2).

Tong-zhi has been used as pen name, the title of a gay novel, and the title for an annual gay conference. Beijing Tong-Zhi is the author of the first Web gay novel "*Beijing Gu Shi*" (*Beijing Story*), which was adapted into the movie *Lan Yu* (Hong Kong 2001) directed by Stanley Kwan. This film features an intergenerational relationship between a semicloseted gay man who pays for sex with the younger and more open Lan Yu, and follows their evolving relationship against the backdrop of the events at Tiananmen Square. Another blockbuster online novel was titled as "*Xiao Yu Tong-Zhi*" by Xiao Hong Xiu, a gay love story which takes place in a **rural** school. The story depicts a love affair between a new teacher and his high school student. After several struggles confronting their feelings, the young teacher left for a big city while the student returned to the straight life. "Chinese Tong-Zhi Conference," promoting homosexual rights specifically for homosexuals of Chinese **ethnicity**, was first held in 1996 in Hong Kong, attended by about 200 Chinese tong-zhi representing 17 countries. It is now an annual event for the global tong-zhi community.

With easy access to the **Internet**, tong-zhi has become slang. Some parents and gay-friendly straight people use it instead of "*tong-xing-lian*" to express either acceptance or just recognition. Despite its acceptance and widespread use, the phrase does not mean that all Chinese homosexuals who identify themselves as "Tong-Zhi" are striving for the same "cause" or view themselves as "comrades." Chinese **lesbian, gay, bisexual**, and **transgender youth** and their older counterparts have different life goals and understanding about sexuality, which is most apparent in this vast, unevenly developing country. In the countryside where people are immersed in deep tradition, for a gay youth to simply remain single may be his primary goal whereas in Shanghai tong-zhi couples are dreaming of the day they can kiss in public and marry.

Bibliography

Chou Wah-shan. 2000. *Tongzhi: Politics of Same-Sex Eroticism in Chinese Societies.* Binghamton, NY: Haworth Press.
Jin Wu. 2003. "From '*Long Yang*' and '*Dui Shi*' to Tongzhi: Homosexuality in China." *The Mental Health Professions and Homosexuality: International Perspectives* 7, nos. 1/2: 117–143.

Web Sites

Chinese Society for Study of Sexual Minorities. Accessed June 11, 2005. http://www.csssm. org. A biweekly Web magazine based in the North America publishing papers on LGBT studies in Chinese in order to help people have a scientific knowledge about LGBT issues. Chinese and English languages.
Institute for Tongzhi Studies. October 2004. Accessed June 11, 2005. http://www.tongzhi studies.org. An English language academic research Web site , based at the City University of New York, for Chinese-speaking educators and researchers engaged in LGBT studies.

Transgender Youth

Brett Genny Beemyn

Adolescence can be a stressful time for most youth, but it is especially difficult for youth who transgress traditional gender boundaries such as cross-dressers, transsexuals, genderqueers, drag kings, drag queens, gender benders, and otherwise masculine women or feminine men. Besides the typical challenges involved in establishing a sense of self, transgender youth face the added burden of how to come to terms with a highly stigmatized **gender identity,** often without support at home or in secondary schools. Becoming economically independent or being able to attend college enables trans youth to have greater control over their lives, but fully entering the adult world comes with its own set of struggles. However, the ability to find information and communicate with others anonymously on the **Internet** and the growing visibility of trans people in **popular culture** are making it easier for trans youth to accept themselves and find support. As a result, more trans youth are **coming out** today and doing so at younger ages.

For many trans people, identifying as a gender different from one's birth gender or desiring to **cross-dress** is especially intense during puberty. Adolescence is also when they are most isolated and most subjected to **harassment** and abuse by family

See also Activism, LGBT Youth; Bullying; Community LGBT Youth Groups; Japan, Gay and Transgender Youth; Legal Issues, Students; Multiple Genders; Reparative Therapy; Residence Life in Colleges; School Safety and Safe School Zones; Secondary Schools, LGBT; Transsexuality.

members, institutional authorities, and peers. Lacking accurate information, many parents fear that a gender nonconforming adolescent is lesbian/gay or mentally ill and will seek a "cure" through punishment or by sending the youth to a therapist, school counselor, or local church official. Frequently, though, the professional knows little more about gender identity issues than the family, resulting in the further mistreatment of the trans person. If the youth continues to display what is perceived as gender inappropriate behavior, family members may become abusive or compel the youth to leave home. Seldom will they provide the adolescent with access to cross-gender clothing and hormone treatment.

Junior highs and high schools rarely provide a supportive environment for students who identify as transgender or who are viewed as gender variant. A 2002 study of 124 trans youth in the **United Kingdom** found that one-third had experienced harassment or persecution by their peers, and as a result, 16 percent feared going to school and 11 percent had dropped out (Cianciotto and Cahill 2003). The **school climate** in the United States may be even worse. In the 2001 National School Climate Survey conducted by the **Gay, Lesbian, and Straight Education Network**, almost 90 percent of self-identified trans youth reported feeling unsafe in school, as compared to 46 percent of the gay and bisexual men and 41 percent of the lesbians and bisexual women in the study (Kosciw and Cullen 2001).

Even though trans youth are more likely than other adolescent groups to experience harassment and violence from peers, they rarely receive support from teachers and **administrators**. On the contrary, school officials often look the other way when a trans youth is taunted or threatened and sometimes even blame the victim or engage in abusive behavior themselves. For example, "Pat Doe," a trans woman attending junior high school in Massachusetts, was prevented by her school's administration from dressing in traditionally female attire. Her family sued. In the first known court case on behalf of a trans student, a Superior Court judge ruled in 2000 that the school had discriminated against her on the basis of sex and violated her right to free expression.

School districts have also largely ignored the hostile atmosphere for trans youth. Few districts provide gender diversity training to their staff and faculty members or have a system in place to address physical and verbal abuse against LGBT students. On the state level, only Minnesota, California, and New Jersey currently have laws that ban harassment against students in public schools based on their gender identity or expression.

With school authorities frequently failing to act, junior high and high school students have taken it upon themselves to confront the virulently anti-LGBT climate at most institutions. In the last fifteen years, LGBT students and their allies have formed more than 2,000 **gay–straight alliances** (GSAs) nationwide to support each other and to educate teachers, administrators, and other students about LGBT issues. But because many GSAs do not specifically address the needs of trans students or focus on gender identity issues, some schools and transgender organizations are beginning to form after-school trans youth groups, such as Chrysalis in O'ahu, Hawaii or the Trans Youth Resources and Advocacy in Chicago. The establishment of New York's Harvey Milk High School, the first accredited public school for LGBT students, has also helped create a supportive environment for trans youth, many of whom had experienced ongoing harassment in the city's other public schools.

These efforts notwithstanding, many trans youth drop out of high school because of relentless abuse and ostracism or because they can no longer suppress their transgender identity to avoid harassment. Trans students who continue on to college can more easily create a supportive social network. College is often the first chance that trans youth have to explore different gender possibilities, and a growing number of college students are identifying as transgendered or genderqueer. Trans people helped start the gay liberation movement during the late 1960s and have always been a part of gay student organizations. Since the 1990s, they have become more visible and insisted on recognition in the names and missions of these groups. They are also beginning to form their organizations at large universities and progressive liberal arts colleges—institutions where there are a significant number of openly transgender students.

Many trans students remain closeted, though, because of the hostile atmosphere for gender-diverse people at most colleges and universities. A study of the environment at fourteen institutions found that 41 percent of the transgender respondents had experienced harassment, including verbal abuse, hostile **graffiti**, threats of violence, or physical assault, in the previous year, as compared to 28 percent of lesbians, gay men, and bisexuals (Rankin 2003). The majority of all survey respondents indicated that trans people were the most harassed group on their campus.

Unfortunately, many colleges and universities have been slow to respond to the needs of trans students. Even campus lesbian, gay, and bisexual leaders and well-meaning student affairs professionals often lack basic knowledge about transgender issues, resulting in policies and practices that further marginalize gender-diverse individuals. For example, it is commonly believed that trans students are lesbian, gay, or bisexual or are planning to undergo gender reassignment surgery. Such **stereotypes** result in **college campus programming** and services that fail to acknowledge heterosexual trans people, cross-dressers, and individuals who are content to remain outside the categories "male" and "female." Similarly, **educational policies** that segregate students by gender, such as restroom designations, residence hall assignments, and rules on who can join most **sports** teams and some student organizations, ignore and stigmatize individuals who transcend binary notions of gender. Likewise, few colleges have addressed the issue of institutional forms that discriminate against trans students by having only "male" and "female" as gender options.

Some colleges and universities, though, are starting to acknowledge how institutional policies and practices discriminate against trans students, often in response to instances of antitransgender bias. Accommodation in public restrooms is one area where trans people experience **discrimination**. The "bathroom issue" is particularly a problem for transsexual women, but butch lesbians and other masculine-appearing women are also often harassed in women's restrooms. To avoid potential confrontations and to make campus restrooms more accessible to gender-diverse individuals, some schools are publicizing the location of single occupancy bathrooms and creating additional gender-neutral facilities. A number of colleges, including American University, New York University, the Ohio State University, and the University of California-Santa Barbara, are including gender-neutral, single-occupancy bathrooms in all new and renovated campus buildings (Beemyn 2005).

Another area where trans students often encounter discrimination is in residence halls, where they may be assigned to a building or have a roommate of the "wrong" gender or be denied access to the appropriate restroom. Some schools, including Wesleyan University, Sarah Lawrence College, the University of Southern Maine, the University of Pennsylvania, and the University of California-Riverside, have addressed this issue by creating gender-neutral housing options, in which students are assigned a roommate regardless of gender (Beemyn 2005).

Relatively more schools have sought to protect the rights of trans students through adding the phrase "gender identity or expression" to their campus nondiscrimination policies. Since the University of Iowa amended its human rights statement to include gender identity in 1996, more than twenty-five colleges and college systems have changed their policies, including Brown University, the University of California system, the Ohio State University, the University of Washington, and Knox College. Many other schools in the United States are in the process of doing so (Transgender Law and Policy Institute 2005).

In the absence of institutional support, trans youth have begun to turn to each other for help, creating communities through student groups, Web sites, publications, and other social and political networks. The **Internet** has been especially important in enabling trans students to develop a sense of community. Even if there are not other out trans people in their schools, they are able to receive advice and build a support system online.

Ever since Christine Jorgensen became a household name in 1952 after news of her "sex change" operation in Denmark reached the U.S. press, transgender people have been regularly featured in the mainstream media. Much of this coverage, though, has been stereotypical and demeaning, such as the sensationalistic representa-

The most well-known and popular Bulgarian transvestite, Ursula is winner of Ms. Bulgaria competitions in 1996 and 1998, and the "Best Dancer" award on Bulgarian musical TV *MM*, in 2000. © Ursula

tions of trans people on television talk shows and the use of improper gender pronouns in many news stories. But as trans communities began to organize politically and demand more accurate portrayals in the 1990s and 2000s, the media's treatment of transgender issues improved. For example, recent **films** such as *Boys Don't Cry* (USA 1999), *No Dumb Questions* (USA 2001), *Just Call Me Kade* (USA 2002), *Southern Comfort* (USA 2001), *Hedwig and the Angry Inch* (USA 2001), and *Better than Chocolate* (Canada 1999) offer more positive images of trans people. Like the Internet, these cinematic representations are enabling trans youth to feel less isolated and to take greater pride in their gender identities.

Bibliography

Beemyn, Brett Genny. 2005. "Ways that Colleges and Universities Meet the Needs of Transgender Students." Accessed June 13, 2005. http://www.transgenderlaw.org/college/index.htm#practices.

Cianciotto, Jason, and Sean Cahill. 2003. *Education Policy: Issues Affecting Lesbian, Gay, Bisexual, and Transgender Youth*. New York: National Gay and Lesbian Task Force Policy Institute. http://www.ngltf.org//library/index.cfm.

Israel, Gianna E., and Donald E. Tarver II. 1997. *Transgender Care: Recommended Guidelines, Practical Information, and Personal Accounts*. Philadelphia: Temple University Press.

Kosciw, Joseph G., and M. K. Cullen. 2001. *The GLSEN National School Climate Survey: The School-Related Experiences of Our Nation's Lesbian, Gay, Bisexual and Transgender Youth.* New York: The Gay, Lesbian and Straight Education Network.

Lees, Lisa J. 1998. "Transgender Students on Our Campuses." Pp. 37–43 in *Working with Lesbian, Gay, Bisexual, and Transgender College Students: A Handbook for Faculty and Administrators.* Edited by Ronni L. Sanlo. Westport, CT: Greenwood Press.

Mallon, Gerald P., ed. 1999. *Social Services with Transgendered Youth.* Binghamton, NY: Harrington Park Press.

Rankin, Susan R. 2003. *Campus Climate for Gay, Lesbian, Bisexual, and Transgender People: A National Perspective.* New York: The National Gay and Lesbian Task Force Policy Institute.

Sausa, Lydia A. 2002. "Updating College and University Campus Policies: Meeting the Needs of Trans Students, Staff, and Faculty." Pp. 43–55 in Addressing Homophobia and Heterosexism on College Campuses. Edited by Elizabeth P. Cramer. Binghamton, NY: Harrington Park Press.

Transgender Law and Policy Institute. 2005. "Colleges and Universities with Non-Discrimination Policies that Include Gender Identity/Expression." Accessed June 13, 2005. http://www.transgenderlaw.org/college/index.htm#policies.

Web Sites

Trans*topia. 2005. Advocates for Youth. Accessed June 16, 2005. http://www.youth resource.com/community/transtopia/index.htm. Provides information and resources specifically for transgender youth, including message boards and personal stories.

Trans Proud. June 2005. The National Coalition for GLBT Youth. Accessed June 16, 2005. http://www.transproud.com Answers questions about transgenderism, trans-coming out stories, message boards, resources for parents whose children have come out as transgender, and other valuable information.

Transsexuality

Brett Genny Beemyn

"Transsexuality"—a term for individuals who identify with a gender different from their biological gender—began to be used by doctors in the late 1940s and entered public consciousness in 1952 through the media sensation over the gender transition of Christine Jorgensen, the first person from the United States to be open about having had a "sex change" operation. But individuals who sought to change their gender existed well before the development of the terminology surrounding transsexuality and the invention of sophisticated surgical techniques. In recent years, the meaning of transsexuality has become less tied to surgical intervention, as many younger trans people have refused to identify as either male or female and challenged the ability of others, particularly some in the medical profession, to define their lives.

See also Adolescent Sexualities; China, LGBT Issues in; Cross-Dressing; Desire; Educational Policies; Gender Identity; Intersex; Japan, Gay and Transgender Youth; Residence Life in Colleges; Sexual Identity; Social Class; LGBT Studies; Transgender Youth.

Contrary to the perception that gender reassignment is a contemporary phenomenon, the earliest known case of transformative surgery involved a female-bodied
man in Germany in 1882. The first complete male-to-female (MTF) genital operation occurred in Germany in 1931, and a number of such surgeries were done in
the country in the early 1930s, before the rise of Nazism. Complete female-to-male
(FTM) genital reconstruction began to be performed in Europe in the late 1940s
and in the United States during the early 1960s, although the media focused almost
exclusively on Jorgensen and other trans women.

The lack of attention given to FTMs, along with the fact that phalloplasty
(plastic surgery to construct a penis) was more complicated and expensive than
vaginoplasty and had limited results, meant that few trans women requested surgery in the 1950s and 1960s. As a consequence, some doctors believed that transsexuality was largely a MTF experience. Even though trans men continue to be less
visible than trans women and female-to-male surgical outcomes are still often considered inadequate, about the same number of MTFs and FTMs approach health
care providers about transitioning from one gender to another.

Gender reassignment surgery (GRS) is plastic surgery, yet the medical establishment imposes restrictions on transsexuals that it does not place on any other group
seeking to alter their bodies. Professionals in the field developed "Standards of
Care," in 1979, that require transsexuals to meet specific criteria before they can
have surgery, and the American Psychiatric Association began listing transsexuality
as a **Gender Identity Disorder** in its *Diagnostic and Statistical Manual of Mental
Disorders* the following year. Doctors have thus been able to limit who has access
to hormones and GRS, giving transsexuals little power over their treatment. Reflecting the genderphobia and **homophobia** of many in the medical profession, this
gate keeping system has meant that transsexuals who could not or would not pass
as the "opposite sex" or who would live as lesbians or gay men after surgery have
often had difficulty obtaining legal hormones and GRS.

Besides the bias of many doctors, the high cost of gender reassignment has prevented many transsexuals, especially trans people of color and trans youth of all
races, from having access to legitimate med-
ical services. Some turn to illicit sources as a
result, such as street dealers of hormones
and unlicensed providers of breast implants
or mastectomies. Since many trans people
cannot afford vaginoplasty and phalloplasty,
they choose to take hormones and have a
mastectomy or electrolysis, but not undergo
"bottom surgery."

Beyond the cost, many younger trans
men and a growing number of younger
trans women do not pursue GRS because
they recognize genitalia is not what makes a
man or woman. They are comfortable being
who they are and do not feel that their gender identities have to be completely aligned
with their bodies. While some doctors and
older transsexuals contend that this lack of
interest in GRS means that they are not

Self-portrait of Tiffany, age 23, from Dublin,
who is a trans woman active in Ireland's youth
group BeLonG To. This image was used widely
as a postcard to promote an exhibition of queer
youth self-portraits in Ireland. © Tiffany

"true" transsexuals, many younger trans people refuse to depend on others to describe their experiences or validate their lives. They are **coming out** and defining a transsexual identity that makes sense to them.

Although more and more youth reject the gender that was assigned to them at birth and openly explore other gender possibilities, generally educators have not acknowledged and address the needs of trans people. Many school officials lack any understanding of transgender concerns and only become cognizant of these issues when a crisis arises, such as a conflict over an MTF using a women's restroom, an FTM being assigned to a residence hall room with a nontrans woman, or someone being the victim of a **hate crime** because of their gender expression. Compounding the problem is the failure of secondary schools and colleges to provide any information about transsexuality. Even the institutions that have lesbian, gay, and bisexual courses and course content typically ignore trans people in their curricula. As a result, secondary schools and colleges today are often not very welcoming to people of all genders.

Bibliography

Benjamin, Harry. 1966. *The Transsexual Phenomenon*. New York: Julian Press.
Califia, Pat. 1997. *Sex Changes: The Politics of Transgenderism*. San Francisco: Cleis Press.
Cromwell, Jason. 1999. *Transmen and FTMs: Identities, Bodies, Genders, and Sexualities*. Urbana: University of Illinois Press.
Denny, Dallas, ed. 1998. *Current Concepts in Transgender Identity*. New York: Garland.
Meyerowitz, Joanne. 2002. *How Sex Changed: A History of Transsexuality in the United States*. Cambridge, MA: Harvard University Press.

Web Sites

Gender Education and Advocacy. 2004. Gwendolyn Ann Smith. Accessed June 16, 2005. http://www.gender.org Web site includes Remembering Our Dead, a memorial to individuals who have been killed because of their gender expression, and an extensive collection of informative handouts. One section of the site provides citations for articles and court cases involving transsexual teachers.
Trans*topia. 2005. Advocates for Youth. Accessed June 16, 2005. http://www.youth resource.com/community/transtopia/index.htm. Provides information and resources specifically for transgender youth. Trans*topia includes message boards, access to Webrings, and personal stories from young transpeople.

U

United Kingdom, LGBT Youth and Issues in

Ian Warwick, Elaine Chase and *Peter Aggleton*

While progress has been made in addressing the needs of **lesbian, gay, bisexual** and **transgender** (LGBT) young people in the United Kingdom (UK), much remains to be done. At the national policy level, the legal and policy contexts across England, Northern Ireland, Scotland, and Wales vary, although steps have been taken to repeal discriminatory legislation, equalize the age of consent, and protect young LGBT people from harm. New national initiatives for young people, in general, often fail to address, or even mention, the needs of young LGBT people. Although there is a national drive to address homophobic **bullying** in schools, some adults working in education, health, and social services remain, at best, unaware of the needs of LGBT youth or, at worst, discriminate against them. Groups for young LGB people exist across the country (few exist for, or include, transgender youth), and while there is an established "scene," young people in **rural** areas, in particular, have limited access to groups and commercial lesbian and gay venues. A vibrant range of Lesbian and Gay Pride events takes place each year. Across the media, the lives of young gay men—but to a much lesser extent those of young lesbians, bisexuals, and transgender young people—are, on occasions at least, portrayed in realistic and informative ways.

The National Survey of Sexual Attitudes and Lifestyles reported, in 2003, the experiences of sixteen to twenty-four-year-olds (Erens et al. 2003). About 4 percent of men have had a same-sex experience, and 2.6 percent have engaged in genital contact with a person of the same gender. Among women the percentage was 9.1 percent and 4.5 percent, respectively. Extrapolated nationally, this would suggest that around 238,000 young men and 454,000 of young women have had some sort of sexual experience with a same-sex partner. These figures do not include young people who feel attracted to others of the same gender but have not acted upon it. Statistics concerning the number of young transgender people in the United Kingdom are unavailable. The Gender Identity Research and Education Society (GIRES) estimates there to be around 1 in 4,000 gender dysphoric adults, with perhaps around 10,000 to 15,000 transgender adults (around one-third dealing with gender conflict, one-third undergoing hormonal treatment and one-third post surgery). Ratios of men to women experiencing gender dysphoria are said to be three to one.

In a national survey, young people (aged fifteen to twenty-four) were more likely than older respondents to recognize that lesbian and gay people faced **discrimination** (55 percent compared to 37 percent) (Citizenship 21 2003). Respondents aged fifteen to forty-four were less likely than those aged forty-five to fifty-four and those over fifty-five to express **prejudice** against lesbians and gay men (9 percent, 19 percent and 31 percent respectively).

Throughout the 1980s and 1990s, national level policy and guidance–especially Section 28 of the 1988 Local Government Act, forbidding local authorities from "promoting" homosexuality—hindered sexuality education, impeded the setting up

See also Britain, Section 28; College Campus Organizing; Community LGBT Youth Groups; Ethnic Identity; Europe, LGBT Youth and Issues in; Heteronormativity; HIV Education; Ireland, LGBT Youth and Issues in; Literature, Secondary School; Sexual Abuse and Assault; Workplace Issues; Youth, At-Risk; Youth Culture.

of supportive youth services for LGBT young people, and contributed to a climate of **homophobia**-related violence and discrimination. However, in 2003, Section 28 was repealed. This was preceded by legislation two years earlier equalizing the age of consent for gay men, lesbians, and heterosexuals (which is sixteen in England, Wales and Scotland, and seventeen in Northern Ireland).

Although there is a duty on schools to protect and promote the welfare of pupils—and as part of this to address homophobic incidents—LGBT issues are most likely to be addressed through sex and relationship education and citizenship classes. The National Union of Teachers recommends ". . . issues surrounding relationships can be explored within Art, English, Drama, History or RE" (NUT 2004, 1). The extent to which this is done is unknown. However, the heteronormative culture of schools generally inhibits helpful discussion of same-sex sexualities (Warwick, Chase, and Aggleton 2004).

As a European Union (EU) member, the United Kingdom is bound by certain legislation. The unacceptability of discrimination on the grounds of **sexual orientation** is specifically mentioned in the most important EU document, its Treaty. Furthermore, the European Convention for the Protection of Human Rights and Fundamental Freedoms and, in the UK, the Human Rights Act 1998, the 1998 School Standards Act, and the 2003 Employment Equality (Sexual Orientation) Regulations, aim to ensure that young people (as well as adults), whether pupils or employees, are legally protected from discrimination and **harassment** on the grounds of their sexual orientation. A key challenge, however, lies in ensuring that this legislation is enforced.

Around 30 to 50 percent of lesbians and gay men report homophobic harassment at school; rates for incidences of general bullying among pupils are around 10 to 20 percent (Rivers 2003; Thompson 2000). Young lesbians and bisexual women

National Union of Students LGB Campaign, London, Nov. 17, 2001.
© Akihiko Komiya

are especially vulnerable to being bullied compared to their heterosexual peers—30 percent, 35 percent and 20 percent, respectively (King and McKeown 2003). Black and Asian young people have been reported to be more likely to experience homophobic physical abuse than sexual minority respondents overall, 57 percent compared to 47 percent (GALOP 1998). Young people from black and minority ethnic communities may find it especially difficult to report homophobic bullying, since **racism** and homophobia can become conflated so as to limit ideas about what constitutes proper and appropriate forms of masculinity and femininity (GALOP 2001).

The Crown Prosecution Service and police forces throughout the country recognize and respond to homophobic and, perhaps to a lesser degree, transphobic incidents. Drawing, in part, on what has been learned from tackling race **hate crimes** and responding to the bombing of a gay pub in the center of London, in May 1999, LGBT people are encouraged to report homophobic incidents. In some areas of the country, particularly in metropolitan areas, police have taken part in LGBT awareness training and how best to respond to such incidents. Hate crimes may increase the legal penalty, depending on the locality and type of incident.

Yet, for too many young people, "coming out" continues to be a difficult process, resulting in physical or sexual assault, becoming estranged from their families and being thrown out of their homes. The range and extent of community youth groups and help lines provide opportunities for young people to talk about feelings of same-sex attraction and, to a lesser extent, to discuss their gender identity. Families and Friends of Lesbians and Gays UK (http://www.fflag.org.uk) provides resources to assist parents and relatives to support better their lesbian and gay children. The Albert Kennedy Trust (http://www.akt.org.uk) gives support to young LGB people who cannot live with their parents and, where needed and possible, provide lesbian or gay foster caregivers. In Scotland, the law prohibiting lesbian and gay households from fostering young people is about to change.

With regard to education, most universities and some colleges of further education have lesbian, gay, and bisexual societies. However, support for younger people of school age generally is available only from out-of-school services. The form and quality of services vary markedly across the United Kingdom. Concerns about teenage **pregnancy**, STIs and HIV, and **AIDS** have contributed to new policies and programs of **sexuality education** in schools. However, these tend to equate sexuality with heterosexuality. Young lesbians have noted that there is little information of relevance to them (YWCA 2004). Despite the impact of HIV and AIDS, there are few opportunities for queer youth to learn about same-sex relationships and safer sex. Further, young transgender people have few opportunities to talk about their gender-related concerns such as their appearance, choice of name, the right sorts of clothes to wear, and medical issues. They face particular challenges whether in or out of school, which can affect their emotional well-being as well as their ability to achieve at school.

Questions have been raised as to whether the club and bar-centered nature of the lesbian and gay scene in the UK—and the opportunities available for alcohol and drug consumption—has an impact on young people's well-being. Some studies suggest that rates of alcohol consumption and other drug use are higher among lesbians and gay men than within the general population (YWCA 2004) and that young gay men's **drug use**, including recreational substances such as ecstasy and alcohol as well as body enhancing substances like steroids, is a cause for concern (Rivers 2003). However, it is difficult to determine whether these are particular concerns for young lesbians and gay men—compared to their older peers—or whether some of the issues identified relate to challenges in drawing representative samples of young LGBT people.

The media and the **Internet** provide LGBT youth with access advice, guidance, and information, as well as opportunities to connect with others outside of the bar scene. *Gay Times* has been published for many years, but newer weeklies and monthlies such as *Boyz* and *Attitude* (chiefly of interest to gay and bisexual men) and *Diva* (advertised as "Europe's only mainstream lesbian magazine") have a more youth focused style. Celebrities appear regularly on their covers, and features about them intermingle with gossip about the lesbian and gay scene, fashion advice, and guidance on matters of sex and relationships. More general youth magazines, particularly those for girls such as *Bliss*, have contained articles or information via problem pages on the subject of same-sex attraction. Through the National Youth Agency's youthinformation.com or through Gaydar (http://gaydargirls.co.uk. and http://gaydar.co.uk/.), young people can browse personal advertisements for friendships and potential girl- or boyfriends. While Gay.com has sections of interest to young lesbians and gay men and is global in ambition, Gay Youth UK (http://www.gayyouthuk.org.uk) and the Queer Youth Alliance (http://www.queeryouth.org.uk) have national coverage and, LGBT Youth Scotland (http://www.lgbtyouth.org.uk) and Gay and Lesbian Youth Northern Ireland (http://www.glyni.org.uk) have a specific country focus. There are also Internet sites for ethnic and religious minorities such as the Safra Project for lesbian, bisexual and/or transgender women who identify as **Muslim** religiously and/or culturally (http://www.safraproject.org/services.htm). Transgender youth find only limited Internet support and there are no UK Web sites exclusively for black or Asian LGB youth.

The Gender Trust and the Gender Identity Research & Education Society offer general information and guidance—some of which will be useful for young Transgender people—with Mermaids (a "Family Support Group for Children and Teenagers with Gender Identity Issues") providing specific information about being young and transgender (http://www.mermaids.freeuk.com).

A number of gay-oriented UK films, documentaries, and television programs have been produced. These include **films**, such as *My Beautiful Launderette* (UK 1985), *Beautiful Thing* (UK 1996) and *Get Real* (UK/South Africa 1998); TV soaps with lesbian, gay, bisexual, and transgender storylines, such as *Brookside*, *Coronation Street*, *Eastenders*, and *Emmerdale*; gay comedians, such as Julian Clary and Graham Norton; and television series like *Metrosexual*, **Queer as Folk** and *Tipping the Velvet*. Participants and winners in the reality show, *Big Brother*, have included lesbians, gay men, bisexual men and women, and a transsexual. Although usually white, characters are generally portrayed positively.

A few contemporary UK authors and playwrights address LGBT themes for young people. However, Shakespeare's *Twelfth Night* continues to generate discussion about gender roles. Other plays, such as *A Taste of Honey*, have lesbian or gay characters. *Why Don't You Stop Talking?*, by Jackie Kay, a Scottish black lesbian, is a selection of short stories, many of which are comic and poignant observations of same-sex attraction between women. Julie Burchill's *Sugar Rush* is a tale of friendship and love between two young women at school. Works from authors outside the UK are also popular. The *Geography Club* (which follows a group of students in the United States who want to form a **gay–straight alliance** in their school), *Boys Like Her* (a series of short stories and poems addressing sexuality and **gender identity**), and *Not the Only One* (an anthology for lesbian and gay young people) are sporadically available to young people at mainstream bookshops or perhaps in local or school libraries across the UK.

Bibliography

Citizenship 21. 2003. *Profiles of Prejudice. The Nature of Prejudice in England: In-Depth Analysis of Findings.* London: Stonewall/Citizenship 21.

Erens, Bob, Sally McManus, Alison Prescott, and Julia Field, with Anne Johnson, Kaye Welllings, Kevin Fenton, Catherine Mercer, Wendy MacDowell, Andrew Copas, and Kiran Nanchahal. 2003. *National Survey of Sexual Attitudes and Lifestyles II: Reference Tables and Summary Report.* London: National Centre for Social Research. Accessed June 22, 2005. http://www.natcen.ac.uk.

GALOP. 1998. *Telling it Like It Is. . . Lesbian, Gay and Bisexual Youth Speak Out on Homophobic Violence.* London: Author.

———. 2001. *The Low Down: Black Lesbians, Gay Men and Bisexual People Talk About Their Experience and Needs.* London: Author.

King, Michael, and Eamonn McKeown, with James Warner, Angus Ramsay, Katherine Johnson, Clive Cort, Oliver Davidson, and Lucienne Wright. 2003. *Mental Health and Social Well-Being of Gay Men, Lesbians and Bisexuals in England and Wales.* London: Mind. Accessed June 22, 2005. Summary available at: http://www.mind.org.uk/News+policy+and+campaigns/Policy/LGB+policy.htm.

National Union of Teachers. 2004. *Supporting Lesbian, Gay, Bisexual and Transgender Students: An Issue for Every Teacher.* London: Author.

Rivers, Ian, and Daniel J. Carragher. 2003. "Social-Developmental Factors Affecting Lesbian and Gay Youth: A Review of Cross-National Research Findings." *Children & Society* 17, no. 5: 374–385.

Thompson, David. 2000. "Bullying and Harassment In and Out of School." Pp. 197–210 in *Young People and Mental Health.* Edited by Peter Aggleton, Jane Hurry, and Ian Warwick. Chichester: Wiley.

Warwick, Ian, Elaine Chase, and Peter Aggleton. 2004. *Homophobia, Sexual Orientation and Schools: A Review and Implications for Action.* London: Department for Education and Skills. Accessed November 2004. http://www.dfes.gov.uk/research.

YWCA. 2004. "Pride Not Prejudice: Young Lesbian and Bisexual Women." *Briefings* 11: 1–8.

Web Sites

Gay's the Word. Accessed April 2005. Accessed June 16, 2005. http://freespace.virgin.net/gays.theword. Booklists of titles relevant to young people.

Stonewall. June 2005. Accessed June 16, 2005. http://www.stonewall.org.uk. A campaigning and lobbying organization that undertakes specific campaigns to promote the rights of young LGBT people.

Urban Youth and Schools

Lance T. McCready

Urban communities and schools offer a range of social/support services that target LGBTQ youth. In the United States, for example, the Hetrick-Martin Institute, home of the Harvey Milk High School (HMI) in New York City (http://gay life.about.com/gi/dynamic/offsite.htm?zi=1/XJ&sdn=gaylife&zu=http%3A%2F%2Fwww.hmi.org%2F), provides a comprehensive continuum of care for LGBTQ youth, ranging

See also Asian American; School Safety and Safe School Zones; Secondary Schools, LGBT; Youth, At-Risk; Youth, Homeless.

Triangle Youth Marching for International Women's Day, 2002. Courtesy of Triangle Program, Toronto

from counseling and access to basic needs to after-school programs such as peer counseling, job exploration, and career readiness. The Albert Kennedy Trust (http://www. akt.org.uk/index.html.), in London, helps place LGBTQ youth who are homeless or living in a hostile environment in LGBTQ caregivers' homes where they can rebuild lives in a safe, affirming environment. Urban Youth, also located in London, offers information, advice, and support for LGBTQ youth under the age of thirty. The Triangle Program (http:// schools.tdsb.on.ca/triangle), in Toronto, provides a classroom where LGBTQ youth can learn and earn credits in a safe, harassment-free, equity-based environment. **Gay– straight alliances** (GSAs) located throughout the United States, aim to make anti-LGBT **bullying, harassment**, and name-calling unacceptable in America's schools while providing support services.

Despite the seeming wealth of resources for LGBTQ youth in urban communities and schools, these programs remain limited in scope because they do not address the new social context of urban communities. For the most part, existing LGBTQ youth programs have been slow to take demographic and economic changes in central cities, such as the rise of the **Latino** population or the flight of middle class families to the suburbs, into account. Moreover, **research** on LGBTQ youth that specifically explores this new urban context of urban communities is virtually nonexistent.

Most of what we know about the physical and **mental health** issues, family dynamics, and school experiences of LGBTQ youth is based on research and narratives drawn from LGBTQ youth who live in metropolitan areas. The tendency to sample LGBTQ youth from metropolitan areas can be attributed to the relative ease that researchers and writers can contact youth through LGBT community centers and organized groups of LGBTQ youth. Since few **rural** communities support such programs, urban LGBTQ youth are oversampled. Paradoxically, research and writing on LGBTQ youth says very little about the specific social and cultural context of an urban community. For example, LGBTQ adolescents are potentially at higher risk for homelessness than heterosexual youths because they are rejected by or run away from families unaccepting of their sexuality (Cochran et al. 2002). Data on LGBTQ runaway or homeless youth are from surveys of youth in large metropolitan cities. City-specific surveys, however, can at best only represent youth within that city, much less youth in other social and cultural contexts.

Another example of research on urban LGBTQ youth that does not address the new social context of urban communities is the rather large number of studies on the life challenges of LGBTQ youth (D'Augelli 2002). These studies suggest that disclosure of homosexuality to family and friends, parents' stance toward homosexuality, worry about HIV infection, **suicide**, and **substance abuse** warrant the need for comprehensive interventions focused on LGBTQ youth. The kinds of interventions offered for these challenges, however, are conceived without regard to the specific political, economic, and demographic dynamics in urban communities.

For example, D'Augelli (2002) suggests that policies should be in place prohibiting victimization based on **sexual orientation**. However, there is no discussion of the inherent challenges in implementing such policies in urban communities where the residents may adhere to cultural values based on a religion or nationality that condemns homosexuality or even discussions of sexual orientation.

The world has experienced unprecedented urban growth in recent decades. In 2000, 47 percent of the world's population lived in urban areas, about 2.8 billion. In the United States, as the nation's white population ages, U.S.-born Asian and Latino children and young immigrants from Asia and Latin America are replacing it. Almost 29 percent of all Londoners are black or Asian. Toronto, with a population of 2.48 million people (five million in the greater Toronto area) is heralded as one of the most multicultural cities in the world. In 2003, 43 percent of Toronto's population reported themselves as being part of a visible minority (e.g. South Asian, Chinese, black, Filipino). One in four children between five and sixteen in the city of Toronto are new immigrants having arrived between 1991 and 2001.

Although metropolitan areas are incredibly diverse, most urban centers have been in decline due to concentrated poverty in the city's core and the consequent disinvestment and flight of the middleclass. Builders, financial institutions, realtors, and developers, supported in part by restrictive racial covenants and reinforced by custom, have promoted segregated housing. Often federal governments aided this process by promoting segregation through the selective construction of public housing and discriminatory tenant placement policies. Middle-class whites flee the inner city when they are assured access to wealth appreciation through a combination of government-assisted private investment and rapidly rising suburban property values. In most cases, these kinds of home ownership advantages have been systematically denied to people of color.

In addition to institutional racism, individual white middle class families have been reluctant to live in the integrated urban communities that civil rights activists imagined (Wells et al. 2004). Middle class whites often fear the quality of schools suffer when they serve large numbers of children who are poor, of color, and/or nonnative speakers of English. When people of color become the majority of a city's population, whites may respond not only with "white flight," but also with a racialized view of "the city," even when they live within the city limits.

Although there is strong consensus regarding the above social dynamics, very little is known about how urban LGBTQ youth experience these economic and demographic changes. Rather, research on LGBTQ youth tends to focus, out of these contexts, on issues such as **coming out, suicide**, substance abuse, harassment, and family acceptance. Even articles that claim to be about, for example, "urban **African American** gay adolescents" focus on incidents of HIV infection without discussing economic and demographic changes that may affect HIV transmission rates. The following are some ways new social contexts of urban communities in the twenty-first century that may affect our conceptualization of urban LGBTQ youth.

The increasing diversity of metropolitan centers due to immigration suggests that many more LGBTQ youth will identify as nonwhite, nonnative speakers of the English who understand their **sexual identity** from a non-Western or at the very least dual cultural frame of reference. The increased visibility of non-white LGBTQ youth does not mean they are more readily accepted within their neighborhoods and schools. For example, black neighborhoods within large cities in the United States became areas of racial and sexual boundary-crossing that supported more visible lesbian and gay activities. However, the presence of such activities within racially segregated neighborhoods did not mean these black GLBTQ youth experienced acceptance as issues of racial segregation and racism persist. Further, many African Americans and African immigrants, influenced by church teachings, disapprove of homosexuality itself while they may approve of LGBTQ individuals and family members (Boykin 1998).

Urban LGBTQ youth who grow up in non-Western countries may understand their sexualities and sexual identities in vastly different ways than Western youth. For example, in some countries in **Africa** and South **Asia** homosexuality is illegal. Non-Western languages may or may not have specific words for nonheterosexual identities that connote the same meanings as the Western sense of **"gay," "lesbian," "bisexual,"** or **"transgender."** Urban LGBTQ youth who are non-white and/or immigrants experience tremendous isolation amidst the wealth of resources for LGBTQ youth when they live in communities that condemn homosexuality for cultural and religious reasons. These youth may also experience isolation when they identify and/or express their sexual identities in Western ways.

In addition to cultural barriers, urban LGBTQ youth in U.S. cities, specifically, are experiencing massive resegregation of public schools due, in part, to segregated housing patterns and the waning commitment of the federal government to enforce court-ordered desegregation. Urban LGBTQ youth who attend segregated schools in poor communities are likely to face a host of problems related to the structure and organization of these schools. For example, one multiracial urban high school in northern California boasts an impressive variety of extracurricular programs and activities (McCready 2001). Most of these programs, including the LGBTQ social/support/activist groups, are racially-defined. At this school, the students who attended **Project 10** tended to be white and female. This racially segregated environment created a **school climate** of racial surveillance that made it difficult for non-white students to participate in clubs and activities outside of their racial group free from the scrutiny of both their same-race and other-race peers.

Racially segregated schools in communities where the median family income is below average are less likely to have programs specifically aimed at LGBTQ youth; there simply are not enough economic resources. Public schools with a weaker residential tax base may attempt to maximize their resources through ability grouping and tracking that puts more money toward students who demonstrate academic potential. In most cases, students with academic potential come from families with more social and cultural capital as several national census studies indicate that in racially diverse communities these families tend to be white or Asian (Noguera 2003). In such environments, black and Latino students tend to be placed in lower-tracked classes where work or "getting a job" is emphasized over issues of college attendance or sexual identity. Access to resources for LGBTQ youth who attend racially segregated neighborhood schools is a needed area of research.

Along with cultural barriers and resegregation, the new social contexts of urban communities likely produces metropolitan areas where larger numbers of LGBTQ youth are at-risk for poverty, homelessness, and foster care placement. Particularly in urban communities where jobs are scarce, LGBTQ youth who escape to develop affirming social/support networks may not find jobs that pay them a living wage in the city. This prospect is diminished even more if the young person is visibly gender nonconforming or identifiably transgender. Rather than return home, many urban LGBTQ youth prefer to live on the street which increases their likelihood of engaging in prostitution and heightens risk for **alcoholism** and **drug use**, violence, suicide, HIV, and other STD infections.

Educational approaches that take into account how immigration, resegregation, and homelessness affect LGBTQ youth programs and services are beginning to appear. Respect Campaign (RC), launched by Out for Equity in eight Saint Paul schools, recognizes that urban school students face multiple forms of oppression and **discrimination** that can make school feel unsafe. RC helps urban educators develop a multidimensional framework of a healthy school climate, one that addresses issues of **homophobia** and **heterosexism**, but also takes into account oppression and discrimination based on **race**, **ethnicity**, **social class**, gender, and religion.

Bibliography

Anyon, Jean. 1996. *Ghetto Schooling: A Political Economy of Urban Educational Reform.* New York: Teachers College Press.

Boykin, Keith. 1998. *One More River to Cross: Black and Gay in America.* New York: Doubleday.

Cochran, Bryan N., Angela J. Stewart, Joshua A. Ginzler, and Ana Maria Cauce. 2002. "Challenges Faced by Homeless Sexual Minorities: Comparison of Gay, Lesbian, Bisexual, and Transgender Homeless Adolescents with their Heterosexual Counterparts." *American Journal of Public Health* 92: 773–777.

D'Augelli, Anthony R. 2002. "Mental Health Problems among Lesbian, Gay, and Bisexual Youths Ages 14 to 21." *Clinical Child Psychology and Psychiatry* 7: 439–462.

———, and Scott L. Hershberger. 1993. "Lesbian, Gay, and Bisexual Youth in Community Settings: Personal Challenges and Mental Health Problems." *American Journal of Community Psychology* 21: 421–448.

McCready, Lance. 2001. "When Fitting In Isn't an Option, or, Why Black Queer Males at a California High School Stay Away from Project 10." Pp. 37–53 in *Troubling Intersections of Race and Sexuality: Queer Students of Color and Anti-Oppressive Education.* Edited by Kevin K. Kumashiro. Lanham, MA: Rowman and Littlefield.

Noguera, Pedro. 2003. *City Schools and the American Dream.* New York: Teachers College Press.

Orfield, Gary, Susan Eaton, and Harvard Project on School Desegregation. 1996. *Dismantling Desegregation: The Quiet Reversal of Brown v. Board Of Education.* New York: New Press.

Pilkington, Neil W., and Anthony R. D'Augelli. 1995. "Victimization of Lesbian, Gay, and Bisexual Youth in Community Settings." *Journal of Community Psychology* 23, no. 1: 33–55.

Ryan, Caitlin C., and Donna Futterman. 1998. *Lesbian and Gay Youth.* New York: Columbia University Press

Schwartz, Wendy. 1994. *Improving the School Experience for Gay, Lesbian, and Bisexual Students.* ERIC Document ED 377 257.

Suarez-Orozco, Carola, and Marcelo Suarez-Orozco. 2001. *Children of Immigration.* Cambridge, MA: Harvard University Press.

Wells, Amy Stuart, Jennifer Jellison Holme, Anita Tijerina Revilla, and Awo Korantemaa Atanda. 2004. *How Desegregation Changed Us.* New York: Teachers College Press.

Web Sites

Family Acceptance Project. March 2005. Accessed June 22, 2005. http://familyproject.sfsu.edu/. A community research and provider training initiative to study the impact of family acceptance and rejection on the health and development of self-identified lesbian, gay, bisexual, and transgender youth. FAB focuses on the experiences of white and Latino LGBTQ youth in the San Francisco Bay Area.

Institute for Urban and Minority Education. June 2005. Accessed June 22, 2005. http://iume.tc.columbia.edu/. The Institute conducts research and evaluations, provides information services, and assists schools, community-based organizations, and parent school leaders in program development and evaluation, professional development, and parent education. The archive contains some articles on LGBTQ youth.

Out for Equity. June 2005. Accessed June 22, 2005. http://outforequity.spps.org. Out for Equity is dedicated to creating safe and affirming school environments for LGBTQ students, families, and staff. The Web site has a link to the RESPECT Campaign.

V

Virtual Schooling

Donovan R. Walling

Virtual schooling is teaching and learning accomplished by electronic **communication**, rather than face-to-face instruction. Such schooling can be an alternative for students who, for one reason or another, are not well served in traditional schools. For **lesbian, gay, bisexual**, and **transgender youth** (LGBT), virtual schooling may be a viable option if traditional school placement becomes untenable, for example, because of **harassment**. Alternatively, virtual schooling could be misused if turning to this alternative allows school officials to avoid addressing **homophobia**.

Virtual schooling is a form of distance education, although actual distance need not be a factor. Such schooling may be used for one or two classes, either as part of or added to the school day; or it may be employed in place of regular schooling. E-learning and e-teaching connote electronic communication and are used synonymously with virtual schooling. The prefix cyber- and any root implies use of the **Internet**; thus the term cyberschooling is used as well. Indeed, the Internet plays a central role in virtual schooling, unlike in the past when distance education was conducted by such means as corresponding, exchanging audio- and videotapes, and telephoning.

Like distance learning, virtual schooling began at the postsecondary level and is gaining widespread acceptance at the high school level. Virtual schooling also has been used in the lower grades. A fair amount of virtual schooling has come about through the home schooling movement. The connection between virtual schooling and alternative education for LGBT youth has not been explored to any extent in the education literature as yet, and so it is unknown how widespread the practice of virtual schooling is for LGBT youth.

Communication between and among students and teachers is at the core of teaching and learning. Many educators believe that whether schools are traditional or "virtual" is less important than whether such communication is effective. The importance of communication is amplified when seeking to provide safe, supportive, and effective education for LGBT youth and children from sexual-minority families. Such children and adolescents often are affected by bias that takes the form of restricting or limiting communication, particularly as related to family and diversity issues as well as the development and expression of self-identity.

Human interaction is at the heart of debates about e-learning and whether virtual schooling is an acceptable replacement for traditional schooling. In the view of many educators, the ideal use of virtual schooling is supplemental, such as electronically connecting one teacher and students in several distant classrooms for a close simulation of face-to-face teaching and learning. A number of schools have demonstrated that this can be advantageous. For example, e-teaching provides a way for small schools to offer specialized classes, such as foreign language, that otherwise might not be economically feasible. Classrooms in different schools, even in different countries, can be connected electronically so that students can converse and "attend" a single virtual classroom.

However, the more common virtual schooling model is one student-one computer. Thus, the question more often debated by policy makers is: Can a one

See also Queer Zines.

student-one computer cyberclassroom provide a learning experience comparable to a real classroom? Most educators agree that comparability cannot be universally achieved. Disciplines such as the arts rely on movement and multisensory interaction. These disciplines are particularly important to LGBT youth because arts teachers typically recognize and encourage individuality and personal expression more than do teachers of the core academics. Visual **arts, music, theater,** and **dance** require tactile and kinesthetic experiences. Students cannot learn to throw pots without getting their hands in the clay or to paint without picking up a brush. Dancers do not learn to dance by staring at a computer simulation or e-chatting with their instructor. Teaching and learning in these disciplines involve "real" doing—handwork, footwork, bodywork. LGBT youth may be disproportionately affected if opportunities for rich, physical learning are reduced by the limitations of virtual schooling.

Most virtual schooling involves use of the Internet, and so there are concerns related to what is accessed online, which is not the case with controlled or monitored use of the Internet in traditional school settings. Unsupervised use concerns some parents and educators because of the potential for students to access inappropriate online content, specifically, explicit sexual content. Although a number of blocking services and software filters are available, some protocols also screen out appropriate information for students. This concern is pertinent to LGBT youth and their parents if screening programs block access to news or articles about homosexuality, **AIDS,** and **HIV education** or screen out Web sites that use the terms such as "gay," "bisexual," "homosexual," and "lesbian."

Another Internet concern is cyber**bullying**. LGBT youth sometimes are the targets of harassment by persons (usually other students) who use the Internet to provoke and torment. For example, cyberbullies often log into chat rooms and interrupt the dialogue with insults and abusive comments. Thus, virtual schooling may not provide an "escape" from harassment if the abuser turns to virtual harassment.

Bibliography

Cate, Fred H. 1998. *The Internet and the First Amendment: Schools and Sexually Explicit Expression.* Bloomington, IN: Phi Delta Kappa Educational Foundation.
Lewin, Larry. 2001. *Using the Internet to Strengthen Curriculum.* Alexandria, VA: Association for Supervision and Curriculum Development.
Perrotti, Jeff, and Kim Westheimer. 2001. *When the Drama Club Is Not Enough: Lessons from the Safe Schools Program for Gay and Lesbian Students.* Boston: Beacon Press.
Walling, Donovan R., ed. 2003. *Virtual Schooling: Issues in the Development of E-Learning Policy.* Bloomington, IN: Phi Delta Kappa Educational Foundation.
Warschauer, Mark. 1999. *Electronic Literacies: Language, Culture, and Power in Online Education.* Mahwah, NJ: Lawrence Erlbaum Associates.

Web Sites

Connections Academy. 2004. Accessed December 21, 2004. http://www.connectionsacademy.com Private operator of K-12 virtual schools with extensive set of resources.
North American Council for OnLine Learning. 2004. Accessed December 21, 2004 http://www.nacol.org/. Includes information on conferences and forums as well as related resources.
Urban 75. On Cyberbullying. Spring 2003. Accessed December 21, 2004. http://www.urban75.org/info/bullying.html. British nonprofit, alternative, youth-oriented e-zine with news, photos, games, bulletin boards, and other features.

White Antiracism

Dominique Johnson

White antiracism is an orientation that empowers white people to dismantle racism. White antiracist identity exists within contexts of white privilege, building an antiracist LGBTQ movement, and most importantly, addressing racism and **homophobia** in educational contexts. Many queer youth organize across boundaries of identities. Some **gay–straight alliances** (GSAs) organize around an antiracism orientation, emphasizing the significance of intersecting identities. In particular, when white queer youth come out, they often struggle with not only the realization of homophobia but with the realities of other oppressions such as racism. These youth come out not only into a queer identity, but may come out into a white antiracist identity as well. The promotion of a white antiracist identity, therefore, is an integral component of LGBTQ education, antioppressive education, and **multicultural education** initiatives.

Race privilege is especially destructive to white LGBTQ youth because it leaves them ill-equipped to negotiate the oppression they encounter as a sexual minority (Russell and Truong 2001). White privilege underlies programs that normalize whiteness, resulting in assimilation-, tokenization-, or exclusion-based educational opportunities. Often white students are most represented in GSAs and many of these groups struggle with the problems brought about by racial separation and segregation as well as the lack of support and resources for youth of color, **transgender youth**, and young women (McCready 2001; Perotti and Westheimer 2001). Additionally, some white GSA advisers and adult **allies** do not acknowledge the significance of race or confront racism as a part of the daily realities of all students. Thus, the work of the GSA is compromised when antihomophobia work is not considered in a broader context of multiple oppressions and marginalized populations.

When the intersections of **sexual orientation** and **racial identity** are not addressed, the educational needs of LGBTQ youth of color, in particular, remain unfulfilled. For example, educational initiatives created to improve the quality of life in school for high school LGBTQ youth such as the groundbreaking counseling program, **Project 10**, have excluded youth of color because of racialized programming (McCready 2001; McCready 2003). Even those multicultural support programs in **secondary schools** like the Harvey Milk School, some believe, should not be separate because "schools must make fundamental changes that work to eliminate racism and homophobia within the dominant educational structure" (Snider 1996, 294).

Understanding white racial identity is crucial for white educators in accepting antiracism and practicing antioppressive education. White racial identity development is a process including stages ranging from obliviousness to racial/cultural issues and whiteness as a race, awareness of the social implications of racism and white privilege and their effects on a personal level, ownership of whiteness and an ability to recognize a personal responsibility to eradicate racism, and an internalization

See also Activism, LGBT Youth; Antibias Curriculum; Discrimination; Identity Politics; Racial Identity.

of a positive, nonracist white identity and world view that seeks to abolish racial oppression (Tatum 1999).

Educators can engage with students in creating antiracist educational contexts, both within entire schools and LGBTQ initiatives, ranging from GSAs to safe zones. Educators can take specific proactive steps by assessing noninclusive curricula or teaching practices. Such noninclusive practices include: teaching lessons that normalize whiteness and assume the perspectives of the dominant group; using **curriculum** or **college campus programming** resources that do not reflect the diversity of cultural and/or linguistic groups among students; employing teaching examples that reinforce **stereotypes** of the cultural and/or linguistic backgrounds of students; and, either intentionally or unintentionally, practicing aversive racism by not acknowledging the diversity among students.

Integrating antiracist curriculum can include the role that LGBTQ people have always had in working within allied movements for social and racial justice, such as the civil rights and **women's movements**. Educators can also introduce white students to white role models who engage in antiracism work through **literature** such as autobiographical memoirs and/or in-class speakers. For example, Becky Thompson's book, *A Promise and a Way of Life: White Antiracist Activism*, presents an account of the last half of the twentieth century based on the life histories of thirty-nine white people who have placed antiracist activism at the center of their lives. Other examples include Eileen O'Brien's *Whites Confront Racism: Antiracists and Their Paths to Action*, which offers interviews with North American female and male white activists of all ages working for racial justice; Mab Segrest's *Memoirs of a Race Traitor* chronicles the life of a white lesbian antiracist activist. Finally, educators can facilitate coalitions of students, especially for students who interact only within a circle of similar people. Here, GSAs and college diversity clubs can play an important role by purposive programming and outreach.

During the 1960s and early 1970s, many gay student activists urged that racism be confronted in order to build a unified social movement. After **Stonewall** and the demise of the Gay Liberation Front, the multi-issue, antiracist coalition politics were often neglected as a generation of mostly white, middle-class men assumed prominent roles in the single-issue gay rights movement both locally and nationally. Similarly, adult service providers imposed single-issue social movement strategies upon LGBT youth organizing and educational spaces. Despite the modern movement claims of "diversity within unity" and "unity in diversity," men and women of color were excluded and continue to be underrepresented in LGBT youth and adult groups. White people who are allies of people of color work within these different contexts for steadfast social change and racial justice by speaking out against systems of oppression and challenging other white people to do the same.

Bibliography

McCready, Lance. 2001. "When Fitting In Isn't an Option, or, Why Black Queer Males at a California High School Stay Away from Project 10." Pp. 37–53 in *Troubling Intersections of Race and Sexuality: Queer Students of Color and Anti-Oppressive Education.* Edited by Kevin Kumashiro. Lanham, MD: Rowman and Littlefield.

———. 2003. "Some Challenges Facing Queer Youth Programs in Urban High Schools: Racial Segregation and De-Normalizing Whiteness." *Journal of Gay and Lesbian Issues in Education* 1, no. 3: 37–51.

O'Brien, Eileen. 2001. *Whites Confront Racism: Antiracists and Their Paths to Action.* Lanham, MD: Rowman and Littlefield.

Perotti, Jeff, and Kim Westheimer. 2001. *When the Drama Club is Not Enough: Lessons from the Safe Schools Program for Gay and Lesbian Students.* Boston: Beacon Press.

Russell, Stephen T., and Nhan Truong. 2001. "Adolescent Sexual Orientation, Race and Ethnicity, and School Environments: A National Study of Sexual Minority Youth of Color." Pp. 113–130 in *Troubling Intersections of Race and Sexuality: Queer Students of Color and Anti-Oppressive Education.* Edited by Kevin Kumashiro. Lanham, MD: Rowman and Littlefield.

Segrest, Mab. 1994. *Memoirs of a Race Traitor.* Cambridge, MA: South End Press.

Snider, Kathryn. 1996. "Race and Sexual Orientation: The (Im)Possibility of These Intersections in Educational Policy." *Harvard Educational Review* 66: 294–302.

Tatum, Beverly D. 1999. *Why Are All the Black Kids Sitting Together in the Cafeteria? And Other Conversations about Race.* New York: Basic Books.

Thompson, Becky. 2001. *A Promise and a Way of Life: White Antiracist Activism.* Minneapolis: University of Minnesota Press.

Vaid, Urvashi. 1995. *Virtual Equality: The Mainstreaming of Gay and Lesbian Liberation.* New York: Anchor Books.

Web Sites

Center for Anti-Oppressive Education (CAOE). December 2004. Accessed December 4, 2004. http://www.antioppressiveeducation.org. Prepares members of educational communities, through curricula, workshops, conferences, professional development, and local advocacy, to create and engage in forms of education that challenge multiple oppressions.

The ERASE Initiative. Accessed December 4, 2004. http://www.arc.org/erase/index.html. Conducts trainings for community-based organizations, publicizes research findings about racism in public schools, develops resource tools for journalists covering No Child Left Behind, and produces a broad range of materials, reports, and other tools for parents, students, teachers, and community activists to expose racism and advance school excellence.

National Gay and Lesbian Task Force (NGLTF) Creating Change Conference. 2004. Accessed December 4, 2004. http://www.thetaskforce.org/ourprojects/cc/index.cfm. The primary educational goal of the annual Creating Change conference is to build an antiracist LGBT activist movement that includes and reflects the perspectives, needs, and priorities of gay, lesbian, bisexual, and transgender activists of all ages, races, ethnic and language origins, spiritualities and incomes through skills and strategy building.

Teaching for Change. Accessed December 4, 2004. http://www.teachingforchange.org. Works with school communities to develop and promote pedagogies, resources, and cross-cultural understanding for social and economic justice in the Americas. The Teaching for Change catalog offers hundreds of K-12 books, videos, and posters for teaching from a social justice perspective, including resources for multiculturalism and antiracism.

Teaching Tolerance. Accessed December 4, 2004. http://www.tolerance.org/teach/about/index.jsp. Supports the efforts of K-12 teachers and other educators to promote respect for differences and appreciation of diversity by offering professional development tools, online forums, grants for implementing antibiased programs, distributing free high-quality antibias materials, and offering classroom resources, activities, and materials (including *Teaching Tolerance* magazine).

Women's Colleges

Kristen A. Renn

Women's colleges are those postsecondary institutions that admit only female students to their undergraduate degree-granting programs. The number of women's colleges declined from a peak of 228, in 1969, to fewer than 80 today, educating just under 1 percent of all women enrolled in postsecondary education (Harwarth 1999; NCES 2002; Women's College Coalition, 2005). Nevertheless, they are important in the historical and contemporary landscape of higher education as well as to the queer community. Intimate relationships between women have existed throughout the history of women's colleges in the United States and remain visible at many of the remaining women's colleges (Faderman 1999; Horowitz 1984). Early leaders in women's higher education lived publicly with other academic women until the 1920s, when the stigma surrounding lesbianism increased. Today some campuses have institutionalized lesbian studies programs and support services for lesbian, bisexual, and transgender students and faculty.

Before Mary Lyon founded Mount Holyoke Female Seminary in 1837 as the first postsecondary institution for women in the United States, she had established an intimate friendship with another woman educator, Zilpah Grant. Later in the nineteenth century, women's colleges were seen as more wholesome environments than coeducational schools, since a woman was less likely to develop an "unwise friendship" with a college man. A college education enabled some white, middle-class women to move outside the domestic setting and to establish relationships of their choosing, thus paving the way for the establishment of women's communities in the women's colleges of the 1880s and 1890s as well as settlement houses of the progressive era.

As participants in the first wave of feminism in the United States, the academic "new women" of the late nineteenth century created a network of relationships among teachers and students at the women's colleges. Katherine Lee Bates and Katherine Coman formed a well-known Wellesley College faculty pair from the 1880s through Bates' death in 1929. M. Carey Thomas assumed the presidency of Bryn Mawr in 1894, living first in a passionate relationship with Mamie Gwinn and later with Mary Garrett. Mary E. Woolley was president of Mount Holyoke College from 1901 to 1936 and lived in the president's house with her former student and Mount Holyoke faculty member Jeannette Marks. Biographers disagree about how to describe these women's relationships, but they concur that romantic friendships were not considered uncommon or unseemly among women academics until after the turn of the century (Faderman 1999; Horowitz 1984; Horowitz 1994).

The prevalence of student "smashes" or **crush**es at women's colleges provides further evidence of women's passion for one another. Students engaged in smashes courted the objects of their emotions, usually an older student or a young teacher, with flowers, poems, and candy. Documented as early as the 1870s at Vassar, smashes were considered normative behavior, innocuous to the participants except in their tendency to disrupt campus life (MacKay 1992).

The pathologizing of lesbianism early in the twentieth century with the popularization of Freudian psychology and the public repute of lesbian novel, *The Well*

See also College Campus Programming; Lesbian Feminism; Residence Life in Colleges; Single-Sex Schools; Teachers, LGBT and History; Women's Movement; Women's Studies.

of Loneliness, interrupted the pattern of women's relationships in academe. Women's colleges and girls' boarding schools in the United States and Britain were judged environments likely to interfere with heterosexual development (Horowitz 1984; Horowitz 1994). This view was sometimes articulated by lesbian faculty and **administrators**. In 1911, for example, Jeannette Marks wrote that "sentimental friendships" were a detriment to a student's health and education. This position was also reflected in the emergence of organizations like the Girl Scouts and the YWCA. Representatives of local Y's visited women's colleges to give talks on "problems," such as homosexuality. In an attempt to prevent intimacy among women, several colleges redesigned student residences to provide single bedrooms for all.

Despite growing antilesbian sentiment, there is evidence that intimate friendships remained part of campus life into the 1920s, and ignorance of its stigma remained (MacKay 1992). For instance, a 1920 Oberlin yearbook featured the Oberlin Lesbian Society, a group devoted to writing poetry, and a 1921 Bryn Mawr senior essay described the passion that students had for one another (MacKay 1992). Mary McCarthy's 1954 semiautobiographical and satirical novel, *The Group*, tells the story of eight Vassar graduates from the class of 1933 who discover that their leader is a lesbian.

After World War II, when many women in the United States returned to their prewar roles of wife and mother, a college education gained renewed importance as a means for women to live independently or in relationships with other women. A fledgling lesbian movement led by the Daughters of Bilitis and its publication, *The Ladder*, paralleled the era of McCarthyism when women's colleges were easy targets for accusations of harboring lesbians. Throughout the 1950s and 1960s women were expelled for being too intensely involved with one another, but women's liberation and the growing gay rights movement eventually gave rise to organized communities of lesbians on campuses.

When elite men's colleges began accepting women in the 1970s and the second wave of **feminism** swept the United States, women's colleges again came under attack for being havens for lesbianism. From 1969 to 2003, three-quarters of these colleges were closed or became coeducational due to economic pressure and declining enrollments. Many that remained were affiliated with the Catholic religious orders or Protestant denominations (Women's College Coalition, 2004).

In the United States, women's colleges are now concentrated in the northeast and nearly all are privately controlled (public institutions, Mississippi University for Women and Texas Woman's University, identify themselves as women's colleges though they are open to male students). Two U.S. women's colleges—Bennett in North Carolina and Spelman in Georgia—are also historically black colleges. Four women's colleges remain in Great Britain (New Hall, Newnham, and Lucy Cavendish at Cambridge University; St. Hilda's at Oxford University), and recent discussions about admitting men to St. Hilda's have involved frank exchanges in the student press about the perception that students at women's colleges are predisposed to lesbianism (Woodward 2003).

Students at some religious colleges maintain student organizations that are not recognized officially by their institutions and many nonreligious women's colleges have organized groups for lesbian, bisexual, transgender, or queer-identified women. Some have specialized groups for women of color or other self-identified communities. As at coeducational institutions, student groups at women's colleges provide a range of programs and services to lesbian, bisexual, and transgender students and to the campus at large.

Women's colleges sponsor LBT **campus resource centers** at about the same rate as their coeducational peers (National Consortium 2004). Owing in part to the relatively small size and operating budgets of these colleges, many campuses do not employ full-time staff as administrators of these centers, relying instead on a combination of part-time staff (or full-time staff in other areas assigned part-time to LGBT issues), student employees, and student volunteers. Some women's colleges partner with other local institutions to provide programs and resources for students.

Even in states with laws prohibiting **discrimination** on the basis of real or perceived **sexual orientation**, private colleges are not required to comply with these laws. However, **antidiscrimination policies** in admissions, employment, and treatment of students, faculty, and staff are about as common at women's colleges as at coeducational liberal arts colleges, though religious institutions are less likely to report such policies (National Consortium 2003). Nondiscrimination policies may operate independently of policies granting domestic partner benefits to same-sex students and employees, and a number of women's colleges offer protection from discrimination in employment and admissions that do not also provide access to same-sex partner benefits (National Consortium 2003).

LGBT or queer studies curricula appear at women's colleges at about the same rate as they appear at coeducational liberal arts institutions. Sometimes linked to a women's or gender studies **curriculum, queer studies** is considered an interdisciplinary field that may be offered as a major (e.g., gender and cultural studies at Simmons College) or a concentration within a major (e.g., Barnard College, Smith College) Like their coeducational peer institutions, no women's colleges have independent departments of queer or **LGBT studies**.

Two contemporary challenges that face every postsecondary institution pose unique issues for women's colleges: competition for resources, including prospective students and financial support from foundations and alumnae, and the increasing population of **transgender youth**. In a society where a majority of men and women believe that affirmative action for women has been a success and gender equity has largely been achieved, making the argument to support single-sex institutions has become especially difficult. Less than 5 percent of all high school women will even consider attending a women's college; less than 1 percent of all college students ultimately do (Harwarth 1999). Although there are several reasons for this phenomenon, **homophobia** framed as concern about the "healthiness" of an all-female environment persists in deterring young women in the United States from considering this educational option (Conway 2001; Harwarth 1999). In response, women's colleges have created programs for returning adult learners, begun aggressive recruiting of international students, and banded together as a group to promote the educational values of single-sex postsecondary education. These efforts have been moderately successful; applications to some women's colleges have increased by as much as 30 percent since 1997 (Women's College Coalition, 2004).

The perception of women's colleges as "hotbeds of lesbianism" and the effects of homophobia influence fundraising at women's colleges (Conway 2001). Whether an institution postures with a defensive approach and denies the presence of LBT students, takes the approach that such students are on every campus in about the same proportion, or asserts the positive influence of LBT students, women's colleges continue to respond to concerns of prospective funders who are hesitant to support an all-female—and thus suspect—institution. The impact of homophobia on fundraising efforts was particularly evident during the 1970s and 1980s, shortly after elite men's colleges began admitting women and women's colleges were challenged to prove their relevance. Nevertheless, Smith, Wellesley, and Bryn Mawr have met this challenge, and are among the most wealthy liberal arts colleges in the nation. LBT alumnae of women's colleges have organized networks that may be formally connected to the institution through the general alumnae association (e.g., Mount Holyoke) or separate from the formal mechanisms of alumnae support (e.g., College of St. Catherine). Institutional outreach to LBT alumnae varies from active inclusion, at events such as LBT alumnae receptions at Mount Holyoke's annual class reunions, to refusal to ally with LBT alumnae networks. The increasing number of transgender students in postsecondary education creates other challenges and opportunities. Like other higher education institutions, women's colleges are examining their gender-based policies, programs, curricula, facilities, and services. Unlike coeducational or all-male institutions, they face foundational questions about what it means to be a college for "women" only. A number of women's colleges have student organizations and other programs and services that have added "transgender" to "lesbian and bisexual" in their titles. However, it is not yet clear to what extent transgender students will be able to participate fully in women's colleges because these are chartered as institutions that admit only female students to degree-granting undergraduate programs. The presence or anticipated attendance of transgender youth on women's college campuses has provoked discussion among students, faculty, administrators, and alumnae about the purposes and continued relevance of women's colleges in the twenty-first century. To date, there is no evidence that a women's college has knowingly admitted a transgender undergraduate.

Bibliography

Conway, Jill Ker. 2001. *A Woman's Education*. New York: Knopf.

Faderman, Lillian. 1999. *To Believe in Women: What Lesbians Have Done for America—A History*. Boston: Houghton Mifflin.

Harwarth, Irene B., ed. 1999. *A Closer Look at Women's Colleges*. Washington, D.C.: U.S. Department of Education. Accessed June 10, 2005. http://www.ed.gov/pubs/Womens Colleges/index.html.

Horowitz, Helen Lefkowitz. 1984. *Alma Mater: Design and Experience in the Women's Colleges from Their Nineteenth-Century Beginnings to the 1930s*. New York: Knopf.

———. 1994. *The Power and the Passion of M. Carey Thomas*. New York: Knopf.

MacKay, Anne, ed. 1992. *Wolf Girls at Vassar: Lesbian and Gay Experiences*. New York: St. Martin's.

National Center for Education Statistics. 2002. *Digest of Education Statistics, 2002*. Accessed June 9, 2005. http://nces.ed.gov/programs/digest/d02/dt217.asp.

National Consortium. 2005, April. *National Consortium of Directors of LGBT Campus Resources in Higher Education*. Accessed June 10, 2005. http://www.lgbtcampus.org/directory.htm.

Women's College Coalition. 2005. *W.C.C.* Accessed June 10, 2005. http://www. womens colleges.org.

Woodward, Will. 2003, March 13. Women Win the Day at St. Hilda's. *The Guardian*. Accessed June 10, 2005. http://education.guardian.co.uk/oxbridge/article/0,5500,913186,00.html.

Web Sites

Stratton, Larry. October 2000. *Universities, Colleges & Other Educational Institutions that Include Sexual Orientation in Their Non-Discrimination Clauses.* Accessed June 10, 2005. http://www.lgbtcampus.org/resources/nondiscrimination.html. Lists postsecondary institutions, including women's colleges, that include sexual orientation in their nondiscrimination clauses.

Younger, John G. February 2005. *University LGBT/Queer Programs.* Accessed June 10, 2005. http://www.people.ku.edu/~jyounger/lgbtqprogs.html. Information about postsecondary institutions, including women's colleges, that offer LGBT/Queer programs, courses, and study abroad programs.

Women's Movement

Susan Birden

As a movement intended to create a society in which women can live a full, self-determined life, the women's movement in the Western world is usually linked to the mid-nineteenth to early twentieth-century struggle for women's suffrage, called the "first wave," and to the resurgence of women's emancipation issues in the 1960s, known as the "second wave." The changes wrought through the women's movement have benefited almost all Western women, but the right to self-determination has been especially important for lesbians. Indeed, many of the most active leaders in the movement were involved in female sexual and/or affectional relationships, or "romantic friendships," as they were called.

In seventeenth-century France, women's salons served as an informal university for the exchange of ideas, as well as readings and critiques of literary works. By the 1750s, some English women, calling themselves "Bluestockings," formed salons, seeking the elevation of women's status through moral and intellectual training. They traveled, studied, wrote for publication, and challenged the **stereotype** of the passive woman.

In eighteenth-century France and England, reformers rallied around egalitarian ideals, but few reformers advocated higher education for women. Abigail Adams wrote to her husband John Adams in 1776, who was attending the Second Continental Congress, begging him to "remember the ladies" by making laws more favorable to women than those in England and by limiting the power of husbands. In 1789, the storming of the Bastille in France stirred Mary Wollstonecraft, who, according to some biographers was **bisexual**, to write *A Vindication of the Rights of Woman*. In it, Wollstonecraft insisted that no fundamental difference in character existed between the sexes and urged identical education for boys and girls. Later feminists, like Emma Willard and Louisa May Alcott, continued to advocate for advances in girls' education.

Democratic ideals were also at the forefront of the movement to abolish slavery in the United States. The Quaker Church, which had advocated equality for all people regardless of **race**, gender, or **social class** since the seventeenth century, was at the forefront of this movement. When Quaker women were excluded from membership

See also Activism, LGBT Teachers; Educational Administration; Johns' Committee; Professionalism; Sexism; Sexual Health, Lesbian and Bisexual Women; Women's Studies.

in public abolitionist groups, they began to form their own societies. Two sisters, Sarah and Angelina Grimke, wrote antislavery articles and addressed women's groups. Soon many others, like the heroic **African American** women Harriet Tubman and Sojourner Truth, were speaking publicly in large mixed audiences, organizing meetings, and carrying on petition drives.

In 1840, eight women planned to attend the World's Anti-Slavery Convention as delegates in London. The male delegates voted to ban their participation. The women claimed that they then understood that, like enslaved African Americans for whose freedom they worked, women had been kept socially and legally inferior to white men. This realization prompted Elizabeth Cady Stanton and Lucretia Mott to organize the 1848 Seneca Falls Convention, which began the serious fight for women in the United States to control their persons and property and to vote. Stanton's "Declaration of Sentiments" used the language of the United States' Declaration of Independence to argue for the inalienable rights of women as well as men. Although enfranchisement took seventy-two years, the women's movement was successful much earlier in changing other laws prohibiting women from holding property and suing in court.

The responsibilities of a husband and children limited the mobility and flexibility of married women in the movement. Thus, even though Stanton planned and organized side-by-side with Susan B. Anthony, it was Anthony who constantly traveled for the cause. Many of the most prominent leaders in the movement were involved in "romantic friendships," such as Susan B. Anthony and Emily Gross; Anthony's niece, Lucy Anthony and Anna Howard Shaw; Alice Stone Blackwell and Kitty Barry.

After the Civil War more women became self-supporting, working in factories or as **teachers**. Women also enrolled in the many **women's colleges** that proliferated during this period, as well as colleges that previously had been exclusively open to men. Romances between female students and female professors were widespread and even more common between female students. In this era before "**sexual identity**," campus women coined terms such as "smash," "mash," and "**crush**" to describe these passionate love relationships. As women entered the professions and became self-supporting, spinsterhood became common, especially between 1885 and 1905. Domestic arrangements between two career women were so commonplace in the East that they were referred to as "Boston marriages," or on college campuses, "Wellesley marriages."

Until the 1890s, the suffrage movement continued to recruit only middle-class women. Many of these women feared that the huge numbers of poor immigrants—Irish, Italian, and Eastern European—would weaken the political power of the established classes. Suffragists turned away from the ideal of equal rights to espouse a narrow and vicious, but persuasive, argument: If women were given the vote, the established class's voting power would be doubled.

However, some women in the movement did take action on behalf of working women. Jane Addams and her first romantic partner, Ellen Starr, founded one of the first settlement houses in the United States, inviting other women college graduates to join them in their work at Hull House, located in a Chicago immigrant neighborhood. Later, Addams, and her second romantic partner, Mary Rozet Smith, pushed for legislation to protect factory women, urging suffragists to realize that working women would strengthen their cause. Other activists included prison reformer Miriam Van Waters and her partner, Geraldine Thompson, and peace and freedom activist Mildred Scott Olmstead and her partner Ruth Mellor.

In 1907, Harriet Stanton Blatch, daughter of Elizabeth Cady Stanton, returned from England where she had worked with Emmeline and Richard Pankhurst in the more militant British women's movement. She initiated women's suffrage parades in New York, outdoor meetings, and attempted to interest trade union women and suffragists in each other. Once factory women began to strike to improve their working conditions, support emerged among middle-class suffragists, an alliance that failed to survive enfranchisement.

In 1920, the Nineteenth Amendment was passed giving women the right to vote, after, according to Carrie Chapman Catt, 56 state referendum campaigns, 480 legislative campaigns for state suffrage amendments, 47 state constitutional conventional campaigns, and 277 state party convention campaigns. What Catt did not say was how many female couples in the movement, including herself and her partner, Mollie Hay, had depended upon their intimate partnerships to support them through years of discouragement.

The women's movement in Germany was thriving by the end of the nineteenth century due in large part to the many lesbians in leadership positions who had worked for years without identifying themselves as lesbians. However, at the end of the nineteenth century when the German homosexual (or as it was more commonly called there—"Uranian") movement emerged under the leadership of **Magnus Hirschfeld** (an ardent support of women's rights), it raised the consciousness of the lesbians within the women's movement about their rights. With the strength of the Uranian movement behind her, in 1904 Anna Rueling publicly chastised the women's movement that had eagerly used the energy of lesbians, but had never acted to improve lesbians' social standing. She called for the women's movement to adopt some of the lesbian issues as their own. Only a few years later the support of the women's movement helped reformers in Germany stall political efforts to make sexual relations between women a criminal offense.

After passage of the Nineteenth Amendment in the United States, the women's rights movement became rudderless. Social conscience fell out of fashion. Lesbian reformers continued to cheer one another on in their endeavors, however, often working through their networks to promote social change.

The Great Depression worsened employment opportunities for women. Twenty-six states prohibited employment of married women, and schools dismissed married female teachers, assuming husbands could support them. Since lesbians had no one to support them, they continued to work and pursue careers. Yet, women professionals struggled in setting up private practice, and few women were winning elections for political office. Women did fare somewhat better in receiving appointments to high political posts, due to a great extent to Eleanor Roosevelt. With the support of the lesbian circle around her, she urged Franklin Roosevelt to appoint women to his administration.

With the exception of a brief respite during World War II, when women's labor power was needed, women's progress in education and the professions continued on its downhill slide through the 1950s. The percentage of women in college professorial and administrative ranks diminished significantly. During this era of the Cold War, homosexual students and professors in American colleges and universities were the victims of witch hunts, and those who continued to work in the public sphere during those times were forced to be much more covert than women had been in the past. Great numbers of college-educated women turned their backs on career aspirations to be a wife and mother. Meanwhile, a handful of lesbians, led by

Phyllis Lyon and Del Martin, formed the Daughters of Bilitis and published the influential magazine, *The Ladder*.

In 1960, John F. Kennedy appointed only nine women to his administration. Eleanor Roosevelt sent the new president a list of women who were qualified to fill administrative slots. Although Kennedy did not change his appointments, at Roosevelt's urging he established the Commission on the Status of Women, which took up the fight of equal pay for equal work. This Commission, the publication of Simone de Beauvoir's *The Second* Sex, Betty Friedan's *The Feminine Mystique,* and the passage of the 1964 Civil Rights Act that prohibited discrimination on the basis of sex, helped launch the second wave of the women's movement.

In 1966, Pauli Murray, a lesbian attorney working with the Commission on the Status of Women, Betty Friedan, and others became convinced that women needed a national nongovernmental organization to promote women's interests. They established The National Organization for Women (NOW), the largest feminist organization in America. In 1971, without the support of Friedan, who called lesbians in NOW "the lavender menace," NOW's national convention confirmed the importance of lesbian energy in its fight for women's rights, resolving to cease evasiveness regarding lesbian issues and urging all women to fight against lesbian oppression.

Lesbians of the second-wave were far different from their predecessors: Their lesbian identity was very consciously chosen. Even though lesbianism continued to be censured, **lesbian feminism** captured the imagination of large numbers of women who saw love between women as a political statement, an antidote to the institutional nature of heterosexuality. The second wave not only challenged public life, as the first wave had, but the organization of personal life: marriage, family, and sexuality. "The personal is political" became the slogan used to raise public awareness of issues like domestic violence and sexual abuse. Women and male **allies** developed health services for women, shelters for battered women, and rape crisis centers. They likewise fought for women's reproductive freedom and threw their sustained support behind the landmark Supreme Court decision, *Roe v. Wade,* brought by a lesbian woman, Norma McCorvey, which gave women the legal right to seek abortions.

Women in the learned professions have increased rapidly since the 1980s, entering medical and law schools in numbers almost as great as male students. Women also serve as ministers in many mainline Protestant churches and as rabbis within Reformed and Conservative Judaism. Furthermore, lesbians such as theologian Mary Daly and Episcopal priest Carter Heyward have made significant contributions to both theology and **feminism**. By 1992 women began achieving positions of political leadership on a significant scale. Currently, 14 percent of both the United States House of Representatives and Senate are women, including one woman who ran for office openly as lesbian.

The United Nations designated 1975 as International Year of the Woman, which was later extended to the International Decade of Women. The 1975 conference, held in Mexico City, made recommendations to promote equality between men and women in all the represented nations. Two years later many nations, including the United States, held national conferences to derive a national plan of action to remove sex barriers. The ratification of the United Nations Convention on the Elimination of All Forms of Discrimination Against Women, in 1981, was a major step forward in women's rights. International women's organizations continue to work for reproductive rights and sexual freedom around the globe, leading the way in countries such as Afghanistan and India, where women have been subject to political policies designed to curtail their freedom.

Bibliography

Blasius, Mark, and Shane Phelan. 1997. *We are Everywhere: A Historical Sourcebook in Gay and Lesbian Politics*. New York: Routledge.

Faderman, Lillian. 1999. *To Believe in Women: What Lesbians Have Done for America—A History*. Boston and New York: Houghton Mifflin.

Faderman, Lillian, and Brigitte Ericksson. 1990. *Lesbians in Germany: 1890's–1920's*. Tallahassee, FL: Naiad Press.

Jay, Karla. 1999. *Tales of the Lavender Menace*. New York: Basic.

Oram, Alison, and Annmarie Turnbull. 2001. *The Lesbian History Sourcebook: Love and Sex Between Women in Britain from 1780 to 1970*. London and New York: Routledge.

Smith-Rosenberg, Carroll. 1985. *Disorderly Conduct*. New York: Knopf.

Web Site

Documents from the Women's Liberation Movement. April 1997. Special Collections Library, Duke University. Accessed December 18, 2004. http://scriptorium.lib.duke.edu/wlm. Extensive digital collection of documents from the first and second Wave of the women's movement.

Women's Studies

Elizabeth Whitney

Women's studies courses grew out of the feminist practice known as "consciousness raising" (CR), an open forum for discussion that ideally provides a safe space for individuals, and particularly women, to speak about patriarchal oppression (McKinnon 1998). Many early women's studies courses were based principally on this model, rather than a more traditional lecture approach to teaching. Women's studies programs have historically offered nontraditional pedagogical approaches to a wide variety of social issues, including; race, social class, gender, sexuality, religion, age, environmentalism. More recently there has been a focus on performativity and the social construction of identity—best understood as the mundane activities (or daily performances) we repeatedly and ritualistically engage in that sediment our identities (Butler 1990). This last point is particularly important, as it alludes to the examination of the very foundations of gender (and by extension, **race**, sexuality, **social class**, and various other aspects of identity). Since women's studies has historically been based on issues concerning the category of "women," contemporary feminists who challenge this category (for example, transgender and transsexual activists) are rapidly changing the face of both women's studies courses and **feminism**. These challenges and changes, in congruency with the advent of postmodernism in women's studies, have been met with mixed reactions by many established feminists. Thus, these developments do not apply unequivocally to all of contemporary women's studies programs.

See also Butler, Judith; Films, Youth and Educators in; LGBT Studies; Men's Studies; Poststructuralism; Psychoanalysis and Feminism; Queer Studies; Women's Movement.

Women's studies courses have generally been synonymous with feminist issues. However, defining feminism is a complex, if not impossible task. There are many different kinds of feminisms, and there is likely as much, if not more, diversity than similiarity among various kinds of feminists. Some examples of feminist thought are liberal feminism, **lesbian feminism**, radicalfeminism, socialist feminism, Marxist feminism, ecofeminism, womanism, transnational (or, global) feminism, and postmodern feminism (or, postfeminism). However, an individual's identification as a feminist may be highly personal and not strictly conform to any particular category. Conflicts over identity are nothing new in feminism or in women's studies. Just as many of the feminists involved with women's studies have disagreed about the potential exclusivity of feminism being limited to the study of biological women, feminism itself is a highly contested category with multiple and subjective meanings (Zimmerman 1997).

Feminism has been historically divided into "waves:" "first wave" feminism (suffrage, Seneca Falls Convention, child labor laws, abolition); "second wave" feminism (lesbian feminist separatism, environmental racism, "women's lib"; ERA), "third wave" feminism (grrrl power, **gender identity**, **queer theory**; **sex work**, global/transnational activism). Women's studies' presence in higher education, for example, is a direct result of second wave feminism, motivated by feminist activists to bring grass-roots ideologies into educational settings. Because second wave feminism brought with it a widespread lesbian movement toward separatism (womynonly spaces), women's studies courses have, at times, been off-limits to nonfemale students. However, with the advent of third wave feminism and interest in the fluidity of (gender) identities, there has been a great deal of conflict over what the nature of women's studies courses should be. Because younger generations' concepts of social categories of identity—such as gender, sexuality, and race—are highly mutable, the notion of separatist spaces, or even the idea that feminism is particular to "women's issues," seems not as useful to queer youth as it did to feminists thirty and forty years ago.

Courses and programs in women's studies programs appeared in universities and colleges, in congruency with radical feminist and lesbian activism, during the early 1960s (Hagen 1993), and even earlier, though they were not overtly stated as such. Within a decade, these existed on many North American college campuses. More recently, women's studies courses have been implemented into **secondary school curricula**. Because feminist activism is usually interrelated with other human rights issues, most women's studies courses are inherently interdisciplinary—largely as a result of an emphasis on postcivil rights, **multicultural education** which, despite continued conservative attacks, persists in many educational systems.

Women's studies instructors have attempted to employ egalitarian teaching methods with similar social structures in mind—egalitarian power structures being a hallmark of feminism. Because many queer youth are committed to questioning established power structures, women's studies courses hold a particular appeal due to the typical women's studies classroom structure. Here, teachers are more likely to facilitate discussion rather than conduct formal lectures, and to emphasize creative scholarship rather than strictly defined rhetorical and/or social science models. While traditional scholarship is often based on **quantitative research** or constructing formal rhetorical arguments, many feminists argue that such models reiterate patriarchal linguistic systems. However, as women's studies programs expand and struggle for disciplinary legitimacy, institutional recognition, and external funding, it is more common to see courses cross-listed outside of the humanities, and more feminist researchers employing traditional methods—at least on university and college campuses.

Students enrolling in women's studies courses are usually self-selected and highly motivated, seeking a classroom outlet for political expression. Typically, women's studies courses have been most popular with feminist and queer-identified students, and have been viewed by nonfeminist and nonqueer students as alienating, particularly by male students. Arguably, this is because women's studies courses generally tend to invert dominant culture power structures and privilege, so they may be the first time a minority student has felt in the majority or vice versa. In addition, due to a consciousness raising ideal of providing safe space for women's voices, some instructors like Mary Daly have—controversially—chosen to close their courses to male students, or at least limit their participation. This naturally becomes problematic in light of postmodern feminist efforts to deconstruct the very foundations of gender and gender categories. How, for instance, does an instructor identify who is or is not a "woman," particularly when students are trans-identified and/or may not wish to embrace what they perceive as an essentialist sex/gender binary (Wilchins 1997).

As women's studies courses are more frequently counted toward general diversity college requirements and cross-listed with basic credit courses in a wider variety of majors, and as definitions of "feminism" are continually broadened and offered in secondary schools, women's studies will attract a wider array of students. For some, this is a cause for celebration. However, many feminists believe that women's studies and feminism, itself, have lost their "original," radical intention of liberating women from patriarchal oppression as they have been "dumbed down" for mass appeal.

Similar assimilationist concerns are expressed in oversimplified popular cultural manifestations of feminism. Although they have provided greater representations of and to queer youth, *Buffy the Vampire Slayer*, for example, portrays same-sex intimacy with a standard liberal feminist representation. More complex renderings can be found in the independent film *All Over Me* (USA 1997), offering a very third wave feminist perspective of queer youth. In international cinema, queer youth have been portrayed in provocative ways through films like *Iron Ladies*, (Thailand 2001, http://www.haro-online.com/movies/iron_ladies.html.) based on the true story of a gay and transgender Thai volleyball team, and the UK film *Bend it Like Beckham* (2002, http://www2.foxsearchlight.com/benditlikebeckham) in which an Indian soccer story which details the relationship between a girl who loves sports (i.e., challenges conventional notions of femininity) and her best gay friend.

Third wave feminists and queer youth, in particular, tend to view **popular culture** as a vehicle for political action rather than an obstacle. Third wave feminism began in the early 1990s, at a time when queer youth were experiencing more freedom and support to come out than any generation had before them. Though the third wave is typically claimed by a young generation, ideology, not chronology, influences political identifications. Thus, some young feminists are committed to maintaining second wave ideals, and many feminists well beyond their thirties identify with the third wave (Hogeland 2001). Third wave feminism is evidenced in "Riot Grrrl" culture, **zines** (locally produced, low budget magazines), the cultural construction and fluidity of **gender identity**, and an increased interest in globalization issues. Zines are a particularly good example of third wave feminism, as they are a creative expression of third wave politics that is produced and circulated totally by the creator. Many zines are specific to queer youth, but it is common for feminist zines to integrate queer subject matter as a matter of course.

As more people, and particularly youth, become increasingly comfortable with gender fluidity and resist sex/gender binaries, many aspects of earlier waves of feminism are less appealing. Women's studies programs and departments recognize this ever expanding concept of feminism by renaming themselves gender studies programs as have some gay studies programs.

As youth activism grows during this third wave feminism, women's studies courses are now offered in many high schools. Introductory courses may include the history of women in the United States, global issues concerning women, feminism and popular culture, **gender roles** and society, the changing structure of family, and courses related to particular racial, ethnic, religious, gendered, and/or sexual identities. Students today have more opportunities than ever to explore feminist themes through their studies, and this has certainly sparked the prevalence of young feminist organizations in many high schools. Students may also create informal social groups based around feminist issues. And some students may enact feminist causes in their lives, although they do not identify primarily as feminist.

Bibliography

Butler, Judith. 1990. *Gender Trouble*. New York: Routledge.

Findlen, Barbara. 1995. *Listen Up: Voices From the Next Feminist Generation*. Seattle: Seal Press.

Hagen, Monys A. 1993. "Equality and Liberation: Feminism and Women's Rights in the Nineteenth and Twentieth Centuries." Pp. 308–317 in *Women's Studies: Thinking Women*. Jodi Wetzel, Margo Linn Espenlaub, Monys A. Hagen, Annette Bennington McElhiney, and Carmen Braun Williams, eds. Dubuque, IA: Kendall/Hunt.

Hogeland, Lisa Marie. 2001. "Against Generational Thinking, or, Some Things That 'Third Wave' Feminism Isn't." *Women's Studies in Communication* 24, no. 1: 107–121.

McKinnon, Catherine. 1998. "Consciousness-Raising." Pp. 165–172 in *Issues in Feminism: An Introduction to Women's Studies*. Edited by Sheila Ruth. 4th ed. Mountain View, CA: Mayfield.

Wilchins, Riki Anne. 1997. *Read My Lips: Sexual Subversion and the End of Gender*. New York: Firebrand.

Zimmerman, Bonnie. 1997. "Feminism." Pp. 147–159 in *Lesbian and Gay Studies: An Introduction*. Edited by Andy Medhurst and Sally R. Munt. London: William Cassell.

Web Sites

Career Opportunities for Women's Studies Majors. November 1998. Accessed June 10, 2005. http://www.msu.edu/~wmstdy/wsmjr1.htm. Michigan State University's women's studies program's annotated bibliography.

Grrrl Zine Network. March 2005. Accessed June 9, 2005. http://grrrlzines.net/writing onzines.htm. Bibliography for articles, Web sites, and books on the subject of feminist zines.

Third Wave Feminist Foundation. November 2004. Accessed June 10, 2005. http://www. thirdwavefoundation.org/. Supports leadership of young women of all sexualities by providing resources, public education, and relationship building opportunities. Site includes news, resources, grant and contact information.

Workplace Issues

Mahoney Archer

The workplace is an environment where an LGBT person spends a considerable amount of their lives. Workplaces, like all facets of life, can be functional, dysfunctional, healthy or unhealthy for those that occupy them. For queer youth and adults, a workplace can potentially be a source of great difficulty and danger. **Homophobia**, homophobic **discrimination**, and punishment motivated by an objection to homosexuality are at the very core of this danger. Specific workplaces can be more threatening than others. Internationally, the workplace experiences of LGBT adults and youth vary, depending upon the different policies and attitudes of governments and communities. **Australia**, for instance, has a long, conservative history with regard to the tolerance of difference. Political and legislative advancements have made some improvements for LGBT workers in this country though schools are still contentious workplaces for LGBT persons.

There are several key issues that many LGBT people experience at work. Centring on discrimination, **sexual harassment**, and the consequences of difference, these are: closeting sexuality; being "out" or "outed" in the workplace; disadvantaged career prospects; emotional/physical violence and intimidation; and, a general sense of fear and caution in the workplace.

Discrimination and harassment can be greatly varied. *The Pink Ceiling is Too Low* (Irwin 1999), a report prepared by the Gay and Lesbian Rights Lobby and the Australian Centre for Lesbian and Gay Research, details numerous types of discrimination experienced by LGBT workers across Australia. Termination of employment, threats of (and actual experiences of) verbal, physical and **sexual abuse**, overt/covert forms of ostracism and exclusion, ridicule, belittling, and homophobic jokes are cited most frequently. Many also reported that their careers had more than likely been restricted because of their homosexuality and the consequences of other people's problems with it.

Findings of this report and others like it reveal that LGBT people often experience some workplace problems stemming from their **sexual** or **gender identity** or the presumption of it. Consequences of this can be serious. Adverse health effects and work performance problems can occur. For queer youth, their age and the frequently transient nature (e.g., fast food industry, shopping centers) of their employment further complicates this problem. Further, they often are not equipped with tools and strategies to protect them from or lessen any threat of harm.

Queer youth are often victimized by other youth in workplaces that primarily hire the young. Their experiences, like those of their adult counterparts, can range from humiliation, intimidation as a result of inappropriate and offensive joke-telling, questioning and name-calling to serious injury and death. These dangers are perhaps most present for those youth who engage in **sex work**. Without concrete perimeters that determine a workplace, the transience of these young prostitutes adds to the risk of their work; they are isolated and often work alone. The potential for physical injury, illness, and **mental health** problems are rife.

See also Career Counseling; Educational Policies; Licensure; Parents, Responses to Homosexuality; Professionalism; South Africa, LGBT Issues in; Youth, At-Risk.

Although not regarded as workers, in the traditional sense of being remunerated for their labor, queer students also labor in schools. They are expected to work, follow rules, and endure consequences of nonadherence, but often are victimized as their education is put at risk. Their workplace safety is exacerbated by the lack of counseling and the general lack of support for queer youth. Schools, with their socially inscribed (Grosz 1994) **heteronormative** meanings and expectations of teachers, the learning process, as well as their peers further complicate workplace experiences.

For LGBT adults many complications also are born of the nature of the school workplace. LGBT teachers, **administrators**, guidance officers, and office staff often experience the workplace as a highly pressured environment where, in some cases, one's employment is contingent upon remaining invisible. In the eyes of other educators and parents, they are viewed as a sexual threat to children or advocates for a depraved lifestyle. Though often not touted, the threat of LGBT school workers is the risk they pose to unsettling the dominant heterosexist discourse. There are very strong pressures to maintain the "face of heterosexuality" in schooling contexts (Spraggs 1994, 180), recreating a heterosexual society that reflects traditional **gender roles** of masculinity and femininity.

While LGBT teachers exist in real terms, pressure is brought to bear upon them to conceal themselves or deny their identity in schooling contexts so that traditional values and beliefs can be preserved. Both colleagues and students perpetuate social rejection and reprisals. Jokes, threats, and abuse are commonplace as the threat of parental and community disapproval looms large. The effects of this can be catastrophic.

LGBT teachers often lament the lack of authenticity or honesty they feel at their workplace. This, too, they feel negatively impacts upon their effectiveness as educators. Even in classrooms where teachers feel a great rapport with students has been achieved, an "absence" in the class dynamic is described. Many feel that a barrier has been erected between them and students—particularly queer youth whom they could **mentor**. Some describe their cautiousness as exhausting, leaving little space for them to relax as classroom facilitators and to offer themselves as resources for learning. The workplace stress is debilitating for LGBT teachers, translating into feelings of sadness and anger and leading to physical and psychological health problems (Ferfolja 1998). This can become too difficult for some LGBT teachers who choose not to remain at the offending school or in the profession.

In Australia, the **Anti-Discrimination** Act (1977) makes unlawful discrimination on the basis of **sexual orientation** and gender identity. However, exemptions exist which lessen its efficacy and effectiveness. When lesbian and gay staff members are terminated from employment at ecclesiastical schools, groups, and private schools, they have little recourse because under Australian law these workplaces may discriminate if the institution is compromised by the presence of such individuals.

Conversely, in line with the Anti-Discrimination Act and the Equal Employment Opportunity in Public Employment Act (1992), government schools have begun to reflect legislative improvements. This is illustrated in the policy documents issued by their State Departments of Education (*Workplace Diversity Document: Education Queensland* and *Workplace Bullying, Harassment and Violence Policy*). These advancements indicate efforts to raise consciousness, outline expectations of behavior, and consequences of (now determined) misconduct. However, LGBT people are not accessing union representation under these policies and still report to interviewers that hostilities toward them continue unabated (Irwin 1999).

Historically, the issues impacting queer youth and teachers were unspoken and certainly not addressed. Australian schools, of late, have introduced numerous strategies and policies that are intended to address **bullying** and harassment at school. In Queensland, *Bullying No Way* (Henderson 2002) is a resource kit for stakeholders, which discusses the foundation of bullying and harassment. Within this, the issue of sexual harassment/homophobic bullying is detailed. Also, anecdotal reports from various Ministerial Advisory Committees indicate that schools are asking for input regarding the accommodation and support of same-sex students. Unions, too, have signaled to gay and lesbian rights groups that the previously poor levels of representation for LGBT members are targeted for improvement.

Bibliography

Ferfolja, Tania. 1998. "Australian Lesbian Teachers: A Reflection of Homophobic Harassment of High School Teachers in New South Wales Government Schools." *Gender & Education* 10, no. 4: 401–415

Grosz, Elizabeth. 1994. *Volatile Bodies: Toward a Corporeal Feminism*. Sydney: Allen and Unwin.

Henderson, Chris. 2002. *Bullying No Way: A National Initiative to Expand Thinking About Harassment and Violence and Their Resolution*. Paper presented at the Roles in Schools in Crime Prevention Conference, September 30–October 1, Melbourne. Available at http://www.aic.gov.au/conferences/schools/henderson.pdf

Khayatt, Madiha Didi. 1992. *Lesbian Teachers: An Invisible Presence*. Albany: State University of New York.

Spraggs, Gillian. 1994. "Coming Out in the National Union of Teachers." Pp. 179–196 in *Challenging Lesbian and Gay Inequalities in Education*: Edited by Debbie Epstein. Buckingham: Open University Press.

Irwin, Jude. 1999. *The Pink Ceiling Is Too Low: Workplace Experiences of Lesbian and Gay Men and Transgender People*. Sydney: Gay & Lesbian Rights Lobby and the Australian Centre for Lesbian & Gay Research, University of Sydney.

Web Sites

Fact Sheets: Work Place Discrimination. 2004. Gay and Lesbian Rights Lobby. Accessed June 22, 2005. http://www.glrl.org.au/publications/fact_sheets/workplace_discrimination.htm. Key research findings from *The Pink Ceiling is Too Low*. Site also includes other publications and fact sheets from this advocacy group.

Workforce Diversity and Equity. December 2004. State of Queensland, Department of Education. Accessed June 22, 2005. http://education.qld.gov.au/workforce/diversity/equity/publications.html. Comprehensive site on workforce issues, including publications on bullying and harassments which outlines responsibilities of employees and administrative staff.

Y

Youth, At-Risk

Laura J. Gambone

"At-risk" designates a child or adolescent who is more likely than peers to fail in school or to manifest other negative emotional or physical outcomes. Originating in the field of medicine, this term is widely used in education, **mental health**, and social policy. Although **lesbian, gay, bisexual,** and **transgender youth** (LGBT) are often left out of the dialogue regarding students "at-risk" for academic failure, most public and mental health **research** on these adolescents has found that they have an elevated risk of being socially rejected and isolated, verbally harassed, and physically victimized at school and at home. Compared to their heterosexual peers, they are also at greater risk for homelessness, sexually risky behaviors, **substance abuse,** and **suicide.** And, LGBT students miss more school, perform more poorly in school, and drop out more often than their heterosexual peers. Many educators and scholars are opposed to the application of the "at-risk" label to any student (Franklin 2000; Swadener 1995). This opposition is grounded in beliefs that the label is culturally biased, as children of color are disproportionately labeled, and results in added stigmatization and lowered teacher expectations and perceptions. Further, using this label locates the problem with the individual and family rather than in social institutions. Finally, labeling a student at-risk fails to acknowledge unique psychological strengths and glosses over those dynamics which reduce risk. For these reasons, most recent LGBT scholarship places an emphasis on **resiliency.**

LGBT youth face emotional and physical harm in schools. A 1995 study (Pilkington and D'Augelli 1995) of 194 LGBT youth reported that 43 percent of males and 54 percent of females had lost one or more friends because of their **sexual orientation** and that about one-third of males and one-quarter of females were less open about their sexual orientation due to a fear of losing friendships. Further, 30 percent of males and 35 percent of females reported experiencing verbal **harassment** based on their sexual orientation; 22 percent of males and 29 percent of females reported being hurt by a peer, and 5 percent of males and 11 percent of females reported being hurt by a teacher. The 2001 Massachusetts **Youth Risk Behavior Survey** (MYRBS), a large-scale study of LGBT and heterosexual adolescents, found that LGBT students were almost twice as likely as their heterosexual peers to have been in a physical fight at school. LGBT youth were also twice as likely to have missed school in the past month due to fear for their safety (Massachusetts Department of Education 2002).

For many LGBT adolescents, fear is not limited to school; the family and the home become fearful places as well. After **coming out,** many LGBT adolescents report being rejected by family members, left out of family activities, blamed for family dysfunction, and verbally and emotionally abused (Savin-Williams and Cohen 1996). In several

See also Adolescent Sexualities; AIDS; Alcoholism; Behavior Disorders; Bullying; Eating Disorders and Body Image; Ethnic Identity; Race and Racism; Racial Identity; Religion and Psychological Development; Rural Youth and Schools; School Safety and Safe School Zones; Sexual Harassment; Sexual Health, Lesbian and Bisexual Women; Sexual Health, Gay and Bisexual Men; Social Class; Urban Youth and Schools; Youth, Homeless.

studies, more than half of LGBT adolescents reporting physical victimization had experienced physical abuse at home (Rivers 2002; Savin-Williams and Cohen 1996). LGBT youth, too, are more likely than heterosexual adolescents to experience **sexual abuse** at the hands of a person of the other gender (Savin-Williams and Cohen 1996).

The mistreatment LGBT students experience at home may result in homelessness, either by choice or by force. It has been estimated that as many as 40 percent of homeless young people on city streets are gay, lesbian, or bisexual (Savin-Williams and Cohen 1996). Youth often find greater acceptance on the street than was available to them at home or in school. **Prostitution** may become the only viable solution to the poverty that comes with homelessness, however, and it brings with it a series of other risks such as **pregnancy** and sexually transmitted diseases (Cochran et al. 2002; Rivers 2002).

Regardless of whether LGBT youth become homeless, social and familial rejection, isolation, and verbal and physical victimization may lead to internalized **homophobia** and/or risk taking behaviors such as unsafe sex, substance abuse, and suicide. In an attempt to prove their heterosexuality, LGBT youth or their sexual partners may become pregnant via unsafe heterosexual sex. Approximately one-fourth of LGBT students who engaged in sexual behavior reported that they or their partner became pregnant, while only 11 percent of heterosexual students who had sex reported pregnancies (Massachusetts Department of Education 2002). Unsafe sex also places LGBT youth at heightened risk for HIV and other STIs.

LGBT youth also have increased risk of alcoholism and illegal **drug use**. In the 1997 MYRBS (the 2001 survey did not compare the drug use of heterosexual and LGBT students), 19 percent of LGBT adolescents reported alcohol use, 49 percent reported marijuana use, and 54 percent reported smoking cigarettes over the course of the last month. LGBT youth compared to heterosexual youth were 3.5 times more likely to drink, 1.7 times more likely to use marijuana in general, more than 2 times more likely to use marijuana in school, and 1.8 times more likely to smoke cigarettes. LGBT youth were nearly 5 times more likely than heterosexual youth to have tried cocaine during their lifetimes (Massachusetts Department of Education 2002).

LGBT adolescents who find it too difficult to cope with their **sexual identity** and its social and familial repercussions sometimes choose suicide. Researchers in the fields of mental and public health have widely recognized successful and attempted suicide as occurring in epidemic proportions among LGBT youth (Russell 2003). In the 2001 MYRBS, 47 percent of LGB youth compared to 19 percent of heterosexual youth had seriously considered suicide in the past year; 31 percent compared to 8 percent had attempted it (Massachusetts Department of Education 2002).

Gender, racial, and ethnic identities of LGBT youth may impact their risks. Lesbian and bisexual females report more experiences of social rejection and physical harm at school as well as more physical, emotional, and sexual abuse at home than do gay and bisexual males (Pilkington and D'Augelli 1995). Individuals of any sex are victimized more frequently if their behaviors do not match the gendered behaviors socially assigned to their sex, suggesting that transgender individuals may be particularly vulnerable to victimization.

Interestingly, white LGBT adolescents' school outcomes appear to suffer more due to the development of a LGBT identity than do those of LGBT youth of color. While less social acceptance, more negative attitudes toward school, lower academic expectations, and lower GPAs than heterosexual peers are reported for LGBT students across racial and ethnic groups, these differences are largest for white students (Russell and Truong 2001). One explanation is that the discovery of a LGBT identity in **adolescence** results in stressors with which white LGBT students, many of whom have never faced stigmatization and discrimination before, are ill-prepared to deal with it. Students of color, on the other hand, are more experienced in coping with **discrimination** (Russell and Truong 2001). Another possibility is that the school performance of students of color may already have declined by adolescence due to previous experiences of stigmatization and discrimination (Franklin 2000).

LGBT adolescents are at-risk for emotional and physical difficulties above and beyond those faced by their peers. The difficulties at school (fear, victimization, isolation) and at home (family rejection and victimization) combined with the negative outcomes that can result from these difficulties (homelessness, alcohol and drug abuse, sexual risk-taking, and suicide) mean LGBT adolescents are more likely than their heterosexual counterparts to be truant, perform poorly academically, and drop out all together (Rivers 2002; Savin-Williams and Cohen 1996).

By the current definition of academically "at-risk," LGBT adolescents qualify for the label. However, applying the "at-risk" label is problematic. Some scholars and educators suggest that the application of the label is classist and racist (Franklin 2000; Swadener 1995). Behaviors labeled as "deviant" and used to justify the "at-risk" label are often only deviant in middle class Euro-American culture. Behaviors considered acceptable or even expected in minority or working class cultures can result in the undeserved labeling of a student. Biases in favor of majority white cultural norms result in higher instances of "at-risk" labels among minority students, a further stigmatization of already stigmatized adolescents.

Consequently, the use of the "at-risk" label within schools may be more harmful than helpful (Franklin 2000; Swadener 1995). The label carries a stigma that negatively impacts teachers' expectations and perceptions of student behavior and achievement. These lowered expectations may result in undeserved poor grading, down tracking, and/or actual declines in student performance. The "at-risk" stigma may also negatively impact students' relationships with peers who are succeeding in school. Thus, paradoxically, designating a student at-risk may increase, rather than decrease, the likelihood of school failure.

Further, this terminology stresses the weaknesses rather than the strengths of students and their families. In so doing, it functions as a "deficit model" and fails to capitalize on potential sources of resiliency in the lives of labeled students (Swadener 1995). Sources of resiliency for LGBT students include support from friends, family, teachers, and LGBT peers, and positive feelings about homosexuality. The deficit model also fails to recognize the reality that most LGBT adolescents mature into healthy adults (Russell 2005).

"At-risk" labeling blames the student and family for any difficulties the student experiences and ignores the role of social institutions and policies that foster a hostile environment for LGBT youth. Scholars argue that a clear understanding of risk in the lives of LGBT adolescents requires examination of personal, interpersonal, and institutional factors, particularly the impact of homophobia, **heterosexism**, and stigma on LGBT youth outcomes (Russell 2005). Ignoring institutional contributions to risk results in a failure to recognize damaging impacts of institutionalized homophobia as well as the ways in which institutional change could contribute to resilience. Another problem inherent in ignoring contextual influences on risk is a failure to identify risk factors unique in the lives of LGBT adolescents, such as feeling isolated due to having an LGBT identity in a homophobic culture, others' negative responses to coming out, and sexuality-based discrimination (Russell 2005).

Bibliography

Cochran, Bryan N., Angela J. Stewart, Joshua A. Ginzler, and Ana M. Cauce. 2002. "Challenges Faced by Homeless Sexual Minorities: Comparison of Gay, Lesbian, Bisexual, and Transgendered Homeless Adolescents with Their Heterosexual Counterparts." *American Journal of Public Health* 92: 773–777.

Franklin, William. 2000. "Students at Promise and Resilient: A Historical Look at Risk." Pp. 3–16 in *Schooling Students Placed at Risk: Research, Policy, and Practice in the Education of Poor and Minority Adolescents*. Edited by Mavis G. Sanders. Mahwah, NJ: Lawrence Erlbaum.

Massachusetts Department of Education. 2002. *2001 Massachusetts Youth Risk Behavior Survey Results*. Accessed June 22, 2005. http://www.doe.mass.edu/hsss/program/ youthrisk.html.

Pilkington, Neil W., and Anthony R. D'Augelli. 1995. "Victimization of Lesbian, Gay, and Bisexual Youth in Community Settings." *Journal of Community Psychology* 23: 34–56.

Rivers, Ian. 2002. "Developmental Issues for Lesbian and Gay Youth." Pp. 30–44 in *Lesbian and Gay Psychology: New Perspectives*. Edited by Adrian Coyle and Celia Kitzinger. Oxford: Blackwell.

Russell, Stephen T. 2003. "Sexual Minority Youth and Suicide Risk." *American Behavioral Scientist* 46: 1241–1257.

———. 2005. "Beyond Risk: Resilience in the Lives of Sexual Minority Youth." *Journal of Gay and Lesbian Issues in Education* 2, no. 3: 5–18.

Russell, Stephen T., and Nhan L. Truong. 2001. "Adolescent Sexual Orientation, Race and Ethnicity, and School Environments: A National Study of Sexual Minority Youth of Color." Pp. 113–130 in *Troubling Intersections of Race and Sexuality: Queer Students of Color and Anti-Oppressive Education*. Edited by Kevin K. Kumashiro. Lanham, MD: Rowman and Littlefield.

Savin-Williams, Ritch C., and Kenneth M. Cohen. 1996. "Psychosocial Outcomes of Verbal and Physical Abuse Among Lesbian, Gay, and Bisexual Youths." Pp. 181–200 in *The Lives of Lesbians, Gays, and Bisexuals*. Edited by Ritch C. Savin-Williams and Kenneth M. Cohen. Fort Worth: Harcourt Brace College.

Swadener, Beth B. 1995. "Children and Families 'At Promise: ' Deconstructing the Discourse of Risk." Pp. 17–49 in *Children and Families "At Promise": Deconstructing the Discourse of Risk*. Edited by Beth Blue Swadener and Sally Lubeck. Albany: State University of New York Press.

Web Site

Advocates for Youth Fact Sheet. January 2003. Meg Earls. Accessed December 18, 2004. http://www.advocatesforyouth.org/publications/factsheet/fsglbt.htm. Information about risk, international news, activism, and issues relevant in the lives of LGBT youth and their parents.

Youth Culture

Valerie Harwood

Youth culture depicts a form of culture that is distinct from "adult" culture and one that is marked by "youthfulness." Depictions of **lesbian, gay, bisexual, transgender,** and **queer** youth cultures include bar and club scenes, raving, and cyberspace.

See also Adolescence; Cartoons; Comics; Critical Social Theory; Popular Music; Queer Studies; Queer and Queer Theory; Queer Zines; Sexual Identity; Youth, At-Risk.

Cinematic portrayals of these youth cultures include the Taiwanese **film** of gay teenagers in *Boys for Beauty* (China 1998), the film of lesbian youth culture in *Go Fish* (USA 1994), of queer youth culture and schools in *Queer Geography: Mapping Our Identities* (USA 2001), and the Icelandic film depicting gay and lesbian teenagers, *Straight Out* (2003, Dir. Hrafnhildure Gunnarsdottir and Thorvaldur Kristinnson). Other depictions of youth cultures include *X/Y Magazine*, television programs such as the American version of **Queer as Folk,** which includes episodes showing the **coming out** of Justin, a white teenager; and Web sites such as queertoday. com and queeryouthtv.org. Scholarship specifically on LGBTQ youth cultures is dominated by North American authors.

Understandings of youth cultures more generally may by considered by drawing on Gordon Tait's (1999, 77–78) suggestion of three perspectives of youth, namely, youth as "stage of life," youth as resistance (especially subcultural theory), and lastly, youth as "part of the process by which youthful identity is constructed." Each of these perspectives present differing views on the way in which youth culture is depicted as different from adult **popular culture.**

Youth cultures generally, and LGTBQ youth cultures in particular, are often characterized by "risk" and "risk-taking." Such portrayals tend to focus on issues such as risky **drug use** and risky sexual behavior and characterize youth cultures as dangerous—something to be monitored and controlled by adults. This emphasis (often sensationalized in the media) has been subjected to critique by youth studies scholars (Kelly 2000). In terms of queer youth cultures, the "risk" emphasis may be linked to threats of not achieving "successful" heterosexual and gender normative outcomes. From this perspective it could be claimed that LGBTQ youth cultures suggest possibilities other than heterosexuality—and in so doing threaten the status quo. This idea of these youth cultures as threatening **heteronormativity** is highly likely to have currency in debates over their presence in school settings.

The perspective "youth as a stage of life" draws on developmental theory, where youth is understood as a developmental process. This perspective is influenced by developmental psychologists (for example Jean Piaget) and has considerable influence in education. Student teachers are frequently taught to understand youth and youth cultures in terms of developmental notions (this influence covers numerous countries including, for example: **Australia, Canada, Japan, China,** Poland, Italy, **New Zealand, United Kingdom,** United States, and **Israel**). From this viewpoint, youth (or **adolescence**) is linked to biological development. This development stage is often characterized as storm and crisis, after **G. Stanley Hall's** notion of the hormonal "storm and stress" of adolescence. Another important influence is Erik Erickson who depicted adolescence as a period of role confusion. **Identity development** theories for homosexuality have also been posited, for example, by Vivienne Cass, Eli Coleman, and Richard Troiden. Thus from a developmental standpoint, youth is seen as a period of change and of immaturity. Viewed from this perspective, youth culture is understood as a stage between **childhood** and adulthood, and as a culture of immaturity. A significant problem with this perspective is that it can devalue youth culture, where positing youth cultures simply as a "transitional stage" can be demeaning.

Developmental perspectives can also have a gendered and heteronormative emphasis. This is especially apparent in narratives of youth as "coming of age." Here developmentalism emphasizes dominant cultural norms where "boys" become "men" and "girls" become "women." Here "men" and "women" are denoted by specific sexual and **gender roles**. This raises questions regarding what "coming of age" may mean if it is not heterosexually and gender normative, and how LGBTQ youth cultures become defined as "other:" nonnormal and problematic, according to this perspective.

David Moore (2002, 19) makes several important points concerning the problems with the developmental model. In particular, he emphasizes what we could call its "monocultural" specificity:

> [T]he universalizing ideological discourses of "adolescence"—of "storm and stress"—becomes the analytical blanket that conceal power relations based on gender, ethnicity/race, sexuality (rarely spelled out but often implicit in the developmental model is the assumption that 'normal development leads to heterosexuality), and social class, and reveals a particularly Western view of subjectivity.

The developmental model is problematic. It tends to homogenize youth cultures by reducing youth's experiences, values, and beliefs to a developmental stage, and linking them to heteronormative and gendered assumptions. This has significant implications for LGBTQ youth cultures, which are diverse in terms of **ethnicity, race, social class**, ability, and genders (Rhoads 1997). For example, how does a developmental understanding of youth cultures depict **intersex** youth, racial minority queer youth, bisexual youth, two-spirited youth, or youth with "**disabilities**" who are questioning their queerness? Arguably, more productive ways to conceptualize youth cultures, and in particular, queer youth cultures are in terms of the latter two perspectives, "youth as resistance" and "youth as the process by which youthful identity is constructed."

The second perspective, "youth culture as resistance," suggests an interpretation of LGBTQ youth cultures as resistance to dominant culture. This could be dominant "heterosexual" cultures or it can be used to consider resistance to experiences of what may be perceived as normative "gay" or "lesbian" cultures. Youth subcultural theory has been influenced by the Centre for Contemporary Cultural Studies (CCCS), Birmingham, England.

David Moore (2002) provides an excellent outline of subcultural theory, including the critiques of the CCCS approach. Briefly, subcultural theory draws on materialist (Marxist) accounts of class difference and considers youth subcultures as a classed resistance to an inequitable status quo. According to Tait (1999), subculture theory emphasizes three key points. First, there is an emphasis on a neo-Marxist perspective that views youth subcultures as concerned with struggles against the dominant culture. Second, importance is given to "generational consciousness," where since the 1950s ". . . youth as a group started to perceive itself to be intrinsically different from the parent generation" (Tait 1999, 76).

The third point draws attention to the idea of "subcultural style" where a subculture will have certain markers. However, these markers are more than aspects such as speech—they can be considered as ". . . a *discourse* constructed from various cultural objects which are appropriated and endowed with new meaning" (Tait 1999, 77 emphasis in original). Thus, subcultural style indicates the ways in which different cultural objects—from "mopeds" to "shoes"—may be taken up and given new meaning by a particular subculture.

Subcultural theory has been subject to critique, particularly in terms of the emphasis that this perspective is argued to place on the "material" (Moore 2002). Yet the idea of subcultures provides a useful way to conceptualize youth cultures, and perhaps, with consideration of questions pertaining to heteronormativity, also queer youth cultures. It may provide ways to understand how LGBTQ youth cultures take up certain practices, or to grasp why they engage in resistance to dominant cultures, including testing categories of "gay" or "lesbian."

The third of Tait's (1999) perspectives "youth as the process by which youthful identity is constructed" departs from the emphasis of subcultural theory by shifting to a consideration of how youthful identities are *constructed*. An example of this is Peter Kelly's (2000, 86) suggestion that ". . . youth can be understood as an artefact of various forms of expertise . . ." This consideration draws attention to how a range of educational and health practices construct youth as individuals who need to be managed, thus requiring expertise of professionals. What we consider to be "youth" is a product of these concerns.

Such perspectives are useful to considerations of queer youth cultures and can draw attention to the way the very idea of a LGBTQ "youth culture" contributes to the construction of LGBTQ youthful identities. Rather than understanding youth culture as a given, the emphasis is on how these identities are constructed and along with them the narratives of risk and riskiness that often underscore deficit depictions of these youth cultures, whether in educational policy, television series such as *Queer as Folk*, or in **film** such as the New Queer Cinema.

Judith Halberstam (2003) signals the import of analyzing (and archiving) queer subcultural forms. Drawing on **Judith Butler**, she makes the point that "style is both the sign of their exclusion and the mode by which they survive nonetheless" (paragraph 3). This point suggests that style can be a signifier of the subculture's exclusion from the dominant or "normative" culture but at the same time be integral to that subculture. For example, Halberstram (2003, paragraph 4) comments that

> Queer punk has surfaced in recent years as a potent critique of hetero- and homoenormativity and dyke punk in particular, by bands such as Tribe 8 and The Haggard, inspires a reconsideration of the topic of subcultures in relation to queer cultural production and in opposition to notions of gay community.

This is an interesting paradox to be alert to in relation to LGBTQ youth cultures. Here it could be suggested that what may be considered problematic in terms of contributing to exclusion may also have a useful purpose for an LGBTQ culture. Extending on the above point by Halberstram, style such as queer punk can call into question notions of homonormativity in what all too easily can be referred to as "gay community." In doing this, it can question assumptions about the "normativity" of "gay" or "lesbian."

These discussions prompt important considerations, including how LGBTQ youth cultures are a product of a dominant "gaze" that stigmatizes difference—and to what extent it is possible (or desirable) to "counterculture" this gaze. And, secondly, how analyses of such youth cultures can explore issues of homogenization, (for example youth as white, male, heterosexual, and middle class), taking into account the heterogeneity of youth and queer youth. In relation to these considerations, it may be useful to draw on aspects of the subcultural approach and on youth as construction of LGBTQ youthful identity. This suggests that those who work with queer youth (and those that seek to understand queer youth culture/s) need to be alert to the ways in which knowledge of young people is heavily influenced by normative assumptions of "youth." This implies that one needs to be cognisant of the ways in which youth is depicted, and importantly, be attentive to the productive effects of queer youth subcultures.

Bibliography

Du Pleiss, Michael, and Kathleen Chapman. 1997. "Queercore: The Distinct Identities of Subculture." *College Literature* 24, no. 1: 45–58.

Halberstam, Judith. 2003. "What's that Smell? Queer Temporalities and Subcultural Lives." *The Scholar and Feminist Online* 2, no. 1. Accessed June 22, 2005. http://www.barnard.edu/sfonline/ps/halberst.htm.

Kelly, Peter. 2000. "Youth as an Artefact of Expertise." Pp. 83–93 in *Researching Youth*. Edited by Julie McLeod and Karen Malone. Victoria: Australian Clearinghouse for Youth Studies.

Moore, David. 2002. "Opening Up the Cul-de-sac of Youth Drug Studies: A Contribution to the Construction of Some Alternative Truths." *Contemporary Drug Problems* 29, no. 1: 13–63.

Ramlow, Todd. 2003. "Bad Boys: Abstractions of Difference and the Politics of Youth 'Deviance'." *Gay and Lesbian Quarterly* 9, nos. 1–2: 107–132.

Rhoads, Robert, A. 1997. "A Subcultural Study of Gay and Bisexual Males: Resisting Developmental Inclinations." *The Journal of Higher Education* 68, no. 4: 460–482.

"Snapshots of Queer Youth." 2003. *The Advocate* (April 15): 60.

Tait, Gordon. 1999. "Youth Cultures, Style and Education." Pp. 75–81 in *Understanding Education, Contexts and Agendas for the New Millennium*. Edited by Daphne Meadmore, Bruce Burnett, and Peter O'Brien. Frenchs Forest, NSW: Prentice Hall.

Walker, Michael. 2003. "Gay Male Youth and the Atlanta Rave Scene." *Lunar Magazine*. Accessed June 22, 2005. http://www.lunarmagazine.com/features/gay_youth.php

---

Youth, Homeless

Suzanne de Castell and *Jennifer Jenson*

Most often overlooked as **youth at risk** of homelessness are sexual minority youth. Whether their **"queer"** sexuality is self-asserted or assigned by others, **lesbian, gay, bisexual,** and **transgender youth** tend to be more likely than their peers to fall through the cracks of existing service provisions for street-based youth. These "throw-away kids" are far more likely than their peers to experience **bullying** and violence at school, to drop out of school prematurely, to suffer bodily violence and **sexual abuse,** to be alienated from family members, to be kicked out of their family homes, and to migrate to street-based survival (Dempsey 1994; Savin-Williams 1994; Travers and Schneider 1996). It is also tacitly understood, though not easily confirmed, that sexual minority youth are an overrepresented population among street-based youth (Dempsey 1994; Novac et al. 2002; Ryan and Futterman 1998). Societal and institutionally entrenched sexual ideologies and orthodoxies, imposed on as well as internalized by schools and community service providers, function to-gether to undermine efforts at effective provision of support and service for youth. Routinely, policies, procedures, and workers themselves often operate in disregard of sexuality as an issue for youth, at best silencing the matter, at worse, prohibiting it.

See also Adolescent Sexualities; LGBT Community Youth Groups; Mental Health; Mentoring; Native and Indigenous LGBT Youth; Parents, Responses to Homosexuality; Prostitution or Sex Work; Race and Racism; Resiliency; School Climate, K-12; Urban Youth and Schools.

Writing on **transsexual** and transgender issues, Viviane Namaste (2000 174), for example, quotes a Canadian **social work**er as saying, "We do outreach with street kids—that's our mandate. We don't serve them [transgender youth]. Well, I guess maybe some of the kids are like that [transgender]. I don't know." Foster care and group homes are notoriously unsupportive of queer and questioning youth, who are scarcely mentioned and rarely taken into account in decisions about care. Within this social service "culture of silence," many queer and questioning youth experience hostility, violence, and sexual abuse while in foster care, where **homophobia** is the norm (O'Brien 1994; Pridehouse Report 2003; Travers and Schneider 1996).

Disregard, denial, and **discrimination** on the part of service agencies and providers render queer and questioning youth more vulnerable to social isolation, damaged self esteem, economic marginalization, and sexual exploitation (Chand and Thompson 1997; Dempsey 1994; Travers and Schneider 1996). These, in turn, increase the risk of street involvement, violence, ill-health, **substance abuse**, HIV infection, and homelessness.

It is from those physical and emotional arenas traditionally held to be safest—parents, family, school, and relationships—that violence in the lives of street-involved queer and questioning youth most often stems. Street-involved youth, for instance, report feeling isolated and rejected at school, unable to access support from teachers, principals, and counselors; the Sexual Information and Education Council of the United States (SIECUS) concluded that LGBTQ youth report experiencing violence at school (SIECUS 2001). For LGBT youth this is especially important given research findings that peer **harassment** is particularly intense at school (Savin-Williams 1994) and that youth felt *the least supported* by school counselors, those individuals designated to mediate precisely those issues (Pridehouse Report 2003). For queer-identified youth on the streets, violence at the hands of the police often exceeds, for both males and females, their experience of violence at the hands of those purchasing sexual services (Pridehouse Report 2003).

The most neglected populations among sexual minority youth are likely to be aboriginal and "of color" transgender youth, those located at the furthest edges of the normative race/gender order (Namaste 2000). For service providers, therefore, the challenge in providing support to the neediest trans youth and youth of color, requires sensitivity to their often ambivalent identifications and dis-identifications with Western signposts of gay culture (Munoz 1999), and being educated about the variety of culturally specific articulations of cross-gender identities that may or may not resemble mainstream queer sexualities, genders, or cultural practices.

Even services specifically oriented to supporting the LGBT community are not necessarily experienced as "gay positive" by ethnic minority youth. Minority respondents, in the Pridehouse Report (2003), for example, did *not* identify mainstream LGBT organizations as their primary service providers, unlike ethnic majority respondents. Instead, ethnic minority youth named aboriginal services, immigrant services, community centers and services, food services and legal aid services not otherwise LGBT positive. With queer identities always on the societal "prohibited list," there are few places where youth can be and fewer yet where they can be safe. Safe and affordable housing and/or transitional housing and/or support targeted specifically toward LGBT street youth, for example, is uncommon in North America, and when found, it is found most typically located in large cities such as Ark House in San Francisco and Supporting Our Youth in Toronto. The most queer-positive places for street-involved youth may often be service industry locations like gay bars and clubs (Pridehouse Report 2003). However, in these settings youth interact with an often predatory culture in an environment predicated on the consumption of drugs and alcohol. Here, sexual exploitation and drug/alcohol addiction can play a mutually reinforcing role, predisposing youth to street involvement.

Because these sites are often as predatory as they are protective to the young, support is needed beyond and outside of them. Homosexual adults, however, themselves often "closeted," have not greatly involved themselves in the care and protection of queer and questioning youth. Although this may be seen as one result of the need to hide their sexuality, there remains the significant consideration that *any* interaction between homosexual adults and youth is often socially stigmatized as "proselytizing" and "recruitment," making LGBT adults extremely wary of offering support. Given the isolation and exclusion of queer and questioning youth in mainstream contexts (homes, family, school community, church), this neglect by their adult counterparts leaves them largely responsible for their own education and socialization—a generation without parents.

When places of greatest support and safety are also the places of greatest harm and danger, and where there are fragile support systems and increased economic marginalization, LGBT youth are at increased risk of homelessness, malnutrition, illness, violence, and sexual exploitation. The state plays a key role here: Unsupported youth, being particularly vulnerable to harm, are placed in the greatest dependency upon the state, yet they are also the group most likely to be overlooked in social safetynet provisions. When budgets for social services to children and families are reduced, the first cut is often to child protection services for older adolescents (under eighteen), leaving youth who face family violence at home due to their sexual identities, or failure to conform to expected **gender roles** unable to turn to the state for protection, with little alternative but homelessness.

Once on the street, it is again stigmatizing and dangerous to self-identify as "queer," particularly for young women, for what appear to be largely economic survival reasons (Pridehouse Report 2003). The affirmation of any particular **sexual identity** is a right with a price tag. That being so, among street-involved homeless youth, fewer women than men declare themselves to be unequivocally "queer" (Novac et al. 2002). In the street-based sex trade, where the customer is male, young women, no matter their personal desires, depend for their survival far more upon heterosexual than homosexual relations. For this same reason, young men are correspondingly more likely to self-identify as queer (e.g., gay, two-spirited, transgender). So in any consideration of homelessness among queer youth, it is essential to recognize how sexuality is regulated by economics of sexual exploitation and sexual exchange.

Sexual minority youth are overrepresented in populations of homeless youth (Gaetz and O'Grady 2002); the percentage of LGBT youth among homeless youth is higher than the 5 to 20 percent identified as LGBT within the general population. In reality, these are far more problematic and contested/contestable categories when mapped onto real bodies, particularly in the case of homeless youth. For those youth, sexuality and the primary means of street-based survival are inseparably intertwined within a sexual economy deformed by poverty, infused across social structures of gender and racial dominance and subordination (Savin-Williams 1994).

Housing policy and practice therefore need to be informed by an understanding of sexuality both more nuanced and more grounded, than traditional identity classifications have been. This means recognizing that the category "queer" does *not* refer to a uniform, compatible, integrated "community of difference," but to a variety of groups whose conditions and constraints, whose sexual behaviors and sexual orientations, whose interests and, therefore, whose needs for housing may not be easily compatible. Differences between and among sexual minority groups make needs, desires, and attitudes very different among the diverse groups of sexual minority youth. There are incompatibilities, discomforts, and even hostilities between and among groups who might seem all to be encompassed by the broad umbrella term, "queer." Discrimination of many, often intersecting kinds, punctuates street life as it does social life, in general, rupturing relations of solidarity among disenfranchised youth themselves, as well as being interwoven in the fabric of a persistently gender-differentiated social service provision.

Thus, in terms of housing, both the determination of housing need and the determination of housing structure must take this social fragmentation seriously into account. For many young women, gender may be a more divisive aspect of lesbian identity than homosexual practice is a basis of unity with their gay male counterparts, just as racial identifications may supercede shared sexual identification for youth of color. Moreover, given the prevalence of drug use and the barriers to accessing addiction services for queer youth, drug use is an important boundary which cuts across sexuality when decisions about appropriate housing structures are being made.

Homeless sexual minority youth themselves may express far less concern about their sexuality than their survival, and voice far less concern with their sexual identification than with the inability of those around them to treat them with respect and acceptance. It might be fair to say that addressing the problem of homelessness for queer and questioning youth is less a response to the special needs of a particular group of youth, than to a generalized societal deficiency in care, respect, and compassion for the young, and a specific abrogation of responsibility for the care and upbringing of queer culture's young by adults whose sexual identification is more far more securely, and more freely accomplished.

Bibliography

Chand, Manjit (Jeet) K., and Lisa B. Thompson. 1997. *You Have Heard This Before: Street Involved Youth and the Service Gaps.* Vancouver: Inter-Ministerial Street Children's Committee.

Cochran, Bryan N., Angela J. Stewart, Joshua A. Ginzler, and Ana Mari Cauce. 2002. "Challenges Faced by Homeless Sexual Minorities: Comparison of Gay, Lesbian, Bisexual, and Transgender Homeless Adolescents with Their Heterosexual Counterparts." *American Journal of Public Health* 92: 773–777.

Dempsey, Cleta L. 1994. "Health and Social Issues of Gay, Lesbian, and Bisexual Adolescents." *Families in Society: The Journal of Contemporary Human Services* 75, no. 3: 160–167.

Gaetz, Stephen, and Bill O'Grady. 2002. "Making Money: The Shout Clinic Report on Homeless Youth and Employment." *Work, Employment and Society* 16, no. 3: 433–456.

Grossman, Arnold H. 1997. "Growing Up with a 'Spoiled Identity:' Lesbian, Gay and Bisexual Youth at Risk." *Journal of Gay & Lesbian Social Services* 6, no. 3: 45–56

Mallon, Gerald P., Nina Aledort, and Michael Ferreras. 2002. "There's No Place Like Home: Safety, Permanency, and Well-Being for Lesbian and Gay adolescents in Out-of-Home Care." *Child Welfare* 80, no. 3: 78–91.

Munoz, Jose E. 1999. *Disidentifications.* Minneapolis: University of Minnesota Press.

Namaste, Viviane. 2000. *Invisible Lives: The Erasure of Transsexual and Transgender People.* Chicago: University of Chicago Press.

Noell, John W., and Linda M. Ochs. 2001. "Relationship of Sexual Orientation to Substance Use, Suicidal Ideation, Suicide Attempts, and Other Factors in a Population of Homeless Adolescents." *Journal of Adolescent Health* 29:31–36.

Novac, Sylvia, Luba Serge, Margaret Eberle, and Joyce Brown. 2002. *On Her Own: Young Women and Homelessness in Canada*. Accessed June 22, 2005. http://www.swc-cfc.gc.ca/pubs/0662318986/200203_0662318986_1_e.html.

O'Brien, Carol-Anne. 1994. "The Social Organization of the Treatment of Lesbian, Gay and Bisexual Youth in Group Homes and Youth Shelters." *Canadian Review of Social Policy* 34: 37–57.

Pridehouse Report. 2003. *No Place Like Home: Final Research Report of the Pridehouse Report*. Suzanne de Castell and Jennifer Jenson. Accessed June 22, 2005. http://www.sfu.ca/pridehouse.

Ryan, Caitlin, and Donna Futterman. 1998. *Lesbian and Gay Youth: Care and Counseling*. New York: Columbia University Press.

Savin-Williams, Ritch C. 1994. "Verbal and Physical Abuse as Stressors in the Lives of Lesbian, Gay Male, and Bisexual Youth: Associations with School Problems, Running Away, Substance Abuse, Prostitution and Suicide." *Journal of Consulting and Clinical Psychology* 62, no. 2: 261–269.

Sexuality Information and Education Council of the United States (SIECUS). 2001. "Lesbian, Gay, Bisexual and Transgender Youth Issues, Fact Sheet." *SIECUS Report 29*, no: 4. Accessed June 22, 2005 http://www.siecus.org/pubs/fact/fact0013.html.

Travers, Robb, and Margaret Schneider. 1996. "Barriers to Accessibility for Lesbian and Gay Youth Needing Addictions Services." *Youth & Society* 27: 356–378.

Youth Risk Behavior Surveys

Geoffrey L. Ream and *Ritch C. Savin-Williams*

The Youth Risk Behavior Survey (YRBS) is part of the Youth Risk Behavior Surveillance System (YRBSS) of the United States Centers for Disease Control (CDC). Several recent studies of **lesbian, gay,** and **bisexual** (LGB) **youth** employ secondary analyses of YRBS data. CDC funds and provides technical support to the program, and state departments of health or education administer the anonymous and confidential in secondary schools. Certain large cities also administer their own Youth Risk Behavior Surveys. The YRBS is not a longitudinal study that follows the same individuals over time. Rather, the purpose of the YRBS is to monitor levels of risk behaviors over time within states and localities.

CDC publishes a questionnaire that states and localities can modify according to their particular needs and interests. Questionnaire items cover violence (including rape and relationship violence), depression, suicide attempts, sexual intercourse (generally with no accompanying definition), substance use, and nutrition. Most states conform closely to CDC's surveys and add some of their own items. This general uniformity of questionnaires among states is particularly advantageous in comparing youth throughout the United States because it ensures that prevalence estimates and other statistics from one state can be directly compared to estimates from others. Basic demographic information included in the questionnaires allows for within-population comparisons by **race**, gender, age, and other factors.

Increasingly, YRBS surveys are including questions about same-sex attractions, same-sex sexual behavior, and LGB identity. State surveys in Massachusetts, Vermont, Wisconsin, Maine, and Oregon, and local surveys in Seattle and San Francisco have at least one item that addresses **sexual identity**, and more may include these items in the

See also Adolescent Sexualities; Research, Quantitative; Youth, At-Risk; Youth, Homeless.

future. Massachusetts (as of 2001) has the most comprehensive set of items on sexual-minority issues, asking about LGB identity as well as same-sex sexual behavior. Maine's 2001 survey asked about **discrimination** based on perceived **sexual orientation** and also had respondents indicate the gender of their sex partners, which allowed reporting of both same-sex and opposite-sex behavior. Vermont (as of 1997) has questions about same-sex sexual behavior. Wisconsin (as of 2001) and Oregon (as of 1999) do not address either sexual behavior or identity, but do ask whether respondents had endured discrimination based on perceived sexual orientation. Items specifically related to transgender youth identity and experiences have not yet appeared.

When studying YRBS sexual-minority respondents, defining the population is an important issue. The Massachusetts YRBS found that 5 percent of respondents either identified as LGB, engaged in same-sex behavior, or both. However, the correspondence between sexual identity and sexual behavior was nowhere near a one-to-one match. More than half (53 percent) of respondents who identified as gay, lesbian, or bisexual had never had any same-sex sexual contact. More than half (55 percent) who had same-sex sexual contact identified as heterosexual, and an additional 8 percent identified themselves as "not sure" of their sexual orientation. Some studies categorize the entire 5 percent of the respondents with either or both of same-sex behavior or LGB identity as sexual minorities and compare them to the "general population" of all other youth. A clearer picture of sexual-minority youth could, however, be achieved through taking advantage of multiple indicators available in the data set—e.g., comparing youth simultaneously in dimensions of both sexually active vs. sexually inactive and straight vs. LGB to discern whether risk behaviors are correlated with sexual activity or LGB identity. In addition to properly identifying cases of sexual minorities within data sets that have these data at all, YRBS data have other limitations. Because their primary purpose is to assess the prevalence of and relationships among risk behaviors, they cannot capture the complete picture of a young person's life. Unless discussions of health risk research results consider context and motivation, they can create the impression that adolescents *are* the sum total of their risk behaviors. Further, YRBS data are collected in schools, which mean that only those who were present in school on the day the survey was conducted can participate. The survey, thus, undersamples frequent absentees, dropouts, homeless, and incarcerated youth. CDC estimates that 5 percent of sixteen and seventeen year-olds are not enrolled in high school. YRBS findings can neither generalize to youth not enrolled in high school nor, because YRBS is a paper-and-pencil survey, to youth who cannot read and write.

The self-report nature of YRBS is another limitation, because self-report data on stigmatized behaviors and sexual identity are never completely accurate or reliable. The sample of youth who identify themselves as same-sex attracted, LGBT identified, or sexually active inevitably excludes some who are unwilling to disclose the information and includes some who identify themselves incorrectly. YRBS does not follow the recommendation of some sexuality researchers to ask the same sensitive question twice in order to assess reliability. In research on sexual-minority youth, nondisclosure is an even more significant complication, because few real cases of sexual minorities are available. The average number of participants in 2001 state surveys was 1,819. If between 4 and 5 percent are sexual minorities, this leaves 73 to 91 sexual minority youth per survey. Once the sample of sexual minorities is divided by sex, if researchers attempt to divide it further (e.g., to compare youth who identify as gay to those who have had same-sex contact but do not identify as gay) they must continually check the valid number of cases for their analyses to ensure they have a statistically viable subsample.

YRBS data on sexual-minority youth, usually from the Massachusetts database, have produced several useful findings. They have confirmed the elevated rates of suicide attempt reports (31 vs. 8 percent), substance use (70 vs. 49 percent used marijuana, 29 vs. 9 percent used cocaine), and other risk behaviors among LGB youth that have been found in clinical and support group populations. These findings are important for policy considerations because they corroborate earlier findings that **discrimination** and internalized **homophobia** that gay youth often encounter in school really does put them at risk, which helps secure funding for programs aimed at improving the environment for sexual-minority youth. The fact that LGB youth in a YRBS sample have been recruited by the same means and with the same sampling strategy and were asked the same questions as all other youth makes it easier to directly compare their outcomes. However, YRBS samples do not include those youth who are most at risk—homeless, incarcerated, and so on.

YRBS data are available from the state and local agencies that administer the surveys. Massachusetts data are available at no cost to researchers, but are currently not being released unless the intended project is sufficiently unrelated to current projects of YRBS staff and associates. Researchers using YRBS data must account for the stratified random sampling strategy used to obtain the data. This technique is used when a truly random sample—one in which all members of a population have an equal chance of inclusion—would be difficult or impractical to obtain; rather, analyses based on the YRBS have to correct for individual cases' unequal probability of inclusion. When this technique succeeds, it approximates a truly random sample, minimizes systematic differences between the sample and the whole population, and ensures that statistics and averages calculated based on the sample accurately describe the population as a whole. It cannot, however, fully make up for the fact that the population actually under study in the YRBS excludes many high-risk youth.

Bibliography

Bontempo, Daniel E., and Anthony R. D'Augelli. 2002. "Effects of At-School Victimization and Sexual Orientation on Lesbian, Gay, or Bisexual Youths' Health Risk Behavior." *Journal of Adolescent Health* 30, no. 5: 364–374.

Brener, Nancy D., Janet L. Collins, Laura Kann, Charles W. Warren, and Barbara I. Williams. 1995. "Reliability of the Youth Risk Behavior Survey Questionnaire." *American Journal of Epidemiology* 141, no. 6: 575–580.

Faulkner, Anne H., and Kevin Cranston. 1998. "Correlates of Same-Sex Sexual Behavior in a Random Sample of Massachusetts High School Students." *American Journal of Public Health* 88, no. 2: 262–266.

Web Sites

Centers for Disease Control. April 2005. Accessed June 16, 2005. http://www.cdc.gov/nccdphp/dash/yrbs/. Homepage of the Youth Risk Behavior Surveillance System, providing questionnaires, recent findings, and other details of the YRBSS.

Massachusetts Department of Education. Accessed June 16, 2005. http://www.doe.mass.edu/hssss/program/youthrisk.html. Questionnaires, recent findings, and information for accessing Massachusetts YRBS data are available here.

General Bibliography

PUBLICATIONS

Books and Reports

Allen, John. 2003. *Gay, Lesbian, Bisexual and Transgender People with Developmental Disabilities and Mental Retardation*. Binghamton, NY: Harrington Park Press.

Baker, Jean M. 2002. *How Homophobia Hurts Children*. Binghamton, NY: Harrington Park Press.

Blount, Jackie. 2005. *Fit to Teach: Same-Sex Desire, Gender, and School Work in the Twentieth Century*. Albany: State University of New York Press.

California Safe Schools Coalition and 4-H Center for Youth Development. 2004. *Safe Place to Learn: Consequences of Harassment Based on Actual or Perceived Sexual Orientation and Gender Nonconformity and Steps for Making Schools Safer*. http://www.casafeschools.org/SafePlacetoLearnLow.pdf.

Canadian Teachers' Federation, ed. 2003. *Seeing the Rainbow: Teachers Talk about Bisexual, Gay, Lesbian, Transgender and Two-Spirited Realities*. Ottawa and Toronto: Canadian Teachers' Federation and the Elementary Teachers' Federation of Ontario.

Caspar, Virginia, and Stephen Schulz. 1999. *Gay Parents/Straight Schools*. New York: Teachers College Press.

D'Augelli, Anthony R., and Charlotte J. Patterson, eds. 2001. *Lesbian, Gay, and Bisexual Identities and Youth: Psychological Perspectives*. New York: Oxford University Press.

Day, Frances Ann. 2000. *Lesbian and Gay Voices: An Annotated Bibliography and Guide to Literature for Children and Young Adults*. Westport, CT: Greenwood Press.

Epstein, Debbie, and Richard Johnson. 1998. *Schooling Sexualities*. Buckingham: Open University Press.

Epstein, Debbie, and James T. Sears, eds. 1999. *A Dangerous Knowing: Sexuality, Pedagogy and Popular Culture*. London: Cassell.

Epstein, Debbie, Sara O'Flynn, and David Telford. 2003. *Silenced Sexualities in Schools and Universities*. Stoke on Trent: Trentham Books.

Fausto-Sterling, Anne. 2000. *Sexing the Body: Gender Politics and the Construction of Sexuality*. New York: Basic.

Gay, Lesbian, Straight Education Network. 2004. *State of the States: A Policy Analysis of Lesbian, Gay, Bisexual and Transgender (LGBT) Safer Schools Issues*. New York: Author.

Gray, Mary L. 1999. *In Your Face: Stories from the Lives of Queer Youth*. Binghamton, NY: Harrington Park Press.

Greene, Beverly, and Gladys L. Croom. 1998. *Education, Research, and Practice in Lesbian, Gay, Bisexual, and Transgendered Psychology: A Resource Manual*. Thousand Oaks: Sage.

Harris, Mary B., ed. 1997. *School Experiences of Gay and Lesbian Youth: The Invisible Minority*. Binghamton, NY: Haworth Press.

Hillier, Lynne, Alina Turner, and Anne Mitchell. 2005. *Writing Themselves In Again: Six Years On, the Second National Report on the Sexuality, Health and Well-Being of Same-Sex Attracted Young People*, Carlton South: Australian Research Centre in Sex, Health and Society, La Trobe University. Available at http://www.latrobe.edu.au/arcshs/downloads/Reports/writing_themselves_in_again.pdf.

Howard, Kim, and Annie Stevens, eds. 2000. *Out & About on Campus: Personal Accounts by Lesbian, Gay, Bisexual, and Transgendered College Students*. Los Angeles: Alyson.

Huegel, Kelly. 2003. *GLBTQ*: The Survival Guide for Queer & Questioning Teens.* Minneapolis: Free Spirit.

Human Rights Watch. 2001. *Hatred in the Hallways: Violence and Discrimination Against Lesbian, Gay, Bisexual, and Transgender Students in U.S. Schools.* http://hrw.org/reports/2001/uslgbt.

Ito Satoru, and Yanase Ryuta. 2001. *Coming Out in Japan.* Translated by F. Conlan. Melbourne: Trans Pacific Press.

Jennings, Kevin, with Pat Shapiro. 2003. *Always My Child: A Parent's Guide to Understanding Your Gay, Lesbian, Bisexual, Transgendered or Questioning Son or Daughter.* New York: Fireside.

Johnson, Suzanne M., and Elizabeth O'Connor. 2002. *The Gay Baby Boom: The Psychology of Gay Parenthood;* New York: New York University Press.

Just the Facts Coalition. 1999. *Just the Facts about Sexual Orientation and Youth: A Primer for Principals, Educators and School Personnel.* Washington, D.C.: National Education Association.

Khayatt, Madiha Didi. 1992. *Lesbian Teachers: An Invisible Presence.* Albany: State University of New York.

Kissen, Rita M., ed. 2002. *Getting Ready for Benjamin: Preparing Teachers for Sexual Diversity in the Classroom.* Lanham, MD: Rowman and Littlefield.

Kosciw, Joseph G. 2004. *The 2003 National School Climate Survey: The School Related Experiences of Our Nation's Lesbian, Gay, Bisexual and Transgender Youth.* New York: Gay, Lesbian, Straight Education Network.

Kumashiro, Kevin, ed. 2001. *Troubling Intersections of Race and Sexuality: Queer Students of Color and Anti-Oppressive Education.* Lanham, MD: Rowman and Littlefield.

Letts, William J., IV, and James T. Sears, eds. 1999. *Queering Elementary Education: Advancing the Dialogue about Sexualities and Schooling.* Lanham, MD: Rowman and Littlefield.

Levine, Judith. 2002. *Harmful to Minors: The Perils of Protecting Children from Sex.* New York: Thunder's Mouth.

Lipkin, Arthur. 1999. *Understanding Homosexuality, Changing Schools: A Text for Teachers, Counselors, and Administrators.* Boulder, CO: Westview Press.

———. 2004. *Beyond Diversity Day: A Q & A on Gay and Lesbian Issues in Schools.* Lanham, MD: Rowman and Littlefield.

MacGillivray, Ian. 2003. *Sexual Orientation and School Policy: A Practical Guide for Teachers, Administrators and Community Activists.* Lanham, MD: Rowman and Littlefield.

Maher, Michael J. 2001. *Being Gay and Lesbian in a Catholic High School: Beyond the Uniform.* Binghamton, NY: Haworth Press.

Martino, Wayne, and Maria Pallotta-Chiarolli. 2003. *So What's a Boy: Addressing Issues of Masculinity and Schooling.* Buckingham: Open University Press.

———. 2005. *Boys' Stuff: Boys Talking about what Matters.* Sydney: Allen & Unwin.

McNinch, James, and Mary Cronin, eds. 2004. *I Could Not Speak My Heart: Education and Social Justice for Gay and Lesbian Youth.* Regina, SK: University of Regina, Canadian Plains Research Centre.

Meezan, William, and James Martin. 2003. *Research Methods with Gay, Lesbian, Bisexual, and Transgender Populations.* Binghamton, NY: Harrington Park Press.

Moran, Jeffery P. 2000. *Teaching Sex: The Shaping of Adolescence in the 20th century.* Cambridge, MA: Harvard University Press.

National Education Association. 2004. *Dealing with Legal Matters Surrounding Student's Sexual Orientation and Gender Identity.* Washington, D.C.: Author.

Owens, Robert E. 1998. *Queer Kids: The Challenges and Promise for Lesbian, Gay, and Bisexual Youth.* Binghamton, NY: Harrington Park Press.

Pallotta-Chiarolli, Maria. 2004. *Coming Out WITH Our Kids: Supporting Same-Sex Attracted Young People in Our Families, Schools and Communities.* Sydney: Finch.

Patterson, Charlotte J., and Anthony R. D'Augelli, eds. 2001. *Lesbian, Gay, and Bisexual Identities in Youth: Psychological Perspectives*. New York: Oxford University Press.

Perez, Ruperto M., Kurt A. DeBord, and Kathleen J. Bieschke. eds. 2000. *Handbook of Counseling and Therapy with Lesbian, Gay, and Bisexual Clients*. Washington, D.C.: American Psychological Association.

Perrotti, J., and K. Westheimer. 2001. *When the Drama Club is Not Enough: Lessons from the Safe Schools Program for Gay and Lesbian Students*. Boston: Beacon.

Pinar, William, F., ed. 1998. *Queer Theory in Education*. Mahwah, NJ: Lawrence Erlbaum.

Plummer, David. 1999. *One of the Boys: Masculinity, Homophobia and Modern Manhood*. Binghamton, NY: Haworth Press.

Rankin, Susan R. 2003. *Campus Climate for Lesbian, Gay, Bisexual and Transgender People: A National Perspective*. New York: National Gay and Lesbian Task Force Policy Institute.

Rasmussen, Mary Lou, Eric Rofes, and Susan Talburt, eds. 2004. *Youth and Sexualities: Pleasure, Subversion, and Insubordination In and Out of Schools*. New York: Palagrave Macmillan

Renold, Emma. 2005. *Girls, Boys and Junior Sexualities: Exploring Gender and Sexual Relations in the Primary School*. London: RoutledgeFalmer.

Ristock, Janice L., and Catherine G. Taylor, eds. 1998. *Inside the Academy and Out: Lesbian/Gay/Queer Studies and Social Action*. Toronto: University of Toronto Press.

Robinson, Kerry, Jude Irwin, and Tania Ferfolja, eds. 2002. *From Here to Diversity: The Social Impact of Lesbian and Gay Issues in Education in Australia and New Zealand*. New York: Harrington Press.

Rottnek, Matthew, ed. 1999. *Sissies and Tomboys: Gender Nonconformity and Homosexual Childhood*. New York: New York University.

Rust, Paula C. Rodriguez, ed. 2000. *Bisexuality in the United States: A Social Science Reader*. New York: Columbia University Press.

Ryan, Caitlin, and Donna Futterman. 1998. *Lesbian & Gay Youth: Care & Counseling*. New York: Columbia University Press.

Sandfort, Theo, Judith Schuyf, Jan Willem Duyvendak, and Jeffrey Weeks. 2000. *Lesbian and Gay Studies: An Introductory Interdisciplinary Approach*. London: Sage.

Sanlo, Ronni L., ed. 1998. *Working with Lesbian, Gay, Bisexual, and Transgender College Students: A Handbook for Faculty and Administrators*. Westport, CT: Greenwood.

Sanlo, Ronni L., Sue Rankin, and Robert Schoenberg, eds. 2002. *Our Place on Campus: Lesbian, Gay, Bisexual, Transgender Services and Programs in Higher Education*. Westport, CT: Greenwood.

Savin-Williams, Ritch C. 1998. *". . . And Then I Became Gay:" Young Men's Stories*. New York: Routledge.

Sears, James T. 1991. *Growing up Gay in the South*. Binghamton, NY: Haworth Press.

———. 2005. *Gay, Lesbian, and Transgender Issues in Education*. Binghamton, NY: Haworth Press.

Sears, James T., and Walter L. Williams, eds. 1997. *Overcoming Heterosexism and Homophobia: Strategies that Work*. New York: Columbia University Press.

Sonnie, Amy. 2000. *Revolutionary Voices: A Multicultural Queer Youth Anthology*. Los Angeles: Alyson.

Spurlin, William J., ed. 2000. *Lesbian and Gay Studies and the Teaching of English: Positions, Pedagogies, and Cultural Politics*. Urbana, IL: National Council of Teachers of English.

van Wormer, Katherine, Joel Wells, and Mary Boes. 2000. *Social Work with Lesbians, Gays, and Bisexuals: A Strengths Perspective*. Boston: Allyn and Bacon.

Wall, Vernon A., and Nancy J. Evans, eds. 1999. *Toward Acceptance: Sexual Orientation Issues on Campus*. Lanham, MD: University Press of America.

Walling, Donovan R., ed. 1996. *Open Lives, Safe Schools*. Bloomington, IN: Phi Delta Kappa Educational Foundation.

925

Book Chapters

D'Augelli, Anthony R. 1998. "Lesbian and Gay Male Development: Steps Toward an Analysis of Lesbians' and Gay Men's Lives." Pp. 118–132 in *Lesbian and Gay Psychology: Theory, Research, and Clinical Applications. Psychological Perspectives on Lesbian and Gay Issues, Vol. 1*. Edited by Beverley Greene and Gregory Herek. Thousand Oaks, CA: Sage.

Davis, James. 1999. "Forbidden Fruit: Black Males' Construction of Transgressive Sexualities in Middle School." Pp. 49–59 in *Queering Elementary Education: Advancing the Dialogue about Sexualities and Schooling*. Edited by William J. Letts IV and James T. Sears. Lanham, MD: Rowan and Littlefield Publishers.

Deaux, Kay, and Abigail, J. Stewart. 2001. "Framing Gendered Identities." Pp. 84–100 in *Handbook of the Psychology of Women and Gender*. Edited by Rhoda K. Unger. New York: Wiley.

Greene, Beverly. 1998. "Family, Ethnic Identity, and Sexual Orientation: African-American Lesbians and Gay Men." Pp. 40–52 in *Lesbian, Gay, and Bisexual Identities in Families: Psychological Perspectives*. Edited by Charlotte J. Patterson and Anthony R. D'Augelli. New York: Oxford University Press.

Harwood, Valerie, and Mary Lou Rasmussen. 2004. "Problematising Gender and Sexual Identities." Pp.413–437 in *Gay and Lesbian Psychology: Australasian Perspectives*. Edited by Damien Riggs and Gordon Walker. Perth: Brightfire Press.

Liu, Peter, and Connie S. Chan. 1996. "Lesbian, Gay, and Bisexual Asian Americans and Their Families." Pp. 137–152 in *Lesbians and Gays in Couples and Families: A Handbook for Therapists*. Edited by Joan Laird and Robert-Jay Green. San Francisco, CA: Jossey-Bass.

Raymond, Diane. 1994. "Homophobia, Identity, and the Meanings of Desire: Reflections on the Cultural Construction of Gay and Lesbian Adolescent Sexuality." Pp. 115–150 in *Sexual Cultures and the Construction of Adolescent Identities*. Edited by Janice M. Irvine. Philadelphia: Temple University Press.

Rivers, Ian. 2002. "Developmental Issues for Lesbian and Gay Youth." Pp. 30–44 in *Lesbian and Gay Psychology: New Perspectives*. Edited by Adrian Coyle and Celia Kitzinger. Oxford: Blackwell.

Rotheram-Borus, Mary Jane, and Kris A. Langabeer. 2001. "Developmental Trajectories of Gay, Lesbian, and Bisexual Youth." Pp. 97–128 in *Lesbian, Gay, and Bisexual Identities and Youth: Psychological Perspectives*. Edited by Anthony R. D'Augelli and Charlotte J. Patterson. New York: Oxford.

Sears, James T. 1997. "Thinking Critically/ Intervening Effectively about Heterosexism and Homophobia: A Twenty-Five Year Research Retrospective." Pp. 13–48 in *Overcoming Heterosexism and Homophobia: Strategies That Work*. Edited by James T. Sears and Walter L. Williams. New York: Columbia University Press.

Journal Articles

Anderson, Andrew L. 1998. "Strengths of Gay Male Youth: An Untold Story." *Child and Adolescent Social Work Journal* 15, no. 1: 55–71.

Atkinson, Elizabeth. 2002. "Education for Diversity in a Multisexual Society: Negotiating the Contradictions of Contemporary Discourse." *Sex Education* 2, no. 2: 119–132.

Baker, Janet G., and Harold D. Fishbein. 1998. "The Development of Prejudice towards Gays and Lesbians by Adolescents." *Journal of Homosexuality* 36, no. 1: 89–100.

Beemyn, Brett Genny. 2003. "Serving the Needs of Transgender College Students." *Journal of Gay and Lesbian Issues in Education* 1, no. 1: 33–50.

Bontempo, Daniel E., and Anthony R. D'Augelli. 2002. "Effects of At-School Victimization and Sexual Orientation on Lesbian, Gay, or Bisexual Youths' Health Risk Behavior." *Journal of Adolescent Health* 30: 364–374.

Cahill, Sean, and Jason Cianciotto. 2004. "Policy Interventions That Can Make Schools Safer." *Journal of Gay and Lesbian Issues in Education* 2, no. 1: 3–17.

Cochran, Bryan N., Angela J. Stewart, Joshua A. Ginzler, and Ana Mari Cauce. 2002. "Challenges Faced by Homeless Sexual Minorities: Comparison of Gay, Lesbian, Bisexual, and Transgender Homeless Adolescents with their Heterosexual Counterparts." *American Journal of Public Health* 92: 773–777.

Consolacion, Theodora B., Stephen T. Russell, and Stanley Sue. 2004. "Sex, Race/Ethnicity, and Romantic Attractions: Multiple Minority Status Adolescents and Mental Health." *Cultural Diversity and Ethnic Minority Psychology* 10: 200–214.

D'Augelli, Anthony R., Neil Pilkington, and Scott Hershberger. 2002. "Incidence and Mental Health Impact of Sexual Orientation Victimization of Lesbian, Gay, and Bisexual Youths in High School." *School Psychology Quarterly* 17, no. 2:148–167.

Diamond, Lisa M. 2000. "Sexual Identity, Attractions, and Behavior among Young Sexual-Minority Women Over a 2-Year Period." *Developmental Psychology* 36, no. 2: 241–250.

Dubé, Eric M., and Ritch C. Savin-Williams. 1999. "Sexual Identity Development among Ethnic Sexual-Minority Male Youths." *Developmental Psychology* 35, no. 6: 1389–1398.

Fann, Rodge Q. 2003. "Growing up Gay in China." *Journal of Gay and Lesbian Issues in Education* 1, no. 2: 35–42.

Fergusson, David M., L. John Horwood, and Annette L. Beautrais. 1999. "Is Sexual Orientation Related to Mental Health Problems and Suicidality in Young People?" *Archives of General Psychiatry* 56: 876–891.

Griffin, Pat, Camille Lee, Jeffrey Waugh, and Chad Beyer. 2004. "Describing Roles that Gay-Straight Alliances Play in Schools: From Individual Support to School Change," *Journal of Gay and Lesbian Issues in Education* 1, no. 3: 7–22.

Goodenow, Carol, Julie Netherland, and Laura Szalacha. 2002. "AIDS-Related Risk Among Adolescent Males Who Have Sex With Males, Females or Both: Evidence from a Statewide Survey." *American Journal of Public Health* 92, no. 2: 203–210.

Hillman, Jennifer, and Renee A. Martin. 2002. "Lessons about Gay and Lesbian Lives: A Spaceship Exercise." *Teaching of Psychology* 29: 308–311.

Holmes, Sarah E., and Sean Cahill. 2004. "School Experiences of Gay, Lesbian, Bisexual, and Transgender Youth." *Journal of Gay and Lesbian Issues in Education* 1, no. 3: 53–66.

Jordan, Karen M. 2000. "Substance Abuse among Gay, Lesbian, Bisexual, Transgender and Questioning Adolescents." *School Psychology Review* 29, no. 2: 201–206.

Letts, Will. 2001. "When Science is Strangely Alluring: Interrogating the Masculinist and Heternormative Nature of Primary School Science." *Gender and Education* 13: 261–274.

Rivers, Ian. Forthcoming. "Bullying and Homophobia at School: A Perspective on Factors Affecting Resilience." *Journal of Gay and Lesbian Issues in Education.*

Russell, Stephen T. 2003. "Sexual Minority Youth and Suicide Risk." *American Behavioral Scientist* 46: 1241–1257.

———. 2005. "Beyond Risk: Resilience in the Lives of Sexual Minority Youth." *Journal of Gay and Lesbian Issues in Education* 2(3): 5–18.

———, Anne K. Driscoll, and Nhan Truong. 2002. "Adolescent Same-Sex Romantic Attractions and Relationships: Implications for Substance Use and Abuse." *American Journal of Public Health* 92, no. 2: 198–202.

———, and Hinda Seif. 2002. "Bisexual Female Adolescents: A Critical Analysis of Past Research, and Results from a National Survey." *Journal of Bisexuality* 2, no. 2/3: 73–94.

Saewyc, Elizabeth M., Linda H. Bearinger, Patricia A. Heinz, Robert W. Blum and Michael D. Resnick. 1998. "Gender Differences in Health and Risk Behaviors among Bisexual and Homosexual Adolescents." *Journal of Adolescent Health* 23, no. 3: 181–188.

Savin-Williams, Ritch C. 2001. "A Critique of Research on Sexual-Minority Youth." *Journal of Adolescence* 24, no. 1: 5–13.

927

Schall, Janine, and Gloria Kauffmann. 2003. "Exploring Literature with Gay and Lesbian Characters in the Elementary School." *Journal of Children's Literature* 29, no. 1: 36–45.

Sears, James T. 1997. "Centering Culture: Teaching for Critical Sexual Literacy Using the Sexual Diversity Wheel." *Journal of Moral Education* 26: 273–283.

———. 2005. "Researching Queer Youth." Special Issue. *Journal of Gay and Lesbian Issues in Education*, 3, nos. 2–3.

SIECUS. 2001. "Lesbian, Gay, Bisexual, and Transgendered Youth Issues." *SIECUS Report Supplement* 29, no. 4: 1–5.

Stacey, Judith, and Timorthy Biblarz. 2001. "(How) Does the Sexual Orientation of Parents Matter?" *American Sociological Review* 66: 159–183.

Szalacha, Laura A. 2003. "Safer Sexual Diversity Climates: Lessons Learned from an Evaluation of Massachusetts' Safe Schools Program for Gay and Lesbian Students." *American Journal of Education* 110, no. 1: 58–88.

Tye, Marus C. 2003. "Lesbian, Gay, Bisexual, and Transgender Parents: Special Considerations for the Custody and Adoption Evaluator." *Family Court Review* 41, no. 1: 92–103.

Walling, Donovan R. 2003. "Gay- and Lesbian-Themed Novels for Classroom Reading," *Journal of Gay and Lesbian Issues in Education*, 1, no. 2: 97–108.

Yep, Gust A. 2002. "From Homophobia and Heterosexism to Heteronormativity: Toward the Development of a Model of Queer Interventions in the University Classroom." *Journal of Lesbian Studies* 6, nos. 3/4: 163–176.

ELECTRONIC RESOURCES

Education & Youth Policy LGBT Organizations

Gay, Lesbian, and Straight Education Network (GLSEN). 2005. http://www.glsen.org/cgi-bin/iowa/all/about/index.html.

International Foundation for Gender Education (IFGE). 2005. http://www.ifge.org.

National Youth Advocacy Coalition. 2005. http://www.nyacyouth.org.

Safe Schools Coalition. 2005. http://www.safeschoolscoalition.org/.

Schools Out. 2005. http://www.schools-out.org.uk/.

Film and Video

Barnes, Lynne (Producer & Director). 2004. *Reaching Out: Library Services for GLBT&Q Teens*. [Videotape].

Cohen, Helen S. (Producer) & Chasnoff, Debra (Producer & Director). 1997. *It's Elementary: Talking About Gay Issues in School* [Film]. (Available from Women's Educational Media, San Francisco, CA).

Cohen, Helen S. (Producer) & Chasnoff, Debra (Director). 1996. *That's a Family!* [Video]. (Available from Women's Educational Media, San Francisco, CA).

Friedman, Jeffrey, and Rob Epstein. 2002. *Paragraph 175* [Videotape]. New York: New Yorker Video.

Gunnarsdottir, Hrafnhildur, and Thorvaldur Kristinsson (Directors). 2003. *Straight Out: Stories from Iceland*. [Film]. Reykjavik: Krumma Kvikmyndir Films.

Jackson, Peter (Director). 1994. Heavenly Creatures [Motion Picture]. New Zealand: Wingnut Films.

National Film Board of Canada (Producer). 2003. *Celebrating Diversity: Resources for Responding to Homophobia* [Videotape].

Rose, Lee (Director). 2000. *The Truth about Jane* [Motion Picture]. United States: Starlight Home Entertainment.

Seitchik, Vickie (Director). 1993. *Queer Son*. [Video]. San Francisco: Frameline.

Public Policy LGBT Organizations

Aguda. http://www.aguda-ta.org.il/content/english.asp.
Bisexual Foundation. 2005. Bisexual.Org—Bringing Bisexuals Together.
    http://www.bisexual.org.
Equality Alliance. 2005. http://www.pfc.org.uk.
Equality for Gay and Lesbians Everywhere (EGALE Canada). 2005. www.egale.ca.
Gender Public Advocacy Coalition (GenderPAC). 2005. http://www.gpac.org.
Homo-Edu. 2005. http://homoedu.free.fr/
Human Rights Campaign. 2005. http://www.hrc.org/.
Human Rights Watch: Lesbian and Gay Rights. 2005. http://hrw.org/doc/?t=lgbt
International Gay and Lesbian Human Rights Commission. 2005. http://www.iglhrc.org.
International Lesbian and Gay Association. 2005. http://www.ilga.org.
Lambda Legal. 2005. http://www.lambdalegal.org.
Lesbian and Gay Equality Project. 2005. http://www.equality.org.za.
National Gay and Lesbian Task Force. 2005. http://www.thetaskforce.org.
National Gay and Lesbian Task Force Policy Institute. 2005.
    http://www.thetaskforce.org/ourprojects/pi/index.cfm.
National Latina/o Lesbian, Gay, Bisexual & Transgender Organization. 2004.
    http://www.llego.org.
National Transgender Advocacy Coalition. 2005. http://www.ntac.org.
Parents, Families, and Friends of Lesbians and Gays. 2005. http://www.pflag.org.
Parents, Families, and Friends of Lesbians and Gays, Canada. 2005.
    http://www.pflagcanada.ca.
Queer Bulgaria Foundation. 2005. http://www.queer-bulgaria.org.
Stonewall: Equality and Social Justice for Lesbians, Gay Men, and Bisexuals. 2005.
    http://www.stonewall.org.uk/stonewall.
Triangle Project. 2005. http://www.triangle.org.za.

Queer Youth Internet Sites

E-jovem. 2005. http://www.e-jovem.com.
ElfBoys. 2005. http://www.elfboys.net.
Gay Youth: A Xanga Blogring. 2005. http://www.xanga.com/blogrings/blogring.
    asp?id=2066.
Gender YOUTH Network. 2004. http://genderyouth.typepad.com/network.
GRRR Zine Network. 2005. http://grrrlzines.net/resources/artandmusic.htm.
Minus18. 2005. http://www.minus18.org.
Outpath Coming Out Archive. 2005. http://www.outpath.com.
Queer Youth Alliance. 2005. http://www.queeryouth.org.uk.
QYWC. 2005. http://www.dogwomble.com/cgi-bin/webapp/mods/showhtml/showhtml.
    pl?url=www.dogwomble.com/html/index.html
Reece's Trans Youth Zine. http://www.teachers.ab.ca/NR/rdonlyres/1BDAA5A1-51B8-
    4DD0-82A3-A7AB501CE085/0/CanadianTransYouthZine.pdf.
soc.support.youth.gay.gay-lesbian-bi. 2002. http://www.ssyglb.org.
Trans Youth Toronto. 2003. http://www.the519.org/programs/trans/transyouthtoronto/
    events.shtml.
Young Gay America. 2004. http://www.younggayamerica.com.

Queer Youth Advocacy Organizations and Projects

BeLonG To Youth Project. 2005. http://www.belongto.org.
CampusPrideNet. 2005. http://www.campuspride.net.
Children of Lesbians and Gays Everywhere (COLAGE). 2005. http://www.colage.org/.

Deaf Youth Rainbow. 2000. http://www.deafqueer.net/cmra/dyr/.
Gay-Straight Alliance Network. 2005. www.gsanetwork.org.
Gay Youth UK. 2005. http://www.gayyouthuk.org.uk/index.phtml.
Genderbridge. 2005. http://www.genderbridge.org.
GLBT Alberta Youth Outreach. 2005. http://www.glbtalberta.com.
GLEE Project. February 25, 2003. http://glee.oulu.fi.
Harvey Milk School. 2005. http://www.hmi.org.
JQYouth.org. 2003. http://www.jqyouth.org/.
LGBT Youth Scotland. 2005. http://www.lgbtyouth.org.uk/.
Lesbian, Gay, and Bisexual Youth Project. 2005. http://www.youthproject.ns.ca.
Lesbians of Undeniable Drive (LOUD). 2004. http://www.space-loud.org/louden.html.
National Coming Out Project. 2005. http://www.comeout.org
Nueva Generación de Jóvenes Lesbianas. 2004. http://www.generacionlesbica.org.
Outlink. 2005. http://outlink.trump.net.au/index.htm.
OutProud. 2005. http://www.outproud.org.
Pace Youthwork Service. 2005. http://www.outzone.org/index.htm.
Project 10. http://www.project10.org.
The Project 10 East. 2005. http://www.project10east.org.
Queer Asian Youth. 2005. http://www.acas.org/QAY.
Queerbodies. 2004. http://www.queerbodies.org.
Rainbow Youth. 2005. http://www.rainbowyouth.org.nz.
School Survival Guide. 2003. http://www.centeryes.org/SIGNS/.
Sexual Minority Youth Assistance League. 2005. http://www.smyal.org/main.htm.
Trans Proud. 2005. http://www.transproud.com.
Triangle Program. 2005. http://schools.tdsb.on.ca/triangle.
YouthCO AIDS Society. 2005. http://www.Youthco.org.
Youth4Youth. 2005. http://www.youth4youth.com.
Youth Guardian Services. 2005. http://www.youth-guard.org.
YouthResource. 2005. http://www.youthresource.com.

Curriculum On-Line Resources and LGBT Professional Education Groups

American College Personnel Association Standing Committee on LGBT Awareness. 2005. http://www.sclgbta.org.
APA Lesbian, Gay, Bisexual Concerns Office. 2005. American Psychological Association. http://www.apa.org/pi/lgbc/office/homepage.html.
Association for Gay, Lesbian, and Bisexual Issues in Counseling (AGLBIC). 2005. http://www.aglbic.org/.
Australian Centre for Lesbian and Gay Research. 2004. http://www.arts.usyd.edu.au/centres/aclgr/.
Center for Anti-Oppressive Education. 2005. http://www.antioppressiveeducation.org/.
Complete Resource for LGBT Families. 2005. http://www.twolives.com.
Gay and Lesbian Educators of BC (GALE-BC). 2005. http://www.galebc.org.
Gender Studies. Voice of the Shuttle, Department of English at University of California at Santa Barbara. 2005. http://vos.ucsb.edu/browse.asp?id=2711.
GLBT Alliance in Social and Personal Psychology. 2005. http://raiders.psych.utah.edu:8180/psych/psych/gasp.
GLSEN Resource Centre, Curricula. Gay Lesbian and Straight Education Network. November 2005. http://www.glsen.org/cgi-bin/iowa/home.html.
Heterosexism Inquirer. 2003. http://www.mun.ca/the.
Lesbian and Gay Addiction Counselors (NALGAP). 2005. http://www.nalgap.org.
Lesbian Herstory Archives. 2004. http://www.lesbianherstoryarchives.org.

Lesbian Information Service. January 2004. http://www.lesbianinformationservice.org.

LGBT/Queer Library Research Guide. 2001. http://www.public.iastate.edu/~savega/lesbigay.htm.

Making Schools Safe for Gay Youth. 2003. http://www.aclu.org/safeschools/safe_schools.html.

National Association of Student Personnel Administrators GLBT Issues Knowledge Community. 2005. http://www.naspa.org/communities/kc/community.cfm?kcid=7.

National Consortium of Directors of Lesbian, Gay, Bisexual, and Transgender Resources in Higher Education. 2005. http://www.lgbtcampus.org/.

National Education Association-Gay, Lesbian, Bisexual, Transgender Caucus. 2005. http://www.nea-glc.org.

National Women's History Project. 2005. http://www.nwhp.org.

Ningen-to-Sei-Kyouiku-Kenkyuu-Kyougikai (The Council for Education and Study on Human Sexuality). 2005. http://www.seikyokyo.org/.

One National Gay and Lesbian Archives. 2005. http://www.oneinstitute.org.

Queer America. 2005. http://www.queeramerica.com.

Queer Culture Center. 2005. http://www.queerculturalcenter.org.

Queer Resources Directory. 2005. http://www.qrd.org/qrd.

QueerTheory.com. 2005. http://www.queertheory.com.

Safe Schools Coalition: Resources for Teachers and Curriculum Specialists. 2005. http://www.safeschoolscoalition.org/blackboard-teachers.html.

Same Sex Attracted Youth Website. Australian Research Centre in Sex, Health and Society. 2004. http://www.latrobe.edu.au/ssay.

Schools Out: Teaching Resources. 2005. http://www.schools-out.org.uk/resources/teaching/contents.htm.

Sexuality Information and Education Council of the U.S. 2005. http://www.siecus.org.

Society for the Psychological Study of Lesbian, Gay, and Bisexual Issues. 2005. http://www.apa.org/divisions/div44/.

Tremblay, Pierre. 2005. A GLBTQ Education Internet Resources. http://www.youth-suicide.com/gay-bisexual/links5.htm.

University LGBT/Queer Programs. 2005. http://www.people.ku.edu/~jyounger/lgbtqprogs.html.

About the Editor and Contributors

EDITOR

James T. **Sears** specializes in research in lesbian, gay, bisexual and transgender issues in education, curriculum studies, and gay history. His scholarship has appeared in a variety of peer-reviewed journals ranging from the *Journal of Homosexuality* and *Sex Education* to the *Journal of Moral Education* and *Educational Policies*. He is the author or editor of sixteen books, including: *Lonely Hunters: An Oral History of Lesbian and Gay Southern Life* (A 1998 finalist for the American Library Association gay nonfiction award); *When Best Doesn't Equal Good* (Outstanding 1995 Research Publication Award, Association for Supervision & Curriculum Development, PA); *Queering Elementary Education* (2000 *Choice* Outstanding Academic Book), *Sexuality and the Curriculum* (cited as one of the 35 most influential sexuality books published since 1970 by SIECUS), *Curriculum, Religion, and Public Education*, and *Overcoming Heterosexism and Homophobia* (Winner of the 1999 GLSEN Award). Dr. Sears has taught curriculum, research, and gay-themed courses in the departments of education, sociology, women's studies, and the honors college at several universities, including: Harvard University, Trinity University, Indiana University, Penn State University, the College of Charleston, and the University of South Carolina. He has also been a research fellow at Center for Feminist Studies at the University of Southern California and at the University of Queensland as well as a Fulbright Senior Research Southeast Asia Scholar on sexuality and culture, and a consultant for the J. Paul Getty Center for Education and the Arts. Sears serves on a variety of editorial boards, was founder of the Gay and Lesbians SIG of the American Educational Research Association, and is a member of the Professors of Curriculum, and the International Academy of Sex Research. Currently, he is the editor of the international *Journal of Gay and Lesbian Issues in Education*. He is the past coeditor (1989–1998) of *Teaching Education Journal*. He was awarded a lifetime achievement award in 2004 from the Curriculum & Pedagogy Conference, which has named its annual award for excellence and scholarship in his name.

Dr. Sears earned an undergraduate degree in history from Southern Illinois University, a graduate degree in political science from the University of Wisconsin, and his doctorate in education and sociology from Indiana University, which awarded him its Outstanding Alumni Award. His professional and personal papers are located at Duke University, Special Collections Library; his award-winning Web site is at www.jtsears.com. Additional biographical information is available through *Who's Who in America* and *Contemporary Authors*.

CONTRIBUTORS

Peter **Aggleton** is professor in education and director of the Thomas Coram Research Unit at the Institute of Education, University of London. He is the author and editor of over thirty books and two hundred articles in the fields of sexuality, sexual health, and education. A senior adviser to UNAIDS, UNESCO, and WHO, he has worked internationally in the field of sexual health for nearly twenty years.

Mahoney **Archer** is a teacher of art and English in Brisbane, Australia. She focused her masters degree research on the motivators for closeted behavior of lesbian teachers and intends to explore this area further in PhD studies in the future.

Nina **Asher** is assistant professor at Louisiana State University. She has published in the areas of postcolonial and feminist theory in education, critical perspectives on multiculturalism, and Asian American education.

Gaynor **Astbury** earned her doctorate from the University of Port Elizabeth, South Africa, in 2001. She currently manages an holistic community-based project in Cornwall, United Kingdom. Her research interests are in pastoral psychology and health psychology.

Pamela K. **Autrey** earned her PhD in curriculum theory at Louisiana State University where she studied gender issues and their effects on learning in elementary schools. She teaches in the public Montessori magnet program in Baton Rouge, Louisiana.

Benjamin **Baez** is associate professor of higher education in the Department of Educational Policy Studies at Georgia State University. He received his law degree in 1988 and his doctorate in higher education in 1997, both from Syracuse University. He recently published *Affirmative Action, Hate Speech, and Tenure: Narratives About Race, Law, and the Academy* (Routledge 2002). He also published with John A. Centra, *Tenure, Promotion, and Reappointment: Legal and Administrative Implications* (Jossey Bass 1995).

Michael **Barron** holds an MA degree in youth and community studies. His dissertation focused on the effects of homophobic bullying on the body images of gay and bisexual young men. He coordinates Ireland's only LGBT youth project and is prominent in LGBT activism.

Timothy **Bedford** is a graduate of Churchill College, Cambridge University. He is currently a high school teacher at Oulun Lyseon lukio and researcher on activist learning and teaching at the University of Oulu, Finland. He directs the European Union's supported GLEE project to overcome homophobia and heterosexism in schools.

Brett Genny **Beemyn** is coordinator of Gay, Lesbian, Bisexual, and Transgender Student Services, the Multicultural Center, at the Ohio State University. Brett has published and spoken extensively on college policies toward transgender students and GLBT history. Brett's most recent publications include "Transgender Issues on Campus" in *New Direction in Student Services: LGBT Issues in Student Affairs* (2005) and a special issue of the *Journal of Gay and Lesbian Issues in Education* on "Trans Youth" (2006).

Kathleen J. **Bieschke** is currently an associate professor of counseling psychology at Pennsylvania State University in the Department of Counselor Education, Counseling Psychology, and Rehabilitation Services. Dr. Bieschke has delivered numerous presentations, written about, and conducted research pertaining to the delivery of affirmative counseling and psychotherapy services to gay, lesbian, and bisexual clients. In addition, Dr. Bieschke has considerable experience working with gay, lesbian, and bisexual individuals in both a college counseling and private practice setting.

Susan **Birden** is assistant professor in the Educational Foundations Department at the State University of New York College at Buffalo. She is author of *Rethinking Sexual Identity in Education* (Rowman & Littlefield, 2005).

Wendy J. **Biss** is finishing her dissertation on equality in lesbian relationships at The University of Memphis.

Mollie **Blackburn** is an assistant professor in literacy, language, and culture in the College of Education at Ohio State University. Her research is critical and activist in nature and works to explore the ways in which youth engage in literacy performances to construct their own identities and work for social change. Her work has been published in such journals as *Teachers College Record* and *Research in the Teaching of English*.

Jackie M. **Blount** is professor of historical, philosophical, and comparative studies in education at Iowa State University. Her latest book, *Fit to Teach: Same-Sex Desire, Gender, and School Work in the Twentieth Century* (SUNY Press 2005), explores the history of LGBT teachers and administrators.

Jodi A. **Boita** is a candidate for the doctoral degree in counseling psychology at Pennsylvania State University. Her research explores issues for lesbian, gay, and bisexual individuals, with particular focus on career and relationship factors.

Barbara **Bolt** is a practicing artist, theorist, and art critic. She lectures in visual media at the University of Melbourne. She has published *Art Beyond Representation: The Performative Power of the Image* (IBTauris 2004), contributed chapters to *Differential Aesthetics: Art Practices and Philosophies: Towards New Feminist Understandings* (Ashgate 2000) and *Unframed: The Practices and Politics of Women's Painting* (IB Tauris 2004), and refereed articles to *Hypatia, Womens Philosophical Review, Social Semiotics* and the online journals *Text, Teknokultura* and *Refractory*.

Deborah P. **Britzman**, professor of education at York University, Toronto, is author of three books: *Practice Makes Practice: A Critical Study of Learning to Teach* (1991); *Lost Subjects, Contested Objects: Toward a Psychoanalytic Inquiry of Learning* (1998); and *After-Education: Anna Freud, Melanie Klein and Psychoanalytic Histories of Learning* (2003), all from The State University of New York Press. Areas of interest are psychoanalysis and education.

Stephen **Brown** is assistant professor of political science at the University of Ottawa, where he also teaches in the program in international development and globalization. He has taught a course on "sexual diversity studies" and published on the LGBT movement in Argentina. His current research focuses on foreign aid, democratization, conflict, and peace building in Africa, topics on which he has published several journal articles and book chapters.

Mary **Bryson** is associate professor of education at the University of British Columbia. She is the (co-)author of numerous articles and chapters on technology, gender, and sexuality, as well as an edited book, *Radical Inventions: Identity, Politics, and*

Differences in Educational Praxis (SUNY Press 1997). In 2000, Bryson received the Canadian Wired Women's "Pioneer in New Media and Technology" award. Her most recent publication is "When Jill Jacks In: Queer Women and the Net," *Feminist Media Studies* (Fall 2004).

JF **Buckley** is associate professor of English at Ohio State University. He has published *Desire, The Self, The Social Critic* (Susquehanna University Press 1997), a study of transcendentalism and queer theory, as well as articles on Ernest Hemingway, Rebecca Harding Davis, and Herman Melville.

Allister H. **Butler** earned his doctorate from the University of Port Elizabeth, South Africa, in 2000. He presently holds tenure as the professional lead in social work at Canterbury Christ Church University, United Kingdom. He has written in the field of international social work practice, gay and lesbian youth, young careers, homophobia, and HIV and AIDS in South Africa. His most recent publication is "Over the Rainbow: Recommendations for Service Provision as Voiced by Post-Apartheid South African Gay and Lesbian Youth," *Child and Youth Care Journal* (Spring 2005).

Brent E. **Cagle** is a doctoral candidate in social work at the University of South Carolina. His dissertation examines the social supports of thriving, same-sex identified male youth in the Carolinas.

Dennis **Carlson** is a professor of curriculum and cultural studies in the Department of Educational Leadership at Miami University of Ohio. He has published widely in educational journals and is the author (most recently) of *Leaving Safe Harbors: Toward a New Progressivism in American Education and Public Life* (RoutledgeFalmer 2003).

Lynne **Carroll** is associate professor of mental health counseling at the University of North Florida. She has published extensively on LGBT issues including ego development, complementarity in gay and lesbian couples, being out versus coming out, and transgender issues in counseling and clinical training. She is currently completing a textbook on LGBT issues in counseling (Merrill/Prentice-Hall).

Yin-Kun **Chang** is a PhD candidate in curriculum and instruction at the University of Wisconsin–Madison where he focuses on queer theory, cultural studies, and critical pedagogy. His dissertation is about queer culture in Taiwan educational field.

Elaine **Chase** is a senior research officer at the Thomas Coram Research Unit at the Institute of Education, University of London. Her work focuses on the health and well-being of children and young people, particularly those who are marginalized or disadvantaged. Recent publications include a review of literature on the commercial sexual exploitation of children and young people; a review of homophobia, sexual orientation, and schools; and a study of teenage pregnancy and parenthood among young people in local authority care.

Mary M. **Clare** is a Professor in the Graduate School at Lewis & Clark College in Portland, Oregon. Her research and scholarship have focused on applications of psychology in schools with particular emphasis on identifying and correcting enculturated systems of oppression. Her book, *Responsive Assessment: A New Way of Thinking About Learning* (Jossey-Bass 1994) is in revision.

Laurel A. **Clyde** is professor of library and information science in the Faculty of Social Science at the University of Iceland. With Marjorie Lobban, she has published a book, *Out of the Closet and Into the Classroom: Homosexuality in Books for Young People* (Port Melbourne: ALIA/Thorpe, 2nd ed, 1996). She has also published books and articles on topics related to information science, information access, and research quality.

Bryan N. **Cochran** received his PhD in clinical psychology from the University of Washington in Seattle. He is currently an assistant professor of psychology at the University of Montana in Missoula. Current areas of research are LGBT mental health, substance abuse treatment, and psychotherapy process. Some of his representative publications appear in the *American Journal of Public Health* and the *Journal of Homosexuality.*

Shawn M. **Coyne** is a graduate student in the clinical–community psychology and the women's studies programs at the University of South Carolina. Her research interests include domestic abuse and sexual assault. She has jointly published two papers on the topic of combining clinical and community psychology as well as a chapter on community organizing, advocacy, and accountability as it relates to youth mentoring programs.

Margaret Smith **Crocco** is associate professor of social studies and education at Teachers College, Columbia University. Her most recent books are *Learning to Teaching in an Age of Accountability* (Lawrence Earlbaum 2004) and *Social Education in the Twentieth Century: Curriculum and Context for Citizenship* (Peter Lang 2004). Her research interests include gender, sexuality, and teacher education in the social studies.

Greg **Curran** earned his PhD in education at The University of Melbourne where he specialized in queer youth studies. He is a casual teacher and academic having worked in the fields of English as a second language, education, and health sciences. Alongside this, he works on community radio (3CR) and is completing postgraduate studies in counseling.

Toby **Daspit** is assistant professor in the Department of Curriculum and Instruction at the University of Louisiana at Lafayette. His most recent coedited books, both published in 2004, are *Science Fiction Curriculum, Cyborg Teachers, and Youth Culture(s)* (Peter Lang) and *Imagining the Academy: Higher Education and Popular Culture* (Routledge/Falmer).

Judy **Davidson** is an assistant professor in the Faculty of Physical Education and Recreation at the University of Alberta in Edmonton, Canada. She teaches about sport and leisure from a cultural studies perspective. Her doctoral dissertation considered the historical emergence of the Gay Games drawing on the work of Michel Foucault and Judith Butler. She is very interested in the cultural production of gender and sexuality in sport and leisure contexts.

Suzanne **de Castell** is a professor in the Faculty of Education at Simon Fraser University. She has published widely on literacy, technology and new media, gender, equity, and queer pedagogy.

Anisa **de Jong** is a researcher and activist on issues relating to sexuality, gender, and law. Her academic background is in human rights and Islamic law. Her previous publications include a guide on LGBT refugees and asylum seekers for ICAR (2003), www.icar.org.uk/content/res/nav/keyiss.html, and an article for Women Living Under Muslim Laws (WLUML) on attacks on the human rights of lesbian, gay, and bisexual people as warning signs of fundamentalism, http://www.whrnet.org/fundamentalisms/docs/doc-wsfmeeting-2002.html.

Jeffery P. **Dennis** is an assistant professor of sociology at Lakeland College. He has written many articles on LGBT youth and popular culture. His book, *All-American Boys: Queering Teen Culture* (Haworth Press) is forthcoming.

Patrick **Dilley** is assistant professor of higher education and qualitative research at Southern Illinois University—Carbondale. He studies the history, cultures, and identities of LGBT college students. Dilley is the author of *Queer Man on Campus: A History of Non-Heterosexual Men in College, 1945–2000* (RoutledgeFalmer 2002).

Joseph A. **Diorio** received his PhD in philosophy and education from Columbia University, and is dean of the Postgraduate Studies Division at Unitec New Zealand in Auckland. He has written widely on educational theory and sexuality education. His recent publications include "Sexuality, Difference, and the Ethics of Sex Education," *Journal of Social Philosophy* (Fall 2001), and "What Does Puberty Mean to Adolescents?" (with Jenny Munro), *Sex Education* (July 2003).

John P. **Elia** is associate professor and associate chair of health education at San Francisco State University. He is associate editor & book review editor of the *Journal of Homosexuality*, and is on the editorial boards of the *Journal of Gay & Lesbian Issues in Education* and *The Educational Forum*.

Kim Jewel **Elliott** is programme leader youth studies at the University of Auckland. She has extensive community experience in the field of sexuality education and has also published in this area. Her most recent publication is "The Hostile Vagina: Reading Vaginal Discourse in a School Health Text" in *Sex Education*. Kim is currently completing a PhD on sexuality and spirituality in Aotearoa/New Zealand.

Nancy J. **Evans** is professor and higher education program co-coordinator in the Department of Educational Leadership and Policy Studies at Iowa State University. She has published six books, including *Beyond Tolerance: Gays, Lesbians and Bisexuals on Campus* (1991) and *Toward Acceptance: Sexual Orientation Issues on Campus* (2001), both published by American College Personnel Administration, as well as numerous book chapters and articles on the impact of the college environment on nondominant student populations.

Qiuxi **Fann,** Ph.D., from mainland China, currently resides in Philadelphia area. He serves as an assistant editor for the *Journal of Gay & Lesbian Issues in Education.*

Tania **Ferfolja** received her PhD in sociology from the University of New South Wales, Australia. Her international publications and current research interests focus on issues pertaining to nonnormative sexualities, particularly in educational contexts. She lectures preservice teachers in the area of social and cultural diversity.

Ana **Ferreira** lectures in English studies at the College of Education of the University of the Witwatersrand, South Africa. She has a postgraduate degree in English literature and a masters degree in English in education. Her areas of interest are critical pedagogy, and film and media studies. She is currently chief language examiner for the country's Independent Examinations Board.

Gloria **Filax** is an assistant professor in sociology and governance and the law with Athabasca University, Canada. Her dissertation, *Queer Youth and Strange Representations in the Province of the Severely Normal*, is under review for publication.

Kevin C. **Franck** is a doctoral student at the University of Maryland–College Park.

Terence P. **Friedrichs**, from suburban St. Paul, Minnesota, privately assesses, teaches, and advocates for students with exceptional learning needs. He earned his PhD from the University of Virginia in gifted education and special education, and is completing his EdD from the University of St. Thomas in critical pedagogy. Over the past twenty-five years, in K–12 and university settings, he has served both gifted and disabled GLBT youth, as teacher, GSA advisor, and researcher.

Linda L. **Gaither** teaches in the Department of Philosophy and Religion at Rowan University, Glassboro, New Jersey. Author of *To Receive a Text* (Peter Lang 1997), she has published numerous articles on hermeneutics and religion studies. She is also an antiracism trainer.

Laura J. **Gambone** is a doctoral student in clinical–community psychology at the University of South Carolina. Her research interests include domestic violence, women's mental health, and LGBT issues.

Michael **Gard** is a senior lecturer in dance, physical and health education at Charles Sturt University's Bathurst campus. He teaches and writes about the human body, gender and sexuality, the shortcomings of biological determinism in all its forms, and the use and misuse of dance within physical education. He is the author of two books: *The Obesity Epidemic: Science, Morality and Ideology*, coauthored with Jan Wright (Routledge 2004) and *Men Who Dance: Aesthetics, Athletics and the Art of Masculinity* (Peter Lang).

André P. **Grace** is an associate professor who works in educational policy studies and inclusive education at the University of Alberta. He initiated Agape, which is an action group in the Faculty of Education that focuses on sex, sexual, and gender differences in education and culture. He is currently conducting a national study of welfare-and-work issues for LGBTQ teachers in Canadian schools. The Social Sciences and Humanities Research Council of Canada is funding this research.

Mary L. **Gray** is assistant professor of communication and culture at Indiana University. Her work examines the production and representation of youth sexualities and genders. She is the author of *In Your Face: Stories from the Lives of Queer Youth* (1999 Haworth Press). Gray's current research explores how young people in the rural United States fashion queer senses of identity through media engagement and how performances of mass-mediated queer identities play out in the public sphere.

Anibal Ribeiro **Guimarães**, Jr. is an independent, nonfunded researcher on sexual minorities, currently writing a book entitled: *Education and LGBT People in Brazil*. He has an LL.B. degree at the Catholic University of Rio de Janeiro, where he helped to found its Human Rights Center. As a member of the International Lesbian and Gay Association, he has been contributing domestically and with international NGOs to the efforts of a resolution on sexual orientation at UNCHR.

Vicki **Harding** is joint author and project manager of the Learn to Include education series. She is very active in the GLBT community in Sydney, was involved in establishing The Women's Library, and is committed to promoting lesbian parenting issues and the importance of educating young people about diversity. She is a mother and has a bachelor of arts degree from the Australian National University.

Valerie **Harwood** is a member of the faculty of education at the University of Wollongong in New South Wales, Australia.

Jeremy P. **Hayes** is assistant director of the President's Office of Diversity Services at Suffolk University. He serves on the executive committee of the National Consortium of Directors of LGBT Resources in Higher Education.

Judy **Hemingway** is a postdoctoral research fellow at the Institute of Education, University of London. Her research is concerned with the interfaces between school and academic geography and makes special reference to recent developments in cultural geography and critical pedagogy. Interested in the lifeworlds of young people, Hemingway hopes to contribute to new and constructive ways of exploring (un)popular culture. Her work focuses on illicit drug-using and sex/ualities.

Todd K. **Herriott** is the ADA compliance officer / coordinator for disability services at Simmons College. He has coauthored two chapters in forthcoming monographs on issues of disability in higher education and has published LGBT related research, "Freshmen Impressions: How Investigating the Campus Climate for LGBT Students Affected Four Freshmen Students" (*Journal of College Student Development*, coauthored with Dr. Nancy J. Evans). He is currently doing original research on LGBT studies' impact on LGBT identity development in college students.

Sharon G. **Horne** is an assistant professor of counseling psychology at The University of Memphis. Her research includes gay, lesbian, bisexual, and transgender youth issues, LGBT spirituality, and queer experience in postcommunist countries.

Pat **Hulsebosch** is professor of education at Gallaudet University. Her teaching and research focus on home–school–community relationships and the role of culture in teaching and learning. Previous publications include "Home–School–Family Collaboration in Deaf Education" (with L. Myers), in *Promising Practices To Involve Families with Special Needs* (Information Age Publishing 2004) and "Responding to Gay and Lesbian Parents in Schools" (with Koerner and Ryan), in *Queering Elementary Schools* (Roman and Littlefield 1999).

lisahunter completed her PhD, *Young People, Physical Education and Transition: Understanding the Middle Years of Schooling*, at The University of Queensland in 2002. She now lectures on, and researches, young peoples' subjectivities, middle schooling, and physical culture at Griffith University. Her most recent publication is "Bourdieu and the Social Space of the PE class: Reproduction of Doxa through Practice." (*Sport, Education and Society*, 9(2), 175–192, 2004).

Francisco **Ibáñez-Carrasco** is an HIV/AIDS community-based researcher in British Columbia, Canada, and faculty at Goddard College. He is the coeditor with Erica Meiners of *Public Acts: Disruptive Readings in Making Curriculum Public* (RoutledgeFalmer 2004). His fiction has been widely published in the United States and Canada. His most recent work, a collection of short stories *Killing me Softly / Morir Amando* was released in 2004 (Suspect Thoughts Press).

Madelaine **Imber** cofounded and facilitates OUTSpoken, a peer resource team that works in schools and universities in addressing LGBTI issues within education and the broader community. She has written a range of papers addressing homophobia and heterosexism in education and is an assistant editor for *The Journal of Gay and Lesbian Issues in Education*. Madelaine is currently teaching senior English in Melbourne, Australia.

jan **jagodzinski** is professor of visual and media education in the Department of Secondary Education, University of Alberta (Canada). He is the author of *The Anamorphic I/i* (Duval 1996), *Postmodern Dilemmas* (Lawrence Erlbaum 1997); *Pun(k) Deconstruction* (Lawrence Erlbaum 1997); *Pedagogical Desire* (Bergin and Garvey 2002); *Youth Fantasies* (Palgrave 2004); *Musical Youth Fantasies* (Palgrave 2005); *Deconstructing the Oral Eye* (Hempsted, forthcoming).

Steven E. **James**, PhD is chair of the Psychology and Counseling Program at Goddard College, Plainfield, Vermont.

Jennifer **Jenson** is an assistant professor of pedagogy and technology in the Faculty of Education at York University. She has published most recently in *Women's Studies International Forum* and *Gender and Education*.

Suhraiya **Jivraj** is the coordinator of the Safra Project, conducting research and providing information on issues relating to lesbian, bisexual, and transgender women who identify as Muslim culturally and/or religiously. Her academic background is in human rights and Islamic law. Her work includes grass roots activism, research and policy in the fields of racism, LGBT rights and gender equality, particularly women's rights in Muslim family laws.

Dominique **Johnson** received her BA degree from Bryn Mawr College and her MA degree from Stanford University and is the founding executive director of The Joseph Beam Youth Collaborative, where she focuses her work on LGBT youth, school safety, mentoring, and antiracism with particular emphasis upon developmental benefits for LGBT youth of color. She is a former staff member of the National Sexuality Resource Center (NSRC) based at San Francisco State University, and The Annenberg Public Policy Center of the University of Pennsylvania.

Rodney **Jones** is an assistant professor in English and communication at City University of Hong Kong. He has researched and published widely in the areas of discourse and AIDS, homosexuality in China, and computer-mediated communication. His work has appeared in such journals as *Culture, Health and Sexuality*, *Discourse and Society* and *Health, Risk and Society*.

Amit **Kama** is an ethnographer of media audiences and has been active in various gay and lesbian organizations since 1982. He has published extensively on gay issues, including his book *The Newspaper and the Closet: Israeli Gay Men's Communication Patterns* (in Hebrew). He earned his PhD at Tel Aviv University in 2001. Amit recently married his spouse of eighteen years, Uzi Even.

Jane **Kenway** is professor of global educational studies in the Education Faculty at Monash University in Australia. Her recent books are *Masculinity Beyond the Metropolis*, with Anna Kraack (Palgrave 2004); Kenway, J., Bullen, E., and Robb, S., Eds. *Art, Humanities and the Knowledge Economy*, with E. Bullen and S. Robb (Peter Lang 2004); and *Globalising public education: policies, pedagogies and politics*, with M. Apple, and M. Singh, M. (Peter Lang 2004).

Didi **Khayatt** is a professor at the Faculty of Education at York University. She is the author of *Lesbian Teachers: An Invisible Presence* (State University of New York Press 1992) and has published numerous articles in books and journals. Her current work looks at how sexual categories used in English-speaking countries are not easily transferable to other cultures.

Amy K. **Kilgard** is an assistant professor of performance studies in the Department of Speech and Communication Studies at San Francisco State University. She is a director and performer currently working on a one-person show about everyday performances of consumerism.

Akihiko **Komiya** is research fellow of the Japan Society for the Promotion of Science. One of his recent publications is "Difficulties Japanese Gay Youth Encounter" (*Journal of Gay and Lesbian Issues in Education* 2003). He is on the editorial board of the Kikan SEXUALITY (Sexuality Quarterly).

Kevin K. **Kumashiro** is founding director of the Center for Anti-Oppressive Education, and senior program specialist in human and civil rights at the National Education

Association. He has authored or edited several books, including *Troubling Intersections of Race and Sexuality: Queer Students of Color and Anti-Oppressive Education* (Rowman & Littlefield 2001) and *Troubling Education: Queer Activism and Antioppressive Pedagogy* (RoutledgeFarmer 2002), which received the 2003 Myers Outstanding Book Award.

Glorianne M. **Leck** is professor emeritus of education at Youngstown State University. Her work with queer theory, feminist theory, and liberation politics have enveloped her career and political activism while also providing many of the insights offered in her teaching and publications.

Will **Letts** is a lecturer in the School of Teacher Education at Charles Sturt University, Bathurst, Australia. He teaches science and technology education and sociology of education, and is associate director of the Centre for Research into Professional Practice, Learning, and Education. His current research interests include the cultural studies of science education, Aboriginal science, and an examination of teachers' desks.

Heidi **Levitt** is an assistant professor of clinical psychology at The University of Memphis. She conducts research that examines the construction and evolution of gender identities and expressions, particularly across gay, lesbian, bisexual, and transgender cultures. As well, she conducts research investigating change processes that span psychotherapeutic orientation and studies the intersection of domestic violence and faith beliefs and practices.

Arthur **Lipkin,** an associate editor of the *Journal of Gay and Lesbian Issues in Education*, is a former instructor at the Harvard Graduate School of Education and taught in the Cambridge Public Schools for twenty years. He is the author of *Understanding Homosexuality, Changing Schools* (Westview 1999) and *Beyond Diversity Day: A Q & A on Gay and Lesbian Issues in Schools* (Rowman & Littlefield, 2004).

Marjorie **Lobban** has worked with children and children's literature throughout her career in education, most recently as a secondary school teacher librarian in Sydney, Australia. She coauthored, with Anne Clyde, *Out of the Closet and Into the Classroom: Homosexuality in Books for Young People* (Port Melbourne: ALIA/Thorpe, 2nd ed. 1996). She continues to read relevant books, write reviews and articles, and speak about the topic.

Loykie Loïc **Lomine** works for University College Winchester (England). His academic background is in sociology, more specifically gay and lesbian studies. He grew up in France and has lived in several countries, including Austria, Australia, and Spain. He has published articles about LGBT issues, and also about e-teaching, tourism, European integration, new queer cinema, and Tintin.

Peggy **Lorah** is director of the Center for Women Students and affiliate assistant professor of counselor education at The Pennsylvania State University. She received her master's degree in community counseling from Shippensburg University in 1989 and her doctorate of education in counselor education from The Pennsylvania State

University in 2001. She is a licensed professional counselor who has specialized in trauma, particularly focusing on sexual assault and relationship violence. She has recently coauthored "Affirmative Counseling for Transgendered Clients" in *Handbook of Counseling and Psychotherapy with Lesbian, Gay, and Bisexual Clients, (2nd ed.* (American Psychological Association, in press).

Karen E. **Lovaas** is assistant professor of speech and communication studies at San Francisco State University. She is on the editorial board of *Journal of Homosexuality* and was coeditor of *Queer Theory and Communication: From Disciplining Queers to Queering the Disciplines* (Harrington Park Press 2003). She is lead editor for an upcoming issue of *Journal of Homosexuality* comparing Queer Theory with LGBT Studies. A reader on sexual identity and communication is also in progress.

Catherine A. **Lugg** is associate professor of education in the Department of Educational Theory, Policy and Administration, at the Graduate School of Education Rutgers University. She is also program coordinator for the Educational Administration Supervision program. Her research areas include educational policy and politics, queer history and politics, and the various intersections of these at the public school site.

Michael J. **Maher** is a lay chaplain at Loyola University Chicago, where he has been part-time faculty and the chaplain to the School of Education since 1996. He has served in ministry at Catholic educational institutions in the U.S. Midwest since 1989. He is the author of *Being Gay and Lesbian in a Catholic High School: Beyond the Uniform* (Haworth Press 2001) and several articles on sexuality, education, and religion.

Connie R. **Matthews** is assistant professor of counselor education and women's studies at The Pennsylvania State University. Her research interests focus on affirmative counseling with gay, lesbian, and bisexual clients and on addiction and recovery in the GLBT population. She is a nationally certified counselor and a licensed professional counselor in Pennsylvania.

Cris **Mayo** is a professor in the Department of Educational Policy Studies and the Gender and Women's Studies Program at the University of Illinois at Urbana Champaign. Her areas of research include gender and sexuality studies and philosophy of education. Her recent book book is *Disputing the Subject of Sex* (Rowman & Littlefield 2004).

Lance T. **McCready** is assistant professor of educational studies at Carleton College in Northfield, MN. His writing focuses on segregation, desegregation, and resegregation in urban schools. His most recent publications focus on the identity formation processes of LGBT youth of color in urban schools that have racially defined academic programs and extracurricular activities.

Ian K. **Macgillivray**, is assistant professor of educational foundations and curriculum at James Madison University. He authored the book *Sexual Orientation and School Policy: A Practical Guide for Teachers, Administrators, and Community Activists* (Rowman & Littlefield 2004).

Paulina **Millán Álvarez** is a psychologist and a sexologist who works as a teacher and a researcher at the Mexican Institute of Sexology. She has published extensively on adolescents and sexual diversity and has coordinated, for seven years, the first support group for young lesbian and bisexual women in Mexico, Nueva Generación de Jóvenes Lesbianas (New Generation of Young Lesbians). Her most recent publication is *Sexualidad: Los Jóvenes Preguntan* (Sexuality: Young People Ask) (Paidos 2004).

George A. **Miller** earned his masters degree in higher education from Florida State University where he specialized in student affairs. He has held administrative posts at several different institutions and currently serves as the director of education and training for the headquarters of Delta Sigma Phi Fraternity.

Ray **Misson** is head of the Department of Language, Literacy and Arts Education and deputy dean in the Faculty of Education at the University of Melbourne. His interests center on the significance of cultural studies for classroom practice, in areas such as popular culture, critical literacy, sexuality studies, narrative, and creativity. He is the coauthor (with Wendy Morgan) of *The Suspicion of Pleasure and Beauty: Towards a Socially Critical Aesthetic in English Teaching*.

Jane **Mitchell** is a senior lecturer in the Faculty of Education at Monash University, Australia. Her research interests are concerned with curriculum, pedagogy and teacher education.

Jesse G. **Monteagudo**, who has a BA in history, is an award-winning freelance writer and journalist who specializes in GLBT issues and culture. His syndicated columns, "Jesse's Journal" and "The Book Nook," appear in newspapers from Pittsburgh to San Diego. Monteagudo's stories and essays have also been published in a variety of fiction and nonfiction anthologies.

Lynda Rae **Myers** is currently a president's fellow at Gallaudet University, and studying for a PhD at The Clinical Social Work Institute of Washington D.C. She is a therapist, community organizer, and advocate in the Deaf community.

Henrique Caetano **Nardi** is professor at the Department of Social Psychology of the Federal University of Rio Grande do Sul. He earned a PhD in sociology and is a medical doctor specializing in social medicine. He is a consultant in the field of public health.

Cynthia D. **Nelson** a senior lecturer at the University of Technology, Sydney in Australia, and teaches and researches in the areas of language and literacy education and research education. She has published extensively on sexual identities in language education, most recently in the *Journal of Language, Identity, and Education* and the *Journal of Curriculum Theorizing*; her ethnographic play, "Queer as a Second Language," has been performed in Australia, Japan, and the United States.

Louis **Niebur** received his PhD from the University of California–Los Angeles in musicology, specializing in electronic music in a popular sphere. He is currently a lecturer at the University of Nevada, Reno, where he teaches music history and film music.

Keiko **Ofuji** is a lecturer in the Department of German, Russian, and East Asian Languages and Literatures at Bates College, Maine. Her research program focuses on "Buraku" (a Japanese minority group) issues and sexual minority issues as well as the current situation and problems of human rights education in Japan. Her recent translations appear in the *Journal of Gay and Lesbian Issues in Education*.

Stacy **Otto** is assistant professor of social foundations at Oklahoma State University. Her work considers the importance of solitude and loss in an individual's decision to pursue a creative life. Otto's writing also includes essays on visual culture. Her recent publication is "Nostalgic for What?: The Epidemic of Images of the Mid-Twentieth-Century Classroom in American Media Culture and What It Means," in the journal *Discourse: Studies in the Cultural Politics of Education* (March 2006).

Gilad **Padva** is a doctoral student at the Shirley and Leslie Porter School of Cultural Studies and the Film & TV Department at Tel Aviv University, Israel. His research is about mainstream and alternative visualizations of sexuality and desire in American and British cinema and television in the 1990s and early 2000s. He published several articles about queer aspects of popular culture and presented many papers in international academic conferences.

Carrie **Paechter** is a professor in education at Goldsmiths College, University of London. Her research interests include the intersection of gender, power and knowledge, the construction of identity, especially with regard to gender, space, and embodiment in and outside schooling, and the processes of curriculum negotiation. Her most recent books are: *Educating the Other: Gender, Power and Schooling* (Falmer Press 1998); *Changing School Subjects: Power, Gender and Curriculum* (Open University Press 2000).

Maria **Pallotta-Chiarolli** is a senior lecturer in social diversity in health and education in the School of Health and Social Development, Deakin University, Melbourne, Australia. Her areas of research and publishing are the interweavings of gender diversity, sexual diversity, and cultural diversity. Her most recent book is *So What's A Boy? Addressing Issues of Masculinity and Schooling* (Open Uni Press 2003), coauthored with Wayne Martino.

Suresh **Parekh** is head of the Department of Psychology and has been teaching psychology both at undergraduate and postgraduate level at M.M.G. College of Arts & Commerce, Junagadh, Gujarat. He has authored several books on subjects such as statistics, behavioral psychotherapy, abnormal psychology, and the Rorschach test, both in Gujarati and English, and has participated international conferences in the United States and in China.

K. Michelle **Peavy** is a PhD candidate in clinical psychology at the University of Montana. She is currently working on research looking at special services provided to GLBT substance abusers.

John E. **Petrovic** is assistant professor at The University of Alabama. He teaches in the areas of philosophy and education, multicultural education, and language policy. He has written a number of articles on gay and lesbian issues in education including "Moral Democratic Education and Homosexuality: Censoring Morality" (*Journal of Moral Education*, 1999) and "Disrupting the Heteronormative Subjectivities of Christian Pre-Service Teachers: A Deweyan Prolegomenon" (*Journal of Equity and Excellence in Education*, 2003).

Voon Chin **Phua** is assistant professor of sociology at Gettysburg College. His research interest is on race, sex, and sexualities. His work has been published in *Journal of Family Issues, Men and Masculinities*, and *Culture, Health and Sexuality*.

William F. **Pinar** teaches curriculum theory at the University of British Columbia, where he holds a Canada Research Chair and directs the Centre for the Internationalization of Curriculum Studies. He is the editor of *Queer Theory in Education* (LEA 1998).

Monika **Pisankaneva** is a NGO-consultant, activist in the LGBT movement, and independent scholar researching Bulgarian LGBT culture. She has a degree in philosophy earned at Sofia University and has further studied comparative European social studies at Amsterdam University.

Alice J. **Pitt** is associate professor and associate dean of pre-service in the Faculty of Education, York University, Toronto. She is interested in the implications of psychoanalysis for questions of learning and pedagogy, research methodology and feminist/critical education. Recent publications include: *The Play of the Personal: Psychoanalytic Narratives of Feminist Education* (Peter Lang 2003); "Reading Women's Autobiography: On Losing and Refinding the Mother" *in Changing English: Studies in Reading and Culture*.

Fernando Altair **Pocahy** is a psychologist who specializes in social and cultural projects related to the LGBT youth issues and member of Nuances–Group for the Free Expression of Sexuality in Brazil.

Susan R. **Rankin** is a senior diversity planning analyst and assistant professor in higher education at The Pennsylvania State University. Her current research focuses on the assessment of institutional climate and providing program planners and policy makers with intervention strategies/initiatives to improve the campus climate for underrepresented groups. She is nationally recognized as a consultant on these issues and has collaborated with a large variety of institutions/organizations in implementing assessments and developing strategic plans regarding social justice issues and concerns.

Mary Lou **Rasmussen** is a lecturer in the school of social and cultural studies in education at Deakin University, Victoria, Australia. In 2004, she will be publishing an edited collection entitled *Youth and Sexualities: Pleasure, Subversion and Insubordination, in and out of Schools* (with Susan Talburt and Eric Rofes and published by Palgrave). Currently, her research interests are focused on the nexus of public pedagogies, popular cultures, and globalization.

947

Victor J. **Raymond** is a Ford predoctoral fellow at Iowa State University in the Department of Sociology. His essay, "Don't Assume You Know What I Am" will appear in *Getting Bi: Voices of Bisexuals Around the World* from the Bisexual Resource Center of Boston, MA.

Geoffrey L. **Ream** is a postdoctoral research fellow at the National Development and Research Institutes. His work focuses on sexual minorities' issues with religion, religion's role in youth development, and youth & young adult risk and resiliency in social, cultural, and subcultural context. He received his Ph.D. in Human Development from Cornell University in 2005.

Michael **Reiss** is professor of science education at the Institute of Education, University of London and editor of the journal *Sex Education*. His most recent book is *Values in Sex Education: From Principles to Practice*, with J. M. Halstead (RoutledgeFalmer 2003).

Kristen A. **Renn** is assistant professor of higher, adult, and lifelong education at Michigan State University. Her research addresses issues of identity in higher education, including the experience of mixed race college students, leadership of identity-based student organizations, and the history of women in higher education. Recent books include *Mixed Race Students in College: The Ecology of Race, Identity, and Community* (SUNY Press 2004) and *Roads Taken: Women in Student Affairs at Mid-Career* (Stylus 2004).

Emma **Renold** is a lecturer in childhood studies at the Cardiff School of Social Sciences, Cardiff University (Wales, UK). Emma's main research interests focus upon school-based sexualities and (hetero) gendered childhoods. She has published widely on children's gender and sexual identities and cultures, gendered and sexualized harassment and researching sensitive topics with children and young people. These key areas are explored in her book, *Girls, Boys and Junior Sexualities* (RoutledgeFalmer 2005).

Penny J. **Rice** is the director of the Margaret Sloss Women's Center at Iowa State University. She is the coeditor and author for *New Directions for Student Services* titled "Meeting the Special Needs of Adult Students."

Eric M. **Richardson** is a lecturer in educational studies at the University of the Witwatersrand, South Africa. He was one of the first South Africans to include sexual diversity issues and criminology theory in teacher education, and has published papers dealing with social justice, gender, and LGBT issues. Eric has addressed the principals of most of the boys' schools in the country on gay issues. He was a school's hostel warden, and has a master's degree.

Kerry H. **Robinson** teaches and researches in the areas of gender, sexuality, and the sociology of childhood. She has written extensively in these areas and is currently coauthoring a book titled *Diversity and Difference in Early Childhood: Implications for Theory and Practice* (Open University Press). Kerry received her PhD in sociology from the University of New South Wales, Australia.

Amardo **Rodriguez** is a professor in the Department of Communication and Rhetorical Studies at Syracuse University. His research and teaching interests explore the potentiality of emergent conceptions of communication to redefine and enlarge current understandings of democracy, diversity, and community. His books include: *On Matters of Liberation (I): The Case Against Hierarchy* (Hampton Press 2001); *Diversity as Liberation (II): Introducing a New Understanding of Diversity* (Hampton Press 2003), and *Essays on Communication and Spirituality: Contributions to a New Discourse on Communication* (Roman & Littlefield 2001).

Jerry **Rosiek** is an associate professor of educational research at the University of Alabama, where he teaches qualitative research methods to teacher education doctoral students, among others. His case study research on teachers knowledge about promoting equity and social justice in schools have appeared in journals such as *Harvard Educational Review, Curriculum Inquiry*, and the *Journal of Teacher Education*. His current writing focuses on the connections between the emotional and cultural dimensions of teachers' pedagogical content knowledge, and the type of teacher professional development infrastructure needed to share that knowledge.

Stephen T. **Russell** is associate professor of family studies and human development at the University of Arizona. Stephen is a William T. Grant Foundation Scholar (2001–2006), and a visiting distinguished professor of human sexuality studies at San Francisco State University. Stephen is an expert on adolescent health, with specific focus on the role of ethnic and sexual identity in adolescent health and well-being.

Ronni **Sanlo** is the director of the Lesbian Gay Bisexual Transgender Center at the University of California–Los Angeles and a lecturer in the UCLA Graduate School of Education. Her doctorate in education was earned at the University of North Florida. Her research area is sexual orientation issues in higher education. Before going to UCLA, she was the LGBT Center director at the University of Michigan. She is the founding chair of the National Consortium of LGBT Campus Resource Center Directors.

Ritch C. **Savin-Williams,** professor and chair of human development at Cornell University, has written *The New Gay Teenager* (Harvard University Press 2005), which follows earlier books on youth and sexuality: *"Mom, Dad. I'm Gay." How Families Negotiate Coming Out* (American Psychological Association 2001,); *". . . And Then I Became Gay." Young Men's Stories* (Routledge 1998); and *The Lives of Lesbians, Gays, and Bisexuals: Children to Adults*, edited with K. M. Cohen (Harcourt Brace 1996).

Debra **Shogan** is a professor in the cultural studies of sport and leisure at the University of Alberta, Canada. Her most recent book is *The Making of High Performance Athletes: Discipline, Diversity, and Ethics* (University of Toronto Press 1999).

John C. **Spurlock** is professor of history at Seton Hill University. He is the author (with Cynthia Magistro) of *New and Improved: The Transformation of American Women's Emotional Culture* (New York University Press 1998) and "From Reassurance to Irrelevance: Adolescent Psychology and Homosexuality in America," *History of Psychology* (2002).

Laura E. **Strimpel** holds a BA in sociology from Arcadia University. She is pursuing a master's degree in student affairs in higher education at Indiana University of Pennsylvania. She is also a hall director at Clarion University of Pennsylvania where she facilitates training sessions for student organizations and residence life staff on sexual orientation and gender identity issues.

Takashi **Sugiyama** is a PhD candidate at Yokohama National University and researcher and a lecturer of the Sei-Kyo-Kyo in Japan. He is also associate editor of the *Journal of Gay and Lesbian Issues in Education*. He was the main editor of a book, *Doseiai: Tayouna Sexuality (Homosexuality and Other Sexualities: How to Teach about Human Rights and Living Together)* (Kodomo-no-Mirai Pubilishing 2002).

Laura A. **Szalacha** earned her doctorate in human development and psychology at Harvard University's Graduate School of Education. As a developmental psychologist and research methodologist, her scholarship focuses on the psychosexual development of LGBTQQI adolescents. She is a research associate at Brown University's Center for the Study of Human Development.

Susan **Talburt** is director of the Women's Studies Institute and associate professor of educational policy studies at Georgia State University in Atlanta. She teaches courses in curriculum, social foundations, and feminist theory. She is the author of *Subject to Identity: Knowledge, Sexuality, and Academic Practices in Higher Education* (Albany: SUNY Press 2000) and coeditor of *Youth and Sexualities: Pleasure, Subversion, and Insubordination in and out of Schools* (Palgrave 2004).

Denise Tse Shang **Tang** is a doctoral candidate at the Hong Kong Polytechnic University. Her research interests include queer women urban spaces in Hong Kong and media culture. She is the Codirector for the Hong Kong Lesbian and Gay Film and Video Festival 2004. Prior to returning to Hong Kong, she was the Director of Community Services at Asian & Pacific Islander Wellness Center, a community-based HIV/AIDS organization in San Francisco, CA.

S. Anthony **Thompson** is an assistant professor of education at the University of Regina. Thompson and colleagues created a certificate in inclusive education, which is soon to include a course on sexualities. His dissertation focused upon the identity work of gay and bisexual men with intellectual disabilities. Thompson's most recent publication is "Operation Special: Interrogating the Queer Production of Everyday Myths in Special Education" in *I Could Not Speak My Heart* (University of Regina Press 2004).

Christopher P. **Toumey** is research associate professor of anthropology at the University of South Carolina. In addition to teaching about alternative genders in his cultural anthropology courses, he studies the cultural dynamics of public scientific and medical controversies, as exemplified in his book *Conjuring Science* (1996 Rutgers). Currently he is working on hermeneutic problems in public reactions to nanotechnology and nanomedicine.

Katherine **van Wormer** is professor of social work at the University of Northern Iowa. She is the author and coauthor of eight books, including: *Social Work with*

Lesbians, Gays, and Bisexuals: A Strengths Approach (Allyn and Bacon 2001); and *Addiction Treatment: A Strengths Perspective and Confronting Oppression, Restoring Justice* (Allyn and Bacon 2003).

Donovan R. **Walling** is director of publications and research for Phi Delta Kappa International. Previously he was a public school teacher and administrator in Wisconsin and Indiana, and taught for the Department of Defense in Germany. His recent books include *Public Education, Democracy, and the Common Good* (PDK 2004), *Virtual Schooling* (PDK 2003), and *Rethinking How Art Is Taught* (Corwin 2000). His latest is *Visual Knowing: Connecting Art and Ideas Across the Curriculum* (Corwin 2005).

Gerald **Walton** grew up in small military communities across Canada and participated in "ex-gay" ministries for most of his twenties. He has since abandoned such ministries and conducted research for his master's thesis on men who identify as both gay and Christian. He now actively promotes health and safety issues of LGBT youth through workshops, publications, media interviews, and his doctoral research. He plans to complete his PhD from Queen's University in Kingston, Ontario, in 2005.

Daisuke **Watanabe** is a student at Tokyo Metropolitan University Graduate School of Humanities doctoral course in pedagogy. He was an editorial member for *Doseiai: Tayoona Sexuality* (Kodomono-Miraisya 2002). He is a member of and serves as a headquarters manager for Sei-Kyo-Kyo.

Ian **Warwick** is a senior research officer at the Thomas Coram Research Unit, Institute of Education, University of London. His work, in the United Kingdom and internationally, focuses on the health and well-being of young people—and the professional development of those who work with them. Recent publications include: a review of homophobia, sexual orientation and schools in the United Kingdom; an evaluation of the National Healthy School Standard in England; a stakeholder analysis to assist the development of a program of continuing professional development for teachers of citizenship; and an evaluation of a peer education sexual health project.

Elizabeth **Whitney** holds a PhD in performance studies and speech communication from Southern Illinois University (2002). Her essay, "When White Girls Act Black: Reconsidering Performances of Otherness" is forthcoming in *Casting Gender: Women and Performance in Intercultural Contexts* (New York: Peter Lang). She tours extensively with her solo performance work and is currently a visiting scholar at Emerson College.

James Anthony **Whitson**, JD, PhD, is associate professor in the School of Education at the University of Delaware, where he teaches curriculum inquiry and social studies. His work includes studies of First Amendment issues in the school curriculum, situated cognition, problem-based learning, and consequences of legally mandated high-stakes testing, and demonstrates the necessity of recognizing curriculum as the course of transformative experience, rather than as a program for producing predetermined learning outcomes.

Shane L. **Windmeyer** is a national LGBT civil rights activist and professional public speaker. He is best known for his pioneering work founding the Lambda 10 Project for LGBT Greek Issues and Campus PrideNet for LGBT Student Leaders. He has written a number of books related to higher education and LGBT issues, including *Out on Fraternity Row: Personal Accounts of Being Gay in a College Fraternity* (Alyson 1998). His latest book is *Brotherhood: Chronicles of Gay Life within the College Fraternity* (Alyson 2005).

Gust A. **Yep** (PhD, University of Southern California) is professor of speech and communication studies and human sexuality studies at San Francisco State University. His research has appeared in numerous interdisciplinary journals and anthologies. He is the lead editor of *Queer Theory and Communication: From Disciplining Queers to Queering the Discipline(s)* (Harrington Park Press 2003) and coauthor of *Privacy and Disclosure of HIV in Interpersonal Relationships* (Lawrence Erlbaum 2003).

Allison J. Kelaher **Young** is an associate professor in the College of Education at Western Michigan University in Kalamazoo, Michigan. Her research interests include the role of motivational beliefs and self-regulated learning in the social contexts of secondary and postsecondary schooling, as well as holistic conceptions of the learner. Her recent work centers on representations of gays and lesbians in education, particularly as these issues intersect the context of teacher education programs.

SWINDON COLLEGE

LEARNING RESOURCE CENTRE

Index